£55.50 for net 2 volumes

Vespers at St. Mark's

Music of Alessandro Grandi, Giovanni Rovetta and Francesco Cavalli

Studies in Musicology

George Buelow, Series Editor

Professor of Musicology
Indiana University

Other Titles in This Series

Vespers at St. Mark's

Music of Alessandro Grandi, Giovanni Rovetta and Francesco Cavalli

Volume One

by
James H. Moore

umi
RESEARCH PRESS

Volume II of this study was prepared for
publication with the aid of a grant from
the Gladys Krieble Delmas Foundation.

Produced and distributed by
UMI Research Press
an imprint of
University Microfilms International
Ann Arbor, Michigan 48106

Library of Congress Cataloging in Publication Data

Moore, James Harold.
  Vespers at St. Mark's.

  (Studies in musicology ; no. 30)
  Bibliography: p.
  Includes index.
  1. Music—Italy—Venice. 2. Church music—History and
criticism. 3. Vespers (Music)—History and criticism.
4. Grandi, Alessandro, d. 1630. Works. 5. Roretta, Giovanni,
ca. 1596-1668. Works. 6. Cavalli, Pier Francesco, 1602-
1676. Works.   I. Title. II. Series.
  ML290.8.V26M66   783'.02'624531   80-39497
  ISBN 0-8357-1143-9 (set)
  ISBN 0-8357-1144-7 (v.1)

O Quam felix, et gloriosa es Urbs beata Venetorum;
quae tam dignum, et gloriosum hodie meruisti suscipere
Patronum, alleluia, alleluia.

Antiphon to the Magnificat
First Vespers of the Feast of the
Translation of the Body of St. Mark

Venice, Biblioteca Correr
Codice Cicogna, 1602, f. 102v

Contents

List of Tables

List of Plates

Acknowledgments

I owe thanks to many people and institutions without whose aid the completion of this work would not have been possible. First, to Frank A. D'Accone, who patiently saw this study through all stages from its inception through the final draft of the manuscript. The chapters based on archival material in particular owe much to his expert guidance as well as to the thorough, professional example set by his own scholarship. Frederick F. Hammond aided me with advice on liturgical questions and with the translations of countless problematic documents; William C. Holmes kindly obtained materials from Venetian libraries which I had been unable to see on my own trips to Venice; and Eleanor Selfridge-Field lent me microfilm copies of a number of archival documents as well as her advice on a number of points. The staffs of the Civico Museo Bibliografico Musicale (Bologna), the Archivio di Stato, Biblioteca Nazionale Marciana, Biblioteca del Civico Museo Correr, and the Fondazione Giorgio Cini (Venice), the Biblioteca Ambrosiana (Milan), and the British Library (London) were exceedingly helpful to me during my periods of work at these institutions. European research for this study was aided by grants from the University of California at Los Angeles (Chancellor's Fellowship), Martha Baird Rockefeller Foundation, and from the Gladys Krieble Delmas Foundation. Indeed, I am particularly grateful to Mrs. Delmas and her husband Jean, not only for their interest in the problems of musical scholarship but also for understanding that such research has its logical fruition in musical performance. And finally, Newell Jenkins and the Clarion Music Society gave me the pleasure of hearing the works I had transcribed in vivid, moving performances, first in Alice Tully Hall (New York) and then, aided by the Città di Castelfranco Veneto, in a number of cities in Northern Italy, culminating in an unforgettable performance in St. Mark's itself.

I

Introduction and Biographical Studies

Introduction: A Seventeenth-Century Venetian School

In the preface to his first set of *Symphoniae Sacrae*, Heinrich Schütz described the new musical fashions he had observed during his Venetian sojourn of 1628:

> Staying in Venice as the guest of old friends, I learned that the long unchanged theory of composing music had in part set aside the ancient numbers to tickle the ears of today with new titillations. To this method I directed my mind and energies, to the end that, in accordance with my purpose, I might offer you something from the store of my industry . . . .[1]

Scholars generally agree that Schütz referred here not merely to the music of Monteverdi but, perhaps even more so, to the works of a generation of younger colleagues who by the 1620s were publishing sacred monodies and small concerted motets in anthologies put out by the presses of Vincenti and Magni.[2] And yet, the very music which confronted Schütz on his second sabbatical trip to Venice—the seminal repertoire for the German *geistliches Konzert* and sacred sister to the continuo madrigal, cantata, and nascent Venetian opera—is nearly unknown today, strangely bypassed in the extensive work already done on the Venetian tradition in sacred music.

To be sure, studies of the Venetian School of the late Renaissance and early Baroque era have been many and diverse. Carl von Winterfeld, Francesco Caffi, Giacomo Benvenuti, Henry Prunières, and more recently Egon Kenton, Denis Arnold, and Denis Stevens all have dealt with aspects of the music at St. Mark's during the late sixteenth and early seventeenth centuries. With the exception, however, of Caffi's work, which chronicles a tradition lasting from 1318 through the fall of the Venetian Republic in 1797, scholars have concentrated almost solely on the century demarcated by the appointment of "Messer Adriano" as *maestro di cappella* in 1527 and the death of Monteverdi in 1643. Monteverdi has usually been considered the *terminus ad quem* of studies in Venetian sacred music, and the subsequent decades of the seventeenth century have been viewed as a decline both in St. Mark's musical establishment and in the artistic significance of the works produced by its composers. For the first view there may well be reason. Documents show that the *cappella marciana* went through several chaotic decades after Monteverdi's death, a situation corrected only by the systematization and regimentation of forces under Giovanni Legrenzi in 1685. There are no grounds, however, for the historical corollary: that the music produced during these years represents a decline in quality from the works of Monteverdi's own epoch. In fact, it would be strange if *seicento* Venice, the center of development of dramatic music, should have produced nothing memorable in the field of church music during the very years when she was the operatic capital of Europe. We know that some of the principal opera composers also worked in Venetian churches, and that Monteverdi, at least, produced a large body of works for St. Mark's which are nearly as important as the 1610 *Vespers*.

That the sacred music of Monteverdi's contemporaries and successors at St. Mark's has received little attention from scholars is due to a number of factors. For one, Leo Schrade put Monteverdi's entire output for St. Mark's in a shadow by insisting that the composer's true interest lay in his secular works and that his attitude toward his Venetian church music was mercenary at best.[3] With the works of the "master" put in this light, certainly the works of smaller figures seemed even less promising territory for investigation. Second, the Venetian opera really did overshadow the church in one important area, that of cold economics. Documents from the 1650s through the 1670s describe the discontent of the chapel's best singers, who repeatedly complained of excessive duties and small salaries. Given the circumstances, it is hardly surprising to learn that St. Mark's was plundered on numerous occasions during these years, not only by operatic impresarios who could offer singers greater financial rewards, but also by a number of foreign courts which could outbid the declining *Serenissima Repubblica*, burdened with the war against the Turk in Candia. Third, much seventeenth-century church music is reactionary and certainly remote from the forefront of musical progress; and in Venice the situation is even more complex than in other parts of Italy. One must, of course, take account of the dichotomy between works in the *prima prattica* and those in the *stile concertato*, a division which holds for sacred works throughout the peninsula. However, a second dichotomy is present in Venetian sacred music, for the tradition of *cori spezzati* exerted a gravitational pull upon composers throughout the seventeenth century. Not only were double-choir psalms in a style derived from that of Willaert sanctioned by the ceremonial rubrics of St. Mark's, but the brilliant polychoral idiom of Croce and the Gabrielis was recalled at climactic moments in works in the *stile concertato* which, otherwise, drew upon the latest techniques from the world of the opera and the cantata. Thus, in a very real sense, Venetian composers drew upon two forms of *stile antico:* the *prima prattica*, which was a common heritage for all Italy; and the polychoral style associated specifically with the composers of St. Mark's. Clearly, a body of music which is retrospective now in one direction, now in the other, fails to attract music historians intent upon discovering only the progressive, the forward-looking, the innovative.

Thus, this study has a dual purpose: first, to fill the gap in our knowledge of Venetian sacred music during the years of development and maturity of Venetian opera; and second, to examine Monteverdi's influence upon the works of his colleagues and successors at St. Mark's. As I gathered and transcribed materials for this study, it gradually became apparent that these two themes would coalesce into a study of the three most prominent figures at St. Mark's during the epoch of Monteverdi and the following few decades: Alessandro Grandi, Monteverdi's *vice-maestro* from 1620 to about 1626 and certainly one of the most important musical figures in Venice during the early 1620s; Giovanni Rovetta, who became *vice-maestro* upon Grandi's departure and who assumed the position of *maestro* upon Monteverdi's death in 1643; and Francesco Cavalli, a singer in the *cappella marciana* from 1616 who passed to the position of second organist in 1639, first organist in 1645, and succeeded Rovetta as *maestro di cappella* in 1668.

Since an examination of the complete sacred *oeuvre* of all three figures would go beyond the scope of a single study, it seemed prudent to survey their music for one liturgical service. To delimit the topic in this way, rather than completing an exhaustive examination of the sacred works of only one of the three composers, might seem to be a denial of a thorough, scholarly approach to the topic. However, from the point of view of cultural history, I think there is more to be gained from a study of a representative section of the output of all three figures. The seventeenth century is certainly not a period of common compositional practice, and Grandi composes in idioms somewhat removed from those of Rovetta and literally worlds away from those employed by Cavalli.

The choice of music for Vespers services as a point of reference was an obvious one for a study of sacred music in the *seicento*, for Vespers music cuts across the stylistic pluralities of the era as well as the vagaries of music publication. Unlike Monteverdi's *Selva Morale e Spirituale* (1640), which contains nearly all of the musical materials for a Vespers service (psalms, hymn, Magnificat, Marian antiphon), most seventeenth-century Venetian collections segregate these materials. Vespers psalms and Magnificats are found in one set of prints; *motetti*, which include psalm antiphons, hymns, and Marian antiphons, are almost invariably found in another set. This division is based not only upon the liturgical types themselves but upon the frequency of use of the materials published. The collections of Vespers psalms and Magnificats (which often contain Mass ordinaries as well) would, of course, be usable throughout the church year. The collections of *motetti* (which in addition to the Vespers materials often contain texts from the proper of the Mass as well as non-liturgical items) encompass material which, on the whole, would be used less often.[4]

The collections of psalms and Magnificats are generally in one of three musical styles: the large-scale *stile concertato*, in which there are parts for vocal soloists, chorus, and instruments; the small-scale *stile concertato*, with parts for one to five vocal soloists and, occasionally, for two violins; and that hybrid idiom for double choir, sandwiched stylistically between true *prima prattica* works and turn-of-the-century polychoral pieces, as exemplified by Monteverdi's *Credidi* and *Memento a 8 voci da Capella (Selva Morale,* 1640) and the *Dixit Dominus a 8 voci alla breve (Messa a quattro voci.... e Salmi,* 1650).[5] The motet collections are almost invariably in the modern *stile concertato*, although the forces are usually fairly modest. Thus, the music for Vespers services encompasses not only the major categories of sacred publications of the seventeenth century but the major stylistic idioms as well.

After a period of work in Venetian archives, it became apparent to me that two additional topics would perforce form important chapters in this study; for the music written for St. Mark's could hardly be divorced from the *cappella marciana*, the musical establishment for which it was created, nor from the special ceremonies and liturgical practices of the ducal chapel. Indeed, the more I worked with the administrative documents of the *cappella* and with the *ceremoniali* and breviaries of the basilica, the more aware I grew that the music of Grandi, Rovetta and Cavalli was not merely the result of artistic currents and trends but the product of practical circumstance and of liturgical necessity. Sacred music in any age is very much the child of its milieu, and the sacred music of the composers of St. Mark's must be understood first and foremost as the artistic expression of a particular musical institution and of unique liturgical customs.

I do not mean to isolate the composers of St. Mark's from the rest of northern Italy, nor to postulate the existence of a unique musical style associated with the basilica. However, if Monteverdi's Venetian sacred works form one segment of the background against which the works of Grandi, Rovetta and Cavalli must be viewed, the history of the *cappella marciana* forms a second crucial segment, and the liturgical and ceremonial life of St. Mark's forms a third. Thus, this study divides quite naturally into five lengthy chapters—indeed, one might say five prolonged essays. The first outlines the biographies of Grandi, Rovetta and Cavalli, tracing their connections with St. Mark's and any evidence of their relationship with Monteverdi. The second contains a discussion of the musical sources of their sacred works and, where known, produces archival documents which elucidate the circumstances of composition and publication. The third chapter is a detailed history of the musical chapel of St. Mark's during the *seicento*, with particular attention paid to the effects of the fortunes of the chapel on performance practice. The fourth chapter is a study of the Vespers liturgy of St. Mark's and its reflection in the Vespers compositions of the composers of the basilica. The final chapter is a study of the musical styles of the Vespers repertoire of St. Mark's, treated not in the abstract but, rather, in relation to the production of Monteverdi, to the history of the basilica's musical institutions and to the demands of its ceremonial life. The core of this repertoire consists of 10 large collections of psalms and Magnificats which roughly span the middle two quarters of the century, from Rovetta's *Salmi concertati* of 1627 through Francesco Cavalli's *Vesperi a otto voci* of 1675. Although motet collections draw our attention back as early as 1610, relevant archival material on the *cappella* spans the century, and the pertinent liturgical documents span several centuries, it is this set of 10 Vespers prints and the period they demarcate—roughly 1625 to 1675—that forms the core of this study.

Alessandro Grandi

The precise date and place of birth of Alessandro Grandi are still unknown.[6] The first documentary material regarding his life is found in the *Catalogo dei Maestri di Cappella dell'Accademia della Morte dal 1594 al 1683 e catalogo dei musicanti d'essa Accademia*, an undated Ferrarese manuscript of the seventeenth century in which Grandi is mentioned twice.[7] He is found first in an undated list of sopranos connected with the Accademia; he later appears in a list of the organization's *maestri di cappella*, with indications that he served in this capacity sometime between the years 1597 and 1604. Just when Grandi assumed the post of *maestro*, however, is open to question. The list of *maestri* is ambiguous and is arranged as follows:[8]

Anno 1594 Il Sig. Hippolito Fiorin, fu anche Maestro di Capella d'Alfonso II, duca di Ferrara.
     1597 Il Sig. Giulio Belli da Longiano, o come altri vogliono Romano.
           Il Sig. Alessandro Grandi.
     1604 Il Sig. Paolo Isnardi Ferrarese

Martin Seelkopf assumes that the year 1597 refers to both Giulio Belli and to Alessandro Grandi, for Belli's first book of Masses, published in January 1600 (1599 *more veneto*),[9] names him as *maestro* of the cathedral of Osimo. However, the catalogue merely states that Grandi served between Belli and Isnardi and, as we shall see below, there is reason to doubt that Grandi assumed this office quite so early in his life.

Until now, the period of Grandi's life from 1604 until the appearance of his first publication in 1610 has been a void. However, I have discovered two new documents from the Venetian State Archives (*Archivio di Stato, Venezia*—hereafter, A.S.V.) which not only throw some light on these missing years but also provide a clue to Grandi's birthdate. The first is a document of 25 July 1604, in which 19 *giovani di coro* are elected to serve in St. Mark's. At the end of the list of electees, we find the following statement (Document 1):

> And although Ales*sandro di* Agustin di Grandi is about eighteen years old and cannot be elected according to the decree of 5 April 1587, which says the *giovani di coro* must be about twenty years old at least, the most Illustrious *Signori* [Procurators] have information about the goodness, good service, and excellence of said Alessandro, who is a good singer and composer, and have decided, said decree notwithstanding, which for this time only may be disregarded, said Alessandro can be elected *giovani di coro*; and he has been so elected.

A second document (Document 2) confirms Grandi's presence in Venice until at least 1607, when seven *giovani di coro*—Grandi among them—who had been dropped from service for having neglected their duties were reinstated upon petition. These two documents are crucial in several respects. First, they show that Grandi spent at least three years of the heretofore "dark period" of his life at St. Mark's. Thus, certain aspects of his biography which have been confusing until now—Caffi's statement that he studied with Giovanni Gabrieli and the appearance of works of Giovanni Croce in Grandi's late collections—no longer demand elaborate explanations. Moreover, we know that as early as age 18, before the publication of any of his works, Grandi was prominent enough as a composer to be cited as such in the Procurators' minutes. And, most important, if Grandi was about 18 years old in 1604, his birthdate can be set sometime in 1586.

To be sure, these documents do pose one problem, for they seem to conflict with a piece of information we already have about Grandi's early life. To wit, if Grandi was born in 1586, he would have been only 11 years old in 1597, the year in which Seelkopf suggests he assumed the post of *maestro* at the Accademia della Morte. It is for this reason that we might assume that Grandi took the post at a slightly later date.[10] To be sure, he still would have been under 18, but it is not impossible that he was appointed at such a tender age. We know from the Procurators' statement that Grandi was a prodigy; after all, they were bending their rules for one time only to admit him. Moreover, the Accademia della Morte, a religious confraternity rather than an intellectual academy, seems to have hired musicians on a part-time basis only to provide music for the funerals of its members,[11] so it is possible that an exceptional adolescent could have been hired to lead them. Moreover, the preface to Grandi's first publication of 1610 speaks of the "giovinezza del mio sapere," a phrase which supports 1586 as a logical birthdate, for such a statement would be out of place for a composer much over 24 years old.[12]

The fact that Grandi was at St. Mark's during the first decade of the century also throws new light on his relationship with Heinrich Schütz. A possible meeting between Schütz and Grandi has traditionally been traced to Schütz's second trip to Venice, that of 1628–29.[13] We know that Schütz must have come into direct contact with Grandi's music, for the motet "O Jesu süss" from Schütz's third book of *Symphoniae Sacrae* is a close parody of the motet "Lilium convalium" from Grandi's second book of *Motetti con sinfonie*.[14] Whether Schütz actually met Grandi has been open to conjecture, for by 1628 Grandi had already left Venice for a position at Santa Maria Maggiore in Bergamo. The discovery of these new Venetian documents on Grandi, however, raises the possibility that Schütz may have met Grandi on his first trip to Venice, which lasted from the spring of 1609 until the spring of 1613. We know Grandi was at St. Mark's until at least 22 July 1607 (see Document 2), and the first indication we have that he had left Venice does not come until 10 March 1610, the date of dedication of his first book of motets, in which he is described as "Maestro di Capella del Spirito Santo in Ferrara."

There are few difficulties with Grandi's biography after 1610, for the steady stream of printed collections of music, supplemented by archival documents, gives us reliable information on Grandi's positions and on other details of his career. In 1610 at the latest, Grandi became *maestro di cappella* of the Accademia dello Spirito Santo, the most significant musical academy of the time in Ferrara.[15] He kept this post at least until 20 August 1614. From the title page of his first book of *madrigali concertati*, however, we learn that by 17 June 1615 he had been named *maestro di cappella* at the cathedral of Ferrara, the highest musical post Ferrara had to offer after the dissolution of the court chapel in 1598. The dedication of this collection shows also that Grandi maintained an artistic relationship with perhaps the most celebrated Ferrarese academy of all time, the Accademia degli Intrepidi.[16]

Grandi kept his position at the cathedral of Ferrara only about two years, for on 31 August 1617 the Procurators of St. Mark's in Venice confirmed him as a singer in the *cappella marciana*. The record of his appointment is preserved in the A.S.V. It reads as follows (Document 3):

31 August 1617

Since the Most Illustrious and Excellent *Signori* [Procurators] have information as to the quality, worth, and sufficiency of Alessandro di Grandi, who has served as *maestro di cappella* in Ferrara, they have determined by ballots that the said Alessandro should be elected to serve in the chapel of St. Mark's, with a salary of eighty ducats per year.

In the following year Grandi was chosen to replace Gasparo Locadello as *maestro di canto* in the seminary (decree of the Procurators, 21 August 1618). For an additional 50 ducats per year (made retroactive to the previous 20 March, when he had assumed his new position), Grandi had the obligation of teaching at the seminary "at least four days per week, bringing proof every two months that he has thus served" (Document 4). Two years later (decree of 17 November 1620), Grandi succeeded Marc' Antonio Negri as *vice-maestro* to Monteverdi, with an annual salary of 120 ducats.

We have few details of Grandi's activities at St. Mark's beyond our general knowledge of the workings of the *cappella*. Arnold has found that he participated in festivities at the Scuola di San Rocco in both 1619 and 1624,[17] and we may assume that these are only two of many occasions on which he worked for other Venetian institutions, as was normal for the singers of St. Mark's. Grandi's years in Venice were fewer than those in Ferrara, however, for on 18 March 1627 he was elected unanimously to the post of *maestro di cappella* at Santa Maria Maggiore in Bergamo.[18]

Grandi's activities in Bergamo are documented more fully than those in either Ferrara or Venice. It seems he enjoyed great respect as *maestro*, for the hour of Vespers was changed after his arrival so that more of the faithful could hear his performances. We know that he taught *canto figurato* to some of the students in the Collegio as part of his duties and that he petitioned the Consorzio, the governing body of the cathedral, on several occasions for higher wages.[19] With the extensive body of *concertato* motets which he had composed during his Venetian years, he must have revolutionized the musical repertoire of Santa Maria Maggiore. An inventory of the music which was handed down to him when he assumed his duties is preserved in the Archives of the Misericordia Maggiore and shows that the musical repertoire was quite conservative. Music for *cori spezzati* by Asola, Croce, Viadana, Vecchi and Giulio Belli existed in abundance, but there was not a trace of the small-scale concerted motet, which had been the center of progressive sacred composition for over 20 years.[20] Grandi died of the plague which was ravaging northern Italy sometime after 28 June 1630, the date of the dedication of his sixth book of motets.[21]

Grandi's musical patrimony is difficult to determine with precision. Caffi's statement that he was the "allievo distino dell'organista Giovanni Gabrieli" is plausible, particularly in view of the new documents which show that Grandi was in the service of St. Mark's during the last years of Gabrieli's life. Although we lack definite evidence to support a pedagogical relationship, the attacks which Renate Günther[22] and Seelkopf launch against Caffi are no longer valid. Indeed, the younger composers who surrounded Gabrieli during the first decade of the *seicento* constitute a virtual school, and it is difficult to believe that Grandi could have escaped the influence of this remarkable circle.

There is, however, more evidence to support a relationship between Grandi and Giovanni Croce, who was *maestro di cappella* at St. Mark's from 1603 to 1609. Two compositions of Croce's find their way into Grandi's publications: an eight-voice *In spiritu humilitatis*, included in the "Aggionta di Motetti di diversi Auttori.... Raccolti da Alessandro Vincenti" in the Venetian edition (1620) of Grandi's *Motetti a cinque voci*, originally published in Ferrara in 1614; and a *Laudate pueri in ecco di Giovanni Croce Chiozotto*, included in Leonardo Simonetti's anthology of Grandi's large sacred works, the *Raccolta Terza.... di Messa et Salmi del Sig. Alessandro Grandi* (Venice: Magni, 1630). Moreover, a madrigal by "Alessandro di Grandi" is included in Croce's fourth book of madrigals (Venice: Vincenti, 1606/07). Seelkopf argues that this is probably not the work of the Grandi in question on the grounds that the "di" is never again used as part of his name in any of Grandi's prints. It is, however, found in a number of documents concerning Grandi in the A.S.V. (as, for example, Documents 1 and 3 cited above). Seelkopf argues further that the inclusion of Croce's works in Grandi's publications is insufficient evidence of a relationship between the two since such inclusions are the work of Vincenti and Simonetti, not of Grandi himself. Be that as it may, the existence of three different musical crossovers seems to indicate some artistic relationship, even if we cannot say for certain that Croce was Grandi's teacher.[23]

Grandi's relationship to Monteverdi is, unfortunately, no clearer than his relationship to Gabrieli or Croce. Indeed, scholars have argued both that Grandi's works unquestionably show the influence of Monteverdi and, conversely, that Grandi was simply a younger colleague whose stylistic resemblance to Monteverdi is nothing more than the reaction of both composers to the new forms, techniques and idioms which made up the common musical language of the early seventeenth century.

Arnold sees Monteverdi as a decisive model for Grandi.[24] He finds a basic change in Grandi's style after his move to Venice in 1617 and attributes this new monodic idiom of dramatic declamation which flowers in Grandi's solo motets to the example of Monteverdi and the influence of the virtuoso singers connected with the chapel of St. Mark's. More specifically, Arnold traces Grandi's "mastery of arioso" to works such as Monteverdi's *Arianna* lament and his setting of *Nigra sum* in the 1610 *Vespers*; Grandi's tuneful *tripla* melodies are likewise said to descend from Monteverdi's setting of *Ave maris stella* in the *Vespers*; and a number of special effects in the works from Grandi's Bergamo period presumably owe much to Monteverdi's examples of the *stile concitato*. While Arnold cites no documentary evidence, he sees the proximity of the two composers and the musical affinity of their sacred works as sufficient signs of some artistic relationship.

Renate Günther[25] sees a similar connection between the two men, but she traces it back to the opening years of the century, when Grandi was still in Ferrara, Monteverdi in Mantua. She cites the close connections which had linked the Ferrarese and Mantuan musical establishments for well over a century and notes the overlapping years of service for the two musicians (Monteverdi in Mantua, 1590–1612; Grandi in Ferrara, ca. 1597–1616). Moreover, she finds Grandi's initial print of 1610 squarely in the musical idiom of Monteverdi. While she does not believe that a teacher-pupil relationship necessarily existed, she does maintain that Grandi was clearly influenced by Monteverdi from the start of his career, not just during the years they spent together in Venice.

Seelkopf, defending the opposite pole from both Arnold and Günther, warns that proximity and contact do not necessarily imply artistic influence. To be sure, he agrees that Monteverdi was in contact with Ferrara, even after the death of Alfonso II; he says, however, that under the circumstances Grandi and Monteverdi could have met only casually, and there is no evidence that Grandi's musical style draws upon Monteverdi's any more than upon the general trends of the epoch. Seelkopf also cites several points of negative evidence. At a time when composers often acknowledge mentors in their early publications (e.g., Monteverdi cites Ingegneri; Schütz, Gabrieli; Giovanni Rovetta, Monteverdi), there is no mention of another composer in any of Grandi's prints. Nor does Grandi figure in Monteverdi's voluminous correspondence. Seelkopf sees the two rather as professionally equal colleagues, and he cites a stanza from Giulio Strozzi's *La Venetia Edificata* as evidence that their contemporaries may have held a similar view.[26]

While Seelkopf is accurate from a purely documentary point of view, one is left, nonetheless, with the fact that Grandi and Monteverdi worked in proximity to each other for a period of no less than 25 years. While their contacts may have been casual during their 15 years in Ferrara and Mantua (ca. 1597–1612), Grandi would certainly have been familiar with Monteverdi's music, at least from the prints and possibly from manuscript copies as well. Moreover, the two composers deal with some of the same institutions; Grandi's first book of madrigals (1615) and Monteverdi's fourth book (1603) both were dedicated to the Accademia degli Intrepidi. In addition, what may have been brief contact in Ferrara and Mantua became a close association in Venice. While Arnold's statement that Grandi was Monteverdi's "own discovery"[27] whom he had personally tempted into Venetian service[28] goes beyond the documentation, the fact that the Procurators' initial decree (Document 3) describes no competitive auditions but cites merely "information as to the quality, worth and sufficiency of Alessandro di Grandi" may indicate that Grandi was invited to join the chapel—perhaps by Monteverdi himself. Certainly Grandi's appointment as *vice-maestro* in 1620 was the result of Monteverdi's own wishes, for in a letter to Alessandro Striggio on 13 March 1620, just a few months before Grandi's appointment, Monteverdi marvels:

> . . . that they accept no singers in the chapel [of St. Mark's] without first asking the *maestro di cappella*, nor do they want reports on matters dealing with singers other than from the *maestro di cappella*, nor do they accept organists or *vice-maestro* if they have not the opinion and report of the *maestro di capella* ....[29]

There can be no doubt that the two composers worked closely in tandem in St. Mark's. Not only was the *vice-maestro* called upon to direct the *cappella* in the absence of the regular maestro, but in the performance of polychoral works, he had the duty of relaying the *maestro*'s beat to the musicians in the first organ loft, the *capo dei concerti* relaying it to those in the second organ loft.[30]

Although Arnold's label "disciple" may be strong, his observations on the stylistic affinity between works of Grandi and Monteverdi are quite accurate. And while one must be wary of assuming causality where it does not exist, one does not overstate the case by saying that Grandi surely worked within Monteverdi's sphere of influence.

Giovanni Rovetta

Less work has been done on Rovetta's life than on Grandi's, and the data we possess come almost entirely from the A.S.V. Neither an exact birth-date nor birthplace has been ascertained. Arnold reports that the *necrol-*

ogio of the *Provvidetori della Sanità* lists Rovetta as 72 years old at his death in 1668; thus Arnold suggests a birthdate of 1596.[31] The *Libro dei Morti* of St. Mark's, however, listed him as being 71 years old on 23 October 1668 (Document 5), which would move his birthdate up to 1597. Since his father, Giacomo Rovetta, was a violinist connected with the *cappella marciana* from 1614 until 1641, it is likely that Rovetta was born somewhere in the Veneto, if not in Venice itself. Caffi cites him as a "cantor di soprano nella sua fanciulezza" at St. Mark's, but we have neither dates nor documentation for this assertion. That Rovetta began his career as a boy soprano is certainly a possibility, for he was hired as a professional bass singer on 2 December 1623, an indication that he may have had previous experience.[32] However, the first record we have of his professional career documents him not as a singer but as an instrumentalist. On 7 December 1614, 11 "sonadori" who had served in St. Mark's on various occasion were put on the regular payroll. They were to be paid 15 ducats per year and to be fined 2 ducats for each occasion on which they failed to appear.[33] Rovetta was one of these instrumentalists. Earlier in the same year, he was an unsuccessful candidate in the *prove* to find a successor for Giovanni Bassano as *capo dei concerti*.[34]

Just what role Rovetta played in the *cappella* after his appointment as a bass singer is not clear. It would seem that he both sang and played, for the preface to his *Salmi concertati* of 1627 (1626 *more veneto*) is an elaborate paean to his work as an instrumentalist and never mentions the fact that he also served as a singer in the *cappella*. The preface is so revealing—not only because of the specific references that Rovetta makes to his life but also because of his remarks about Venetian musical politics—that it is worth quoting in full (Document 7):

> Kind Readers: For many years now it has been my profession to play every sort of instrument, both strings and winds; and while I have toiled quite a bit in this area, I have not neglected the study of composition. [In fact], since I wanted to employ my talent in this field, I got the Most Illustrious and Excellent Procurators to appoint me to a musical post in St. Mark's. I hoped, moreover, to be able to fill the office of *vice-maestro* in the absence of the *maestro di cappella*; and my hope did not prove groundless, for since this need came up shortly after I entered, I was honored by the Most Illustrious and Excellent Procurators, my Patrons, who asked that I exercise the [office of *vice-maestro*] until they could make a new decision [to fill the office permanently]. Although certain people have found it fantastic that I have passed so quickly from the profession of instrumentalist to that of composer and director of music on diverse feasts, they have used poor judgment [in declaring that] I could not compose sacred music. Since I realize that such opposition could very quickly make a bad impression on people who do not know me, I have taken the expedient of printing these sacred songs, so that the Most Illustrious and Excellent Procurators should see that, although they were kind to me, I am supported by the same foundation [of musical skill] as anyone else who has been appointed in the past. And let it be known, moreover, that

these are really my compositions, and not those of others; and anyone who believes otherwise should be ready to offer every sort of proof. And let no one wonder that I was first a player and then set myself to be a composer, for Striggio, Priuli, Valentini, and almost the entire best school of composers have worked in such a manner. In fact, because of this experience, I am truly qualified for the position of *vice-maestro di cappella* of St. Mark's, since in this Most Serene Service there are not only over thirty singers, but over twenty instrumentalists, both winds and strings. Therefore, Virtuous Gentlemen, if you should find in these compositions of mine something which is not entirely pleasing to your taste, you will excuse me from blame, [since] I have told you the necessity which forced me to have them printed, and I shall not fail to prepare something else which will please you. And live happily, etc.

Apart from its polemics, the preface is significant because it eluci- dates the chronology of Rovetta's early years in the *cappella* with disarm- ing candor. According to his own remarks, Rovetta had been a professional instrumentalist and had studied composition long before his appointment at St. Mark's. He sought to be named to the *cappella* with the particular aim of using his compositional talent in the office of *vice-maestro*. Shortly after he entered the *cappella* the position of *vice-maestro* became vacant (because of Grandi's departure for Bergamo), and Rovetta was named to the post temporarily until the Procurators could decide upon a permanent candidate. To insure that he be given the post permanently, and to quell rumors that he was a mere performer and could not compose, Rovetta was now publishing these *Salmi concertati*.

Evidently Rovetta's publication pleased the Procurators, for on 22 November 1627 they appointed him as Grandi's official successor with an annual salary of 120 ducats per year.[35] His salary was increased by 40 ducats on 22 March 1635, by another 20 ducats on 28 March 1640, and to 200 ducats on 1 March 1642.[36]

We have records of few of Rovetta's activities during his years as *vice-maestro*. The most important is his supervision of the music per- formed in San Giorgio Maggiore to honor the birth of Louise XIV of France. The dedication of Rovetta's *Messa e Salmi* of 1639, a collection printed to commemorate the event, is addressed to Louis XIII and reads as follows (Document 8):

I was commanded by Monsignor di Housaij, Counsellor of State, and Ambassador of Your Majesty, to assist in the celebration of thanks on [the occasion of] the birth of the Grand Dauphin, which was celebrated with regal display of music in the Basilica of San Giorgio of Venice.

This little service, for which I was honored by receiving public praise from this gentleman, emboldens me to dedicate to you these sacred musical efforts of mine so that I may immortalize my obligation in print and make myself known in that world of France as a servant of Your Majesty.

Rovetta's dedication does not state whether the works he was publishing were those actually performed in San Giorgio or whether the print was merely a commemoration of the event. Nor does the elaborate ceremonial written by one Fausto Ciro and printed in November, 1638, solve the problem.[37] Ciro describes Rovetta's participation as follows (Document 9):

> For the composition of the music, and for *maestro di cappella*, Signor Rueti [*sic*] was chosen from the many [musicians] who live in Venice; for this occasion, he was expressly asked to engage all of the singers and instrumentalists to be found in the city, to do justice to the great concept of His Excellency, who wanted the most festive and solemn music which could be found.

While Ciro goes on to describe an elaborate celebration of the Mass, he makes no mention of music for Vespers. (The ceremonies are discussed in more detail below, Chapter III, pp. 89-91.)

Rovetta also had connections with the Venetian *ospedali* during these years. We find him as *maestro di musica* at the Ospedale dei Derelitti ("Ospedaletto") in 1635 with a salary of 24 ducats per year.[38] He held a similar position at the Ospedale dei Mendicanti from 1639 on.[39] Rovetta also organized musical festivities at the Chiesa dello Spirito Santo at Pentecost in 1640.[40]

On 21 February 1644 Rovetta was promoted to the office of *maestro di cappella* by a decree which only gently alludes to the flurry of activity which preceded his appointment (Document 10).[41] In their decree, the Procurators describe how, before electing a successor to Monteverdi, they had written to Pietro Ottoboni in Rome, to Vienna, to the governors of the Venetian provinces on *Terrafirma*, and to the Venetian Residents in various cities to solicit nominations for the post. However, since no one of "qualità e virtù" other than Giovanni Rovetta sought the position, they decided that Rovetta should be offered the post with a salary of 300 ducats per year. This was 100 ducats below Monteverdi's final salary, though Rovetta was also offered the usual gratuities as well as the *maestro*'s residence in the rectory, with a promise that it would be "accommodated with the necessary fittings." Indeed, this last statement was more than just a token promise, for the financial records of the basilica record the following payment of 17 June 1644 (Document 11):

> For expenses for lodgings: in cash sixty ducats fourteen grossi exactly, to diverse *maestri* for materials and labor done in the apartment in the rectory in which Don Zuane Rovetta *maestro di cappella* has gone to live, as was decreed last February 21st.

A few weeks later, the following is recorded (Document 12):

> For expenses for lodgings: in cash ten ducats exactly, to Bartolo Maragon for labor and materials for having put window-shutters on the pergolas in the apartment occupied by the *maestro di cappella*.

The responses to the Procurators' inquiry from Venetians in various parts of Europe are preserved in the A.S.V.[42] To be sure, the decree cited above hints only at the vague outlines of the search, for a number of possible candidates were recommended: one Antonio della Tavola, *maestro di cappella* of the basilica of St. Anthony of Padua; Francesco Turini, organist at the cathedral of Brescia; one Buzatti, *maestro di cappella* at Milan;[43] Giovanni Battista Crivelli, *maestro* at Santa Maria Maggiore in Bergamo; and Giacomo Carissimi, *maestro* of the Collegio Germanico in Rome.[44] The figure who seems to have been the Procurators' first choice was Orazio Benevoli, *maestro di capella* of San Luigi dei Francesi in Rome. Indeed, the election of the new *maestro*, which the Procurators had originally scheduled for the end of January 1644, was put off to the fourth or fifth of February so that Benevoli and the rest of the contestants could come to Venice. Arnold hypothesizes that the *prove* finally took place on 15 February. However, he seems to have overlooked a letter of Romano Micheli of 13 February 1644[45] which states that the auditions were to be held on the twenty-first, as well as the actual decree of the twenty-first naming Rovetta as *maestro*. This latter document implies that when the day arrived no audition took place at all. Thus, while Rovetta was finally given the position without opposition, it appears that his 16 years of service as *vice-maestro* were not sufficient to guarantee him Monteverdi's post.

A few special events in Rovetta's career stand out during his tenure as *maestro di cappella*. The most interesting of these—though frustrating because no music survives to illuminate the bare historical facts—surround the composition of his two operas, *Ercole in Lidia* (1645) and *Argiope* (1649). Libretti were printed for both works and provide us with the essential information.[46]

Ercole in Lidia, to a libretto by Count Maiolino Bisaccioni, was performed in 1645 in the Teatro Novissimo in Venice. Rovetta's position as *maestro di cappella* was evidently considered a drawing card, for he is specified as the composer of the opera in the published libretto, a somewhat unusual honor for the period:

La Musica è del Signor Giovanni/Rovetta Mastro [*sic*] di Capella/della Serenissima Re-/publica.

In addition to the statistics from the libretto, we have John Evelyn's description of the visual aspect of the performance:

This night, having . . . taken our places, we went to the Opera, where comedies and other plays are represented in recitative music, by the most excellent musicians, vocal and instrumental, with variety of scenes painted and contrived with no less art of perspective, and machines for flying in the air, and other wonderful motions; taken together, it is one of the most magnificent and expensive diversions the wit of man can invent. The history was, Hercules in Lydia; the scenes changed thirteen times.[47]

The circumstances surrounding *Argiope* are more problematic; indeed, despite a published libretto which explains the manner of its composition, we have no clear documentation that it ever was performed. The libretto was written by P. Michiel and Giovanni Battista Fusconi and dedicated to Anna Renzi,[48] one of the most illustrious singers of the century, in 1645. However, it was not published until 1649, when the rather confused authorship was explained in these two passages (Documents 13 and 14):

> I hope, nonetheless, that the diversity of the [verbal] style, [which is] unfortunately apparent, will be rendered uniform by the incomparable music (although diverse) of the Gentlemen Giovanni Rovetta and Alessandro Leardini, Princes of Modern Musicians, and that the excellence of the most famous voices of the century will cover the faults of my own pen.

> To those who have read [the libretto]: Errors which take place in printing are the children of a Mother who, unfortunately, can be in error herself. For this reason, at the time that they should be corrected, they are indulged still more. The unforeseen events which change the essence of things in a moment, having deprived our Drama of its second glory, which would have been the music of Giovanni Rovetta joined with that of Leardini, will let you enjoy the harmony of a single Orpheus, whereas I had prepared you for [the harmony of] two.

Apparently *Argiope* was originally to be the work of four persons: the two Fusconis, Rovetta and Leardini. For some unknown reason, Rovetta was unable (or chose not) to provide his part of the music, and the entire work was completed by Leardini. Caffi's suggestion that Rovetta's election to the office of *maestro* made him decide to abandon the opera cannot be correct since the election took place five years earlier. We do not know why he abandoned the work.

We do know, of course, that even as *maestro* his work was not confined to St. Mark's. The most complete description of Rovetta's work in other churches is found in the collection of letters written during the years 1647–48 by the young German composer Paul Hainlein to his patron in Nuremberg, Lukas Friedrich Behaim. Two Vespers services for which Rovetta composed (and presumably conducted) the music are described in detail: one in Ss. Giovanni e Paolo, described in a letter of 11 October 1647; and another in San Francesco della Vigna, detailed in a letter of 13 December 1647. Even with the wealth of material from St. Mark's which survives from the seventeenth century, these are among the most detailed descriptions of religious services for the period.[49]

Rovetta was an ordained priest and served first in the church of San Fantino, later in the Congregazione di San Silvestro. San Silvestro was the church in which the instrumentalists' guild met, but we have no record of Rovetta's having any special connection with the guild through his post at San Silvestro. He also held certain additional posts both before and after being appointed *maestro* at St. Mark's. Repeated payments during the 1640s and 1650s are listed for "Zuanne Rovetta" in various capacities: "guardian alle portelle" (24 ducats per year); "guardian di chiesa" (also 24 ducats); and "guardian di procuratia" (20 ducats per year).[50] The payments are listed among those to petty employees of the church and when totaled up, they give Rovetta an extra 68 ducats per year, over one-fifth the salary he received as *maestro*.

Rovetta's will is preserved in the A.S.V.[51] It was drawn up on 16 July 1667 and registered with the notary Francesco Ciola on 2 August of the same year. Most of the will is predictable and unremarkable; Rovetta's property and savings were to be divided between his sister Elena and his nephew Giovanni Battista Volpe *detto* Rovettino. Particularly intriguing, however, are Rovetta's careful plans to have his Requiem Mass for double choir performed in perpetuity both in St. Mark's and in San Silvestro.[52] The type of composition involved, the methods of financing the performance, and the conditions for payment to the singers recall immediately the similar provisions in Cavalli's better known will of eight years later, in which Cavalli took great pains to insure the performance of a double-choir Requiem in his memory in both St. Mark's and San Lorenzo.

Rovetta's plan was quite simple, yet ingenious (Document 16). He left a capital sum of 1,000 ducats to the Procurators which, when invested, would render an income of 45 ducats per annum or 22½ ducats every six months. One half of this sum was to be distributed among the singers and canons of the chapel who, in return, were obliged to sing Rovetta's double-choir Requiem, composed earlier in Bologna, and his motet *Ad Dominum cum tribularer* in St. Mark's.[53] This was to take place during the first half of a given year. During the second half of the year, the other half of the income accruing from the capital sum was to be used to finance a performance of the same work by the same forces in San Silvestro. Rovetta rigidly specified that those singers who did not participate in the performance were not to be paid. Moreover, if at any time the canons and singers failed to perform the Mass, it was to be sung by the sacristans of St. Mark's, who would then receive the 22½ ducats assigned to the others. (Cavalli's Requiem, slightly more expensive, was to be performed at a cost of 30 ducats per occasion, with still more elaborate instructions as to how the money was to be divided up between singers and clergy.)

Rovetta died on 23 October 1668 and was succeeded almost immediately by Cavalli as *maestro di cappella*.[54]

In determining the musical influences which affected Rovetta's compositions, we are in a better position than with Grandi, although the information is still slight. Most important is the preface from his very first
publication, the *Salmi concertati* of 1627, where he states that in these
earliest efforts he has "sought to follow the footprints of a new living
Apollo, upon whose green Mount (.... sovra'l cui verde Monte....) the
true Muses try to take shelter to learn the tones of the exquisite harmon-
ies."[55] Thus the pedagogical relationship between Monteverdi and Rovetta, which would seem implicit under the circumstances, is clarified—
albeit metaphorically—in print. On the other hand, as was the case with
Grandi, there is no mention of Rovetta by name in the vast body of Monteverdi's correspondence which has survived. The one oblique reference
to him comes from a letter to Alessandro Striggio of 10 September 1627,
in which Monteverdi, while describing the benefits of his Venetian service,
mentions that there is a *sotto maestro* to aid him in his work.[56] Since the
letter was written during the period when Rovetta was serving as interim
vice-maestro, before his appointment as Grandi's official successor, he is
clearly the person to whom Monteverdi is referring; but the statement is
brief, vague and not very instructive.

The nature of Rovetta's relationships with Grandi and Cavalli is still
more elusive. As stated above, Seelkopf suggests that a rivalry may have
existed between Rovetta and Grandi, basing his claim on inferences in the
preface to the 1627 *Salmi concertati*. But the evidence is ultimately in-
conclusive. Neither does the dedication to Cavalli of Rovetta's third book
of *Madrigali concertati* (Venice: Vincenti, 1645)[57] define their relationship,
for the collection was assembled by Rovetta's nephew Giovanni Battista
Volpe, for whom Cavalli evidently acted as patron. And although Volpe
also cites Rovetta in the dedication, one cannot tell exactly what role
Rovetta had in preparing the print, nor how he viewed Cavalli. Whatever
the influences on Rovetta, we do know that his reputation lasted well
beyond his death. In fact, a *Messa a Cappella a quattro voci* by Rovetta,
preserved in the Biblioteca Nazionale Marciana, Cod. It. IV-1134 (-10949),
contains a rubric saying that it was performed on Maundy Thursday and
on the Feast of St. Nicholas until the fall of the Venetian Republic in
1797 (Document 17).

Francesco Cavalli

Cavalli's biography is more nearly complete than those of Grandi and
Rovetta. Indeed, his life in the theater has, by now, been documented so

extensively that it will suffice here to provide a description of his activities in the sphere of sacred music alone.[58]

Pietro Francesco Caletti-Bruni was born and baptized in the parish of San Benedetto in Crema on 14 February 1602. The third of nine children, he most probably received his earliest musical education from his father, Giovanni Battista Caletti, *maestro di cappella* at the cathedral of Crema. Giovanni Battista was a fairly skilled composer, for he published a set of *Madrigali a cinque voci* (Venice: Amadino, 1604) and had two works included in Giovanni Battista Leonetti's *Primo Libro de madrigali a cinque voci* (Venice, 1617), which, significantly enough, is dedicated to Federigo Cavalli, Venetian *podestà* in Crema. It was this same Federigo Cavalli who, evidently admiring the voice of young Pietro Francesco, had already taken him to Venice in 1616.

On 18 December 1616 "Pietro Franc.o Bruni cremasco" was accepted as a soprano in the *cappella marciana* and presented to the Doge the following 18 February (Documents 18 and 19). We know that he entered the chapel with the blessing of Monteverdi, for the decree of the Procurators reads as follows:

18 December 1616

Let the *soprani* listed below, one of whom is a eunuch,[59] be admitted as singers in the church of St. Mark's, as they have been heard by the Most Excellent *Signori* [Procurators] and also received a report from the *maestro di cappella* [stating] that they are suitable for the service of the church, with a salary of 80 ducats each, at the consent of the Most Illustrious *Signori* [Procurators].

Pietro Francesco Bruni cremasco
Felice Cazzeleri da pistoia eunuco

On 1 February 1627, "Pier Francesco Caletti" was re-confirmed as a tenor in the *cappella*, and on 1 January 1635 his salary was raised to 100 ducats per annum, the top salary for a singer.

When Giampietro Berti, the second organist of St. Mark's, died, Cavalli participated in the competition for the position with three other contestants. A report of 23 January 1640 states that the Procurators "had the *maestro di cappella* write out some sonatas in *canto fermo* taken from a book brought out from the sacristy" (Document 20), but this is probably an erroneous description of what actually took place. Most probably, rather than playing a written-out work, Cavalli was asked to improvise a four-part sonata on a *cantus firmus*, putting the plainchant successively in each of the four voices and accompanying it with imitative entries in the other three—one of the three traditional tests for an organist at St. Mark's (Document 20, second paragraph).[60]

An overview of all the pertinent documents suggests that Cavalli was made first organist of St. Mark's upon the death of Carlo Fillago in 1645. The accuracy of this date has been open to question. Caffi insists that Massimiliano Neri, who entered the *cappella* on this date, became first organist immediately and that Cavalli did not receive the post until January 1665. This conclusion, however, seems to be based on too literal a reading of the Procurators' decree of 18 December 1644, which states that Neri was elected "organista in Chiesa di San Marco in luoco del *quondam* Carlo Fillago." Caffi, as well as most later scholars, assumed that since Neri was elected "in luoco del q*uondam* Carlo Fillago," who was first organist at the time, Neri immediately became first organist himself.[61] The payment records, overlooked until now, clearly show the opposite. Admittedly, the case is somewhat confused. Neri's first payment was retroactive for "mesi 4 giorni 12"; Cavalli received a pay raise on 19 February 1645 and then was absent from the pay lists for a number of months. However, when the two finally appear on the lists together (29 October and 22 December 1645),[62] Cavalli is always listed first at a salary of 180 ducats per year, Neri second with 150 ducats per year.

During these early years, Cavalli's fame as a singer and organist seems to have equaled his renown as a composer. In the dedication of Rovetta's third book of madrigals (1645), cited above, Giovanni Battista Volpe praises Cavalli's compositional skill in warm terms (Document 22):

> the perfection of your most celebrated compositions is such that you enrapture the souls of all, in churches, in private homes, and in the theater.

But he devotes equal space to Cavalli's versatile achievements as a performing musician:

> The organ of St. Mark's, made divine by the gifted hand of Your Lordship, is [but] the least proof which you make of your great worth . . . and, truly, since three eminent qualities converge in you, [in that] you know how to give [musical] subjects noble clothing, sing them incomparably, and accompany them with graceful care on the instrument, I believe that Your Lordship would not do wrong to put your best compositions to press, [since] the other two privileges you possess—that of singing and accompanying them well—are living treasures, impossible to print.

Similarly, E. G. Zittio, quoted in Nicolò Doglioni's *Le cose notabili, et meravigliose della città di Venetia* (Venice, 1655) praises all three of Cavalli's musical skills:

> Francesco Cavalli truly has no peers in Italy, in the perfection of his singing, in the worth of his organ-playing, and in his exceptional musical compositions, of which those in print bear witness to his merit.[63]

Paul Hainlein, in his letters on the Venetian musical scene in the late 1640s, gives high praise to Cavalli's organ playing. He compares Cavalli favorably with Frescobaldi and complains that he is not heard often enough in Venetian churches.[64]

We have a number of documents concerning Cavalli's activities outside St. Mark's during his years as singer and organist. Arnold has documented his activity as organist at Ss. Giovanni e Paolo, with a salary of 30 ducats per year, from 18 May 1620 until the height of the great plague, sometime in 1630. There are also records of Cavalli's having served as a solo singer for the Feast of St. Roche at the Scuola di San Rocco in 1627.[65] Hainlein's letters tell us that Cavalli played one of three positive organs in a Vespers service at San Francesco della Vigna as well as for a Sunday service in San Geremia, both in 1647. Additional records show Cavalli's organizing musical festivities at the Chiesa dello Spirito Santo for Pentecost in 1637 and serving as the organist at the Fondamenta Nuove for the Feast of Santa Caterina in 1646.[66]

Perhaps the most important religious celebration outside St. Mark's in which Cavalli participated occurred in January 1660, when the Venetian state commemorated the Peace of the Pyrenees. This treaty, which ensured several years of peace between France and Spain, also provided, as a tangible sign of good will, for the marriage of Louis XIV and the Infanta Maria Teresa of Spain, which took place on 8 November 1659. The Venetian state honored the occasion with the performance of a Mass and Te Deum in St. Mark's on 20 January 1660, probably conducted by Rovetta. On the following 25 January, however, the French ambassador Georges d'Ambusson ordered a second Mass and Te Deum to be performed in Ss. Giovanno e Paolo under the direction of Cavalli. The ambassador reported that the music was:

> composed of two different choirs on *palques* or moveable tribunes, composed of thirty of the best voices from the chapel of St. Mark's and of the most celebrated musicians who have come here to sing in the opera this carnival, and of fifteen instruments: *violes*, violins, cornetts, and certain trumpets adjusted to the music, on the order of Monsieur Cavalli, the first man in Italy in his art.

And in a letter to Mazarin, the ambassador continued:

> The music of the Te Deum and of the Mass which I had performed was so excellent that I am truly dismayed that the King cannot have the equal in France, for it would be necessary to bring not only Monsieur Cavalli, a music master held in the highest regard in his art, but also all of the virtuosi who have come here to sing in the operas, and that is not possible.[67]

Cavalli's commission to perform these works was due not only to his reputation in Venice but, no doubt, also to the fact that he had already accepted an offer to go to Paris to compose a festival opera as part of Louis XIV's wedding festivities. Since Cavalli, as organist at St. Mark's, was in the employ of the Doge, his leave had to be approved by the highest governing bodies of the state, and the French ambassador petitioned the Doge before the Full Senate in the following terms (Document 23):[68]

11 April 1660

Since His Majesty wishes to make a magnificent display of joy as part of the solemnities surrounding his marriage to the Most Serene Infanta of Spain, he is searching all over for the most celebrated persons in every perfection, and since he has learned that *Signor* Cavalli, organist in St. Mark's, is a man excellent in composing operas in music, he has commanded me to entreat Your Serenity to concede him the permission to make a journey to France, so that he may employ his talents on this occasion; but since this employment is for a brief time, His Majesty hopes that it please Your Serenity to guarantee him his position and privileges in the church of St. Mark's for the period of time that he will serve in these solemnities.

The Doge's response was short but affirmative, and the Procurators of St. Mark's concealed Cavalli permission to leave the very same day (Document 24).

11 April 1660

Let Francesco Cavalli, organist, be allowed to depart for France when it is requested by the said Ambassador for the solemnities of the marriage of the Most Christian King, and let him remain there until the end of the said solemnities, with the assurance that his position and salary will be retained until his return to this city: this is also the public will of the Most Excellent Senate.

Further on in the decree, two of the singers in the *cappella*, a soprano and a tenor, were granted permission to accompany Cavalli:

Let Giovanni Calegari and Giannagostino Poncelli be allowed to go with the organist Cavalli to serve the Most Christian King on the forthcoming occasion of his nuptials, as the said Cavalli has been allowed.

It was decided that Giovanni Volpe, the nephew of Rovetta and a student of Cavalli, would substitute for him during his absence.

On 20 November 1668, Cavalli was named Rovetta's successor as *maestro di cappella* of St. Mark's. The mode of election was quite a contrast from that employed at the death of Monteverdi, for there is no record of a general search beyond the confines of Venice itself. On 17 November 1668 a notice was put on the large door of St. Mark's, saying that anyone who wanted to compete for the post of *maestro* should declare his candidacy (Document 25). Cavalli was the only contestant, and so three days later he was named the new *maestro* by the Procurators

(Document 26). He was hired at Rovetta's current salary, which was 400 ducats per year, the same fee which Monteverdi had been paid. The extant documents belie the common view that Cavalli was given the post of *maestro* late in his life as a final honor for his service to music in Venice. On the contrary, his election seems to have followed the established rules of St. Mark's, and while there is no evidence that anyone else was considered, neither does Cavalli's election differ from many others in the century. Only the Procurators' description of Cavalli as a

> servant of the Ducal Chapel as organist, to great acclaim and universal satisfaction . . . whose virtue, diligence and merit promise every profit in public service and the advancement of his glory . . .

suggests that the appointment might have held any sentimental value for the church.

Cavalli died sometime between the fourteenth and the twenty-fifth of January, 1676.[69] He was buried at the church of San Lorenzo, in the tomb of the Bishop of Pola, Claudio Sozomeno, his mother's uncle. Cavalli wrote his will on 12 March 1675 and presented it to the notary Demenico Garzoni Paulini on 14 January 1676. This is the will quoted by Caffi and Prunières, which was published complete by Taddeo Wiel in 1914.[70] An earlier will, drawn up before Cavalli's journey to France and nullified in 1675, has not come down to us.

Cavalli's will is elaborate and lengthy—12 pages in the original manuscript. While the majority of its provisions do not concern us here, two passages are of great importance for this study. The first involves the fate of Cavalli's musical manuscripts:

> To *Signor* Zuanne Calliari, my disciple and delegate, I leave the entire furnishings of my study, just as it is, with the bed, paintings, mirror, table, chairs—in sum, everything in the study, which is the ninth room above the alley-way; in addition, all of the original copies of [my] theatrical works, except for those bound in red leather and embossed in gold, and I also leave him the rest of the music, both for private gatherings and for the church.[71]

There is no trace of the manuscripts left to Giovanni Cagliari, and their loss is much to be regretted. They surely contained numerous sacred and chamber works which have not survived in other copies. Moreover, the missing autographs of Cavalli's operas might well have shed more important light on the performance practices of the time than do the extant copies, though a few of these latter are autographs as well. The volumes "bound in red leather and embossed in gold" are, of course, those tomes which found their way into the library of Marco Contarini and, eventually, into the Biblioteca Nazionale Marciana.

The second important passage from the will deals with the performance of Cavalli's Requiem Masses (Document 27). In this matter, Cavalli went a step beyond Rovetta; not only did he provide for a Requiem Mass "à due Chori" to be performed every six months, alternately in St. Mark's and San Lorenzo, but he also established the organizational framework for a large Requiem "in musica concertata" to be performed in San Lorenzo a week after his death.

The large concerted Requiem was to be performed by the "best singers and instrumentalists of the chapel of St. Mark's" and conducted by the new *maestro*, the *vice-maestro*, or some other virtuoso. The total cost was set at 75 ducats; of this sum, 60 ducats were to be paid to the musicians, and the remaining 15 would be spent on "two platforms for the music, the little catafalque, candles on the altar, two candles on the catafalque, and the alms to the priest for the sacrifice of the Mass...." Cavalli specified the following instrumentation for the work: two violins, four *viole*, two cornetts, two theorbos, trombones, *fagotto*, a *violon grosso* which was to be played by Signor Paolo Mancin, three organs, and "singers for the *ripieno*, [chosen] from those in the chapel, as is needed" (Plate 1). It is not clear whether this Requiem was to be a composition by Cavalli himself or the work of another Venetian composer. The specification of exact musical forces has led to the assumption that this Requiem was, indeed, a gargantuan lost work of Cavalli.[72] In his will, however, Cavalli never actually said that it was his own composition. In fact, while discussing the distribution of payments, Cavalli warned the sacristans to give "suitable recognition to that *maestro di cappella*, or other musician, who had the task of the composition of the Mass."[73] To be sure, this is a puzzling statement. Was Cavalli really referring to the work of another composer, or did "the composition of the Mass" mean merely assembling the forces and conducting the performance? The will fails to resolve these questions.

The second Requiem, "à due Chori," was actually composed by Cavalli and has been preserved.[74] It was to be performed twice a year in perpetuity at six-month intervals, once in San Lorenzo and once in St. Mark's. All of the canons of St. Mark's as well as the singers in the chapel were to take part, and each performance would be financed by a sum of 30 ducats. Of this amount, 15 ducats would be given to the *maestro di coro* to divide among the canons; similarly, 15 ducats would be given to the *maestro di cappella* to divide among the musicians. The two *maestri* were to receive double shares, and special provisions were made for the officiating priest, the deacon and sub-deacon, the *custode dei libri*, and for Paolo Mancin, the *violone*-player named also in conjunction with the concerted Requiem, who was to reinforce the bass line.

Plate 1   Cavalli's autograph will, A.S.V., Archivio Notarile, Busta 488
(Testamenti Garzoni Paulini Domenico), no. 206.

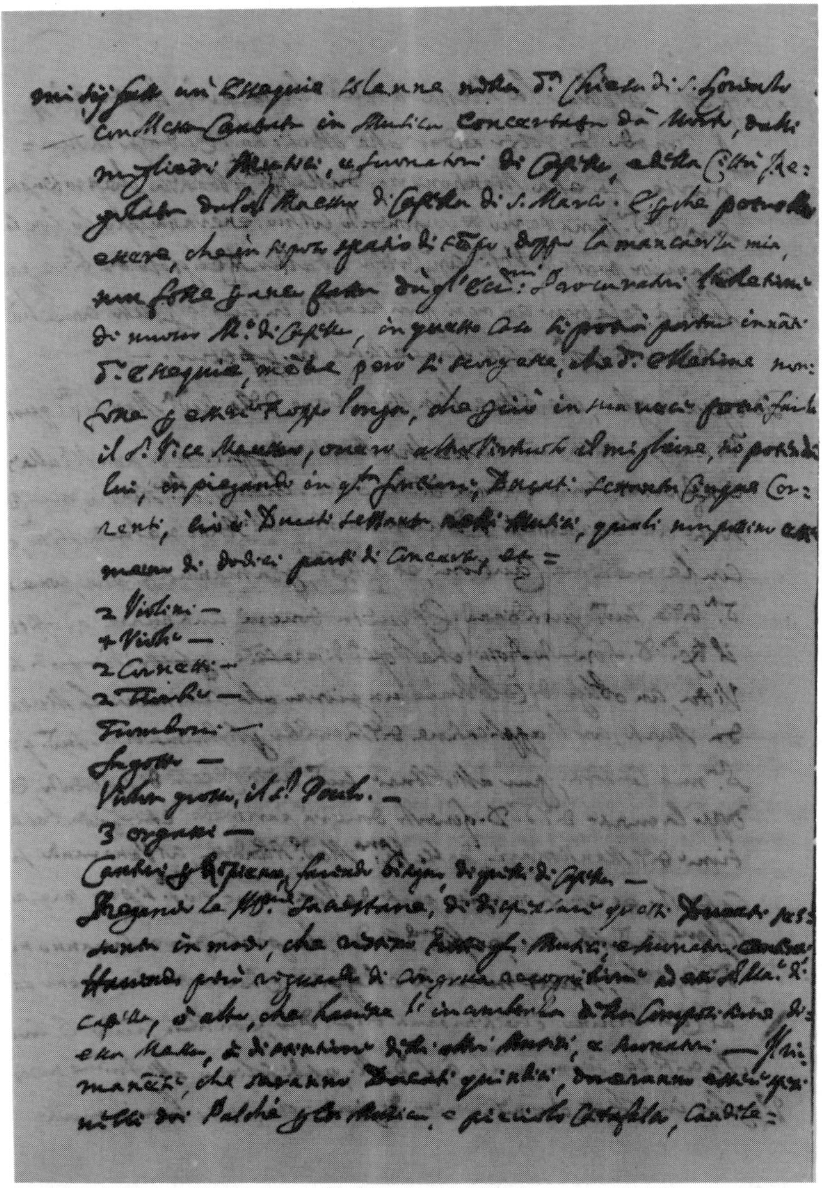

Cavalli's plans for these two Requiems may well have originated in 1667, the date of Rovetta's will. We know, in any case, that they go back at least three years, for the plans are discussed in an extant fragment of yet another will, dated 8 March 1673 (Document 28). This fragment reveals that Cavalli's plans for the two Requiems had originally been somewhat different. In 1673, Cavalli had calculated a sum of 94 ducats for the performance of the Requiem Masses, a figure half again as large as that prescribed in 1676. Of this sum, 54 ducats were to finance a performance of a Requiem "in musica concertata" in San Lorenzo, and six months later the remaining 40 ducats were to finance the Requiem "à due Chori" in St. Mark's. *Both* of these Requiems were to be performed in perpetuity, one every six months. Evidently this plan proved too ambitious, for as we have seen, Cavalli finally requested only one performance of a concerted Requiem and let the simpler double-choir work ensure his immortality.

It should not be forgotten that the biographical outline just presented represents only one facet of Cavalli's life. Far more of his time and energy was expended in the area of opera, for in the thirty-year period between 1639 and 1669 Cavalli wrote no fewer than 32 different works.[75] Although his work in opera took him out of Venice on only one extended occasion (his stay in Paris from 1660 until 1662 for the productions of *Serse* and *Ercole amante*), he also composed works for Milan (*L'Orione*, 1653) and Florence (*Presa d'Argo e gli Amori di Linceo con Hipermestra*, 1658), which may have involved shorter trips for which no documentation survives. In any case, the extant payment lists of the *cappella marciana* for the 1640s and early 1650s indicate that he was away from St. Mark's much of the time. Often his name is absent from the records for as long as six months before he appears to pick up, in a single lump sum, half a year's salary "che non hebbe." While this does not mean that Cavalli was out of the service of the basilica during these periods, the fact that he picked up his salary at such irregular intervals suggests that his attention was clearly directed elsewhere.

Just how extensive Cavalli's commitments to the theater must have been is indicated by a surviving contract between Cavalli and the Venetian impresario Marco Faustini, dated 24 July 1658.[76] The contract bound Cavalli for a three-year period. During this time, Cavalli was to provide Faustini with one new opera each year; he would be paid 400 ducats for each work, the same figure he was later to be paid as *maestro di cappella*. For this sum, he was expected not only to compose the opera, but to copy out all of the necessary parts for the performance, to attend all the rehearsals, to alter or amplify the score if necessary, and to play "first instrument" (i.e., the principal keyboard part) in all of the performances.

Cavalli must have been a facile, instinctive musician to hold down a demanding position at St. Mark's in the midst of ceaseless operatic commitments.

Whether Cavalli was actually a student of Monteverdi or merely a younger colleague is open to question. Monteverdi does not mention Cavalli in his correspondence, nor does Cavalli speak of Monteverdi in the few letters preserved in the A.S.V. In fact, all assumptions regarding their relationship are based upon only two documents: Vincenti's posthumous publication of Monteverdi's late sacred works, the *Messa a quattro Voci, et Salmi* (1650) and the Venice manuscript of Monteverdi's *L'Incoronazione di Poppea*. Materials of both composers are juxtaposed in each source.

Vincenti's collection is noteworthy for its inclusion among the works of Monteverdi of a *Magnificat a 6 voci et due violini*, "Del Signor Francesco Cavalli Organista di San Marco."[77] The presence of this work has led to the assumption that, as Monteverdi's student, Cavalli edited the collection and inserted a composition of his own. While this is a possibility, Vincenti's preface is noncommittal. Moreover, if Cavalli did edit the collection, he was certainly more self-effacing than many editors of the period. One will recall that Giovanni Battista Volpe proclaimed his role as editor vociferously on the title page of Giovanni Rovetta's third madrigal book; and Leonardo Simonetti did the same in the several collections he edited for Vincenti.

One should also note that Cavalli's Magnificat is not an extraneous addition to the collection but completes it liturgically. The bulk of the volume (after the opening Mass in *stile antico*) consists of two sets of psalms—the first for feasts of Our Lord and of Apostles and Evangelists, the second for feasts of the B. V. M., of Virgins, and of Holy Women. The variety of musical styles represented and the varying number of settings for different psalms suggest that the collection was a true "grab bag," i.e., a random group of Vespers compositions which Vincenti arranged in liturgical order without much attention to the resultant stylistic unity. Of course, a Magnificat would be necessary to complete the collection, and it is possible that Vincenti chose Cavalli's work for want of a large-scale Magnificat by Monteverdi; for he states that he had collected these works "non senza miracolo" after Monteverdi's death.

The Venice manuscript of *Poppea* (Biblioteca Nationale Marciana, Cod. t. IV-439 [-9963] is potentially more revealing yet ultimately more confusing. Cavalli's hand is found throughout the manuscript, a fact which led Wolfgang Osthoff to postulate that the Venice manuscript is the heavily edited score for a revival of *Poppea* which Cavalli mounted in 1646.[78] While this may be the case, it does not elucidate the relationship between the two men with any certainty. Nor can we deduce anything conclusive from the fact, also noted by Osthoff, that Cavalli used the bass-line from the opening *sinfonia* of *Poppea* as a foundation upon which to build the *sinfonia* for his own *Doriclea* in 1645.

It is, nonetheless, difficult to deny that Cavalli must have grown up under the musical tutelage of Monteverdi. We have noted above that Monteverdi personally approved Cavalli's entrance into the *cappella* (Document 18) and also supervised the auditions for second organist in 1640 (Document 20). The style of Cavalli's Magnificat in Monteverdi's collection of 1650 draws freely upon the idiom of the older composer's works for St. Mark's. Moreover, whatever the significance of Cavalli's hand in one of the *Poppea* sources may be, it would be difficult to conceive of the bulk of Cavalli's operas of the 1640s and 1650s without the monumental examples of *Poppea* and *Ulisse*. As was the case with Grandi and Rovetta, there is no irrefutable documentation for Monteverdi's musical influence upon Cavalli. The circumstances argue for it, however, and so do the remarkable compositions which the two men wrote for St. Mark's.

II

The Sources of the Music

A study of the Vespers music of Grandi, Rovetta and Cavalli entails the examination of four categories of sources: printed collections of their psalms and Magnificats; printed collections of their motets; printed sacred anthologies of the period, which contain isolated motet compositions of the three composers; and manuscript sources.

Most important are the composers' 10 printed collections of psalms and Magnificats, which span the middle two quarters of the century—1627 to 1675, to be exact. Except for Rovetta's first published collection, hastily put together to ensure him the post of *vice-maestro di cappella*, and Grandi's final collection, a somewhat haphazard volume assembled by Vincenti, the collections are not random assemblages but rather discrete musical breviaries from which one can extract the psalms prescribed for a number of complete services. Thus, these collections provide well-defined sets of the most important music for Vespers. Although the performing forces and musical style vary strikingly from print to print, their uniformity within a single collection ensures that the psalms and Magnificats for any given service can be performed by a stable, fixed body of musicians.

These 10 prints form the core of the musical repertoire of Vespers at St. Mark's during the mid-seventeenth century and are the basis for the chapter on the musical repertoire of the basilica which closes this study. They do not encompass all Vespers music, however, for a number of liturgical items are conspicuously absent: hymns, psalm antiphons, Magnificat antiphons and Marian antiphons.[79] As mentioned above, these items are found in the motet collections of the period, which also contain items from the Proper of the Mass and from the lesser offices as well as a host of non-liturgical pieces. Fifteen of these motet collections have been examined: 11 of Grandi and 4 of Rovetta. Cavalli published no independent motet collections, although he published a number of motets in his *Musiche Sacre* of 1656.

Because of the extent of the material—25 printed collections devoted exclusively to the sacred music of Grandi, Rovetta and Cavalli—I have not examined the remaining two categories of sources in exhaustive detail: the sacred anthologies of the period and the manuscript sources, both of which contain a few isolated compositions. For the works of Grandi and Rovetta in these sources, I have taken the researches of others as my basis and done as much "spot checking" as possible with the sources themselves.[80] On the other hand, for Cavalli, who occupies such a central position in this study, I have searched out every isolated sacred work, no matter what its source.

Alessandro Grandi

The sources of Grandi's music pose greater problems than those of Rovetta or Cavalli for two reasons: first, his three psalm collections were all published after he became *maestro di cappella* at Santa Maria Maggiore, Bergamo and, thus, must be examined carefully to determine their relationship to the traditions of St. Mark's; and second, the motet collections form several series which are a bibliographic tangle.

Grandi's three collections of psalms and Magnificats appeared during the last years of his life, one in 1629 and two in 1630. The fact that his published sacred works consisted entirely of motet collections during his years in Ferrara and Venice has led Arnold to insist that these three collections of psalms and Magnificats represent music written during the last three years of his life for Santa Maria Maggiore in Bergamo.[81] However, it is by no means certain that all of the works in these prints were written during Grandi's Bergamo years, despite the dates of their publication. On the contrary, only the composition of the *Messa e Salmi concertati a tre voci* (Venice: Vincenti, 1630) can definitely be ascribed to Grandi's years in Bergamo. Nor can we accept Arnold's argument that Grandi may have sought out the position in Bergamo expressly to be able to write large-scale music for Mass and Vespers—opportunities presumably denied him in his post as *vice-maestro* at St. Mark's. This argument appears less persuasive in light of the knowledge that Rovetta published three elaborate collections of Mass and Vespers music during his years as *vice-maestro*.

Grandi's first collection of Vespers music was published as follows:

(RISM G 3453) .... SALMI / A OTTO BREVI / CON IL PRIMO CHORO/CONCERTATO./DEL SIGNOR ALESSANDRO GRANDI/MAESTRO DI CAPPELLA IN SANTA MARIA/MAGGIORE DI BERGAMO./Raccolti, et nuovamente dati in luce da Alessandro Vincenti, Et dedicati Al Molto Illustre, et Reverendissimo/P. D. AURELIO POLICANTI DA VERONA. ABBATE GENERALE/DELLA CONGREGATIONE CAMALDOLENSE. CON LICENZA DE'

SUPERIORI, ET PRIVILEGIO./(device)/IN VENETIA./Appresso Alessandro Vincenti. MDCXXIX.

TAVOLA DELLI SALMI/A OTTO BREVI/CON IL PRIMO CHORO CONCER-TATO./DI ALESSANDRO GRANDI.[82]

Domine ad adiuvandum.	1
Dixit Dominus. Primi Toni.	1
Confitebor tibi Domine. Secundi Toni.	3
Beatus vir qui timet Dominum. Tertij Toni.	5
Laudate pueri Dominum. Quarti Toni.	6
Laudate Dominum. Sexti Toni.	8
In exitu Israel de Aegyptu. Proprij Toni.	8
Laetatus sum in quae. [sic] Secundi Toni.	11
Nisi Dominus. Quinti Toni.	13
Lauda Ierusalem Dominum. Octavi Toni.	15
Credidi propter. Quarti Toni.	16
In Convertendo Dominus. Secundi Toni.	17
Domine probasti. Primi Toni.	19
De profundis Clamavi. Septimi Toni.	22
Beati omnes. Primi Toni. Senza intonazione.	23
Memento Domine. Tertij Toni.	24
Magnificat. Secundi Toni. Senza intonazione.	26
Dixit Dominus Domino. A 10.	28
Magnificat Anima mea. A. 10.	31

Partbooks: I: C, A, T, B; II: C, A, T, B; Basso continuo
Location:
    Kremsmünster, Benediktiner-Stift: complete
    Bologna, Civico Museo Bibliografico Musicale: complete
    Bologna, Archivio di San Petronio: complete
    Spoleto, Archivio del Duomo: I: B; II: A, T, B; Basso continuo
    Piacenza, Archivio del Duomo: Basso continuo[83]
    Vercelli, Archivio del Duomo (Biblioteca Capitolare):
        I: A, T, B; II: C, A, T; Basso continuo

(RISM G 3454) reprint: 1640

Location:
    Naples, Archivio Musicale della Comunità Oratoriana dei Padri Filippini: complete
    Rome, Archivio di San Giovanni in Laterano: complete
    Wroclaw, Biblioteka Uniwersytecka: I; B; II: C, A, B.

The works in this collection are for two four-part choirs and basso continuo. The parts for the first choir (".... il primo choro concerato....") are written in a soloistic style and were surely meant to be sung by individual singers, with massed voices performing the music of the second choir.[84] Two works in the collection—the final *Dixit Dominus* and Magnificat—have parts for an obbligato violin and trombone. Roche has shown that these instruments were the very two included in the permanent chapel of Santa Maria Maggiore at the time and, on that basis, suggests that the entire collection was written for Bergamo.[85] Similarly, Seelkopf considers the compositions to have been intended for Bergamo because of the designation "brevi," their relative simplicity, the intonations and the choice of psalms.[86] All of these statements can be challenged.

First of all, Roche's indication that the final *Dixit* and Magnificat were written for the forces at Bergamo does not mean that the remainder of the collection, works scored for somewhat different forces, was intended for the same church. In fact, the two final pieces may well have been *addenda* to a body of works already in existence, for the 15 settings without instruments are a complete set in themselves, covering the most important Vespers services for the church year. Moreover, the fact that the collection was edited not by Grandi but by Vincenti may indicate that the contents were not composed in a single sweep; on the contrary, the works may have been written at various times and only collected by Vincenti in 1629, with or without Grandi's assistance.

Seelkopf's allegations are still more questionable. The fact that these works are *salmi brevi* does not necessarily identify them exclusively with Bergamo, since Monteverdi, Rovetta and Cavalli all wrote *salmi brevi* for St. Mark's. Indeed, all of the works by these latter composers show the relative simplicity, the uniformity of texture, and the use of intonations which Seelkopf associates with a simpler *milieu* than that of the ducal chapel. Documentary evidence also suggests that such relatively simple music for double choir may have had a special place in the repertoire of the *cappella marciana*. A passage in a *ceremoniale* of 1678, which lists the days and services at which the musicians of the *cappella* must appear, states that "every time that the Pala [d'oro] is opened, the [singers and organists] are obligated to perform Vespers in two choirs, with psalms set for eight voices . . . ." (Document 29). Thus, there was a perennial need for simple, double-choir settings of the psalms for Vespers, and Grandi's 1629 psalm collection may have been designed expressly to fill this need.

Similarly puzzling is Seelkopf's statement that the choice of psalm links the collection to Bergamo. While he assigns some of the psalms to Vespers and some to Lauds (which strictly speaking is not incorrect), there is actually no psalm in the collection that is not a part of the Roman Vespers service. Although the liturgy of St. Mark's differed in subtle ways from the Roman rite, all of the psalms set here by Grandi can be found in the lavish printed psalter for St. Mark's published in 1609 under the direction of *maestro di coro* Giovanni Stringa.[87] Thus, from a liturgical point of view, there is really no indication that these works could not have been used in St. Mark's. Indeed, the very medium for which the major part of the collection is scored—two four-part choirs, one of which is a choir of soloists—is a medium which has an important place in the history of psalmody at St. Mark's. Bartolomeo Bonifacio's *Rituum Ecclesiasticorum Ceremoniale*, a work which was the authority for ceremony in St. Mark's from its first redaction in 1564 through 1677, tells us that the standard method of performing double-choir psalms is to have the singers "divided into two choirs, that is, four singers in one choir, and all the rest in the other."[88]

Two psalm collections by Grandi were published in 1630. The first was edited by Grandi himself:

(RISM G 3458) .... MESSA, E SALMI/CONCERTATI/A TRE VOCI/DI ALESSANDRO GRANDI/MAESTRO DI CAPELLA IN SANTA/MARIA MAGGIORE DI BERGAMO./NOVAMENTE COMPOSTI ET DATI IN LUCE./Con licenza de' Superiori, et Privilegio./DEDICATI/Alli Molto Illustri miei Signori Osservandissimi/IL MOLTO REVER.do SIG. D. PIETRO CANONICO./ET IL SIG. PAOLO FRATELLI MORANDI./(device)/IN VENETIA. Appresso Alessandro Vincenti. MDCXXX.

TAVOLA DELLA MESSA E SALMI/CONCERTATI A TRE VOCI./DI ALESSANDRO GRANDI

<table>
<tr><td>MESSA.</td><td>1</td></tr>
<tr><td>Dixit Dominus Domino meo.</td><td>7</td></tr>
<tr><td>Confitebor tibi Domine.</td><td>9</td></tr>
<tr><td>Beatus vir qui timet Dominum.</td><td>11</td></tr>
<tr><td>Laudate pueri Dominum.</td><td>14</td></tr>
<tr><td>Laetatus sum in his quae dicta.</td><td>16</td></tr>
<tr><td>Nisi Dominus aedificaverit domum.</td><td>16</td></tr>
<tr><td>Lauda Hierusalem Dominum.</td><td>21</td></tr>
<tr><td>Laudate Dominum omnes gentes</td><td>22</td></tr>
<tr><td>Magnificat.</td><td>23</td></tr>
</table>

Partbooks: C I, C II, B; Basso per l'organo
Location:
　　Bologna, Civico Museo Bibliografico Musicale: complete
　　Rome, Biblioteca Apostolica Vaticana (Casimiri): B

(RISM G 3459) reprint: 1637

Location:
　　Wroclaw, Biblioteka Uniwersytecka: C I, C II
　　Chapel Hill (USA), University of North Carolina Music Library: C II

This collection is the only one of Grandi's three psalm collections whose contents were definitely composed during his years in Bergamo. In the dedication, Grandi says that the works date from his sojourn, two years before, at the home of Pietro and Paulo Morandi in Val Breno, an area just northeast of Bergamo.

Grandi's third set of Vespers psalms was edited by Leonardo Simonetti, a singer in the chapel of St. Mark's. This was not the first time Simonetti had occasion to edit Grandi's works; in 1619, he edited Grandi's fifth book of motets and six years later included four works of Grandi in his celebrated anthology of sacred monody, the *Ghirlanda Sacra* (Venice: Magni, 1625). The title page of Grandi's Vespers collection reads as follows:

(RISM G 3460) .... RACCOLTA/TERZA/Di Leonardo Simonetti Musico nella Capella/della Serenissima Republica./DE MESSA ET SALMI/DEL SIG. ALESSANDRO GRANDI/Et Gio. [Croce] Chiozotto à 2. 3. 4./con Basso continuo./Aggiontovi li Ripieni à beneplacito./Con Licenza de' Superiori./ET PRIVILEGIO./ (device)/STAMPA DEL GARDANO./IN VENETIA M. DC. XXX./Appresso Bartholomeo Magni.

TAVOLA./Della Messa et Salmi di Alessandro Grandi à 2. 3. 4./con il Basso continuo, et con li ripieni à be-/neplacito, con un Laudate à 4. in/Ecco di Gio: Croce Chiozotto.

Messa	A 3 overo à 4	1
Dixit	A 4	4
Dixit in ritornelo	A 3	6
Confitebor	A 3	11
Beatus vir	A 4	13
Laudate Pueri	A 3	16
Laudate Pueri in ecco di Gio: Chiozotto	A 4	18
Laudate Dominum omnes gentes	A 2	20
Laudate Pueri 4. Toni	A 4	21
Nisi Dominus	A 4	23
Beatus vir	A 4	24
Laetatus sum	A 4	25
Lauda Hierusalem	A 4	28

Partbooks: C, A, T, B; Basso continuo; 6 books of "ripieni de voci overo instrumenti," marked A through F. (C, A, T, B, Basso continuo all published in 1630; parts for "ripieni" published in 1632).

Location:
Bologna, Civico Museo Bibliografico Musicale: complete

(RISM G 3461) reprint, in several installments: A, T, and B reprinted in 1635; C and Basso continuo reprinted in 1636; parts for *ripieni* reprinted in 1647.

Location:
Vienna, Bibliothek der Gesellschaft der Musikfreunde: complete
Glasgow, Euing Musical Library, University of Glasgow: S
Wroclaw, Biblioteka Uniwersytecka: S; Basso continuo

The unity of Grandi's two preceding psalm collections is not found in Simonetti's *Raccolta*, which forms neither a liturgical whole nor a body of music set for a stable combination of musical forces. On the contrary, the absence of a Magnificat, the inclusion of two settings of *Dixit Dominus* and three of *Laudate pueri* (one by Giovanni Croce) suggests that the set was not conceived as a whole but rather put together by Simonetti from a number of sources that happened to be available to him.

The musical settings—two to four *obbligato* voices supplemented by a number of optional vocal or instrumental parts—are representative of the trend to make any sacred collection adaptable to as many performing situations as possible. The immediate ancestor of this practice is Giovanni Ghizzolo's collection of *Messa, Salmi, Letanie.... a 5 ò 9* (1619), whose contents can be performed by either one choir of five voices or two choirs totalling nine voices. And the tradition has its origins in such collections as Viadana's *Salmi a quattro chori* (Venice: Giacomo Vincenti, 1612), whose contents can be performed either by two or by four choirs, and Giovanni Croce's *Sacrae cantilene concertate a tre, a cinque, et sei voci, con i suoi ripieni a Quattro voci* (1610), whose compositions call for three to six *obbligato* solo voices as well as an optional four-part choir.[89]

Two of the works in Simonetti's collection of 1630 can be linked with Grandi's years in Bergamo. The *Laudate pueri a 3*, set for two tenors and bass, is the same as the *Laudate pueri* that appears in a setting for two sopranos and tenor in the *Messa e Salmi concertati a tre voci*, also of 1630. Moreover, the use of a single violin or cornetto as the *obbligato* instrument for the *Confitebor a 3* does suggest the make-up of the chapel at Bergamo, with its single violin and single trombone.

Grandi's 11 collections of motets were not published in a single series. Instead, they were segregated into two groups—motets with *obbligato* instrumental parts and motets for voices with basso continuo alone—and were printed as two numbered series and two miscellaneous prints.

The largest group are the motets for two to eight voices without *obbligato* instrumental parts. These span Grandi's entire creative life—1610 to 1630—and were printed in the following collections:

(RISM G 3417) .... IL PRIMO LIBRO/DE MOTETTI/A Due, Tre, Quattro, Cinque, et Otto Voci, con una/Messa à Quattro Voci/Accommodati per cantarsi nell'Organo, Clavicembalo,/Chitarrone, ò altro simile Stromento./Con il Basso per sonare/DI ALESSANDRO GRANDI/Maestro di Cappella Del Spirito/Santo in Ferrara./Nuovamente dati in luce./CON PRIVILEGIO./(device)/IN VENETIA. /Appresso Giacomo Vincenti. MDCX.

Partbooks: C, A, T, B; Basso continuo
Location:
   Bologna, Civico Museo Bibliografico Musicale: C, A, T, B
   Bologna, Archivio di San Petronio: B
   Parma, Biblioteca Palatina (Conservatorio Arrigo Boito): S (incomplete copy)

(RISM G 3418) reprint: 1617
Location:
Oxford, Library of Christ Church College: complete
Bologna, Civico Museo Bibliografico Musicale: Basso continuo
Bologna, Archivio di San Petronio: C, A, T

(RISM G 3419) reprint: 1618
Location:
Regensburg, Proskesche Musikbibliothek: complete
Bologna, Civico Museo Bibliografico Musicale: A
Ferrara, Biblioteca comunale Ariostea: complete

(RISM G 3420) reprint: 1621, Alessandro Vincenti
Location:
Brussels, Bibliothèque Royale Albert ler: complete[90]
Münster, Bischöfliches Priesterseminar und Santini Sammlung: complete

(RISM 3421) reprint: 1628
Location:
Paris, Bibliothèque nationale: complete
Oxford, Library of Christ Church College: complete
Bologna, Civico Museo Bibliografico Musicale: complete
Naples, Archivio Musicale della Comunità Oratoriana dei Padri Filippini: complete
Rome, Archivio di San Giovanni in Laterano: complete
Wroclaw, Bibliotecka Uniwersytecka: complete set, but C partbook incomplete

(RISM G 3422) .... IL SECONDO LIBRO/DE MOTETTI, A DUE TRE/ET QUAT-
TRO VOCI./Con il suo Basso per sonar nell'Organo./DI ALESSANDRO
GRANDI/Maestro di Capella nello Spirito/Santo in Ferrara./Nuovamente dati in
luce./CON PRIVILEGIO/(device)/IN VENETIA./APPRESSO Giacomo Vincenti.
MDCXIII

Partbooks: C, A, T, B; Basso continuo
Location:
Bologna, Civico Museo Bibliografico Musicale: B

(RISM G 3423) reprint: 1617[91]
Location:
Regensburg, Proskesche Musikbibliothek: complete
Bologna, Civico Museo Bibliografico Musicale: C; Basso continuo

(RISM G 3424) reprint: 1619, Alessandro Vincenti
Location:
Brussels, Bibliothèque Royale Albert ler: complete[92]
Münster, Bischöfliches Priesterseminar und Santini Sammlung: B
Cesena, Biblioteca comunale Malatestiana: C, B; Basso continuo

(RISM G 3425) reprint: 1623
Location:
Münster, Bischöfliches Priesterseminar und Santini Sammlung: C, A, T; Basso
continuo
London, British Library: C
Bologna, Civico Museo Bibliografico Musicale: complete
Siena, Biblioteca dell'Accademia Musicale Chigiana: C, A, T; Basso continuo

(RISM G 3426) reprint: 1628
Location:
Paris, Bibliothèque nationale: complete
Oxford, Library of Christ Church College: complete
Naples, Archivio Musicale della Comunità Oratoriana dei Padri Filippini: complete
Wroclaw, Biblioteka Uniwersytecka: complete

(RISM G 3436) .... IL TERZO LIBRO/DE MOTETTI A DUE, TRE,/ET QUATTRO VOCI/Con le Letanie della B. V. à Cinque Voci/et il suo Basso per l'Organo/DI ALESSANDRO GRANDI/Musico della Serenissima Signoria di/Venetia in S. Marco/Novamente con ogni diligenza corrette, et ristampata./CON PRIVILE-GIO./(device)/IN VENETIA./Appresso Giacomo Vincenti MDCXVIII.

Partbooks: C, A, T, B; Basso continuo
Location:
Regensburg, Proskesche Musikbibliothek: complete
Ferrara, Biblioteca comunale Ariostea: complete
Bologna, Civico Museo Bibliografico Musicale: complete

(The first edition of this collection was printed in 1614. The only known surviving copy was destroyed in Berlin during the Second World War.)

(RISM G 3437) reprint: 1621, Alessandro Vincenti
Location:
Brussels, Bibliothèque Royale Albert ler: complete
Münster, Bischöfliches Priesterseminar und Santini Sammlung: complete
London, British Library: C
Naples, Archivio Musicale della Comunità Oratoriana dei Padri Filippini: complete

(RISM G 3438) reprint: 1636
Location:
Paris, Bibliothèque nationale: complete
Bologna, Civico Museo Bibliografico Musicale: complete
Wroclaw, Biblioteka Uniwersytecka: A, T, B

(RISM G 3431) .... IL QUARTO LIBRO/DE MOTETTI/ A DUE TRE QUATTRO/ ET SETTE VOCI/Con il Basso Continuo per sonar nell'Organo./DI ALESSAN-DRO GRANDI/Maestro di Capella nel Duomo di Ferrara./Dedicati All'Illustrissimo, et Reverendissimo Signor Cardinal Leni/Vescovo di Ferrara:/(device)/IN VENE-TIA, Apresso Giacomo Vincenti. 1616.

Partbooks: C, A, T, B; Basso continuo
Location:
London, Westminster Abbey: complete
Bologna, Civico Museo Bibliografico Musicale: complete
Verona, Biblioteca Capitolare (Cattedrale): B

(RISM G 3432) reprint: 1618
Location:
Regensburg, Proskesche Musikbibliothek: complete
Bologna, Civico Museo Bibliografico Musicale: A, T; Basso continuo

(RISM G 3433) reprint ("quinta impressione" [*sic*]): Palermo: Giovanni Battista Maringo, 1620
Location:
   Naples, Archivio Musicale della Comunità Oratoriana dei Padri Filippini: complete

(RISM G 3434) reprint ("quinta impressione" [*sic*]): 1621, Alessandro Vincenti
Location:
   Münster, Bischöflisches Priesterseminar und Santini Sammlung: C, A, T; Basso continuo continuo
   Paris, Bibliothèque nationale (fonds du Conservatoire de musique): Basso continuo
   London, British Library: C
   Bologna, Civico Museo Bibliografico Musicale: C, T,
   Cesena, Biblioteca comunale Malatestiana: A, T; Basso continuo (two copies)
   Ferrara, Biblioteca comunale Ariostea: complete
   Washington, Library of Congress: C, A, T, B.

(RISM G 3435) reprint ("quinta impressione" [*sic*]): 1628
Location:
   Munich, Bayerische Staatsbibliothek: T
   Oxford, Library of Christ Church College: C, A, T, B; Basso continuo
   Vercelli, Archivio del Duomo (Biblioteca capitolare): complete
   Wroclaw, Biblioteka Uniwersytecka: A, B

(RISM G 3439) .... CELESTI/FIORI/DEL SIG./ALESSANDRO GRANDI/LIBRO QUINTO/De suoi/Concerti à 2. 3. 4. Voci. Con alcune/Cantilene nel fine./Raccolti da Lunardo Simonetto Cantor nella/Capella di S. Marco in Venetia./CON PRIVILEGIO./Stampa del Gardano./In Venetia Appresso Bartolomeo Magni. 1619.

Partbooks: C, A, T, B; Basso continuo
Location:
   Regensburg, Proskesche Musikbibliothek: complete
   Bologna, Civico Museo Bibliografico Musicale: complete
   Cesena, Biblioteca comunale Malatestiana: B; Basso continuo

(RISM G 3440) reprint: 1620
Location:
   Bologna, Civico Museo Bibliografico Musicale: A, T; Basso continuo

(RISM G 3441) reprint: 1625
Location:
   Paris, Bibliothèque nationale (fonds du Conservatoire de Musique): Basso continuo
   London, British Library: complete
   Bologna, Civico Museo Bibliografico Musicale: complete

(RISM G 3442) reprint: 1638
Location:
   Oxford, Library of Christ Church College: complete
   Naples, Archivio Musicale della Comunità Oratoriana dei Padri Filippini: complete
   Wroclaw, Biblioteka Uniwersytecka: C, A, B; Basso continuo.

(RISM G 3455) .... IL SESTO LIBRO/DE MOTETTI/A DUE, TRE, QUATTRO VOCI/DI ALESSANDRO GRANDI/Maestro di Cappella in S. Maria Maggiore di Bergamo/DEDICATI/All'Eminentissimo, et Reverendissimo Prencipe/IL SIGNOR CARDINAL FRANCESCO DIETRICHSTAIN./OPERA VIGESIMA./Con licenza de' Superiori, et Privilegio./(device)/IN VENETIA,/Appresso Alessandro Vincenti. MDCXXX.

Partbooks: C, A, T, B; Basso continuo
Location:
    Oxford, Library of Christ Church College: complete
    Bologna, Civico Museo Bibliografico Musicale. A, T, B, Basso continuo
    Orvieto, Archivio musicale del Duomo: B

(RISM G 3456) reprint: 1637
Location:
    Bologna, Civico Museo Bibliografico Musicale: C (incomplete)
    Naples, Archivio Musicale della Comunità Oratoriana dei Padri Filippini: complete
    Orvieto, Archivio musicale del Duomo: B
    Wroclaw, Biblioteka Uniwersytecka: A, T, B; Basso continuo

(RISM G 3457) reprint: Liber sextus motectorum duabus, tribus, et quatuor vocibus cantandorum, cum basso continuo . . . opus vigesimus. Antwerpen, les héritiers de Pierre Phalèse, 1640.
Location:
    London, British Library: T

A second series of numbered volumes begins with Grandi's arrival in Venice. These are works for one, two or four voices and continuo with *obbligato* parts for two violins. The series consists of three collections, two published during the years of Grandi's service at St. Mark's, one during his years in Bergamo:

(RISM G 3445)[93] .... MOTETTI/A UNA, ET DUE/VOCI/Con Sinfonie d'Istromenti Partiti per cantar, et/sonar co'l Chitarrone/DI ALESSANDRO GRANDI/Vice Maestro di Capella della Serenissima Signoria/di Venetia in S. Marco./Novamente dati in luce./CON PRIVILEGIO./Dedicati All'Illustrissimo, et Reverendissimo Monsignor/Gio: Francesco Morosini Abbate di Leno, et Canonico di Padoa. [Libro Primo]/(device)/In Venetia, Appresso Alessandro Vincenti. 1621.

Partbooks: C I, C II, Vl I, Vl II; Basso per l'organo.
Location:
    Bologna, Civico Museo Bibliografico Musicale: C I, C II; Basso per l'organo
    Milan, Biblioteca del Conservatorio "Giuseppe Verdi": Vl I, Vl II

(RISM G 3446) reprint: 1626
Location:
    Munich, Bayerische Staatsbibliothek: C II
    Paris, Bibliothèque nationale: Vl I, Vl II; Basso per l'organo
    London, British Library: C I
    Piacenza, Archivio del Duomo: VI, I, VI II[94]

Wroclaw, Biblioteka Uniwersytecka: Vl I, Vl II

(RISM G 3447) reprint: 1637
Location:
Bologna, Civico Museo Bibliografico Musicale: Vl I, Vl II; Basso per l'organo

(RISM G 3448) .... MOTETTI/A UNA, DUE,/E QUATTRO VOCI/Con Sinfonie d'Istromenti Partiti per cantare, et sonar co'l Chitarrone./DI ALESSANDRO GRANDI/Nuovamente ristampati, et corretti./CON PRIVILEGIO./LIBRO SECONDO./(device)/IN VENETIA,/Appresso Alessandro Vincenti./MDCXXV.

The first edition of this collection is not known to be extant. It appeared sometime between 1621 and 1625.

Partbooks: C I, C II, Vl I, Vl II; Basso per l'organo
Location:
Munich, Bayerische Staatsbibliothek: C II
Lodi, Biblioteca comunale Laudense: Vl I, Vl II
Milan, Biblioteca del Conservatorio "Giuseppe Verdi": Vl I, Vl II
Wroclaw, Biblioteka Uniwersytecka: Vl I

(RISM G 3449) reprint: 1637[95]
Location:
Bologna, Civico Museo Bibliografico Musicale: complete

(RISM G 3450) .... MOTETTI/A UNA, ET DUE VOCI/CON SINFONIE/DI DUE VIOLINI/Et il Basso Continuo per l'Organo./DI ALESSANDRO GRANDI/Maestro di Capella in Santa Maria Maggiore di Bergamo/Nuovamente composti, et dati in luce./LIBRO TERZO./CON LICENZA DE' SUPERIORI, ET PRIVILEGIO./(device)/IN VENETIA,/Appresso Alessandro Vincenti. MDCXXIX.[96]

Partbooks: C I, C II, Vl I, Vl II; Basso continuo
Location:
Bologna, Civico Museo Bibliografico Musicale: complete
Vercelli, Archivio del Duomo (Biblioteca capitolare): Vl I, Vl II
London, British Library: C I
Oxford, Library of Christ Church College: complete

(RISM G 3451) reprint: 1637
Location:
Bologna, Civico Museo Bibliografico Musicale: complete

(RISM G 3452) reprint: Cantiones sacrae una, duabus, quatuor, quinque vocibus, et duobus violinis, cum basso continuo ad organum . . . liber tertius. Antwerpen, les héritiers de Pierre Phalèse, 1639.
Location:
The Hague, Gemeentemuseum, Muziekafdeling: C II
Washington, Library of Congress: C II

Two additional collections of motets were published independently without being assigned to a series. The first was edited by Placido Marcelli, the dedicatee of Grandi's *Primo Libro de Motetti* of 1610. After Grandi moved to Venice, the entire collection was reprinted twice in 1620. The first reprint was by Magni; the second was by Vincenti and included an *aggionta* of six more motets—two by Alvise Grani, one by Giovanni Croce, and three by Grandi himself.

(RISM G 3427) Motetti a cinque voci, con le letanie della Beata Vergine.... raccolti da Placido Marcelli. Ferrara, Vittorio Baldini, 1614.

Partbooks: C, A, T, B, Quintus; Basso continuo
Location:
Bologna, Civico Museo Bibliografico Musicale: T, B, Quintus

(RISM G 3428) reprint: 1620, Bartholomeo Magni
Location:
Piacenza, Archivio del Duomo: A, T, B, Quintus; Basso continuo[97]

(RISM G 3429) reprint: .... MOTETTI/A CINQUE VOCI/CON LE LETANIE DELLA/BEATA VERGINE/DEL SIGNOR/ALESSANDRO GRANDI/Novamente ristampati corretti dal medesimo/Con l'Aggionta di Motetti di diversi Auttori./A 2. 3. 4. et Otto Voci/Con il Basso Continuo per sonar nell'Organo./Raccolti da Alessandro Vincenti./Con Privilegio, et licenza de' Superiori./(device)/IN VENETIA. Appresso Alessandro Vincenti. 1620.

Location:
Bologna, Civico Museo Bibliografico Musicale: complete
Piacenza, Archivio del Duomo: A, T, B, Quintus; Basso continuo[98]
Siena, Accademia Musicale Chigiana: T
Spello (Perugia), Archivio di Santa Maria Maggiore (Collegiata): Basso continuo
Vercelli, Archivio del Duomo (Biblioteca capitolare): C, A, T, B, Quintus
Uppsala, Universitetsbibliotek: A, B, Quintus[99]

The second independent volume is Grandi's only collection devoted exclusively to motets for solo voice:

(RISM G 3443) .... DEL SIGNOR/ALESSANDRO/GRANDI/V. MAESTRO DI CAPELLA/Della Serenissima Signoria/Di Venetia./MOTETTI A VOCE SOLA/CON PRIVILEGIO/DEDICATI/ALL'ILL. MO ET REV. MO SIG.or/MARC'ANTONIO CORNARO/Abbate Primiciero di S. Marco/(device)/STAMPA DEL GARDANO./IN VENETIA M DC XXI/Appresso Bartholomeo Magni./

Partbooks: one single volume, vocal line plus basso continuo in score
Location:
London, British Library

(RISM G 3444) reprint: 1628, Bartholomeo Magni
Location:

Durham, Cathedral Library
Oxford, Library of Christ Church College
Trieste, Biblioteca civica
Wroclaw, Biblioteka Uniwersytecka

Those works of Grandi preserved in sacred anthologies of the period and in contemporary manuscripts do not add anything to the canon of his Vespers compositions. Out of the 17 compositions which Seelkopf discovered in sacred anthologies published in Italy from 1619 to 1629, and which do not appear in the prints of Grandi's works alone, not one is identifiable as a Vespers composition.[100] Moreover, of the more than 50 compositions by Grandi which Seelkopf has found in German and English anthologies of *concerti* printed between 1613 and 1672, all can be traced to the Italian prints of Grandi's works.[101]

Similarly, the manuscript copies of works by Grandi reveal no new music for Vespers. The compositions are, rather, merely transcriptions into score of works published in the Italian partbooks.[102]

Giovanni Rovetta

The printed sources of Rovetta's sacred music are considerably less complex than those of Grandi. There are nine collections in all—five of psalms and Magnificats, four of motets. Only one of the psalm collections was ever reprinted, and although each of the motet collections was re-issued in Antwerp, only two were republished in Venice itself.

Of the five psalm collections, the first stands somewhat apart from the other four. Whereas each of Rovetta's four later collections forms a liturgical unit, is stylistically uniform throughout, and can be performed by a stable body of musicians, the first collection is a conglomeration from every point of view. The contents include both works in the modern *stile concertato* and retrospective works to be sung *alla breve*. Of the *salmi concertati*, some have *obbligato* violin parts while others are purely vocal. In no case can a complete liturgical service be assembled from the psalms set in any one style. In fact, the five most common Vespers psalms—*Dixit Dominus, Confitebor tibi Domine, Beatus vir, Laudate pueri,* and *Laudate Dominum omnes gentes*—would cut across three stylistic categories if assembled solely from this collection. Every facet of the collection underlines Rovetta's statement that the publication was rushed into print to insure him the post of *vice-maestro di cappella*. Indeed, he seems to have been most eager to show the Procurators that he had mastered every style of composition used by the ducal chapel.

The collection was published as follows:

(RISM R 2962) .... SALMI/CONCERTATI/A CINQUE ET SEI VOCI/Et Altri Con Doi Violini, Con Motetti/à Doi è Tre Voci./Et Alcune Canzoni per Sonar à Tre è quattro Voci/Con Basso Continuo./DI/GIO: ROVETTA: Opera Prima./Novamente Stampati Con Privilegio, et Licentia de Superiori .... /(device)/STAMPA DEL GARDANO./IN VENETIA M DC XXVI./Appresso Bartolomeo Magni.

TAVOLA Delli Salmi[103]

Concertati A 5. Voci
Dixit Dominus	2
Beatus vir	6
Lauda Ierusalem Dominum	8

Per Cantar alla Breve con le parte Radoppiate Se piace.
Confitebor tibi Domine	10
Nisi Dominus	12

A 6. Voci
Credidi propter	14

Concertati A 5. Voci, et due Violini.
Laudate Pueri.	16
Laetatus sum	20
Nisi Dominus	23
Beatus vir	26
Laudate Dominum omnes gentes	30

A 6. Voci, et due Violini.
Magnificat	32

Motetti.
Conditor alme syderum	dui Soprani, et due Violini	36
O intemerata	à due Bassi, et due Violini	38
Ave Regina Caelorum	à 3. due Tenori, et Basso.	40
Salve Regina	à due Tenori.	42

Canzon per Sonar.
Canzon Prima	à 3. due Violini, et una Violetta da Brazzo	50
Canzon Secondo	à 3. due Violini, ò Corneti, e Tromb.	54
Canzon Terza	à 4. due Violini, et due Viole da Brazzo	57
Canzon Quarta	à 4.	59

Partbooks: C, A, T, B, Quintus; Vl 1, Vl 2; Basso continuo
Location:
    Bologna, Civico Museo Bibliografico Musicale: all except Vl 2

(RISM R 2963) reprint: 1641
    Location:
    Vienna, Gesellschaft der Musikfreunde: complete
    London, British Library: complete
    Wroclaw, Biblioteka Uniwersytecka: complete

Rovetta's next psalm collection was not published until 1639. It is a much more orderly, unified body of music than the collection of 1627. Dedicated to Louis XIII of France, the publication of 1639 commemorated the ceremonies held in the basilica of San Giorgio Maggiore on the occasion of the birth of Louis XIV. Set for two four-part choirs and two violins (forces which are reduced only slightly for a number of works), these works are on a larger scale than those in any other collection of Rovetta. The print was published as follows:

> (RISM R 2966) .... MESSA, E SALMI/Concertati A Cinque, Sei, Sette, Otto Voci,/E Due Violini./DI GIOVANNI ROVETTA,/Vice Maestro di Capella/DELLA SER-ENISSIMA REPUBLICA/Opera Quarta./DEDICATA/ALLA MAESTA/ CHRISTIANISSIMA/DEL GLORIOSISSIMO/RE/DI FRANCIA, ET DI NAVAR-RA/LUIGI XIII./IL GUISTO/Con Privilegio/(device)/IN VENETIA. Appresso Alessandro Vincenti. M, DC. XXXIX.
>
> TAVOLA

Kyrie	A 5.	2
Gloria	à 6.	4
Credo	à 7.	8
Dixit Primo.	à 7.	13
Confitebor	à 7.	17
Beatus	à 8. Senza Violini	21
Laudate pueri. Primo	à 6.	24
Laudate Dominum omnes.	à 6.	29
Credidi	à 5.	32
Memento	à 6.	36
Dixit Secondo	à 7.	40
Laudate Pueri Secondo.	à 6. Senza Violini	45
Laetatus sum	à 6.	49
Nisi Dominus	à 5.	52
Lauda Ierusalem	à 6.	56
Magnificat	à 8.	61

> Partbooks: C I, A, T I, B I: C II, T II, B II et Ottava parte; Vl I, Vl II, Basso continuo.
>
> Locations:
>
> Bologna, Civico Museo Bibliografico Musicale: complete
>
> Naples, Archivio Musicale della Comunità Oratoriana dei Padri Filippini: complete; second copy: C I, A, T I; C II, T II, B II et Ottava parte; VI I, Basso continuo
>
> Orvieto, Archivio musicale del Duomo: C II; Vl II.
>
> Lübeck, Bibliothek der Hansestadt Lübeck: T I, B I; C II; Vl II.
>
> Wroclaw, Biblioteka Uniwersytecka: all except Basso continuo

A third collection of psalms was published in 1642. Not only was it the last such collection Rovetta published as *vice-maestro* of St. Mark's, but it was also his last psalm collection involving independent instrumental parts:

> (RISM R 2971) .... SALMI/A TRE, ET QUATTRO VOCI/Aggiontovi un Laudate pueri A 2. et Laudate Dominum omnes gentes/A voce sola, et nel fine un Kyrie, Gloria, et Credo pur à tre voci/Tutto Concertato con doi Violini, ò altri Instromenti

Alti/DI GIO: ROVETTA/Vice Maestro di Capella della Serenissima Republica./OPERA SETTIMA./CON PRIVILEGIO./(device)/IN VENETIA./Apresso Alessandro Vincenti. M D CXXXXII.

TAVOLA

Partbooks: C, A, T, B; Vl I, Vl II; Basso continuo
Location:
  Bologna, Civico Museo Bibliografico Musicale: complete
  Venice, Biblioteca Nazionale Marciana: B
  Wroclaw, Biblioteka Uniwersytecka: all except T
  London, British Library: Vl II
  Regensburg, Proskesche Musikbibliothek: C, A, T, B; Basso continuo

Rovetta's fourth and fifth psalm collections (1644, 1662) both consist of compositions for two four-part choirs and basso continuo. While less elaborate than the earlier collections from a purely musical standpoint, they are nonetheless important because of their liturgical organization. They contain not only the psalms for all major feasts of the Roman rite but also a number of psalms which are associated strictly with the special liturgy of St. Mark's. Both collections contain the psalms *Lauda anima mea Dominum* and *Laudate Dominum quoniam bonus est*, two texts which make possible the performance of a special Vespers service all five of whose psalms begin with a form of *laudare: Laudate pueri, Laudate Dominum omnes gentes, Lauda anima mea Dominum, Laudate Dominum quoniam bonus est*, and *Lauda Jerusalem*. As we shall see below, this series of psalms was dubbed the "Vespero delli Cinque Laudate" and occupied a special place in the liturgy of the basilica on the vigils of major feasts. The collection of 1662 also contains the unusual psalms *Ad te levavi, Levavi oculos meos*, and *Laudate nomen Domini*. In modern Roman sources, these texts appear as ferial psalms only,[104] but in the liturgy of St. Mark's, they formed the basis of a Vespers service for the Saturday after Pentecost.

A number of other factors prove that these two collections were printed for the private use of the *cappella marciana* rather than for commercial distribution. In the dedication to the 1644 print, Rovetta states that as a sign of gratitude for his appointment as *maestro di cappella* he has "finished up some compositions of which I felt the Most Serene Royal Chapel of St. Mark's had the greatest need."[105] It seems, in fact, that Rovetta had to obtain special permission to publish these works, for on 3 January 1644, the Procurators gave Rovetta a *licenza* to publish certain unnamed materials (Document 30), a statement which almost certainly refers to the 1644 collection, since Rovetta's next sacred collection did not appear until 1648. The evidence for the 1662 collection is stronger still. The title pages describe the contents as "Secondo l'uso della Serenissima Capella Ducale di *San* Marco," and Rovetta's dedication states that "since [these psalms] would easily be lost and worn out if they existed in only a few manuscript copies, and since the use and necessity of these [texts] is very frequent . . . I have decided to put them into print, so we will have the benefit of many copies of longer durability . . ." (Document 31). Moreover, it seems that Rovetta actually financed the publication of the 1662 collection himself, for on 7 January 1663, the Procurators voted to reimburse him 150 ducats for his expenses in publishing the partbooks and for his excellent service to the church (Document 32).[106]

These two final collections were published as follows:

(RISM R 2972) .... SALMI/A OTTO VOCI/DI GIO: ROVETTA/Maestro di Capella della Serenissima Republica,/OPERA OTTAVA/DEDICATI/All'Illustrissimi, et Eccellentissimi Signori/PROCURATORI/DELLA CHIESA DI S. MARCO/CON PRIVILEGIO./(device)/IN VENETIA. /Apresso Alessandro Vincenti. MDCXXXXIIII.

TAVOLA

Dixit Dominus	3
Confitebor tibi Domine	5
Beatus vir	8
Laudate pueri	12
Laudate Dominum omnes	15
In exitu	16
Laetatus sum	20
Nisi Dominus	22
Lauda Ierusalem	25
Lauda anima mea Dominum	27
Laudate Dominum quoniam bonus	29
Credidi propter	32
In convertendo Dominus	33
Domine probasti	37

Partbooks: I: C, A, T, B; II: C, A, T, B; Basso continuo
Location:
  Bologna, Civico Museo Bibliografico Musicale: complete
  Lucca, Biblioteca del Seminario: complete (two sets)[107]
  Wroclaw, Biblioteka Uniwersytecka: complete
  Bologna, Archivio di San Petronio: complete
  Frankfurt, Stadt- und Universitätsbibliothek: complete

(RISM R 2979) .... DELLI SALMI A 8. VOCI/Accommodati da cantarsi alla Breve/Secondo l'uso/DELLA SERENIS.ma CAPELLA DUCALE DI S. MARCO/DI GIO: ROVETTA/Maestro di detta Capella./Opera Duodecima./(device)/IN VENETIA M. DC. LXII. Apresso Francesco Magni detto Gardano

TAVOLA

Partbooks: I: C, A, T, B; II: C, A, T, B; Basso continuo
Location:

Bologna, Civico Museo Bibliografico Musicale: complete
Cividale del Friuli, Archivio Capitolare: complete
Vienna, Gesellschaft der Musikfreunde: complete

Rovetta's four collections of *motetti concertati* were all published during the middle years of his career, two during his tenure as *vice-maestro* and two during his first years as *maestro di cappella*:

(RISM 2964) .... MOTETTI/CONCERTATI/A Due, Tre, Quattro, et Cinque Voci/CON LE LITANIE DELLA MADONNA, Et Una Messa Concertata à Voci Pari/DI GIO. ROVETTA/Vice Maestro di Cappella della Serenissima Republica/OPERA TERZA./CON PRIVILEGIO./(device)/IN VENETIA,/Appresso Alessandro Vincenti. MDCXXXV.

Partbooks: C, A, T, B; Basso continuo
Location:
  Bologna, Civico Museo Bibliografico Musicale: complete
  Naples, Archivio Musicale della Comunità Oratoriana dei Padri Filippini: complete
  Regensburg, Proskesche Musikbibliothek: C, A, T
  Pesaro, Biblioteca comunale Oliveriana: Basso continuo
  Rome, Archivio di San Giovanni in Laterano: complete

(RISM R 2965) reprint: 1640
Location:
  Regensburg, Proskesche Musikbibliothek: B; Basso continuo
  Paris, Bibliothèque Sainte-Geneviève: complete
  Wroclaw, Biblioteka Uniwersytecka: A, B; Basso continuo
  London, British Library: C, A, T

(RISM R 2975) reprint: 1648; the works for two voices and basso continuo reprinted as:
BICINIA SACRA/SIVE/CANTIONES SACRAE/DUABUS VOCIBUS,/SUAVISSIME CONCERTANTIBUS/Cum Basso Generali/CANENDAE/AUTHORE/IOANNES ROVETTA/VICE-MAGISTRO CAPELLAE/SERENISSIMAE VENETIARUM/REIPUBLICAE./LIBER TERTIUS./(device)/ANTVERPIAE,/Apud Haeredes PETRI PHALESII/Typographi Musices./M.DC.XLVIII./

Partbooks: C I, C II; Basso continuo
Location:
  Brussels, Bibliothèque Royale: Basso continuo[108]
  Durham, Cathedral Library: complete
  Gaesdonck, Collegium Augustinianum: complete
  Oxford, Library of Christ Church College: complete

(RISM R 2976) reprint: 1668, a new printing of the above Phalèse edition.
Location:
  Oxford, Library of Christ Church College: complete

(RISM R 2977) reprint: 1649; the works for three, four and five voices and basso continuo reprinted as:

GEMMA MUSICALIS/DIVERSIS CANTIONIBUS SACRIS/TRIBUS, QUA-
TUOR, ET QUINQUE/VOCIBUS, Uti varijs speciosis coloribus preciosa,/In
Lucem edita/Cum Basso Continuo/PER IOANNEM ROVETTA/VICE-
MAGISTRUM CAPELLAE/SERENISSIMAE VENETIARUM/REIPUB-
LICAE/LIBER QUARTUS./(device)/ANTVERPIAE,/Apud Magdalenam Phale-
siam et cohaeredes./M.DC.XLIX./
Partbooks: C, A, T, B; Basso continuo
Location:
    Gaesdonck, Collegium Augustinianum: C, A; Basso continuo
    Oxford, Bodleian Library: complete
    Oxford, Library of Christ Church College: complete
    London, British Library: complete
    Lier, Eglise St. Gummarus: A, T, B (incomplete)

(RISM R 2967) .... MOTETTI/CONCERTATI/A DUE, E TRE VOCI/Con le Letanie
della Madona à Quattro/DI GIO: ROVETTA/Vice Maestro di Capella della Serenissima Republica./DEDICATI/ALL'Illustrissimo Signore/BATTISTA NANI/OPERA
QUINTA/CON PRIVILEGIO./(device)/IN VENETIA,/Appresso Alessandro Vincenti. MDCXXXIX.

Partbooks: C, A, B; Basso continuo
Location:
    Paris, Bibliothèque Sainte-Geneviève: complete
    Bologna, Civico Museo Bibliografico Musicale: A, B; Basso continuo
    Regensburg, Proskesche Musikbibliothek: complete
    Wroclaw, Biblioteka Uniwersyteka: complete
    London, British Library: B; Basso continuo

(RISM R 2968) reprint: 1640, as:
MOTETTA/CONCERTATA/DUABUS, ET TRIBUS VOCIBUS,/adiunctis Litanijs
Beatae Virginis/Quatuor vocibus./AUTHORE/IOANNE ROVETTA/VICE MAG-
ISTRO CAPELLAE SERENISSIMAE/REIP. VENETAE./OPUS QUINTUM,/In
his Partibus nunquam ante hac editum,/in hac nostra impressione à multis men-
dis / emundatum. / (device) / ANTVERPIAE, Apud Haeredes PETRI
PHALESII/Typographi Musices./M.D.C.XL

Partbooks: C, A, B; Basso continuo
Location:
    Uppsala, Universitetsbibliotek: complete[109]

(RISM R 2969) reprint: 1648, by Phalèse
Location:
    Gaesdonck, Collegium Augustinianum: C, A; Basso continuo

(RISM R 2970) reprint: 1648, by Vincenti
Location:
    London, British Library: complete

(RISM R 2973) .... MOTETTI/CONCERTATI/A DUE E TRE VOCI/LIBRO
TERZO/DEL SIGNOR/GIO. ROVETTA/Maestro di Capella della Serenissima Re-

publica,/RACCOLTI/DA GIO: BATTISTA VOLPE/ET DEDICATI/Al Molto Illustre, et Reverendiss. Signore et Patrone/COLLENDISSIMO/ MONSIGNORE/GIOANNI POMELLI/PIOVANO DI S. FANTINO, CANONICO DUCALE,/Arciprete della Veneranda Congregatione di S. Polo, /OPERA DECIMA./(device)/IN VENETIA/Appresso Alessandro Vincenti. MDCXXXXVII.

Partbooks: C I, C II, B; Basso continuo
Location:
    Bologna, Civico Museo Bibliografico Musicale: complete
    Wroclaw, Biblioteka Uniwersytecka: complete

(RISM R 2974) reprint: 1648, as:
MANIPULUS/E MESSE/MUSICUS/DUARUM,/ET TRIUM VOCUM/ CONCERTANTIUM,/AUCTORE IOANNE ROVETTA/Collectore verò/Ioan. BAPTISTA VELPIO./(device)/ANTVERPIAE./Apud haeredes Petri Phalesij, Typhographi Musices/ad insigne Davidis Regis./M.DC.XXXXVIII.

Partbooks: C, A, B; Basso continuo
Location:
    Gaesdonck, Collegium Augustinianum: C, A; Basso continuo
    Paris, Bibliothèque nationale: A, B; Basso continuo
    Brussels, Bibliothèque royale: Basso continuo[110]

(RISM R 2978) .... MOTETTI/A DUE, TRE, E QUATTRO/DEL SIGNOR GIO: ROVETTA/Maestro di Capella della Serenissima Repubblica/DEDICATI/Al Molto Reverendo P. D./BATTISTA CONTI/Dottor in Sacra Teologia Prior Dignissimo/di Santa Maria dalle Carceri./LIBRO QUARTO./OPERA UNDECIMA./CON PRI-VILEGIO./(device)/IN VENETIA./Appresso Alessandro Vincenti. M. DC. L.

Partbooks: C, A, B; Basso continuo
Location:
    Wroclaw, Biblioteka Uniwersytecka: complete
    Modena, Biblioteca Estense: A
    San Francisco, De Bellis Collection of California State University at San Francisco: B
    Assisi, San Francesco: complete[111]
    Tokyo, Nanki Music Library, Ohkù Collection: C, A; Basso continuo

(RISM R 2979) reprint: 1653, as:
    Novi Concentus sacrae philomelae, Duarum, Trium ac Quatuor Vocum. Cum Basso Continuo . . . Antverpiae, Haer. P. Phalesius, 1653.

Partbooks: C, A, B; Basso continuo
Location:
    Antwerp, Musée Plantin: A
    Brussels, Bibliothèque royale: C, B; Basso continuo[112]

A large number of works of Rovetta are included in sacred anthologies of the period or preserved in manuscript. While it has not been possible to check every isolated composition, a survey of this body of music suggests that, on the whole, it offers no significant additions to the canon of Rovetta's Vespers compositions. The unique exception is a *Magnificat a 4 e 5 voci* included in Cod. It. IV-1134 (-10949) of the Biblioteca Nazionale Marciana, Venice.[113] This manuscript is a nineteenth-century copy of four works of Rovetta which are not found among his printed compositions. The copy of the Magnificat is possibly an *unicum*; there is no known concordance with a seventeenth-century source. My own supposition, however, is that the original may be found among a collection of 15 choirbooks which are housed in the archive of the Procurators of St. Mark's but are generally inaccessible to scholars. I was allowed only the briefest access to these volumes and found that they do contain a number of works of Rovetta.[114] The Magnificat is an important work, for it is one of the few surviving Vespers pieces of Rovetta in pure *stile antico*. Stylistically, it is quite similar to the four-part Mass from Monteverdi's *Selva Morale*.[115]

Francesco Cavalli

Cavalli's Vespers music is essentially reducible to only two psalm collections, a Magnificat printed in Monteverdi's *Messa a quattro Voci e Salmi* (1650), a *Confitebor* preserved solely in manuscript and a number of motets. Unlike Grandi and Rovetta, he did not publish separate motet collections. He included, rather, a number of Vespers motets in his major publication devoted to sacred music, the *Musiche Sacre* of 1656. A number of miscellaneous motets of Cavalli are extant in sacred anthologies of the period, but none is identifiable as a Vespers composition.

We know that the extant sacred music of Cavalli represents only a part of his total production, for there are records of a number of works that seem not to have survived. Principal among these are the works listed by Caffi in his inventory of the musical archive of St. Mark's, dated 25 September 1720: three Masses; six books of motets; a book of hymns; and two Requiem Masses (or, possibly, two copies of one Mass). Presumably these were all in manuscript. It is possible that Cavalli also composed a large concerted Requiem for his own funeral (see above, p. 24. We know furthermore of a Mass and Te Deum performed in Ss. Giovanni e Paolo on 25 January 1660 (see above, p. 21). The financial records of St. Mark's show that the Procurators paid 272 ducats to Lorenzo Rossi, a priest, to copy the following works after Cavalli's death: two hymns, one for the Feast of the Nativity of St. John the Baptist, the other for the Feast of the Apparition of the Body of St. Mark; two Masses, one of four and one of five voices; two motets, one for the Finding of the Holy Cross, and one for St. Nicholas; a Magnificat for four voices; and a Requiem

Mass for eight voices.[116] Rossi also was paid 24 ducats for copying certain "Messe solenne" for Christmas of 1671, 1672, and 1673 as well as a Vespers service for 1671, all compositions of Cavalli. The Christmas Vespers may be the service which eventually found its way into Cavalli's *Vesperi* of 1675 as the *Vespero delli Cinque Laudate* (Document 33). There is no way of knowing whether any of these works were contained in the manuscript materials cited by Caffi.

The publication of so little of Cavalli's sacred music is partially explained in the foreward to his most elaborate collection, the *Musiche Sacre* (Document 34):

> My talent has always been far from the presses; and I have consented to let my weak creations travel where fortune may carry them by means of the pen rather than by means of the printing press. Finally, however, I let myself be persuaded by the entreaties of Signor Alessandro Vincenti, who—after I had long persisted in my own frame of mind—succeeded in winning me over and making me bold to expose to the universe the weak outlines of my notes. If you receive pleasure from them, the credit goes to him. And similarly, if you find them tedious, do not complain to me, for I did not mean to bring you this nuisance for any purpose other than to gratify a friend, who persuaded me with his kindness.

We do not know why Cavalli was so reluctant to publish even those works which Vincenti finally coaxed into print. It is possible that his involvement with the erratic exigencies of stage performance made him balk at the finality of a printed declaration of his musical intentions. And certainly a number of the extant scores of his operas show the signs of elaborate revision which one expects of theatrical works.[117] It is also possible that he considered his sacred work to be the special property of St. Mark's; we have seen that the Procurators spent a considerable sum to have a number of his compositions copied out after his death. One must note, however, that neither Monteverdi, Grandi nor Rovetta had shown compunctions about publishing their own music for St. Mark's. It may well be that Cavalli merely fell victim to the decline in musical publication which occurred in Venice after 1650. At any rate, Vincenti never persuaded Cavalli to give him materials for a second collection. Cavalli's double-choir *Vesperi* of 1675 were published by Vincenti's rival, the house of Gardano. Despite a promise that "other works of this most Excellent Virtuoso will go to press immediately,"[118] Vincenti published no more of Cavalli's compositions.

Cavalli's extant music for Vespers service is contained in two collections. The first and most important of the two was published in 1656 as follows:

(RISM C 1565) .... MUSICHE/SACRE/CONCERNENTI/Messa, e Salmi Concertati con Istromenti Imni Antifone et/Sonate, A Due 3. 4. 5. 6. 8. 10. e 12.

Voci/DI/FRANCESCO CAVALLI/Organista Della Serenissima Republica, in S. Marco./CONSACRATE/AL SERENISSIMO/GIO. CARLO/CARDINAL, DE MEDICI/CON PRIVILEGIO/(device)/IN VENETIA/Appresso Alessandro Vincenti MDC LVI.

TAVOLA

Partbooks: I: C, A, T, B; II: C, A, T, B; Vl I, Vl II, Violoncino, Basso continuo
Location:
Bologna, Civico Museo Bibliografico Musicale: complete

Bologna, Accademia Filarmonica: complete
Wroclaw, Biblioteka Uniwersytecka: C II, Vl II, Violoncino
Regensburg, Proskesche Musikbibliothek: complete

The *Musiche Sacre* form an exceptional collection from every point of view. Liturgically, they are an unusually elaborate compendium of the most important music for the church year. They contain a concerted Mass, Vespers psalms for the most important cycles of feasts (the feasts of Our Lord, of the Virgin Mary and of Apostles and Evangelists), five hymns from the Common of the Saints, a Magnificat, all four Marian antiphons, and six church sonatas. The mixture of independent instrumental sonatas with vocal liturgical works, while not unheard of in *seicento* Italy, is exceptional for a sacred collection from the middle of the century. Similarly, the mixture of motets (hymns, Marian antiphons) with psalm and Magnificat settings is unusual for the period. Few collections from mid-century are quite as broad in scope as the *Musiche Sacre*, though Monteverdi's *Selva Morale* does match the vastness of Cavalli's collection and may well have served as its prototype.

The forces demanded by the different works in the *Musiche Sacre* vary in the extreme. They range from a modest setting of *Ave regina caelorum* for two voices and basso continuo, to an extravagant Magnificat for two four-part choirs, eight vocal soloists, two violins, *violoncino*, basso continuo, and three trombones.[119] The largest portion of the volume, however, consists of works conceived for relatively small forces. Indeed, out of 22 vocal compositions, only 5 call for vocal *ripieni*; the remaining 17 are conceived for soloists. The existence of so many works for a small number of musicians has led Arnold to suggest that the contents of the collection might not really have been destined for St. Mark's at all. He postulates, instead, that they date from the 1620s and were written for Ss. Giovanni e Paolo during Cavalli's tenure as organist there.[120]

This supposition can be challenged on several grounds. First, it is not true, as Arnold maintains, that the smaller works in the *Musiche Sacre* are "quite unlike the more grandiose music which belongs to the tradition of San Marco." On the contrary, the most superficial examination of Monteverdi's *Selva Morale* reveals a number of works for modest forces: a *Confitebor* for three voices, two violins, and basso continuo; a number of hymns for solo voice, two violins and continuo; settings of the *Salve Regina* for one, two, and three voices and continuo; and four solo motets. Thus, the supposition that grandiose works were destined for cosmopolitan centers while modest works were for provincial churches is totally unfounded.

Second, as we shall see below, the *cappella marciana* went through some lean years after the death of Monteverdi. During the 1650s the singers of St. Mark's grew more and more discontented with their lot, and a steady exodus of musicians began which would not cease until the 1680s. Indeed, by 1653 the number of singers in the *cappella* had fallen to a mere 28. Under these circumstances, it seems reasonable to suppose that St. Mark's welcomed works of small dimensions because of their practicality.

Finally, the entire question of the provenance of the *Musiche Sacre* is, in a very real sense, somewhat beside the point. The major Venetian churches shared musical forces so completely that it is doubtful whether any published collection (other than those which contained works for the special liturgy of St. Mark's) was the property of any one Venetian church to the exclusion of the others. We know that the *cappella marciana* as a body accompanied the Doge on his visits to various churches in the city. More specifically, we know that the chapel sang in Ss. Giovanni e Paolo, San Francesco della Vigna, Santa Maria dei Frari, the Chiesa del Redentore, San Giorgio Maggiore, and San Zaccaria, to name only the most prominent churches. Furthermore, individual members of the *cappella* were hired by smaller churches and by the *scuole* on innumerable occasions. Thus, much of the music written for the *cappella marciana* would soon have found its way into other churches of the city, and it is doubtful that the composers associated with St. Mark's had the ducal chapel exclusively in mind when they penned their sacred works.

Cavalli's second collection of Vespers music, on the other hand, is one of these exceptional publications which may have been intended for use in St. Mark's alone. For it not only contains the *Vespero delli Cinque Laudate* associated with the liturgy of the ducal chapel, but it is written in the simple idiom for eight-part choir and organ found in Rovetta's psalm collections of 1644 and 1662—a style which, as we have indicated above, may have been especially important for the observance of the traditions of St. Mark's. The collection was published the year before Cavalli's death as follows:

(RISM C 1566) .... VESPERI/A OTTO VOCI/DI FRANCESCO CAVALLI/Maestro Di Capella della Serenissima Republica in S. Marco/CONSACRATI/AL SERENIS.mo PRENCIPE/NICOLO SAGREDO/DOGE DI VENETIA/(device)/IN VENETIA 1675. Stampa Del Gardano.

VESPERO DELLA B. V. M.

Dixit	2
Laudate pueri	5
Laetatus sum	7
Nisi Dominus	9
Lauda Ierusalem	11

VESPERO Delle Domeniche, et altri Salmi

VESPERO Delli Cinque Laudate

Partbooks: I: C, A, T, B; II: C, A, T, B; Basso continuo
  Location:
    Bologna, Civico Museo Bibliografico Musicale: complete

The *Vesperi* of 1675 are more complete from a liturgical point of view than the *Musiche Sacre*, which cover only major feasts. In fact, of the Vespers collections covered in this study, only Rovetta's final collection of 1662 encompasses a broader field of psalms than Cavalli's 1675 print. Cavalli's *Vesperi* differ from most Vespers prints of the period in being organized into three discre te services: a Marian Vespers, a Sunday Vespers, and the *Vespero delli Cinque Laudate* of St. Mark's. Most Vespers collections of the era are organized along different lines: each psalm is set only once, and various Vespers sequences can be assembled from the collection by selecting the correct psalms for a given feast. Cavalli, on the contrary, resets a psalm text every time it appears in a new Vespers sequence. Thus, the collection of 1675 represents a rare instance of a composer's conceiving of a Vespers service as a discrete musical entity rather than as a collection of individual items each of which might serve in a number of services. As previous research has shown, collections such as Cavalli's are unusual in the seventeenth century, Monteverdi's 1610 *Vespers* notwithstanding.[121]

In addition to the works contained in his two printed collections, a small number of Cavalli's sacred works are preserved in printed anthologies of the period and in manuscript. Of these, two are identifiable as Vespers compositions: a Magnificat included in Monteverdi's *Messa a quattro Voci e Salmi*; and a *Confitebor* preserved in manuscript only:[122]

> Magnificat A 6. voci e due violini Del Sig. Francesco Cavalli Organista di S. Marco, in: (RISM 1650/5) .... MESSA/A QUATTRO VOCI,/ET/SALMI/A Una, Due, Tre, Quattro, Cinque, Sei, Sette, et Otto Voci,/Concertati, e Parte da Cappella, et con le Letanie della B.V./DEL SIGNOR/CLAUDIO MONTEVERDE/Gia Maestro di Cappella della Serenissima/Republica di Venetia./DEDICATI/AL R.MO P. D. ODOARDO/BARANARDI/Abbate di Santa Maria delle Carceri della Congregatione/Camaldolense./(device)/IN VENETIA,/Appresso Alessandro Vincenti. M DC I.

> Partbooks: I: C, A, T, B; II: C, A, T, B; Basso continuo
> Location:
>   Rome, Biblioteca Casanatense: complete
>   Berlin, Deutsche Staatsbibliothek: I: A, B
>   Munich, Bayerische Staatsbibliothek: II: A
>   Bologna, Civico Museo Bibliografico Musicale: I: S, T, B; II: A, T, B, Basso continuo

> Confitebor tibi Domine à 5, 2 Violin*i*, 2 Cant*i*, Basso è Continuo del Sig*no*r Francesco Cavalli.

> Location:
>   Berlin, Staatsbibliothek der Stiftung Preussicher Kulturbesitz

The body of music of Grandi, Rovetta and Cavalli in the preceding inventory represents a large and variegated assemblage. From Grandi's first publication of motets (1610) to Cavalli's valedictory *Vesperi* (1675), the prints span a rather ungainly period of 65 years, during an era which saw some startling changes in musical style. In 1610, Giovanni Gabrieli was still alive, and neither his *Canzoni e suonate* (1615) nor his second set of *Symphoniae Sacrae* (1615) had yet appeared in print; by 1675, the young Alessandro Scarlatti was in his teens, soon to produce his first opera. Moreover, the forces demanded by the 25 prints considered in this study vary in the extreme: from a single voice with basso continuo to multiple choirs, instruments and an aggregate of soloists. Similarly, in terms of musical idiom the pieces range from retrospective works notated *alla breve* to compositions in the most modern vocal and instrumental language.

Nonetheless, this is still a unified body of music. The unity has neither a temporal nor a stylistic basis; it is, rather, a unity of place and of purpose. For all these works were written to fill the liturgical requirements of a Vespers service; and while not destined exclusively for the musical chapel of St. Mark's, they all were associated primarily with that body of musicians. Thus, these compositions form a solid fabric against which one can chart the musical history of the most important chapel in northern Italy during the seventeenth century.

III

The Musical Chapel of St. Mark's in the Seventeenth Century

Archival Sources

In his study of Monteverdi, Henry Prunières presented a tantalizing invitation to further investigation of the documents surrounding music at St. Mark's:

> It would be exceedingly interesting to write a history of the musicians of St. Mark's. All the details could be found in the files of the *Procuratia di Sopra* of the *Cancelleria Inferiore*. Historians of music seem, up to the present, to have ignored this rich source of information. See, in particular, *Cancelleria Inferiore*: T. 79, f. 108, T. 80, f. 24, 65, 102, 203, 230, 249 and f. 45; T. 81, 123; T. 82, f. 20.[123]

While some of the bibliographical details are faulty,[124] Prunières' statement is essentially correct. There is, indeed, a wealth of information in the Venetian State Archives and—apparently unknown to Prunières—in the Biblioteca del Civico Museo Correr which supplements the scanty, sometimes inaccurate figures given by Caffi and the frustratingly brief summary provided by Prunières himself.

Curiously, Prunières's suggestion has never been followed up in full. About a decade after his book appeared in print, René Lenaerts examined some of the documents in the *Procuratia de Supra* in his study of St. Mark's during the epoch of Adrian Willaert.[125] More recently, Denis Arnold has drawn upon the same series of volumes in a number of articles and a book on music at St. Mark's during the early seventeenth century,[126] and Eleanor Selfridge-Field has sketched an expert summary of the documents on instruments in the archive.[127] However, the documents in the *Procuratia de Supra* have never been scrutinized to the extent they might be, nor have the documents Prunières cites in the *Cancelleria Inferiore* been touched except for a few minor references.[128] The material in the Biblioteca Correr has been cited only selectively,[129] and the extant *ceremoniali* which discuss the place of music in the ritual of the basilica have been examined only superficially.[130] Clearly, it is time for a more thorough examination of these sources, not only to chronicle the history of the *cappella marciana*—easily the most important musical chapel in seventeenth-century Italy—but also to solve the myriad performance problems posed by the vague specifications in contemporary Venetian prints of sacred music.

The first step, of course, must be an annotated listing of the extant archival sources, a step which has been omitted—or deemed inessential—in earlier studies of the *cappella*.[131] Some knowledge of the government and ecclesiastical hierarchy of the basilica is also necessary in order to understand the significance of the documents. This will be discussed in greater detail below; for the moment it will be sufficient to grasp a few basic principles.

The government of St. Mark's was under the direction of nine *procuratori*. These nine positions fell into three bodies: the *procuratia de supra*, *procuratia de citra* and *procuratia de ultra*.[132] Of these, the three *procuratori de supra* were in charge of the government of the church itself: administering its funds, choosing clergy and engaging musicians. The other two bodies were in charge of the church's domains within Venice; the *procuratori de citra* controlled those on the same side of the Grand Canal as St. Mark's, the *procuratori de ultra*, those on the far side of the canal. Ostensibly, the Doge was the true head of the basilica—"ecclesiae Sancti Marci nostrae capellae solus patronus et Dominus" was the inscription emblazened upon ducal decrees. In reality, however, the Doge was largely a figurehead, as he was in most areas of Venetian life, and the extensive series of ducal decrees dealing with the basilica are little more than token ratifications of decisions made by other bodies. The Doge did have the right, however, to appoint the *primicerio*, who headed the 26 canons of the church and presided over the religious ceremonies. Under the *primicerio* in the ecclesiastic hierarchy came the *maestro di coro* or *maestro delle ceremonie*, canons and subcanons, deacons and subdeacons, sacristans and subsacristans, the chorus of priests, clerics connected with the church and the seminary, and a number of miscellaneous posts. During the seventeenth century, the musical hierarchy was headed by the *maestro di cappella* and *vice-maestro*; it consisted of singers, two organists, a caretaker for the organs, a *maestro dei concerti* and instrumentalists.

The major source of information on the basilica is the archive of the *Procuratia de Supra*, which was transferred to the A.S.V. from St. Mark's itself after the fall of the Republic in 1797. Several types of documents are preserved. First, there are series of *registri* kept by the various administrative bodies within the basilica, which are more or less in their original state. Second, there are single documents, both originals and transcriptions, occasionally bound into volumes but sometimes still unbound and only randomly gathered in *buste*. Finally there are transcriptions of documents from the *registri*, gathered together according to the topics treated, and thus forming an annotated index of the extant documents on various aspects of the basilica.

Documents relating to musical matters are contained in the following series in the *Procuratia de Supra*:[133]

A. *Giornali Cassier*

> Archival designations: Registri d'Amministrazione[134]
> Registri per conto chiesa
> Giornali Cassier

Volumes covering the seventeenth century:[135]
Registro 5 — 1592–1603
      6 — 1603–1610
      7 — 1610–1614
      8 — 1614–1622
      9 — 1623–1628
      10 — 1628–1633
      11 — 1633–1639
      12 — 1639–1648
      13 — 1648–1659
      14 — 1659–1663
      15 — 1663–1674
      16 — 1674–1684
      17 — 1684–1695
  missing — 1695–1704

The *Giornali Cassier* cover the period from 1318 to 1797. Records kept after the fall of the Republic are still located in the parochial archive in St. Mark's itself. The *Giornali Cassier* are lists of funds paid out by the Procurators for services rendered by various employees of the church or by people hired for special occasions. These are payments to individuals for one-time services only. Employees on the general payroll of the basilica are not included in these records unless they were paid for some extraordinary service. The payments to those employees on the general payroll of the basilica are represented in these records only by a lump sum at the end of each two-month period, with no indication of how this sum was distributed among the church employees. However, for the single decade spanning 24 May 1642 to 28 February 1652, complete lists of bi-monthly payments survive, which are itemized into payments for individual priests, musicians, and other employees; these give us a model for the breakdown of the large payroll sums during the central years of this study.

B. *Libri di Scontro*

> Archival designation: Registri d'Amministrazione
> Registri per conto chiesa
> Scontro

> Volumes covering the seventeenth century:
> missing — 1579–1611
> Registro 29 — 1611–1614
> 30 — 1614–1623
> 31 — 1623–1628
> 32 — 1628–1633
> 33 — 1633–1639
> missing — 1639–1648
> 34 — 1648–1658
> missing — 1658–1674
> 35 — 1674–1684
> 36 — 1684–1695
> 37 — 1695–1699

The *Libri di Scontro* are nothing but a second copy of the *Giornali Cassier* made as a control to keep track of funds. While giving no new information, they are generally a fair copy of the original figures and, thus, are useful tools in solving paleographic problems in the *Giornali Cassier*.

C. *Quaderni Chiesa*

> Archival designation: Registri d'Amministrazione
> Registri per conto chiesa
> Quaderni

> Volumes covering the seventeenth century:
> missing — 1567–1614
> Registro 52 — 1614–1638
> 53 — 1639–1663
> 54 — 1663–1678
> 55 — 1678–1707

The *Quaderni* are summary volumes in which the individual payments from the *Giornali Cassier* and *Scontro* are categorized and totaled up. The *Quaderni*, while less useful than the former two series, do give us the figures for the total expenditures of the church and, thus, help us to gauge the place of music in the economic hierarchy.

D. *Chiesa Actorum*

> Archival designation: Decreti e Terminazioni della Procuratia de Supra
> Collezione degli Atti della Procuratia

Volumes covering the seventeenth century:
Registro 139— 1598–1607
140— 1607–1614
141— 1614–1620
142— 1620–1629
143— 1629–1637
144— 1637–1648
missing— 1648–1655
146— 1655–1674
147— 1675–1690
148— 1675–1694
149— 1694–1700

The *Chiesa Actorum* (also referred to as the *Decreti e Terminazioni*) are the minutes of the Procurators' weekly meetings and, thus, exact records of their deliberations. They contain decisions regarding virtually every aspect of music within the basilica. Appointments of musicians are recorded, often with records of the balloting itself. Salary increases are voted upon and registered. Augmentation or diminution of musical personnel is determined. Firings or resignations are recorded. Special attention is given to the question of leaves of absence, both for short periods of time and for lengthy trips, such as the records surrounding Cavalli's trip to Paris, discussed above. The *Chiesa Actorum* are particularly valuable for filling an important void in the records of the *Giornali Cassier*; in the ten-year period when they contain payment lists for the entire *cappella*, the *Giornali Cassier* almost never specify voice types or instruments. To be sure, the *Chiesa Actorum* provide this information only irregularly, but between hirings, firings, and numerous salary adjustments, we can determine the performing medium for the majority of musicians in the chapel.

E. *Rubricari delle Terminazioni della Procuratia*

> Archival designation: Disciplinare pella Procuratia, Decreti e Terminazioni della stessa

Terminazioni della Procuratia
Rubricari

Materials covering the seventeenth century:
Busta 4, Processo 49, Fascicolo 3 — 1589–1630
4 — 1630–1654
5 — 1655–1674
6 — 1675–1692

The *Rubricari delle Terminazioni* are brief summaries of the documents in the *Chiesa Actorum* which have been arranged according to topic. Thus, decrees dealing with the different ecclesiastical and musical offices of St. Mark's are segregated, and one can follow the historical progression of a single office more clearly than from the original *Terminazioni* themselves. As was the case with the *Libri di Scontro*, the *Rubricari* are useful for deciphering difficult writing in the original decrees. However, since the *Rubricari* are, after all, mere summaries of the originals, they cannot be relied upon completely. There are also documents in the *Chiesa Actorum* which, strangely enough, do not find their way into the *Rubricari* and, moreover, a few cases in which the summaries are inaccurate and the information is misconveyed.

F. *Cariche ed Impiegati di Chiesa*

Archival designations and relevant *buste:*

Cariche ed Impiegati di Chiesa
   Cariche ed Impiegati del Clero

Primicerio	Busta 88, Processo 190
Canonici	191
Sotto Canonici	192
Titolati Diaconi	193
Suddiacono	194
Ceremoniere	195
Sacrestani	196
Sottosacrestani	197
Capellani delli Procuratori	198
Capo coro	Busta 89, Processo 199
Maestro di Canto	200
Maestro di Grammatica	201
Giovani di Coro	202
Chierici	203

Cariche ed Impiegati di Capella
    Maestro di Capella   Busta 90, Processo 204
    Sotto Maestro di Capella   Busta 91, Processo 205
    Appuntator di Capella   206
    Organisti   207
    Musici e Suonatore   208
    Alza Mantici   209

These four *buste* were assembled sometime during the eighteenth century (in any case, after 1730) and are transcriptions of documents dealing with the various offices of the basilica, both clerical and musical. The transcriptions are primarily from the *Chiesa Actorum* and, thus, form a second check for the deliberations of the Procurators. These *buste* are a more important source than the *Rubricari*, however, because they contain actual transcriptions, not merely summaries, of primary documents. Certain of the transcriptions appear to be of documents which are no longer extant and are, thus, highly valuable for historians. The very nature of the transcriptions, however, has caused problems; musicologists have relied too uncritically on the understandably tempting phenomenon of fair copies of the most important documents on the basilica already categorized by topic. Unfortunately, the transcriptions are not always accurate, and certain lists and tables of church officials which appear in the *buste* alongside the transcriptions reflect these inaccuracies. It appears that both Winterfeld[136] and Caffi based their studies on the transcriptions in these *buste*, and some of their information reflects this practice.[137] Nor has a blind trust in these transcriptions stopped with Caffi and Winterfeld. In a recent encyclopedia article on Cavalli, one of these transcriptions is actually reproduced in a photograph as if it were a primary document.[138]

In addition to the transcriptions, these *buste* contain a number of original documents, largely neglected by music historians: letters, records of special hearings of the Procurators, documents advertising positions available, and a few official printed documents which describe the duties of musicians.

G. *Ristauro Organi*

    Archival designation: Ristauro Chiesa e Palazzo Ducale
                       Ristauro Organi

Busta 78, Processo 183

This *busta* contains both transcriptions and original documents dealing with the adjustment and repairing of the famous organs of St. Mark's. The documents span the period 1389 to 1749, and the transcriptions are in the same hand as those in the *buste* of *Cariche ed Impiegati di Chiesa*.[139]

Several other archives in the A.S.V. outside the *Procuratia de Supra* series are of major importance for this study.

Cancelleria Inferiore

Archival designation: Cancelleria Inferiore
                                    Atti dei Dogi
Volumes covering the seventeenth century:
    Registro 78 — 1595–1605
          79 — 1605–1615
          80 — 1615–1623
          81 — 1623–1645
          82 — 1645–1655
          83 — 1655–1663

    The series *Atti dei Dogi* of the *Cancelleria Inferiore* is a set of *registri* kept by the ducal secretary which contain records of the Doge's decisions and decrees. Since the Doge's powers were quite limited in the political areas of Venetian life, the few domains in which he was allowed a voice appear quite prominently in these records. One of these areas was that of music, both within the basilica itself and in the context of ceremonies in the ducal palace. Theoretically, any new musician who came into the chapel was formally presented to the Doge, and these presentations are recorded among the ducal decrees. Thus, if one cannot find the Procurators' record of a musician's appointment, the presentation records will often suggest when he entered the service of the basilica. Occasionally musicians approach the Doge with grievances or petitions dealing with the conduct of musical affairs. The most significant instance is the establishment of the *Compagnia di San Marco*, an organization of the singers in the *cappella* for the purpose of self-government on those occasions when they went out into the city to sing at other churches.

    Two other *fondi* in the A.S.V. are important to us. They are not directly concerned with St. Mark's, but they do preserve valuable information on Francesco Cavalli and his career outside the basilica.

    Scuola di San Marco (Buste 188, 194). These two *buste* contain the papers of Marco Faustini, one of the most important Venetian opera impresarios of mid-century Venice. Included among the documents are letters, performance contracts, and a few lists of payments to instrumentalists for specific opera performances.[140]

    San Lorenzo di Venezia (Buste 23, 24). San Lorenzo was Cavalli's parish church, and many of his personal papers were deposited in its archive at his death. Most important are the copies of his wills, cited above, and a large group of documents connected with his real estate dealings both in Venice and *Terrafirma*.[141]

Moving out of the A.S.V. altogether, we find two other Venetian libraries which hold important sources on the *cappella marciana*: the Biblioteca del Civico Museo Correr and the Biblioteca Nazionale Marciana.

Codici Cicogna (Biblioteca del Civico Museo Correr, Venice). The Cicogna codices are a vast set of prints and documents compiled under the direction of Emmanuele Cicogna, a nineteenth-century Venetian patriot and bibliophile. These materials relate to various aspects of Venetian history and culture, and among them are *buste* containing copies of documents dealing with the musical chapel of St. Mark's. In many cases, the originals can be traced to the archive of the *Procuratia de Supra*, A.S.V. Other copies in these codices seem to be *unica*, however, and thus of extreme importance. Included among these materials are lists of musical employees, letters to and from the Procurators regarding the government of the chapel, and decrees of the patriarch of Venice regarding liturgy.

Archival documents among the *Codici Cicogna:*

> Codice Cicogna 3118, fascicoli 44–56: copies of musical documents, primarily from the 1650s plus a large number from 1677; lists of singers' demands; list of "defections" from the *capella*; list of days and services at which musicians must appear.
> Codice Cicogna 2711, fascicolo 2: uses of the campanile in the Piazza San Marco, c. 1665.
> Codice Cicogna 2583, f. 119: patriarchal decrees on music in the liturgy—1595, 1628, 1633.[142]
> Codice Cicogna 801: "Accenni ai musici de la cappella di San Marco": a list of the ecclesiastical and musical hierarchy drawn up in 1714.
> Codice Cicogna 3081: transcriptions from the A.S.V., *Cancelleria Inferiore*, documents of 1612, 1628, 1651.

> *Francesco Caffi, Musica Sacra in Venezia. Appunti per aggiunte alla "Storia. . . ."* (Biblioteca Nazionale Marciana, Cod. It. IV-762 [-10467])

The manuscript in the Biblioteca Nazionale Marciana which touches the *cappella marciana* most closely is a secondary source: the *aggiunte* compiled by Francesco Caffi after the publication of his monograph on music in St. Mark's. While some of the material in the manuscript merely duplicates that in the published volumes, other items exist only in this source. Some of the material is traceable to volumes in the archive of the *Procuratia de Supra*, but other material—for example, the brief catalogue of works in the musical archive of St. Mark's—is entirely Caffi's own work, and the information is not available elsewhere.

A final group of sources cannot be isolated in any one library or archive. These are Venetian *ceremoniali* and come in two major formats. The most important are the large manuscript volumes which describe in minute detail the ceremonial life of the basilica. Less important but often extremely helpful are the small printed pamphlets which describe the ceremonies for specific, one-time events, such as the funeral service for Cosimo II de' Medici in 1621 or the festivities surrounding the birth of Louis XIV of France in 1638.

Ceremoniali (A.S.V., Biblioteca del Civico Museo Correr, Biblioteca Nazionale Marciana, Biblioteca Querini-Stampaglia [Venice]; Biblioteca Ambrosiana [Milan]).

Titles and archival designations:

1. Biblioteca Ambrosiana, Milan. MS A. 328 inf.
   CEREMONIALE MAGNUM/ sivè/Raccolta Universale di tutte le Ceremonie spettanti/Alla Ducal Regia Capella di S. Marco.... Dal Rev:do P. Gio: Battista Pace.... 1678.[143]

2. Biblioteca Nazionale Marciana. Cod. It. VII-1269 (-9573).
   CEREMONIALE MAGNUM/Sive/Raccolta Universale di tutte le Ceremonie spettanti alla Ducal/Regia Capella di San Marco.... Dal R:do P. Gio: Battista Pace.... 1678.

3. Biblioteca Nazionale Marciana. Cod. It. VII-396 (-7423).
   CEREMONIALE MAGNUM/sivè/Raccolta Universale di tutte le Ceremonie/Spettanti alla Ducal Regia Capella di S. Marco . . . . DAL REV:DO P. GIO: BATTISTA PACE.... 1678. Same hand as item 11 below. Copy made ca. 1732.

4. Biblioteca del Civico Museo Correr. Codice Cicogna 2769.
   CEREMONIALE MAGNUM sive/Raccolta Universale di tutte le Ceremonie/spettanti alla Ducal Regia Capella/di San Marco/Distinte di Mese in Mese/Con Cronologia de fatti in quest'occorrenti./[1695]

5. Biblioteca Correr. Codice Cicogna 2770.
   CEREMONIALE MAGNUM.... copy made ca. 1745. Same hand as Cicogna 1295.

6. Biblioteca Correr. Codice Cicogna 1295.
   CEREMONIALE MAGNUM.... copy made ca. 1745. Same hand as Cicogna 2770. Frontispiece: "Codice copiato circa 1745 da Agostino Prezzato.... "

7. Biblioteca Nazionale Marciana. Cod. Lat. III-172 (-2276)
   Caeremoniale rituum sacrorum ecclesiae S. Marci Venetiarum, partim latine, partim itale, ex pluribus libris accurate compilatum opera Bartholomaei Bonifacii Caeremoniarum magistri. 1564.

8. Biblioteca Correr. Codice Cicogna 2768.
   Ceremoniale di San Marco. Incomplete manuscript, labeled 1564.

9. A.S.V., Consulatore in Jure, Registro 555
   Rituum Ecclesiasticorum Ceremoniale iuxta Ducalis Ecclesiae Sancti Marci/Venetiarum consuetudinem, et vetustissimis Ecclesiae Codicibus/quam diligentissime undique collectum, ac in ampliorem formam et ordine novissime renovatum. Anno Domini M. D./lxiiij, Pio iiij, Pontifice Maximo Apostolice/....[144]

10. A.S.V., San Marco, Procuratia de Supra, Registro 98
    Rituum Ecclesiasticorum/CERIMONIALE/Iuxta Ducalis Ecclesiae S. MARCI consuetudinem/ex Vetustissimis eiusdem Ecclesiae Codicubus quam diligentissime undique/collectum et in ampliorem formam et ordinem novissime renovatum./Anno Domini MDLXIV. Includes "Aggiunte Posteriori estratte dall'Antico Cerimoniale" written in 1713, and a second *aggiunta*, in a different hand, of events from 1713 to 1770.

11. A.S.V., San Marco, Procuratia de Supra, Registro 99
    COMPILAZIONE/De Cerimoniali Essistenti/Nella Cancellaria secreta/Nella Cancellaria Ducale/NELLA PROCURATIA DI/SUPRA/Con una copia fedelissima/Dell'Antico Cerimoniale/Della Chiesa di San Marco/Aumentato con aggiunta/Di moltissime Annotazioni e casi occorsi/NELLE PUBBLICHE ECCLESIASTICHE/FUNZIONI/estratti da Scritti Auttentici/De' Maestri di Cerimonie di detta Chiesa/con numerosi Decreti/Attinenti all'Ecclesiastica Officiatura/Fatta da/P. Zuanne Gavazzi Maestro di Coro e di/Cerimonie/Per Commando/

DELLA SERENISSIMA SIGNORIA/Con Terminazione 23. Gennaro 1752./ANNO AB INCARNATIONE DOMINI MDCCLV.

Title page of the "antico Ceremoniale": Rituum Ecclesiasticorum/Ceremoniale/juxta Ducalis Ecclesiae Sancti Marci/ Consuetudinem ex yetustissimnis ejusdem Ecclesia./Codicilibus, quam diligentissime undique collectum,/et in ampliorem formam et ordinem/novissime renovatum/A P. BARTOLOMEO BONIFACIO CERIMONIARUM/MAGISTRO./ANNO DOMINI. MDLXIV.

12. A.S.V., San Marco, Procuratia de Supra, Registro 100
CEREMONIALI PUBLICI/TOMO II/Scritto Da D. Giovanni Verdura/Maestro di Ceremonie/della Ducal/di S. Marco/ COMINCIA NOVEMBRE/MDCCLVII.

13. Biblioteca del Civico Museo Correr. Codice Cicogna 559.
NUCLEUS CEREMONIA-/RUM./Sivè/Ristretto di tutte le Ceremonie, e Riti,/ che si pratticano nella Ducal Basilica di/S. Marco.... /Da Padre Gio: Battista Pace.... /In Venetia. 20. Luglio. M.DC.LXXVII.

14. Biblioteca Nazionale Marciana. Misc. 134.9 and 2619.8.
RACCONTO/DELL'APPARATO,/ET SOLENNITA/FATTA NELLA DUCAL CHIESA/de San Marco di Venetia./Con l'occasione dell'Inventione, et espositione del Sangue Pretiosissimo/del Costato di Christo, del Latte della Beata Vergine,/con altre santissime Reliquie./Li 28. Maggio. 1617./DI GIULIO CESARE VERGARO/Canonico, et Maestro delle Cerimonie/ nella stressa Chiesa./.... IN VENETIA, M. DC. XVII./Appresso Antonio Pinelli, Stampator Ducale.

15. Biblioteca Querini-Stampaglia, I.A. 725
ESEQUIE/FATTE IN VENETIA/DALLA NATIONE/ FIORENTINA/AL SERENISSIMO /D. COSIMO II/QUARTO GRAN DUCA/DI TOSCANA/Il dì 25 di Maggio/1621./IN VENETIA Appresso il Ciotti.

16. Biblioteca Nazionale Marciana. Misc. 134.17.
VENETIA FESTIVA/PER GLI POMPOSI SPETTACOLI/ FATTI RAPPRESENTARE/Dall'Illustriss. et Eccellentiss. Sig. d'Husè/Ambasciatore di S. M. Christianissima,/PER LA NASCITA/ DEL REAL DELFINO DI FRANCIA./A

MONSIEUR DU HUSSAY/Conseiller d'Estat Intendant, et Controolleur [*sic*]/General de ses Finances./.... IN VENETIA, MDCXXXVIII./Appresso Andrea Baba.

While 16 items are listed in this category, only 7 different texts are actually represented; for items 1 through 6 are copies of a single source, and items 7 through 11 are, likewise, copies or partial copies of a sole text. These items represent the known extant copies of the two great *ceremoniali* of the sixteenth and seventeenth centuries: that of Bartolomeo Bonifacio, first copied in 1564, and that of Giovanni Pace, copied in 1678. These volumes have scarcely been tapped by scholars of Venetian music, and they contain a wealth of information on the integration of music into the ceremonial life of St. Mark's.

Giovanni Battista Pace's gigantic compendium (item 1) is nearly 500 pages in length. Pace, a canon of St. Mark's, outlines the scope of his work in a prefatory passage (Document 35). He aims to describe the chronology and history of the ducal chapel, the rites and ceremonies of the church, the privileges and duties of the clerical hierarchy, as well as the duties of the singers, organists and bell-ringers of St. Mark's. This information, he tells us, has been drawn from "various authors, chronicles, diverse manuscripts, and doctors' writings in the secret ducal files [and has been] summarized in this *Ceremoniale perpetuo* through a long and laborious effort" over a period of 38 years.[145]

A glance at the table of contents, however, shows us that the compendium is really much more. In addition to an elaborate ecclesiastical calendar describing the day-to-day ceremonies of the basilica, there is an index of obsolete ceremonies drawn from the "antico Ceremoniale"; a *rubrica generale* of office items in the *Orationale*, the special breviary for St. Mark's; and then elaborate descriptions of special ceremonies, meetings, ballotings—in short, a complete guide to every aspect of the life of the basilica. At least six copies of this document exist. Item 2 contains the same hands as are found in item 1; it may well have been copied at the same time. Of the additional copies, item 3 was made in 1732, item 4 in 1695. Items 5 and 6 date from ca. 1745, judging both from the dated inscription in no. 6 and of one new ceremony inserted into the volumes, which is dated 1745.[146]

The most important *ceremoniale* for St. Mark's before Pace's volume is the work which Bartolomeo Bonifacio, the third *maestro delle ceremonie*, assembled in 1564. About Bonifacio himself we have little information.[147] Giovanni Stringa mentions him briefly in his 1604 revision of Sansovino's *Venetia città nobilissima* (Document 36):

> The third master of ceremonies was named Bonifacio, who lived until the year 1564. This was the man who composed and wrote with his own hand, to much praise, the *Ceremoniale*, which contains all of the ceremonies which are customarily practiced in this church.

Giovanni Pace also cursorily cites Bonifacio in his own *Ceremoniale Magnum* (Document 37):

> 1564. P. Bartolamio Bonifacio *maestro di coro* composed the *Ceremonial Antico* under Pope Pius IV, and Doge Gerolamo Priuli, drawn from very ancient and primitive rites, now [made] majestic and venerable, and enlarged and altered in such a manner, with respect to the place they are performed, in the presence of the Public Majesty, that the old ceremonies can scarcely be distinguished from the new ones.

Bonifacio's text is found in five copies in Venetian libraries (items 7 through 11) and is referred to over and over as "l'antico ceremoniale della chiesa di San Marco," to distinguish it from Pace's later *ceremoniale*. Item 7 is clearly the earliest exemplar of the text. It is in a sixteenth-century hand, and the many cancellations and marginal notes give it a rather "scruffy" appearance. Indeed, this is very possibly the copy which Stringa says Bonifacio wrote out "di suo proprio pugno," and which he described in a letter of 1609 as "falling apart, written over, and confused."[148] The volume is prefaced by documents signed by the *maestri di coro* of the *cinquecento* and *seicento*, confirming their receipt of the volume as they took office. These statements go right up to 1678 (Document 38), the year Pace finished his own *ceremoniale*, and they suggest that Bonifacio's volume was used as a liturgical authority for the first three-fourths of the seventeenth century. Several other documents attest to the use of the "antico ceremoniale" through the first part of the *seicento*. The first book listed among the items given to Giorgio Minaccia when he became *maestro di coro* in 1631[149] is "Il Ceremonial coperto di Carta peccora scritto a pena," a statement which undoubtedly refers to item 7, since Minaccia is among the *maestri* who signed statements upon receiving the volume. Moreover, one of the later copies of the *ceremoniale*, item 10, contains a statement to the effect that Minaccia presented the volume to the Inquisition on 27 June 1646 (Document 39). In all probability, the same volume was the source from which Minaccia copied documents into one of the ducal *ceremoniali* three days earlier (Document 40). The most specific document, however, is the decree naming Rocco de Bruni to the post of *maestro di coro e delle ceremonie* in 1601 (Document 41). On this occasion, the Procurators instructed him

> that in virtue of Your election by us, you must . . . exercise and put into execution the Book and Ceremonial of the ecclesiastic rites which was consigned to you at the time of your election, which is entitled thus:

Rituum Ecclesiasticorum Cerimoniale iuxta Ducalis Ecclesiae
Sancti Marci Venetiarum . . . Anno Domini: 1564 . . .
neither altering nor changing any of these sacred rites.

The three other complete copies of the *ceremoniale* are clearly derived from item 7 and form a neat, simple genealogical stemma. No. 9 has the same contents as no. 7 except for two new documents, clearly labeled "copia," which are dated 1589 (f. 186v) and a notice of approval of the volume signed by Doge Marino Grimani in 1602 (f. 187r). No. 10, the volume sent to the Inquisition by Minaccia in 1646, has all of this material in a single hand—i.e., the body of the text, the two documents from 1589, and the confirmation of Doge Grimani—along with an *aggiunta* of seventeenth-century ceremonies in a new hand, the copy of which is dated 1713. No. 11 in turn has the complete contents of no. 10 plus a second *aggiunta* of various ceremonies from the sixteenth through eighteenth centuries. It was copied out between 1752 and 1755.

Although it does not fit into the stemma, we can tentatively identify the fragmentary copy of Bonifacio's *ceremoniale* in the Biblioteca Correr (item 8). In his letter to the Procurators of 1609 (see below, note 148), Giovanni Stringa reviews his past liturgical publications and outlines his plans to publish three additional volumes, "and these are the *Ceremoniale*, the Psalter, and the Missal, according to the custom of this Church, which differs from the Roman rite in many respects." He adds, moreover, that "it is most necessary and fitting that, since the *Ceremoniale* is presently falling apart, written over, and confused, it be re-copied, re-ordered and reformed in many places by my own hand, which the Most Serene Prince has asked me to do, and which task I have already begun."[150] Evidently, it never got out of the preliminary stages, for of the three projected publications, only the psalter found its way into print as the *Psalterium Davidicum* of 1609. The *ceremoniale* and missal were never published.[151]

The remaining *ceremoniali* are independent volumes. Item no. 12, begun in the late 1750s, is a loosely organized volume. It contains miscellaneous descriptions of events from 1758 through 1792, nearly to the fall of the Republic. An additional *ceremoniale* may have been compiled at this time, for the *Indice e Repertorio Generale* of acts passed by the governing bodies of Venice states that a compilation was ordered on 28 April 1759 and that the volume was to contain ceremonies both within and outside St. Mark's (Document 42). Moreover, on 31 May 1759 the Serenissima Signoria asked that the "tre uniformi Libri Ceremoniali" which they had ordered be placed in the Cancelleria Secreta, the Procuratia de Supra, and with the *maestro delle cerimonie* (Document 43). Despite the disparity in dates, item 12 may indeed be the volume referred to here, for it is mysteriously labeled "Tomo II," although it appears to be autonomous in content.

The remaining four volumes are smaller in scope. The first, no. 13, is another work of Giovanni Pace, a detailed ecclesiastical calendar which describes ceremonies for much of the church year. It may well have been a sketch for the calendar included in the *Ceremoniale Magnum*, though the two are far from identical. Item no. 14 is a pamphlet which describes the ceremonies which accompanied the display of relic of the blood of Christ in St. Mark's in 1617. Item no. 15 is the celebrated print describing the Requiem Mass for Cosimo II de' Medici, performed in Ss. Giovanni e Paolo in 1621. Item no. 16 describes the ceremonies in November, 1638, ordered by the French ambassador to commemorate the birth of Louis XIV of France.

At least one printed ceremonial for the Roman rite must be considered in this context: Clement VIII's *Ceremoniale Episcoporum*, first published in 1600 and then reprinted a number of times during the early years of the century.[152] While the extensive material which survives from St. Mark's itself might seem to render such a general source superfluous, we do know that the basilica owned a copy; for the volume is one of three works dealing with the Roman liturgy which were purchased by the Procurators in 1620 (Document 44).[153] The other two volumes bought at this time can also be identified. The first is Giovanni Guidetti's *Directorium Chori ad usum sacrosanctae Basilicae Vaticanae et aliarum Cathedralium*, first published in Rome in 1582, which had gone through five printings in Rome and Munich by 1620. The second is clearly the Roman martyrology of Pope Gregory XIII, first published in 1584.

It is difficult to say what role Clement VIII's *ceremoniale* would have played in St. Mark's. It is never referred to in any of the documents dealing with ceremony in the basilica, which cite instead the manuscript sources from St. Mark's as the authorities for ceremonies. Moreover, Venice's struggle with the papacy was at its height during the early *seicento*, and countless documents insist that the ceremonies in St. Mark's take place according to the ancient rite of the basilica, without changes or innovations. However, since the *Ceremoniale Episcoporum* is quite a general book which does not go into as much detail as the *ceremoniali* of St. Mark's, it may have been used as a general reference and authority while the sources from St. Mark's served as the guide for the details of the services. It is difficult to believe that it could have occupied a position equal in importance to the volumes of Pace and Bonifacio, which are cited continuously as the ultimate authorities on the rite of the ducal chapel.

The Era of Maestro Claudio Monteverdi

The most striking event in the history of the *cappella marciana* during the seventeenth century was surely Monteverdi's appointment as *maestro* on 19 August 1613. Rather than seeking out a Venetian to fill the post vacated by Giulio Cesare Martinengo, the Procurators finally adopted the procedure suggested by Procurator Federico Contarini back in 1603 and looked outside the Veneto for "a mature individual, not only in terms of age but also in terms of his lifestyle and habits,"[154] a man truly able to follow in the tradition of Willaert, Rore and Zarlino, the legendary triumvirate invoked throughout the first decade of the seventeenth century as a virtual symbol of the lost glories of the *cinquecento*. While Monteverdi's arrival heralded the beginning of a new age of disciplined music-making in St. Mark's, his appointment was actually part of a series of moves on the part of the Procurators to upgrade musical standards at the basilica, and in order to understand the period of Monteverdi's tenure as *maestro di cappella*, one must understand some of the currents present in the musical life of the basilica during the decades preceding his appointment.

The 1590s were a difficult time for the *cappella*. Standards had fallen under *maestro* Baldissare Donati, who could neither maintain discipline nor attendance at services among the members of the choir.[155] The choir consisted of only 13 singers in the mid-1590s, when a list was drawn up of the members and of Donati's appraisal of their vocal gifts (Document 45):[156]

In reverent obedience to the order given me by the Most Illustrious Serene (Procurator), in a manner and form to show my good faith, I report that in the chapel of St. Mark's there are the following singers:

Sopranos
Antonio Spagnol: lovely and good voice, but not very secure
Guielmo Francese: secure and confident singer, but not so refined a voice

Contraltos
Zuanne Chiozotto: sufficient singer, and where his voice lacks refinement, he makes
    up for it with lovely singing
Hieronimo de Carmeni: not much of a voice
Bernardo di Frari: his voice is not of bad timbre, but he has never trained it
Battista da San Pantazzo: he has a large voice and is very secure

Tenors
Zuanne Antonio Fiamingo: has always had a good voice and been a good singer, but
    because of his age, he will soon decline
Augustin Fazuol: good voice and a good singer
Paulo Roman: his voice is not of bad timbre, and he sings well

Basses
Fabritio di Frari: good voice .
Giacomo Ant*onio* di Corsenieri: good voice
Sigismondo da S*an* Zanepolo: good voice
Augustin di Foscari: good voice, but sings timidly

A campaign to bolster the vocal resources of St. Mark's had already begun in early 1595, when the Procurators decreed that the Venetian ambassadors in various parts of Italy and the Austro-Hungarian empire should be contacted and asked to search for possible singers for the chapel. Evidently all voice types were needed, for the Procurators stated that they wanted "in particular, soprano eunuchs, basses, tenors and contraltos" (see Document 46). The Procurators emphasized three points in trying to woo singers to St. Mark's: first, that the singers would have security of employment for their entire life; second, that they did not have to sing on ferial days; and third, that there were many opportunities to earn extra money by singing in other churches in the city. These points are important, for they were clearly the factors which made employment at St. Mark's so attractive during the early seventeenth century; and when the *cappella* ran into severe problems in the 1650s and then again in the 1670s, the difficulties stemmed precisely from the fact that St. Mark's could no longer offer these generous working conditions. Responses came in from the Ambassadors in Prague, Rome, Verona and Paris.[157] The first three did not have much luck in their searches. The Ambassador from Prague could not find any *castrati* although he found out about two basses in Innsbruck who might want to come to Venice. The Ambassador in Rome was only able to put his hands on a Spanish *castrato* whom he had known previously and who was coming to Venice anyway for personal business. The Ambassador from Verona was able to speak to the two basses in Innsbruck, recommended by the Ambassador to Prague, but they would not give him a firm commitment. Only the Parisian Ambassador was successful; he found a marvelous eighteen-year-old bass at Notre Dame who "sings as far down as singers can, and has such a large voice that it makes the whole church respond, which is four times larger than St. Mark's."[158] The Ambassador was also able to persuade a French *castrato* to come to Venice, and the singers were accepted into the *cappella* on 23 December 1597 at 100 ducats per year, the figure which remained the top fee for singers throughout the seventeenth century. There were 12 singers on the payroll at the time the Frenchmen entered the chapel.[159]

The *cappella* grew steadily during the next few years. In January of 1597, the singers were interviewed by the Procurators to get their opinion of the state of the *cappella* and the names of possible candidates for auditions; Guglielmo *francese* reported the vocal distribution at this time as "four basses, five tenors, five contraltos including myself, one boy singer, three sopranos, and the priest from Brescia who just left, who can be used as a baritone, that is, who can sing three vocal parts."[160] These 18 singers had grown to 22 by 22 November 1601, when they petitioned the Doge to let them incorporate themselves as a *compagnia* with certain privileges and benefits (Document 47).

The organization of the company of singers was a move to insure discipline and organization on those occasions when the singers went out of St. Mark's to sing in other churches of the city. Of course, they regularly did this as part of their normal duties. They followed the Doge to San Nicolò on the Lido for the Feast of the Ascension, to Palladio's church of the *Redentore* on the annual comemoration of Venice's delivery from the plague of 1576, and to a number of other Venetian churches on their appropriate feast days. The company, however, was designed to govern them on those occasions when they were not under the auspices of the basilica but, rather, sang in the churches and *scuole* of Venice for extra fees. The singers had initially organized for this purpose in 1579 under Doge Nicolò da Ponte, and the Doge Marino Grimani authorized a renewal of the charter in 1601.[161] The charter is reproduced in the ducal records.[162] The company was headed by Giovanni Croce, from whom authority passed to a *vice capo*, and then to the singers in order of their seniority.[163] The administration of the company was carried out by officers, arranged in an elaborate hierarchy of responsibility which probably never functioned in actuality. It is worth nothing, however, that a careful pay scale was established for Vespers services, based on the portion of a service for which a singer was present. If he was on time and sang the entire service, he naturally received full pay. If he had not yet arrived at the time the second psalm was begun, he lost one third of his fee; if he was not present for the beginning of the third psalm, he lost two thirds; and if he had not arrived for the fourth psalm, he was not paid at all (Document 48).

While the company of singers ran smoothly during the first decade of the century, problems began during the second. Gasparo Locadello, elected *capo* in 1612, ran into conflict with the *vice-maestro* of St. Mark's, Marc'Antonio Negri, who felt that he should retain his status as *vice-maestro* when the company went out to sing at other churches. The case was brought before Doge Marc'Antonio Memo on 27 August 1613, and he decided in favor of the company, stating that Negri's authority "according to his election is in the chapel of St. Mark's and nowhere else." (Document 49)[164] Thus, the company achieved a major victory, and its autonomy outside of St. Mark's became a factor with which Monteverdi had to deal more than once.

The story of the company during the next decades is one of power struggles, both from within and without. In 1614, two *procuratori* elected by the company appeared before the Doge. They reported that some of the singers were "very arrogant and without any fear, scorning the rules and refusing to obey them," and they asked the Doge to help maintain order within the group "in order that all the singers of the Company of St. Mark's obey the bylaws and decrees" of the organization.[165] Difficulties persisted, however, and on 13 January 1617 an elaborate hearing took place before Doge Giovanni Bembo (Documents 52 and 53). First the Doge heard Monteverdi and one group of singers from the company, who complained that singers from outside St. Mark's were gradually taking over the company. The Doge then heard a second group of singers, including some from outside St. Mark's, who wanted the *status quo* maintained with Monteverdi kept out of the group. The singer Domenico Aldegatti testified that the entire company should be dissolved, while another, Paulo Veraldo, spoke in favor of its continued existence. The Doge retained the company but established a new set of rules. According to his decision, only the singers from the *cappella* of St. Mark's could be members of the Company of St. Mark's when it went out to other churches. Outside singers might be brought in on days when the company had two services in remote parts of the city, but these singers were not to be permanent members. A new set of officers was established, old elections were invalidated, and new ones were to take place. Moreover, Monteverdi and his successors as *maestro di cappella* could not be members of the company nor were they to have any voice in its affairs. Finally, all singers were to be free to accept tips if they were offered.

While the Doge's decision was clearly a compromise—he allied the company more closely with St. Mark's by excluding outside singers, yet he also refused to let Monteverdi participate—it did not establish stability within the group. The singers had overreached themselves, and only six months later two of the company's officers approached the Doge for more help (Document 54). They were filled with remorse and had seen the error in their judgment, for they spoke as follows:

> To tell the truth, there is a great difference between the office of *maestro di cappella* and that of a singer, from which it is born. With [only] weak success, to our great mortification, we have seen and experienced all too keenly the public opinion of our music going up in smoke in this city. This is a great blow to us, and we fear much worse, since we face the competition of many other companies, filled with ambitious men.

Thus, they asked the Doge to allow them

> to elect by ballot someone outside of our organization, some valorous man known and
> beloved by the city, who will use his power and authority in our interest [by] directing
> our music, marking the beat and giving us new compositions according to our need.

The Doge accorded them this privilege. Just who this "valorous man" was intended to be we do not know. It may have been Monteverdi himself, however, for on 20 October 1620, the new Doge Antonio Prioli decreed that the office of *maestro di cappella* and that of *capo* of the company of singers should be merged and held by a single person (Document 55). Thus, Monteverdi was finally made the head of the singers of the chapel both within and outside St. Mark's. Similarly, the Doge decreed that the *vice maestro di cappella* of St. Mark's would be *vice capo* of the singers outside the basilica; Negri was *vice-maestro* at the time of this decree, but Grandi assumed this double position a month later. The Doge also created a sort of "steering committee" of the *maestro, vice-maestro*, and the two most senior singers, which could accept singers from outside the *cappella* into the company.

Still, the company seems to have been beset with problems. In 1622, the Doge instituted a series of fines for disobeying the bylaws of the company, citing continuous difficulties between the *capo, vice capo*, and the singers (Document 56). Later the same year, he forbade the singers to go into the churches of Venice unless they were under the auspices of the company or had his special permission (Document 57). Other problems developed between the company and the guild of instrumentalists, headquartered in the church of San Silvestro. After the guild had tried on a number of occasions to make those singers of St. Mark's who played instruments pay dues to the guild, the Doge intervened, decreeing that the singers of St. Mark's should be entirely free from the strictures of the instrumentalists at San Silvestro. The singers were to be responsible to the Doge alone and were allowed to play instruments as well as sing in any of the churches of Venice and to teach both playing and singing in the schools of the city. They were forbidden only to play for dancing[166] (Document 58).

The difficulties surrounding the Company of St. Mark's are only one example of the legacy which Monteverdi inherited from the early years of the century. If we examine the documents of the first decade of the *seicento*, we find a number of signs that discipline was growing thin within the ranks of the *cappella*. On 6 July 1603, the Procurators noted that the singers were not attending the services faithfully; on 9 July, Procurator

Federico Contarini cited the need for a strong *maestro* to maintain order; and on 13 July a system of fines was instituted which established a framework for financial control over attendance which lasted the entire century. The system provided that one singer should be responsible for taking attendance for a period of two months. He was to report those missing from any service, and their salary for the service would be taken and divided up among those singers actually present (Document 59).

While we have no lists of the exact vocal personnel of the *cappella* for the first decade of the century, there are no signs that it deviated from the 20 or so singers listed on the company's charter of 1601. We know, of course, that the vocal forces were somewhat greater on the major feasts. While later in the century extra musicians seem to have been hired only on Christmas and the Ascension (for the ceremonies surrounding the marriage of Venice to the sea), within the first decade we find records for Christmas, Ascension, Epiphany, the Annunciation, and the Feasts of St. Isidore and St. Mark. Sometimes the hired body of singers was actually quite large; for example, 14 singers were hired for Vespers on the Vigil of Ascension in 1604: 3 boy sopranos, 3 altos, 4 tenors, 3 basses, and 2 unspecified voices (Document 60).

Documents indicate also that as early as the first decade of the century certain singers were hired specifically for their skill as soloists. When the Procurators renewed the contract of tenor Stefano Rivieri in 1606, they mentioned their satisfaction at having "heard him several times, singing both in the chorus and as a soloist with the organs."[167] Determining the distribution of voices in the *cappella* is not possible during these years, but one can make a statistical estimate. Of the 31 singers who entered the *cappella* between 1600 and Monteverdi's appointment on 19 August 1613, 7 were basses, 6 altos, 8 tenors, and 4 were sopranos, 3 of whom were specified as *eunuco* or *voce mutata*. (The voice types of the remaining 6 are not given). While these figures can provide only the vaguest approximation of the proportions of voice types, we do know that there were only 3 sopranos in the *cappella* around 1605.[168] This shortage of high voices would exist throughout the century, and it only became worse after 1650 when the operatic stage drew the best voices from the chapel. It is worth noting, however, that one of the *castrati* to enter the chapel during this period was Leonardo Simonetti, the man who would eventually edit the popular *Ghirlanda Sacra*, the definitive anthology of the Venetian sacred monody during the 1620s, as well as Grandi's final Vespers collection.[169]

The singers of the *cappella* were not the only singers of the basilica. In his description of the ecclesiastical hierarchy of St. Mark's in 1604,

Giovanni Stringa speaks of the duties of a number of employees who made up the plainchant choir of St. Mark's.[170] The nucleus of the choir consisted of about 30 *giovani di coro*, singers who were required to be present every day to sing and to recite psalms.[171] There is also some evidence that the *giovani* may have sung Masses in the *stile antico* on ferial days when the singers of the *cappella* were not present. The 10 resident canons of the church recited the canonical hours every day and intoned Vespers on major feasts; the subcanons intoned them on minor feasts and ferial days.[172] On certain very elaborate feasts, two other groups were present in the choir: 14 *piovani*, or non-resident canons, and the clerics from the seminary.

The instruments used in St. Mark's during the first decade of the *seicento* can be determined with less certainty because the permanent nucleus of players was small and many instrumentalists were hired for special feasts.[173] Instrumentalists in the basilica can be traced back to 1568, when Girolamo dalla Casa and his two brothers were hired to play in the organ lofts. By 1601, when Dalla Casa was succeeded by Giovanni Bassano, the nucleus of players within the basilica seems to have been only four *cornetti* and trombones.[174] The payments for individual players brought in ad hoc for special feasts are many, however, and they show that the body of players was considerably greater on many occasions. For example, on Christmas of 1602, 14 extra instrumentalists were paid for performing in the basilica: 6 trombones, one of whom doubled on bassoon, 3 *cornetti*, 2 violins and 1 *violone*.[175] On Christmas of 1603, a similar contingent was called in: 5 trombones, 4 *cornetti*, 1 bassoon, 2 violins, and a *violone*.[176] Other records showing ad hoc payments to instrumentalists exist for the feasts of the Epiphany, the Annunciation, St. Isidore and St. Mark.[177] Most of the instrumentalists were the same as those hired at Christmas, although there is a payment to one "*Padre Lorenzo dalla tiorba*" in a list covering a number of feasts in 1603-4.

Another group of instruments which played in the basilica on certain occasions was the company of *piffari e tromboni* who accompanied the Doge on important state occasions.[178] This group consisted of six players who, at least at the opening of the seventeenth century, seem usually to have played *cornetti* and trombones. While they do not seem to have played in St. Mark's on a regular basis, we do know that they were present for important occasions. Bonifacio tells us that *piffari* (and he specifies *cornetti* here) played during Mass at the Elevation on the day when a new Doge was elected and presented to the populace (Document 61). He also states that the players performed on the anniversary of the Doge's ascension to the dogate.

Both groups of instruments were officially incorporated a few years after Monteverdi became *maestro di cappella*. The instrumentalists connected with the church were put on a regular payroll, paid 15 ducats per year, and required to play in the basilica on 26 different occasions during the year. There were 16 members of the ensemble at this point, and although they cannot all be identified, we know that there were at least 3 violins, 3 trombones, and a *violone contrabasso*.[179] The *piffari e tromboni* were also organized more tightly at this time, although in their case this organization took place at their own request. Jealous over the success which the singers were having with their Company of St. Mark's, the Doge's *piffari* decided they would be well advised to form a company of their own; and on 24 November 1614, Giovanni Bassano presented the Doge with a request to declare his *piffari e tromboni* a "union of instrumentalists" with the privilege of playing "both in the churches and the *scuole grande* within and outside of Venice" (Document 62). The instrumentalists seem to have had better luck with their company than the singers and did not have the constant disputes which plagued the Company of St. Mark's. On 22 October 1616, the bylaws of the union of instrumentalists was drawn up and recorded in the ducal records (Document 63). The union would actually consist of three separate companies of instrumentalists, to be headed by Giovanni Bassano, by Francesco Bonfante, who would later succeed Bassano as *maestro de' concerti* of St. Mark's, and by Nicolo da Udene. The three companies were to be of the same size and were to take up the opportunities to play on different feasts in turn, the company to play on the first such occasion to be chosen by ballot. The engagements which they could accept were defined as Mass, Vespers, Compline and the *Quaranta hore*, i.e. the Mass, processions and other services taking place during the 40 hours the Blessed Sacrament was displayed in church. The discipline of the three companies was governed by regulations only slightly less convoluted than those governing the Company of St. Mark's. The union of instrumentalists seems to have functioned efficiently, for it practically disappears from the ducal records once its bylaws are drawn up. The charter of the union was reconfirmed by the Doge on 27 September 1625, and on 9 March 1645, the members were excused from having to pay dues demanded by the other instrumentalists of the city, so the union seems to have been functioning as late as mid-century.[180]

The other elements of instrumental music at St. Mark's were, of course, the two large organs, the traditional "first" organ above the chapel of St. Peter, and the smaller "second" organ above the chapel of St. Clement. Stringa describes both in detail—the larger first organ which, at the time of his writing, was played by Paolo Giusti and the sweeter sounding second organ, about which Stringa writes:

> The sound of this organ is most refined; and it is all the more refined when it is played by the finest organist which Italy has today; and this is Giovanni Gabrieli, worthy of the highest praise for his rare and unique skill which he possesses in this profession.[181]

It has been suggested that the larger first organ may have been used as a continuo organ for large choral works, since its sound seems to have been less refined, and that the second organ was used for the virtuoso repertoire of the well-known organists connected with the basilica. These were not the only instruments in the basilica, however. Two chamber organs (*organetti*) were used during the seventeenth century. One belonged to the Seminario Gregoriano in Castello and was constantly carted back and forth, but both instruments were moved around St. Mark's for certain major feasts. A number of documents record the moving of the *organetti* from their places of storage to the so-called *nicchie* of the church and back again. (These *nicchie* or "niches" are the small arches which separate each of the choirlofts from the main body of the church.) The use of the *organetti* was two-fold. They were often used to accompany instrumental sonatas, for Pace reports that on Easter Day, "double-choir music is sung to the accompaniment of the large organs and sonatas to the small ones."[182] Moreover, the *organetti* were the instruments which would eventually accompany the small concerted motets which were popular in St. Mark's from the 1620s onward. A number of singers were hired from the first decade of the century onward with the dual duties of singing "both in the choir and in *concerti* accompanied by the organs and the theorbo."[183] Although the documents do not specify whether these organs are the large ones in the lofts or the *organetti* in the *nicchie,* iconographic evidence points to the latter; for an anonymous painting now in the Ca' Morosini in Venice of a musical performance in the basilica on 7 May 1690 clearly shows three solo singers standing in one of the *nicchie,* next to a theorbo and just below one of the *organetti* (see Plate 5).[184] It seems, moreover, that a bass instrument was used to reinforce the sound of the *organetti,* for when Paulo Mancin was hired to play *violone* on 25 July 1655, he was accepted "as an instrumentalist to play the *violone* with the *organetti* and elsewhere in the church of St. Mark's."[185] Indeed, there is an instrument which might be a *violone* in the lower *nicchia* next to the violins in the Ca' Morosini painting. Players for the *organetti* were hired *ad hoc* at the beginning of the century, but in 1645, Giovanni Battista Volpe, Rovetta's nephew, and Giovanni Battista Gualtieri were hired to play them whenever the *maestro di cappella* thought it necessary (Document 64).

It is worth noting that two other continuo instruments were present in St. Mark's in the seventeenth century. The theorbo has been cited once, and while it is not mentioned prominently, it is recorded regularly in the documents. Indeed, on 4 January 1618, a payment was made to one "Franceschino, son of the *maestro di cappella*, who sang the prophecies with the theorbo on Christmas Eve and Christmas Day."[186] This Franceschino is, of course, Francesco Monteverdi, who may still have been a boy soprano at the time; five years later; he joined the *cappella* as a tenor.[187] Pace tells us, moreover, that a harpsichord was used at Matins in Holy Week, although we do not know whether it was used in the regular music of the basilica.[188]

We have one list of the entire *cappella* from the middle of the second decade of the century which can sum up this discussion so far (Document 65). While it is undated, I have been able to date it quite accurately through its contents. The list must have been drawn up after 5 March 1616, the day Zorzo Gardassin was accepted into the chapel, since his name is included. Moreover, it must have been written before 24 August 1616, when the *maestro*'s salary was raised from 300 to 400 ducats per year. Thus, in mid-1616, the *cappella* consisted of a *maestro* and *vice-maestro* (Monteverdi and Marc'Antonio Negri), 24 singers, 2 organists (Giusto and Savii), 2 *maestri di concerti* (Giovanni da Udine and Giovanni Bassano), and 16 rank-and-file players. While not all of the voice types can be identified, the distribution seems almost equal between the four standard voice parts. Of the instrumentalists, most are not identifiable from other documents, but those who are seem to have played bowed strings and trombones. This list represents the *cappella* about three years into Monteverdi's period of tenure as *maestro di cappella*, and it is clear that the *cappella* was quite a healthy body from a purely numerical point of view.

Monteverdi is said to have brought about a number of reforms in the *cappella* during his first years as *maestro*, and some of these are clearly mirrored in the documents. That he bolstered the soprano voices by auditioning and admitting a number of *castrati* is clear. While only three *castrati* had been accepted into the chapel during the first decade of the century, Monteverdi accepted six between 1613, and 1620: Giovanni Battista Calceta, Bortolo Arabali, Felice Casselen, Antonio Grimani, Giovanni Francesco Dalmatin and Prospero Arigon.[189] Thus, there were skilled voices to sing the solo and duo motets which Grandi would compose during the early 1620s.[190]

Another reform which Monteverdi supposedly instigated upon his appointment as *maestro* was the revival of *cinquecento* polyphony through insistence upon Masses in *canto figurato* for ferial days as well as for feasts. One of Monteverdi's first acts as *maestro* was to have the Procurators order prints of Masses in the *stile antico* for use on ferial days (Document 67).[191] On 6 April 1614, stating that there were few good collections of music for ferial use, when the services had to be brief, and that it would be too expensive to have works copied out in manuscript, the Procurators concluded an agreement with the Gardano firm to buy copies of six books of Masses for four, five, six and eight voices. Monteverdi's choice of repertoire is surprising in historical hindsight, for the names of obscure figures are found alongside those of the greatest composers of the *cinquecento*:

> Palestrina's second and fifth books of Masses for four, five and six voices; the first book for four voices of Francesco Soriano; the Masses for six and eight voices of Orlando Lasso; a book of Gerolamo Lambardi for four voices; and the first book of Paolo Paciotto for four and five voices. . . .

It has been asserted that Monteverdi was reviving a lost tradition of *stile antico* performance with this gesture. It seems, however, that he was merely updating the repertoire rather than resurrecting a lost practice; for on 22 April 1607, six years before Monteverdi's arrival in Venice, the Procurators had discussed the problems of obtaining copies of sixteenth-century polyphony for performance (Document 68). A comparison of the contents of these two documents is informative. All of the items in Monteverdi's list can be identified with prints published in Rome, Venice or Munich during the two decades 1590–1610.[192] Although Palestrina's Second Book of Masses was originally published in 1567 (RISM P 660), it was reprinted three times at the turn of the sixteenth century: first by Angelo Gardano in Venice, 1598 (RISM P 662); and then twice in Rome by Nicolo Mutii, 1599 and 1600 (RISM P 662 and 663). Palestrina's Fifth Book was printed by Francesco Coattino in Rome, 1590 (RISM P 670), then reprinted twice, first in Venice by the "erede di Girolamo Scotto," 1591 (RISM P 671) and later in Rome by Mutii, 1599 (RISM P 672). Soriano's First Book was published by Robletti in Rome, 1609, and Pietro Paolo Paciotto's First Book was also printed in Rome by Alessandro Gardano in 1591 (RISM P 39). The "Masses for six and eight voices of Orlando Lasso" must refer to the posthumous collection printed in Munich by Nicolaus Heinrich in 1610 (RISM L 1024).

The document of 1607 deals with music which is, in general, a generation or more older than that ordered by Monteverdi. Three collections of music printed in Antwerp are mentioned: a book of 8 Masses of Lasso, Rore, Crequillon and Josquin; a book of 10 Masses of Clemens non Papa, Crequillon and Lasso; and a book of motets of Isaac and Josquin. The first two publications can be identified. The first one seems to be described erroneously in the document, for it is almost certainly the *Octo Missae Quinque, sex et septem vocum* of George de la Hèle, 1578 (RISM L 285), which contains 4 parody Masses à 5 on motives of Lasso, Rore and Crequillon, 2 à 6 on motives of Lasso, and 2 à 7 on motives of Josquin.[193] The second print is Phalese's anthology of 1570 (RISM 1570/1), which contains 4 Masses of Clemens non Papa, 2 of Crequillon, 3 of Lasso, and 1 of Gerardus Turnhout. The collection of motets of Isaac and Josquin cannot be identified with any known source. These three collections had been performed in the basilica and been judged "bone, dottissime, et breve"—the brevity of the settings seems to have been an important factor in their suitability. It seems, therefore, that Monteverdi was continuing a tradition already established in the basilica, but he systematically replaced the older repertoire with works of Palestrina and his Roman followers.

The performance of sixteenth-century polyphony in St. Mark's lasted throughout the entire period of Monteverdi's tenure as *maestro*. As late as 30 June 1640, funds were allocated to have manuscript copies of Magnificats and hymns of Morales bound in leather (Document 69).[194] Later in the same year manuscript copies of Masses of Monteverdi and Palestrina were ordered (Document 70). Moreover, the stylistically retrospective works of Giovanni Croce were performed well into the 1640s. A document of 21 April 1642 orders manuscript copies of "due Compiete; una del Maestro Monteverde, et l'altra del Chiozoto," and a decree of 31 March 1645 orders "due copie vespri a 8. voci in stampa del Chiozotto...." (Documents 71 and 72). The Compline service of Monteverdi is a missing work, heretofore unrecorded in the literature.[195] The two collections of Croce are almost certainly the *Compietta a otto voci* of 1591 (RISM C 4428) and the *Vespertina omnium solemnitatum psalmodia octonis vocibus decantanda*, first published by Vincenti in 1597 (RISM C 449–452).[196]

There were no dramatic changes in the constitution of the *cappella* during the remainder of Monteverdi's term as *maestro*. Although musical activities were curtailed during the plague of 1630–31 and all hiring ceased for a short while, the *cappella* rebounded to full strength shortly thereafter. Alessandro Grandi, then Giovanni Rovetta were appointed *vice maestri* in 1620 and 1627 respectively; Carlo Fillago, Giampietro Berti, and Cavalli were appointed organists; and the position of *maestro dei concerti* passed significantly from a wind player (Giovanni Bassano) to a violinist (Francesco Bonfante).[197] A number of important musical occasions occurred during Monteverdi's tenure as *maestro*. The festivities for the discovery of the relic of the blood of Christ in 1617, the Requiem for Cosimo II de' Medici which took place in Ss. Giovanni e Paolo in 1621, and the Mass of Thanksgiving after the plague of 1631 are all described in print and have been discussed elsewhere.[198]

One event which has not been discussed is the ceremony for the setting of the first stone for the church of Santa Maria della Salute at the conclusion of the plague in 1631. The large *ceremoniale* of seventeenth- and eighteenth-century events in the A.S.V. describes the proceedings in minute detail (see Document 73). Originally planned for the feast of the Annunciation (25 March), the ceremonies were postponed because of rain and finally took place on 1 April 1631. Boats were moored in the Grand Canal from the end of the Calle da Cà Giustiniano near San Moisè (now called the Calle dei Tredici Martiri) to the projected site in Dorsoduro, and planks had been placed across them, forming a temporary pontoon bridge. On the building site had been erected a church of wooden planks in the form of a cross, which could accommodate a thousand people. Above the door was painted a portrait of Mary with a dove, symbolizing the Holy Spirit. The choir was decorated with golden hearts; on the right sat the Doge and the *Signoria* while on the left was a door leading to the pit where the first stone was to be set. The boys of the Seminario Gregoriano, the *giovani di coro* and the singers of St. Mark's led the procession from St. Mark's to the building site singing litanies.[199] No instruments are mentioned, and it is impossible to determine whether plainsong or *canto figurato* was sung. It is possible that some type of double-choir litany was performed, for Bonifacio mentions the singing of both litanies and the *Te Deum* in two choirs, and he describes the manner in which double-choir works were sung in processions, with the larger choir of singers in front and a smaller choir of soloists in back.[200] During the actual setting of the stone, the singers sang "hymns and psalms to the Lord" and participated in the celebration of the Mass.

One of the final events of Monteverdi's era was the attempt to reinstate the *cornetto* in the instrumental ensemble of the *cappella*. On 8 July 1640, the Procurators noted that the *cornetto* had been absent from the ensembles both in St. Mark's and elsewhere in Venice for some years. Citing the difficulty of playing the instrument, they offered stipends of 15 ducats a year to two members of the *cappella*, the singer Marco Coradini and the instrumentalist Pietro Furlan, to play *cornetto* in St. Mark's and to work to perfect their performance on the instrument (Document 74). Perhaps Coradini and Furlan played in some services in the early 1640s, but neither appears on the pay lists of the *cappella* which began in 1642.[201] The Procurators' next attempt to train cornettists occurred on 25 October 1643, when they hired Marco Pellegrini, a violinist in the church, to teach *cornetto* for an extra 20 ducats per year (Document 75). His first two students were Giovanni Babin and Domenico dei Martini, who were paid

9 ducats on 27 July 1644 to buy music books and instruments (Document 76). Babin and Martini must have been facile musicians, for the first was accepted into the chapel on 24 April 1645, less than a year after he began his study, and the second was accepted a year later on 23 April 1646 (Documents 77 and 78).

We do not know exactly how the *cornetto* was used in the music of the basilica. Certainly there were independent *cornetto* parts in the instrumental ensemble music of this period, as in the elaborate sonatas in Massimiliano Neri's Opus 2 (1651).[202] Their use in concerted sacred music, however, is more conjectural. They may have been used to double vocal parts, doubling the upper voices of a choir whose lower voices were doubled by trombones. For example, the preface to Cavalli's *Musiche Sacre* states that three trombones may double the lower three voices of the second choir and that similar doublings may be used for other vocal parts. A *cornetto* could easily have doubled the top voice of that choir. The other possible role of the *cornetti* would be to play the two violin parts in large concerted works. Certainly *cornetti* are listed as the standard alternate instruments on many violin publications of the period. Moreover, a manuscript copy of the Kyrie and Gloria movements from Rovetta's *Messa e Salmi* (1639) is preserved in Uppsala, in which the parts originally written for violin have been designated "cornettini."[203] A few very large works of the era may have had *obbligato* parts for violins and *cornetti* both; pairs of both instruments are specified by Cavalli in the orchestra for the concerted Requiem to be performed after his death (see Document 27). However, this seems to be a rather anachronistic orchestration, and one has to go back to Gabrieli to find additional works which are scored for this combination of instruments. (See, for example, the setting of *Surrexit Christus* from the second book of *Symphoniae Sacrae* [1615].)

The precise use of *cornetti* must remain conjectural because of the ambiguous nature of the documents. Although both Babin and Martini were accepted into the *cappella* in the mid-1640s, never do both names appear together on the bi-monthly lists of payments to the members of the chapel. This might signify that a single *cornetto* was used above three trombones to complete a four-part ensemble; however, it could also mean that Marco Pellegrini, though paid as a singer, also played *cornetto* in the instrumental ensemble and that only one student at a time was needed to form a duo. At any rate, the *cornetto* was still not prominent in Venice in the 1640s, for in a letter of 11 October 1647, Paul Hainlein remarks that "we hear almost nothing of *cornetto* players."[204]

About a year before Monteverdi's death, bi-monthly payment records for the entire *cappella* begin to appear in the *Giornali Cassier*. Just why the lists suddenly appear at this time is difficult to say. However, their appearance might be connected with a document of 1 July 1642, which reports that Francesco Badoer, one of the financial administrators of the *procuratia*, had been reimbursed during 1641 for certain funds which he was to use to pay musicians' salaries but which, in fact, had never been used for this purpose (Document 79). The lists extend from 24 May 1642 to 28 February 1652; they are not lists of the full *cappella* but, rather, lists of people who appeared to pick up their salary on the appointed days. Nonetheless, despite the few names which are occasionally omitted and then inserted with double salary on the following list, they give us a good idea of the size of the *cappella* during these years.

The list of salaries paid out for March–April 1643 is one of the most complete (see Plate 2), and it is typical of the lists for the entire decade. The format for payment is always the same. The *maestro* and *vice-maestro* are listed first, and they are followed by the roster of singers. The list of March–April 1643 contains the names of 35 singers, the first organist Carlo Fillago, the second organist Francesco Caletto (that is, Caletto *detto* Cavalli), the organ custodian Bartolomeo Papafonda, and the *maestro dei concerti* Francesco Bonfante with the names of 14 other instrumentalists. Most of the other lists for the decade are approximately of these dimensions, i.e. slightly more singers and slightly fewer instrumentalists than were specified by Rovetta's "non tanto trenta, e più Cantori, ma venti, e più Instrumenti da fiato, e da arco," in the preface to his *Salmi concertati* of 1627. Not all of the voice types can be identified, but the distribution on this and the other lists of the decade is more-or-less equal between the four voice parts with a slight tendency towards a "bottom-heavy" choir with more basses, tenors and contraltos than sopranos. Of the 15 instrumentalists on this list, we can identify 9: 5 violins, 2 *violoni* and 2 trombones. We know from the minutes of the Procurators' meetings, however, that bassoons, theorbos and *cornetti* were also members of the instrumental staff. Moreover, although the acceptance of players of *viola* or *violetta* was not common until the 1650s, it seems logical that many violinists might have doubled on viola as players do today. Indeed, Rovetta mentions his versatility on a number of instruments in the preface to his collection of 1627, and in 1617 three players were accepted into the *cappella* with the stipulation that they had to play any of the instruments they knew how to play if the *capo dei concerti* or *maestro di cappella* should ask them.[205]

The Era of Maestro Giovanni Rovetta

Although Giovanni Rovetta did not succeed Monteverdi until 21 February 1644, his "era" in the *cappella marciana* may be said to date from late

Plate 2 Salary payments for the *cappella marciana* for March–April, 1643. A.S.V., San Marco, Procuratia de Supra, Registro 12 (Giornali Cassier, 1639–48).

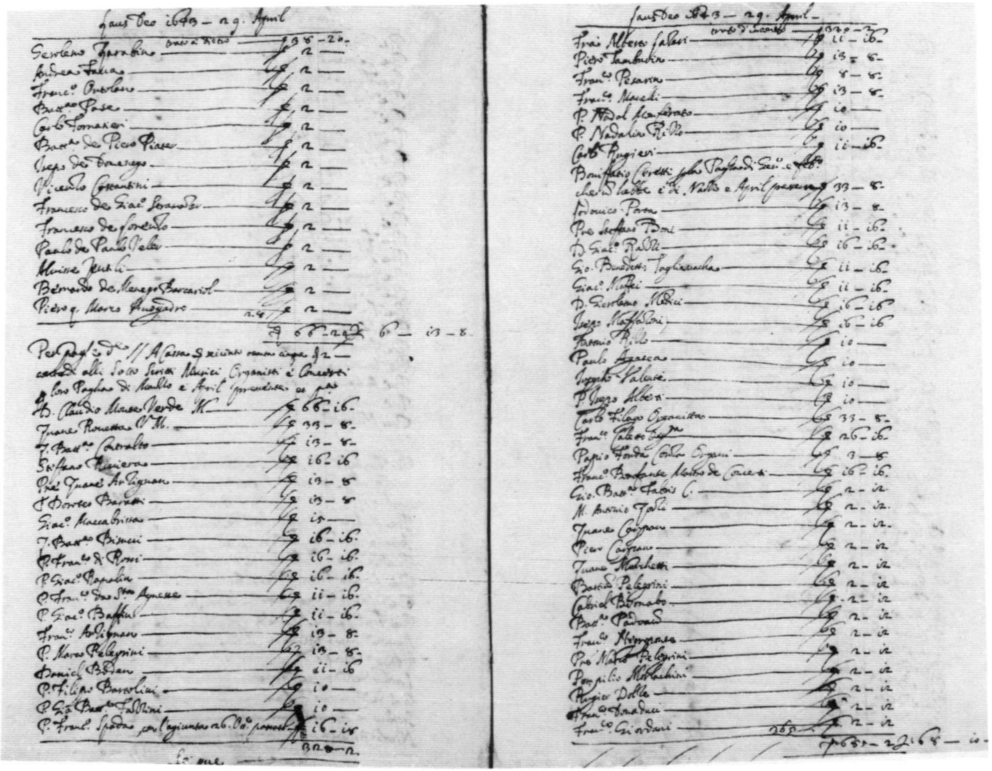

Reproduced by permission of the Venetian State Archives (A.S.V.)

1638, when he was chosen by the French Ambassador Hamelot de la Houssaye to compose and conduct the music in San Giorgio Maggiore for the celebration of the birth of Louis XIV of France. To judge from the description of Fausto Ciro in his pamphlet *Venetia Festiva*, the service which took place was one of the most sumptuous of the century. Large risers (*palchi*) were built between the columns of the church to support the musicians (Document 80). The Doge, *Serenissima Signoria*, French Ambassador, and their retinue traveled from the Doge's palace to the island of San Giorgio in a procession of 60 gondolas. At their arrival, trumpets and drums were sounded as well as some sort of music with string and wind instruments (Document 81; Ciro is somewhat vague in his description of musical events). A large concerted *Te Deum* was the first musical item in the service (Document 82) after which a concerted Mass was performed (Document 83). During the Mass, some sort of solo motet was performed by a singer known as "il Mantovano"; it was clearly a virtuoso display, and Ciro's description is one of the best we have of the effects of *seicento* vocal technique on an audience (Document 84). It is most frustrating that we do not know who this fabulous "Mantovano" was. One "Don Antonio mantoano" was accepted as a tenor in the *cappella* on 20 January 1620, but he does not seem to have drawn an extraordinary salary, nor do we know much more about him. It is possible that "il Mantovano" was actually Monteverdi's son Francesco, who might have been called by that nickname, who was indeed a member of the *cappella*, and who had sung the affecting *O vos omnes* in the Requiem service for Cosimo II de' Medici in Ss. Giovanni e Paolo in 1621. Whoever he was, he clearly was a complete virtuoso, and Ciro's description shows the effect which the innocuous-looking motets of Simonetti's *Ghirlanda Sacra* could have had when properly performed. A lutenist named Bernardello also caused considerable excitement. At the conclusion of the service, the psalm *Omnes gentes plaudite manibus* was performed (Document 84). Music accompanied a banquet in the ducal palace that evening (Document 85), and fanfares continued in the courtyard (Document 86). All in all, it was quite a day!

Perhaps such an event was a lucky start for Rovetta, for the 1640s seem to have been a good time for the *cappella*. The payment lists which stretch from 1642 through 1652 show that the size of the *cappella* was constant during these years. Moreover, a number of special, elaborate services occurred, cluminating in the special ceremonies for the feast of St. Anthony of Padua in 1652. The description by *maestro di coro* Giorgio Minaccia tells of the nighttime arrival of the relics of St. Anthony via the Burchiello, the elaborate ship which sailed up and down the Brenta canal, and the procession which issued from St. Mark's to meet the boat; the

Gregorian seminary, the singers of St. Mark's and the *giovani di coro* formed part of the procession. The following day, the *scuole grandi* and the clergy of St. Mark's again processed to Santa Maria della Salute where "the Mass was sumptuously sung, directed by *Maestro* Rovetta with elaborate music."[206] The ceremonies ended with a *Salve Regina*. Additional ceremonies took place on 13 June 1652, again with the singers from St. Mark's.

It is difficult to tell how long after Monteverdi's death the *cappella* operated at full strength, for the payment lists stop abruptly in February, 1652. Certainly, the penultimate list (24 January 1651 [*more veneto*]) shows little evidence of a decline, for the full complement of forces is present: *maestro di cappella*, *vice-maestro*, 29 singers, two regular organists, the two players of the *organetti*, the caretaker of the organs, the *maestro dei concerti*, and 12 additional instrumentalists. While the number of instrumentalists is smaller than in the peak years, the salary lists vary so widely from month to month (depending on just who happened to take the trouble to be present on payday) that a drop to 12 players is not really significant.

However, the final list in the *Giornali Cassier* is a different case. To be sure, there were meager lists in the past, which often signified nothing but a poor turn-out on payday and were rectified during the following months either by special payments to musicians in the daily records or by double and triple salaries recorded in the bi-monthly lists. However, the list for 28 February 1651 (*more veneto*) is meager in the extreme. Neither *maestro* nor *vice-maestro* is present, only 16 singers, 1 organist, the caretaker of the organs, the pumpers of the organ bellows, and a mere 5 instrumentalists. The fragmentary nature of this final payment record is a fitting prelude to the history of the *cappella* in the next three decades.

A number of documents from the 1650s onward show that the singers of St. Mark's were highly discontent with their lot and that a decline in the *cappella* was certainly in evidence before the middle of the decade. The sources of this discontent are simple: small salaries, increased duties, and the progressively richer fields offered by both foreign chapels and the Venetian operatic stage. Indeed, by 1653 the membership of the *cappella* had fallen off so sharply that the Treasurer of the Procurators asked Rovetta to write out a recommendation, stating what size establishment he thought could reasonably be maintained under the circumstances. To this, he responded (Document 87):

Most Illustrious and Excellent Procurator, Treasurer

Since Your Excellency commanded me, Giovanni Rovetta, *Maestro di Cappella* and requested expressly that I write out what is in order and necessary for the good service of music at St. Mark's, I say that, since at present there are no more than twenty-eight salaried singers, that is

8 Basses
9 Tenors
5 Altos
3 Mezzo sopranos
2 Falsettists
1 Soprano
———
28

And, since there were forty singers at other times, it would be well to reach at least the number of 32, that is, eight per part, so that the *concerto* as well as *servicio continuo* will take place with dignity in this same church, and to the satisfaction of Your Excellency, to whom I, the above-mentioned, bow.

Rovetta's request for a *cappella* of 32 singers was clearly a makeshift recommendation, made under pressure and certainly not his view of the ideal size of musical forces for the basilica. That it was written under duress is underlined by a second document, presented to the Procurators at the same time, which speaks for itself (Document 88):

1653

Duties added for the singers of St. Mark's after the plague [of 1630–31] without increase in salary, which they are rigorously fined for missing—

The processions of all Saturdays, in which almost the entire morning is used up
number 52
Processions to [Santa Maria della] Salute ... 1
Funeral Masses in St. Mark's ... 12
Three offices for the [feast of] St. Laurence ... 3
For the [feast of the] above saint at [San Pietro di] Castello ... 1
Processions for the [feast of] St. [Anthony] of Padua, to [Santa Maria della] Salute, morning and evening ... 2
Mass at St. Paternian ... 1

The fines, which used to be divided among those present, [and] which were an incentive for good service, have been taken away to make vestments for the clerics.
Two times for the exposition of the Holy Sacrament, three days per time, with the two processions in the evening, which are offices ... 8

Others at the will of the *Serenissimi*
———
80 offices in all

The singers regret that the fines, which for the most part were divided among them, as is still done with the canons, have been taken away to make the cassocks and vestments for the clerics;
That in addition to the ordinary duties, which reach the number of 525 have been added 80 offices, as can be seen above.

These documents did not really precipitate a crisis, for the *cappella* seems to have proceeded normally during the 1650s and into the 1660s. Only in 1677, after Cavalli's term as *maestro*, would the cumulative effects of the discontent really be felt. If there is any major trend in the *cappella* during the fifties and sixties, it is felt in the instrumental component, for the middle-register strings (*viola*, *violetta*) were first accepted with regularity during these years; while not felt in the works of Rovetta and Cavalli for St. Mark's, this trend was certainly seen in works of Legrenzi, such as the *Sacri e Festivi Concenti* of 1667, in which middle-range strings have a prominent role. Salary levels also rose during Rovetta's tenure as *maestro*, but only for players of bassoon or theorbo who, necessary for the basso continuo, might receive as much as the singers were paid.

The Era of Maestro Francesco Cavalli

Francesco Cavalli was elected to the post of *maestro* on 20 November 1668. At the end of a successful operatic career, albeit one that had peaked in the fifties and was now waning, he was perhaps the obvious choice. The "era" of Cavalli lasted only a little over seven years. By and large, it seems to have been uneventful, and the *cappella* remained more-or-less the same in size as it had under Rovetta. A few important players came into St. Mark's during Cavalli's tenure. Benedetto di Carli dall'Arpa entered on 17 January 1669, the only harp player ever recorded in the basilica; he probably functioned as a continuo player. Moreover, Pietro Andrea Ziani returned to Venice from the imperial court in Vienna to serve as an organist.[207] In general, however, Cavalli's tenure was uneventful, and the significance of his years as *maestro* was not fully felt until the great crises of 1677.

A number of old traditions were kept alive in St. Mark's during the years Cavalli served as *maestro*. One of these was the performance of a *Messa della Battaglia* or, as it later came to be called, *Messa della Caccia*, on Carnival Thursday. We have records for the copying of "motteti della messa della Caccia" on 27 February 1670 and of the Mass itself on 11 January 1671 (Documents 89 and 90). It is difficult to identify this work precisely. Its performance goes back to at least 1564, for Bonifacio describes it in his *ceremoniale*:

> On the Thursday cited above [i.e., Carnival Thursday] the singers always sing some joyful Mass, and it used to begin with *Kyrie eleison*. Today they sing the Mass which is called *della Battaglia*, which was composed for the victory of the Most Christian King of the French over the Swiss, and this is said at the hour of Terce with Gloria, Credo, with candles, cross and the incensing of the altar as in *feriae* of double rank.

The Mass cited above is [also] said for our victory over the patriarch of Aquileia, etc. as well as [for the commemoration of] other victories. (Document 91)

Although Bonifacio's statement is a bit confused, he is almost certainly describing Jannequin's *Missa super la Bataille*, a parody Mass based on his chanson *La Guerre*, which described the victory of Francis I over the Swiss. The chanson model, in fact, was entitled "La Bataille ou la défaite des Suisses à la journée de Marignan" in Susato's *Dixième Livre* (1545), where it appeared with a fifth voice added by Verdelot.[208] A copy of this Mass exists in manuscript in the Biblioteca Nazionale Marciana.[209]

When Pace describes the same ceremony in 1678, however, there is some doubt that he is discussing the same composition (Document 92):

On Carnival Thursday a High Mass is sung at the hour of Terce, which was composed by a German over very lively imitative figures on the organ, and it is called the *Messa della Battaglia*, although they refer to it as the *Messa della Cazza* at the present. This was composed for the victory of the king of France over the Swiss. It is sung with Gloria, Credo, candles, and every other device *more duplici*.

Is Pace describing the same Mass as Bonifacio? It is possible that he is; certainly repertoire of the *cinquecento* was still sung at this date, for a book of Palestrina's Masses was touched up by the copyist Lorenzo Rossi in 1671.[210] However, the statement that the Mass was composed by a German ("composta da un Todesco") and that it had an *obbligato* organ part seems to indicate that a seventeenth-century work may have been performed. In any case, the tradition of performing a *Battaglia* composition towards the end of Carnival season lasted well over a hundred years.

Ever since the singers had protested to the Procurators during the period of Giovanni Rovetta—complaining that they were paid too little for too many duties—there had been discontent in the *cappella*. Despite the discontent, the daily musical life of the basilica proceeded more-or-less in an orderly fashion. Pressure grew gradually, however, and by 1677 it was clear that the small difficulties which had occurred year by year had finally precipitated a musical crisis in the *cappella*. A body of documents which exist in duplicate copies in the A.S.V. and the Biblioteca Correr detail the degree of the crisis and the helplessness with which the Procurators watched the shrinking *cappella*.[211] First, a list was drawn up of 23 singers who had left the service of the ducal chapel between 1665 and 1677, i.e. in the brief space of 12 years (Document 93).[212] There was little pattern in the manner of departure or in the singers' destinations; any court which could offer a better salary and more gracious working conditions would do. Within Italy, singers left St. Mark's for positions in

Loreto, Parma, Modena, Padua, Naples, Rome, Bergamo and Verona. Foreign courts which raided the *cappella* included those of Saxony, Brandenburg, the imperial court in Vienna, Poland, Brunswick, Naiburg and England.[213]

It is difficult to know where the blame should fall for the problems of the *cappella* during these years, but we are faced with the fact that out of the 23 defections, 18 occurred during Cavalli's term as *maestro di cappella*, although the exodus had started under Rovetta. At any rate, a lengthy "master plan" for the *cappella* was drafted by Alessandro Contarini, the treasurer of the basilica.[214] Contarini complained that the quality of singing in the *cappella* was low and that, in particular, there were not good *soprani* and *castrati*. He cited the 23 singers who had left since 1665 and also blamed the "comedie et opere in Musica" for wooing the best voices away from the *cappella*—Cavalli had clearly been playing both sides of this game. Contarini also attacked the infamous decree of 10 April 1677, which declared that all singers who had entered the *cappella* during the previous 12 years would have to undergo new auditions. This, said Contarini, had caused "confusione pericolissima," and he urged other measures to insure the quality of the *cappella*. Other courts, he maintained, gave their singers security of employment and did not penalize them for absenteeism, conditions which made employment at such courts more attractive than a position at St. Mark's.

A solution to the problem was not found immediately. Gradual reforms took place which culminated in a complete re-organization of the *cappella* by Giovanni Legrenzi. A fixed distribution of players for the orchestra was established in 1685 and a fixed number of singers for the choir, in 1686.[215] However, if one reviews the history of the *cappella* during the first three quarters of the seventeenth century, one is struck not by the difficulties of the last few decades but, rather, by the continuity of tradition. The performance ideal seems to have stayed the same for much of the century: an orchestra of *viole da braccio*, trombones and *cornetti*, bassoons and *violoni*, with organs and theorbos as the continuo instruments. This seems to have been the ideal in 1670 as much as in 1610. To be sure, there is a greater emphasis on strings than on winds after 1620 or so, and the emphasis on middle-register *viole* in the 1650s and 1660s is a development rather contrary to the polarized ensemble of the early decades of the century. But the real changes in the orchestra had to wait until many years after Cavalli's death and even postdated the reforms of Legrenzi. The first oboe did not enter until 1698, the first trumpet not until 1685.[216] The ensemble which would have played for Grandi and Rovetta in 1625 was essentially the same as that which would play for Cavalli in 1675.

The Orchestration of Vocal Works

A survey of the instrumental and vocal forces employed in St. Mark's at various points in the *seicento* enables us to determine the probable forces which performed the published Vespers compositions. While every detail of performance practice cannot be resolved, we have nonetheless a sufficient body of information to make intelligent decisions in virtually every area.

Some of the pieces are really not too problematic. The small-scale *concertato* motets of Grandi and Rovetta, for example, were clearly performed by small groups of solo singers accompanied by the *organetti* or by theorbo. When the *organetti* were used, a *violone* was placed alongside to strengthen the bass line. This may also have been done for the theorbo—certainly many modern singers find it difficult to perform music of this period to the accompaniment of plucked strings without some firm reinforcement on the bass line—but even if this occurred occasionally, it probably was not a regular practice. Indeed, several singers in the *cappella* were also theorbo players,[217] and it is doubtful that they would have given up the intimate freedom of singing to their own accompaniment in order to coordinate their singing with a *violone*.

The *salmi spezzati*, i.e. the works for two four-part choirs and basso continuo published by Grandi in 1629, Rovetta in 1644 and 1662, and Cavalli in 1675, are more of a problem. They are scored for two four-part choirs and basso continuo without any further instructions in most of the prints. Grandi's *Salmi a otto brevi* is the one exception, for the basso continuo part is cued to show where the first and second choirs are singing; thus, it seems that for this collection performance with two organs—one with each choir—was a possibility, and with a few marks in the basso continuo part, the other collections could be performed in this manner as well. One must note, however, that Grandi's collection is not set for two equal choirs; on the contrary, it is subtitled "con il primo choro concertato," and the musical idiom shows that the first choir is clearly a choir of soloists. Thus, the designations for the two choirs in the basso continuo part might well be used for a single organist to adjust his registration, or at least the style of his continuo realization, in order to support the large choir sufficiently yet not to drown out the choir of soloists.[218]

The medium for which Grandi set his *Salmi a otto brevi* may be more significant than scholars have realized so far, and the other three collections of *salmi spezzati* under consideration—Rovetta's *Salmi a otto voci* (1644) and *Delli Salmi a otto voci* (1662) as well as Cavalli's *Vesperi* (1675)—may also have been performed by mixed solo and choral forces, even though there are no definite signs in the prints that such forces were demanded.[219] All four of these collections are in an archaic idiom which allies them with the double-choir tradition of Willaert's *salmi spezzati*; and the description in Bonifacio's *ceremoniale* of the performance of such double-choir psalms makes it clear that they were not, strictly speaking, music for two equal choirs. On the contrary, documents state that the first choir was a solo choir consisting of only four singers—sometimes specified as "four of the best singers"—and the other was a ripieno choir consisting of all the remaining singers in the *cappella*. The most important document is one which Bonifacio included twice in his *ceremoniale*, and it deals with the singing of psalms on all feasts of the year (Document 94):

> On the singing of psalms in all solemnities: In all solemnities, the psalms used to be sung by the small chapel and by the singers who sing from memory. It is thought, and it is said that they were sung more georgiano. Today this mode of singing has gone out of use, and the singers of the large chapel sing all the psalms and all the other items; and they sing these psalms divided into two choirs, namely, four singers in one choir and all the rest in the other, since the small chapel no longer exists.[220]

This document is copied into the three later exemplars of this *ceremoniale*, and thus appears a total of eight times in the volumes in the A.S.V. and the Biblioteca Nazionale Marciana. It is not, however, the only document to describe this sort of performance. In a description of Vespers on the Vigil of Pentecost, Bonifacio writes (Document 95):

> After the midday meal, at the usual hour, when the *Pala d'oro* has been opened ceremoniously, Vespers are sung with the greatest decorum, as is indicated in our books. The psalms all begin with *Laudate* and are said under this antiphon: *Veni Sancte Spiritus*; and the singers sing these psalms divided into two choirs, namely four singers in one choir, and all the rest in the other, as is the custom in solemnities.

This manner of performance was used in processions, both inside and outside the church, no less than in services where the singers were stationary. In describing the order of the procession for Corpus Domini, Bonifacio writes:

> then come the singers, singing in two choirs *Pange lingua gloriosi*, the group in front and then the four. . . .[221]

Moreover, in descriptions of two processions in supplication to the Madonna and of a procession on Holy Saturday, Bonifacio is always careful to distinguish between the *ripieno* choir and the four soloists.

Procession with the Madonna to pray for rain or peace:

then the priests, *giovani*, deacons, and subdeacons, then the singers, the group, then the four singers, *maestro di cappella*, and the *maestro di coro* . . .

Procession with the Madonna in times of plague and death:

then the *giovani*, and the group of singers, then the four singers, then the subcanons . . .

Procession for Holy Saturday:

then the deacons and subdeacons, then the singers with their robes, then the four singers . . .[222]

The significance of these documents cannot be overestimated. They show that the practice of pitting a solo quartet against a *ripieno* choir was not the invention of the early seventeenth century but was practiced in St. Mark's well before the *concertato* works of Croce and the late works of Gabrieli. Indeed, the prints of Croce and Gabrieli merely make explicit a practice which was already considered a tradition in 1564 and may well have been used as early as Willaert's *salmi spezzati* of 1550. While Pace does not describe this mode of performance in his own *ceremoniale*, this does not mean that it went out of use in the seventeenth century. On the contrary, it may have been so well established that it did not need to be mentioned. Moreover, the fact that at least two collections in a retrospective style seem to be designed for this medium may indicate that the other collections in this style were also to be performed in this manner. I would certainly suggest that the three *salmi spezzati* in Monteverdi's Venetian collections—the *Credidi* and *Memento* in the *Selva Morale* and the second *Dixit Dominus* in the *Messa a quattro voci e Salmi*—could have been performed in this way.

We do not know whether works such as these would have required— or even allowed—the instrumental doubling of vocal parts. Certainly the bass line could have been doubled by a string instrument, for there is a *violone* part written into the score of Cavalli's double-choir Requiem, a work which is in a style very similar to that of the *salmi spezzati* of the mid-seventeenth century. I would tend to view the negative evidence of the partbooks as a sign that instrumental doubling was probably not used in these works—certainly not for the choir of soloists at any rate. However, there is really no clear evidence on this practice. We know that instrumentalists were in church on certain days on which *salmi spezzati* were used, but as I shall show in Chapter V, they may have played independent instrumental music on these occasions; their mere presence does not indicate that they doubled vocal lines.

We have more complete information on the use of instruments in the works in the *stile concertato*, although the prints still leave many ambiguities which must be filled in by information gleaned from the archives, the *ceremoniali* and iconographic sources. Perhaps the best print to use as a "test case" for the application of these sources to actual performance practice is Cavalli's *Musiche Sacre* of 1656. This is the most elaborate of the Venetian sacred collections, along with Monteverdi's *Selva Morale* and *Messa a quattro voci e Salmi* and Rovetta's *Messa e Salmi* of 1639. Although it contains copious instructions for performance, it also offers some of the most irksome problems. The *Musiche* are printed in 12 part-books whose contents are summarized in Table III-1: canto, alto, tenor and basso for each of two choirs; two parts for violins; a part for *violoncino*, which can also be used for bassoon or theorbo, and a basso continuo part for unspecified instruments. The alto, tenor and bass partbooks of the second choir contain parts for three trombones in certain ritornelli, and there are parts for three *viole* in one work, the *Laetatus sum*.[223]

Despite Cavalli's designation of a number of specific instruments, he leaves so many ambiguities and offers so many alternatives that one is at a loss to determine the exact size or make-up of the forces which would have performed these works in St. Mark's if one works from the print alone. While Cavalli says that they may be performed either with or without vocal *ripieni*, there is no statement of how many voices might constitute the *ripieni*. While he says that the three trombones can double the vocal parts in the *tutti* sections *si placet*, they can also be left out entirely, as can the three *viole* in *Laetatus sum*. Cavalli sanctions instrumental doublings of the other vocal parts, but he does not suggest specific instruments. He also admits that the *violoncino* part can be played on bassoon or theorbo or be omitted entirely. Indeed, in case of necessity, even the largest of the works could be performed by only 11 musicians. Of course, this very versatility is part of Cavalli's plan, for he designed the collection to meet as many performing situations as possible. Nonetheless, by collating information from a number of sources, one can determine with some certainty how such large works would have been performed in St. Mark's.

The basic archival material on the *cappella marciana* provides most of the information one needs, although three sources which deal with specific works might also be used. The first is Hainlein's description of the Vespers service which took place in San Francesco della Vigna in 1647, for which he says that the orchestra consisted of four violins, two *viole da braccio*, four trombones, and three organs.[224] The second is Cavalli's autograph will (Document 27), in which he lists the instruments for his own Requiem: 2 *violini*, 4 *viole*, 2 *cornetti*, 2 *tiorbe*, *tromboni*,

Table III-1
Partbooks for Cavalli's *Musiche Sacre*

1. CANTO Primo Choro	5. CANTO Secondo Choro
2. ALTO Primo Choro	6. ALTO Secondo Choro, trombone[a], viola[b]
3. TENOR Primo Choro	7. TENOR Secondo Choro, trombone[a], viola[b]
4. BASSO Primo Choro	8. BASSO Secondo Choro, trombone[a]

9. VIOLINO PRIMO
10. VIOLINO SECONDO
11. VIOLONCINO, viola[b]
      (fagotto)
      (tiorba)

12. BASSO CONTINUO

---

[a] Parts for sinfonie and ritornelli in *Messa Concertata* and *Magnificat*.

[b] Parts for *Laetatus sum à 3 con due violini e tre viole se piace.*

fagotto, violon grosso, and 3 *organi.* The third are Monteverdi's works for St. Mark's in the *Selva Morale* and the *Messa a quattro Voci e Salmi.* While these works have their own ambiguities, they at least show the instrumental rubrics for a collection in the *stile concertato* written more-or-less for the same forces as Cavalli's. Monteverdi's works call for a pair of violins, up to four trombones and *viole da braccio,* and bassoon. With this information, one begins to see how Cavalli's pieces could have been orchestrated in St. Mark's, and I would suggest the distribution of forces listed in Table III-2.

A point-by-point discussion should explain the various facets of the solution. As mentioned above, Cavalli suggests that three trombones double the three lower parts of choir II and states that any other vocal part can similarly be doubled by an instrument. One might surmise that the canto of choir II was also doubled by a trombone because of the choir of four trombones specified for the Vespers service in San Francesco della Vigna as well as the four trombones called for in some large works of Monteverdi. However, the upper limit of the highest member of the trombone family is given by Praetorius as d'', and the highest note of the canto II part is e''. Thus, a *cornetto* might have been the preferred instrument for doubling this part, and the lack of a suitable instrument to play such parts above a choir of trombones may have been the main reason the Procurators encouraged *cornetto* players in the early 1640s. That choir I would have been doubled by strings is suggested not only by the prepon-

Table III-2
Suggested Musical Forces for the *Musiche Sacre*

Singers	
Choir I	Choir II
16 *ripieno* voices	16 *ripieno* voices
4 soloists	4 soloists

Doubling Instruments	
Choir 1	Choir II
C viola I	C (cornetto)
A viola II	A trombone I
T viola III	T trombone II
B violoncello I	B trombone III

Obbligato Instruments		
violin I		cornetto I
violin II	and/or	cornetto II
violoncello II		bassoon

Basso Continuo
1 or 2 large organs
1 or 2 chamber organs
theorbo
violone

derance of strings in the *cappella*, but also by the four *viole* mentioned in Cavalli's will, the four *viole da braccio* listed in the titles of some of Monteverdi's late works, and the presence of three parts for *viole* in *Laetatus sum*. That two *cornetti* and a bassoon might have been used instead of, or in addition to, the two violins and *violoncino* is suggested by their alternate use in instrumental sonatas and by their appearance in

Cavalli's will. Since four organs were available at St. Mark's and three are specified in Rovetta's service as well as in Cavalli's will, one would assume that at least three could be used for the *Musiche Sacre*. The problems of the number and sizes of organs are complex, for they have as much to do with where the musicians were placed as with the size and identity of musical forces. It seems quite probable, however, that the two large organs were used to accompany the large choirs of *ripieno* singers while the two portable *organetti* accompanied the two quartets of vocal soloists. The theorbo was also part of the basso continuo contingent and seems to have played both with solo voices and with obbligato instruments; for it is specified in the ritornelli of some of the hymn settings as well as in one psalm and two Marian antiphons which do not employ obbligato instruments. The presence in the *cappella* of Paulo Mancin, who played the *violon grosso*, clearly implies the use of some sort of contrabass instrument as part of the basso continuo.

Eight vocal soloists would have been drawn from among the best voices in the *cappella*. The 2 sopranos as well as the 2 altos could have been *castrati*, for *cantori eunuchi* were hired at St. Mark's for both voice types. Since Rovetta implied in his report of 1653 that the optimum size of the *cappella* was 40, and the 8 best singers would have been used as soloists, the two *ripieno* choirs would have consisted of 16 singers each— 4 per part—under the best conditions.

The Placement of Musicians in the Basilica

Three principal sites for music-making are mentioned in the documents from St. Mark's: the choirlofts above the chapels of St. Peter and St. Clement; the *nicchie* into which the small *organetti* were moved on certain feasts, which are located next to the choirlofts and adjacent to the rood screen which separates the altar area from the rest of the church; and an octagonal platform known as the *bigonzo* or "tub," which was located on the floor of the church across from the double-tiered pulpit from which the Gospel and Epistle were sung. All three structures are visible in Plate 3. The choirloft above the chapel of St. Peter is at the upper right of the photograph, where the organ pipes are visible. One of the *nicchie* is seen just to the left of the loft, above the large wooden cross on the rood screen; the little balcony in the arch just below it would also have been used. The *bigonzo* is in the foreground, in the lower right-hand corner of the plate.

The location in the basilica which is mentioned most often as the site for musical forces is, interestingly enough, not the choirlofts but rather

Plate 3   Interior of St. Mark's; view of the principle structures in which musicians were placed.

the octagonal *bigonzo*. Often referred to as the "pergola dei musici," the *bigonzo* is described best by Giovanni Stringa (Document 96): [225, 226]

> Opposite the two pulpits just described, in which as I said the Gospel and Epistle are sung, is found the pergola of the musicians. This is in an octagonal form and it is supported by seven columns of the finest stone; two lower [columns which are] against the wall also help to support it. In this [pergola] the musicians sing high Mass and the Divine Office of Vespers on almost all the ordinary days and especially on those solemn feasts when the *Signoria* comes to church.

Stringa's emphasis on important musical events' taking place in the pergola seems somewhat strange to historians brought up on the theory that the double choirlofts which housed the two organs were the site of the most important music-making in the basilica. Nor is Stringa the first person to mention the use of the *pergola*. In 1589, a dispute arose during Vespers on the Feast of the Dedication of the Church of St. Mark's over whether or not double-choir music should be sung, and a Procurators' inquest was held to resolve the problems. It is clear from the testimony that Vespers were being sung from the pergola, not from the choirlofts.[227] Moreover, Giovanni Pace describes the singing of Vespers from the *bigonzo* on the Vigil and Feast of Epiphany (Document 99):

> The Vigil of Epiphany: the *Pala d'oro* is opened on this day as well as on both offices of the feast itself. Vespers are celebrated *in quinto* [i.e., officiated by a canon and four other priests], and psalms for eight voices are sung by the singers in two choirs in the *bigonzo*.

While this seems in some ways a strange statement—certainly at variance with the myth of *salmi spezzati* being tossed back and forth, verse by verse, between the choirlofts—it is not the only piece of evidence showing that double-choir music was sometimes done from the *bigonzo*. A large ecclesiastical calendar of 1761[228] describes the performance of Vespers for a number of feasts as "Vespero à due Cori con Palla nel Bigonzo," i.e. the *Pala d'oro*, the large gold altarpiece of the church, is to be opened and Vespers sung by two choirs from the "tub."

While this may sound strange at first, it is not really so preposterous in view of the fact that the documents in Bonifacio's *ceremoniale* tell us that one of the choirs in the performance of *salmi spezzati* was a choir of soloists. In fact, iconographic evidence proves rather conclusively that this sort of performance was perfectly possible. In the vast *oeuvre* of Canaletto on Venetian themes, there survive nine works depicting the interior of St. Mark's—paintings, drawings and fragmentary sketches.[229] Of these, three paintings and two drawings show musicians; and while they all date from the mid-eighteenth century, they all illustrate the use of the "pergola delli musici" described by Stringa. Two of the works—items 556 and 577 in Constable's catalogue—do not show sufficient detail to enable us to determine specific numbers of musicians or methods of performance. We see merely a crowd of singers in the *pergola* without instruments. Since the floor of the church below is filled with people, this is presumably a major feast. Two other works—items 578 and 579—give us more information. The singers are not only present in the *pergola* but are singing from a large choirbook which is placed on a stand against the wall of the church. This could presumably be any of the volumes in large format we know from the archives: the large antiphonaries in the *Procuratia de Supra*, the large choirbooks housed in St. Mark's itself, or even the *Psalterium Davidicum*.

The most helpful work of Canaletto is the pen-and-ink drawing which he made in 1766, at the age of 68, "Cenzza Ochiali"—without his glasses (Constable, item 558; see Plate 4). Here we can distinctly make out 11 figures in the *pergola*; again, they are reading from a large choirbook, though it is not possible to determine whether it contains plainchant or *canto figurato*. The drawing may represent one of a number of occasions for which the *Tavola* of 1761 specifies "Messa a Capella in Bigonzo" or "Vespero à due Cori con Palla nel Bigonzo." At any rate, it shows clearly that nearly a dozen people could squeeze into the "bigonzo" with ease, and thus, that double choir music could indeed be performed from the structure if one of the choirs consisted of only four people. While this information does not annihilate the myth of *cori spezzati* spaced far from each other in the double choir lofts—after all, the information here is all from the seventeenth and eighteenth centuries—one cannot overlook the fact that the medium of four soloists and a *ripieno* choir is described as early as 1564, and Stringa refers to Vespers in the *bigonzo* as early as 1604.

Other works of art provide information on the placement of musicians for the large *concertato* compositions of the seventeenth century. Perhaps the most important piece of iconographic evidence on performance practice in St. Mark's is the painting housed in Ca' Morosini of a musical performance in the basilica on 7 May 1690[230] (Plate 5). The portion of the basilica shown in the painting is that behind the rood screen which separates the apse from the rest of the church, and the service and its music seem directed entirely to the people in the apse rather than to those below in the nave. The *Serenissima Signoria* are present, seated in the choir; women are seated behind them, just below the *cantoria*. The distribution of musicians is informative. Eight singers are standing in the choirloft, at the upper left of the painting. To the right, on the same level, is an oblong object which may be one of the *organetti*. Below this, in the double-

Plate 4   Canaletto, pen-and-ink drawing of the interior of St. Mark's, 1766. (W. G. Constable, *Canaletto: Giovanni Antonio Canal, 1697–1768* [Oxford: Clarendon, 1962], item 558).

Plate 5   Anonymous painting, housed in Ca' Morosini, Venice, showing ceremonies in St. Mark's on 7 May 1690. Reproduced in Ferdinando Ongania, ed., *La Basilica di San Marco a Venezia* (Venice, 1888) VII, facsimile 109.

tiered arch (or *nicchia*, as it is called in the documents) are two groups of musicians. On the upper level are three *viole da braccio* and a *violone*. On the lower level are three singers and a plucked string instrument.

While one hesitates to read too much into such a painting, the musical forces are precisely those called for in some of the larger works of Monteverdi, Rovetta and Cavalli; indeed, this painting may represent the precise position of musicians for large-scale *concertato* works throughout the *seicento*. The eight singers in the *cantoria* are probably a *ripieno* choir; the three on the lower level of the *nicchia* are probably soloists, with a plucked string instrument next to them for support. The identity of this instrument is somewhat of a mystery; theorbos are the instruments which archival documents and printed sources suggest for the realization of the continuo although the instrument in the painting looks more like a Spanish guitar, or even a plucked treble viol—a clear impossibility! The three *viole da braccio* might be three violins or, possibly, two violins and a viola; the *violone* could be any of a number of bass string instruments. Thus, nearly all the forces associated with collections such as Cavalli's *Musiche Sacre*, Rovetta's *Messa e Salmi* (1639) or Monteverdi's Venetian sacred works are present; we lack only *tromboni* and a *fagotto*. However, there certainly would be room for several *tromboni* in the *cantoria*; and *tromboni* often did double vocal parts, after all. Moreover, a *fagotto* could easily be placed next to the *organetto*, or it could replace the *violone* next to the *viole da braccio*. To coordinate all these forces, the *maestro di cappella* might stand in the opposite *cantoria*, or even in the opposite *nicchia*; in either of these positions, he would be visible to all of the musicians.

Table III-3 illustrates the way the forces needed for the large *concertato* works in Cavalli's *Musiche Sacre* might have been placed in the church if the arrangement in the Ca' Morosini painting were duplicated in the second choirloft and second set of *nicchie* in a mirror image of the painting. All of the forces which Cavalli requires are accounted for in this plan, and nothing is assumed which we do not know from either archival documents or iconographic sources. To coordinate the whole affair, it is quite likely that the *maestro di cappella* stood in one loft and that his beat was relayed to the musicians in the other loft by the *vice-maestro*. Indeed, we know that the office of *vice-maestro* was created in 1607 for just this purpose.[231]

One final point should be understood from the Ca' Morosini painting and the arrangement of musical forces for large *concertato* works which I have suggested. The music is clearly directed *not* to the populace in the nave of the church, but to the *Signoria* in the apse. Contemporary listeners who are disappointed by the acoustics of the basilica in concerts

Table III-3
Suggested Placement of Musicians for the *Musiche Sacre*

Choirloft Above the Chapel of St. Peter	Choirloft Above the Chapel of St. Clement
Conductor I *(vice-maestro)*	Conductor I *(maestro-dei concerti)*
Ripieno choir I (16 voices)	*Ripieno* choir II 16 voices)

Doubling instruments
  C viola I
  A viola II
  T viola III
  B violoncello
	Doubling instruments
	  C (cornetto)
	  A trombone I
	  T trombone II
	  B trombone III

First organ	Second organ

Nicchia I	*Nicchia* II
Top level: organetto I	Top level: organetto II

Middle level: violin I
          violin II
          violoncello
          violone
	Middle level: —

Lower level: soloists: C A T B
          theorbo
	Lower level: soloists: C A T B
	          theorbo

in which the players are placed before the main altar and the audience is on folding chairs in the nave would be well advised to note the Ca' Morosini painting. The acoustics of the church must work quite differently when the musicians and listeners are in such proximity. This is, no doubt, the acoustical setting for which the elaborate, virtuoso vocal lines of the *Selva Morale* and the *Musiche Sacre* were designed.

IV

The Vespers Liturgy of St. Mark's

Introduction: Printed and Manuscript Sources

On 1 October 1644, a little over seven months after he was named *maestro di cappella*, Giovanni Rovetta published a set of psalms for double choir whose dedication, directed to the Procurators of St. Mark's, contains the following puzzling passage (Document 100):

> Scarcely had I been honored by the kindness of Your Excellencies with this noble duty than, feeling within myself the stimulus of gratitude and of duty, I finished up several compositions of which I thought the service of the Most Serene Royal Chapel of St. Mark's had the greatest need.

Surely, this is a strange introduction to a psalm collection. Why would another setting of the standard Vespers psalms for the church year be considered a collection of which St. Mark's would have "the greatest need"? A look at the *tavola*, however, may illuminate Rovetta's statement, for there is, indeed, something irregular about the contents of this collection.[232]

Most of the psalms in the print are the standard texts set in collections designated "per tutte le sollenità dell'anno," a type of publication which became rather common during the last decades of the sixteenth century and whose archetype is the famous 1550 print of Willaert and Jachet of Mantua (RISM 1550[1]).[233] However, two of Rovetta's psalms are unusual: *Lauda anima mea Dominum* and *Laudate Dominum quoniam bonus est*. While these two psalms had been published in Giovanni Croce's *Vespertina omnium solemnitatum* of 1597, they are absent from most such collections of the period. Moreover, just what role such psalms would have played in the Vespers liturgy is not answered by standard Roman sources. The *Breviarium Romanum* of Urban VIII (Rome, 1632), which represents the last major reform of the breviary before Rovetta's publication, lists these as ferial psalms for Saturday, but they form no part of the liturgy for any feast. All of the other psalms in Rovetta's collection are associated with a number of different feasts.

Rovetta's 1662 collection of double-choir psalms is a bit more specific
in this matter; for the psalms *Lauda anima mea Dominum* and *Laudate
Dominum quoniam bonus est* are included at the head of the collection in
a special Vespers service with its own Magnificat.[234] The remainder of
this service employs three other psalms which begin with a form of the
Latin verb *laudare: Laudate pueri, Laudate Dominum omnes gentes* and
Lauda Jerusalem. While the *tavola* shows how the two strange "laudate"
psalms fit into a Vespers service, it also contains three other strange
psalms whose liturgical function is dubious: *Ad te levavi, Levavi oculos
meos* and *Laudate nomen Domini*. Again, these texts are found as ferial
psalms in the reformed breviary of Urban VIII, but they form no part of
the Vespers of any feast. Rovetta's entire collection, however, has the
subtitle "Secondo l'uso della Serenis*si*ma Capella Ducale di S*an* Marco,"
an indication that some of these psalms may have had a special place
within the ceremonies of St. Mark's that they did not have in the Roman
rite as practiced outside the basilica.

Cavalli's *Vesperi* of 1675 are still more specific. The five "laudate"
psalms are grouped together at the end of the print as a special service
with the designation "Vespero delli Cinque Laudate ad uso della Capella
Di S*an* Marco." Indeed, this "Vespero delli Cinque Laudate" is just the
tip of the iceberg. It is merely one of a number of special services which
were used in St. Mark's, and its existence hints at an important point:
St. Mark's had its own liturgy from the late Middle Ages onward. While
this liturgy seems never to have been given a specific name, it appears to
be a liturgical dialect of the old Aquileian rite, the primatial rite of the
Veneto. And this rite was jealously guarded in the face of the reforms in
Roman Catholic liturgy which were taking place during the last decades
of the sixteenth century and the first of the seventeenth.

Any discussion of liturgy during the decades from the 1560s through
the 1630s is fraught with difficulties, for one must deal with the various
reforms of the Roman breviary which took place during the decades following the Council of Trent.[235] Three important volumes resulted from
these successive reforms. The first was the *Breviarium Romanum ex decreto sacrosancti Concilij Tridentini restitutum*, published under the auspices of Pope Pius V in 1568.[236] According to the papal bull of 1568,
Quod a nobis, the adoption of the new breviary was mandatory unless a
church could prove that its litu*r*gy was over 200 years old—an "escape
clause" which St. Mark's exploited fully. Although Pius V's breviary was
meant to be sacrosanct, his immediate successors added a number of
feasts and changed the texts of a number of prayers. Gregory XIII, Six-
tus V and Clement VIII all endorsed modifications of Pius V's text, and
Clement VIII published his own version of the breviary in 1602: *Breviar-*

ium Romanum ex decreto sacrosancti Concilij Tridentini restitutum, Pii V., Pont. Max., iussu editum et Clementis VIII. auctoritate recognitum.[237] The most extreme reformer, however, was Urban VIII, who not only added a number of feasts but also amended the texts of the hymns to conform to contemporary concepts of classical Latin prosody. Urban VIII's breviary was published in 1632: *Breviarium Romanum ex decreto Sacrosancti Consilii Tridentini restitutum; Pii V Pont. Max. jussu editum, et Clementis VIII primum, nunc denuo Urbani VIII. PP. auctoritate recognitum.*[238] This was the most influential of all the new breviaries, for the new hymn texts found their way into other prayer books and were part of the modern liturgy until the latest reforms of the Second Vatican Council. The Desclée editions of the *Antiphonale Romanum*, the *Breviarium Romanum*, the *Vesperale Romanum* and the *Liber Usualis* all print the hymns from Urban VIII's revised breviary. (The *Antiphonale Monasticum* and the *Liber Responsorialis* print the older versions).

The liturgy of St. Mark's, however, seems to have been virtually untouched by these reforms. Indeed, in the preface to his *Ceremoniale Magnum*, Giovanni Pace invokes the bull *Quod a nobis* and states that since the liturgy of St. Mark's was over 200 years old in 1568, the basilica was allowed to retain it (Document 101). This is only the most emphatic of a number of documents from the *seicento* which describe the preservation of the special liturgy of St. Mark's in the face of Roman liturgical reform. On 27 June 1628, for example, Doge Giovanni Cornaro ordered Cesare Vergaro, the *maestro di coro*, to see that the Mass and Divine Office be celebrated in St. Mark's "according to the rite, form, and ancient use of this Church, without the slightest innovation" (Document 102). An undated letter to the Doge, possibly dating from the fourth decade of the seventeenth century, recounts that the "Royal Chapel of Your Serenity has retained its most ancient practice, which has since become its prerogative, of not allowing any [liturgical] alterations," although it proceeds to warn the Doge that in the future he may have to cede the "prerogative of not admitting any reforms in Your Chapel"[239] (Document 103). The Doge, however, did not cede. On the contrary, his proclamation of 10 June 1630 seems to have echoed through the two following centuries: "in the celebration of the Divine Office in this Church, one must observe the rubrics, rites, usages and ceremonies described in the book entitled *Orationale*" (Document 104).

What is this *Orationale*? Clearly it was a volume of major importance in the ceremonial life of the basilica, for it is referred to in extant documents on a number of occasions. Indeed, both Bonifacio and Pace mention it prominently in their *ceremoniali* as the prime liturgical authority for the basilica; and Sansovino cites it as one of the two guides to the basilica's liturgy: "the book of ceremonies and that other one called *Orationale*, with its rubrics."[240] The *Orationale* was the special breviary for St. Mark's which maintained its role as the source of the liturgy of the Divine Office right through the years of Roman reform.[241] It is but one of a number of special liturgical books for St. Mark's which are mentioned again and again in the documents of the seventeenth century. In addition to the *Orationale*, St. Mark's had its own antiphonary, gradual, missal and hymnal. In short, an entire liturgical library existed in St. Mark's during the sixteenth, seventeenth and eighteenth centuries which outlined a rite differing from the Roman rite in many respects. The rite seems not to have been confined to St. Mark's; it was also used in the four churches of Venice under direct ducal jurisdiction: Santa Maria in Broglio, Ss. Filippo e Giacomo, San Giacomo di Rialto and San Giovanni Nuovo di Rialto. Moreover, it was used whenever the Doge or the *Serenissima Signoria* went on one of the "andate diverse" to various churches in the city.[242] Indeed, only when St. Mark's became the cathedral of Venice in 1807 does it seem to have dropped its special rite and adopted the Roman liturgy.[243]

Some preliminary work on the sources of the liturgy has already been done. In the nineteenth century, Emmanuele Cicogna listed the known printed sources in his *Bibliografia veneziana*, [244] but he made no attempt to catalogue manuscript sources. More recently, a few of the sources have been cited in specialized studies, but no comprehensive list of such material was compiled.[245] The following list is the most extensive bibliography of primary sources on the liturgy of St. Mark's which has been compiled to this date:

1. Biblioteca del Civico Museo Correr. Codice Cocogna 1602.
   Orationale ad usum Basilicae Ducalis Sancti Marci Venetiarum. MDCCLIX. This is a sixteenth-century manuscript with an eighteenth-century title page attached (1759) and a number of additional texts added at the end of the volume in an eighteenth-century hand. Cicogna's notes on the preliminary pages state that the volume was copied, notated and illuminated by a Brescian priest, Giovanni di Vitale, in 1567.

2. Oxford Bodleian. MS Canon. Liturg. 323.
   Ordo Orationalis secundum consuetudinis Ecclesiae Sancti Marci de Venetis. Undated manuscript; Bodleian catalogue dates it as 1514 while describing it erroneously as a Roman breviary.[246]

3. Biblioteca del Civico Museo Correr. Codice Cicogna 163.
   Breviarium Manuscriptum. A *pars aestivalis* of a manuscript

breviary. The presence of special feasts and texts associated solely with St. Mark's marks this as a partial third copy of the *Orationale*.

4. British Library. Department of Printed Books. IA. 19878. *Breviarium secundum ritum et consuetudinem alme ecclesiae Aquileiensis.* Franciscus de Hailbrun: Venetijs, 1481.

5. Biblioteca del Civico Museo Correr. Codice Cocogna J 31. Biblioteca Nazionale Marciana. Incunabula Veneta 854. *Breviarium secundum usum Aquileiae.* Andreas de Torresanis de Asula: Venetijs, 1496. (in two volumes, one in each library)

6. Biblioteca Nazionale Marciana 230. d. 26. A.S.V., San Marco, Procuratia de Supra, Registro 106. PSALTERIUM/DAVIDICUM,/PER HEBDOMADAM DIS-POSITUM/AD USUM ECCLESIAE DUCALIS SANCTI MARCI VENETIARUM/Cum omnibus, quae pro Psalmis, Hymnis, et Antiphonis,/in Divinis Officijs, necessaria sunt./Nec non cum Officio Defunctorum, ac Indice Psalmorum, Hymnorum*que*; omnium in fin./PRAECIPUA NUPER CURA EMENDA-TUM ET EXCUSSUM. (device)/VENETIIS. M DC IX./Apud Franciscum Rampazettum, Typographum Ducalem.

7. Biblioteca Nazionale Marciana. 80. d. 122. OFFICIUM/IN NOCTE/NATIVITATIS/DOMINI/AD MATU-TINUM,/Secundum consuetudinem Ducalis Ecclesiae/Sancti Marci Venetiarum./(device)/VENETIIS, MDCCXXII./Ex Typographia Andreae Poleti.[247]

8. Biblioteca Nazionale Marciana. 80. d. 122. BENEDICTIO/AQUAE/Quae sit in Nocte Epiphaniae,/JUXTA CONSUETUDINEM/ECCLESIAE DUCALIS/SANCTI MARCI/VENETIARUM/(device)/VENETIIS, MDCCXXII./ Ex Typographia Andreae Poleti.[248]

9. Biblioteca Nazionale Marciana. 80. d. 122. LITANIAE/Secundum Consuetudinem/Ducalis Ecclesiae/ SANCTI MARCI/VENETIARUM./VENETIIS, MDCCXIX/ Ex Typographia Pinelliana.[249]

10. Biblioteca Nazionale Marciana. 163. d. 175. Officia propria/FESTI SANCTI/MARCI APOSTOLI, ET EVANGELISTAE,/CUM OCTAVA:/NECNON TRANSLA-

TIONIS,/et Apparitionis Corporis eiusdem./RECITANDA EX
ANTIQUA/Consuetudine in Ducali eius Ecclesia; . . . /Per R.
D. Ioannem Stringa eiusdem Ecclesia Canonicum . . ./
(device)/VENETIIS, M. D. C. II./Apud Franciscum de Pa-
trianis, ad signum Hercu. V.[250]

11.   Biblioteca Nazionale Marciana. 171. D. 199.
      OFFICIUM/Hebdomadae   Sanctae,/Secundum   consuetudi/
      nem Ducalis Ecclesiae/S. MARCI/VENETIARUM./Dominica
      Palmarum / usque ad dien Pascha / inclusive. / AD ANTI-
      QUUM/ritum et integritatem/restitutum./VENETIIS 1716./
      Typis Ioseph Prodocini.[251]

12.   Biblioteca Nazionale Marciana. Misc. 134.10 and 134.5
      SUPPLICATIONES/Ad Sanctissimam/VIRGINEM MAR-
      IAM./TEMPORE BELLI./Secundum consuetudinem Ducalis
      Basilicae S. Marci Venetiarum./(device)/VENETIIS, M. DC.
      XCV./Apud Io: Antonium Pinellium/Impressorem Ducalem. A
      second edition was published in 1715.[252]

13.   Biblioteca del Civico Museo Correr. Codice Cicogna 596.
      SUPPLICATIONES ad GLORIOSISSIMAM VIRGINEM
      MARIAM pro variis necessitatibus Ad usum DUCALIS BA-
      SILICAE SANCTI MARCI VENETIARUM. ANNO DOM-
      INI: MDCCLXXXVIII. A manuscript containing miscellaneous
      Marian ceremonies.[253]

14.   Biblioteca del Civico Museo Correr. Codice Cicogna 1595.
      Ordines. Sixteenth-century manuscript with eighteenth-
      century additions at the end.

15.   Biblioteca del Civico Museo Correr. Codice Cicogna 1605.
      Modus et ordo offici fiendi in ecclesia beati Marci . . . .

16.   Biblioteca del Civico Museo Correr. Codice Cicogna 1006.
      Rituale per la Chiesa di S. Marco di Venezia. Fourteenth-
      century manuscript; eighteenth-century additions at end of the
      manuscript.

17.   A.S.V. San Marco. Procuratia de Supra. Registri 113-118
      Libri corali. Choirbooks filled with plainchant settings of the
      special texts for the liturgy of St. Mark's. Fifteenth century, but
      with an eighteenth-century index attached to each volume.

18. A.S.V. San Marco. Procuratia de Supra. Registro 119.
    Uffizio della Beata Vergine. Marian offices from St. Mark's.

19. A.S.V. San Marco. Procuratia de Supra. Registro 122.
    Breviario gottico. A fourteenth-century breviary with sections
    of musical notation. Possibly used as a model for the later copies
    of the *Orationale.*

20. A.S.V. San Marco. Procuratia de Supra. Registri 120 and 121.
    Biblioteca Nazionale Marciana. Cod. Lat. III-44 (-2742)
             Cod. Lat. III-45 (-2444)
             Cod. Lat. III-46 (-2099)
             Cod. Lat. III-47 (-2100)
             Cod. Lat. III-48 (-2291)
             Cod. Lat. III-111(-2116)
    A set of missals from the fourteenth through sixteenth centuries
    used in St. Mark's. Only one volume (Cod. Lat. III-111 [-2116])
    contains the special feasts and liturgy of the basilica. The others
    are Roman missals adapted for use in the church by the addition
    of materials at the end, or by the amplification of their calendars.
    Those in the Biblioteca Nazionale Marciana were deposited
    there in 1786.

Of all of the extant sources, items 1 and 2 are certainly the most
important, for they are the two surviving copies of the *Orationale*, the
special breviary of St. Mark's which, as demonstrated above, is referred
to in documents at least through the era of Pace's *Ceremoniale Magnum.*
The eighteenth-century title page of item no. 1 (1759) and the added eighteenth-century folios at its end suggest that this volume was used in services throughout the eighteenth century as well. There are also signs that
item no. 2 was used long after the assumed date of copying, 1514; for the
feasts of certain saints who had not yet been canonized appear on the
liturgical calendar—notably St. Francis de Sales, who was not born until
1567 and not canonized until 1665. Similarly, Lorenzo Giustiniani was not
canonized until 1690, although he appears under his feast day, 8 January.
To be sure, Lorenzo Giustiniani appeared on Venetian calendars before
his canonization in Rome, but it is significant that the first list of days and
services for musicians on which his feast appears is that of 1677. Both
Francis de Sales and Lorenzo Giustiniani appear in the calendar of item
no. 2 in a different hand from the remainder of the feasts, and no special
liturgy for either appears within the *Orationale.* Thus, it would seem that
they were added to the calendar late in the seventeenth century, a sign
that the volume was still used at that time.[254]

Item no. 3 is a smaller volume, the *pars aestivalis* of a complete breviary. The details of the liturgy connect it with St. Mark's, i.e. it is half of a third copy of the *Orationale*. Documents in the A.S.V. state that two *orationales* were copied out by Giovanni Battista Vitale in 1567, one large and one small. Item no. 3 may well be the smaller of these two volumes.

Items 4 and 5 are the only published breviaries for the Aquileian rite, the early rite of the Veneto, which seems to be the source for a number of special ceremonies from the rite of St. Mark's.[255]

Item 6 is the basic psalter for the rite of the ducal chapel. It was assembled in 1609 by the indefatigable Giovanni Stringa, the *maestro di coro* who not only revised Sansovino's *Venetia* in 1604 but also edited a number of liturgical prints for the basilica. It includes the psalms and antiphons for ferial use and the hymns for major feasts. Documents tell us that the psalter was printed at this time because the manuscript copies were in "pessimo statto," only one was in usable condition—and that one, only barely. Since the cost of copying the texts out would have been 50 ducats per volume, and the cost of a printing would be only 200 ducats, the Procurators decided to have Stringa edit the materials for press and paid him 50 ducats for his efforts. Fifty copies of the psalter were printed. (See Documents 108 and 109.)

Items 7 through 13 are special prints and manuscripts which deal with important individual feasts: Matins on Christmas Day, the ceremony of the Blessing of the Waters on Epiphany, special litanies, the office for the three major feasts of St. Mark, the office for Holy Week, and special supplications to the Virgin, in wartime and on a number of other occasions.[256] A number of these prints date from the eighteenth century, though at least three—items 10, 11, and 12—were published in the seventeenth as well. In some cases we can be fairly sure of the manuscript sources from which these prints were drawn. For example, items 7, 9, 10 and 11 all contain texts found in the *Orationale*. The contents of item 10, however, may not have been drawn directly from the *Orationale* but rather from Biblioteca Nazionale Marciana, Cod. Lat. II-93 (-2925), a sixteenth-century manuscript which contains the office liturgy for the three major feasts of St. Mark celebrated in the basilica. Indeed, the printing of the office texts for the feasts of St. Mark seems to have been a gesture toward the Procurators, who in 1600 gave Giovanni Stringa 25 ducats to print his newly written life of St. Mark, provided that he also print the "officio della vita di San Marco" and give a copy of each volume to the members of the Senate (Document 110).

Items 14, 15 and 16 are liturgical manuscripts which Cicogna dated from the fourteenth through sixteenth centuries. Items 14 and 16, however have additional folios in an eighteenth-century hand, suggesting that these volumes were used well into the eighteenth century, just like the *orationales*. Item 14 contains ceremonies for receiving the Patriarch in St. Mark's, for Ascension, for the Feast of the Purification, for Ash Wednesday, and for Palm Sunday. Item 15 is limited to Holy Week texts; and item 16 includes services for both Christmas Eve and Holy Week. These manuscripts are of the utmost importance, because they contain the texts to certain special ceremonies not included in the *Orationale* which were set by the composers of the basilica.

Item 17 is a set of fifteenth-century choirbooks which contain plainchant settings of many of the texts from the *Orationale* as well as certain other texts—namely, texts associated with Matins—which were left out of the *Orationale*. These are almost certainly the volumes to which Bonifacio refers over and over in connection with the *Orationale* as the antiphonaries of St. Mark's.[257] A similar set of books is presently housed in St. Mark's near the *loggia dei cavalli*, and documents state that these were executed in the 1550s by Giovanni di Vitale, the same copyist and illuminator who made the copy of the *Orationale* in the Biblioteca Correr.[258] Each of the volumes in the A.S.V. has an eighteenth-century table of contents at the end, a sign that the set was used for centuries after it was first copied.

Items 18 and 19 are two manuscripts containing texts used in the basilica. The first is a collection of various ceremonies for Marian feasts, the second a fourteenth-century breviary which may well have been the model for the later copies of the *Orationale*.

Item 20 is a set of eight missals associated with St. Mark's. Those in the Biblioteca Nazionale Marciana have been dated tentatively as manuscripts from the fourteenth through sixteenth centuries.[259] While these volumes were brought to the Marciana from St. Mark's in 1786, according to the inscription on the inside cover of each tome, it is difficult to determine whether the missals were actually being used in the basilica at this date. The missals fall into three broad categories. Some are purely Roman missals with no signs that they were actually used in St. Mark's except for the inscription from 1786. Others are Roman missals whose calendars have been amplified by the addition of feasts which were celebrated only in St. Mark's, appended at the end of each volume. Only one tome, the elaborately illuminated Cod. Lat. III-111 (-2116), contains the special liturgy for St. Mark's as an integral part of the missal.

This set of volumes is described in Valentinelli's Marciana catalogue merely as "Missale Romanum, olim ad usum Ecclesiae Sancti Marci."

Why would Roman missals have been used in the basilica? Although the liturgy for the Mass at St. Mark's is an area which still awaits detailed research, preliminary work suggests that it agreed much more closely with that of Rome than did the liturgy for Vespers. Joan Ann Long has found that none of the motets of Willaert which she could identify with Mass texts differed from Roman sources.[260] Moreover, Bonifacio mentions that many Masses are to be sung "secundum Curiam Romanum," stating that some Masses at St. Mark's differ from Rome only in the Epistle and Gospel.[261] Since the copying of liturgical books was very expensive, it is logical that St. Mark's would have made as much use as possible of Roman missals rather than having its own missals copied out for the sake of those feasts for which it had a special Mass liturgy.[262]

Several of the items in this bibliography are alluded to in an inventory of the manuscripts given to Giorgio Minaccia on 30 January 1631, when he was elected *maestro di coro* of St. Mark's.[263] Included in the list are "Il Rational coperto di Veluto," (cf. items 1 and 2), "Un libro in Carta Bergamina scritto a pena coperto di Cartoni roani, intitolato Suplicationis ad Gloriosissimam Verginam Mariam," (cf. items 12 and 13, which no doubt contain many of the same texts as the volume given to Minaccia), "Un libro in foglio di carta pergamina scritto a penna, con cartoni coperto de ciro roan scuro, intitolato Ordo, sivè officium ad benedicendum aquam in nocte Epiphaniae," (cf. item 8), and "Un libro coperto di brocadelo per l'officio et cerimonie del Venerdi Santo" (cf. item 11, which would have incorporated the cermonies for Good Friday).

The *ceremoniali* of St. Mark's mention a number of other liturgical books which seem not to have survived. Bonifacio speaks of a "Hymnarium Magnum" as well as of certain "magnis libris negris" which preserve the ceremonies for All Saints' Day, a "libretto rosso" which preserves litanies, a special "Libro Passionario" for Good Friday and a general liturgical source called the "Ordinarium."[264]

In comparing the liturgy of St. Mark's with that of the Roman rite, three Roman sources have been used. The first is a Roman breviary printed in Venice in 1562, which represents the Roman rite as practiced in Venice just prior to the Tridentine reforms. Since the *Orationale* is a pre-Tridentine source, this breviary provides a more precise tool than seventeenth-century Roman service books:

Biblioteca Nazionale Marciana. 32. D. 227.

Breviarium Romanum optime/recognitum: in quo Commune sancto-/rum cum suis psalmis, Nonnulle octa-/ve, Tabula parisina, Officium/nominis Jesu, Desponsatio-/nis Mariae, et alia multa-/quae in caeteris desidera-/bantur, nuper sunt/accomodata. (on p. 384:) Venetijs apud Joannes Va-/riscum, et Socios. 1562./Mense Maius.

The second is the breviary of Clement VIII, which represents Roman practice from 1602 through 1632:

Biblioteca Nazionale Marciana. 209. C. 9.
BREVIARIUM/ROMANUM,/Ex decreto Sacrosancti Concilij/Tridentini restitutum, Pij Quinti Pont. Max. iussu editum./ET/CLEMENTIS VIII./auctoritate recognitum./PARISIIS/Sumptibus Dionysij de la Noüe via/Iacobea sub signo Nominis IESU./A.O IUBILAEI, M. DC. XXV.

And the third is the reformed breviary of Urban VIII:[265]

Biblioteca Nazionale Marciana. 150. D. 211-214.
BREVIARIUM/ROMANUM./EX DECRETO SACROSANCTI/CONCILII TRI-DENTINI/RESTITUTUM./PII. V. PONT. MAX. IUSSU EDITUM./ET CLEMEN-TIS VIII. PRIMUM./nunc denuo URBANI PP. VIII./auctoritate recognitum./IN QUATUOR ANNI TEMPOR./DIVISUM./PARISIIS, E TYPOGRAPHIA REGIA. M. DC. XLVII.

The reformed breviaries were not unknown in the basilica. In early 1602, *maestro di coro* Rocco da Bruni drew up a list of necessities for the church, among which he specified not only "missals, breviaries, and psalters according to the rite of St. Mark's" but also "at least six reformed breviaries, provided that [those cited] above are made according to the rite of St. Mark's." Although Bruni does not specify the exact use of these reformed breviaries, they may have been employed as a symbolic bow to Roman practice on the occasions when an authority outside St. Mark's officiated at Mass; for one of the later items on the list is "a reformed Pontifical, for the [occasions] on which some Prelate officiates at Mass; this is a pressing need, for [the lack of such a volume] is a great shame."[266]

The liturgy of St. Mark's has not been ignored entirely in the literature on the basilica. As early as 1739, in his *Ecclesiae venetae antiquis monumentis*,[267] Flaminio Corner briefly discusses liturgical practices. He cites the old *ceremoniale* of Bonifacio as well as Stringa's *Psalterium Davidicum*, and he notes that St. Mark's has a number of unique texts (such as those for the Office for Christmas, Holy Week and for the Feast of St. Mark) as well as certain feasts of its own (such as the Translation and Apparition of the Body of St. Mark). However, he asserts that essentially nothing is found in the liturgy of the basilica which cannot be found in the Roman rite prior to the Tridentine reforms.[268] He then launches a brutal attack against Sansovino, who had stated that the liturgy of St. Mark's was derived from the Byzantine liturgy although it resembled the Roman rite.[269] Marco Foscarini echoes Corner's attack on Sansovino in his monumental *Della letteratura veneziana* (1752), stating that

Venetian writers tended to trace the origin of anything they did not understand to Byzantium or to Greece.[270] Nineteenth-century studies by Giovanni Diclich and Antonio Pasini[271] are more meticulous in their examination of liturgical documents. However, they side with Corner and Foscarini in asserting that there is no connection between the rite of St. Mark's and that of Byzantium. They affirm, moreover, that the tradition which traces the rite of St. Mark's to that of the early church in Alexandria is a myth which cannot be substantiated.[272]

The rite which both Pasini and Diclich do cite as the origin for the liturgy of St. Mark's is the primatial rite of the Veneto, called variously the *rito patriarchino, rito gradese* or the *rito aquileiese* in the literature.[273] Centered in the patriarchates of Grado and Aquileia, and used at one time throughout much of Northern Italy, the rite was supplanted by the Tridentine reforms and officially surpressed in major centers during the last three decades of the sixteenth century.[274] However, a liturgical dialect of the rite was retained in St. Mark's as the special liturgy of the ducal chapel. Indeed, a comparison of Aquileian breviaries, the *Orationale* of St. Mark's, and Roman sources shows that the liturgy of the basilica was very much a cross between those of Aquileia and of Rome, although it occasionally included texts of its own which appeared in neither rite. Corner's statement that the rite of St. Mark's contained nothing that was not found in pre-Tridentine Roman breviaries is simply untrue. While the basic form of the liturgy is clearly that of the Roman church, the textual content of the liturgy in St. Mark's differs from Rome in countless details, many of which can be traced to Aquileian sources.

Venice and Aquileia

Connections between Venice and Aquileia extend back to the early Middle Ages.[275] Indeed, according to one tradition, St. Mark actually wrote his gospel in Aquileia itself, and thus can be considered the founder of the Aquileian church. By stealing the relics of St. Mark from Alexandria ca. 828-829, Venice effectively usurped Aquileia's patron saint, an act commemorated by the three feasts of St. Mark in the Venetian liturgy: that of the saint himself, that of the translation of his relics from Aquileia, and that of their subsequent disappearance and miraculous apparition. Before the translation, St. Theodore had been the patron saint of the city and a symbol of Byzantine sovereignty over Venice; he was ousted by the arrival of the relics of Mark. In subsequent centuries, Venice acquired the relics of a number of Aquileian saints connected with Mark: those of Anianus, whom Mark had healed and consecrated bishop of Alexandria, as well as those of Ss. Hermagoras and Fortunatus. Venice also received relics of the four so-called "Aquileian Virgins," Euphemia, Dorothea, Thecla and Erasma. All of these figures were the subjects of important feast days on the Aquileian calendar and held a similar rank in the liturgy of St. Mark's.

Aquileia had long had designs to become one of the chief patriarchal sees of Christianity; its bishops wanted to be recognized as the successors to St. Mark just as those of Rome were to be the successors of St. Peter. These designs had been thwarted when the so-called Aquileian schism took place and the patriarchate split into two bodies, with its rival Grado attempting to usurp Aquileia's claims. From the tenth through the twelfth centuries, Grado and Aquileia battled for ecclesiastical dominance, and Venice fought to maintain her domination over both. The result was somewhat of a political see-saw. While Grado was supreme in the synod of 967, she was invaded by Aquileia in 1024. Venice intervened to restore Grado's rights, and by the privilege of Benedict IX in 1044, Grado was recognized as the see of the true patriarchate and symbolically renamed *Nova Aquileia*. Then in 1164, Ulric of Aquileia attacked Grado and forced her to renounce certain claims in a compromise of 1180. Throughout all of this, Venice sought to retain her dominance over both of the powers and actually succeeded. From 1156 onward, the patriarch of Grado resided in Venice, and from 1177 that of Aquileia did as well. Finally, in 1451, the patriarchate itself was transferred to Castello and, in 1807, to St. Mark's itself. In short, Venice had supported Aquileia's claim as the center of a North Adriatic church founded by St. Mark himself; then she had supported Grado's claim as the successor to Aquileia; and finally she had usurped Grado by stealing St. Mark's relics for herself.

In view of the strong historical connections between Venice and Aquileia, it is not surprising that there are strong links between the rite of St. Mark's and the Aquileian rite. Some scholars insist, in fact, that the early rite of St. Mark's was the Aquileian rite itself.[276] Whatever its origins, however, the liturgy of St. Mark's would logically have had close ties with that of Aquileia, and the Aquileian breviary is, thus, the logical "check" when items from St. Mark's do not agree with parallel items from Rome. Indeed, an examination of the calendar of the basilica and of the individual items of the Vespers liturgy makes this evident.

The Liturgical Year at St. Mark's

Neither the liturgical calendar which opens Giovanni Variscum's *Breviarium Romanum* of 1562 nor that which opens the *Orationale* is a completely reliable source for the liturgical year as celebrated in the Roman rite or in St. Mark's during the mid-sixteenth century. Variscum's calendar, which

prefaces a Roman breviary published in Venice for Venetian use, is filled
with a number of local saints who do not appear in the body of the
breviary. For example, the feasts of the Translation and the Apparition of
the Body of St. Mark (31 January, 25 June) as well as that of Ss. Hermagoras and Fortunatus (12 July) appear on the calendar although they
are not mentioned within the breviary. Similarly, the calendars in the two
complete *orationales* were expanded after they were originally copied,
and thus contain a number of feasts not found within the volumes themselves.[277] Therefore, the actual bodies of the breviary and the *Orationale*
are more certain guides to the feasts celebrated during the church year.
Moreover, the contents of the *Orationale* can be checked against certain
other documents which describe the church year at St. Mark's at a specific time and which do not seem to have been polluted by later hands:

1.   A.S.V., San Marco, Procuratia de Supra, Registro 98 (Ceremoniali), f. 62r and
     following. Bonifacio's *ceremoniale* contains a liturgical calendar at this point.

2.   Ibid., f. 58v–60v: "De Sanctis qui habent Orationes in nostro Orationali." Boni-
     facio's list of saints important enough to have at least a collect of their own.

3.   Biblioteca Ambrosiana, MS A. 328 inf., f. 187v–194r. An elaborate church cal-
     endar in Pace's *ceremoniale*, including a number of saints whose feasts had been
     added since the *orationales* were copied and containing additional information on
     ranks of feasts, commemorations, etc. This is the definitive statement on the
     calendar of the late seventeenth century.[278]

A comparison of the liturgical calendars of Bonifacio and Pace shows
that St. Mark's successfully resisted the attempts of the Council of Trent
to simplify the *Sanctorale* by the elimination of the feasts of local saints.
The calendar of St. Mark's remained almost untouched between 1564 and
1678. In fact, Venice as a whole fought the adoption of the reformed
Roman calendars. When Patriarch Giovanni Tiepolo ran into difficulties
with the Sacred Congregation of Rites regarding the idiosyncrasies of the
Venetian calendar, the Senate ordered him to "have the calendar published immediately without changes or innovations, according to the old,
established practice."[279] And when Patriarch Gianfrancesco Morosini
had a calendar printed which adopted certain reforms, the Senate ordered
him to "abolish that calendar and have the ducal printer make another
immediately, according to the old practice, without innovations."[280] The
effort to retain the old Venetian calendar was, of course, only one facet
of the political tug-of-war between Venice and the papacy during the first
part of the *seicento*. It is difficult to know what effect the retention of the
old calendar had on the liturgy of Venetian churches outside St. Mark's,
however, for it is not clear how local saints' days were celebrated in

Venetian churches before the Tridentine reforms. As elaborate as the prefatory calendar to Variscum's *Breviarium Romanum* may be—and it contains even more saints than the crowded calendar of the *Orationale*— none of the saints of purely local importance is provided with a special liturgy for his feast day. Indeed, none is even provided with a collect, the minimal liturgical item for a commemoration. Thus, if such feasts were celebrated as an integral part of Mass or Vespers, all items of the liturgy, including the collect, must have been drawn from the appropriate Common.

Table IV-1 (p. 155) contains all those feasts for which the *Orationale* provides at least one proper liturgical items—even if it be merely a collect—and for which Variscum provides no proper liturgy at all. In other words, these are the feasts which were considered more significant in the liturgy of St. Mark's than in the Roman rite. A little over half of them are cited in Variscum's calendar nonetheless, and about one fourth of them can be traced to Aquileian brevaries.[281] It is not difficult to determine why these feasts held an important position in the liturgy of the basilica, for they fall into a number of clear categories.[282]

In the first category are those feasts which are related to St. Mark and to figures associated with him. While the feast of St. Mark was celebrated in the rites of both Rome and St. Mark's, the basilica also celebrated the feasts connected with the arrival of Mark's relics in Venice, those of the Translation and the Apparition of the Body of St. Mark.[283] The feast of the Dedication of the Church of St. Mark's was a corollary to these feasts, celebrating the erection of a basilica over the relics of the saint. St. Mark's also observed the feast of Anianus, who succeeded Mark as bishop of Alexandria, and that of Ss. Hermagoras and Fortunatus, disciples of Mark in Aquileia.

A second category of saints who had their own liturgy in St. Mark's are figures whose relics lie in Venice. Venice always has been particularly rich in this respect, and in 1617 Patriarch Giovanni Tiepolo praised her as "not only a terrestrial paradise, due to the wisdom of your leaders, but a celestial paradise as well, due to the many relics you contain."[284] Relics of about one-fourth of the saints in Table IV-1 lie in Venetian churches. The body of St. Isidore of Chios is in St. Mark's—in fact, Bonifacio lists his feast as that of "*Sancti* Isidorij m*artyris* cuius corpus habemus." The bodies of St. Athanasius and St. Zachary are in San Zaccaria, that of St. Alban in a parochial church on Murano, that of St. Marina in Santa Maria Formosa and that of St. Anianus in San Tomà. The body of St. Ligorius was once at San Lorenzo, that of St. Magnus was at St. Geminiano, and two churches claim to have the body of St. Barbara. Relics of a number of other saints from the table are found within the city: Syrus, Mary of Egypt, John Chrysostom, Dorothy, Gerard of Csanad, Hermagoras and Fortunatus, Fosca, John the Almsgiver, Margaret, Hermolai and Simeon. St. Peter's Chair at Antioch is preserved in San Pietro in Castello.

A third category involves saints from Aquileia. The most important of these are, again, Hermagoras and Fortunatus, Ss. Euphemia, Dorothea, Thecla and Erasma, Ss. Cantius, Cantianus and Cantianella, and St. Maurus from Trieste. Saints venerated on the Adriatic coast were also important in the basilica: Paternian, bishop of Fano; Liberal; Bassus of Cupra Marittima; Severus, bishop of Ravenna, and closer to Venice, Eliodorus, patron saint of Torcello.

A number of saints connected with Byzantium and the East found their way into the liturgy of the basilica. Many of these were already venerated in areas of the West (e.g., Ravenna) and did not come directly from the East into Venetian liturgy. Among these can be counted Sabas, Lazarus, Hilary, John Chrysostom, Apollonia, Mary of Egypt, Helena, Alexander, Daniel the Stylite, Antoninus, James Intercisus, Athanasius and Basil. Other feasts at St. Mark's honored saints connected with monastic orders in the area of the lagoon: Scholastica, Gregory, Louis and Stephen. And still others were connected with saints from neighboring areas of Northern Italy: Proculus, who suffered martyrdom at Bologna; Faustinus and Jovita, patron saints of Brescia; Gaudentius, bishop of Brescia; Vigilius, bishop of Trent; Nicholas of Tolentino from Sant'Angelo; Zeno, bishop of Verona; Prosdocimus, bishop of Padua.

Thus, the political and religious history of Venice was reflected in Venetian hagiography. Venice's connections with the East, the Adriatic coast, and with Northern Italy, her role as a maritime power, and her possession of the relics of so many important figures—all of these are reflected in the liturgical calendar of St. Mark's, and thus in the liturgy of the basilica. The unique points of the calendar, however, are limited to the *Sanctorale*. The *Temporale* follows the outline of the Roman rite, and the *Commune Sanctorum* contains the same categories as do Roman liturgical books. If one examines the actual texts used for specific liturgical items on various feasts, however, one finds variants between the Roman rite and that of St. Mark's throughout all three sections of the breviary. In many cases, the texts used in St. Mark's can be traced to Aquileia; in others, however, there is no Aquileian analogue and the texts seem to represent idiosyncrasies in the liturgy of St. Mark's itself.

Before beginning an examination of the variants between the Vespers liturgies of St. Mark's and Rome, it would be well to summarize briefly the liturgical components of a Vespers service at St. Mark's.

The basic format of Vespers in St. Mark's was similar to that of the

Roman rite. Vespers began during most of the year with the standard versicle *Deus in adiutorium meum intende* and the response *Domine ad adiuvandum me festina.* During Easter week, however, the ceremony began with *Kyrie eleison—Christe eleison—Kyrie eleison.*[285] This formula is found during the same period, Easter Sunday through Low Sunday, in Aquileian breviaries, and it was also used in a number of other medieval liturgies.[286] The central portion of the service consisted of the recitation of five psalms, each one framed by a proper antiphon for the day. This basic pattern was changed on only a few occasions during the year. During the octave of Epiphany, on the *feriae* and Sundays after Easter, and on the Vigil of Pentecost the psalms were sung under a single antiphon. On Holy Saturday, a full complement of five antiphons was sung over the single psalm *Laudate Dominum omnes gentes.* And on Easter Sunday, the first three psalms were said under one antiphon while the remaining two were recited *after* the Magnificat under a second antiphon and followed by a *second* performance of the Magnificat text. After the recitation of the psalms, the chapter was said. This was followed by the singing of the hymn for the day and by the recitation of a versicle and response. The final large item of the service was the Magnificat, preceded and followed by the antiphon for the feast or by some non-liturgical substitute.[287] This was followed by a collect (*oratio*) and by any commemorations for the day. Thus, the formal structure of Vespers at St. Mark's followed that used by the Western church as a whole. The differences between the liturgies are found, rather, in the textual contents of the liturgical items.

The Psalter of St. Mark's

When Giovanni Stringa edited the *Psalterium Davidicum* for publication, he tacitly affirmed that the psalter of St. Mark's differed from the Roman psalter in crucial ways. Some of these differences were recorded as early as 1739 by Flaminio Corner, who printed parallel versions of Psalms 1, 3, 4, 5, 6 and 7, first as they appear "Ex Psalterio Communi," and then "Ex Psalterio ad usum Basilicae S. Marci." Although Corner does not cite a particular psalter from St. Mark's, he is almost certainly drawing his material from Stringa, for the psalms he quotes are all from Sunday Matins, the first texts to be found in Stringa's volume.

The *Psalterium Davidicum* is the basic ferial psalter for the basilica, and it agrees with the Roman psalter in its general form. That is, the psalter begins on Sunday with Psalm 109 (*Dixit Dominus*) and goes through the psalms in numerical order at the rate of five per day, with a few omissions, as follows:[288]

Domenica ad Vesperis

Dixit Dominus	Psalm 109
Confitebor	110
Beatus vir	111
Laudate pueri	112
In exitu Israel	113

Feria II

Dilexi quoniam exaudiet Dominus	114
Credidi	115
Laudate Dominum omnes gentes	116
Ad Dominum cum tribularer	119
Levavi oculos meos	120

Feria III

Laetatus sum	121
Ad te levavi oculos meos	122
Nisi quod Dominus	123
Qui confidunt	124
In convertendo	125

Feria IV

Nisi Dominus	126
Beati omnes	127
Saepe expugnaverunt	128
De profundis	129
Domine non est exaltatum	130

Feria V

Memento Domine David	131
Ecce quam bonum	132
Laudate nomen Domini	134
Confitemini	135
Super flumina Babylonis	136

Feria VI

Confitebor . . . quoniam audisti	137
Domine probasti me	138
Eripe me Domine	139
Domine clamavi ad te	140
Voce mea ad Dominum clamavi	141

Sabbato

Benedictus Dominus	143
Exaltabo te Deus meus	144
Lauda anima mea	145
Laudate Dominum quoniam bonus	146
Lauda Jerusalem	147

One should note that although the rites of St. Mark's and of sixteenth-century Rome are in agreement, there is a vast difference between the Vespers psalter of the time and that in the modern *Liber Usualis*.[289]

In the intervening centuries, four psalms have been dropped from the sequence, nos. 116, 134, 145 and 146; similarly, four have been "split" to form two psalms for the purposes of Vespers: nos. 135, 138, 143 and 144. Thus, the modern *Liber Usualis* is of little use as a control source for the rite of St. Mark's.

Although the sequence of psalms for ferial days at St. Mark's is the same as that of the Roman rite, the actual texts of the psalms differ somewhat from the standard Vulgate used by Rome. The differences are seldom great; they involve only nuances in the rendering of certain terms or phrases. Nonetheless, discrepancies are sprinkled through nearly all the psalms of the psalter, and examples from some of the psalms for Sunday Vespers will serve to illustrate the point. (See Table IV-2, p. 158).The origins of this translation of the psalms are obscure. It is neither the standard Vulgate nor the version which St. Jerome made from the Hebrew. Pasini has suggested that it represents the *Itala* version of the psalter, that is, the *Vetus Latina* which existed prior to St. Jerome's revisions of 383 (the *Psalterium Romanum*) and 392 (the *Psalterium Gallicum*, which became the Vulgate).[290] At any rate, these versions of the psalms must have been used on ferial days only, for none of the prints of *canto figurato* by the composers in St. Mark's during the seventeenth century reproduces these variants.[291] Even Rovetta's Vespers prints of 1644 and 1662 and Cavalli's print of 1675, collections published expressly for the use of the *cappella marciana*, revert to the standard Vulgate translation.

While the *Psalterium Davidicum* gives us the psalm texts as used at St. Mark's, we must turn to the *Orationale* to find the psalm sequences used for various feast days throughout the year. And, indeed, in this area the liturgy of the ducal chapel deviates from Roman practice in a number of crucial cases. The first major variant occurs early in the liturgical year, at the end of Advent. In the *Orationale*, the following texts are prescribed for Vespers on the Vigil of Christmas:[292]

In vigilia Nativitatis Domini. Ad Ve*speras*.
*antipho*na. Rex pacificus magnifica*tus* est, cuius vultum desiderat universa terra.
p*salmu*s. Laudate pueri D*omi*num.
*antipho*na. Magnificatus est rex pacificus super omnes reges universae terrae.
p*salmu*s. Laudate Dominum *omn*es gentes.
*antipho*na. Levate capita vestra ecce appropinquabit redemptio vestra.
p*salmu*s. Lauda *a*nima mea D*omi*num.
*antipho*na. Scitote, quia prope e*st* regn*um* Dei, amen dico vobis, quia non tardabit.
p*salmu*s. Laudate D*omi*num q*uoniam* bonus est psalmus.
*antipho*na. Completi su*nt* dies Mari*a*e, ut pareret filium suu*m* primogenitum.
p*salmu*s. Lauda Jerusalem.

The antiphons are the familiar texts from the Vespers of the Christmas Vigil in the Roman rite,[293] but the psalms are not the standard texts of the male *cursus*;[294] instead, the *Orationale* lists those very five psalms which Cavalli labeled the *Vespero delli Cinque Laudate*[295] (Plate 6). The service was used not only on the Vigil of Christmas but on a bewilderingly large number of other feasts: the Vigils of Epiphany, Ascension and of Pentecost, Second Vespers for Corpus Christi and for its Octave, First Vespers for the Purification, and the Vigils of the Assumption, of the Nativity and Conception of the B. V. M. and of All Saints' Day. At one time, the sequence had also been used for Vespers on Holy Saturday.[296] Thus, the service would have been one of the most prominent sequences of Vespers psalms of the entire church year.

The *Vespero delli Cinque Laudate* can clearly be traced to the Aquileian rite. The Aquileian breviaries describe the psalm sequence as the standard one for First Vespers on all feasts of double rank for which other psalms are not assigned (Document 112). Thus, the sequence was used even more often in Aquileia than in St. Mark's; it is found on the following feasts in the Aquileian rite, for which St. Mark's used other sequences of psalms: the Vigils of the Feast of the Holy Trinity and of the Annunciation, First Vespers for Ss. Philip and James and for the Finding of the Holy Cross, the Vigils of St. John before the Latin Gate, the Feast of St. John, the Apostles Peter and Paul, the Visitation, the Transfiguration of Our Lord, Ss. Hermagoras and Fortunatus, and St. Laurence. The use of the *Cinque Laudate* for First Vespers of the Common of Apostles, of the Common of Martyrs, and of the Common of Virgins brings it into use on virtually every important saint's day of the year.[297] It is clear that the *Vespero delli Cinque Laudate* was a third major psalm sequence for Aquileia whose importance equaled that of the male *cursus* and female *cursus*.

A survey of pre-Tridentine breviaries reveals that Aquileia and St. Mark's were not the only early liturgies to include the *Cinque Laudate*. In fact, the service was very widespread. It is found in all three of the major English breviaries—those for the Sarum rite and the rites of Hereford and York—as well as in a number of monastic and special breviaries, among which are those for the Augustinian rite, the Dominican rite, the rite of the Church in Salzburg and the Carmelite rite.[298] Nor was St. Mark's the only rite to retain them after the Trent reforms. They were retained by the Dominicans and the Carmelites, among others. Nonetheless, it seems clear that the psalms came to St. Mark's through Aquileia and that by the mid-seventeenth century, they were associated exclusively with the basilica in the minds of its composers.

Cavalli was certainly not the only composer at St. Mark's to set the *Vespero delli Cinque Laudate*, although he seems to be the only one to have given the service this name. Neither Bonifacio nor Pace has a special title for the service; they refer to it merely by indicating "Psalmi omnes

Plate 6 The *Orationale* of St. Mark's, showing the liturgy for the Virgil of Christmas. Biblioteca Correr, Codice Cicogna 1602, f. 12v–13r.

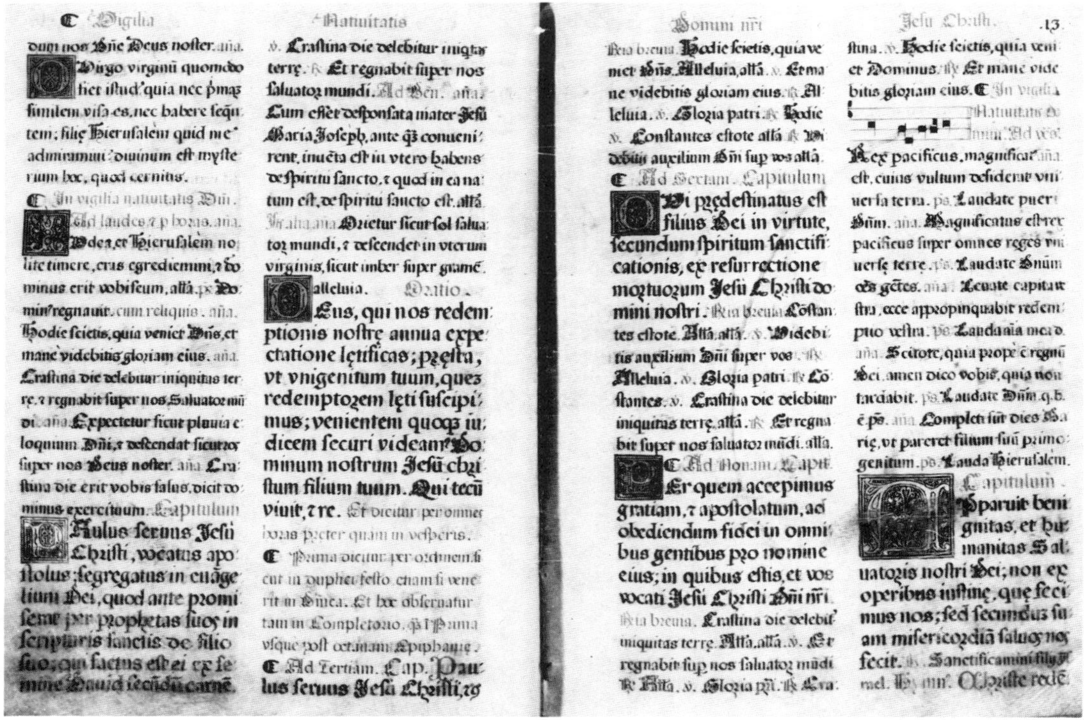

Reproduced by permission of the Biblioteca del Civico Museo Correr, Venice.

Laudate" or "Li salmi sono tutti Laudate" for various feasts. As mentioned above, Rovetta set the sequence as a unified series in his psalm
collection of 1662, although one can also assemble the sequence from his
collection of 1644 by combining the two special *Laudate* psalms which
he sets—*Lauda anima mea* and *Laudate Dominum quoniam bonus est
psalmus*—with the three more usual psalms which appear in other Vespers sequences as well—*Laudate pueri, Laudate Dominum omnes gentes*
and *Lauda Jerusalem*. A number of other composers from St. Mark's
"set" the *Vespero delli Cinque Laudate* in this way, i.e., by providing
settings of these two special *Laudate* psalms in their Vespers collections.
Croce included them in his *Vespertina omnium solemnitatum* (1597), and
Willaert seems to have set them as well, for Zarlino includes them in a
list of Willaert's psalm compositions to be studied as examples of coun-
terpoint for more than three voices (Document 113).[299] We do not know
with what frequency these psalms were set after Cavalli's *Vesperi*. The
entire service was set in the *Salmi brevi a otto voci* (Bologna: Monti,
1675) of Natale Monferrato, the *vice-maestro* of St. Mark's who would
soon succeed Cavalli as *maestro di cappella*; however, a thorough survey
of eighteenth-century Venetian sacred music is still to be undertaken.
Nonetheless, the service is cited in liturgical manuscripts from St. Mark's
as late as 1788, when "Psalmi omnes Laudate" are specified as the sequence for First Vespers on the Feast of the Nativity of the B. V. M.[300]
Moreover, the musical archives of St. Mark's contain a set of *Laudate*
psalms by Baldassare Galuppi which are scored for double choir and
include the texts *Laudate Dominum quoniam bonus est* and *Lauda anima
mea Dominum*. The last of these is dated 1789.[301, 302]

A second Vespers sequence unique to St. Mark's is that for the Vigil
of the Feast of the Holy Trinity. Bonifacio describes the service as follows:

> Saturday after Pentecost. In this Vigil and on the day [i.e., the following day, the Feast
> of the Holy Trinity] the psalms are sung with the greatest decorum . . . the psalms in
> First Vespers are: *Levavi oculos meos, Ad te levavi, De profundis, Memento, Laudate
> nomen Domini*. (Document 114)[303]

In this case, there is no analogue in the Aquileian rite, which used the
Cinque Laudate for this feast. Composers seem not to have bothered to
set this service in *canto figurato* until Rovetta set those three psalms
which are not part of other Vespers sequences—*Levavi oculos meos,
Ad te levavi*, and *Laudate nomen Domini*—in his collection of 1662. Moreover, a set of documents from 1600 confirms that the psalms had not been
composed by any *maestro* during the sixteenth century. As part of an
inquest held in August, 1600 to determine whether Rocco da Bruni should
be reappointed to the post of *maestro di coro*, Giovanni Croce was called

before the Procurators and asked, among other things, whether Rocco da Bruni had made any alterations in the ceremonies of the Divine Office. To this, Croce responded as follows (Document 115):

> He made changes in the ceremonies for First Vespers of the Most Holy Trinity, which he wanted sung with two choirs; but double-choir settings do not exist for these psalms, nor were they ever composed by any of the *maestri di cappella*; so as not to cause a scandal, we sang them in *falsobordone*, and a Senator, whose name I do not now remember, spoke to me and asked me about this innovation of singing *falsobordone* in the *cappella* of St. Mark's.

A third special Vespers sequence from St. Mark's is that used for Second Vespers on the Feast of the Dedication of the Church of St. Mark's (October 8th).[304] While this sequence involves no psalms which are not found in collections designed "per tutte le solennità" in the Roman rite, the choice and order of texts is unique to St. Mark's:

Credidi
Laetatus sum
Nisi Dominus
Confitebor tibi Domine quoniam audisti
Lauda Jerusalem

The origin of the series can be traced to Aquileia, where it appears as Second Vespers for the Dedication of the Church of Aquileia and for the Transfiguration of Our Lord. Although we have double-choir settings of these psalms by both Rovetta (1662) and Cavalli (1675), this service seems never to have been performed in double-choir music before the start of the seventeenth century. To be sure, the documentation is somewhat ambiguous on this point. The feast is found on Bonifacio's list of days on which the *Pala d'oro* was opened and double-choir psalms were sung.[305] However, the feast is also mentioned in two lengthy inquests of 1589 and 1600, in which the singers insist that the psalms were never meant to be sung, nor indeed ever had been sung, in double-choir settings.[306]

The details of the inquests are interesting for the insight they give us into the musical life of the basilica; they are also quite amusing. On 8 October 1589, there had been a disturbance during Second Vespers for the Feast of the Dedication of the Church of St. Mark's, and the singers had climbed down from the pergola and marched right out of the church. During the inquest, it became apparent that the *maestro di coro* had asked the singers to sing double-choir music on a day for which it was not specified on the large ecclesiastical calendar which hung in the sacristy. They responded that they were not obligated to sing in two choirs for this feast, that the psalms for the day had never been sung in double-choir settings, and that one psalm had never even been set for two choirs. The text of some of the testimony on this last point is instructive (Documents 116 and 117):

(From the testimony of Bernardo Andeli)

Question: Which Vespers was being celebrated on that day?
Answer: That of the feast of [the Dedication of] the Church of St. Mark's.
Question: Was it customarily sung in one or in two choirs?
Answer: In one choir, for in the twenty-five years that I have served, it never has been sung by two choirs, nor have the past *maestri di cappella*, which have been Messer Adrian, Messer Ciprian and the Reverend Father Isepo Zerlino, ever set one psalm which is missing.

(From the testimony of Baldissare Donati)

Question: Since this sign [to sing in two choirs] was posted by the *maestro di cappella*, who is the chief, and since the sign was there and the *maestro di coro* had ordered it, why did you not sing and obey?
Answer: Because it is not the custom to sing [this service] in two choirs, nor does the psalm exist [in a double-choir setting] as do [those for] all the other Vespers services, set by the hand of Messer Adrian. If this had been the custom, since only one psalm was missing, he would have set it. However, his successor Messer Ciprian did not set it either; nor did the present maestro Messer Padre Isepo [Zarlino], and if he had wanted it sung by two choirs, he would have set it.

The problematic missing psalm was clearly the *Confitebor Angelorum*, a psalm which has a very limited use in the Roman rite on a number of feasts of angel saints and which had been omitted from the large 1550 psalm collection of Willaert and Jachet of Mantua. The text does not seem to have been set as a result of this inquest, however, for the same problem came up in the inquest of 1600. Again, the situation is outlined by an excerpt from the testimony (Document 118):

(From the testimony of Guglielmo *francese*, a soprano)

Questioned whether the *maestro* [Rocco da Bruni] had made changes in the ancient ceremonies of the office.
Answered: In this connection, he had the psalms sung in *falsobordone* the day of the feast [of the Dedication of the Church of St. Mark's], something which is no longer done, and he shouted at the *maestro di cappella* [asking him] why he had not set these psalms, and the *maestro di cappella* answered that since neither Adrian, nor Ciprian had ever set them, nor Zarlino either, he did not know why [the *maestro di coro*] wanted him to set them, since this was not the custom.

The testimony in this final document is a bit confusing, since by this date an eight-voice setting of the *Confitebor Angelorum* had appeared in print in Croce's *Vespertina omnium solemnitatum psalmodia* of 1597. There may, however, have been a custom of using only the psalm compositions of the *maestro di cappella* for major Vespers services at this time. Certainly there had been more composers on the staff of the basilica than "Messer Adrian, Messer Ciprian e'l Reverendo Padre Isepo Zerlino," although these are the only names cited in support of the tradition of *not* setting this Vespers service for two choirs. It is perhaps significant that, when queried about *maestro* Bruni's changes in the ceremonies, Croce did not cite this feast at all but mentioned instead the First Vespers of the Feast of the Holy Trinity.

A fourth psalm sequence from the *Orationale* which is not found in Roman sources is that for Second Vespers on the Feasts of Ss. Hermagoras and Fortunatus (12 July) and of St. Clement (23 November):[307]

Dixit Dominus
Confitebor
Beatus vir
Credidi
Eripe me Domine ab homine malo

The "exotic" psalm in the series, *Eripe me Domine* (Psalm 139) seems never to have been set by composers connected with St. Mark's. It did have a use in the Roman liturgy, however, for it is found in a sequence of psalms used on both Maundy Thursday and Good Friday:[308]

Credidi
Ad Dominum cum tribularer
Eripe me Domine ab homine malo
Domine clamavi ad te
Voce mea ad Dominum clamavi

The psalm also occurs as part of the Second Vespers for the Common of Martyrs in Aquileia:

Dixit Dominus
Beatus vir
In convertendo
Eripe me Domine ab homine malo
Lauda Jerusalem

There are a number of other important variants between the distribution of the psalter in Vespers services in St. Mark's and in the Roman rite. (These variants, as well as those discussed above, are summarized in Table IV-3, p. 159.) These variants do not involve special sequences of psalms but, rather a redistribution of the standard psalm sequences to new feasts. For example, the psalms for Vespers on Christmas Day *(Dixit Dominus Confitebor, Beatus vir, De profundis, Memento)* are used on four occasions in St. Mark's where the Roman rite prescribes other psalms: Second Vespers of Epiphany, both Vespers of the Octave of the Epiphany, and Second Vespers of the Purification. This practice is traceable to Aquileia for all four occasions; Rome uses the *cursus* of Sunday psalms for Epiphany and its Octave *(Dixit Dominus, Confitebor, Beatus vir, Laudate pueri, In exitu)* and the female *cursus* for the Purification. For First Vespers on the Feast of St. Agatha, St. Mark's uses a *cursus* which is used by Rome for the dedication of a church: *Dixit Dominus, Confitebor, Beatus vir, Laudate pueri, Lauda Jerusalem*; the Roman rite uses the female *cursus* for this service. On the Vigil of the Nativity of St. John the Baptist, St. Mark's uses a *cursus* employed by Rome for the Feast of a Confessor Bishop: *Dixit Dominus, Confitebor, Beatus vir, Laudate pueri* and *Memento*; Rome uses the male *cursus* here. For Second Vespers on the Feast of the Transfiguration of Our Lord, St. Mark's uses the *cursus* of Sunday psalms; Rome uses the male *cursus*. And for both First and Second Vespers on the Feasts of St. Mark and of Ss. Peter and Paul, St. Mark's uses the psalms of the Common of the Apostles: *Dixit Dominus, Laudate pueri, Credidi, In convertendo, Domine probasti me*;[309] Rome uses these psalms for Second Vespers only and uses the male *cursus* for First Vespers. In none of these cases can the variants between St. Mark's and Rome be traced to the Aquileian rite; these represent practices unique to the basilica.

The Cycle of Hymns

The principal hymns for the liturgy of St. Mark's are set forth in the central section of Stringa's *Psalterium Davidicum*, f. 107v–137v. The same titles are given in the *Orationale* with the same liturgical designations although the *Orationale* does not give the full texts of the hymns. It is clear, therefore, that there was no revision of the hymnal in St. Mark's between 1567, the date of the copying of the *Orationale*, and 1609, the date of Stringa's *Psalterium*, although two reforms of the Roman breviary took place between these dates.

The hymns for St. Mark's can be divided into three distinct groups: independent hymns from the liturgy of the basilica which are not found in the Roman rite; hymns which correspond with a Roman text but have a different liturgical use in the basilica from that in the Roman rite; and hymns whose texts and liturgical positions are the same in both rites.

Stringa himself cites three hymns which are unique to St. Mark's. For the Feast of the Ascension, he states that the hymn *Jesu nostra redemptio* is sung "secundum Curiam Romanam," but that St. Mark's uses the hymn *Festum nunc celebre*; for the Feast of St. Mary Magdalene, Stringa cites *Pater superni luminis* as the Roman hymn and *Maria Mater Domini* as the hymn for St. Mark's; and for the Feast of the Transfiguration of Our Lord, *Quicumque Christum quaeritis* is the Roman text and *Fons pietatis culmina* the hymn for St. Mark's.[310] Of these three hymns, only one can be traced to Aquileia; the hymn *Festum nunc celebre* is the Vespers hymn in Aquileian breviaries. The hymns for St. Mary Magdalene and the Transfiguration seem to be independent texts from St. Mark's without Aquileian roots.

Although Stringa cites only three hymns which diverge from Roman practice, a comparison of his *Psalterium* with the breviary of Clement VIII, which had been published just seven years before, reveals several others. For Palm Sunday, St. Mark's uses the hymn *Magno salutis gaudio*; the Roman hymn is *Vexilla regis prodeunt*.[311] For the Annunciation, St. Mark's has the special hymn *Deus qui mundum crimine*; Rome uses the general Marian hymn *Ave maris stella*. For the Feast of St. Mark, St. Mark's would naturally have a special hymn, *Athleta Christi belliger*; Rome uses *Triste erant apostoli* from the Common of Apostles. And for the Commemoration of St. Paul, St. Mark's has two hymns; the first, *Doctor egregie Paule*, is also used in the Roman rite; the second, *Iam bone pastor* is found in the Roman rite only as a Lauds hymn on the Feast of Ss. Peter and Paul. *Iam bone pastor* is found as the Vespers hymn for the commemoration of St. Paul in the Aquileian rite and is, in fact, the only one of the above hymns for St. Mark's which can be traced to Aquileia.[312]

The Roman hymns for Lent are shuffled around in St. Mark's. The major hymn for Lent in St. Mark's is *Aures ad nostras deitatis preces*, which also appears in Variscum's *Breviarium Romanum*. A second hymn for Lent in St. Mark's, *Sicter quaternis trahit*, is traceable neither to Rome nor to Aquileia, while a second Roman hymn, *Audi benigne conditor*, is shifted to Lauds in St. Mark's.

Stringa's *Psalterium* is really not a complete hymnal for St. Mark's, for a glance through the *Orationale* reveals several more hymns which are unique to the basilica. For the feasts of the Holy Innocents, St. Helen, St. Blaise, the Translation and the Apparition of the Body of St. Mark, Ss. Hermagoras and Fortunatus, and Ss. Euphemia, Dorothea, Thecla and Erasma, the basilica had its own hymns, all of which differed from those of the Roman rite and none of which can be traced to Aquileia. (The occasions on which the Vespers hymn varied between the rite of St. Mark's and that of Rome are summarized in Table IV-4, p.162.)

The composers of St. Mark's do not seem to have taken a uniform approach to the publication of hymn texts. The five hymns in Cavalli's

Musiche Sacre (Iste confessor, Ave maris stella, Jesu corona virginum, Exultet orbis and *Deus tuorum militum)* are settings of the reformed texts of Urban VIII, a clear move to make the publication eligible for the commercial market by avoiding the texts from the *Psalterium Davidicum.* However, the settings in Monteverdi's *Selva Morale (Sanctorum meritis, Deus tuorum militum, Iste confessor, Ut queant laxis)* use the texts from the *Psalterium Davidicum* which would have been sung in St. Mark's rather than the reformed texts which would have been used by the Roman world at large.[313] Grandi and Rovetta publish a few hymns in their motet collections. Both set the *Ave maris stella,* but since this is one of the hymns which were not touched by Urban VIII's scholars, and since Grandi and Rovetta did not group it with any other hymns whose texts *did* change, we have no hint of their textual source. Rovetta does set one additional hymn text, *O Gloriosa Domina,* which is used as a Lauds hymn for the Office of the Virgin in both St. Mark's and in Rome. He sets the earlier version of the text; it was altered in Urban VIII's breviary to *O Gloriosa Virgina.* However, since the motet was published in 1635, it may well have been an earlier work written before the reform took place.[314]

It is not clear just why Monteverdi's *Selva Morale* and Cavalli's *Musiche Sacre* differ in their choice of hymn texts. Certainly 1640, the year of publication of the *Selva,* was not too early a time to publish the reformed texts, for the new hymns had been set by Filippo Vitali in his *Hymni* of 1636. The fact that Vincenti published Cavalli's collection while Magni published Monteverdi's may be significant, but I would attach greater significance to the prefatory material of the publications. Cavalli's print is clearly designed for the commercial world and for musical performance. There are prefatory remarks in all of the partbooks on the performance of the pieces, and a number of alternatives are explained in detail to insure that the collection would have the widest possible use. On the contrary, the only prefatory material in the *Selva* is an obsequious homage to Eleonora Gonzaga, and the print is filled with ambiguities concerning the performance of a number of pieces. It seems quite plausible that the *Selva* may have been designed more as an homage to Monteverdi, St. Mark's and the city of Venice—not to mention the Gonzagas—much as the early prints of operatic scores were designed to glorify the Medici or the Gonzagas. As such, it is only natural that the special hymns for St. Mark's would have been included rather than their Roman counterparts. While it is possible that the *Selva* was published for the use of the *cappella marciana* itself, there are no signs in the score nor documents in Venetian archives to support such a hypothesis.

At any rate, there seems to have been no effort in the seventeenth century to publish the special hymns of St. Mark's for the various feasts of the church year, nor even to publish the Roman cycle as Willaert had done. The extant settings are not as limited as they might seem, however, for such settings were often designed to be used for any hymn in a given poetic meter. For example, the first setting of *Sanctorum meritis* in the *Selva Morale* had the rubric "on the *aria* [of this hymn] one can sing other hymns, as long as they are in the same meter."[315] The seven settings in the *Selva Morale* plus the five in the *Musiche Sacre* cover a variety of Latin poetic meters, and the special hymns from St. Mark's could easily have been accommodated by these settings.

The Psalm Antiphons of St. Mark's

There are extensive variants between the sets of psalm antiphons used in St. Mark's and those prescribed for the Roman rite. While these are primarily found in the *Sanctorale*, which contains many special texts for those saints' days not celebrated by Rome, a number appear in the *Temporale* and in the *Commune Sanctorum*. Though not as extensive as the variants in Magnificat antiphons, for which St. Mark's seems to have had its own text on almost every major feast, they nonetheless comprise a formidable body of texts associated solely with the ducal chapel.

Before examining the antiphons of the *Temporale*, the *Sanctorale* and the *Commune Sanctorum*, which are preserved in the *Orationale*, I must cite a few variants from the antiphons for ferial use, which are given by Stringa in the *Psalterium Davidicum*, ff. 83r and following. While the antiphons for the *feriae* themselves agree with the breviary of Clement VIII, there are some deviations in Sunday Vespers. The five basic antiphons for use on Sunday in St. Mark's agree with those used by Rome:

> Dixit Dominus Domino meo, sede a dextris meis
> Fidelia omnia mandata eum; confirmata in saeculum saeculi
> In mandatis eius cupit nimis
> Sit nomen Domini benedictum in saecula
> Nos qui vivimus, benedicimus Domino

However, Stringa lists four additional texts alongside the first, second, fourth and fifth antiphons, which are to be used between Septuagesima Sunday and Palm Sunday:

> Sede a dextris meis, dixit Dominus Domino meo
> Magna opera Domini
> Excelsus super omnes gentes Dominus
> Domus Jacob de populo barbaro

While none of these is found in the Roman breviary, two are the equivalent psalm antiphons for Sunday Vespers in Aquileia: *Sede a dextris meis* and *Domus Jacob de populo barbaro.*

The Temporale

There are nine sets of psalm antiphons from the Proper of the Time for which the version in the *Orationale* does not correspond with that in Variscum's *Breviarium Romanum*. Some of the variants are slight and involve the reordering of psalms within a service or the shifting of entire psalm sequences to new feasts. On the Vigil of Christmas, for example, the third and fifth antiphons for St. Mark's, *Levate capita vestra* and *Completi sunt dies Mariae*, are switched from their Roman position as the fifth and third antiphons for the feast. On the Vigil of the Circumcision, St. Mark's repeats the antiphons for the Second Vespers of Christmas (*Tecum principium, Redemptio misit Dominus, Exortum est in tenebris, Apud Dominum*, and *De fructu ventris tui*) while Rome introduces a new set on this feast (*O admirabile commercium, Quando natus es, Rubum quem viderat, Germinavit radix Jesse, Ecce Maria genuit*). On the Vigil of Epiphany, St. Mark's introduces the set used by Rome for the Circumcision, while Rome introduces another set (*Ante luciferum, Venit lumen tuum Hierusalem, Aperis thesauris, Maria et flumina, Stella ista sicut flamma*).

The other variants within the *Temporale* are more extensive and involve sequences of antiphons which do not appear in the Roman rite at all. On Holy Saturday, the Roman rite prescribes that the single psalm *Laudate Dominum omnes gentes* be sung under a single antiphon, *Alleluia, alleluia, alleluia*; St. Mark's, on the other hand, prescribes a full set of five antiphons (*Vespere autem Sabbati, Et ecce terraemotus factus, Angelus autem Domini, Erat autem aspectus eius, Prae timente autem*) the first of which is used as the Magnificat antiphon for Holy Saturday by Rome. Similarly, on the Vigil of Pentecost, the liturgy for St. Mark's prescribes a single antiphon, *Veni sancte spiritus, reple tuorum corda fidelium*, while the Roman rite prescribes a complete set of five antiphons (*Dum complerentur, Spiritus Domini, Repleti sunt omnes spiritu, Fontes et omnia, Loquebantur*). On the Vigil of Ascension as well as in Second Vespers for both Trinity Sunday and Corpus Christi, the texts from St. Mark's do not overlap with those of Rome. (See Table IV-5, p. 164.)

One of the most unusual services in the *Temporale* is that for Vespers on Easter Day at St. Mark's. While the Roman rite uses a normal set of five antiphons and the Sunday psalms, the service for St. Mark's does not follow the standard framework for Vespers at all.[316] The service begins with the invocation *Kyrie eleison—Christe eleison—Kyrie eleison*, a formula which, as we have seen, was used throughout Easter Week in place of the *Deus in adiutorium—Domine ad adiuvandum*. Then the single antiphon *Vespere autem Sabbati* is intoned, under which are said the first three psalms for Sunday, *Dixit Dominus, Confitebor* and *Beatus vir*. At this point, the antiphon *Vespere autem Sabbati* is repeated. After several versicles and responses, the antiphon to the Magnificat, *Post passionem Domini*, is intoned, after which the Magnificat is sung and the antiphon repeated. Then a procession to the baptismal font begins, during which is sung the antiphon *In die resurrectionis*. When the procession has arrived at the font, the antiphon *Alleluia, alleluia, alleluia* is intoned, and only now are the two remaining psalms for Sunday recited, *Laudate pueri* and *In exitu Israel*. They are followed by a repetition of the single antiphon, *Alleluia, alleluia, alleluia*. At this point, a second Magnificat antiphon is sung, *Cito euntes dicite discipulis*, the Magnificat is performed a second time, and the antiphon is repeated. The service ends with a number of special prayers and ceremonies.[317] The outlines of this service come from Aquileia, both in the substitution of the *Kyrie* for the opening versicle-response and in the presentation of the first three psalms as one unit and the last two as another.[318]

The Sanctorale

The psalm antiphons from the *Sanctorale* of the *Orationale* differ in some manner from those in Variscum's *Breviarium Romanum* on 32 feasts during the liturgical year. These range from feasts for which St. Mark's and Rome used the same texts but varied their order, through feasts on which there is a partial overlap of texts, to those feasts whose liturgy is entirely different in the two rites.

There are nine feasts which are not even mentioned within Variscum's *Breviarium* for which the *Orationale* provides a full set of psalm antiphons for at least one Vespers service:

Translation of the Body of St. Mark (31 January)
St. Gerard of Csanad (23 February; also listed as 25 September)
St. Helen the Queen (21 May)
Apparition of the Body of St. Mark (25 June)
Ss. Hermagoras and Fortunatus (12 July)
Ss. Euphemia, Dorothea, Thecla and Erasma (3 September)
St. Victor Maurus (18 September)
Dedication of the Church of St. Mark's (8 October)
St. Brice (13 November)

These figures were all listed earlier in the discussion of the calendar of St. Mark's, but it is interesting to note which feasts were deemed important enough to be given a full liturgy. The feasts of the Translation and Apparition of the Body of St. Mark as well as of the Dedication of the Church of St. Mark's are central to Venetian religious mythology and would logically have elaborate texts of their own. Indeed, the Vespers liturgy for the feasts of St. Mark is nothing short of a detailed description of the theft of the relics from Alexandria, their appearance on the Rialto in 828/29, and their loss and miraculous reappearance; the services culminate in Magnificat antiphons which are nothing less than paeans to the glory of the Venetian state:

> O what a blessed city, home of the Venetians, in which the glorious remains of St. Mark are buried . . .

> O how happy and glorious you are, blessed city of the Venetians, who today have earned the right to accept such a worthy and glorious patron, alleluia, alleluia.[319]

The other figures on the list are connected with Venice in various ways. St. Gerard of Csanad was a monk at San Giorgio Maggiore early in life, and after his martyrdom in Hungary his body was brought to San Donato on Murano. St. Helen, mother of Constantine the Great, occupied an important position in the Eastern church, and her body was eventually brought to Venice from Constantinople. Euphemia, Dorothea, Thecla and Erasma as well as Hermagoras and Fortunatus were central figures in Aquileian hagiography. Victor Maurus was the patron saint of Milan, and his name formerly adorned the Venetian church of San Moïsè. St. Brice clearly finds his way into St. Mark's through Aquileia, where his feast day was observed. The psalm antiphons used in St. Mark's are identical with those used in Aquileia on four of these feasts: the Translation of the Body of St. Mark, St. Helen, Ss. Euphemia, Dorothea, Thecla and Erasma, and St. Brice. On the feast of Ss. Hermagoras and Fortunatus, three antiphons agree with those of Aquileia—two from First Vespers and one from Second Vespers.

There are nine feasts which are found within Variscum's breviary with a collect but without a special Vespers liturgy, for which the *Orationale* lists at least one complete set of psalm antiphons:

St. Nicolas of Bari (6 December)
St. Thomas the Apostle (21 December)
Ss. Fabian and Sebastian (20 January)
St. Gregory the Great (12 March)
St. Benedict (21 March)

St. Matthew (21 September)
Ss. Cosmas and Damian (27 September)
St. Theodore (9 November)
St. Martin of Tours (11 November)

In almost all cases the psalm antiphons are unique to St. Mark's; only those for St. Benedict are taken from the Aquileian liturgy.

Again, many of these figures had a special significance for Venice. St. Nicolas of Bari had been venerated since his relics were brought to Venice from Asia Minor, and a church and monastery in his honor existed on the Lido as early as 1053. This church was the site of the ceremony of Venice's marriage to the sea, which took place every year on the Ascension. The relics of St. Thomas are in Venice at the church of San Tomà, those of St. Fabian at Santa Maria della Salute, and those of St. Sebastian at San Sebastiano. The body of St. Cosmas lies in San Giorgio Maggiore, and the relics of St. Martin are in San Giovanni Evangelista. St. Theodore was, of course, the patron saint of Venice before the translation of the body of St. Mark. Ss. Gregory, Benedict, and Matthew have more tenuous connections with Venice although the city has had churches named after all of these saints at one time or another.

It is certainly no surprise that almost all of the saints in the above two categories figure prominently in the iconographic program of the mosaics of the basilica.[320] Scenes from the life of St. Mark occur in numerous places in the church, particularly in the Zeno chapel and in the chapel of St. Peter. Scenes depicting the translation of his body from Alexandria are on the facade of the church and above the choirloft over the chapel of St. Clement. The disappearance and apparition of the body are depicted in a small nave on the south side of the building. St. Gerard originally appeared on the north side of the church where St. Nicolas now stands. St. Hermagoras is represented in the Zeno chapel, in a mural in the nave, in the chapel of St. Peter, and he also stands in the apse below Christ Pantocrator along with Nicholas, Peter and Mark as one of the four great protectors of Venice. The four Aquileian virgins, Euphemia, Dorothea, Thecla and Erasma, are found in the cupola of the Holy Sacrament. St. Nicolas is found on the facade on the north side of the church above the *loggia*, in the cupola of the Holy Sacrament, in the apse, in the chapel of St. Isidore, and near the door to the *piazzetta*. St. Thomas the Apostle is in the central gallery and in the cupola over the baptismal font. Ss. Fabian and Sebastian are in the choirloft over the chapel of St. Clement. St. Gregory is in the cupola of St. John and in the cupola over the main altar. St. Matthew is found in the central cupola, in the cupola over the baptismal font and in the small nave on the south side of the church along with Ss. Cosmas and Damian. St. Theodore is pictured in the chapel of St. Peter, in the sacristy and in an arch next to the baptismal font. Not all of these figures are among the earliest mosaics in the church. Indeed, a number date from the seventeenth century: St. Gerard (1640); the figure of St. Mark in the mural in the nave (1646–48); and the figure of St. Theodore in the arch next to the baptismal font (1674). The iconographic pattern of the mosaics (or at least of those sections based on the New Testament) can, in fact, be viewed as a projection of the liturgy of the basilica, and both mosaics and liturgy can be seen as parallel expressions of the religious mythology of the Republic.[321]

There are nine feasts for which Variscum gives at least one set of psalm antiphons which differ in their entirety from those given in the *Orationale*:

Conversion of St. Paul
Annunciation
St. Mark
Ss. Peter and Paul
St. Mary Magdalene
Transfiguration of Our Lord
Assumption of the Virgin
All Saints' Day
St. Clement[322]

Only those antiphons for the Vigil of the Assumption can be traced to Aquileia; two of them are used on the Assumption, and three are found as part of First Vespers for the Nativity of the B. V. M. The texts of these antiphons are most significant, for while the antiphons for the Roman rite describe the Assumption of Mary and only one is drawn from the Song of Songs, those from St. Mark's are almost all drawn from the Song of Songs, both for First and Second Vespers. Thus, the identification of Mary with the lover in the Song of Songs, a point which is clear from the many centonized motet texts which combine the Old Testament text with invocations to the Virgin, is merely a reflection of the traditional liturgy of the basilica.

There is a partial correspondence between Variscum's *Breviarium* and the *Orationale* on three feasts. On the Vigil of the Nativity of St. John the Baptist, three of the antiphons used by St. Mark's agree with Rome and two do not. On the feast of the Dedication of the Basilica of St. Michael the Archangel and on the feast of St. Cecilia, four out of the five antiphons in the *Orationale* agree with Rome; in both cases, the fifth antiphon can be traced to Aquileia. On the feast of the Beheading of St.

John the Baptist and the feast of the Exaltation of the Holy Cross, the same antiphons are used by St. Mark's and Rome, but the order of the texts varies.

The Commune Sanctorum

Not only do the psalm antiphons of St. Mark's differ from those of Rome on a number of individual saints' days, but the Common of the Saints also has different psalm antiphons for five of its services. All of these antiphon sequences seem to be unique to St. Mark's; none are taken from Aquileia.

While the same antiphon texts are used by St. Mark's and Rome for First Vespers for the Common of Martyrs, St. Mark's has its own texts for Second Vespers (*Iustorum autem animae, Tanquam aurum, Si coram hominibus, Spiritus et animae, In caelestibus regnis*).[323] Similarly, St. Mark's has its own sequence for Second Vespers of the Common of Virgins (*Veni sponsa Christi, Haec est virgo sapiens quam Dominus, Veni sponsa prudens, Virgines Domini, Prudentes virgines*)[324] as well as a special sequence for First Vespers of a Confessor Bishop (*Ecce sacerdos magnus, Beatus ille servus, Fidelis servus et prudens, Serve bone et fidelis, Ecce vere Israelita*).[325]

There are two occasions for which the *Orationale* lists two sets of psalm antiphons for a single service. In Second Vespers for the Common of a Martyr, the *Orationale* specifies that the antiphons of Lauds are to be used, for which St. Mark's and Rome share identical texts. However, a second set of texts is listed in the *Orationale* which is unique to the basilica (*Iustum deduxit Dominus, Amavit eum Dominus, Qui mihi ministrat, Si quis per me intraverit, Qui perdiderit animam suam*). In Second Vespers for a Confessor Bishop, the same phenomenon occurs. The *Orationale* first specifies the Lauds antiphons (which agree with Roman texts) and then lists a special set used in St. Mark's (*Virgam virtutis tuae, In consilio iustorum, Potens in terra, Venientes autem venient, Sacerdotes tui induantur*).

The Magnificat Antiphons of St. Mark's

From a purely numerical point of view, textual variants between the liturgies of St. Mark's and Rome are most prominent in the area of Magnificat antiphons. If one takes the *Temporale* for the period between Advent and Corpus Christi as a control—a portion of the breviary in which the general organization is alike for both liturgies and in which one need not account for special days which occur only on the calendar of St. Mark's—

one finds that out of *circa* 150 Magnificat antiphons listed in the *Oration-ale*, St. Mark's has its own text for nearly one-third of the occasions. Of these textual variants, about one in four can be traced to Aquileia; the others are unique to St. Mark's.[326]

Beyond this mere calculation, it is difficult to find a pattern in the variants. *Feriae* and feasts claim their own antiphons in St. Mark's with about equal frequency. Some shifting of texts does occur between the two liturgies. Psalm antiphons from St. Mark's crop up as Magnificat anti-phons for Rome and vice versa. Commemorative antiphons for Rome occasionally are found as Magnificat antiphons for St. Mark's. And the Magnificat antiphons for the Sundays after Pentecost are generally shifted by one week, i.e., St. Mark's uses the texts one week later than does Rome. However, such shifts are not systematic. The feasts for which St. Mark's provides a special Magnificat antiphon include those of the Holy Innocents, St. Thomas, and St. Silvester, the Vigil of the Circumcision, Holy Saturday and Easter Sunday, Low Sunday, the Vigil of Ascension, both Vespers of Pentecost, and Second Vespers of both Trinity Sunday and Corpus Christi. To this, one can add Septuagesima, Sexagesima and Quinquagesima Sundays, three of the Sundays in Lent, two additional Sundays after Easter and two in Advent, plus a number of *feriae*.

One area of particular interest is the final octave of Advent, the period of the year in which the so-called Greater Antiphons are used. While there are seven such antiphons in the Roman rite—*O sapientia, O Adonai, O radix Iesse, O clavis David, O oriens, O rex gentium* and *O Emanuel*—St. Mark's adds an eighth text, *O virgo virginum*, an antiphon which is also found in the Sarum rite. This probably came into the liturgy of the basilica through Aquileia, though the Greater Antiphons for Aquil-eia are even more numerous. Eleven texts were used in Aquileia, the eight above plus *O Gabriel, O rex pacifice*, and *O Hierusalem*. While the Greater Antiphons begin on 17 December in the Roman rite, so that the seven texts can be performed between 17 and 23 December, St. Mark's begins the antiphons two days earlier. This accommodates the extra *O virgo virginum* and, moreover, allows St. Mark's the idiosyncrasy of plac-ing *none* of the Greater Antiphons on the Fourth Sunday in Advent.[327]

The exact use of the Greater Antiphons is also unique in St. Mark's. Unlike Rome, St. Mark's does not use these texts as Magnificat antiphons but as special commemorative antiphons *in addition* to the Magnificat antiphon. The Magnificat antiphons which St. Mark's uses during this period are not found in the Roman rite. Like the Greater Antiphons, the date of their performance is a function of the calendar and varies from year to year; unlike the Greater Antiphons, however, the actual texts of these Magnificat antiphons as well as their position on the calendar vary according to the year.

The *Sanctorale* contains 49 feasts during the year for which at least one of the Magnificat antiphons of St. Mark's differs from the Roman rite. Of these feasts, however, fully 30 were mentioned above in connection with the psalm antiphons of the *Sanctorale*; for only 2 feasts in the church year, the Annunciation and the feast of St. Martin, does St. Mark's provide a special set of psalm antiphons yet fail to provide its own Magnificat antiphon. The additional 19 feasts for which St. Mark's provides its own Magnificat antiphon for at least one of the Vespers services are the following:

St. Andrew (30 November)
St. Bassus (5 December)
St. Basil (1 January)
St. Anthony Abbot (17 January)
Ss. Philip and James
Finding of the Holy Cross (3 May)
Ss. John and Paul (26 June)
St. Apollinaris of Ravenna (23 June)
Our Lady of the Snow (5 August)
St. Laurence (10 August)
Ss. Tiburtius and Sisona (11 August)
Ss. Hippolytus and Cassianus (13 August)
St. Bartholomew (24 August)
St. Francis (4 October)
St. Luke (18 October)
Ss. Simon and Jude (28 October)
St. Leonard (6 November)
St. Maurus (21 November)
St. Catherine (25 November)

These figures have tenuous connections with Venice if any at all, although St. Apollonaris, an Adriatic saint, and St. Basil, whose relics lie in San Giorgio dei Greci, fit into the categories discussed earlier. Of the 19 figures listed here, only 2 (St. Andrew and St. Maurus) have Magnificat antiphons which can be traced to Aquileia; and of the full 49 feasts whose Magnificat antiphons differ from those of Rome in some way, only 14 texts can be traced to Aquileia.

Of the services in the *Commune Sanctorum*, those for Apostles, One Martyr, Several Martyrs, and for Virgins have Magnificat antiphons for both Vespers services which do not agree with Rome. Only the antiphons for First Vespers of Apostles and First Vespers of Virgins can be traced to Aquileia. It is also striking to find that the Roman Magnificat antiphon for the Marian Common, *Sancta Maria succurre miseris* is not used for the Common in St. Mark's; it appears instead as the Magnificat antiphon for Our Lady of the Snow (5 August).

The Musical Settings of Antiphons and the Role of Non-Liturgical Motets

A comparison of the texts for psalm antiphons and Magnificat antiphons from the rite of St. Mark's with the motet compositions of Grandi, Rovetta and Cavalli yields a correspondence that is far from complete. Only a small portion of the texts from the *Orationale* seem to have been set. Moreover, even if one broadens the search to include antiphons from the Roman rite, only a small group of motets can be identified with specific liturgical items. Many of these do not quote the texts *verbatim* but, rather, set a textual paraphrase, a gloss, or a centonized text which draws upon a number of sources.

Table IV-6 (p. 166) lists those motets of Grandi and Rovetta which set a complete antiphon from either the rite of St. Mark's or of Rome. Some of the settings involve paraphrased texts and a few involve other texts which are combined with the antiphon text, but in each case the antiphon text forms the essential kernel of the motet. Cavalli's five independent motet settings are not included, for none of them can be identified with a liturgical antiphon.[328]

If the information one gleans from the table is primarily negative, it tells us nonetheless some important facts about the relationship between music and liturgy in St. Mark's. To take the psalm antiphons first, it is clear that no attempt was ever made to set all of the antiphons of a feast as a sequence or even to set them cumulatively over the years in various publications. The closest one comes to a complete set of five antiphons for a feast is the set of four antiphons for the Feast of Pentecost which Grandi included in his *Terzo Libro* (1614). Four antiphons are also set by Rovetta for First Vespers of the Feast of Philip and James, but he combines the texts in a single motet. Otherwise, the antiphons which are set appear to be chosen at random, although it is worth noting the presence of *Veni Sancte Spiritus*, a paraphrase of the single antiphon used on the Vigil of Pentecost in St. Mark's. It is also striking that one antiphon is set which is not part of the liturgy of the basilica: *Non est inventus*, the second antiphon for the Roman Common of a Confessor Bishop, which Grandi sets as an independent motet in his *Secondo Libro* (1613) and as the second half of the motet *Ecce sacerdos magnus*, which appears in two settings, in the *Motetti a voce sola* (1621) and the third book of

Motetti con sinfonie (1629). While the first and third of these books date from Grandi's years in Ferrara, the *Motetti a voce sola* (1621) falls squarely in his Venetian period. The presence of a Roman text in a book of motets published during Grandi's Venetian years hints not so much at the infiltration of the rite of St. Mark's by that of Rome—documents argue rather cogently against that supposition—but, rather, at a para-liturgical use for many of these motets, even perhaps those whose texts correspond with liturgical items. This point will be discussed further below. Three of the antiphons from the *Orationale* which do not appear in the Roman rite are set by Grandi. *Tota pulchra es*, the third antiphon for the Feast of the Assumption, appears in both the *Motetti a voce sola* (1621) and the first book of *Motetti con sinfonie* (1621). And *Haec est virgo*, a motet which combines two antiphons from the Common of Virgins, is found in the *Quarto Libro* (1616).

The range of Magnificat antiphons in the motet collections is greater than that of the psalm antiphons, and there seems to have been a more concentrated plan to cover the major feasts, at least on the part of Grandi. Grandi sets Magnificat antiphons for the following feasts, for which St. Mark's and Rome use the same text: Second Vespers of the Nativity of the B. V. M., the Common of a Confessor Bishop, the Feast of the Circumcision, All Saints' Day, the Purification, Corpus Christi, the Common of Doctors, and the Exaltation of the Holy Cross. One Roman antiphon is set twice: *Virgo prudentissima*, the Roman antiphon for First Vespers of the Assumption, is set in the *Motetti a voce sola* (1621) and the third book of *Motetti con sinfonie* (1629). One Magnificat antiphon not found in the Roman rite is also set, that for St. Victor.

If such a small fraction of the texts of Grandi's and Rovetta's motets can be correlated with the Vespers antiphons of the *Orationale* or of Roman breviaries, the logical question which poses itself is the identity of the textual sources of the remaining motets and, more important, the liturgical functions they might have served. Several categories of motets are not problematic. A certain number can be identified with the Proper of the Mass (or with paraphrases of Proper texts). Another group is composed of Marian antiphons.[329] Indeed, Rovetta includes 20 settings of the 4 Marian antiphons in his 4 books of motets: 5 of *Alma redemptoris mater*, 4 of *Ave regina caelorum*, 7 of the *Salve Regina* and 4 of *Regina caeli laetare*. The large number of Marian antiphons stems not only from the veneration of Mary in Venice but also from the fact that the *Salve Regina* seems to have been used as a general ceremonial motet in honor of the Virgin, quite apart from its role as the final item in Vespers (or Compline). It is for this reason, I think, that there are 5 extant settings of the *Salve Regina* by Monteverdi yet none of any of the other Marian antiphons.

The motet texts which pose liturgical problems are of several kinds. Some are merely centonized texts which draw upon a number of sources related to the same theme. A good example is Rovetta's setting of *Nigra sum* published in Magni's *Sacra Corona* of 1656. The text of the motet is as follows:

> Nigra sum sed formosa filiae Ierusalem
> Ideo dilexit me Rex et introduxit me in cubiculum suum.
> Trahe me post te curremus in odorem unguentorum tuorum.
> Veni sponsa Christi accipe coronam quam tibi Dominus praeparavit in aeternum.
>   Alleluia.

The text of the motet is actually a combination of antiphons from two different Marian feasts with a third text which cannot be identified. The first two lines—"Nigra sum . . . cubiculum suum"—form the third antiphon from both First and Second Vespers of the Marian Common for both Rome and St. Mark's. The line starting "Trahe me post te" is a paraphrase of the fifth antiphon for the Feast of the Immaculate Conception in the modern Roman liturgy, but it finds no place in the Roman liturgy of the sixteenth and seventeenth centuries nor in that of St. Mark's. The final line—"Veni sponsa Christi . . ."—is the Magnificat antiphon for the Common of Virgins in Rome, although it is the first psalm antiphon in St. Mark's.

A second category of motet texts are those which are connected with the feast of a saint but do not draw upon any of the antiphon texts of the day. The name of the saint is usually placed over a capital letter N. ("nomen"), which indicates that any saint's name can be substituted at that point. Thus, these motets maintain total liturgical flexibility and can be used at virtually any point in the *Sanctorale*.

A third category consists of Marian motets on texts which are paraphrases of sections of the Song of Songs.[330] Indeed, the texts of these works are quite formulaic, consisting of the same phrases and epithets assembled in an ever-changing order. Also included is a group of motets which are drawn from the Song of Songs but do not attempt to invoke Mary. However, the connections between the Song of Songs and the liturgy of the Assumption at St. Mark's, which were cited above, suggest an implicit connection even when the text does not make the relationship explicit.

There is little question that the general import of many of the non-liturgical texts would make them appropriate for performance at Vespers on certain feasts. Moreover, we have the indirect evidence of Monteverdi's 1610 *Vespers*, in which small motets are placed between the psalms, and the *Sonata sopra Sancta Maria* is placed after the final psalm and before the hymn. There is, moreover, a Vespers collection published in 1619 by Paolo Agostini[331] in which two motets are associated with each psalm, one a liturgical motet from the Marian Common, the other a non-liturgical motet. In fact, four of the six motets which are associated with the psalms in Agostini's collection are on texts also set by Grandi or Rovetta.[332] The *Antiphonae, seu Sacrae Cantiones* (1613) of Giovanni Francesco Anerio also contains a number of motets which seem to be conflations of several textual sources rather than a single liturgical unit.[333] All of this evidence is indirect, however, and Venetian sources provide much more exact information on the problem of non-liturgical music.

There is ample evidence for the use of extra-liturgical motets at several points in Vespers at St. Mark's, although the question of whether the motets actually replaced liturgical items or merely embellished the service is one which cannot be answered conclusively. Pace mentions the singing of *Quem terra* and *O Gloriosa Domina* as special processional hymns during Vespers on the Vigil of the Assumption (Document 119)[334] and the singing of *Laudate Dominum de caelis* as a motet during Vespers of All Saints' Day (Document 120). He mentions, moreover, that on the days when the *Pala d'oro* is opened a motet is to be sung as a required part of the service, even if the Doge is not present (Document 121). Bonifacio mentions the use of a motet for the *Deo gratias* at the end of Vespers,[335] although Pace does not.

Certainly extra-liturgical motets were popular in Venice during the 1620s and 1630s, for alongside the profusion of motet publications of these years, we find warnings from the Patriarch of Venice that departures from Holy Writ are not to be tolerated. In 1628, Patriarch Giovanni Tiepolo warns those officiating in the churches of Venice that "in the music performed in their churches, oratories and chapels, no words are to be sung but those from the Holy Scriptures allowed by the Holy Roman Catholic Church, which should follow one after the other as they appear in the text itself, without transpositions in their order or the interpolation of words gathered from different sections of Holy Scripture, Breviaries or Missals" (Document 122). Indeed, his statement is a rather exact description of many of the centonized texts set by Grandi and Rovetta. A similar decree in 1633 was directed against the use of non-liturgical texts in ceremonies in convent churches, a practice tolerated only if the texts had been approved by the Patriarch himself (Document 123; see points 1 and 2).

Despite the patriarchal warnings, non-liturgical motets continued to be published, and in 1639 the *Provveditori di Commun* tried to bar such motets from services in the *scuole*. They did allow motets in certain liturgical contexts, however, for they decreed that in the music for reli-

gious services, the heads of the *scuole* should not permit "transpositions
in the order of words, or texts with made-up words which are not found
in holy books, except that during the Offertory, and the Elevation, and
after the Agnus Dei, and similarly between the psalms at Vespers, one
can sing motets on pious, devout texts which are taken from holy books"
(Document 124). The reference to the practice of singing motets between
Vespers psalms is of the utmost importance; it is the first statement I have
found in a Venetian source which indicates that the order of the materials
in the print of Monteverdi's 1610 *Vespers* represents a single liturgical
sequence. While this document does not refer to a church service, two
excerpts from the letters of Paul Hainlein, a German composer living in
Venice in the late 1640s, show that this practice was also followed in the
churches of the city. In his description of a Vespers service at Ss. Giovanni
e Paolo, Hainlein relates that "a sonata or motet was always performed
between the psalms, among which was a *Romanesca*, sung by a bass and
by boy singers in a lovely manner." Similarly, in a description of a service
at San Francesco della Vigna, he states that "between the psalms a motet
or sonata was performed, by a bass and soprano among others; one piece
was a *Romanesca*, one a text to the *Madonna*, and one involved words
from the forty-sixth psalm, with the implication that [the Venetians] should
destroy the Turks' power, break their bows and shields, burn their ships
and galleys, and throw their entire might into the abyss of the sea."[336]
(Clearly, the war in Candia had entered the liturgy in a more graphic form
than the mere singing of the *Te Deum* for naval victories.)

A number of documents give us more specific information on the role
which the many motets on Marian texts may have played in services. In
1695, a set of *Supplicationes Beatae Mariae Virgine in tempore belli*, or
Marian supplications for wartime, was published "according to the custom of the Ducal Basilica of St. Mark's in Venice." The volume contains
a series of prayers to Mary, and it includes a special Marian litany, each
item of which invokes some attribute of the Virgin (*Sancta Maria Mater
Christi Sanctissima . . . Sancta Maria Virgo Virginum . . . Sancta Maria
Dei Genitrix Virgo . . . Sancta Maria Mater innupta . . .* etc.). The litany
consists of 41 such Marian invocations; it seems to be a distillation of a
similar litany in the Aquileian rite which consisted of 91 (!) invocations
of the Virgin's aid.[337] Although the texts of this volume do not match
those of the Marian motets, it is possible that many of the motets were
intended as non-liturgical *supplicationes in tempori belli*, for Venice was
deeply involved with the war in Candia during the middle of the century,
and documents in the A.S.V. describe numerous services celebrating naval victories or asking for divine aid.[338]

Another use to which Marian motets were no doubt put was that of commemorations of the Virgin. The cult of Mary had been intimately tied to Venice from the very earliest times. In fact, the city itself was supposedly founded on the Feast of the Annunciation. Commemorations of Mary are prescribed in the *Orationale* for all days during Advent which do not contain feasts of double rank, and then are liberally sprinkled through the rest of the church year.[339] Motets had long been used for commemorations in St. Mark's, and it is quite probable that the Marian motets published in the 1620s, 1630s and 1640s served the same purpose. Commemorative motets occurred at the very end of Vespers, following the Magnificat.

One can sum up the essential points on the liturgy of St. Mark's as follows. The legends surrounding the founding of Venice as well as the religious history of the Veneto gave rise to a church calendar which differed markedly from that of Rome. A special breviary, special psalter and a number of other liturgical books preserve a rite which, similarly, can differ from the Roman rite in the case of almost every liturgical item for Vespers. The psalms were drawn from a translation outside the Vulgate. The sequences and arrangement of psalms differed throughout the year. St. Mark's had its own hymns for a number of important feasts in the *Temporale* as well as for a number of special saints' days in the *Sanctorale*. Certain special psalm and Magnificat antiphons were unique to the basilica. Many of these items seem to stem from the early rite of Aquileia, although the majority were found in St. Mark's alone. And while some of the variants between St. Mark's and Rome can be traced to feasts which had a special place in the religious mythology of Venice, many of them seem to follow no such distinct program.

Not all of these special liturgical items were mirrored in the musical settings of the composers of the basilica. By the mid-*seicento*, the special version of the psalms, for example, must have been limited to plainchant services. Similarly, we have no extant settings from the *seicento* of the special hymns and a limited number of settings of the psalm and Magnificat antiphons. Nonetheless, the special psalm sequences were an important part of the musical repertoire of the basilica, and the setting of the *Cinque Laudate* by Galuppi certainly illustrates the strength and longevity of the liturgical tradition.

Since politics, ceremony and religion were intimately interwoven in Venice, and the resplendent ceremonial life of St. Mark's was considered a symbol of the state, it is logical that the liturgy would be regarded with special pride by the *Serenissima Signoria*. With the city under siege by Paul V and his Venetian interdict at the opening of the century and by the Turks later on, it is no wonder that the liturgy would have assumed symbolic proportions in the *seicento*; the Senate's attempts to retain the Venetian calendar and the Doge's attempt to conserve the *Orationale* were certainly symbolic acts in the truest sense. It was not a question of an antiphon or a saint's day but, rather, of the preservation of the cultural identity and political independence of the *urbs beata Venetorum*.

Table IV-1
Feasts for Which the *Orationale* Has At Least One Proper Liturgical Item but Which Have No Proper Liturgy In Variscum's *Breviarium Romanum*

Feast	Date	Present on *Variscum's Calendar*	Observed in *Aquileia*
Ansanus	1 December	x	
Anianus	2		
Barbara	4	x	x
Bassus	5		
Sabas	5		
Zeno	8		
Proculus	9		
Syrus	9	x	x
Damasus	11	x	x
Lazarus	17	x	
Basil	1 January	x	
Julian	7		
Hilary of Poitiers	13	x	
Maurus, Abbot	15		
John Chrysostom	27	x	x
Geminianus	30	x	
Translation of the Body of St. Mark	31	x	x
Severus	2 February	x	
Simeon	4	x	
Dorothy	6	x	x
Apollonia	9	x	x
Scholastica	10		
Fosca and Maura	13	x	
Faustinus and Jovita	15	x	
Juliana	16	x	x
Peter's Chair at Antioch	22	x	x
Gerard of Csanad	23		
Herculanus	1 March	x	
Julian	6		
Thomas Aquinas	7	x	x
Pope Julius I	14		
Hilary and Tatianus	16		
Mary of Egypt	2 April	x	x
Ambrose	4	x	
Vincent Ferrer	5	x	
Euphemia	13		
Translation of St. Isidore	16		

Feast	Date	Present on *Variscum's Calendar*	Observed in *Aquileia*
Pope Leo IX	19	x	
Liberal	27		
Jeremiah	1 May		
Athanasius, Patriarch of Alexandria	2		
Florian	4		x
Gothard	5		
Victor and Corona	14		
Barbarus	15		
Isidore of Chios	15	x	
Ubald of Gubbio	16	x	
Bernardine of Siena	20	x	
Eustace	20	x	
Helena	21	x	x
Nicomedes	31		
Cantius, Cantianus and Cantianella	31	x	x
Alban of Mainz	21 June	x	
Ten Thousand Holy Martyrs	22	x	
Apparition of the Body of St. Mark	25	x	
Vigilius	26	x	
Eliodorus	3 July		
Paternian	10		
Hermagoras and Fortunatus	12	x	x [a]
Foca	14	x [b]	
Quiricus and Iulita	15	x	
Rofilus	16		
Marina	17	x	
Alexis	17	x	
Margaret	20	x	x
Christopher	25	x	
Hermolai	27		
Seven Holy Sleeping Martyrs	27		x
Eusebius of Vercelli	2 August	x	
Eleutherius and Rusticus	9		
Clara	12	x	
Louis of Anjou	19	x	
Magnus	19		
Genesius the Comedian	25		
Alexander	26	x	
Rufus	27		
Pelagius	27		x
Daniel the Stylite	28		x
Felix	30	x	

Feast	Date	Present on *Variscum's Calendar*	Observed in *Aquileia*
Egidius	1 September		
Antoninus of Apamea	2	x	
Euphemia, Dorothea, Tecla, Erasma	3	x	x^c
Moses	4	x	
Zachary	6		
Nicolas Tolentino	10	x	
Ligorius	13		
Victor	18	x	
Eustace	20	x	x
Tecla	23	x	
Leodegarius	2 October		
Magnus	6	x	
Dedication of the Church of St. Mark	8		
Gaudentius	14		
Gall	16	x	x
Amandus	26		
Cesarius	1 November		
Justus	2		
Leonard of Noblac	6	x	x
Prosdocimus	7		
John the Almsgiver	12		
Brice	13	x	x
Stephen	20	x	
Maurus	21	x	x
James Intercisus	27	x	
Saturninus	29	x	

a. Celebrated on 8 July in Aquileia, according to Biblioteca Correr, Codice Cicogna J 31.

b. Listed under 5 March in Variscum's breviary.

c. Celebrated on 19 September in Aquileia.

Table IV-2
Variants between the Psalms from the *Psalterium Davidicum* of St. Mark's and Variscum's *Breviarium Romanum*

Beatus vir

St. Mark's: Beatus vir qui timet Dominum: in mandatis eius *cupit* nimis.
Roman: Beatus vir qui timet Dominum: in mandatis eius *volet* nimis.

St. Mark's: In memoria aeterna erit justus: ab *auditu malo* non timebit.
Roman: In memoria aeterna erit justus: ab *auditione mala* non timebit.

St. Mark's: Paratum cor ejus sperare in Domino, confirmatum est cor ejus: non
           commovebitur donec *videat* inimicos tuos.
Roman: Paratum cor ejus sperare in Domino, confirmatum est cor ejus: non
           commovebitur donec *despiciat* inimicos tuos.

In exitu Israel

St. Mark's: Facta est Judaea sanctificatio ejus, Israel *regnavit in ea.*
Roman: Facta est Judaea sanctificatio ejus, Israel *potestas ejus.*

St. Mark's: Quid est tibi mare quod fugisti: et tu Jordanis, *quare* conversus es retrorsum.
Roman: Quid est tibi mare quod fugisti: et tu Jordanis, *quia* conversus es retrorsum.

St. Mark's: A facie Domini *commota* est terra, a facie Dei Jacob:
Roman: A facie Domini *mota* est terra, a facie Dei Jacob:

St. Mark's: Qui convertit *solidam* petram in *stagnum aquae* . . .
Roman: Qui convertit petram in *stagna aquarum* . . .

St. Mark's: Deus autem noster in caelo *sursum: in caelo et terra* omnia quaecumque
           voluit, fecit.
Roman: Deus autem noster in caelo: omnia quaecumque voluit, fecit.

St. Mark's: Manus habent, et non palpabunt: pedes habent, et non ambulabunt.
           Non clamabunt in gutture suo: *neque enim est spiritus in ore ipsorum.*
Roman: Manus habent et non palpabunt: pedes habent, et non ambulabunt: non
           clamabunt in gutture suo.

St. Mark's: Dominus memor fuit nostri, et benedixit *nos:* benedixit *domum* Israel,
           benedixit *domum* Aaron.
Roman: Dominus memor fuit nostri, et benedixit *nobis:* benedixit *domui* Israel,
           benedixit *domui* Aaron.

St. Mark's: Benedixit *omnes timentes se* Dominus: *pusillos* cum maioribus.
Roman: Benedixit *omnibus qui timent* Dominum: *pusillis* cum maioribus.

Table IV-3

Variants between the Psalm Sequences for Vespers in St. Mark's
(*Orationale*) and Those in the Roman Rite (Variscum's *Breviarium Romanum*)

Feast	St. Mark's	Rome	Aquileia
Vigil of Epiphany	Cinque Laudate	Male *cursus*	Cinque Laudate
Vigil of Ascension	Cinque Laudate	Male *cursus*	Cinque Laudate
Vigil of Pentecost	Cinque Laudate	Male *cursus*	Cinque Laudate
Corpus Christi, Second Vespers	Cinque Laudate	Dixit / Confitebor / Credidi / Beati omnes / Lauda Jerusalem	Dixit / Confitebor / Credidi / Beati omnes / Lauda Jerusalem
Purification, First Vespers	Cinque Laudate	Female *cursus*	Cinque Laudate
Vigil of Assumption	Cinque Laudate	Female *cursus*	Cinque Laudate
Vigil of Nativity of B. V. M.	Cinque Laudate	Female *cursus*	Cinque Laudate
Vigil of Conception of B. V. M.	Cinque Laudate	Female *cursus*	Cinque Laudate
Vigil of All Saints' Day	Cinque Laudate	Male *cursus*	Cinque Laudate
Holy Saturday (formerly)	Cinque Laudate	—	—
Holy Saturday (at present)	Laudate Dominum omnes gentes	Laudate Dominum omnes gentes	Laudate Dominum omnes gentes

Feast	St. Mark's	Rome	Aquileia
Feast of Holy Trinity, First Vespers	Levavi oculos meos Ad te levavi De profundis Memento Laudate nomen Domini	*Male cursus*	Cinque Laudate
Dedication of the Church of St. Mark's, Second Vespers	Credidi Laetatus sum Nisi Dominus Confitebor Angelorum Lauda Jerusalem	Dixit[a] Confitebor Beautus vir Laudate pueri Lauda Jerusalem	Credidi[b] Laetatus sum Nisi Dominus Confitebor Angelorum Lauda Jerusalem
Ss. Hermagoras and Fortunatus, Second Vespers and St. Clement, Second Vespers	Dixit Confitebor Beatus vir Credidi Eripe me Domine	—	Dixit Beatus vir In convertendo Eripe me Domine Lauda Jerusalem
Epiphany, Second Vespers and Octave of the Epiphany, First and Second Vespers	Dixit Confitebor Beatus vir De profundis Memento	*Sunday cursus*	Dixit Confitebor Beatus vir De profundis Memento
Purification, Second Vespers	Dixit Confitebor Beatus vir De profundis Memento	*Female cursus*	Dixit Confitebor Beatus vir De profundis Memento

St. Agatha, First Vespers	Dixit Confitebor Beatus vir Laudate pueri Lauda Jerusalem	Female *cursus*	Ferial psalms
Vigil of Nativity of St. John the Baptist	Dixit Confitebor Beatus vir Laudate pueri Memento	Male *cursus*	Cinque Laudate
Feast of the Transfiguration, Second Vespers	Sunday *cursus*	Male *cursus*	Credidi Laetatus sum Nisi Dominus Confitebor Angelorum Lauda Jerusalem
Feast of St. Mark, First Vespers, and Feast of Ss. Peter and Paul, First Vespers	Dixit Laudate pueri Credidi In convertendo Domine probasti me	Male *cursus*	Cinque Laudate

[a] Psalms for Second Vespers of the Dedication of a Church.

[b] Psalms for Second Vespers of the Dedication of the Church of Aquileia.

Table IV-4
Variants Between the Cycle of Hymns Used in St. Mark's
(*Orationale, Psalterium Davidicum*) and That Used in the Roman Rite
(Breviary of Clement VIII)

Feast	St. Mark's	Rome	Aquileia
Ascension	Festum nunc celebre	Jesu nostra redemptio	Festum nunc celebre
St. Mary Magdalene	Maria Mater Domini	Pater superni luminis	Votiva cunctis
Transfiguration	Fans pietatus culmine	Quicumque Christi quaeritis	—
Palm Sunday	Magno salutis gaudio	Vexilla regis	Vexilla regis
Annunciation	Deus qui mundus crimine	Ave maris stella	Ave maris stella
St. Mark	Athleta Christi belliger	Tristes erant Apostoli	Vita sanctorum
St. Paul	Iam bone pastor / Doctor egregie	Doctor egregie	Iam bone pastor
Hymns for Lent	Aures ad nostras dietatis preces / Sicter quaternis trahit	Audi benigne conditor	Aures ad nostras deitatis preces
Holy Innocents	Caterua matrum personat	Sanctorum meritis	Rex gloriose martyrum
St. Helen	Regina sancta Helena	—	—

Feast	St. Mark's	Rome	Aquileia
St. Blaise	En festum sancti Blasij	—	
Translation of the Body of St. Mark	Natos recolens pristinos	—	
Apparition of the Body of St. Mark	Hodie festum piem celebremus	—	
Ss. Hermagoras and Fortunatus	Omnes ad haec Christicolae	—	
Euphemia, Dorothea, Thecla and Erasma	Virginum Christi	—	Paterno splendor luminis

Table IV-5
Variants between the Psalm Antiphons Used in the *Temporale* at
St. Mark's (*Orationale*) and Those Used in the Roman Rite
(Variscum's *Breviarium Romanum*)

Feast	St. Mark's	Rome
Vigil of Christmas	Rex pacificus Magnificatus est Levate capita vestra Scitote quia prope est Completi sunt dies Mariae	Rex pacificus Magnificatus est Completi sunt dies Mariae Scitote quia prope est Levate capita vestra
Vigil of Circumcision	Tecum principium Redemptio misit Dominus Exortum est in tenebris Apud Dominum De fructu ventris tui	O admirabile commercium Quando natus es Rubum quem viderat Germinavit radix Jesse Ecce Maria genuit
Vigil of Epiphany	O admirabile commercium Quando natus es Rubum quem viderat Germinavit radix Jesse Ecce Maria genuit	Ante luciferum Venit lumen tuum Hierusalem Aperis thesauris Maria et flumina Stella ista sicut flamma
Holy Saturday	Vespere autem Sabbati Et ecce terraemotus factus Angelus autem Domini Erat autem aspectus eius Prae timore autem eius	Alleluia, alleluia, alleluia
Easter Sunday	Vespere autem Sabbati Alleluia, alleluia, alleluia	Angelus autem Domini Et ecce terraemotus factus Erat autem aspectus eius Prae timore autem eius Respondens autem angelus
Vigil of Ascension	Sublevatis oculis Pater manifestavi Pater sancte serva eos quod Pater iuste mandus Pater sancte serva oes in	Viri galilae Cunque intereventur Elevatis manibus Exaltate regem regum Videntibus illis elevatus
Vigil of Pentecost	Veni sancte spiritus	Dum complerentur Spiritus Domini replevit Repleti sunt spiritus Fontes et omnia Loquebantur

Feast	St. Mark's	Rome
Feast of the Holy Trinity, Second Vespers	Benedicta sit sancta Trinitas	Gloria tibi Trinitas
	Tibi laus tibi gloria	Laus et perhennis gloria
	O vera summa sempiterna	Gloria laudis resonet
	Te iure laudant	Laus Deo patri
	Benedicta sit creatrix	Ex quo omnia
Corpus Christi, Second Vespers	Cenantibus apostolis	Sacerdos in aeternum
	Accipite et comedite	Miseratur Dominus
	Similiter et calicem	Calicem salutaris accipiam
	Ego sum panis vivus	Sicut novellae olivarum
	Caro mea vere est	Qui pacem ponit fines

Table IV-6

Psalm and Magnificat Antiphons Set by Grandi and Rovetta

Text incipit and printed source	Liturgical Function in the Roman Rite	Liturgical Function in St. Mark's
	Alessandro Grandi	
Nativitas tua (*Motetti, Libro Primo*, 1610)	Magnificat antiphon Second Vespers Nativity of the B. V. M.	Same as Rome
Non est inventus (*Motetti, Libro Secondo*, 1613)	Second antiphon Vespers Common of a Confessor Bishop	—
Magnum haereditatis (*Motetti, Libro Secondo*, 1613)	Magnificat antiphon Second Vespers Circumcision	Same as Rome
Quam gloriosum (*Motetti, Libro Secondo*, 1613)	Magnificat antiphon Second Vespers All Saints' Day (centonized with a second text)	First Vespers
Dum complerentur (*Motetti, Libro Terzo*, 1614)	First antiphon Vespers Pentecost	Second Vespers

Juravit Dominus (*Motetti, Libro Terzo*, 1614)	First antiphon Second Vespers Common of Apostles	First Vespers
Spiritus Domini (*Motetti, Libro Terzo*, 1614)	Second antiphon Vespers Pentecost	Second Vespers
Repleti sunt (*Motetti, Libro Terzo*, 1614)	Third antiphon Vespers Pentecost	Second Vespers
Da pacem Domine (*Motetti, Libro Terzo*, 1614)	Commemorative Antiphon for Peace	One of the *Antiphonae Machabeorum* for Saturdays after Pentecost at the Magnificat
Fontes et omnia (*Motetti, Libro Terzo*, 1614)	Fourth antiphon Vespers Pentecost	Second Vespers
Dum esset (*Motetti, Libro Terzo*, 1614)	Magnificat antiphon Second Vespers Common of a Confessor Bishop	Same as Rome
Dabit ei Dominus (*Motetti, Libro Terzo*, 1614)	Fourth antiphon Second Vespers Purification	Magnificat antiphon Saturday before the Fourth Sunday in Advent
O sacrum convivium (*Motetti, Libro Quarto*, 1616)	Magnificat antiphon Second Vespers Corpus Christi	Same as Rome
Haec est virgo (*Motetti, Libro Quarto*, 1616)	—	First and second antiphons Common of Virgins

Text incipit and printed source	Liturgical Function in the Roman Rite	Liturgical Function in St. Mark's
	Alessandro Grandi	
O magnum sacramentum (*Celeste Fiori*, 1619)	Magnificat antiphon, Second Vespers, Corpus Christi (paraphrase of *O sacrum convivium*)	Same as Rome
Diem festum (*Celesti Fiori*, 1619)	Refrain of the motet is the Magnificat antiphon for Vespers of the Common of Doctors	Same as Rome
Virgo prudentissima (*Motetti a voce sola*, 1621) (*Motetti con sinfonie, Libro Terzo*, 1629)	Magnificat antiphon, First Vespers, Assumption	—
Ecce sacerdos magnus (*Motetti a voce sola*, 1621) (*Motetti con sinfonie, Libro Terzo*, 1629)	First and second antiphons, Second Vespers, Common of a Confessor Bishop	First antiphon only (second part of the motet is not found in the *Orationale*)
Tota pulchra (*Motetti con sinfonie, Libro Primo*, 1621) (*Motetti a voce sola*, 1621)	—	Third antiphon, plus a paraphrase of the first antiphon, First Vespers, Assumption
O Beate Hieronime (*Motetti con sinfonie, Libro Secondo*, 1625)	Magnificat antiphon (paraphrase), Vespers, Common of Doctors	Same as Rome
Memoriam fecit (*Motetti con sinfonie, Libro Primo*, 1621)	Magnificat antiphon, Second Vespers, Corpus Christi (*O sacrum convivium* centonized with other texts)	Same as Rome

Motet		
Hic est vere Martyr (*Motetti con sinfonie, Libro Secondo*, 1625)	—	Magnificat antiphon First Vespers St. Victor
Veni Sancte Spiritus (*Motetti con sinfonie, Libro Terzo*, 1629)	—	Sole antiphon (paraphrase)[a] First Vespers Pentecost
O crux splendidior (*Motetti, Libro Sesto*, 1630)	Magnificat antiphon First Vespers Exaltation of the Holy cross	Second Vespers

Giovanni Rovetta

Motet		
O pretiosum et admirabile convivium (*Motetti concertati, Libro Primo*, 1635)	Magnificat antiphon Second Vespers Corpus Christi (paraphrase of *O sacrum convivium*)	Same as Rome
Domine ostende (*Motetti concertati, Libro Secondo*, 1639)	First through fourth antiphons First Vespers Ss. Philip and James	First through fourth antiphons First Vespers Ss. Philip and James OR Magnificat antiphon Vespers Ss. Philip and James (centonized with other texts)

[a]Grandi also sets the *Veni Sancte Spiritus* which is the sequence for Pentecost (*Motetti, Libro Sesto*, 1630).

V

The Musical Repertoire

The Celebration of Vespers at St. Mark's

We know more about the performance of the Mass in the ducal chapel than we do about the celebration of Vespers. While Bonifacio and Pace describe the ceremonies of the Mass in great detail, they often state merely that Vespers are to be sung or give a pithy, one-sentence description of the ceremony which clearly meant more to clerics in the *seicento* than it does to us today. Nonetheless, by gathering isolated facts from various sources, one can paint a fairly complete picture of the ceremony, even if all the details cannot be filled in.

The beginning of Vespers was announced to the public by the ringing of the campanile in the piazza.[340] We do not have a record of the exact hour at which Vespers were sung. Pace constantly refers to their taking place "dopo pranzo," i.e. after the mid-day meal, though this presumably means after the afternoon siesta as well. Bonifacio similarly refers to Vespers' taking place "post prandium." The total length of the service must have varied greatly according to the style of music being performed and the amount of extra-liturgical music included. Coryat refers to a service at the Scuola di San Rocco which lasted from five until eight in the evening, one clearly embellished with extra music to judge from his description. The services conducted by Rovetta which Hainlein describes in his letters[341] were said to last until one and three "in the night" respectively, although these figures are a bit misleading. In Venice and certain other parts of Italy, *ventiquattro ore* was a flexible hour which coincided with sundown each day. Thus, "one in the night" meant one hour after sundown, "three in the night," three hours after sundown. The service which lasted until three seems to have been performed almost entirely in *canto figurato*, since Hainlein describes the elaborate musical forces for the various psalms and adds that a motet or sonata was performed between them.

Vespers were celebrated "in quinto" according to Pace; that is, the officiant was a canon, and he was assisted by four other priests.[342] The service began during most of the year with the standard versicle *Deus in adiutorium meum intende* and the response *Domine ad adiuvandum me festina*. This opening portion of the service seems usually to have been performed in plainchant, intoned by one of the canons and continued by the rest of them.[343] There is only one polyphonic setting of the *Domine ad adiuvandum* in the 10 psalm collections by Grandi, Rovetta and Cavalli—the one in Grandi's *Salmi a otto brevi* of 1629.[344] While some *falsobordone* formula may occasionally have been used, the singers of St. Mark's felt that *falsobordone* was beneath the dignity of "una capella del Serenissimo Principe," as they testify in the records of an inquest held in August, 1600.[345]

The central portion of the service followed the basic outlines of Roman Vespers, i.e. five psalms were recited, each one framed by a proper antiphon for the day. The exact procedure during this portion of the service depended on the solemnity of the feast. On ferial days or on minor feasts when the singers, instrumentalists and organists were not present, the antiphons and psalms were intoned by a canon and continued by the *coro* responsible for singing plainchant.[346] Special procedures were prescribed in the event that anything went wrong in this part of the service. If the wrong psalm were intoned, the chorus which responded was to complete the verse of the psalm which had been erroneously intoned; then the proper psalm was to be intoned and sung. If the wrong psalm tone were used, the members of the choir were instructed to use the tone which had been initiated, lest the public see that an error had been committed.[347] While antiphonal psalmody between two choirs seems to have been the norm for services in plainchant, *alternatim* performance between choir and organ was also used in the early seventeenth century. On 18 October 1624, the Procurators decreed that organists Carlo Fillago and Giovanni Pietro Berti were to be present in St. Mark's on all Sundays and on other feasts when requested and to respond verse by verse to all of the psalms (Document 125).

On more important feast days, the singers were required to be present in church and some type of *canto figurato* was used for the service. While the style of music performed was no doubt a function of the importance of the feast, it also depended on certain liturgical requirements which were tightly interwoven with Venetian political history. One of the glories of the church of St. Mark's was the *Pala d'oro*, a large gold altarpiece which is, in some ways, the central jewel of the basilica (Plate 7). Constructed in Constantinople in 976, the *Pala* was enlarged by gold panels commissioned between 1102 and 1117. It was enlarged again in the thirteenth century and finally placed in its present frame in 1345.[348] On ferial days and on minor feasts, the *Pala d'oro* was kept out of sight; it was

Plate 7   The *Pala d'oro* of St. Mark's.

covered by a second altarpiece, painted by Paolo Veneziano and his sons
in 1345. On major feasts, however, the *Pala d'oro* was opened by an
elaborate system of wheels and pulleys which folded up the ferial altarpiece, hoisted it above the *Pala d'oro* at the same time as it unfolded the
Pala d'oro to display it fully to the populace. This ceremonial opening of
the *Pala d'oro* was clearly coordinated with music in a suitably impressive
style, for Pace tell us that "every time the *Pala d'oro* is opened, the
singers must sing Vespers in two choirs with psalms set for eight voices."[349]
We do not know exactly when this practice began. Pace's explanation is
quite vague: "The singers used to be obligated to sing the *Te Deum*; the
Most Excellent Procurators freed them from this duty on the condition
that they should sing psalms for eight voices, in two choirs, every time
the *Pala d'oro* was opened."[350] Certainly the custom was well established
by the time Bonifacio drew up his *ceremoniale* in 1564, for he states that
while the psalms had once been performed in plainchant on major feasts,
they were now done in settings for two choirs.[351]

Thus, there were three possibilities for the performance of the five
psalms which formed the central portion of Vespers. On ferial days they
were recited to plainchant formulas, no doubt read right out of Stringa's
Psalterium Davidicum. On the days when singers attended the service but
the *Pala d'oro* was not open (more or less all the feasts with the rank of
Lesser Doubles on the calendar of the *Orationale*), they were sung in
canto figurato in settings for a single choir. And on those days when the
Pala d'oro was opened (mainly feasts with the rank of Greater Doubles),
they were to be sung in settings for two four-part choirs. The performance
of the other items in this portion of the service, i.e. the antiphons which
were required before and after the psalms, is considerably less clear. Certainly on ferial days the antiphons would have been done in plainchant.
The *giovani di coro* and the *canonici residenti* were required to attend
Vespers every day to "cantare e salmeggiare," and the plainchant settings
of the special antiphons for the basilica are preserved in the large antiphonaries in the A.S.V. It is clear, moreover, that the antiphon sung before
each psalm would be abbreviated according to the usual Roman practice,
for the *Psalterium Davidicum* prints only the incipit of the antiphon before
each psalm and the complete antiphon after the psalm.

On the feasts where *canto figurato* was used, however, the problem
is more complex. Let us summarize the information we have, for much
of it is really quite sketchy, and it will be necessary to distinguish the
information we have about St. Mark's from that we have about other
churches in Venice or about Catholic liturgical practices in general. Let
us start with general Roman Catholic liturgical procedures.[352]

The modal agreement of antiphon and psalm in plainchant services is a tradition which dates back to the Middle Ages. That such modal agreement was still important in plainchant services in the seventeenth century is shown by manuals such as Adriano Banchieri's *L'Organo suonarino*. Banchieri presents all eight psalm tones, all eight Magnificat tones, and eight formulas for *falsobordone* so that, using his materials, an organist could direct an *alternatim* performance of a psalm or Magnificat in whatever mode its accompanying antiphon might appear. However, while Banchieri's instructions would work for a service in plainchant or in *falsobordone*, a problem arises in services employing fixed psalm settings in *canto figurato*; for a polyphonic setting of a psalm is in a fixed mode and, theoretically, can be used only if the accompanying antiphon happens to fall in the same mode. We know, however, that antiphons did not need to be performed on all occasions. Another organist's manual of the period, Giovanni Battista Fasolo's *Annuale* (Venice, 1645) states that an organ work could substitute for the performance of the antiphon after the Magnificat. Moreover, we know that vocal motets on non-liturgical texts were sometimes used as substitutes for Proper items of the Mass. Stephen Bonta has taken the above information and developed an elegant argument to suggest that such liturgical substitutions could have been used to solve the problem of modal agreement between antiphon and psalm in elaborate services employing *canto figurato*. Simply stated, he argues that a sonata, organ work or non-liturgical motet would have been performed after a psalm or Magnificat in place of the plainchant antiphon. Since modal agreement would not be necessary between such vocal or instrumental works and a psalm or Magnificat setting, the use of these pieces as antiphon-substitutes would free any psalm or Magnificat composition to be used for any service. Bonta argues further that the four *sacri concerti* and the *Sonata sopra Sancta Maria* from Monteverdi's 1610 *Vespers* are probably antiphon-substitutes and would take the place of plainchant antiphons in a Vespers service using the music from this collection.

Venetian sources corroborate much of Bonta's data. A statement in Michele Bauldry's *Manuale Sacrarum Caeremoniarum iuxta Ritum S. Romanae Ecclesiae*, a Roman *ceremoniale* published in Venice in 1689 says that an organ work may be used after a psalm is sung as long as the text of the antiphon is recited in a clear voice in the middle of the choir (Document 126). Moreover, we have evidence that the organ was played in St. Mark's after each of the first three psalms on Easter Day,[353] and the performance of motets and sonatas between the Vespers psalms at San Francesco della Vigna, as well as the performance of non-liturgical motets between Vespers psalms in the *scuole piccole*, was mentioned in the last chapter. Moreover, as we have shown, there is a large repertoire of non-liturgical motets composed by the composers of St. Mark's, and if only a few of them are actual settings of the antiphon texts connected with the basilica, many of them are closely related in theme to the liturgical antiphons of St. Mark's. (One thinks particularly of the motets on centonized texts from the Song of Songs and the antiphons for the Feast of the Assumption.)

Nonetheless, it is difficult to believe that such motets or sonatas could actually have displaced liturgical antiphons in St. Mark's. After the material presented in the preceding chapter, it should hardly be necessary to emphasize the place which the liturgy of St. Mark's occupied in the collective psyche of Venice, and one might only add that the antiphons for the psalms and the Magnificat are the central items of that liturgy for many feasts. The feast of St. Mark is perhaps the most telling case, for while the psalms of First Vespers are merely the usual ones from the male *cursus*, the antiphons dramatically describe the translation of Mark's relics from Alexandria to Venice and end in lofty praise of the Venetian state. The liturgy for the feasts of the Translation and Apparition of the Body of St. Mark is similarly dramatic and patriotic. The plainchant settings of these antiphons are in the antiphonaries in the A.S.V., and it seems inconceivable that, after fighting with Rome to retain their own calendar and liturgy, the Doge and Procurators would have allowed these texts to be hidden behind innocuous, non-liturgical items.

If the plainchant antiphons connected with the liturgy of the basilica were indeed performed, two questions must be answered. First, what was their relationship with the non-liturgical motets? And, second, how was modal unity retained between the antiphons and the polyphonic settings of psalms and Magnificats? The first question is the easier to answer, for there is evidence that antiphons *and* their non-liturgical substitutes could both actually have been performed. While Michele Bauldry states that organ music can substitute for the antiphon *after* a psalm on a major feast, he insists that the antiphon *before* the psalm be performed in chant (Document 127). This is not a unique statement, for Clement VIII's *Ceremoniale Episcoporum* (Rome, 1600), a book which the Procurators of St. Mark's purchased in 1620, made the same demand (Documents 128 and 129).[354] Thus, it is not impossible that liturgical plainchant antiphons found a place in the service before a psalm or Magnificat, and their non-liturgical substitutes were performed afterwards.

The second question—that of modal agreement between psalm and antiphon—is a more subtle one. We do know that the problem was at least recognized by composers in St. Mark's, for Giovanni Croce published a set of Magnificats in every mode in 1605.[355] Moreover, although those works in the *stile concertato* created by composers connected with St. Mark's never have modal designations, the simpler double-choir works which could be performed when the *Pala d'oro* was open are all labeled according to the system of psalm tones and transpositions given by Adriano Banchieri in his *L'Organo suonarino* and *Cartella musicale*.[356] However, there seems to be no particular pattern to the modes in which composers choose to set the psalms nor any attempt by them collectively to cover all the possible modes for each psalm text. Since this is a crucial point, I should like to explain it in a bit more detail.

In each of the four collections of simple, double-choir *salmi spezzati*,[357] the mode of each composition is listed in the basso continuo part. Only Grandi's collection of 1629 gives the modes of the compositions in the table of contents, and the other collections are inconsistent in their listing of mode in partbooks other than the basso continuo. The fact that the modal plan of an entire collection can be grasped at a glance in only one instance suggests that choice of mode is an incidental issue rather than an important part of the plan or liturgical function of these collections. Moreover, multiple settings of a single psalm, which would allow a choice of settings in different modes to co-ordinate with the antiphons of the day, are almost non-existent in these prints. Where psalms are set more than once, they are part of complete Vespers services which are meant to be performed intact: for example, the Marian Vespers in Cavalli's *Vesperi* of 1675 and the settings of the *Vespero delli Cinque Laudate* by Cavalli (1675) and Rovetta (1662).

That the modes of the psalms and Magnificats in these collections have been chosen without regard to any fixed liturgical function is evident, for there is almost no consistency in the mode chosen for a given psalm from print to print. It is true that there are certain patterns; the old custom of setting the first five psalms of a collection in modes I through V is echoed in the Marian Vespers from Cavalli's *Vesperi* and in the first four psalms from Grandi's 1629 print. Beyond this, however, there seems to be little rationale in the choice of mode. For example, in the two settings of the *Vespero delli Cinque Laudate* by Cavalli and Rovetta, only one item is set in the same mode by both composers:

	Cavalli 1675	Rovetta 1662
Laudate pueri Dominum	[Secundi Toni]	[2. Tuono][358]
Laudate Dominum omnes gentes	Octavi Toni	5. Tuono
Lauda anima mea	Quarti Toni	Primo tuono
Laudate Dominum quoniam bonus es	Tertij Toni	8. Tuono
Lauda Jerusalem	Quinti Toni	4. Tuono
Magnificat	Tertij Toni	[Primo tuono]

This lack of correspondence is still more startling when one compares the modal choices for all of the psalms from these four collections (see Table V-1, p. 209). It is true that some correlation exists among the collections: all four settings of *Confitebor* are in mode II, three of the settings of *Beatus vir* are in mode III, and three of the settings of *In convertendo* are in mode VIII. The setting of *In exitu* in a *misto tuono*, i.e. the *tonus peregrinus* which wanders between different reciting tones, is a tradition which extends back to the Middle Ages; the agreement of all four collections has no special significance in this case. Indeed, about the only point on which the four collections do agree is their use of Banchieri's system of transpositions, for all of the settings of Grandi, Rovetta and Cavalli agree with the pitch of the psalm tones which Banchieri presents in *L'Organo suonarino* and the ecclesiastical modes he gives in the *Cartella musicale*.

It is not impossible that the problem of modal concordance was actually ignored. While Banchieri, Fasolo and others give a prominent place to the discussion of mode in their manuals for organists, one must not forget that they are discussing services for plainchant choir and organ or, at their most elaborate, in *falsobordone* alternating with organ settings— all media for which the agreement of mode between psalms and antiphons would have posed no great problem. We really have no incontestable proof that such modal unity was necessary in services employing *canto figurato*, let alone those employing the more lavish forms of the *stile concertato*. This is not to say that psalms and antiphons would have been allowed to clash violently, but the agreement may have been a looser one than scholars have assumed.

We do know that psalm tones were freely transposed in St. Mark's. In an aside in *L'Organo suonarino*, Banchieri describes a practice which he heard at St. Mark's, in which the organists Giovanni Gabrieli and Paolo Giusti transposed all of the psalm tones so that they would end on *D la sol re* (Document 130). Banchieri does not say if antiphons were transposed as well; one assumes they must have been if modal consistency were to be maintained. In any case, Banchieri's description proves that plainchant was transposed rather freely in the basilica; his realization of this practice employs key signatures from two flats to two sharps. Considering this fact, it is not inconceivable that plainchant antiphons could have been transposed in services employing double-choir music or large works in the *stile concertato* so that the final note of the antiphon agreed with the tonic of the psalm or Magnificat to follow, or at least so that an egregious clash in tonalities was avoided. While it is true that such a transposition would not bring the antiphon into the actual mode of the psalm, such a total theoretical agreement may not have been necessary in the mid-*seicento*, when the modal system itself was gradually dissolving. Moreover, one must admit that the connection between the eight ecclesiastical modes and the eight plainchant psalm tones associated with them is rather tenuous in certain cases.

The final section of the service began with the reading of the chapter and continued with the singing of the appropriate hymn for the day. The texts of the hymns for the major days of the year are reproduced in the *Psalterium Davidicum* while those other hymns mentioned in the *Orationale* were presumably in the *Hymnarium Magnum* of which Bonifacio speaks but which seems not to have survived. Since we have so few settings of hymn texts from the seventeenth century, it is possible that the hymns were often done in plainchant, even on major feasts. As mentioned above, however, the hymn settings of Monteverdi and his colleagues were designed to be used for any text in the requisite meter, so the few surviving settings may actually have done yeoman's duty for virtually all the texts in the hymnal. At any rate, when the hymns were performed in *canto figurato*, they seem to have been performed consistently by small forces. Most of the settings from the first half of the seventeenth century involve but one to three solo voices, basso continuo, and sometimes a pair of violins. While all of the verses of the hymn may have been sung to the melodic framework provided for a single verse, alternatim performance was also used. For example, Rovetta's setting of *Ave maris stella* in his first book of *Motetti concertati* (1635) indicates that only the odd-numbered verses are to be sung in *canto figurato*. The even-numbered verses are to be represented by organ interludes, as Rovetta states in his rubric at the end of the musical setting:

> Here the organ plays a bit, and this serves for the following verse; then one repeats from the top, beginning at the proportion, and one does the same for the other verses.[359]

Rovetta does not actually write out music for the organist. It is probable that the player merely realized the bass line of the setting, either in full or in a truncated form. Cavalli's setting of *Ave maris stella* in the *Musiche Sacre* follows just such a pattern; the written-out ritornelli are based on a telescoped version of the bass for the stanzas of the text, adopting the phrases for the first, second, third and sixth lines of each stanza and dovetailing them to create a single span of music.[360]

After the performance of the hymn, there was a versicle and response (presumably sung by the canons and the *giovani di coro*) and then the Magnificat was sung. On ferial days, the Magnificat was recited to plainchant formulas, but it was sung in *canto figurato* on greater feasts. Presumably it was sung in double-choir settings along with the psalms on those days the *Pala d'oro* was opened, for the collections of Grandi, Rovetta and Cavalli which contain double-choir psalms for the most important Vespers sequences also contain Magnificats for the same musical forces. The problem of the manner of performance of the Magnificat antiphon is similar to the problem of the psalm antiphons, but the fact that we have a much more significant body of motets on texts drawn from the Magnificat antiphons of the *Orationale* indicates that the plainchant antiphon after the Magnificat must have been replaced by a motet on a number of occasions. The Magnificat coincided with the incensing of the altar on most feasts, although other liturgical actions accompanied it on special occasions. On the Vigil of the Apparition of the Body of St. Mark, holy water was sprinkled in the church during the Magnificat,[361] and at First Vespers of the Feast of St. Mark, the Doge was permitted by Pope Alexander III to hold a special candle in a silver holder inlaid with gold while the Magnificat was sung.[362]

After the Magnificat and its accompanying antiphon and/or motet, the collect of the day was read and commemorative antiphons were sung or motets were performed in their place. Motets might also be performed for the *Deo gratias* at the end of Vespers. The usual pattern of singing the Marian antiphon at the end of Vespers if Compline were not to follow immediately seems to have been observed in St. Mark's, but the basilica also had a number of other services which served as a liturgical supplement to Vespers. The most elaborate of these occurred on Easter.[363] The rather unusual Vespers for Easter Day has already been described; three psalms were sung in *canto figurato*, then the Magnificat was sung; after a procession to the baptismal font, the remaining two psalms were sung in plainchant (Document 131) and the Magnificat repeated. However, the service did not end here; a second procession took place which took the clergy of St. Mark's to the crypt for additional prayers; during this procession the singers were to sing *Surrexit Christus* in two choirs, with eight *alleluias* after each stanza.[364] Occasionally, Vespers ended with the singing of litanies. This practice was connected with Marian feasts in particular, and Pace tells us that litanies were sung at the end of Vespers on the Visitation, the Conception and the Presentation of the Virgin although the practice may have involved other Marian feasts as well (Documents 132, 133 and 134). Litanies seem to have been done in three ways. A document of 1630 describes a performance by two choirs (Document 135), while one of 1644 describes a performance by four solo singers (Document 136). Moreover, the fact that no litany setting has survived from the seventeenth century with the full text demanded by the liturgy of the basilica or with the text of the special Marian litany sung in the church suggests that litanies were often sung in plainchant. The four-voice setting sung in 1644 may well have been the composition which Rovetta published in his second book of *Motetti concertati* (1639), since none of the other settings by the major composers connected with St. Mark's during the 1630s and 1640s is for this medium. The litany from Monteverdi's *Messa a quattro Voci e Salmi* is for six voices, the two litanies by Grandi are both for five, and Rovetta's other litany is for three. There is no surviving double-choir litany by composers connected with St. Mark's during this period, although such works were composed in the preceding century.

Despite a lack of extensive documentation—both Pace and Bonifacio are rather unconcerned with non-liturgical items—we can be fairly sure where independent instrumental music was used in the Vespers service. Hainlein's description of the Vespers at St. Francesco della Vigna related that the music between the psalms consisted of "ein Motetten oder Sonata," thus suggesting that either vocal or instrumental music might be used after each liturgical item except the hymn, either merely embellishing the service or actually substituting for an antiphon. Stephen Bonta has noted that a number of seventeenth-century Vespers collections end with some sort of instrumental work after the Magnificat, reinforcing the idea of liturgical substitution for the Magnificat antiphon.[365] Indeed, two of the Vespers collections in this study contain such sonatas. Rovetta's *Salmi concertati* of 1627 contains four *canzoni* along with one non-liturgical motet, *O intemerata*. It is dangerous to read too much into the numerical significance of these items, for Rovetta's collection was assembled rapidly and he seems to have been more intent on showing his compositional versatility than providing a collection which would be workable from a liturgical point of view. Cavalli's *Musiche Sacre* is different, however, for he seems to have wanted to provide the consumer with a concerted Mass plus all the materials for the major Vespers services of the year. And Cavalli has provided six sonatas at the end of his collection, set for progressively greater forces: 3, 4, 6, 8, 10 and 12 parts. There is no statement by Cavalli telling us exactly where these sonatas might have been played, but one cannot ignore the fact that the six works would fit a solemn Vespers service perfectly—one after each psalm, and the grand *Sonata à 12* after the Magnificat.[366]

Thus, by drawing upon a number of sources—and using a bit of liturgical intuition—one can reconstruct the outlines of a Vespers service at St. Mark's in the mid-seventeenth century. It is clear, however, that a number of the details are missing from the picture I have presented. And many of the missing details are not in the area of actual practice but, rather, in the temporal location of liturgical and musical events. When was plainchant used? When was the *Pala d'oro* opened and double-choir music appropriate? When would the elaborate repertoire in the *stile con-*

certato have been sung? And, most crucial, when would the various printed collections of Vespers psalms which survive from the mid-seventeenth century have been used in St. Mark's? The answer to the first question can be gleaned from archival documents which tell us the days and services at which singers in the *cappella* were required to be present in the basilica. The answer to the second can be found on the *tariffa*, the official list which hung in the sacristy and enumerated the days on which double-choir music was required. To answer the third question, one must collate all of this information with the textual contents of the various published psalm collections and the texts prescribed by the *Orationale* for Vespers on various feasts.

The Tariffa of the Basilica

Question: Do you know that there is a chart in the sacristy on which are listed all of the Vespers which the singers must sing, be they in a single choir or in two choirs?

Answer: Yes sir, I know it.

Question: Did you see that there are certain signs which indicate when the singers must sing in two choirs?

Answer: I saw certain signs, but I did not think much about them.

Question: Did you hear the *maestro di coro* order that the Vespers be sung in two choirs?

Answer: When the Vespers had been intoned, I heard the *maestro di coro* tell the singers to sing, and they all answered that they were not obligated to sing according to the *tariffa*.

Question: What *tariffa* are you talking about?

Answer: There is a chart in the sacristy on which a special sign appears when double-choir music is required.

The documents above are excerpts from the Procurators' inquest of 1589 into the disturbances at Vespers on the Feast of the Dedication of the Church of St. Mark's (see Documents 137 and 138). The arguments centered around the question of whether double-choir music was required for that day, and the details of the testimony tell us exactly how the daily obligations were conveyed to the singers. A chart was displayed on the wall of the sacristy, and all of the days on which the singers were required to be present in the basilica were listed. Those days on which double-choir Vespers were to be sung were marked with a special sign.

Although the *tariffa* from the seventeenth century does not seem to have survived intact, we have five detailed lists of "days and services" for the singers in the *cappella marciana*: one for the sixteenth century (1515); two for the seventeenth (1677, 1678) and two for the eighteenth (1755, 1761). It is not surprising that there are so few extant lists of these duties; most of the copies are from large manuscript *ceremoniali* which were used for decades on end without revision, and only one list—the one published in 1761—seems actually to have been designed for display. The lists are found in the following sources:

1. The list of 1515 was copied into Bonifacio's *ceremoniale*. Although the list is labeled 1515, it must have been updated before being inserted into this *ceremoniali* of 1564. Since the list was copied without change into A.S.V., San Marco, Procuratia de Supra, Registro 98, it is probable that it reflects accurately the duties of the singers as late as 1646 (Document 139).

2. The list of 1677 is included in Biblioteca Correr, Codice Cicogna 3118, fascicoli 44-50; the folios of the busta are unpaginated (Document 140).

3. The list of 1678 is from Pace's *Ceremoniale Magnum*, Biblioteca Ambrosiana, MS A. 328 inf., f. 163r–165v (Document 141).

4. The list of 1755 is from the *Compilazione* of earlier *ceremoniali* ordered in 1752, A.S.V., San Marco, Procuratia de Supra, Registro 99, f. 163r–165v (Document 142).

5. The list of 1761 is the only one intended for display. It is a single large printed folio, "Stampata per li Figliuoli del q*uondam*.... *Zuanne* Antonio Pinelli, Stampatori Ducali." It reverts ultimately to the list of 1515, which it gives as its original source, stating that copies were displayed in 1515, 1661 and 1694 before the final revision and publication in 1761. At least two manuscript copies of this list survive: A.S.V., San Marco, Procuratia de Supra, Registro 100, f. 358r–361v and 365v–368r (Document 143).

Clearly, the lists of 1677 and 1678 are the most important for this study, although the collation of all five lists which is found in Appendix 2 emphasizes the sanctity of tradition within the basilica. The place of music in the liturgy does not change appreciably over two-and-one-half centuries. Indeed, the days and services which were added over this period of nearly 250 years are limited to those quasi-religious, quasi-civic feasts which were so important to the Venetian calendar: the *festa del Redentore*, which commemorated the end of the plague of 1576; the feast of Santa Maria della Salute, celebrated on the Presentation and commemorating the end of the plague of 1630–31; the feast of St. Giustina, on which the Venetians celebrated their victory over the Turks in the Battle of Lepanto in 1571; the feast of St. Lorenzo Giustiniani, the first patriarch of Venice; and that of St. Peter Orseolo, a Venetian seaman and Doge. The list of 1677 totals 210 Vespers services at which the singers were required to be present every year. In general, *canto figurato* was required at one or both Vespers on all feasts of Double rank in the *Orationale* (both Lesser and Greater Doubles).

The feasts at which the singers were required to be present, according to the seventeenth-century sources, are listed in Table V-2 (p. 210). These feasts fall into three main categories: the major feasts of the *Temporale* which, naturally, would require elaborate music; the major feasts of the Roman *Sanctorale*, particularly the major Marian feasts, which held a special place in the liturgy of St. Mark's; and the feasts of a number of saints connected specifically with Venice as well as the politico-religious holidays mentioned above. In general, the singers' duties involved both Mass and Vespers and, as one can see from the tabulation in Table V-2, *canto figurato* was required at both Vespers on most of the important feasts. Occasionally the duties were extended to other ceremonies. The most important of these were the processions which took place either within the church or in the piazza on certain selected days. These are the events represented in Gentile Bellini's famous painting of the Corpus Domini procession and in Mattio Pagan's woodcut of the procession for Palm Sunday.[367] A number of these processions involved "supernumeraries" from outside the church; documents record payments to extra persons for the processions of St. Isidore, St. Giustina, the Presentation, Good Friday, Corpus Domini, Ss. Vitus and Modestus and the Apparition of the Body of St. Mark.[368] The singers also sang at Compline on the Annunciation as well as on all the Sundays during Lent; it was probably for these occasions that Rovetta included a set of Compline psalms in his Vespers collection of 1662. Further duties abounded. The members of the *cappella* sang the Passion during Holy Week, and they sang at Matins of the Triduum. They performed motets all day long on those occasions during the year when the Most Holy Blood of Our Lord was displayed.[369] Moreover, the *cappella* performed in the Bucintoro, the large boat which took the Doge and the *Serenissima Signoria* to San Nicolo on the Lido for the ceremony of the marriage of Venice to the sea on the feast of the Ascension. Litanies were sung just before the blessing of the sea, a "certo Madrigal allegro" during the crossing to the Lido, and "qualche cosa d'allegro" during the return to Venice.[370]

At least some of the singers seem to have sung Mass on ferial days during Monteverdi's term as *maestro di cappella*. It is difficult to tell whether this practice lasted after Monteverdi's death and whether the entire *cappella* had to come to these ferial services. We know that Monteverdi bought prints of sixteenth-century Masses for ferial use shortly after he was appointed *maestro*, and when Marc'Antonio Negri's status changed from that of a simple singer to that of *vice-maestro*, he was excused "dall'obligo di andar à cantar in capella nelli giorni feriali, et altri feste ordinarie...."[371] Moreover, three singers who entered the *cappella* in 1621 and 1622 were accepted with the stipulation that they serve "ogni giorno."[372] However, the lists of duties of the singers never specify ferial days. It may well be that only part of the *cappella* had to meet this obligation, and that such services were attended on a rotating basis; it seems unlikely that the entire *cappella* would have sung the ferial Masses.

While we have a plethora of data on the services which singers were required to attend, we lack such a definitive list of duties for instrumentalists. Selfridge-Field has used the large calendar in Busta 91 of the Procuratia de Supra (reproduced here as Document 143) as her guide, and with some justification, since many elements of the table agree with similar documents from earlier periods. The problem, however, is that this calendar was published in 1761, and although the rubrics state that it goes back to 1515 and was displayed in both 1661 and 1694, we do not know what revisions might have been made at these dates. Certainly the information on specific services at which instrumentalists played cannot apply to the mid-seventeenth century; for the table is weighted heavily toward instrumental participation at Mass rather than at Vespers, and the most cursory glance at the sacred publications connected with St. Mark's during the mid-*seicento* shows that Vespers was the service which called for the more elaborate instrumental forces. It is probable, however, that the feasts listed on the large printed calendar as demanding instrumental music are more or less the same as those which required instruments in the seventeenth century. As Selfridge-Field has pointed out, the feasts which demanded instruments were generally those on which the Doge attended services in the basilica.[373] We know that in the seventeenth century the Doge attended services on close to 30 days each year.[374] We know, moreover, that when the orchestra of St. Mark's was first drawn up as a unit in 1614, the instruments attended services on 26 days a year, and special mention was made of the fact that they had to play at the entry of the Doge.[375] While documents do not state that the instrumentalists must be in church every time the Doge attends services, it seems that this is a relatively good guide to the occasions on which they may have been used.

We are far more fortunate in the case of those feasts on which the *Pala d'oro* was opened and double-choir psalms performed. There are at least six sources from which one can glean this information:

1. Biblioteca Correr. Codice Cicogna 3118, fascicoli 44–50.
   A list of duties of the singers of St. Mark's in which "Palla" is inserted in the left margin for certain feasts. Dated 1677 (Document 140).

2. Biblioteca Ambrosiana, MS A 328 inf.
   Although Pace does not give a list of these dates, one can search through his description of the church year and compile such a list by taking the information from his descriptions of individual feasts. 1678.

3. Biblioteca Nazionale Marciana. Cod. Lat. III-172 (-2276), f. 114r.
   The original copy of the *ceremoniale* of Bonifacio contains among a number of supplementary materials included as an *addendum* a list of days on which double choir psalms are sung. This list was supposedly "taken from the schedule of *maestro di cappella* Iseppo Zerlino." Undated, it falls in the volume between documents dated 1588 and 1591 (Document 144).

4. A.S.V., San Marco, Procuratia de Supra, Registro 98, f. 69v–70r.
   A later, more readable copy of a list contained in item 3 above on f. 46r. Since Registro 98 seems to have been copied in 1646, one can assume that the days on which the *Pala d'oro* was opened did not change between 1564 and 1646 (Document 145).[376]

5. A.S.V., San Marco, Procuratia de Supra, Registro 99, f. 409r–413r.
   An ecclesiastical calendar of 1755 on which the opening of the *Pala d'oro* is marked (Document 142).

6. A.S.V., San Marco, Busta 91, large unpaginated folio.
   The ecclesiastical calendar printed in 1761, on which the opening of the *Pala d'oro* is marked (Document 143).

A collation of the information in these six sources reveals, yet again, the sanctity of tradition within the basilica.[377] By and large, the *Pala d'oro* was to be opened on the major feasts of the *Temporale* as well as certain feasts in the *Sancorale* which held particular importance for the Catholic church as a whole or for St. Mark's in particular. These feasts are almost all ranked as Greater Doubles on the calendar of the *Orationale*. On the whole, the feasts did not change greatly between 1564, the date of the model from which the list of 1646 was taken, and 1761. A few notable changes did occur. The feasts of St. Isidore, Ss. Vitus and Modestus, St. Marina and the Transfiguration were eventually dropped from the list. Important quasi-religious feasts of a civic nature were added: the *festa del Redentore*, which celebrated the end of the plague of 1576; and the Feast of the Presentation, on which the end of the plague of 1630–31 was celebrated by a procession to the votive church of Santa Maria della Salute. Corpus Domini was the only important feast from the *Temporale* to be added to the list.[378]

The Liturgical Year and the Printed Psalm Collections

I have waited until now to discuss the liturgical propriety of the collections of psalms and Magnificats published by Grandi, Rovetta and Cavalli not out of a perverse sense of the dramatic but out of sheer necessity. At St. Mark's liturgical function was determined by more factors than were significant in most churches in Italy, and one must take three elements into account rather than merely match texts and feasts:

1. The archival lists of days and services at which the singers of the *cappella* were required to be present in the basilica

2. The psalms which the *Orationale* specifies for these days

3. The days on which the *Pala d'oro* was opened and double-choir music was required

These elements have been correlated, and the results are displayed in Table V-4 (p. 216). Each feast for which the singers' presence was required is listed, and the presence of the Doge as well as the opening of the *Pala d'oro* is noted. The psalms prescribed by the *Orationale* are then listed for each Vespers at which *canto figurato* was sung. Finally, those collections of Grandi, Rovetta and Cavalli which satisfy all of the requirements for the feast are named.[379]

As might be expected, the results of such a tabulation are far from random. The *Orationale* prescribes 14 different sequences of psalms for the various feasts of the church year, and the published psalm collections are organized rather ingeniously so that they can accommodate 12 of these sequences both on occasions when the *Pala d'oro* is to be opened and when the *Pala* remains closed. The two remaining sequences involved special liturgical considerations and did not need to be sung in their entirety in *canto figurato*. These 14 sequences are treated below, one by one.[380]

Sequence I: Dixit Dominus, Confitebor,
Beatus vir, Laudate pueri, Laudate Dominum omnes gentes

The so-called male *cursus* is used in St. Mark's for First or Second Vespers, or both, on a number of major feasts of male saints. Since it is not part of the Common of Apostles and Evangelists, as it is in the Roman rite, it is used less often than it would be in the Roman liturgy; however, the *Orationale* specifies the male *cursus* on First Vespers of certain saints' days which would normally use the psalms in the Common of Apostles and Evangelists, so the use of the male *cursus* is not really as limited as one might be led to suspect. In fact, this is still the most important sequence in the *Orationale*. Its uses, however, are largely confined to the *Sanctorale*; while it has many uses in the *Temporale* of the Roman rite, these functions have been taken over by other sequences in St. Mark's.

When the *Pala d'oro* was closed, the psalms could be provided by the following collections: Grandi 1630/1, Grandi 1630/2, Rovetta 1627, Rovetta 1639, Rovetta 1642 and Cavalli 1656. These occasions included some of the most important saints' days in the church year, and it was clearly for such occasions as these that the most lavish music was written. Most of the items in Monteverdi's *Selva Morale* could also have been used on these days, although the largest works would surely have been performed only on the very few most important feasts.

On the four feasts which used this psalm sequence under an open *Pala d'oro* (First Vespers of the Nativity of St. John the Baptist, St. Magnus and St. Theodore; Second Vespers of the Ascension), the psalms could have been supplied by the following collections: Grandi 1629, Rovetta 1644, Rovetta 1662 and Cavalli 1675.

Sequence II: Dixit Dominus, Laudate pueri,
Laetatus sum, Nisi Dominus, Lauda Jerusalem

The female *cursus* was used in St. Mark's for at least one Vespers service on many feasts of the Virgin and for both Vespers on most feasts of female saints. It was displaced by the *Vespero delli Cinque Laudate* on First Vespers of four important Marian feasts: the Purification, the Assumption, the Nativity and the Immaculate Conception of the B. V. M. The female *cursus* was certainly the most important psalm sequence in St. Mark's after the male *cursus*; however, it seems to have been performed under the *Pala d'oro* more often than were the psalms for male saints. First and Second Vespers of the Annunciation, the Visitation, the Presentation and the Feast of St. Mary Magdalene, as well as Second Vespers of the Assumption, the Nativity and the Immaculate Conception of the B. V. M. all demanded the female *cursus* performed in double-choir settings. Single-choir settings were reserved for lesser Marian feasts or for the feasts of other female saints.

The female *cursus*, when performed without opening the *Pala d'oro*, could have been drawn from the same collections as the male *cursus*: Grandi 1630/1, Grandi 1630/2, Rovetta 1627, Rovetta 1639, Rovetta 1642 and Cavalli 1656. The psalms might also have been drawn from among the works in Monteverdi's posthumous *Messa a quattro Voci e Salmi*. If the *Pala d'oro* were opened, the psalms of the female *cursus* could be drawn from any of the following four collections: Grandi 1629, Rovetta 1644, Rovetta 1662 or Cavalli 1675.

Sequence III: Dixit Dominus, Laudate pueri,
Credidi, In convertendo, Domine probasti me

The *Orationale* prescribes these psalms for both Vespers of the Common of Apostles and Evangelists, although within the body of the *Sanctorale* these psalms are replaced by the male *cursus* on First Vespers of a number of feasts of these saints. If required without the opening of the *Pala d'oro*, these psalms could have been supplied by only one collection, Cavalli's *Musiche Sacre*. When the *Pala d'oro* was open, however, a number of collections could have provided the necessary psalms: Grandi 1629, Rovetta 1644, Rovetta 1662 or Cavalli 1675.

Sequence IV: Dixit Dominus, Confitebor,
Beatus vir, Laudate pueri, Credidi

These are the psalms from Second Vespers of the Common of One or More Martyrs in St. Mark's. First Vespers was usually supplied by the psalms of the male *cursus*. If the *Pala d'oro* were not open, the psalms might be drawn from any of three collections: Rovetta 1627, Rovetta 1639 or Cavalli 1656. If it were open, these psalms could be drawn from those four collections which have provided double-choir psalms for the sequences discussed previously: Grandi 1629, Rovetta 1644, Rovetta 1662 and Cavalli 1675. These psalms can also be found in Monteverdi's *Selva Morale*, but the settings involve both double-choir and single-choir idioms.

Sequence V: Dixit Dominus, Confitebor,
Beatus vir, Laudate pueri, Memento Domine David

The psalms for Second Vespers of the Common of a Confessor Bishop were used only six times during the church year. When the *Pala d'oro* was closed, the psalms could be drawn from only one source, Rovetta's *Messa e Salmi* of 1639. If the *Pala* was open, any of the four major sources of double-choir psalms could supply settings of the appropriate texts: Grandi 1629, Rovetta 1644, Rovetta 1662 and Cavalli 1675.[381] Like the psalms from the Common of Martyrs, these psalms can all be drawn from Monteverdi's *Selva Morale*, though in settings that mix single- and double-choir idioms.[382]

Sequence VI: Dixit Dominus, Confitebor,
Beatus vir, De profundis, Memento Domine David

These are the psalms for Second Vespers of Christmas. They are used on a number of feasts during the Christmas season—St. Stephen's Day, the feasts of St. John, the Holy Innocents and St. Silvester—and while they drop out of use in the Roman rite after the Feast of the Circumcision, St. Mark's retains them for Epiphany and repeats them as late as Second Vespers of the Feast of the Purification. Since there is no setting by Grandi, Rovetta or Cavalli (or, for that matter, by Monteverdi) of the *De profundis* for a single choir, one can produce a full service in *canto figurato* for double choir only. It can be drawn from any of the four large collections of double-choir psalms: Grandi 1629, Rovetta 1644, Rovetta 1662 or Cavalli 1675. All of the feasts for which this sequence is required demand the opening of the *Pala d'oro* except for the feasts of the Holy Innocents and St. Silvester. However, since the *De profundis* does not seem to have been set for a single choir at this time, double-choir settings may have been used on these two days as well.[383]

Sequence VII: Dixit Dominus, Confitebor,
Beatus vir, Laudate pueri, In exitu Israel

These are the psalms for Sunday, and they were also used for Second Vespers on major feasts which fell on Sundays, e.g. Easter, Ascension and Pentecost. The only collections from which all five psalms can be drawn are the four collections of psalms for two choirs: Grandi 1629, Rovetta 1644, Rovetta 1662 and Cavalli 1675. Certainly these collections were used on Easter, Ascension and Pentecost. We have no way of knowing, however, whether these settings would have been used regularly on ordinary Sundays. It is true that the singers were required to come to the basilica on Sundays, so some sort of *canto figurato* was probably used. However, the *Pala d'oro* was not opened on ordinary Sundays, and while double-choir psalms were required for those services sung under the *Pala d'oro*, it is difficult to tell whether such settings were restricted to those three dozen occasions per year when the *Pala d'oro* was opened. While the singers balked at singing *canto doppio* on the Feast of the Dedication of the Church of St. Mark's in 1589 and 1600, it is clear that their true objection was against singing *falsobordone* for the one psalm that had not been set for two choirs. Moreover, if the singers did not sing the Sunday psalms in double-choir settings, we must postulate the existence of single-choir settings for which we have no evidence.

Sequence VIII: Dixit Dominus, Confitebor
Beatus vir, Laudate pueri, Lauda Jerusalem

The psalms for First Vespers for the Dedication of the Church of St. Mark were sung but once a year, under the *Pala d'oro*. While the texts can be found in any of the prints of Grandi, Rovetta or Cavalli, the settings used were no doubt taken from the four double-choir collections.

Sequence IX: Credidi, Laetatus sum,
Nisi Dominus, Confitebor Angelorum, Lauda Jerusalem

This is the service which caused all the confusion in 1589 and to which the Procurators alluded in their inquest of 1600: Second Vespers for the Feast of the Dedication of the Church of St. Mark. Clearly, the service was not sung under the *Pala d'oro* at that time, although Pace states that the *Pala* is to be opened for both Vespers of this feast.[384] The psalms of this sequence are all found in two of the prints containing double-choir settings: Rovetta 1662 and Cavalli 1675.

Sequence X: Dixit Dominus, Confitebor,
Credidi, Beati omnes, Lauda Jerusalem

This sequence is used only once a year, on First Vespers for Corpus Christi. It is sung under the *Pala d'oro* and can be drawn from Grandi 1629, Rovetta 1644, Rovetta 1662 and Cavalli 1675.

Sequence XI: Levavi oculos meos, Ad te levavi,
De profundis, Memento Domine David, Laudate nomen Domini

This sequence for First Vespers of the Feast of the Holy Trinity was sung under the *Pala d'oro* during the seventeenth century, although the Procurators' inquest of 1600 revealed that it probably had not been sung that way in the sixteenth century.[385] Double-choir settings of the psalms can be found in only one publication, Rovetta's print of 1662.

Sequence XII: Laudate pueri, Laudate Dominum omnes gentes,
Lauda anima mea Dominum, Laudate Dominum quoniam bonus est,
Lauda Jerusalem

The *Vespero delli Cinque Laudate* was performed on the Vigils of Christmas, Epiphany, Ascension, Pentecost, the Purification, the Assumption,
the Nativity and Conception of the B. V. M. and of All Saints' Day; it
was also used for Second Vespers of Corpus Christi. It was always sung
under the *Pala d'oro*. The psalms are found in three collections only:
Rovetta 1644, Rovetta 1662 and Cavalli 1675.

Sequence XIII: Benedictus Dominus, Exaltabo te Deus meus,
Lauda anima mea, Laudate Dominum quoniam bonus est, Lauda
Jerusalem

These psalms are the ferial psalms for Saturday. They would have been
sung by the singers of the *cappella* during Lent, when they were required
to sing Saturday Vespers. Not all of these psalms exist in polyphonic
settings. The final three are, of course, part of the *Vespero delli Cinque
Laudate*, and double-choir settings of them exist by Rovetta and Cavalli.
There are no settings of the first two. However, during the Procurators'
inquest of 1600, when the singers were asked why they did not want to
sing four psalms in *canto figurato* and one in *falsobordone*, a number of
them replied that *falsobordone* was not used in the basilica except during
Lent (Documents 146 and 147). This is an important statement, for if
falsobordone was admissible during Lent, it could have been used to
perform those two psalms from Saturday Vespers which were not set in
canto figurato in the seventeenth century. Indeed, *Benedictus Dominus*
and *Exaltabo te Deus meus* may well have been the only two psalms for
which *falsobordone* was used in St. Mark's, although since the *Pala d'oro*
remained closed during Lent and Rovetta's and Cavalli's settings of the
three *Laudate* psalms are for double choir, it is possible that all five psalms
were chanted to *falsobordone* formulas.

Sequence XIV: Dixit Dominus, Beatus vir,
In convertendo, Eripe me Domine, Lauda Jerusalem

This sequence, which is used at Second Vespers on the feasts of Ss.
Hermagoras and Fortunatus and St. Clement, is the only one prescribed
for a major saint's day which cannot be drawn from the printed psalm
collections. The problematic text is, of course, the psalm *Eripe me Domine*, which seems not to have been set by composers from the basilica,

at least during the seventeenth century. However, singers were not required to be present at these two services, so all of the psalms must have been recited in plainchant on these occasions.

The import of this discussion should be clear. While there was a definite correspondence between the rank of a feast at St. Mark's and the style of music which was appropriate for that feast, the most important days of the year did not necessarily demand the most elaborate music. It was, rather, on these central days of the church year that the continuity of the musical tradition of the basilica was emphasized by the performance of psalms for double choir. The more elaborate settings in the *stile concertato* certainly had a prominent role in the ceremonial life of the basilica, for they would have been used on the many saints' days which dotted the calendar of the *Orationale*. Moreover, it is worth noting that the most elaborate service of the year, First Vespers on the Feast of St. Mark, was one on which the *Pala d'oro* was *not* opened but the treasury of the basilica displayed instead. Thus, the full resources of collections such as Monteverdi's *Selva Morale* or Cavalli's *Musiche Sacre* would have been appropriate for this service, and there is little doubt that the large pieces in these collections were probably composed for this very day. On the most solemn days of the year, however, the pull of tradition seems to have been more telling than elaborate display, and the greatest tribute which the *cappella marciana* could pay the city of Venice was to invoke the brilliant days of "Messer Adrian, Messer Ciprian, e'l Reverendissimo Padre Iseppo Zerlino" and to "cantare à due Chori con li Salmi à 8. li Vesperi."

Lest the reader complain that the above argument has been a bit too tight, a bit too rigid, and that all ambiguities in the documents have been dispatched in too cavalier a manner, I should hasten to add that the closed system I have outlined is no doubt an oversimplification and oversystematization of what in reality may have been a less rigid practice. I have taken the documents at face value and tried to come up with the simplest, most logical interpretation of the data in terms of extant musical sources. There are, however, certain lacunae in the information we possess on the use of music in the ceremonial life of the basilica, as well as certain ambiguities. Lest I be taken to task for ignoring these, let me outline some of the factors one might take into account if one had certain additional information, and some of the ways in which my scheme might be modified were one to take less of a "strict constructionist" view toward the documents.

The major lacuna with which one must contend is the lack of a definitive list of days and services for instrumentalists during the seventeenth century. For this information, we are dependent on the large calendar in Busta 91 of the archive of the Procuratia de Supra (A.S.V., San Marco), drawn up in 1515 and then revised in 1661, 1694 and 1761 (Document 143). As I have stated above, the information on the services at which the instrumentalists played cannot be considered accurate for the seventeenth century because of the focus upon the Mass rather than upon Vespers. While Selfridge-Field has noted that instrumentalists were generally present when the Doge attended services—and the Doge's presence or absence has been noted in Table V-4—this principle can be used as a guide in only the most general sense. However, we do have payment records for the employment of extra instrumentalists on a few major feasts of the year, and the correlation of these records with the psalm settings proper to the days in question indicates that the presence of instruments in church did *not* necessarily indicate that large *concertato* psalms with obbligato instrumental parts were performed.

The most blatant example involves music on the Vigil of the Ascension. Documents from the 1640s indicate that extra singers and instrumentalists were brought in regularly for First Vespers of the Ascension (see Documents 148 through 152). We know, however, that the *Pala d'oro* was opened for this service and that double-choir music was necessary. Moreover, the *Orationale* tells us that the *Cinque Laudate* were required for the service, and all of the extant settings of these psalms from the seventeenth century are for two four-part choirs and basso continuo, *without* parts for obbligato instruments. It seems, furthermore, that extra instrumentalists were also hired for First Vespers of Christmas, another feast for which the *Pala d'oro* was opened and the *Cinque Laudate* were sung.[386] There is nothing illogical about this situation; the instrumentalists could certainly have been brought in to participate in the large ensemble sonatas written at this time by some of the composers of the basilica— the large works which were eventually published in Massimiliano Neri's Opus 2 (1651) or Cavalli's *Musiche Sacre* are the most obvious possibilities. At any rate, the evidence suggests that the mere presence of instruments in the basilica on a specific feast does not necessarily indicate that musical settings involving instruments were used for the psalms.

Another piece of information we lack is an explanation of just what Pace meant by his phrase "cantare à due Chori con li Salmi à 8. li Vesperi." I have interpreted this phrase quite literally to refer to works for two four-part choirs and basso continuo. Certainly this is the only type of double-choir music written by the composers connected with St. Mark's which could have supplied settings for an entire Vespers service on the various occasions when the *Pala d'oro* was opened. The three extant settings by Rovetta and Cavalli of the *Cinque Laudate* are set for this medium, and we know from the *Orationale* and various liturgical calendars that all of the feasts for which the *Cinque Laudate* were required were also feasts on which the *Pala d'oro* was opened. It is clear, therefore, that the three simple, double-choir settings of these psalms by Rovetta and Cavalli were written for performance under the *Pala d'oro*, and it stands to reason that the other items in the collections—all composed for the same forces and in the same style as the *Cinque Laudate*—were also written for these occasions. However, these might not be the only compositions which could have been performed under the *Pala d'oro*. There are isolated compositions by Grandi, Rovetta and Cavalli—as well as by Monteverdi—which can be considered double-choir music in a more general sense; these pieces may have filled the bill for Pace as "Salmi à 8," although they certainly have little to do with the idiom of *salmi spezzati* developed by Willaert and echoed in the double-choir Vespers collections of Grandi, Rovetta and Cavalli.

The works of which I am speaking are of two types. Some are large *concertato* works which, almost incidentally, happen to be set for eight voices, obbligato instruments and basso continuo. In this category fall the two settings of *Dixit Dominus*, two of *Laudate Dominum omnes gentes*, and one of the Magnificat from Monteverdi's *Selva Morale*; the first setting of *Dixit Dominus* from Monteverdi's *Messa a quattro Voci e Salmi* (which also appears, recomposed, as one of the settings in the *Selva Morale*); the Magnificat from Rovetta's *Messa e Salmi* of 1639; and the settings of *Dixit Dominus, Confitebor, Laudate Dominum omnes gentes, Lauda Jerusalem* and the Magnificat from Cavalli's *Musiche Sacre*.[387] The others are works for four voices and basso continuo with an optional four-part choir which can be used *ad libitum*. Settings of *Dixit Dominus, Beatus vir, Laudate pueri, Laudate Dominum, Nisi Dominus* and *Lauda Jerusalem* from Leonardo Simonetti's *Raccolta Terza* of the music of Grandi are all in this category. Could works such as these be used to satisfy the liturgical need for double-choir psalms on those occasions when the *Pala d'oro* was opened? Clearly, the answer to this question is complex, and the two categories of compositions must really be considered separately.

The main barrier to using the works in the first category to satisfy the requirements for double-choir music is the fact that no composer seems to have set a complete Vespers service in this style. The most complete service could be drawn from Cavalli's *Musiche Sacre*, in which the first, second and last psalms of the male *cursus* ·as well as the Magnificat are set in this style. One can also draw the first and last psalms of the female *cursus* from Cavalli's print, and the first and last psalms of the male *cursus* as well as the Magnificat from Monteverdi's *Selva Morale*. Perhaps the performance of the first and fifth psalms plus the Magnificat in large *concertato* settings for double choir was considered a sufficient "tip of the hat" to the polychoral tradition of St. Mark's to allow these settings to be performed on the days when the *Pala d'oro* was opened. The intermediate psalms, however, would have had to be performed in single-choir settings, for we know of no double-choir settings in this style of *Beatus vir*,[388] *Laetatus sum, Nisi Dominus* or *Laudate pueri*—to mention only those psalms necessary to fill out the male and female *cursus*. While one must consider the possibility that not all Vespers psalms were performed in *canto figurato* on every feast, we have no archival data stating that such mixed performances were a feature at St. Mark's as they were at such provincial churches as San Petronio, Bologna, or Santa Maria Maggiore, Bergamo.[389]

The psalms in the second category share the problem of incompleteness for the male *cursus* only; Simonetti has included the complete female *cursus* in settings for four obbligato voices and four voices which constitute a *ripieno* choir to be used *ad libitum*. Certainly, these are "salmi à 8" in the strictest sense, but they have little to do with the traditional idiom of *salmi spezzati* since the obbligato choir sings throughout and the second choir enters only at climactic moments to "far maggior li ripieni"—to use a phrase of Cavalli. On the surface, it seems that a collection such as this would be optimum for St. Mark's, for the works could be adjusted to single-choir or double-choir settings according to the dictates of the church calendar. However, since collections such as this were popular throughout Northern Italy in the early seventeenth century, there is some doubt that the idiom was chosen with the liturgical requirements of St. Mark's in mind.

One further point needs to be discussed here. There are actually two types of Vespers collections published during the seventeenth century, and one must distinguish between them in discussing the liturgical propriety of an entire publication. The first type is a collection which is clearly designed as a liturgical unit in terms of the texts set, of the musical forces employed, and of the musical style of the compositions. The collections of double-choir psalms published by Rovetta in 1644 and 1662 and by Cavalli in 1675 are the purest examples of this genre, though Grandi's 1629 collection also fits in if one discounts the two psalms in the *stile concertato* which form a supplement to the basic body of the print. Grandi's *Messa e salmi concertati a tre voci* (1630) and Rovetta's *Salmi a tre a quattro voci* (1642) are also conceived as liturgical units. Moreover, one can include Rovetta's large *Messa e Salmi* (1639) if one forgives one stylistically anomalous *Beatus vir*; and one can include Cavalli's *Musiche Sacre* which, despite the disparity of the forces for which its contents are scored, is a stylistically unified body of music.

The second type of collection is one which seems to have been assembled out of miscellaneous items for varying forces and in various musical styles which probably never rubbed shoulders in an actual Vespers service—at least not in a church where musical style had the implications it did in St. Mark's. These collections are not easy to detect from their tables of contents, for publishers tried to assemble works which would form a liturgical unit, even if they crossed stylistic categories. Rovetta's *Salmi concertati* (1627) is in this category, for it was rushed into print when he became a candidate for *vice-maestro di cappella*, and while the individual items were certainly part of the repertory of St. Mark's, it is doubtful that an entire service was drawn from the volume. Similarly, Monteverdi's *Selva Morale* and *Messa a quattro Voci e Salmi* are not stylistically unified and combine works which probably would not have formed a single service in St. Mark's. This is obvious in the case of the *Messa a quattro Voci e Salmi*, for Vincenti states that these are miscellaneous works which he was able to collect "non senza miracolo" after Monteverdi's death. The works in the *Selva Morale* form less of a stylistic hodge-podge, but certainly the settings of *Credidi* and *Memento Domine David*, labeled "a 8 voci da Capella," were not combined with the more elaborate works to form Vespers for the Commons of Martyrs and of Confessor Bishops. Most likely these two works were combined with other compositions in the same style to form complete services for double choir which could have been used when the *Pala d'oro* was open. While Giuseppe Biella has pointed out that the inclusion of these two psalms makes the collection a complete compendium of the psalms from the Commons for the major saints' days,[390] I doubt that the psalms were ever combined in this manner in St. Mark's and would suggest, rather, that these two psalms were included to make a liturgically complete collection, all of whose works were by Monteverdi.[391]

Because of its stylistic heterogeneity, Rovetta's collection of 1627 could really have been omitted from Table V-4. Similarly, Grandi's *Messa e salmi concertati a tre voci* (1630) could have been omitted, for it is the one collection we are sure he composed after he left St. Mark's and, as we shall see below, it represents a medium not commonly found among psalm settings for the basilica. I have included these two collections merely for the sake of having all 10 psalm collections of Grandi, Rovetta and Cavalli represented in the table. Indeed, they do satisfy the requirements of St. Mark's for a number of feasts, although I feel it is unlikely they were actually used in the basilica.

Musical Style and Liturgical Function

The stylistic plurality of sacred music of the early *seicento* is a phenomenon which seems to have baffled theorists of the time no less than it fascinates scholars today. Italian theorists appear to have ignored the problem almost entirely, something which is not surprising since much seventeenth-century Italian theory is retrospective in the fullest sense and pays only lip service to musical developments which cannot be explained in terms of Zarlino. Writers who did try to grapple with the problems of genre and terminology, such as Praetorius, often found that the imprecision of descriptive titles of sacred works—*concerti ecclesiastici, motetti concertati, symphoniae sacrae*—did not allow for a system of strict Aristotelian categorization. And, indeed, discussions of sacred music in the seventeenth century which go beyond a mere list of generic titles are few.

Perhaps the best of the early attempts to impose a theoretical order on the world of sacred music in the *seicento* came from Marco Scacchi, *maestro di cappella* in Warsaw from 1628 to 1649, although an Italian by birth and training. While his system was later elaborated by theorists such as Angelo Berardi in Italy and Christoph Bernhard in Germany, Scacchi's is the earliest major attempt to categorize the entire spectrum of styles present in sacred music of the seventeenth century.[392] Scacchi's largest division contains the three basic categories of music for church, music for the chamber and music for the theater. Each of these categories is then divided into smaller ones, with church music divided into four different styles:[393]

1. Masses, motets and similar works for four, five, six and eight voices without organ

2. The same types of works with organ or for several choirs and organ

3. The same types of works *in concerto*

4. Motets written according to the modern style

Scacchi gives a set of principles for composing in each of his four styles, although his view of the idioms is rather strict and academic.

To a certain extent, Scacchi's categories can be applied to the music composed for the liturgy of St. Mark's, although their essential ambiguity causes certain difficulties. In a certain sense, no composition of the early *seicento* at St. Mark's fits into Scacchi's first category, for every work in the published collections of Grandi, Rovetta, Cavalli and Monteverdi has

an organ part, even if it be merely a *basso seguente*. If one modifies
Scacchi's category a bit to include works which are clearly in the *stile
antico* tradition and notated *alla breve* even if they do contain an organ
part (and from the compositional principles he enumerates, this does seem
to be the type of work which Scacchi has in mind), a number of works
fall into this category. The two *stile antico* Masses from Monteverdi's
Selva Morale and *Messa a quattro Voci e Salmi* are the two most obvious
examples; indeed, the *Selva Morale* Mass fits Scacchi's rigid, limited description of the style rather closely. One could also include Monteverdi's
Magnificat secondo a quattro voci in genere da Capella (Selva Morale),
the Magnificat à 5 of Rovetta preserved in manuscript in Biblioteca Nazionale Marciana,[394] and the settings of *Confitebor* and *Nisi Dominus*,
both marked "A 5 voci alla breve," from Rovetta's *Salmi concertati* of
1627. From this point, one begins to run into difficulties. Since Scacchi
allows works in the first category to be as large as eight voices, one could
presumably include the setting of *Credidi à 8 voci da Capella* from the
Selva Morale as well as the *Dixit à 8 voci alla breve* from the *Messa a
quattro Voci e Salmi*. Similarly, one could include the works from Rovetta's *Delli Salmi à 8. voci/Accomodati da cantarsi alla Breve*. What does
one do, however, with the Magnificat which ends this collection as well
as the *Memento à 8 voci da Capella* from Monteverdi's *Selva Morale*, or
Rovetta's entire psalm collection of 1644? All of these works are notated
for eight voices, but they are notated *alla semibreve* (Scacchi says that
all compositions in his first category are to be notated *alla breve*); moreover, they are in a style decidedly more modern than the rest of the
compositions mentioned above. Perhaps these would fall into Scacchi's
second category along with a number of works of Monteverdi which,
although they do not involve soloists or double-choir distribution, are
nonetheless notated *alla semibreve* and are not nearly as austere as the
works in the true *stile antico*; the *Laudate pueri secondo* from the *Selva
Morale* and the *Laudate pueri a 5 voci da Capella* from the *Messa a
quattro Voci e Salmi* are the clearest examples.

There are similar ambiguities in Scacchi's third and fourth categories
when applied to the music of St. Mark's. In short, while it is easy enough
to identify motets in the modern soloistic vocal style (virtually any of the
motets in Rovetta's four books) and works *in concerto* (virtually any of
the large works for vocalists and instruments in Monteverdi's *Selva Morale* or Cavalli's *Musiche Sacre*), the two styles are hardly mutually exclusive. Indeed, a work such as the *Nisi Dominus* from the *Musiche Sacre*,
which is scored for four solo voices, two violins, *violoncino* and basso
continuo, and which uses the most extreme chromaticism and dissonance
for the alto-tenor duet on "Qui manducatis panem doloris," is very much

a work *in concerto* which uses all of the harmonic license which Scacchi attributes to works in the modern vocal style.[395] In other words, this is a composition which straddles Scacchi's last two categories completely. Of course, Scacchi does not say that a composition must fall into only one category; his system is more of an abstract typology of style. Nonetheless, the ambiguity shows that one cannot really use his system as a guide for examining the music connected with St. Mark's, although his categories certainly have much to offer insofar as they focus our attention on certain key compositional elements.

One element which must clearly have higher priority in a stylistic typology designed expressly for music at St. Mark's is the basic medium of a work. The most important consideration, of course, is the simple question of single-choir or double-choir setting; for the basic medium in these cases would have determined the entire range of feasts for which a psalm setting was suitable. However, the distinction between large-scale *concertato* works and small-scale motets—a distinction suggested but never made entirely clear in Scacchi's system—is equally important, for such considerations would have determined the place in the church from which the work could have been performed. Thus, I would suggest the following typology for the music of the composers of St. Mark's during the middle decades of the *seicento*:

Works Involving Two Choirs

1. Large-scale *concertato* works à 8

    Works such as the *Dixit Dominus, Laudate Dominum* and Magnificat settings from Monteverdi's *Selva* and *Messa.... e Salmi*; the same items plus *Lauda Jerusalem* and *Confitebor* from Cavalli's *Musiche Sacre*; and the Magnificat from Rovetta's *Messa e Salmi* of 1639. In the 10 psalm collections of Grandi, Rovetta and Cavalli as well as the 2 Venetian sacred collections of Monteverdi, there are only 13 compositions of this magnitude.

2. *Salmi spezzati*, i.e. works for two four-part choirs and basso continuo; these can be divided into two groups:

    a. Works notated *alla breve*

        Rovetta's collection of 1662; Cavalli's *Vesperi* of 1675; the second *Dixit* from Monteverdi's *Messa.... e Salmi* and the *Credidi* from the *Selva Morale*.

b.   Works notated *alla semibreve*

Grandi's collection of 1629; Rovetta's collection of 1644; the *Memento* from Monteverdi's *Selva Morale*; in both Grandi's and Rovetta's collections, the idioms of the two choirs are distinct, one choir of soloists, one *ripieno* choir.

Grandi's setting of *Nativitas tua* (*Motetti, Libro I*, 1610)

3.   Works with *ad libitum* choirs

Grandi's works in Simonetti's *Raccolta Terza* of 1630; the *Confitebor Primo à 3 voci con 5 altre ne' ripieni* in Monteverdi's *Selva Morale*. I think, moreover, that the *Lauda Jerusalem à 3 voci* from Monteverdi's *Messa.... e Salmi* may originally have had a *ripieno* choir which was omitted in publication.

Works Involving a Single Group of Musicians

4.   Large-scale *concertato* works à 6 and à 7

Nisi Dominus à 6 and the two settings of *Beatus vir* à 6 and à 7 from Monteverdi's late collections; the *Credidi* à 6 and the Magnificat à 6 from Rovetta's collection of 1627; and almost the whole of Rovetta's collection of 1639. Cavalli's 1651 Magnificat. Monteverdi's *Letaniae della Beata Vergine* (*Messa.... e Salmi*) and motet *Cantate Domino* (Bianchi's *Motetti, Libro I*, 1620).

5.   Small-scale concertato works à 2 to à 5 with *sinfonie* for instruments

Smaller settings from the two late collections of Monteverdi and from Cavalli's *Musiche Sacre*; Rovetta's entire collection of 1642, with the exception of the monodic *Laudate Dominum*.

Grandi's motets from the 1620s; hymn settings by Cavalli.

6.   Small-scale *concertato* works à 2 to à 5 without *sinfonie* for instruments

Grandi's *Messa e salmi concertati a tre voci* (1630); *Dixit, Beatus vir, Lauda Jerusalem* from Rovetta's collection of 1627; *In convertendo* from Cavalli's *Musiche Sacre*; smaller settings without instruments from the two late collections of Monteverdi.

Grandi's motets before the 1620's and his *Sesto Libro* (1629); Rovetta's four books of *motetti concertati*; Monteverdi's motets published in anthologies; many Marian antiphon settings by all four composers.

7. Choral compositions for a single choir

    a. Works notated *alla breve*

        Monteverdi's *Magnificat secondo* in the *Selva Morale*; Rovetta's manuscript Magnificat in the Biblioteca Nazionale Marciana.

    b. Works notated *alla semibreve*

        Large motets of Monteverdi's in anthologies which seem to be clearly choral in idiom; the most obvious are *Domine ne in furore* à 6, *Christe adoramus te* à 5, and *Adoramus te Christe* à 6, all from Bianchi's *Motetti*, Libro I, 1620. Less clearcut cases: *Laetatus sum* à 5 (*Messa.... e Salmi*), *Laudate pueri secondo* à 5 (*Selva Morale*).

8. Liturgical monodies

    Monteverdi's *Pianto della Madonna* and solo *Laudate Dominum* settings, as well as miscellaneous solo hymns from anthologies; Grandi's *Motetti à voce sola* (1621) plus solo motets from other collections of the 1620s; Rovetta's solo *Laudate Dominum* from the psalm collection of 1642; Cavalli's *O quam suavis* and *Cantate Domino*, printed in anthologies.

Examples of works in all eight of the stylistic categories discussed above are included in the body of transcriptions which forms Volume II of this study. The complete contents of this volume are tabulated in Table V-5 (p. 229), not in the order in which the transcriptions appear but, rather, according to the eight categories of musical style which summarize the idioms employed by the composers of the basilica in the *seicento*.

The basic truth which one can draw from the stylistic typology which I have postulated, and from the tabulation of representative works in each group, is quite simple. The kaleidoscope of musical idioms used by the composers associated with the basilica were not drawn upon in a random or haphazard manner. While a collection like the *Selva Morale* might seem to be a stylistic hodge-podge, there is an underlying rationale for its stylistic plurality, and that rationale is liturgical function. Moreover, this factor seems to have been a crucial determinant of musical style on a temporal basis as well. That is, there were two elements which any composer connected with the basilica had to consider before setting a Vespers text: first, the liturgical identity of the text and how it would fit into the service; and, second, the temporal propriety of the composition and how it would fit into the liturgical year as a whole. This principle is not as self-evident as it might sound, for while liturgical function is an obvious determinant of musical style in certain other repertoires—plain-chant, for example—its role as a guide to composers in St. Mark's in the *seicento* has been camouflaged by the nature of the most important collections of the period, Monteverdi's *Selva Morale* and *Messa a quattro Voci e Salmi*. That the latter collection is not a liturgical unit is obvious, for it was a posthumous publication assembled by Vincenti. However, despite Giuseppe Biella's insistence that the *Selva Morale* represents a unified body of materials for use on the feasts of major saints, the jarring juxtaposition of elaborate works in the *stile concertato*, many of them in settings for a single body of musicians, with *salmi spezzati* for days when the *Pala d'oro* was opened argues against the actual use of this collection as a whole within the liturgical strictures of St. Mark's. While other composers occasionally published such stylistically heterogeneous collections (Rovetta's *Salmi concertati* of 1627 is the best example), there usually seems to have been some external set of circumstances to prompt such a publication. The majority of collections associated with St. Mark's are unified from both a stylistic and liturgical point of view. The two Venetian sacred collections of Monteverdi are, indeed, atypical; the collections of Grandi, Rovetta and Cavalli give us a more accurate picture of the position of music in Venetian liturgy.

The segregation of liturgical items in the nine categories of my typology is more complete in the large-scale idioms than in the smaller ones. Of the large-scale *concertato* works for eight voices (category 1), all are settings of psalms or of the Magnificat. It is particularly significant that the other liturgical items are never set in this manner. Hymns, Marian antiphons, and psalm and Magnificat antiphons were always set for smaller, more intimate forces. The elaborate settings of Magnificat antiphons which one finds in the works of Giovanni Gabrieli and the elaborate double-choir setting of *Ave maris stella* from Monteverdi's 1610 *Vespers* are among the last large-scale settings of these items, not only by composers from St. Mark's but among northern Italian composers on the whole.[396] Similarly, after the first decade of the century, the medium of two four-part choirs and basso continuo (category 2) is limited to settings of psalms and Magnificats. Grandi's *Nativitas tua*, a setting of the Magnificat antiphon for the Feast of the Immaculate Conception of the B. V. M., appears here as the last relic of a dying genre. It recalls the double-choir idiom of Croce and the earlier works of Giovanni Gabrieli and it is significant that the work was published in Grandi's first motet collection (1610) and, thus, might well have been composed under the tutelage of Croce or Gabrieli during the period when Grandi was a *giovane di coro* at St. Mark's. None of the later motets of Grandi nor any of the motets of Rovetta or Cavalli employs the idiom of *cori spezzati*. This idiom survives into the late seventeenth century at St. Mark's, but only associated with psalm and Magnificat texts, i.e. only to fulfill the liturgical requirements of singing "à dui Cori con li Salmi à 8" on the occasions when the *Pala d'oro* is opened. Indeed, the perfunctory character of the works of Rovetta's collection of 1662 or Cavalli's of 1675 seems to indicate that both composers were fully aware of the fact that they were fulfilling a liturgical duty by composing music in a deliberately archaic style for a medium which was no longer in vogue.

The medium of solo voices combined with a *ripieno* choir (category 3) is also one which is limited to settings of psalms and Magnificats in St. Mark's. In this case, the liturgical limitation is but a reflection of the practice outside Venice, for important psalm collections of Viadana, Giacobbi, Ghizzolo and Ignazio Donati all employ this medium. Moreover, within St. Mark's, Giovanni Croce and Marc'Antonio Negri had composed important collections of psalms for this flexible combination of forces. Like the large motets written for *cori spezzati*, this idiom was somewhat out of vogue in St. Mark's after the first years in the century. Rovetta and Cavalli never touched it, and we have only one work of Monteverdi which is definitely in this idiom, the *Confitebor Primo à 3 voci con 5 altre ne' ripieni* from the *Selva Morale*. I would suggest, however, that a second work of Monteverdi was originally written for soloists and a *ripieno* choir but that only the solo parts survive. The *Lauda Jerusalem à 3 voci* from the *Messa.... e Salmi* is written in a suspicious refrain form, a formal structure which is often employed in works with optional *ripieno* choirs, where the extra choir is brought in to bolster the refrain while the soloists have the non-repetitive episodes to themselves. In Monteverdi's setting of *Lauda Jerusalem*, there are eight musical sections. The odd-numbered sections employ a virtuoso solo idiom associated with the *concertato* madrigal and early Venetian opera, and new musical material is used for each section of the text. The even-numbered sections, on the contrary, have musical material which is virtually identical, varied only to accommodate the text and to insure a weighty final cadence at the end of the doxology. The music in these sections consists of sustained block chords, an idiom more suited to performance by an ensemble which has more than one voice to a part. Moreover, many of the chords are incomplete, lacking either the third or the fifth above the bass. It is precisely in passages such as these that *ripieno* choirs tend to be added to bolster the texture, and I would suggest that Monteverdi's *Lauda Jerusalem* may have originally been composed as just this sort of work. Since its publication was posthumous, Vincenti was certainly free to present the work with only the essential musical parts intact.

Thus, double-choir settings are always associated with the central items of Vespers in St. Mark's during the 1620s and the following decades. Be they pieces in the large-scale *concertato* idiom, the old-fashioned medium of *salmi spezzati*, or the mixed medium "with detachable parts," they are used only for the texts of psalms or Magnificats, never for other liturgical items. As I demonstrated above, a composer's choice among these idioms was probably dictated by the liturgical calendar, and if an entire Vespers service was to be set for two choirs, the anachronistic idiom of *salmi spezzati* was inevitably the one to be chosen. On the other hand, the settings in the *stile concertato* for eight voices are generally limited to only four items: *Dixit Dominus*, the opening psalm of both the male and female *cursus*; *Laudate Dominum omnes gentes*, the final psalm of the male *cursus*; *Lauda Jerusalem*, the final psalm of the female *cursus*; and the Magnificat. Cavalli's setting of the *Confitebor* is the one exception to this rule, although it is perhaps significant that while Cavalli sanctions vocal *ripieni* for his settings of the other works in this style, the *Confitebor* is specifically marked "senza ripieni e senz'altri Istrumenti."

The works set for a single choir—or, to be more accurate, a single body of musicians—encompass a greater variety of liturgical items; and yet, here too there is a strong correlation between specific musical styles, specific mediums and the liturgical position of the texts that are set. Most of the large works for six and seven voices in the *stile concertato* (category 4) are still psalms and Magnificats. Monteverdi has one setting of *Nisi Dominus* and two of *Beatus vir* for these forces. Moreover, Rovetta's *Credidi* and Magnificat from his collection of 1627 are both *concertato* works in six parts, and almost the entirety of his *Messa e Salmi* of 1639 is set for these forces. A few motets are set for these forces as well: Monteverdi's impressive litany setting (*Messa.... e Salmi*) and his *Cantate Domino* from Bianchi's anthology (1620). These, however, are somewhat exceptional; motet texts are generally reserved for smaller forces still.

The division between "large-scale" and "small-scale" *concertato* works is, naturally, somewhat arbitrary. However, I have set six voices as the lower limit of the "large" and five voices as the upper limit of the "small" for specific reasons. In Cavalli's *Musiche Sacre*, there seems to be a determined effort to contrast large, eight-voice settings for the first psalm, last psalm and Magnificat with smaller settings for the middle three psalms. The middle three psalms are all set for three, four and five voices. Moreover, five voices is the upper limit for all of Grandi's motets, except for the early *Nativitas tua* discussed above. The small *concertato* pieces scored for two to five voices, either with or without obbligato instruments, form the categories which are the most inclusive from a liturgical point of view (categories 5 and 6). Psalms and Magnificats are set for these forces, as is the bulk of the motet repertoire of Grandi and Rovetta. Hymns and Marian antiphons are also set in this style, although the hymns almost always involve instruments which play *ritornelli* between the verses (which, as we have seen, may sometimes take the place of stanzas of text) whereas the Marian antiphons are traditionally set as austere motets for voices and basso continuo which seldom involve obbligato instruments.[397]

Category 7 is small and consists of but a few single-choir works whose idiom is clearly choral rather than soloistic. The only works notated *alla breve* are the two simple Magnificats by Monteverdi and Rovetta. There is a broader variety of texts set *alla semibreve* in this style. The para-liturgical motets by Monteverdi are actually somewhat exceptional. We have no equivalent works in this style by Grandi, Rovetta or Cavalli, and Monteverdi's style in these large five- and six-voice works is really closer to that of the 1610 *Vespers* than to the styles in his Venetian sacred collections.

The liturgical monodies (category 8) cannot all be dated, but those in Grandi's collections seem to date primarily from the 1620s. Arnold has suggested that the vogue for the solo vocal motet at this time was related to the increase in the number of virtuoso *castrati* hired by the *cappella marciana* during these years,[398] although like the other mediums current at the time, the solo motet was not used indiscriminately but was considered particularly appropriate for certain items in the liturgy. Along with the many non-liturgical items which were set as monodies as well as the hymns in Monteverdi's *Selva Morale*, there are two rather unusual settings of *Laudate Dominum omnes gentes*, the final psalm in the male *cursus*. One is a setting by Monteverdi for bass and continuo, which appears in 1651 in both the *Messa.... e Salmi* and in Gasparo Casati's *Raccolta di motetti à 1, 2, 3 voci*. The other is Rovetta's setting for alto, two violins and continuo in his collection of 1642.[399] Both settings are virtuoso display pieces and are totally out of character with the psalms which precede them in the collections. It is almost certain that these psalms were not used as the final item in a normal Vespers service but, rather, for the special Vespers of Holy Saturday which consisted of this single psalm sung under a full set of five antiphons.[400] The organization of Rovetta's collection supports this view, for it is liturgically complete without this extra setting of *Laudate Dominum*. Documents also support this hypothesis, for the Vespers of Holy Saturday are not found on the extant lists of singers' duties until 1755. If any sort of concerted music were to be used for *Laudate Dominum* on Holy Saturday, it would have to be for some medium which did not involve the full *cappella*, and a setting for a single voice would certainly have filled the requirements in the easiest manner.

The foregoing material can be summarized succinctly by a number of principles which, while not without exceptions, were generally valid in St. Mark's during the mid-seventeenth century. Psalms and Magnificats could be set in virtually any style: in the large-scale *concertato* for single or double choir; in the small-scale *concertato* for a single group of voices and instruments; as *salmi spezzati* either in a retrospective style notated *alla breve* or in a more contemporary style notated *alla semibreve*; and as works for a set of soloists plus an *ad libitum* choir. Magnificats were also set for a single choir notated *alla breve*, and at least one psalm, *Laudate Dominum omnes gentes*, was regularly set as a monody. Motets were never set for double choir after the opening of the century and seldom set for large forces at all. The most common distribution of parts was for two to five voices, either with or without obbligato instruments—almost always specified as two violins. While such items as psalm or Magnificat antiphons might be set as any sort of motet, special traditions existed for hymns and Marian antiphons. The former almost always were set with instrumental *ritornelli* between the verses; the latter seldom incorporated obbligato instrumental parts. While the style of motets does not seem to have varied much with the liturgical calendar, the style of psalms was totally dependent on the exigencies of liturgical temporality. The major dichotomy was, of course, one between works for a single body of musicians and those for double choir, mediums which would have been appropriate on entirely different sets of feasts during the year. Thus, the *Orationale* really wielded more power than its modest size would ever suggest; for its contents determined not only which texts would be set by the composers of the basilica but, in a very real sense, the forces for which they would be set and the musical styles which could be employed.

Thus, all of the elements of a Vespers service at St. Mark's were correlated: liturgy, ceremony, art and music. The service was clearly a *Gesamtkunstwerk* in the fullest sense. And yet, it was a special kind of art work in which the past was evoked at every turn. One has only to reflect, for example, that when the *Vespero delli Cinque Laudate* was performed under the *Pala d'oro* in settings for *cori spezzati*, the entire Venetian cultural heritage was on display. A liturgy taken from Aquileia was performed under the sign of artwork taken from Byzantium using a style of music which recalled the greatest days of the Venetian musical establishment. And surely, in the minds of the Venetians for whom the *seicento* was a politically and economically unsettling time to live, the entire service was a comforting symbol of the past glories of the *Serenissima Repubblica*.

Table V-1
Modal Designations for Compositions
in the Four Collections of *Salmi Spezzati*
of Grandi, Rovetta and Cavalli

Liturgical Item	Grandi 1629	Rovetta 1644	Rovetta 1662	Cavalli 1675
Domine ad adiuvandum	[1]ᵃ	—	—	—
Dixit Dominus	1	8	[8]	1, 5
Confitebor	2	2	2	2
Beatus vir	3	3	3	5
Laudate pueri	4	1	[2], 5	2, 4, [2]
Laudate Dominum omnes	6	4	5, 1	3, 8
In exitu	P	P	P	P
Laetatus sum	2	4	6	3
Nisi Dominus	4ᵇ	1ᶜ	1	4
Lauda Jerusalem	8	2	4, 8	5, 5
Credidi	4	6	2	2
In convertendo	2	8	8	8
Domine probasti me	1	5	[1]	5
De profundis	7	4	4	7
Beati omnes	1	8	6	6
Memento	3	5	1	1
Lauda anima mea	—	8	1	1
Laudate Dominum quoniam	—	6	8	3
Confitebor Angelorum	—	—	—ᵈ	8
Magnificat	2	3	2	6, 5, 3

ᵃFigures in brackets represent modes which are not designated in the print but which can be determined from the musical setting.

ᵇListed as *Quinti toni* in the print, but seems to be mode IV from musical analysis.

ᶜListed as *Sesto Tuono* in the print, but seems to be mode I from musical analysis.

ᵈFour psalms appear in this print without basso continuo and, hence, without modal designation: *Confitebor Angelorum*, *Lévavi oculos meos*, *Ad te levavi*, and *Laudate nomen Domini*.

Table V-2

Days on Which the Singers Were Required
to Attend Services in St. Mark's

Feast	Mass	Vespers	Procession	Doge
Circumcision (1 January)	x	1, 2		x
Epiphany (6 January)	x	1, 2		x
Lorenzo Giustiniani (8 January)	x	1, 2		x
St. Anthony, Abbot (17 January)	x	1, 2		
Ss. Fabian and Sebastian (20 January)	x	1, 2		
Conversion of St. Paul (25 January)	x	1, 2		
Translation of the Body of St. Mark (31 January)	x	1, 2		
Purification (2 February)	x	1, 2		x
St. Peter's Chair at Antioch (22 February)	x	1, 2		
Gerard of Csanad (24 February)	x	2		
St. Matthias (25 February)	x	2		
St. Gregory (12 March)	x	1, 2		
St. Joseph (19 March)	x	1, 2		
St. Benedict, Abbot (21 March)	x	1, 2		
Annunciation (25 March)	x	1, 2	—[a]	x
Third Thursday in March (Most Holy Blood)			—[b]	
Translation of St. Isidore (16 April)	x	1, 2	x	x
St. George (23 April)	x	1, 2	x	x
St. Mark (25 April)	x	1, 2		x
Ss. Philip and James (1 May)	x	1, 2		x
Finding of the Holy Cross (3 May)		1	—[c]	
St. John before the Latin Gate (6 May)	x	1, 2		
Apparition of St. Michael, Archangel (8 May)	x	1		
Nativity of St. Isidore (15 May)	x	1, 2		
St. Bernardine of Siena (20 May)	x	1, 2		
St. Barnabas (11 June)	x	1, 2		
St. Anthony of Padua (13 June)	x	1, 2	x	x
Ss. Vitus and Modestus (15 June)	x	1, 2	x	x
Nativity of St. John the Baptist (24 June)	x	1, 2		
Apparition of the Body of St. Mark (25 June)	x	2[d]	x	x
Ss. John and Paul (26 June)	x		x	
Ss. Peter and Paul (29 June)	x	1, 2		
Commemoration of St. Paul (30 June)	x			
Visitation (2 July)	x	1, 2		
St. Paternian (10 July)	x			
Ss. Hermagoras and Fortunatus (12 July)	x	1		
St. Marina (17 July)	x	1, 2	x	x
St. Mary Magdalene (22 July)	x	1, 2		
St. James (25 July)	x	1, 2		

Feast	Mass	Vespers	Procession	Doge
St. Anne (26 July)	x	2		
Third Sunday in July *(Redentore)*			—e	
St. Peter's Chains (1 August)	x	1		
Our Lady of the Snow (5 August)	x	1, 2		
Transfiguration of Our Lord (6 August)	x	1, 2		
St. Lawrence (10 August)	x	1, 2		
Assumption (15 August)	x	1, 2		x
St. Roche (16 August)	x	1, 2		
St. Bartholomew (24 August)	x	1, 2		
St. Augustine (28 August)	x	1, 2		
Beheading of St. John the Baptist (29 August)	x	2		
Nativity of the B. V. M. (8 September)	x	1, 2		x
Exaltation of the Holy Cross (14 September)	x	1, 2		
St. Victor (18 September)	x	1		
St. Matthew (21 September)	x	1, 2		
Dedication, Church of St. Michael Archangel (29 September)	x	1, 2		
St. Jerome (30 September)	x	2		
St. Francis (4 October)	x	1, 2		
St. Magnus (6 October)	x	1, 2		
St. Giustina (7 October)	x	—f	x	
Dedication of the Church of St. Mark (8 October)	x	1, 2		x
Sergius and Bacchus (9 October)	x			
St. Luke (18 October)	x	1, 2		
Ss. Simon and Jude (20 October)	x	1, 2		
All Saints Day (1 November)	x	1, 2		x
All Souls Day (2 November)	x		x	
St. Leonardo (6 November)	x	1, 2		
St. Theodore (9 November)	x	1, 2		
St. Martin (11 November)	x	1, 2		
Presentation (21 November)	x	1, 2	x	x
St. Clement (23 November)	x	1		
St. Catherine (25 November)	x	1, 2		
St. Andrew (30 November)	x	1, 2		
St. Nicholas (5 December)	xg	1, 2		
St. Ambrose (7 December)	x			
Immaculate Conception of the B. V. M. (8 December)	x	1, 2		
St. Lucy (13 December)	x	1, 2		
St. Thomas (21 December)	x	1, 2		
Christmas (25 December)	xh	1, 2		x
St. Stephen (26 December)	x	2		
St. John the Evangelist (27 December)	x	2		
Feast of the Holy Innocents (28 December)	x	2		
St. Silvester (31 December)	x	2		

Feast	Mass	Vespers	Procession	Doge
All Sundays of the year	x	2		
All Sundays of Lent	x	2	—[i]	
All Saturdays which require a Mass of the Virgin	x			
All Saturdays of Lent		2		
Palm Sunday	x	2	—[j]	x
Tuesday in Holy Week			—[k]	
Wednesday in Holy Week			—[l]	
Maundy Thursday	x		—[m]	
Good Friday	x		x[n]	
Holy Saturday	x			
Easter Sunday	x	2	x	x
Easter Monday and Tuesday	x	2	x	
Low Sunday	x	2	x	x
Entire octave before and after Ascension		2		
Monday and Tuesday before Ascension	x		x	
Vigil of Ascension	x	2		x
Ascension	x[o]	2		x
Vigil of Pentecost	x	2		x
Pentecost	x	2		x
Monday and Tuesday of Whitsun Week	x	2		
Feast of the Holy Trinity	x	1, 2		x
Corpus Christi	x	1, 2	x	x

[a] Singers also sing at Compline on the Annunciation.

[b] Singers attend the Ceremony of the Display of the Most Precious Blood.

[c] Singers attend the Ceremony of the Display of the Most Precious Blood.

[d] Despite its importance as a Venetian feast, First Vespers of the Feast of the Apparition of the Body of St. Mark was displaced by Second Vespers of the Feast of the Nativity of St. John the Baptist. See Pace's elaborate rationale for this practice, Biblioteca Ambrosiana, MS A. 328 inf., f. 51r, and Bonifacio's description of the service, A.S.V., Consulatore in jure, Registro 555, f. 62v.

[e] Motets sung in Palladio's *Chiesa del Redentore*.

[f] There is some question as to whether Second Vespers of St. Giustina or First Vespers of the Dedication of the Church of St. Mark were celebrated on the evening on October 7th. See Table V-4, entry of 8 October.

[g] Mass is said at the church of San Nicolò on the Lido.

[h] Singers are present at two Masses, that of the Christmas Vigil and that of Christmas Day.

[i]Singers also sing at Compline on these Sundays.

[j]Singers also sing Compline and sing the Passion at Mass.

[k]Singers sing the Passion at Mass.

[l]Singers are present at Matins.

[m]Singers also are present at Matins and for the Display of the Most Precious Blood.

[n]Singers are also present at Matins.

[o]Mass is said at the church of San Nicolò on the Lido as part of the ceremony of the marriage of Venice to the sea. The singers are also required to sing in the Bucintoro on the way to the Lido.

Table V-3

Feasts on Which the *Pala d'oro* Is Opened and Double-Choir Psalms Are Sung

Feast	1588-91	1646	1677	1678	1755	1761
Circumcision	1, 2	1, 2		1, 2	1, 2	1, 2
Epiphany	2	1, 2	(1, 2)	1, 2	1, 2	1, 2
Translation of the Body of St. Mark		1, 2		1, 2	1, 2	1, 2
Purification of the B. V. M.	1, 2	1, 2	(1, 2)	1, 2[a]	1, 2	1, 2
Annunciation	1, 2	1, 2		1, 2	1	1
Translation of St. Isidore		2				
St. Mark	1, 2	1, 2			2	2
Nativity of St. John the Baptist	2	1, 2	(1, 2)	1, 2	1, 2	1, 2
Apparition of the Body of St. Mark	2	2	(2)		2	2
Ss. Peter and Paul	2	1, 2	(1, 2)	1, 2	1, 2	1, 2
Visitation of the B. V. M.	2	1, 2		1, 2	1, 2	1, 2
Festa del Redentore					1, 2	1, 2
St. Marina		2				
St. Mary Magdalene		2			2	2
Transfiguration of Our Lord		1, 2			1, 2	1, 2
St. Salvatore	1, 2			1, 2		
Assumption	1, 2	1, 2	(1, 2)	1, 2	2	2
Nativity of the B. V. M.	1, 2	1, 2		1, 2	1, 2	1, 2
St. Magnus		1, 2		1, 2	1, 2	1, 2
Dedication of the Church of St. Mark	2	1, 2		1, 2	2	2
All Saints Day	1, 2	1, 2		1, 2		
St. Theodore		1, 2	(1, 2)	1, 2	1, 2	1, 2
Santa Maria della Salute			(1, 2)	1, 2	1, 2	1, 2
Conception of the B. V. M.	2	1, 2	(1, 2)	1, 2	1, 2	1, 2

Feast	1588-91	1646	1677	1678	1755	1761
Christmas	1, 2	1, 2	(1, 2)			2
St. Stephen	2	2	(2)			2
St. John the Evangelist	2		(2)			2
Easter Sunday	2	2			2	2
Easter Monday	2	2	(2)		2	2
Easter Tuesday	2	2	(2)		2	2
Low Sunday		(2)				
Ascension	1, 2	1, 2	1	1, 2	2	2
Pentecost	1, 2	1, 2	1	1, 2	1, 2	1, 2
Monday of Whitsun Week	2	2	(2)	2	2	2
Tuesday of Whitsun Week	2	2	(2)	2	2	2
Trinity Sunday	2	1, 2	1	1	1, 2	1, 2
Corpus Christi		1, 2	1, 2		1, 2	1, 2

a The Purification is not given as a feast on which the *Pala d'oro* is opened in Pace's *Ceremoniale Magnum*, but it is described as such in his earlier work, the *Nucleus Ceremoniarum*. See Biblioteca Correr, Codice Cicogna 559, f. 7v.

Table V-4
Appropriate Psalm Collections of Grandi, Rovetta and Cavalli
for Those Feasts of the Church Year Celebrated
with *Canto Figurato* at St. Mark's

Circumcision (1 January)   Pala   Doge
   1st Vespers: Dixit, Confitebor, Beatus vir, De profundis, Memento
     Grandi 1629, Rovetta 1644, Rovetta 1662, Cavalli 1675
   2nd Vespers: same

Epiphany (6 January)   Pala   Doge
   1st Vespers: Cinque Laudate
     Rovetta 1644, Rovetta 1662, Cavalli 1675
   2nd Vespers; Dixit, Confitebor, Beatus vir, De profundis, Memento
     Grandi 1629, Rovetta 1644, Rovetta 1662, Cavalli 1675

Lorenzo Giustiniani (8 January)   —   Doge
   1st Vespers: Dixit, Confitebor, Beatus vir, Laudate pueri, Laudate
   Dominum
     Grandi 1630/1, Grandi 1630/2, Rovetta 1627, Rovetta 1639,
     Rovetta 1642, Cavalli 1656
   2nd Vespers: Dixit, Confitebor, Beatus vir, Laudate pueri,
   Memento
     Rovetta 1639

St. Anthony Abbot (17 January)   —   —
   1st Vespers: Dixit, Confitebor, Beatus vir, Laudate Pueri, Laudate
   Dominum
     Grandi 1630/1, Grandi 1630/2, Rovetta 1627, Rovetta 1639,
     Rovetta 1642, Cavalli 1656
   2nd Vespers: same

Ss. Fabian and Sebastian (20 January)   —   —
   1st Vespers: Dixit, Confitebor, Beatus vir, Laudate pueri, Laudate
   Dominum
     Grandi 1630/1, Grandi 1630/2, Rovetta 1627, Rovetta 1639,
     Rovetta 1642, Cavalli 1656
   2nd Vespers: Dixit, Confitebor, Beatus vir, Laudate pueri, Credidi
     Rovetta 1627, Rovetta 1639, Cavalli 1656

Conversion of St. Paul (25 January)   —   —
   1st Vespers: Dixit, Confitebor, Beatus vir, Laudate pueri, Laudate
   Dominum
     Grandi 1630/1, Grandi 1630/2, Rovetta 1627, Rovetta 1639,
     Rovetta 1642, Cavalli 1656
   2nd Vespers: Dixit, Laudate pueri, Credidi, In convertendo,
   Domine probasti me
     Cavalli 1656

Translation of the Body of St. Mark (31 January)   Pala   —
   1st Vespers: Dixit, Laudate pueri, Credidi, In convertendo, Domine
   probasti me
      Grandi 1629, Rovetta 1644, Rovetta 1662, Cavalli 1675
   2nd Vespers: same

Purification (2 February)   Pala   Doge[a]
   1st Vespers: Cinque Laudate
      Rovetta 1644, Rovetta 1662, Cavalli 1675
   2nd Vespers: Dixit, Confitebor, Beatus vir, De profundis, Memento
      Grandi 1629, Rovetta 1644, Rovetta 1662, Cavalli 1675

St. Peter's Chair at Antioch (22 February)   —   —
   1st Vespers: Dixit, Confitebor, Beatus vir, Laudate pueri, Laudate
   Dominum
      Grandi 1630/1, Grandi 1630/2, Rovetta 1627, Rovetta 1639,
      Rovetta 1642, Cavalli 1656
   2nd Vespers: Dixit, Confitebor, Beatus vir, Laudate pueri,
   Memento
      Rovetta 1639

St. Gerard of Csanad (24 February)   —   —
   1st Vespers: Dixit, Confitebor, Beatus vir, Laudate pueri, Memento
      Rovetta 1639
   2nd Vespers: Dixit, Confitebor, Beatus vir, Laudate pueri, Credidi
      Rovetta 1627, Rovetta 1639, Cavalli 1656

St. Matthias (25 February)   —   —
   1st Vespers: Dixit, Laudate pueri, Credidi, In convertendo, Domine
   probasti me
      Cavalli 1656
   2nd Vespers: same

St. Gregory (12 March)   —   —
   1st Vespers: Dixit, Confitebor, Beatus vir, Laudate pueri, Laudate
   Dominum
      Grandi 1630/1, Grandi 1630/2, Rovetta 1627, Rovetta 1639,
      Rovetta 1642, Cavalli 1656
   2nd Vespers: same

St. Joseph (19 March)   —   —
   1st Vespers: Dixit, Confitebor, Beatus vir, Laudate pueri, Laudate
   Dominum
      Grandi 1630/1, Grandi 1630/2, Rovetta 1627, Rovetta 1639,
      Rovetta 1642, Cavalli 1656
   2nd Vespers: same

St. Benedict, Abbot (21 March)   —   —
   1st Vespers: Dixit, Confitebor, Beatus vir, Laudate pueri, Laudate
   Dominum
      Grandi 1630/1, Grandi 1630/2, Rovetta 1627, Rovetta 1639,
      Rovetta 1642, Cavalli 1656
   2nd Vespers: same

	Pala	Doge
Annunciation (25 March)	Pala	Doge

Annunciation (25 March)
1st Vespers: Dixit, Laudate pueri, Laetatus sum, Nisi Dominus,
Lauda Jerusalem
    Grandi 1629, Rovetta 1644, Rovetta 1662, Cavalli 1675
2nd Vespers: same

Translation of St. Isidore (16 April)   —   Doge
1st Vespers: Dixit, Confitebor, Beatus vir, Laudate pueri, Laudate
Dominum
    Grandi 1630/1, Grandi 1630/2, Rovetta 1627, Rovetta 1639,
    Rovetta 1642, Cavalli 1656
2nd Vespers: same

St. George (23 April)   —   —
1st Vespers: Dixit, Confitebor, Beatus vir, Laudate pueri, Laudate
Dominum
    Grandi 1630/1, Grandi 1630/2, Rovetta 1627, Rovetta 1639,
    Rovetta 1642, Cavalli 1656
2nd Vespers: Dixit, Confitebor, Beatus vir, Laudate pueri, Credidi
    Rovetta 1627, Rovetta 1639, Cavalli 1656

St. Mark (25 April)   —[b]   Doge
1st Vespers: Dixit, Confitebor, Beatus vir, Laudate pueri, Laudate
Dominum
    Grandi 1630/1, Grandi 1630/2, Rovetta 1627, Rovetta 1639,
    Rovetta 1642, Cavalli 1656
2nd Vespers: Dixit, Laudate pueri, Credidi, In convertendo,
Domine probasti me
    Grandi 1629, Rovetta 1644, Rovetta 1662, Cavalli 1675

Ss. Philip and James (1 May)   —[c]   Doge
1st Vespers: Dixit, Confitebor, Batus vir, Laudate pueri, Laudate
Dominum
    Grandi 1630/1, Grandi 1630/2, Rovetta 1627, Rovetta 1639,
    Rovetta 1642, Cavalli 1656
2nd Vespers: Dixit, Laudate pueri, Credidi, In convertendo,
Domine probasti me
    Cavalli 1656

Finding of the Holy Cross (3 May)   —   —
1st Vespers: Dixit, Confitebor, Beatus vir, Laudate pueri, Laudate
Dominum
    Grandi 1630/1, Grandi 1630/2, Rovetta 1627, Rovetta 1639,
    Rovetta 1642, Cavalli 1656

St. John before the Latin Gate (6 May)   —   —
1st Vespers: Dixit, Confitebor, Beatus vir, Laudate pueri, Laudate
Dominum
    Grandi 1630/1, Grandi 1630/2, Rovetta 1627, Rovetta 1639,
    Rovetta 1642, Cavalli 1656
2nd Vespers: Dixit, Laudate pueri, Credidi, In convertendo,

Domine probasti me
  Cavalli 1656

Apparition of St. Michael, Archangel (8 May)   —   —
  1st Vespers: Dixit, Confitebor, Beatus vir, Laudate pueri, Laudate
  Dominum
    Grandi 1630/1, Grandi 1630/2, Rovetta 1627, Rovetta 1639,
    Rovetta 1642, Cavalli 1656

Nativity of St. Isidore (15 May)   —   —
  1st Vespers: Dixit, Confitebor, Beatus vir, Laudate pueri, Laudate
  Dominum
    Grandi 1630/1, Grandi 1630/2, Rovetta 1627, Rovetta 1639,
    Rovetta 1642, Cavalli 1656
  2nd Vespers: Dixit, Confitebor, Beatus vir, Laudate pueri,
  Memento
    Rovetta 1639

St. Bernardine of Siena (20 May)   —   —
  1st Vespers: Dixit, Confitebor, Beatus vir, Laudate pueri, Laudate
  Dominum
    Grandi 1630/1, Grandi 1630/2, Rovetta 1627, Rovetta 1639,
    Rovetta 1642, Cavalli 1656
  2nd Vespers: same

St. Barnabas, Apostle (11 June)   —   —
  1st Vespers: Dixit, Laudate pueri, Credidi, In convertendo, Domine
  probasti me
    Cavalli 1656

St. Anthony of Padua (13 June)   —   Doge
  1st Vespers: Dixit, Confitebor, Beatus vir, Laudate pueri, Laudate
  Dominum
    Grandi 1630/1, Grandi 1630/2, Rovetta 1627, Rovetta 1639,
    Rovetta 1642, Cavalli 1656
  2nd Vespers: same

Ss. Vitus and Modestus, Martyrs (15 June)   —   Doge
  1st Vespers: Dixit, Confitebor, Beatus vir, Laudate pueri, Laudate
  Dominum
    Grandi 1630/1, Grandi 1630/2, Rovetta 1627, Rovetta 1639,
    Rovetta 1642, Cavalli 1656
  2nd Vespers: Dixit, Confitebor, Beatus vir, Laudate pueri, Credidi
    Rovetta 1627, Rovetta 1639, Cavalli 1656

Nativity of St. John the Baptist (24 June)   Pala   —
  1st Vespers: Dixit, Confitebor, Beatus vir, Laudate pueri, Memento
    Grandi 1629, Rovetta 1644, Rovetta 1662,Cavalli 1675
  2nd Vespers: Dixit, Confitebor, Beatus vir, Laudate pueri, Laudate
  Dominum
    Grandi 1629, Rovetta 1644, Rovetta 1662, Cavalli 1675

Apparition of the Body of St. Mark (25 June)   Pala   Doge
    2nd Vespers: Dixit, Laudate pueri, Credidi, In convertendo,
    Domine probasti me
        Grandi 1629, Rovetta 1644, Rovetta 1662, Cavalli 1675

Ss. Peter and Paul (29 June)   Pala   —
    1st Vespers: Dixit, Laudate pueri, Credidi, In convertendo, Domine
    probasti me
        Grandi 1629, Rovetta 1644, Rovetta 1662, Cavalli 1675
    2nd Vespers: same

Visitation of the B. V. M. (2 July)   Pala   —
    1st Vespers: Dixit, Laudate pueri, Laetatus sum, Nisi Dominus,
    Lauda Jerusalem
        Grandi 1629, Rovetta 1644, Rovetta 1662, Cavalli 1675
    2nd Vespers: same

Ss. Hermagoras and Fortunatus (12 July)   —   —
    1st Vespers: Dixit, Confitebor, Beatus vir, Laudate pueri, Laudate
    Dominum
        Grandi 1630/1, Grandi 1630/2, Rovetta 1627, Rovetta 1639,
        Rovetta 1642, Cavalli 1656

St. Marina (17 July)   —   Doge
    1st Vespers: Dixit, Laudate pueri, Laetatus sum, Nisi Dominus,
    Lauda Jerusalem
        Grandi 1630/1, Grandi 1630/2, Rovetta 1627, Rovetta 1639,
        Rovetta 1642, Cavalli 1656
    2nd Vespers: same

St. Mary Magadalene (22 July)   Pala   —
    1st Vespers: Dixit, Laudate pueri, Laetatus sum, Nisi Dominus,
    Lauda Jerusalem
        Grandi 1629, Rovetta 1644, Rovetta 1662, Cavalli 1675
    2nd Vespers: same

St. James, Apostle (25 July)   —   —
    1st Vespers: Dixit, Laudate pueri, Credidi, In convertendo, Domine
    probasti me
        Cavalli 1656
    2nd Vespers: same

St. Anne, Mother of the B. V. M. (26 July)   —   —
    2nd Vespers: Dixit, Laudate pueri, Laetatus sum, Nisi Dominus,
    Lauda Jerusalem
        Grandi 1630/1, Grandi 1630/2, Rovetta 1627, Rovetta 1639,
        Rovetta 1642, Cavalli 1656

St. Peter's Chains (1 August)   —   —
    1st Vespers: Dixit, Confitebor, Beatus vir, Laudate pueri, Laudate
    Dominum

Grandi 1630/1, Grandi 1630/2, Rovetta 1627, Rovetta 1639,
Rovetta 1642, Cavalli 1656

Our Lady of the Snow (5 August)   —   —
   1st Vespers: Dixit, Laudate pueri, Laetatus sum, Nisi Dominus,
Lauda Jerusalem
      Grandi 1630/1, Grandi 1630/2, Rovetta 1627, Rovetta 1639,
      Rovetta 1642, Cavalli 1656
   2nd Vespers: same

Transfiguration of Our Lord (6 August)   —   —
   2nd Vespers: Dixit, Confitebor, Beatus vir, Laudate pueri, In exitu
      Grandi 1629, Rovetta 1644, Rovetta 1662, Cavalli 1675

St. Lawrence, Martyr (10 August)   —   —
   1st Vespers: Dixit, Confitebor, Beatus vir, Laudate pueri, Laudate
Dominum
      Grandi 1630/1, Grandi 1630/2, Rovetta 1627, Rovetta 1639,
      Rovetta 1642, Cavalli 1656
   2nd Vespers: Dixit, Confitebor, Beatus vir, Laudate pueri, Credidi
      Rovetta 1627, Rovetta 1639, Cavalli 1656

Assumption of the Virgin (15 August)   Pala   Doge
   1st Vespers: Cinque Laudate
      Rovetta 1644, Rovetta 1662, Cavalli 1675
   2nd Vespers: Dixit, Laudate pueri, Laetatus sum, Nisi Dominus,
Lauda Jerusalem
      Grandi 1629, Rovetta 1644, Rovetta 1662, Cavalli 1675

St. Roche (16 August)   —   —
   1st Vespers: Dixit, Confitebor, Beatus vir, Laudate pueri, Laudate
Dominum
      Grandi 1630/1, Grandi 1630/2, Rovetta 1627, Rovetta 1639,
      Rovetta 1642, Cavalli 1656
   2nd Vespers: same

St. Bartholomew, Apostle (24 August)   —   —
   1st Vespers: Dixit, Laudate pueri, Credidi, In convertendo, Domine
probasti me
      Cavalli 1656
   2nd Vespers: same

St. Augustine (28 August)   —   —
   1st Vespers: Dixit, Confitebor, Beatus vir, Laudate pueri, Laudate
Dominum
      Grandi 1630/1, Grandi 1630/2, Rovetta 1627, Rovetta 1639,
      Rovetta 1642, Cavalli 1656
   2nd Vespers: Dixit, Confitebor, Beatus vir, Laudate pueri,
Memento
      Rovetta 1639

Beheading of St. John the Baptist (29 August)   —   —
   2nd Vespers: Dixit, Confitebor, Beatus vir, Laudate pueri, Credidi
      Rovetta 1627, Rovetta 1639, Cavalli 1656

Nativity of the B. V. M. (8 September)   Pala   Doge
   1st Vespers: Cinque Laudate
      Rovetta 1644, Rovetta 1662, Cavalli 1675
   2nd Vespers: Dixit, Laudate pueri, Laetatus sum, Nisi Dominus,
   Lauda Jerusalem
      Grandi 1629, Rovetta 1644, Rovetta 1662, Cavalli 1675

Exaltation of the Holy Cross (14 September)   —   —
   1st Vespers: Dixit, Confitebor, Beatus vir, Laudate pueri, Laudate
   Dominum
      Grandi 1630/1, Grandi 1630/2, Rovetta 1627, Rovetta 1639,
      Rovetta 1644, Cavalli 1656
   2nd Vespers: same

St. Victor (18 September)   —   —
   1st Vespers: Dixit, Confitebor, Beatus vir, Laudate pueri, Laudate
   Dominum
      Grandi 1630/1, Grandi 1630/2, Rovetta 1627, Rovetta 1639,
      Rovetta 1644, Cavalli 1656

St. Matthew (21 September)   —   —
   1st Vespers: Dixit, Confitebor, Beatus vir, Laudate pueri, Laudate
   Dominum
      Grandi 1630/1, Grandi 1630/2, Rovetta 1627, Rovetta 1639,
      Rovetta 1644, Cavalli 1656
   2nd Vespers: Dixit, Confitebor, Beatus vir, Laudate pueri, Credidi
      Rovetta 1627, Rovetta 1639, Cavalli 1656

Dedication of the Church of St. Michael, Archangel (29 September)   —   —
   1st Vespers: Dixit, Confitebor, Beatus vir, Laudate pueri, Laudate
   Dominum
      Grandi 1630/1, Grandi 1630/2, Rovetta 1627, Rovetta 1639,
      Rovetta 1642, Cavalli 1656
   2nd Vespers: Dixit, Confitebor, Beatus vir, Laudate pueri,
   Confitebor Angelorum
      —[d]

St. Jerome (30 September)   —   —
   2nd Vespers: Dixit, Confitebor, Beatus vir, Laudate pueri, Laudate
   Dominum
      Grandi 1630/1, Grandi 1630/2, Rovetta 1627, Rovetta 1639,
      Rovetta 1642, Cavalli 1656

St. Francis (4 October)   —   —
   1st Vespers: Dixit, Confitebor, Beatus vir, Laudate pueri, Laudate
   Dominum
      Grandi 1630/1, Grandi 1630/2, Rovetta 1627, Rovetta 1639,
      Rovetta 1642, Cavalli 1656

St. Magnus (6 October)   Pala   —
 1st Vespers: Dixit, Confitebor, Beatus vir, Laudate pueri, Laudate
 Dominum
  Grandi 1629, Rovetta 1644, Rovetta 1662, Cavalli 1675
 2nd Vespers: Dixit, Confitebor, Beatus vir, Laudate pueri,
 Memento
  Grandi 1629, Rovetta 1644, Rovetta 1662, Cavalli 1675

Dedication of the Church of St. Mark (8 October)[e]   Pala   Doge
 1st Vespers: Dixit, Confitebor, Beatus vir, Laudate pueri, Laudate
 Dominum
  Grandi 1629, Rovetta 1644, Rovetta 1662, Cavalli 1675
 2nd Vespers: Dixit, Confitebor, Beatus vir, Laudate pueri,
 Memento
  Grandi 1629, Rovetta 1644, Rovetta 1662, Cavalli 1675

St. Luke (18 October)   —   —
 1st Vespers: Dixit, Confitebor, Beatus vir, Laudate pueri, Laudate
 Dominum
  Grandi 1630/1, Grandi 1630/2, Rovetta 1627, Rovetta 1639,
  Rovetta 1642, Cavalli 1656
 2nd Vespers: Dixit, Laudate pueri, Credidi, In convertendo,
 Domine probasti me
  Cavalli 1656

Ss. Simon and Jude (28 October)   —   —
 1st Vespers: Dixit, Laudate pueri, Credidi, In convertendo, Domine
 probasti me
  Cavalli 1656
 2nd Vespers: same

All Saints (1 November)   Pala   Doge
 1st Vespers: Cinque Laudate
  Rovetta 1644, Rovetta 1662, Cavalli 1675
 2nd Vespers: Dixit, Confitebor, Beatus vir, Laudate pueri, Credidi
  Grandi 1629, Rovetta 1644, Rovetta 1662, Cavalli 1675

St. Leonardo (6 November)   —   —
 1st Vespers: Dixit, Confitebor, Beatus vir, Laudate pueri, Laudate
 Dominum
  Grandi 1630/1, Grandi 1630/2, Rovetta 1627, Rovetta 1639,
  Rovetta 1642, Cavalli 1656
 2nd Vespers: same

St. Theodore (9 November)   Pala   —
 1st Vespers: Dixit, Confitebor, Beatus vir, Laudate pueri, Laudate
 Dominum
  Grandi 1629, Rovetta 1644, Rovetta 1662, Cavalli 1675
 2nd Vespers: Dixit, Confitebor, Beatus vir, Laudate pueri, Credidi
  Grandi 1629, Rovetta 1644, Rovetta 1662, Cavalli 1675

St. Martin (11 November)   —   —
   1st Vespers: Dixit, Confitebor, Beatus vir, Laudate pueri, Laudate
   Dominum
      Grandi 1630/1, Grandi 1630/2, Rovetta 1627, Rovetta 1639,
      Rovetta 1642, Cavalli 1675
   2nd Vespers: Dixit, Confitebor, Beatus vir, In convertendo,
     Memento
      Rovetta 1639

Presentation of the B. V. M. (Santa Maria della Salute)   Pala   Doge
   1st Vespers: Dixit, Laudate pueri, Laetatus sum, Nisi Dominus,
   Lauda Jerusalem
      Grandi 1629, Rovetta 1644, Rovetta 1662, Cavalli 1675
   2nd Vespers: same

St. Clement (23 November)   —   —
   1st Vespers: Dixit, Confitebor, Beatus vir, Laudate pueri, Laudate
   Dominum
      Grandi 1630/1, Grandi 1630/2, Rovetta 1627, Rovetta 1639,
      Rovetta 1642, Cavalli 1675

St. Catherine (25 November)   —   —
   1st Vespers: Dixit, Laudate pueri, Laetatus sum, Nisi Dominus,
   Lauda Jerusalem
      Grandi 1630/1, Grandi 1630/2, Rovetta 1627, Rovetta 1639,
      Rovetta 1642, Cavalli 1675
   2nd Vespers: same

St. Andrew (30 November)   —   —
   1st Vespers: Dixit, Confitebor, Beatus vir, Laudate pueri, Laudate
   Dominum
      Grandi 1630/1, Grandi 1630/2, Rovetta 1627, Rovetta 1639,
      Rovetta 1642, Cavalli 1656
   2nd Vespers: Dixit, Laudate pueri, Credidi, In convertendo,
   Domine probasti me
     Cavalli 1656

St. Nicholas (6 December)   —   —
   1st Vespers: Dixit, Confitebor, Beatus vir, Laudate pueri, Laudate
   Dominum
      Grandi 1630/1, Grandi 1630/2, Rovetta 1627, Rovetta 1639,
      Rovetta 1642, Cavalli 1656
   2nd Vespers: Dixit, Laudate pueri, Credidi, In convertendo,
   Domine probasti me
     Cavalli 1656

Immaculate Conception of the B. V. M. (8 December)   Pala   —
   1st Vespers: Cinque Laudate
     Rovetta 1644, Rovetta 1662, Cavalli 1675
   2nd Vespers: Dixit, Laudate pueri, Laetatus sum, Nisi Dominus,
   Lauda Jerusalem
      Grandi 1629, Rovetta 1644, Rovetta 1662, Cavalli 1675

St. Lucy (13 December) — —
1st Vespers: Dixit, Laudate pueri, Laetatus sum, Nisi Dominus,
Lauda Jerusalem
   Grandi 1630/1, Grandi 1630/2, Rovetta 1627, Rovetta 1639,
   Rovetta 1642, Cavalli 1656
2nd Vespers: same

St. Thomas (21 December) — —
1st Vespers: Dixit, Confitebor, Beatus vir, Laudate pueri, Laudate
Dominum
   Grandi 1630/1, Grandi 1630/2, Rovetta 1627, Rovetta 1639,
   Rovetta 1642, Cavalli 1656
2nd Vespers, Dixit, Laudate pueri, Credidi, In convertendo,
Domine probasti me
   Cavalli 1656

Christmas (25 December) Pala Doge[f]
1st Vespers: Cinque Laudate
   Rovetta 1644, Rovetta 1662, Cavalli 1675
2nd Vespers: Dixit, Confitebor, Beatus vir, De profundis, Memento
   Grandi 1629, Rovetta 1644, Rovetta 1662, Cavalli 1675

St. Stephen (26 December) Pala —
2nd Vespers: Dixit, Confitebor, Beatus vir, De profundis, Memento
   Grandi 1629, Rovetta 1644, Rovetta 1662, Cavalli 1675

St. John the Evangelist (27 December) Pala —
2nd Vespers: Dixit, Confitebor, Beatus vir, De profundis, Memento
   Grandi 1629, Rovetta 1644, Rovetta 1662, Cavalli 1675

Holy Innocents (28 December) — —
2nd Vespers: Dixit, Confitebor, Beatus vir, De profundis, Memento
   Rovetta 1639

St. Silvester (31 December) — —
1st Vespers: Dixit, Confitebor, Beatus vir, De profundis, Memento
   Rovetta 1639

Sundays through the year — —
Vespers: Dixit, Confitebor, Beatus vir, Laudate pueri, In exitu
   Grandi 1629, Rovetta 1644, Rovetta 1662, Cavalli 1675[g]

Saturdays during Lent — —
Vespers: Benedictus Dominus, Exaltabo te Deus meus, Lauda
anima mea, Laudate Dominum quoniam bonus, Lauda Jerusalem
   Rovetta 1644, Rovetta 1662 and Cavalli 1675 contain the last three
   psalms; there are no settings of the first two in Vespers
   collections. However, the inquests of 1589 and 1600 reveal that
   falsobordone was used during Lent, and it may well have been
   used precisely for the first two psalms of this service
   (Documents 146 and 147).

	Pala	Doge
Palm Sunday Vespers: Dixit, Confitebor, Beatus vir, Laudate pueri, In exitu Grandi 1629, Rovetta 1644, Rovetta 1662, Cavalli 1675	—	Doge
Easter Sunday Vespers: Dixit, Confitebor, Beatus vir, Laudate pueri, In exitu[i] Grandi 1629, Rovetta 1644, Rovetta 1662, Cavalli 1675	Pala	Doge[h]
Easter Monday Vespers: Dixit, Confitebor, Beatus vir, Laudate pueri, In exitu[j] Grandi 1629, Rovetta 1644, Rovetta 1662, Cavalli 1675	Pala	—
Easter Tuesday Vespers: Dixit, Confitebor, Beatus vir, Laudate pueri, In exitu Grandi 1629, Rovetta 1644, Rovetta 1662, Cavalli 1675	Pala	—
Low Sunday Vespers: Dixit, Confitebor, Beatus vir, Laudate pueri, In exitu Grandi 1629, Rovetta 1644, Rovetta 1662, Cavalli 1675	Pala	Doge
Eight days before and eight days after the Feast of the Ascension Vespers: Dixit, Confitebor, Beatus vir, Laudate pueri, Laudate Dominum[k] Grandi 1630/1, Grandi 1630/2, Rovetta 1627, Rovetta 1639, Rovetta 1642, Cavalli 1656	—	—
Ascension 1st Vespers: Cinque Laudate Rovetta 1644, Rovetta 1662, Cavalli 1675 2nd Vespers: Dixit, Confitebor, Beatus vir, Laudate pueri, Laudate Dominum Grandi 1629, Rovetta 1644, Rovetta 1662, Cavalli 1675	Pala	Doge
Pentecost 1st Vespers: Cinque Laudate Rovetta 1644, Rovetta 1662, Cavalli 1675 2nd Vespers: Dixit, Confitebor, Beatus vir, Laudate pueri, In exitu Grandi 1629, Rovetta 1644, Rovetta 1662, Cavalli 1675	Pala	Doge[l]
Monday in Whitsun Week Vespers: Dixit, Confitebor, Beatus vir, Laudate pueri, In exitu[m] Grandi 1629, Rovetta 1644, Rovetta 1662, Cavalli 1675	Pala	—
Tuesday in Whitsun Week Vespers: Dixit, Confitebor, Beatus vir, Laudate pueri, In exitu Grandi 1629, Rovetta 1644, Rovetta 1662, Cavalli 1675	Pala	—
Feast of the Holy Trinity 1st Vespers: Levavi oculos meos, Ad te levavi, De profundis, Memento, Laudate nomen Domini Rovetta 1662 2nd Vespers: Dixit, Confitebor, Beatus vir, Laudate pueri, Laudate	Pala	Doge

Dominum
   Grandi 1629, Rovetta 1644, Rovetta 1662, Cavalli 1675

Corpus Christi   Pala   Doge
   1st Vespers: Dixit, Confitebor, Credidi, Beati omnes, Lauda
Jerusalem
   Grandi 1629, Rovetta 1644, Rovetta 1662, Cavalli 1675
   2nd Vespers: Cinque Laudate
   Rovetta 1644, Rovetta 1662, Cavalli 1675

---

[a] The Doge and the *Serenissima Signoria* hear Vespers in Santa Maria Formosa; half the singers go with them, and the other half sing Vespers in St. Mark's.

[b] While Bonifacio says that the *Pala d'oro* is opened at both Vespers services, all of the later sources state that it is opened at Second Vespers only on the Feast of St. Mark; for the gold and jewels from the treasury of the basilica were displayed at First Vespers. Cf. Documents 144 and 145 with Documents 140, 142 and 143.

[c] Singers split into two groups; half sing in St. Mark's, and half in Ss. Filippo e Giacomo.

[d] There is no published collection by Grandi, Rovetta or Cavalli—or, for that matter, by any composer connected with St. Mark's during the sixteenth or seventeenth centuries—which contains all of the psalms for this service in settings for a single choir. The problematic text is the *Confitebor Angelorum*, which is found in Rovetta 1662 and Cavalli 1675 in double-choir settings only. However, single-choir settings of this text must have existed in the sixteenth century; for in the Procurators' inquest of 1589, discussed in Chapter IV, the singers insisted that Second Vespers for the Feast of the Dedication of the Church of St. Mark's, which contains this psalm, was to be sung *ugnolo*, i.e. in settings for a single choir. They make it clear, moreover, that this psalm had never been set for two choirs and that the service was not customarily sung in *falsobordone*. Because of the uncertainty over the manner in which this sequence of psalms was performed, I have left it out of the schema of 14 psalm sequences discussed on the pages following this table. Theoretically, however, this could constitute a 15th sequence.

[e] The documents are contradictory at this point in the church year. They all agree that Vespers services with the *Pala d'oro* open occurred on the evenings of 7 and 8 October, but there seems to be some disagreement as to just which services were performed. The list of duties of 1677 (Biblioteca Correr, Codice Cicogna 3118, fascicoli 44–56) lists the feast of St. Giustina under 7 and 8 October, with the singers' coming to both Vespers services but the *Pala d'oro* remaining closed. Pace, on the other hand, describes the feast of St. Giustina but does not say that the singers participated in Vespers, only at Mass. He then says that First *and* Second Vespers of the Feast of the Dedication of the Church of St. Mark are celebrated, with the *Pala d'oro* open and double-choir music for *both* services. I am following Pace in this chart, assuming that the two Vespers services were both connected with the Dedication of the Church and the singers' participation for the feast of St. Giustina was limited to Mass and a procession. The question is a difficult one, for both feasts were important to Venice; the victory over the Turks in the Battle of Lepanto (1571) was commemorated on the feast of St. Giustina every year, so First Vespers of the Feast of the Dedication would not necessarily have precedence. At any rate, it is certain that

Second Vespers of the Feast of the Dedication were celebrated under the *Pala d'oro* with double-choir music in the seventeenth century; this is an important point, for the service was one of those unique to the basilica. It is also the service which caused the brouhaha with the singers in 1589 and 1600 over whether or not double-choir psalms were to be sung. (See A.S.V., San Marco, Procuratia de Supra, Busta 91, f. 12r–24v; Busta 88, Processo 195, f. 53r–62v).

ᶠ Doge attends Vespers at San Giorgio Maggiore; however, this is a plainchant service sung by the canons of the church; the musicians from St. Mark's sing Vespers in the basilica as usual. See Sansovino-Martinioni, p. 505; cf. Biblioteca Ambrosiana MS A. 328 inf., f. 66v.

ᵍ These four collections do not satisfy all of the theoretical requirements for ordinary Sundays, since they contain only double-choir psalms and the *Pala d'oro* is not opened on Sundays unless a feast occurs. However, these are the only collections from which the Sunday psalms can all be drawn. Moreover, Cavalli's *Vesperi* of 1675 contain a group of pieces specifically designated as "Vespero delle Domeniche, et altri Salmi". Thus, there is little doubt that double-choir psalms were admitted into the Sunday liturgy.

ʰThe Doge goes to San Zaccaria with half of the singers; the other half sing Vespers in St. Mark's.

ⁱOnly the first three psalms are performed in *canto figurato;* the other two are performed in plainchant. (See Document 131.)

ʲ Psalms not listed in *Orationale;* service identified in A.S.V., San Marco, Procuratia de Supra, Registro 98, f. 22v: De II, et III Fer*iae* post Pascha.

ᵏSee A.S.V., San Marco, Procuratia de Supra, Registro 98, f. 23v: De diebus 8. ante, et 8. post diem Ascensionis Dom*ini*.

ˡThe Doge is present on the Vigil only.

ᵐSee A.S.V., San Marco, Procuratia de Supra, Registro 98, f. 26v: De Die Sanctissimo Pentecostes.

Table V-5
Compositions Contained in Volume II,
Arranged According to Stylistic Categories

Works involving two choirs

---

1. Large-scale *concertato* works à 8

    Francesco Cavalli. Dixit Dominus. *Musiche Sacre* (1656)
      Volume II, no. 1
    Francesco Cavalli. Lauda Jerusalem. *Musiche Sacre* (1656)
      Volume II, no. 5
    Francesco Cavalli. Magnificat. *Musiche Sacre* (1656)
      Volume II, no. 7

2. *Salmi spezzati*

    a. Works notated *alla breve*

        Giovanni Rovetta. Dixit Dominus. *Delli Salmi a otto* (1662)
          Volume II, no. 12
        Giovanni Rovetta. Domine probasti me. *Delli Salmi a otto* (1662)
          Volume II, no. 13
        Francesco Cavalli. Dixit Dominus. *Vesperi a otto voci* (1675)
          Volume II, no. 21

    b. Works notated *alla semibreve*

        Giovanni Rovetta. Beatus vir. *Salmi a otto voci* (1644)
          Volume II, no. 18
        Alessandro Grandi. Deus in adiutorium. *Salmi a otto brevi* (1629)
          Volume II, no. 11
        Alessandro Grandi. Beautus vir. *Salmi a otto brevi* (1629)
          Volume II, no. 15

3. Works with *ad libitum* choirs

    Alessandro Grandi. Laudate Dominum. *Raccolta Terza* (1630)
      Volume II, no. 16

Works involving a single group of musicians

---

4. Large-scale concertato works à 6 and à 7

   Francesco Cavalli. Magnificat. *Messa a quattro Voci et Salmi.... del Signor Claudio Monteverdi* (1651)
   Volume II, no. 22

5. Small-scale concertato works à 2 to à 5 with *sinfonie* for instruments

   Francesco Cavalli. Laudate pueri. *Musiche Sacre* (1656)
   Volume II, no. 2
   Francesco Cavalli. Laetatus sum. *Musiche Sacre* (1656)
   Volume II, no. 3
   Francesco Cavalli. Nisi Dominus. *Musiche Sacre* (1656)
   Volume II, no. 4
   Francesco Cavalli. Ave maris stella. *Musiche Sacre* (1656)
   Volume II, no. 6

6. Small-scale concertato works à 2 to à 5 without *sinfonie* for instruments

   Francesco Cavalli. Salve Regina. *Musiche Sacre* (1656)
   Volume II, no. 8
   Francesco Cavalli. In convertendo. *Musiche Sacre* (1656)
   Volume II, no. 20

7. Choral compositions for a single choir

   a. Works notated *alla breve*

       Giovanni Rovetta. Magnificat a 4. e 5. voci. Biblioteca Nazionale Marciana, Cod. It. IV-1134 (-10949)
       Volume II, no. 19

   b. Works notated *alla semibreve*
       _____

8. Liturgical monodies

   Francesco Cavalli. O quam suavis. *Motetti a voce sola di diversi Eccelentissimi Autori* (1668)
   Volume II, no. 10
   Giovanni Rovetta. Salve Regina. *Motetti concertati* (1647)
   Volume II, no. 14
   Giovanni Rovetta. Laudate Dominum. *Salmi a tre e quattro voci* (1642)
   Volume II, no. 17

Appendix I

Documents

Chapter I

Doc. 1: A.S.V., San Marco, Procuratia de Supra, Registro 139 (Chiesa Actorum, 1598–1607)

1604. 25. Luglio in Lozetta

Et perche Alessandro di Agustin di Grandi è di età di anni 18. in circa, et non poscia esser ballotato rispetto la terminazion 1587 5. April la qual vuole, che le Zoveni di coro habbino almeno anni vinti in circa, Et havendo SS. SS. Illustrissime informatione della bonta, buon servitio, et virtu del detto Alessandro il qual è buon cantore et comporre, hanno à bossoli et balloti terminato che non ostante la detta termination la qual per questa volta tanto sia in questo suggetto disposta possi esser ballotato al carico di Giovene di coro, et cosi ballotato il detto Padre Allessandro fù nel bossolo.

Doc. 2: A.S.V., San Marco, Procuratia de Supra, Registro 140 (Chiesa Actorum, 1607–16)

1607. 22. Luglio

L'Illustrissimi Signori Procuratori oltrascritti tutti tre hanno à bossoli et balloti terminato ut infra.

Volendo SS. SS. Illustrissime devenir à ellettione de Zoveni di coro in chiesa di San Marco per la cassation fatta de Zuan Battista Bonamin, Zuane Bertoluzzi, Francescco Domici, Alessandro Grandi, Ettor Zanberti, Gerolimo Tagia, Lunardo Dotian, et altri dipenati di paga in virtù di terminazion de 23 Ottobre 1594, per non haver prestato il debito loro servitio in chiesa di San Marco, et essendo comparsi li sopradetti con una scrittura letta à SS. SS. Illustrissime, richiedendo che per gratia siano descritti per Zoveni di coro, promettendo di non esser contumaci come fin hora sono stati. Pero intesa la sopradetta instantia, et benignamente procedendo, ha proposto l'Illustrissimo Signor Procurator Contarini Cassier che atesa la sopradetta richiesta siano et s'intendono reeletti li sopradetti per Zoveni di coro con il salario, modi, et condition solite, et consuete, la qual termination non s'intendi presa se non con tutte le balloti.

Doc. 3: A.S.V., San Marco, Procuratia de Supra, Registro 141 (Chiesa Actorum, 1614–20), f. 78v

1617. 31. Agosto

Havutta SS. SS. Ill*ustrissi*me, et Ecc*ellentissi*me informatione, della qualità, Valor, et sufficientia, d*i* Allessandro d*i* Grandi, qual ha servito p*er* maestro di Capella in Ferrara han*n*o à boss*oli* et ball*otti* ter*mina*to ch*e* sia elletto il d*etto* Alessandro per servir in capella di S*an* M*a*rco, co*n* salario d*i* d*uca*ti ottanta all'an*n*o.

Doc. 4: A.S.V., San Marco, Procuratia de Supra, Registro 141 (Chiesa Actorum, 1614–20), f. 97

1618. 21. Agosto

Havendo m*esser* P*adre* Gaspar*o* Locadelo renonciato il carico di maestro di ca*n*to del sem*inario* fin marzo passatto, et volendo SS. SS. Ill*ustrissi*me far ell*etio*ne in loco suo, havutta informat*io*ne d*e*l valor, et sufficienza d*i* m*esser* Alless*andro* di Grandi già elletto al ser*vizi*o d*e*lla capella in S*an* M*a*rco, han*n*o, à boss*oli* et ball*oti* ter*mina*to, ch*e* sia elletto il d*etto* m*esser* Alless*andro* p*er* maestro di canto d*e*l d*etto* sem*inario* co*n* sal*ario* d*i* d*uca*ti cinqua*n*ta, come havea il sud*etto* Locadelo, co*n* obligo di andar quatro g*ior*ni alla settimana almeno, portando fede ogni doi mesi di haver servito il qual sal*ario* d*e*bba principar à 20 Marzo passato, ch*e* principiò servir in d*etto* carico d*e*l ordine d*i* SS. SS. Ill*ustrissi*me.

Doc. 5: A.S.V., San Marco, Procuratia de Supra, Busta 90, Processo 204 (Maestro di capella), f. 58r

1668

Facio fede Io P*ad*re Antonio Rossi Curato nella Ducale di S*an* M*a*rco, come nel Libro dei Morti di d*etta* Chiesa si ritrova l'infras*critt*a nota, cioè.

à 23 Ott*obre* 1668

Il Sig*nor* Gio*vanni* Roeta Mastro di Capella Ducale d'anni 71 in e*t*a amalato mesi doi in e*t*a da febre, e cattivo, ettico, Medico l'Ecc*ellentissi*mo Fasol
Data di Chiesa sud*etta* 14 Gen*naro* 1668

Io sud*etto* di mano propria

Doc. 6: A.S.V., Cancelleria Inferiore, Atti dei Dogi, Registro 81 (1623–45), p. 5

1623. à 24. D*icembr*e
Venuto in Cam*era* dal Ser*enissi*mo D. D. France*sc*o Contarinj Duce di Vene*zi*a il R*everen*do p*adre* Cesare Vergaro maestro di Choro della chiesa di S*an* M*a*rco, per nome (come disse) delli ecc*ellentissi*mi Sig*nor*i Procurator*i* di detta chiesa dinotò alla Seren*i*tà

sua; come dettj Sig*nori* Procu*rato*ri havevano à 17. dell ista*n*te fatta elettione delli
sott*oscritti* ministrj in detta chiesa. Li quali di ordine, et p*er* nome di dettj Sig*nori*
Procu*ratori* prese*n*tava personalme*n*te alla Ser*enissima* sua giusta l'ordinario. Facendo
istanza à me Cancel*liere* che ne facessi la p*rese*nte Seren*i*ta sua et sono li sottoscrittj.
civi.—

    P*adre* Giovan Maria Tagiapietra p*er* diacono.
    P*adre* Franc*esc*o Sgobba. et
    P*adre* Pietro Gavioni p*er* Giovine di choro.
    et m*esser* Giovanj Rovetta p*er* cantore....

Doc. 7:   Giovanni Rovetta, *Salmi concertati* (Venice: Magni, 1626 [*more veneto*])

Gia per molti anni à dietro è stato sempre mia professione il Sonar ogni sorte
d'Istromento, si da arco, come da fiato, et se bene m'affaticava non poco intorno à
questi, non però tralasciano lo studio della Compositione, et desideroso d'impiegare in
questo'l talento, procurai appresso gl'Illustrissimi, et Eccellentissimi Signori Procuratori
d'essere connumerato fratello trà gl'altri Signori Musici di lor Eccelenze in S*an* Marco
del che ne fui fatto degno, sperando doppo di poter in mancamento del Signor Maestro di
Cappella escercitar il carico del Vice Maestro, essendo già per avanti vacato detto luogo;
ni vano in ciò mi riuscì il pensiero, poi che occorso il bisogno poco doppo entrato, da
gl'Illustrissimi et Eccelentissimi Signori Procuratori miei Padroni fui honorato sino à lor
nova determinazione che esercitassi tal carico. Ma essendo parso ad alcuni cosa
stravagante, che in un instante io sia passato dalla professione de gl'Instrumenti à quella
del comporre, e reggere in diverse Feste varie Musiche; hanno fatto mal fondato giuditio,
che tali Musiche Ecclesiastiche non potessero da me essere state composte. Per lo che
prevendendo io, che tali oppositioni haverebbono potuto in breve tempo forse far alcuna
mala impressione in quelli, da' quali non son conosciuto; hò preso espediente di mandar
alle Stampe questi Canti Ecclesiastici, acciò che gl'Illustrissimi, et Eccellentissimi Signori
Procuratori veggano in effetto, che havendo procurato io la gratia di qual si voglia altro,
c'habbia per l'innanzi procurato detto luogo, et insieme sia conosciuto, che effetivamente
sono mie Compositioni, et non d'altri, non ricusando di farlo alla giornata apparire con
ogni sorte di prova à qual si voglia, che altrimenti credesse: et non sia, chi si maravigli,
che prima habbia esercitato il Sonare, e poi postomi ad esercitar il Comporre, che il
Signor Striggio, il Signor Priuli, il Signor Valentini, et quasi tutta la miglior scola de'
Compositori hanno in tal maniera operato. Anzi per questa tal cognitione, giustamente
poss'io pretendere il detto carico de Vice Maestro di Cappella in S*an* Marco per trovarsi
à questo Serenissimo Servitio non tanto trenta, e più Cantori, ma venti, e più
Instrumentisti da fiato, e da arco. Si che dunque Signori Virtuosi se in tali miei
Compositioni trovasti, cosa, che non fosse al tutto grata al vostro gusto, mi haverete per
iscusato incolpando la necessità narrata, che mi hà sforzato mandarle al presente in luce,
non mancando io fra tanto di mettere qualch'altra cosa all'ordine che, vi possa esser à
grado, et vivete Felici etc.

Doc. 8: Giovanni Rovetta, *Messa e Salmi* (Venice: Vincenti, 1639)

    .... Io fui comandato da Monsignor di Housaij Consigliere di Stato, et Ambasciador di
Vostra Maestà, à solennizzar nella neascita del gran Delfino il rendimento di quelle gratie,
che si celebrò con regal apparato di Musiche nella Basilica di S*an* Giorgio di Venetia.

Questo poco di servitio, per lo quale io fui honorato di riceverne da esso Signore
publica lode, mi rende animoso a consegrarle queste mie sacre fatiche musicali, per
eternar con la stampa le mie obbligationi, e per farmi conoscer in cotesto Mondo della
Francia per servidore della Maestà Vostra....

Doc. 9: Biblioteca nazionale marciana. Misc. 180. 17. *Venetia Festiva* (Venice: Baba,
1638), p. 24

Per la compositione della Musica, ò per Mastro di capella fù scielto fra tanti che
visono in Vinetia il Si*gn*or Rueti; al quale fù espressamente imposto di pigliare quanti
cantori et instrumenti Musicali si trovassero nella Città, per corrispondere à i concetti
magnanimi di S*u*a Ec*c*e*ll*en*z*a il quale desiderava la più celebre e solenne Musica, che si
potesse ritrovare.

Doc. 10: A.S.V., San Marco, Procuratia de Supra, Registro 144 (Chiesa Actorum,
1637–48)

1643: adì 21: Febraro [*more veneto*]

Volendo l'Ill*ustrissi*mi et Ecc*ellentissi*mi Si*gn*o*ri* Procuratori, devenir all'ellettione di
Mastro di Capella della Chiesa di S*an* Marco in luogo del q*uondam* Don Claudio
Monteverde ultimam*en*te mancato di vita; et essendo di già statto scritto conforme al
solito di ord*in*e di SS: SS: Eccellentissime, à Roma all'Ill*ustrissi*mo et R*everendissi*mo
Ottobon Aud*itor* di Rotta, à Viena, à Tutti li Rettori di T*erra Firma*, et alli Ressid*en*ti
Veneti p*er* haver informatione de soggetti qualifficati in quella professione, che
inclinassero al serv*iti*o sud*et*to, dalle risposte de quali havendosi inteso non ve ne esser di
qualità, et virtù, che inclini; Ne essendo comparsi altri che Gio*vann*i Rovetta Vice Mastro
di Capella, le virtù, e degne condition del quale essendo statte da SS: SS: Ill*ustrissi*me,
et Ecc*ellentissi*me ben considerate, Hanno à bossoli, et ballotte questo elletto in d*et*to
carico con salario de ducati tresento all'anno, et regalie solite, et consuette; dovendo
etia*m* haver la Casa in Canonica giusta all'ord*ina*rio, da esserli consegnata accomodata
delle cose necessarie.

Doc. 11: A.S.V., San Marco, Procuratia de Supra, Registro 12 (Giornali Cassier, 1639–48)

[1644] 17. Giugno

Per spesi per le Case//a Cassa *ducati* sessanta quattro *grossi* 14—, contadi a diversi
maestri per robbe e fatture fatti nella casa in cannonica, nella qual'è andato ad'habitar D.
Zuane Rovetta maestro di cappella, et è per term*inazio*ne di 21 Febru*ar*o passato....

Doc. 12: A.S.V., San Marco, Procuratia de Supra, Registro 12 (Giornali Cassier, 1639–48)

[1644] 9. Luglio

Per spese per le Case//à Cassa ducati diese contadi à Bartolo Maragon tra fatture e robbe
d'haver fatto gelosie alli pergoli nella casa habitata dal Maestro di Cappella giusta la
term*inazio*ne di 3. del corrente, polizza numero 77.

Doc. 13: P. Michiel and Giovanni Battista Fusconi, libretto to *Argiope* (Venice: Pinelli, 1649), pp. 6–7

Spero nondimeno che la diversità pur troppo apparente dello stile verrà resa uniforme dalla musica impareggiabile (anchorche diversa) delli Signori Giovanni Rovetta, e Alessandro Leardini Prencipi de Musici Moderni, e che l'eccellenza delle più famose voci del secolo coprirà i mancamenti della mia penna.

Doc. 14: P. Michiel and Giovanni Battista Fusconi, libretto to *Argiope* (Venice: Pinelli, 1649), p. 96

A chi haverà letto.

Gli errori, che avvengono nella stampa, sono figli d'una Madre, che pur troppo ne sà esser seconda. Perciò nel medesimo tempo, che quegli doveano venire da te emendati saranno stati ancora compatiti. Gli accidenti, che mutano l'essere alle cose in un istante, havendo privato della seconda gloria il nostro Dramma, la quale sarebbe stata le musica del Signor Rovetta, unita a quella del Signor Leardini, ti lasceranno godere dell' armonia d'un solo Orfeo, mentre io te ne havea apparecchiata quella di due.

Doc. 15: A.S.V., San Marco, Procuratia de Supra, Registro 146 (Chiesa Actorum, 1655–74)

Adi 28. Maggio 1663

Di più hanno gl'Illustrissimi et Eccellentissimi Signori Procuratori soprascritti terminato, che de danari della Cassa della Chiesa siano dati ducati vintidoi grossi sedese correnti ad Giovanni Rovetta Maestro di Capella per sotisfare la spesa dell'opera ligatura et carta reale della messa da morto posta in Musica per detto Maestro di carte trenta per servitio della Chiesa di San Marco....

Doc. 16: A.S.V., Archivio Notarile, Testamenti, Busta 281 (Francesco Ciola), Testamento numero 113

Laus Deo Adi. 16. Luglio 1667 in Venetia

.... Mi ritrovo ducati mille di Capitale dati da me à livello alla Procuratia di supra, delli quali ne ricano annualmente di prò ducati quarantacinque in rate doi, cioè ogni sei mesi ducati vinti doi e mezo. Voglio, che il prò sodetto sia impiegato in questo modo cioè li primi ducati vinti dui, e mezo, che matureranno doppo la mia morte siano riscorsi dal Basilicano del Capella di San Marco, et dal più vecchio cantor Sacerdote di detta Ducale, con obligo alli Signori Canonici, et cantori dell'istessa Ducale nel primo giorno non impedito subito fatta la riscorsione del denaro di farmi un esequie nella medesima Chiesa di San Marco, nel qual dovrà esser cantato da cantori la Messa da Morto à due Chori composta da me, e scritta à Bologna con il mottetto, ad Dominum cum tribularer, dovendo il denaro esser diviso (levatare l'elemosina per il sacrificio) metà alli Signori Canonici et l'altra metà alli Signori Cantori da esser divisi inter presentes, et non in altro modo, non intendendo, che alcuno delli sopradetti participano di questo denaro, se non saranno stati *presen*ti, et haveranno cantato la detta Messa. Per la pontuale essecutione di questo essequie sive Messa cantata instituisco *per* commisiarij il Sig*nor* Maestro di Capela, che saranno pro tempore alli quali dovrà esser dato doppia parte.

L'altra rata poi, che maturerà delli altri ducati vinti doi, e mézo voglio pure, che sia riscorsa dalli sopradetti Basilicano, et Cantor più vecchio Sacerdote con obligo similm*en*te alli Sig*no*ri Canonici, et Cantori di celebrarmi, et cantar la med*esi*ma messa nel primo giorno non impedito doppo fatta la riscorsione, nella Chiesa però di S*an* Silvestro, dove sarà sepolto il mio corpo, da esser il sopradetto dinaro diviso (levatare l'elemosina per il Sacrificio) solamente inter presentes come sopra ho dichiarito.

Nelle altre rate poi, che anderanno maturando sia praticato il mede*si*mo, cioè il primo dinaro impiegato nella celebratione et canto della Messa in S*an* Marco, et l'altro nella celebratione et canto della Messa in S*an* Silvestro, decadino ogni volta, che mancassero dal beneficio della metà della portione à loro come sopra destinata, et quella vadi alli Sig*no*ri Sacristani della detta Chiesa Ducale, che pro tempore saranno, divisa trà loro egualmente, essendo mia ferma, et risoluta volontà, che volendo godere li sopradetti beneficiati del detto dinaro, sijno anco obligati di celebrare et cantare puntualm*en*te la Messa sod*ett*a, et non altrim*en*ti, dovendo li Sig*no*ri Basilicano et Cantor più vecchio Sacerdote conservar sempre il libro di detta Messa, et occorrendo rifarlo spender quanto bisognerà delli sodetti denari acciò si possi perpetuam*en*te cantar....

Doc. 17: Biblioteca Nazionale Marciana, Cod. It. IV-1134 (-10949)

Questa Messa si cantava il Giovedì Santo al Tempo della Veneta Repubblica, cioè sino all'Anno 1797. Si cantava pure il Giorno di S*an* Nicolò li 6 Dicembre nell'Oratorio posto a latere della Scala dè Giganti in presenza del Serenissimo Doge, e del minore Collegio.

Doc. 18: A.S.V., San Marco, Procuratia de Supra, Registro 141 (Chiesa Actorum, 1614–20). Also reproduced in Glover, *op. cit.*, 165

1616 adi 18 *Dicem*bre

Che siano condutti *per* cantori in ch*ies*a in S*an* Marco l'infras*cri*tti soprani, uno d*ei* quali Eunuco quali sono statti sentiti da SS. SS. Ecc*ellentissi*mi, et anco havutta relaz*io*ne dal Maestro di capella, ch*e* sono à proposita *per* servizio dalla ch*ies*a c*on* salario d*i* d*uca*ti ottanta *per* cad*aun*o, et à beneplacido d*i* SS. SS. Ill*ustrissi*mi.

Piero Franc*esc*o Bruni cremasco.
Felice Cazzeleri da pistoia eunuco.

Doc. 19: A.S.V., Cancelleria Inferiore, Registro 80 (Atti dei Dogi, 1615–23), p. 74

1616. 18 Febr*uaro* [*more veneto*]

Venuto in Cam*er*a di sua Serenità il Sig*no*r Guglielmo Maffei nod*ari*o delli ecc*ellentissi*mi Sig*no*ri Procu*ratori* di Supra pres*en*tò a sua Serenità li sotto*scri*tti tre cantori novamente *per* detti Sig*no*ri Procu*ratori* eletti; et destinati *per* la Capella di S*an* Marco cioè.

Pietro Francesco Brunj cremascho
Felice Cazzelleri da Pistoia
Antonio Grimanj Ennrico
Dal qual Serenissimo ben vedutj: et amonitj di virtuosamente vivere, et attendere al carico loro gli mando à Monsignor Primicerio in San Marco giusta l'ordinario. Comandando à me suo cancelliere che ne facessi la presente nota....

Doc. 20: A.S.V., San Marco, Procuratia de Supra, Registro 144 (Chiesa Actorum, 1637–48)

1638 23 Gennaro [*more veneto*]

Essendo ridotti li Eccellentissimi Signori Procuratori in Chiesa di San Marco, per sentir la prova di Organista sopra l'organo picciolo in locco del quondam Giovanni Pietro Berti, fecero scriver dal Signor Maestro di Capella alcune sonate di canto fermo fatte levar da un libro mandato à pigliar in Saghrestia, et fatti li bollettini delli concorenti, et quelli cavati à sorte toccò per ordine come qui sotto—

Padre Niccolo Fontei.
Francesco Caletto detto Cavalli.
Padre Nadal Monferato.
Giacomo Arigoni.

Et sentiti tutti quattro SS: SS: Eccellentissime si riddussero à Lozetta, et ballottarono à bossoli coperti, et rimase elletto con tutte tre le balle de si il sopradetto Messer Francesco Caletto detto Cavalli con salario de ducati cento quaranta all'anno.

Doc. 21: A.S.V., San Marco, Procuratia de Supra, Busta 91, Processo 207 (Organisti), f. 1r

Prova solita per esperimentar li Organisti che pretendono di concorrer a L'Organo nella Chiesa di San Marco in Venetia

Primo si apre il libro di Capella, et a sorte si trova un principio di Kirie, o vero di Motetto, et si copia mandandolo al l'Organista che concorre, il quale sopra quel sugetto ne l'istesso Organo vacante deve sonar di fantasia regolatamente, non confondendo le parti, come che quattro Cantori cantassero.

Secondo si apre il libro de canti fermi pur a sorte, et si copia un canto fermo, o d'introito o d'altro, et si manda al detto organista, sopra il quale deve sonar cavando le tre parti, facendo il detto canto fermo una volta in Basso l'altra in Tenore, poi in contralto, et soprano, cavando fughe regolatamente et non semplici accompagnamenti.

Terzo si fa cantar la Capella de Cantori, qualche Versetto di compositione non troppo usitata, la quale deve imitare et rispondergli, si in tuono come fuori di tuono: et queste cose fatte d'improviso dar chiaro indicio del valor de l'Organista facendole bene.

Doc. 22: Giovanni Battista Volpe, dedication of Giovanni Rovetta's *Madrigali concertati*
.... *Libro Terzo* (Venice: Vincenti, 1645). Also reproduced in Glover, *op. cit.*, p. 165

.... L'Organo di San Marco reso divino dalla dotta mano di Vostra Signoria e la minor
prova, ch'ella fa del suo molto valore.
   Posciache l'esquisitezza delle sue celebratissime compositioni à tale, ch'ella rapiace
con esse loro e nelle Chiese, e nelle Camere, e ne' Teatri gli animi di tutti....
   E Veramente mentre concorrono in lei tre qualità esimie, ch'ella, e sa vestire
nobilmente i soggetti, e impareggiabilmente cantarli, e accompagnarli con la leggiadra
accuratezza su l'istrumento, credo io che non voglia Vostra Signoria far torto con metter
alla stampa le sue ottime compositioni, all'altre due prerogative ch'ella possiede, di ben
cantarle et accompagnarle, che sono vivi tesori incapaci della stampa.

Doc. 23: A.S.V., San Marco, Procuratia de Supra, Busta 91, Processo 207 (Organisti),
       f. 68r.

Desiderando Sua Maestà di far magnifiche demostrationi d'allegrezza nelle sollennità del
suo Matrimonio con la Serenissima Infanta di Spagna, cerca da tutte le parti le persone
più celebri in ogni perfettione, et havendo saputo, che il Signor Cavalli Organista di
San Marco è un Huomo Eccellente er la Compositione d'opere in Musica mi hà
comandato supplicar Vostra Serenità di concedergli la permissione di far un viaggio in
Francia à fine di servirsi de suoi talenti in quest'occasione, ma essendo quest'impiego per
breve tempo desideraria Sua Maestà che piacesse alla Serenità Vostra di conservargli la
sua Carica nella Chiesa di San Marco con li suoi assegnamenti per il tempo che lò servirà
in queste sollennità.

Disse il Serenissimo Prencipe. E affare questo di poco rilievo, sarà facile incontrar le
sodisfattioni che desidera. Questi Signori vi haveranno riflesso, e tutto si farà per le
sodisfationi della Maestà Christianissima in riguardo anco all'intercessioni di Vostra
Signoria, che viene da noi singolarmente amata.

Doc. 24: A.S.V., San Marco, Procuratia de Supra, Registro 146 (Chiesa Actorum,
       1655–74)

Adi 11 Aprile 1660.

Sia concesso a Francesco Cavalli organista che parta per Francia quando sarà per detto
Signor Ambasciatore ricercato per le solennità del matrimonio del Re Christianissimo, et
ivi si trattenga sino al fine di dette solennità, con sicurezza che gli sarà riservato il luoco
ed emolumento suo fino al suo ritorno in questa Città: cosè anche essendo la pubblica
intentione dell'Eccellentissimo Senato. Dovendo trà tanto impiegarti nella funtione
d'organista in luogo di detto Cavali Don Giovanni Battista Volpe come egli stesso si è
offerto senza altra mercede, che di acquistar merito col ben servire.
Sia Concesso a Giovanni Calegari *soprano* e Giannagostino Poncelli *tenore*, che possano
andar con l'organista Cavalli per servire al Re *Christianissimo* nella vicina occasione delle
nozze, come s'è conceduto al detto Cavalli.

Doc. 25: A.S.V., San Marco, Procuratia de Supra, Busta 90, Processo 204 (Maestro di Cappella), f. 59r

1668. 20. Novembre

Fu d'ordine dell'Eccellentissimi Signori Procuratori per Victorio Polani custode di Procuratia chiamato e stridato sulla porta d'essa Procuratia, che se v'è alcuno, che voglia concorrer alla Carica di Maestro di Capella della Ducal Chiesa di San Marco, debba darsi in nota, volendo dette Eccellentissime, venir all'elettione in luoco del quondam D. Zuane Roeta Defonto.

.... Comparse D. Francesco Caletti, et si diede in nota

in margin: 1668: a dì: 17 novembre fu publicato per me Carlo Foresti Comandador de detta procuratia sopra la porta grande de la Chiesa di San Marco.

Doc. 26: A.S.V., San Marco, Procuratia de Supra, Registro 146 (Chiesa Actorum, 1655–74)

1668: 20: Novembre

Essendo in questi ultimi giorni passato à miglior vita D. Zuane Roeta Maestro di Capella della Ducal Chiesa di San Marco, et dovendosi provedere d'altro soggetto valevole à sostenere tal Carico, fatti per ciò farli proclami alli lochi soliti, che chi prettende concorrer à detta fontione debba nel termine de giorni trè prossimi comparer alla Procuratia Nostra à darsi in nota come dalla relatione de Carlo Foresti Publico Commandador di 17: instante appar. Ne essendo comparso altri, che D. Francesco Caletto detto Cavali, hora serviente la stessa Ducal Chiesa per organista, con molta sua Laude e sodisfattione universale; hanno gl'Illustrissimi et Eccellentissimi Signori Procuratori infrascritti.... a bossoli et ballotte eletto il sudetto D. Francesco Caletto, detto Cavalli, Maestro di Capella della medesima Ducal Chiesa in loco del sudetto Roveta deffonto, con tutti li Carichi, obligationi, salario, et godimento di Casa nella Canonica in tutto, et per tutto come haveva et godeva il predetto Roeta, promettendosi dalla sua virtù, diligenza, e valore ogni buon frutto, per il Publico servitio, et avanzamento di sua gloria così.

Doc. 27: A.S.V., Archivio Notarile, Busta 488 (Testamenti Garzoni Paulini Domenico), numero 206. Also reproduced in Wiel, *op. cit.*, pp. 144–45

Voglio in oltre, che nel termine di giorni otto, doppo la mia morte, mi sij fatto un'Essequie solenne nella detta Chiesa di San Lorenzo con Messa Cantata in Musica Concertata dà Morto, dalli migliori Musici, e Suonatori de Capella e della Città regolata dal Signor Maestro di capella di San Marco. E perche potrebbe essere, che in si poco spatia di tempo, doppo la mancanza mia, non fosse per anco fatta da gl'Eccellentissimi Procuratori l'Ellettione di nuovo Maestro di Capella, in questo Caso si potrà portar innanti dette Essequie, mentre però si scorgesse, che detta Elletione non fosse per esser troppo longa, che per ciò in sua vece potrà farla il Signor Vice Maestro, overo altro Virtuoso il migliore, non potendo lui, impiegando in questa fontione, Ducati settanta

Cinque correnti, cio è Ducati sessanta nelli Musici, quali non possino esser meno di dodici parti di Concerto, et

2 Violini
4 Viole
2 Cornetti
2 Tiorbe
Tromboni
Fagotto
Violon grosso, il *Signor* Paulo
3 Organi
Cantori per Ripieno, facendo bisogno, di quelli di Capella.

Pregando le Ill*ustrissi*me Sacrestane, di dispensare questi Ducati sessanta in modo, che restino tutti gli Musici, e Suonatori Contenti. Havendo p*erò* riguardo di congrua recognitione ad esso *Signor* M*aestr*o di Capella, ò altro, che havesse l'incombenza della Compositione di essa Messa: à distintione delli altri Musici, e Suonatori. Il rimanente, che saranno Ducati quindici, doveranno esser spesi nelli doi Palchi *per* la Musica, e picciolo Catafalco, Candele sopra gl'Altari, doi Torchi al Catafalco, et l'Elemosina al Sacerdotte *per* il sacrifitio della Messa, Diacono, Sodiacono, et cetera.

Voglio in oltre, che mi siano instituiti doi altri essequii all'anno in p*er*petuo, il p*rim*o nella Ducal Chiesa di S*an* M*ar*co, il *secon*do nella d*et*ta Chiesa di S*an* Lorenzo, et così successiva*men*te in p*er*petuo, con la distanza però di mesi sei l'uno dall'altro, nelli giorni più comodi, et à proposito, come dovrà esser stabilito dalli *Signo*ri Cantori della giornata destinata p*er* questa fontione. Ne quali essequii se dovrà cantare una Messa dà morto, dà me Composta à due Chori, che sarà apparecchiata, e scritta a questo fine, e possino intervenire à questi doi Essequii, tutti gli Canonici di essa Chiesa di S*an* M*ar*co, et tutti gli Cantori di Capella, *per* li quali esseguii, intendo, et voglio ch*e* si*jn*o destinati Ducati sessanta da lire 6 soldi 4 per Ducato all'anno in p*er*petuo, cioè la meta che saranno D*uca*ti 30 per Cadaun di essi Essequii, da farli il p*rim*o in Chiesa di S*an* Marco, siano, Consegnati Ducati quindici al *Signo*r M*aestr*o di Choro, overo al Degano di esso Capitollo *per* dover dividere, detratta l'elemosina per il sacrifitio, che no*n* dovrà esser meno di D*uca*to mezzo al Sacerdotte, e mezzo trà il Diacono, e Sodiacono, il rimanente, de ciò, dividere con essi *Signo*ri Canonici inter presentes. Et altretanti D*uca*ti 15, similmente Consegnarli al *Signo*r M*aestr*o di Capella overo à due Cantori più Vecchi, p*er* dover dividere trà tutti li Musici parimente inter presentes datta p*er* ò doppia parte à d*et*ti S*igno*ri M*aest*ri di Choro e di Capella. Et p*er*chè à questa mia Messa che desidero si*j* Cantata, si conviene per necessità un Istromento grave per Basso Continuo, voglio che si*j* Chiamato fin che vive, et può, il Signor Paulo Mansina col Violone, al quale sia datto, p*er* candauna volta, un Ducato da lire 6 soldi 4 del Corpo delli sopra*det*ti Ducati quindici assignati à S*igno*ri Musici come sopra. E voglio anco sia dato una meza parte di quello toccherà à Cadaun Musico al Chierico, over Custode di Libri, quale havrà obligo di far Consapevole, come di sopra ho d*et*to, tutti gli *Signo*ri musici otto giorni innanti, acciò no*n* habbino à dolersi di no*n* haverlo saputo, obligando, *per* espresso, essi *Signo*ri Cantori à dover Cantare la Messa, da me sopra nominata, altrimenti contrafacendo, decadino ogni volta dal benefi*ci*o della mettà della lor portione, come sopra destinatale, qual mettà in tal Caso, vada in benefi*ci*o delli *Reveren*di Sacrestani di d*et*ta Ducal Chiesa, che fossero presenti, divisa fra di loro, essendo così mia intentione, e non in altro modo. Dovendo à questo effetto dal sud*et*to Chierico, over Custode di Libri con special Cura essere Conservato il Libro di d*et*ta M*es*sa p*er* no*n* haver occasione di apportar spesa per accomodarlo, o rifarlo, perche quando venisse il Caso, si dovrà spendere delli sopra*det*ti Denari assignati come sopra à Cantori, p*er* rifarlo, et accomodarlo, acciò si possi perpetuamente Cantare essa Messa; Et così voglio sij continuato in perpetuo a far questi doi Essequii ogn'Anno, Uno in San Marco, e l'altro in San Lorenzo, con la distanza però Come sopra, di mesi sei, da uno all'altro, et con l'esborso del denaro, nel modo, e quantità, in tutto, e per tutto come hò detto di sopra, che dovrà esser Cavato dalle Entrate et prò del mio Residuo.

Doc. 28: A.S.V., San Lorenzo di Venezia, Busta 23, fascicolo 21 (L), ff. 15r–20r

Laus Deo Anno 1673, adi 8 Marzo
In Venetia....

Il Rimanente poi delli Prò sopradetti, che saranno ducati 94 in circa ordino e voglio, che subito maturati sij fatto un essequie solenne in detta Chiesa di San Lorenzo per l'anima mia con messa cantata in musica concertata da morto dalli migliori Musici, et suonatori della Città, et regolata dal Signor Mastro di Capella di San Marco, che prò tempore sarà, overo non potendo lui dal Signor Vice Mastro, ò da altro Virtuoso il più perfetto, assegnando per questa funtione ducati cinquanta quattro grossi 14 del corpo delli sopradetti che rimangono, compresa in essi l'ellemosina, che per il sacrificio doverà esser data alli Reverendi Capellani, il resto doverà esser diviso trà detti Musici, e Suonatori, secondo parerà all'Illustrissime Sacristane di San Lorenzo, havuto però riguardo di congrua recognitione ad'esso Signore Mastro di Capella, ò Vice Mastro, ò a quello havesse l'incombenza della compositione della Messa sopradetta a distintione de altri musici, e suonatori. Lò restanti poi ducati quaranta delli prò sopradetti voglio, che sijno consignati alli Reverendo Basilicano, et più Vecchio Cantor Sacerdote della Ducal Chiesa di San Marco ogn'anno in perpetuo per l'anima mia, havendosi però mira, che li essequij sopradetti sijno fatti con distanza di mesi sei l'uno dall'altro, così che ogn'anno tutti due sijno celebrati, nel qual secondo essequie in Chiesa di San Marco si doverà cantare una messa da morto dà mè fatta à due cori, che sarà apparecchiata e scritta à questo fine, e possino intervenire tutti gli Cantori di Capella, tutti gli Cannonici, e sotto Canonici di essa Ducal Chiesa, assegnando la metà, che sono ducati 20 al Signor Mastro di Coro per dover dividere, detratta prima l'ellemosina per il sacrificio, con essi Signori Cannonici et sotto Cannonici inter presentes; et l'altra metà, che sono pure ducati 20 sijno assegnati al Signor Mastro di Capella per dover dividere con tutti gli musici però inter presentes; datta però dopia parte sempre à detti Signori Maestri di Coro, e di Capella.

Et perche à questa mia messa, che desidero sij cantata in tal giorno se gli conviene per neccessità un Instromento grave per Basso Continuo voglio, et intendo, che sij chiamato fino che vive, e che può il Signor Paulo Mancina col Violone, alquale gli sij datto per cadauna volta un ducato da lire 6 soldi 4 del corpo delli sopra detti ducati 20 assegnati à Signori musici come sopra Desiderando, che gli due Maestri di Coro e di Capella s'abbocchino prima assieme per apuntare il giorno commodo à tutti per questa Pia funtione all'hora di terza: al qual effetto sarà tenuto il Chierico de Libri di far avvertiti tutti li Signori Cantori della giornata destinata per questa functione, e per la sua fatica gli doverà esser datto del corpo di questi ultimi ducati 20 una meza parte di quello toccherà à cadaun de Signori Musici: havendo l'obligo di fare avvertiti otto giorni innanti tutti essi Signori Cantori, accio non habbina à dolersi di non haverlo saputo. Obligando per espresso essi Signori Cantori dover cantare la messa da mè sopra nominata, altrimente contrafacendo decaino ogni volta dal beneficio della loro positione come sopra destinatali, e l'altra vadi in beneficio delli Reverendi Sacristani di detta Ducal Chiesa, che fossero presenti divisa frà di loro, essendo così mia intentione, et non altrimenti, dovendo à quest'effetto dal detto Chierico con special cura esser conseniato il libro di detta messa, per non haver occasione d'apportar spesa per acconciarlo, e riffarlo, mà quando venirà il caso si doverà spendere delli sopradetti denari: per riffarlo, ò accomodarlo, acciò si possi perpetuamente cantarla: pregando pure la detta Illustrissima Abbadessa, et Illustrissime Sacristane di San Lorenzo, che saranno prò tempore haver loro questo impaccio perche sijno riscossi li prò sopradetti alli suoi tempi, e quelli far sborsare così alli detti Reverendi Sacerdotj sempre con la certezza delle Officiatura, come alli detti Reverendi Basilicano, e più vecchio Cantor Sacerdote di San Marco per le funtioni sopradette.

Chapter II

Doc. 29: Biblioteca Ambrosiana, MS A. 328 inf., f. 164v

Ogni volta, che si apre la Palla sono obligati Cantare à due Chori con li Salmi à 8. li Vesperi, et alle Messe cantar un Motetto nell'Organo.

Doc. 30: A.S.V., San Marco, Procuratia de Supra, Registro 144 (Chiesa Actorum, 1637–48)

1643. 3 Genaro [*more veneto*]

Che sia concessa licenza à D: Giovanni Rovetta Vice Mastro di Capella di poter stampar le cose nominate nella sua supplica hoggi presentata.

Doc. 31: Dedication to *Delli Salmi a 8. Voci* of Giovanni Rovetta (Venice: Magni, 1662)

ALL'ILL.MI ET ECC.MI SIG.RI PROCURATORI DI SUPRA

Doppo le compositioni dalle mie vigilie partorite, di Hinni, Motetti, e Messe, che s'attrovano in manuscritti diversi al bisogno della Regia Capella di S. MARCO: sono stati da altre mie non meno serie fatiche formati al canto, secondo l'uso di detta Capella anco li Salmi di tutto l'anno. E perche di facile rimarrebbono smarriti, e consunti, se solamente ad alcuno esemplare di penna fossero raccommandati: cadendo molto frequente l'uso, e necessità di quelli: Tanto maggiormente, che l'opere di servitio della Publica Maestà, quanto più odorano da perpetuità, tanto più incontrano la profonda Mente Regale: Propria perciò resolutione m'è parsa rassegnarli alle stampe: dalle quali s'ha il beneficio e di molteplici copie, e di durabilità più costante, la qual'intentione all'hora però si riputarà conseguita, che dalli Nomi deli Ecc. VV. quasi Numi immortali di tutte le Virtù saranno alla perpetuità sublimati. Dunque dovotissimo le supplico ammettere all'udito dell'Eccelsa loro Begnignità la presente mia Opera, et in argomento validissimo della mia suisceratezza al Publico servitio, et in ossequosissimo Tributo à VV. Ecc: delle quali viverò sempre.

Doc. 32: A.S.V., San Marco, Procuratia de Supra, Registro 146 (Chiesa Actorum, 1655–74)

Adi 7. Genaro 1662 [*more veneto*]

Havendo il Maestro di Capella Gio*vanni* Rovetta fatta stampare alcune messe, et salmi necessarij per la Capella di San Marco: mentre gl'antichi manuscritti erano dal tempo consunti, et impossibile à più servirsene. Pero essendo conveniente oltre il rimborsarlo della spesa considerabile di riconoscere il suo diligente impiego gl'Ill*ustrissi*mi et Ecc*ellentissi*mi Sig*no*ri Proc*urato*ri infras*crit*ti.... Hanno terminato, ch*e* de danari della Cassa della Chiesa siano al medesimo dati ducati cento e cinquanta, nei quali il sopra più della spesa serva p*er* testimonio del gradimento, e p*er* aletamento à chi serve la Chiesa, et questa Procuratia....

Doc. 33: A.S.V., San Marco, Procuratia de Supra, Registro 146 (Chiesa Actorum, 1655–74)

Adi 8. Aprile 1674

Gl'Ill*ustrissi*mi et Ecc*ellentissi*mi Sig*no*ri Proc*urato*ri.... hanno terminato che de denari della Cassa della Chiesa sian pagati ducati vintiquatro a P*ad*re Lorenzo Rossi in sodisfatione delle copie fatte delle Messe solene in musica servirono per il Natale de gl'anni 1671, 1672, et 1673, et Vespero per detto anno, 1671 compreso la carta composte da nove dal Maestro di Capella della medesima giusto la sua poliza sottoscritta dal detto Maestro....

Doc. 34: Preface to Francesco Cavalli, *Musiche Sacre* (Venice: Vincenti, 1656)

L'AUTORE A CHI LEGGE

LETTORE. Il mio Genio è stato sempre lontano dalle stampe: et hò più tosto aconsentito à lasciar correre le mie debolezze dove le partò la fortuna col mezo della penna, che con quello de Torchi. Al fine però mi sono lasciato persuadere dalle instanze del Signor Alessandro Vince*n*ti, che, doppo lunga persistenza nella mia Opinione hà saputo vincermi, e darmi ardire di esponere all'universo i deboli tratti delle mie Note. Se tu ne riceverai gradimento siane egli il benemerito; come pure, se ne incontri tedio non dolerti di me, che à recarti questo incommodo per altro fine non mi sono condotto, solo che per compiacere un amico, che con le sue cortesie hà saputo persuadermi.

Chapter III

Doc. 35: Biblioteca Ambrosiana, MS A. 328 inf., unpaginated folio from dedicatory passage, "Serenissimo Prencipe"

.... Di più si haverà la Cronologia di molti fatti spettanti alla detta Ducal Capella, oltre le Riti della Chiesa e fontioni tutte le Ceremonie del Ser*enissi*mo nella Chiesa, et Palazzo con suoi Privilegi, et auttorità, quello si deve apparecchiar nella Sacristia quando cala il Ser*enissi*mo Le Ceremonie spettanti alli Ecc*ellentissi*mi Proc*urato*ri et Privilegi. Li Privilegi della Capella med*esi*ma, le di lei essentioni, et delle Dimissorie p*er* l'ordinatione del suo Clero, et Chiese annesse. Li Privilegi del Primicerio, essentioni de Can*oni*ci, de Sacristani. Le obligationi de Cantori, Organisti, e del Campanil di S*an* Marco, et altre cose tutte di curiosità ripiene tratte da varij auttori, da Croniche diverse mansucritte, e da Scritture de Dottori essistenti nella Secreta Ducale, ridotte nel presente Ceremoniale perpetuo con lunga et laboriosa fatica.

Quest'è quanto hò potuto raccogliere in anni 38. di servitù prestata con essatezza dovuta à questa sua Regia Capella....

Doc. 36: Giovanni Stringa, revised edition of Sansovino's *Venetia città nobilissima* (Venice, 1604), f. 82v

Il terzo si chiamava Bartolomeo Bonifacio, che visse sino all'anno 1564. Questi [*sic*] fu quello, che compose; e scrisse di suo proprio pugno con molta sua lode il Libro, detto Cerimoniale, che contiene tutte le cerimonie, che usar si sogliono in questa Chiesa.

Doc. 37: Biblioteca Ambrosiana, MS A. 328 inf., f. 207r

1564. P. Bortolamio Bonifacio Maestro di Coro compose il Ceremonial Antico sotto Pio 4.o Pontefice, et Ger:mo Priuli Doge, tratto da Riti antichiss*i*mi, et rudi; hora Maestosi, et venerabili, e di maniera accresciuti et alterati rispetto al luoco, ove si fan*n*o, alla presenza della Publica Maestà, ch'à pena le vecchie Ceremonie si riconoscono dalle nuove.

Doc. 38: Biblioteca Nazionale Marciana, Cod. Lat. III-172 (-2276), f. 2v

Adi 16 Gen*n*aro 1677 [*more veneto*]

Io Franc*esc*o Zuliani Can*oni*co et Vic*ari*o Ducale ho consignato il presente libro chiamato Ceremoniale della Chiesa di S. Marco al M. Rev*erendo* Sig*nor* D. Giacomo Giulani Cass*ier* e Maestro di Choro, questo di eletto Maestro dalli Ill*ustrissi*mi et Ecc*ellentissi*mi Sig*no*ri Procuratori di Supra in loco del q*uondam* Ecc*ellentissi*mo D. Zuane Viani.

Doc. 39: A.S.V., San Marco, Procuratia de Supra, Registro 98 (Ceremoniali), verso of title page (unpaginated)

Copia: 1646. 27 Junij

Presens liber pr*ae*sentatus fuit per D: D: Georgium Minaccia Magistrum C*ae*remoniarum Ecclesi*ae* Sancti Marci in obedientia preceti relaxati de. mandato magnificorum Dominorum Inquisitorum Promissionis Ducalis occasione obitus Serenissimi Principis Ervizzi ad instantiam heredum predicti Ser*enissi*mi Principis.

Doc. 40: A.S.V., Collegio, Ceremoniali, III, f. 123v

1646. 21 Giugno.

Copia tratta dal Cerimonial della Ducal Chiesa di San Marco. Atta fatta da me Padre Zorzi Minaccia Maestro di Choro della sodetta Chiesa.

Doc. 41: A.S.V., San Marco, Procuratia de Supra, Registro 139 (Chiesa Actorum, 1598–1607)

1601: 26. Luglio

Noi Procuratori de Supra della Chiesa di San Marco facciamo intender et saper à voi Messer Padre Rocco de Bruni Maestro di Coro, et delle Cerimonie in Chiesa di San Marco, che in virtù della Vostra ellettione per noi fatta, dobbiate nel vostro Carico predetto essercitar, et metter in essecutione il Libro, et Cerimoniale delli Riti Ecclesiastici che vi fù consignato al tempo di detta vostra ellettione il quale è intitulatto cosi:

Rituum Ecclesiasticorum Caerimoniale iuxta Ducalis Ecclesiae Sancti Marci Venetiarum consuetudinem, ex Vetustissimis eiusdem Ecclesiae Codicibus, quam diligentissime undique collectum, ac in ampliorem formam et ordinem novissime renovatum Anno Domini: 1564: Pio 4.o Pontifice Maximo Apostolice sedis sceptra Tenente; Hieronimo quae Priolo Rempublicam Venetam optime gubernante Sacrarum Caerimoniarum Ecclesiae Divi Marci Evangelistae Libri Tres Videlicet, Dominicale, Sanctuarium, et extraordinarium.

Non alterando, ne innovando, niuno di essi ritti sacri, et Cerimoniali, quelli esseguendo giusta l'antica consuetudine osservata; et se vi fosse persona tanto ardito, che volesse impedirvi nel vostro Carico, significarete à noi quanto in tal material occorerà, a ciò che possiamo preveder quel ispediente, che giudicaremmo necessario: Et se altramente farete provederemo come si convenirà all'innobedientia vostra.

Doc. 42: Biblioteca del Civico Museo Correr. MS Donà delle Rose 68: INDICE E REPERTORIO GENERALE/DELLE LEGGI/STATUARIE DEL S.M.C. ECCE.O SENATO/COLLEGIO, ET ECC:O DI X.E..... f. 258v

1759: 28 Aprile in Signoria

Resta commesso al Maestro di Coro e di Ceremonie Don Zuanne Vardure, di formar la proposita Compilatione e Registro delle Cerimonie tutte, e nella Chiesa di San Marco, e fuori di essa.

Doc. 43: Biblioteca del Civico Museo Correr. MS Donà delle Rose 68, f. 258v

31 Maggio in Signoria

Che li tre uniformi Libri Cerimoniali della Chiesa Ducal di San Marco, in ordine alla Terminazione della Serenissima Signoria 28 Aprile passato siano risposti uno in Secreta, uno in Procuratia di Supra, e l'altro resti appresso il Maestro di Ceremonie pro tempore.

Doc. 44: A.S.V., San Marco, Procuratia de Supra, Registro 141 (Chiesa Actorum, 1614–20)

1619. Primo Genaro [*more veneto*]

Essendo necess*a*rio comprar un ceremonial chiamato Cerimoniale Episcoporu*m* ordinato dalla Santità di Clemente Ottava p*er* osservar qua*n*to si deve in esse cerimonie, et cosi un directoriu*m* chori, et martirologio Romano; Però SS. SS. Ill*u*strissi*m*e et Ecc*ell*entissi*m*e han*n*o à boss*oli* et ball*oti* ter*mina*to ch*e* sia comprato il d*etto* libro, il qual sia ligato in cuore, come si ricerca, et sia tutto consignato al Maestro delle Cerimonie.

Doc. 45: A.S.V., San Marco, Procuratia de Supra, Busta 91, f. 56r. Also reproduced in Arnold, *Gabrieli/Venetian High Renaissance*, 32–34

Per obedir rivere*n*temente all'ordine impostomi da V*o*stra S*er*enissima Ill*u*strissi*m*a nel modo, et forma, che la è molto bene con Sapevole.
                                        Dico
Che nella Capella di S*an* Marco si ritrovano li infras*cri*tti cantori.

Soprani
Antonio Spagnol: Bella, et buona voce, ma no*n* troppo sicuro.
Guielmo Francese: Sicuro, et franco ca*n*tor, ma no*n* così delicata voce.

Contralti
P*adre* Zuanne Chiozotto: sufficient*issim*o cantor, e dove manca la delicatezza della voce supplisse co'l bel cantare.
Fra Hier*oni*mo de Carmeni: no*n* è di molta voce.
Fra Bernardo di Frari: no*n* è la sua voce di cattivo metale ma no*n* l'ha saputa mai accomodare
Batt*ist*a da S*an* Pantazzo: ha gran voce, et honestame*n*te sicuro

Tenori
Zuanne Ant*oni*o Fiame*n*go: è stato sempre di buona voce, et bel cantante, ma p*er* la vechiezza convien declinar.
Fr*a* Agustin Fazuol: buona voce, et buon cantore.
Paulo Roman no*n* ha cattivo metal di voce, et canta honestamente.

Bassi
Fr*a* Fabritio di Frari buona voce
Fr*a* Giacomo Ant*oni*o di Corsenieri buona voce
Fr*a* Sigismondo da S*an* Zanepolo honesta voce.
Fr*a* Agustin di Foscari honesta voce, ma ca*n*ta polito.

Doc. 46: A.S.V., San Marco, Procuratia de Supra, Busta 91, Processo 208, fascicolo 2, f. 26r

1594. 7. Genaro [*more veneto*]

L'Ill*u*strissi*m*i Sig*no*ri [Procuratori]....han*n*o a boss*oli*, et ball*o*tti ter*mina* to ut infra
Che sia scritto all'Amb*assado*r Veneto app*re*sso sua Maestà Cesarea et ad altri Amb*assado*ri come sarà dall'Ill*u*strissi*m*o Cassier ordinato, ch*e* desiderando noi haver

cantori Eccelenti per la capella della chiesa nostra di San Marco, et in particolar di soprani Eunuchi, Bassi Tenori, et contralti, siano contenti usar ogni diligentia aciò quelli cantori di tal conditione, che si ritrovassero in quelli lochi, o contorni, sappino, et siano fatti certi da S. S. Illustrissime che venendo da qui, et essendo le loro voci bone, et sufficienti per la capella nostra, saranno accettatti, et stipendiati in vita loro, in maniera tale che restaranno sodisfattissimi, et li sarà pagato la spesa del viaggio, à quali sarà datto il salario anco in caso di malatia et sempre di doi mesi in doi mesi, facendoli sapere che li cantori nostri non sono obligati tutti li giorni della settimana, come sono nelle corti d'altri Principi, et che gli utili d'incerti, che hanno nell'occassioni di cantar in tempo di solennità nelle altre chiese di questa città sono molti....

Doc. 47: A.S.V., San Marco, Procuratia de Supra, Busta 91, Processo 208, fascicolo 1, f. 61v

Registro de Signori Cantori che sono al presente

Il Reverendo Padre Giovanni Croce Chiozzoto capo mag.to
Messer Guielmo Francese
Padre Frate Agostin Fasuolo
Padre Frate Agostin Basso
Messer Zuane Battista contralto
Messer Paolo Veraldo Romano
Messer Nicolo Vandali Romano
Messer Nicolo Cheggia
Messer Lutio Mora
Messer Christofor Porro Basso
Messer Antonio Bonhuomo
Messer Padre Zuane Francese
Messer Padre Piero Francese
Messer Padre Bortolamio Conte
Messer Padre Vicenzo Spontoni
Messer Padre Rocco Zambelli
Messer Stefano Riveri
Messer Francisco Castigliano
Messer Padre Huomo Bon Basso
Messer Padre Felician Contralto
Messer Zuanne Arzignan
Messer Baldissera Dotto Basso
Messer Mutio Facini Basso

Data de Procuratia de supra ali 22 Novembre 1601.

Doc. 48: A.S.V., Cancelleria Inferiore, Registro 78 (Atti dei Dogi, 1595–1605), f. 55r

Et acciò che ogn'uno sij sollecito alli carichi suoi, sij puntato ogn'uno mentre mancasse dell'officio suo, cioè chi non venirà al principio del terzo salmo di terza, perda un terzo di quello potrebbe guadagnare in quella mattina, finito terza et che non sia al principio della processione, perdi la mità dell'istesso guadagno ut supra, et non venendo inanzi, che sia finita la gloria della Messa, perdi il tutto ut supra. Del Vespero si tenghi l'istesso ordine con l'istessa limitatione, cioè non essendo al secondo salmo perdi ut supra. Al principio del terzo salmo non vi essendo perdi ut supra, Al quarto salmo non vi essendo al principio perdi ut supra ne ardisca sij chi si voglia d'impiantar all' officio et beneficio, mà doppo finito avisar il capo nostro maggiore, overo essecutori, la caggione che voglia partire, acciò si possi rimediare à tal inconveniente.

Doc. 49: A.S.V., Cancelleria Inferiore, Registro 79 (Atti dei Dogi, 1606–15), f. 108r

Marco Antonio Memo DEI gratia Dux Venetiarum et cetera atque Ecclesiae Sancti Marcj nostrae capellae solus patronus et Dominus.

Udito padre Marc'Antonio Negri Veronese, uno delli cantori, et in hoc Vice maestro delli cantorj di detta Capella, co'l suo avocato: Dimandante che per noi sij Terminato, che nelle Musiche, ch'occoreranno farsi nelle chiese, et altri lochj della Città con i cantori predetti gli sij conservato il suo luoco et grado di Vice maestro, si come tiene nella predetta chiesa di San Marco, in virtù della sua elettione fatta per li Signori Procuratori di detta Chiesa, et da noj confirmata. Non essendo di publico decoro, et dignità ch'esso Vice maestro nelle musiche, che si fanno fuori della nostra predetta Capella habbia loco inferiore à quello ch'ha in quella. Nella quale senza dubbio doppo il maestro tiene il primo loco da una. Et dall'altra udito Padre Gasparo Locatello capo della compagnia delli cantori della predetta nostra capella con il suo avocato dicente: il sopradetto Vice maestro in San Marco dover esser licenciato per più ragioni et cause dette, dedotte, et alegate. Stante massime, che'l suo luoco per la forma della sua elettione è nella capella di San Marco solamente et non altrove; si come in quella chiaramente si legge. Nec non stante l'elettione di lui Padre Gasparo in Capo di detta compagnia per essa fatta di tutti li sufragij, servata in tutto la forma delli capitoli stabiliti sotto la felice memoria del Serenissimo Duce Grimanj; anco da noi ultimamente confirmatj. Veduto, et il tutto maturamente considerato chiamato il nome di nostro Signore Gesu Christo unica luce di Pace, et di Giustizia, habbiamo sententiato, et sententiando licenciato detto Padre Marco Antonio, dovendo in conseguenza detto Padre Gasparo continuare l'officio suo di capo della predetta compagnia giusta la forma dell'elettione sua di 30 maggio 1612. Commandando all'infrascritto nostro cancelliero che così notar e publicar dovesse.
.... die 27 Augusti 1613....

Doc. 50: A.S.V., Cancelleria Inferiore, Registro 79 (Atti dei Dogi, 1606–15), ff. 138r–v

[1614] Adi 3. Dicembre

Serenissimo DD. Marc'Antonio Memo per la Dio gratia Duce di Venezia et cetera. Udito il tenore, et continenza della sottoscritto et anco li capi de cantori nominati in quella, istantemente ricercantj l'espedittione del negotio in essa contenuto: sentendosi molto occupato in publici et in privati affarj ha rimesso, et commesso l'ispeditione di tale controversia à monsignore Illustrissimo Primocerio di San Marco il quale ser.tis ser.dis et aud: audien termini, et prononcij quanto stimerà conveniente.

Tenor scriptur

Serenissimo Principe:

Essendo comparsi inanti la Serenissima Vostra alcuni cantori quali adimandavano taglio
de alcune costitutionj, decretj, et capitoli del Serenissimo Ponte, [138v] confirmati
susseguentemente da tuttj gl'altrj suoi successorj, et dall'altra il resto da tuttj gl'altri
cantorj, quali adimandavano la confirmatione, et approbatione d'essi decretj, et ordinj.
Aldiche le parti con molte ragioni si da una come dall'altra parte: invocando il nome
d'Iddio la Serenissima Vostra approbò, et confirmò dette costitutionj, et ordinj; volendo,
che quelli sijno inviolabilmente osservatj. Ma essendo alcunj tanto arrogantj senza alcuno
timore, sprezzando non tenendo conto alcuno di dettj ordenj siamo statj astrettj per non
atediar la Serenissima Vostra comparir inanti monsignore Illustrissimo et Reverendissimo
Primicerio à dimandarli à quello suffraggio d'uno m:to, acciò che tutti gli cantori della
Compagnia di San Marco obediscano detti ordeni, et decretj. Et così ottenuto, et à tuttj
intimato messer padre Zan Battista detto Calcetta per via alla Serenissima Vostra
suspese detto m.to quanto alla persona sua sino ad altro ordine. Hora vedendo la
compagnia nostra esser gravemente da questo, et da altrj danizata, reduta nel solito loco
hanno terminato sotto di 27. novembre 1614 di elegger dui procuratori quali habbino
facultà di comparer inantj sua Serenità et altri superiori nostrj quali da detta compagnia
furono eletti il Reverendo messer padre Pietro Savollj compagni della detta compagnia.
Noi adunque procuratorj reverentemente compariamo inanti la Serenità Vostra
supplicandola sufragar detta compagnia acciò suoj fidelissimi servitori non sijno più da
questi talj oppressi et danizatj ma con la sua solita benignità faci si, che questi tali
transgressorj, quali vogliono viver liberi, et non sottoposti à detti ordinj, et decretj
confirmatj da molti Serenissimi Principi etiam dalla Serenissima Vostra sotto di xi agosto
1613 sijno astrettj, et obligatj alla osservatione di quelli, come fanno tutti gl'altri
compagni.
Noi Marc'Antonio Memmo per Gratia di Dio Doge di Venetia et cetera.

Doc. 51: A.S.V., Cancelleria Inferiore, Registro 79 (Atti dei Dogi, 1606–15), f. 140v

Marcus Antonius Memo Dei gratia Dux Venetiarum et cetera. A 3. del passato
rimettessimo, et commettessimo l'ispeditione d'una controversia vertente fra Padre
Vicenzo Spontonj, et Padre Pietro Savollj capi (come dissero) della compagnia de cantori
nostri in detta Capella da una: et Padre Giovanni Battista Cattabenj detto Calcetta uno
delli cantori della medesima capella dell'altra, à monsignore Primicerio in San Marco:
atteso che si ritrovavimo occupati in publici, et in privatj affarj. Hora mò [sic], che si
ritroviamo alquanto disoccupatj; annullando motu proprio la predetta remissione, et
commissione Avochiamo à noi detta controversia: Volendo quella ben intendere et con la
solita nostra maturità benignamente terminare à consolacione, et beneficio della capella
nostra predetta. Commandando all'infrascritto nostro Cancelliero che cosi notare, et
publicare dovesse.
.... ix Januarius 1614.

Doc. 52: A.S.V., Cancelleria Inferiore, Registro 80 (Atti dei Dogi, 1615–23), f. 24r

1616. à 27. maggio.

Venuto in Camera di sua Serenità monsignore Illustrissimo Primicerio di San Marco,
espose: che li cantori di detta chiesa; che li mesi passatj furono più volte avantj la

Serenità sua in contrad:o sopra certa dificoltà fra loro vertente in proposito delle loro utilità incerte da mettersi in commune: erano questj prossimi passati giornj comparsi avantj di lui, et tutta via erano in cittacione per detta, o altra simil causa: istando ch'egli non proferischa la sentenza. Per tanto ne haveva voluto dar conto alla sublimità sua; accio che circa ciò la commandasse quanto era di gusto et voler suo. La Serenità sua gli rispose. Che dovesse in tutto astenersj dall'udire, et giudicare detti cantorj perche voleva egli intendere et definire questa materia, et queste dificoltadj. Le quali ha avocado, et avoca à se per giustissime cause, et rispettj. Comandando, che cosi sij fatto intendere à dettj Cantori; accioche venghino quanto primo per l'espeditione.

Doc. 53: A.S.V., Cancelleria Inferiore, Registro 80 (Atti dei Dogi, 1615–23), pp. 64–68

Ioannes Bembo DEI gratia Dux Venetiarum et cetera atque ecclesiae Sancti Marcj nostrae Capellae solus patronus et Dominus. Udito per avantj più volte il maestro della nostra capella di San Marco; et anco [p. 65] alquantj delli cantori di quella con li loro avocatj: Dimandante et dimandantj: Ch'essendo stata istituita dal Serenissimo Ponte, et stabilita dalli Serenissimi Grimanj et Memo precessori nostri di felice memoria una unione et compagnia fra li cantori di detta Capella. la qual unione da certo tempo in qua viene grandemente perturbata da una parte delli cantorj di essa nostra capella. che accordatj, et unitj con alcunj cantorj estranej, novamente à detta compagnia aggregatj hanno fatto, et fanno elettione delli capi, et dello officialj di quelle persone, che non sono di detta capella; et altre novitadj contrarie affatto all'unione, et alla Pace di detta compagnia: Fosse da noj detta unione, et compagnia confirmata; Levandogli però quella tal qual autorità, ch'hanno di poter in quella assummere et aggregare Cantorj estranej. Con aggiongere et dechiarire: Che'l Maestro della Capella di San Marco; come sopra intendente à detta compagnia dovesse de cetero intervenire alla riducionj, et alli trattamentj di quella; et haver voce attiva et passiva come haver possono li cantorj di quelli per più ragionj, et cause dette, et considerate.

Uditij anco un'altra parte delli cantori di detta nostra capella unitamente con alcunj cantori estranej, che pur sono dellj aggregati à quella: Dicente che le cose recercate non dovevano esser essaudite; anzi che restando l'unione, et compagnia con li suoj capitoli, come sta, et giace il Maestro di Capella doveva esser licentiato per più ragionj, et cause da essj, et dalli loro avocatj dette alegate, et considerate. Di più udito messer Dominico Aldegattj uno delli cantori della sudetta unione, et compagnia; nec non delle costitucionj, et decretj in tal materia fattj: Desiderando egli di essere dal vinculo di quelli affatto libero giusta la forma della sua elettione; la quale si offerisse di produre; et per alte e più ragioni et cause da luj dette, et considerate. Vedute le scritture [p. 66], capitoli, costitucionj, et attj in proposito di detta compagnia fattj; et circa la presente materia oportunj. nec non la scrittura over dimanda avantj noj presentata per il capo, et procuratorj elettj dalla compagnia predetta, contra alcuni delli medesimi contorj, che contrariavano à quella sotto di 20 Genaro 1615 del tenor, come in quelle. Et il tutto maturamente considerato; sedendo in Catedra nella Camera della solita nostra ressidenza: Chiamato il nome di Dio padre di Pace, di Carità, et di Giusticia per tenore delle presenti prononciando, et sentenziando laudiamo l'unione, et compagnia predetta ordinata dal Serenissimo Ponte; Et insieme confirmiamo li capitolj am [sic] essi, et decretatj per li Serenissimi Grimanj, et Memo in tutte le sue partj. eccetto che nelle cose infrascritte le quali à quelli aggiongendo vogliamo che s'habbino per corrette, et in questo modo decchiarite. cioè.

*Prim*o che la detta unione, et compagnia sia, et s'intendi essere istituita, et stabilita à comodo, pace, et beneficio delli soli cantorj, che sono, et che p*er* tempo sara*n*no iscrittj, et stipendiatj nella capella n*ost*ra di S*an* Marco; et no*n* di altri per modo alcuno.

2.o Debbano li cantorj della pred*ett*a n*ost*ra capella di tempo in te*m*po ridursj insieme giusta la forma dellj loro capitoli alli p*res*enti no*n* repugnantj, et elegere à bossoli, et ballote il loro capo, over capi, il vice capo, o vice capi, li sindicj, li sotto sindicj, il cassiero, li essecutorj, et il cancell*iero* Nelle qual riduttionj siano al meno dui terzi del corpo di tutti li cantori di essa n*ost*ra capella. Et li eletti à detti carichi no*n* si possino publicare rimasti se nel bossolo bianco no*n* havera*n*no conseguito più della metà delle balle delli perciò, come di sopra congregatj.

3.o Debanno gl'officiali, che come di sopra sara*n*no p*er* tempo elettj esseguire et far in tutte le sue parti osservare li p*res*enti et cadaunj altri loro capitoli alla p*res*ente correttione, et dechiaratione no*n* repugnantj. In pena di danarj, et altro ad abritrio n*ost*ro tante volte quante contrafara*n*no.

4.o Comandando, che tutte le elettioni di capi, et d'altri officiali fin'hora in altra maniera, che nella sudetta fatte siano p*er* de cetero mille, et di niun valore.

5.o Vogliamo in oltre; che detti cantori di S*an* Marco debbano interv*en*ire [p. 67] di giorni otto prossimi futuri ridursj insieme ad numero, et modo di sopra dechiarito; et eleger il loro capo, over capi, et gl'altri tuttj loro officialj; Accioche co'l nome dello sp*irit*o santo riccevino l'uso et il godimento della Pace da loro desiderata....

6.o Vogliamo, che'l Maestro della capella n*ost*ra di S*an* Marco et li successori suoj, che p*er* tempo sara*n*no no*n* possano p*er* modo alc*un*o ne in tempo alcuno esser capo di detta compagnia; ne participare d'alcuna delle cose appartinentj à quella: Essendo che egli nelle cose della musica è in capella loro superiore giusta la forma delle costitutionj, et ordinj in tal materia disponentj.

7:mo Satuimo in oltre; ch'in ogni occasione, et caso, ch'à detti n*ost*ri cantori occorerà, ch'in un medesimo giorno habbino à far doi, o più musiche nelle chiese, et altri lochi rimotj della Città; et che il lor numerò non sarà bastante p*er* supplire à tanto bisogno: possano tuor [*sic*] quali, et quantj musicj estranej, ch'à loro più piacerà tante volte quante farà bisogno. Facendo però à quelli il guadagno eguale, come tocherà ad essi et più, et meno, come saranno d'accordo. Non se intendendo p*er* ciò, ne p*er* altra maniera questi estranej cantori essere ne poter essere del gremio di detta unione, et compagnia, et cose appartinentj à quella.

8.o Di più vogliamo che se fatti li mercatj delle p*re*detti nostri cantori à chi spetta co*n* le chiese, lochi pij, et altrj li festizantj vora*n*no oltra esso mercato overo mercati dare, et donare q*u*alche cosa ad alcuno delli cantorj, che gli servira*n*no, o siano di capella, overo delli estranej: Quella sij tutta libera, et espedita di quel tale, o di quelli tali à quali la sarà stata data, overo donata senza contradittione [p. 68] et diminucione alcuna tante volte, quante occorerà....

. . . Die xiij Janua͞rij indict*ur* XV. M.D.C.XVJ . . .

Doc. 54: A.S.V., Cancelleria Inferiore, Reigstro 80 (Atti dei Dogi, 1615–23), pp. 102–3.

1617. à 14. Luglio.

La sottoscritta supplicatione fu presentata in proprie manj del Serenissimo DD. Giovanni
Bembo Duce di Venezia per messer Mattio Facino, et messer Padre Bortolo Strambalj
sindici della compagnia de cantori di San Marco per nome loro et di tutti (come dissero)
li cantori della detta Capella. Il qual Serenissimo havendo quella benignamente letta, et
considerata ha dettj cantori per le cose in quella contenute licentiato. Quelli viva voce
ammonendo et essortando alla debita essecutione, et obedienza delli Terminationj, et
decretj da lei fin'hora in tale proposito fattj, approbati, et publicattj. et in tutto come in
quelli, alli quali s'habbia sempre relacione....

Tenor supplicatur

Serenissimo Principe

Quel benigno Zelo ch'ha sempre regnato nella Serenità nostra dell'utile, et riputazione di
noj divotissimi et humilissimi servi et cantorj suoj quell'istesso ci affida al presente in
occasione non meno importante di qual altra si fosse maj alla professione et interesse
nostro à comparerle davantj. Ci fo con solo fine, et fondamento d'utilità, et honor apunto
con l'ultimo decreto di Vostra Serenità prohibito di prevalersj d'estranej cantori, et capi.
Al che con sommo gusto habbiamo asuntito, elegendo fin'hora fra da noj stessj chi
regesse le musiche nostre. Ma per che per dir il vero ci è gran diferenza dall'officio di
maestro di Capella all'officio di cantore di qui è nato, che con tenue riuscita, et con
qualche nostro mortificatione habbiamo coll'esperienza veduto pur troppo chiaro cremarsi
nella Città il concetto della nostra musica, con gran nostro danno, et con tema di molto
peggio rispetto alla concorenza che ci fanno molte altre compagnie rette da huominj
molto intendentj. Al qual nostro manifesto danno, desiderando pure di trovar qualche
rimedio, sapendo ch'all'espettacione et al grido della musica di San Marco non pure ci è
bisogno di chi regoli; ma di chi sia con la regola e col valore adeguato, et proportionato
à quella; massime nelle solennità grandj che si fanno per la città, alla presenza di tutta la
nobilità, col concorso d'infiniti gentilhuominj, e ben spesso principi forestieri. Per ciò
prostrati à piedi della Serenità Vostra riverente la supplichiamo che in atto di gratia, et
dispensa particolare ci conceda, che possiamo elegersj à più balle una persona fuori
del nostro numero valorosa, conosciuta, et amata dalla Città, che intenta con la virtù, et
autoritade all'interesse nostro ci rega le nostre musiche, batendo la batuda, et
amministrandocj nove composicionj secondo il bisogno. Dalla qual gratiosa dispensa si
possiamo certamente assicurare che ci sarà conferito quell'utile, et quell'honore, che la
Serenissima Vostra istessa come prencipe benignissimo et gratiosissimo ci ha sempre
desiderato.

Doc. 55: A.S.V., Cancelleria Inferiore, Registro 80 (Atti dei Dogi, 1615–23), pp. 203-204.

1620. à 26 Ottobre.

Havendo il Serenissimo DD. Antonio Prioli Duce di Venezia più volte inteso dal maestro
de cantori della sua chiesa, overo Capella di San Marco, et anco da alcunj di essi cantorj
la causa de diversj disgustj, et disordinj, ch'alle volte occorono fra di essi causa delle
musiche; che ben spesso occorono farsj fuori di detta capella nelle chiese di questa Città.

Et desiderando la Serenità sua di conservare fra essi pace, et unione: Veduto ciò, ch'altre volte è stato dallj Serenissimi suoi precessori circa la presente materia terminato. Et il tutto maturamente considerato: Havuto anco circa ciò il parer delli eccellentissimi Signori Giovanni Cornaro, et Antonio Barbaro procuratori della chiesa sua predetta. Ha terminato et per la presente aggiongendo, et decchiarando termina, convide, et commanda;

Che'l maestro della predetta sua Capella al quale appartiene il governo di quella sij anco loro capo, et governatore nellj affari musicalj ch'occoreranno farsi per dettj cantorj fuori di detta capella; non altrimentj di quello, che sij in detta sua capella. Dovendo in ogni caso di disparere per mancamento di essi cantorj venir lui personalmente di giorno in giorno à darne conto particolare alla Serenità sua; accioche possa farne quelle provisionj, ch'alla prudenza sua pareranno convenientj.

Et se occorerà, che'l detto maestro di capella sij da alcuna particolar persona ricercato di dover intervenire à qualche solenne Musica fuori di detta capella nelle chiese di questa Città: suo Serenità contenta, che gli possi andare; con darne pero prima conto à lei, et da ricceverne licenza particolare di volta in volta, et non altrimentj, ne in altro modo.

In oltre termina et commanda che'l Vice maestro della detta nostra capella sia, et s'intendi anco fuori della detta capella sempre Vice capo delli cantori di quella: Se che habbia l'istessa autorità, ch'havrebbe il capo, et governatore predetto se vi fosse presente.

Et occorrendo nelle musiche che sj facessero di furoi di detta Capella aggregare, et aggiongere per qual si voglia causa uno, o più musicj che [p. 204] non fussero di capella al numero delli predettj cantori di detta capella: Habbino autorità il maestro, et il Vice maestro predetti insieme con li duoj più vecchj cantorj di detta Capella di farne l'elettione, come meglio à loro quatro, o alla maggior parte di essi parerà. Salve in resto cadaune constitucionj et ordinj; ch'in tal materia fussero alla presente non repugnantj....

Doc. 56: A.S.V., Cancelleria Inferiore, Registro 80 (Atti dei Dogi, 1615–23), p. 230

Antonius Priolus DEI gratia Dux Venetiarum et cetera Essendocj pervenuto all'orecchie; che ben spesso vertiscono delle difcultà fra il capo, il vice capo, et li cantorj della Capella nostra di San Marco per occasione, et causa di diversj abbusj, et alla giornata vengono da alcunj di loro introdottj contra la forma del loro capitolare, confirmato, et regolato dalli Serenissimi Precessori nostri fo; et che da noi anco è sommamente desiderata: Per tenore delle presenti commettemo al capo, al Vice capo, et à cadauno delli cantori di detta nostra capella presentj, et futurj; che debbano inviolabilmente osservare, et esseguire, et far osservar, et esseguire in tutte le sue partj le regole, et ordinj contenutj nel capitolare della loro compagnia; et in cadauna anco delle costitucionj, confirmationj, et regolationj Ducalj fin'hora fatte in questa materia. Et ciò in pena (olim le pene in detto capitolare, et regolationj statuite) de ducati cinque. à [lire] 6 [soldi] 4 per ducato ogni volta, che contrafaranno. Da essergli in remissibilmente tolta; et applicate alle monache del monasterio delle convertite alla Zudeca di questa Città. Et in pena anco (se occorerà) di esser privi della detta compagnia per quel tempo, che parerà alla Giustizia; et anco di refar la detta compagnia d'ogni danno che per causa della loro trasgressionj, o disobedienza fosse seguito, o che seguir potesse....

. . . vij. martij. 1622.

Doc. 57: A.S.V., Cancelleria Inferiore, Registro 80 (Atti dei Dogi, 1615–23), p. 249

16. Luglio [1622]

De mandato del Serenissimo D.D. Antonio Prioli Duce di Venezia et cetera per debita essecutione delle costitucionj Ducalj in tal materia disponentj se intima et commette à voj cadauni Cantori della chiesa di San Marco sua capella: che nell'avenire non dobbiate cantare, ne andare à cantare messe, o altri divini officij in alcuna chiesa, o altro loco pio di questa Città, et suo dogarolo fuori della vostra ordinata compagnia de cantorj di detta chiesa; se non haverete espressa licenza in scrittura dalla Serenità sua. Et questo in pena di prigione, et altro ad arbitrio à quella.

Doc. 58: A.S.V., Cancelleria Inferiore, Registro 81 (Atti dei Dogi, 1623–45), p. 123

1633. Die 29 Ottobris

Essendo pervenuto à notizia de Sua Serenità certa tal qual pretensione della scola de sonadori eretta nella chiesa di Sancto Silvestro di questa Città di voler aggregare in essa loro scola di Cantori della Cappella della Chiesa di Sancto Marco, il che riuscirebbe a poca riputatione di essi Cantori già eleti, e che si elegeranno dalli Illustrissimi Signori Procuratori, et impossessati della suprema auttorità della Serenità Sua. Perciò invigilando alla Conservatione della Ducal Giurisditione et al giusto sollievo et honorevolezza di essi Cantori. Terminando hà terminato, che tutti li Cantori di essa Capella presenti, et che saranno de caetero eleti, siano et s'intendino assolutamente liberi, et essenti di essa scola et non debbino conoscere altro Magistratto superiore in tal matterial che'l Serenissimo Principe suo Padrone, et Prottettore. Terminando in oltre Sua Serenità che essi Cantori di detta Cappella possino oltre il Canto, sonare qualunque instromento musicalmente, in qualunque chiesa, et luoco di questa Città, et parimente insegnare di sonare, et Cantare si nelle proprie sue scole. come nelle case de particolari (musicalmente) ne possino sonare di ballo nelle feste publiche, et private mercenariamente)....

Doc. 59: A.S.V., San Marco, Procuratia de Supra, Registro 139 (Chiesa Actorum, 1598–1607)

Fu terminato sotto 6 del presente mese che per il buon servitio della chiesa di San Marco siano posti in destribution parte delli salarij, che hanno li diaconi suddiaconi Giovani di coro, Zaghi, et cantori di essa chiesa et come in essa terminatione alla qual s'habbi relation, nella qual essendo sta terminato che li medesimi deputati à tenir conto delli Canonici, Sagrestani e Sotto Canonici per la loro distribution cotidiana siano anco deputati à tenir conto delli sopradetti, et considerando, che sarà di molto maggior servitio che il sudetto conto sia tenuto da ogn'uno dell'istessi interessatti. Hanno à bossoli et balloti terminato che del numero di Cantori sia cavato à sorte uno di loro di due in due mesi, il qual habbi à tenir conto delli negligenti apontando quelli giusta la continentia della sopradetta terminatione 6 Luglio, li quali tutti ponti siano poi distribuiti tra quelli, che saranno diligenti pro rata delli loro salarij con pollizza, che sarà portata in Procuratia et sottoscritta dal Reverendo Vicario, come quelle di Canonici et SottoCanonici Et l'istesso modo sia osservato dalli Diaconi, et Suddiaconi uniti insieme et delli Gioveni di coro, et Zaghi similm*en*te uniti insieme tra loro, delli quali Zaghi no*n* sia admesso a tenir co*n*to se no*n* di quelli che parera al R*everen*do Vicario esser habili à questo effetto.

Doc. 60: A.S.V., San Marco, Procuratia de Supra, Registro 6 (Giornali Cassier, 1603–10)

1604 adi 3 Maggio

P*er* spese ditte//à Cassa ducati otto *lire* 11 *grossi* 8 contadi alli sotto scritti cantori aggionti al vespero della Vigilia della Sensa à *lire* 3 *denari* 10 l'uno cioè P*ad*re Zorzi Basso, P*ad*re Andrea Basso, P*ad*re Roman Basso, P*ad*re Gasparetto Tenor, P*ad*re Francesco Tenor, P*ad*re Zuane Tenor, P*ad*re Camille Tenor, P*ad*re Antonio Alto et Torquato Alto, P*ad*re Giulio Alto, P*ad*re Cesare Alto, tre putti sopranij, P*ad*re Nicoletto, et P*ad*re Domenego come per polizza del sopra ditto.

Doc. 61: A.S.V., San Marco, Procuratia de Supra, Registro 98 (Ceremoniali), f. 103v.

E se li canta una bella Messa della Trinità con l'or*ati*one de San Marco, e del Dose, id est pro famulo nominando el nome, et la Casa dal Vicario, overo Can*oni*co che tocca, e li Sonatori sonano li Piffari, dapoi l'Ep*isto*la diedo all'Altar Grande, et all'Elevazion sonano cornetti, over altri Instrum*en*ti, et in questa et in ogni solennità mazor se canta negli Organi dalli Cantori over si sona dalli Sonatori.

.... Poi ogn'anno el di del suo Annual el vien in Chiesa a Messa Grande etc. Se li canta la sopras*critt*a Messa della Trinità con l'Or*ati*one di S*an* Marco, et pro Duce con li 8. Sonatori del Pr*inci*pe con Instrum*en*ti con con il Cantori, et in Org*an*o all'Ep*isto*la et Eleva*zio*n, et all'Offert*ori*o.

Doc. 62: A.S.V., Cancelleria Inferiore, Registro 79 (Atti dei Dogi, 1605–15), ff. 135v–136v.

Adi 24. nov*em*bre [1614]

Davantj il Ser*enissi*mo D. D. Marc'antonio Memo p*er* la Dio gr*ati*a Duce di Ven*ezi*a etc. comparse m*esser* Pasqualin Savioni p*er* nome (come disse) de m*esser* Zuane Bassan, et compagni sonatorj suoj, et pre*se*ntò una scrittura del tenor infras*crit*to: humilm*en*te supplicando la Sere*ni*tà sua à voler ponar à qu*ell*a il suo Ducale decreto affine che co*n* l'autorità, et sotto il felice auspicio della Serenissima sua sortisca il desiderato fine d'unione, et di Pace fra detti sonadorj. La Sere*ni*tà sua veduta essa scritt*ur*a, et il tutto ben inteso: sentendosi molto occupata in publ*i*ci et in particolarj affari ha rimesso, et p*er* tenor della pre*se*nte rimette, et com*m*ette la pred*ett*a richiesta à mons*ignore* Ill*ust*rissimo Primoc*er*io di S*an* Marco accioche in vece sua veduto et considerato quanto si deve et uditi li pred*ett*i sonadorj debba circa ciò terminare, et prononciare quanto li parerà giusto et conveniente....

Tenor Script*ur*

Ser*enissi*mo Pr*inci*pe:

Io Zuanne Bassano capo de concertj de Vostra Serenità insieme con li altri cinque miei compagni sonatori di Vostra Serenissima cioè Nicolo da Udene, Lorenzo Cittera, Giacomo Roeta, Francesco Bonfante e Piero Loschj tutti noi sej sonatori nominati trombonj e piffari di Vostra Serenità habbiamo finalmente conosciuto esser vero quanto da me già molti, e molti anni sempre è stato ricordato, che ciò è la vera unione de instrumenti musicj consiste prima nel buon aiuto accordato insieme et che da questa nostra unione sempre ne haveria sentito contento il Serenissimo Patrone. Hora cosi ispirati da nostro Signore Iddio vogliono, e si contestano tuttj loro, che sotto scrivendo questa mia scrittura che dividiamo tutti li utilj, che si acquistera con le nostre fatiche della nostra professione de sonadori di musica, si nelle chiese, come nelle scole grande in Venezia et fuori di Venezia, eccetuando però li nostri salarij, che habbiamo annualmente di Vostra Serenità et da la procuratia de supra. Il sesto tutto se intenda unito egualmente insieme obligandosj l'uno per l'altro in accidente d'infirmità aiutarsi fin'al fin di nostra vita. Però tutti noi sei sonadori, et fedelissimi servitori di Vostra Serenissima la supplichiamo humilmente che si degni approbar questa nostra scrittura de unione gia, che ancora il Serenissimo Principe Nicolo da Ponte fece un decreto de cantorj della chiesa di San Marco de unione sotto l'anno 1579 lodato ancora dal Serenissimo Principe Marino Grimanj, come si vede nel decreto de Cantorj per lo che speriamo ancora noi sei suoj sonatorj ricever la giusta approbatione di questa nostra scrittura da la Serenissima Vostra. Obligandosi noj di pregar il Signore per la vera et compita felicità di Vostra Serenità....

Noi Marc'Antonio Memmo per Gratia de Dio Doge de Venetia.

Doc. 63: A.S.V., Cancelleria Inferiore, Registro 80 (Atti dei Dogi, 1615-23), pp. 54–59

Primo. Sia sempre intesa la unione delli sej Sonatorj di sua Serenità con l'aiuto concorde insieme, se ben saranno divisi questi sei sonatorj in tre corpi di compagnie. cioè la compagnia delli Bassanj, la compagnia delli Udenj, et la compagnia delli Bonfantj. Et questi tre capi possino formar nelli bisogni di molte festività la quarta, et la quinta compagnia, secondo, che à loro parerà ricercar il bisogno.

2:do Che'l capo maggiore sij, et s'intendi essere il Signor Giovanni Bassano durante la sua vita; et doppo lui dovendosi far elettione d'un altro tal elettione sij fatta dalli sei sonatorj publicj, che saranno pro tempore nella persona di uno, che sia del numero delli sei medesimj, et cosi di tempo in tempo.

3:o Che le difficultà, che nascerano sopra gl'interesssj della compagnia, over compagnie siano terminate dal capo maggiore con li doj altri capi. Et quando alcuno non volesse star al loro giudicio possi haver ricorso alli suoi superiorj.

4:o Che siano formate le tre compagnie d'uno istesso numero di sonadori per cadauna; accio che quelli che spendeno [sic] nelle loro festività si possino servir egualmente di qual si voglia compagnia; trovandosi in tutti tre il numero eguale di Sonatorj, et il valore di essi anco diviso egualmente.

5:to Che fermata una festa dalli tre sindicj siano poste tre ballote in un bossolo, con l'inscrittione del nome ad ogn'una di quelle della sua compagnia. Et la prima festa sij cavata à sorte, restando le doi altre imbossolate. Cavandone une per la 2:da festa; et la terza per la terza festa e cosi sempre sia osservato quest'ordine di rotolo.

6.o   Che se alcuno vora altri sonatori, oltra à quelli della compagnia, che li sarà toccata per sorte in tal caso si debba procurar di darli sodisfattione co'l consento di tutti tre li capi.

7.o   Che siano fatti tre sindicj uno per compagnia per far i mercatj delle festività occorentj; et che ogni compagnia faccia separatamente l'elettione del suo. Et non potendo in caso di qualche impedimento trovarsj cosi per apunto tutti tre insieme; se ben sarà stabilito da loro il quando, et l'hora; mancando il terzo, doj di loro possino fare i mercatj, ne altri, che quelli tre sindici [p. 55] possino far mercatj. Et questo si fa, accioche tutte le compagnie restino con l'aiuto sinciero; essendo interessati li tre capi delle tre compagnie.

viij.o   Che doppo fatti li mercatj li donativj, che saranno fattj dalli Vardianj delle scole, et altri, o allj capi delle compagnie, o ad altri siano di quelli alli quali saranno dattj, senza obligo di metterli in compagnia.

ix.o   Che siano divisi insieme tuttj gl'utilj, che si faranno nelle chiese di Venezia et scole grandj, et piccole si nella Città, come fuori della Città di Venezia cosi di messe, Vesperi, compiete, et delle Quaranta hore, che si sogliono fare la Quadragesima in molti luoghi della Città, et sposari, che si fanno con musica in chiesa; eccettuando quelli, che servissero annualmente in qualche chiesa con salario annuo. Dovendo esser quel beneficio di quello, che serve. Con questo però; ch'in occasione di bisogno di lui nella sua compagnia egli procuri di accommodarsj con un'altro compagno in suo luogo, overo haver licenza dal suo capo: et quel utile sia suo particolare.

x.mo   Che parimente gl'utilij che non siano di cose di Chiesa, overo delli specificatj, come di sopra siano d'ogn'uno in particolare, secondo, che si affaticherà; non havendo obligo di metterlj in compagnia.

xj:mo   Che niuno compagno che partisse in disgratia di una delle tre compagnie unite non possi esser accettato in alcuna delle altre doj, o più compagnie.

xij.o   Che sia in libertà d'ogn'uno delli tre capi di dar licenza alli suoj campagni per otto giornj più, et meno per andar fuori della Città. Havendo riguardo cadauno capo di non dar licenza in tempo di qualche bisogno grande di festività. Et se alcuno andasse fuori della Città con utile di musica, quale tale non debbj participar delle guadagni di questi della Città.

xiij.o   Che siano agiustatj li amalatj delle tre compagnie. Pregando tuttj noi, che'l Signore ne conservij sani in suo santo servitio. Et quando piacesse à sua divina maestà di visitar alcuno di noj in una, in doj, o in tutte tre le compagnie, in quel numero che le piacesse se le conceda la sua portione fino al fine della sua vita. Ma racquistando le forze questi talj debbano in loro conscienza andar nelle suo compagnie ad essercitare la loro professione. Et se di questo numero alcuno fingere di esser amalate per suoi comodj, o capricj in [p. 56] tal caso se li manderà uno medico, il quale farà fede se quel tale stij bene, o male. Quando male: haverà agiuto. Quando bene venirà anch'esso ad affaticarsi con gl'altrj.

xiiij:o   Che trovandosi due, o tre compagnie insieme niuno delli capi permetta, che si suonj instrumento di sorte alcuna solo. Altrimentj volendo alcuno sonar solo contra l'ordine del suo capo, quel tale case serà in disgratia della sua compagnia.

xv:o   Ch'ogn'uno delli compagni habbia autorità di dimandar riduttione alle tre compagnie. Et possino tutti racordar per beneficio delle compagnie di pigliar altri compagni in occasione, che mancasse il numero de sonatorj, o per accrescer portione di parte ad alcunj compagni.

xvj.o   Che nelle riduttionj, che si faranno non si possi deliberar cosa alcuna, se non vi si troveranno presenti in esse la maggior parte di compagni. Potendo li capi che chiameranno la riduttione metter pena alli compagni secondo che à loro parerà; affine che si riduchino.

xvij:o   Che tuttj li compagni delle dette tre compagnie habbino voto nelle riduttionj, che si faranno per trattar le materie spettantj all'interesse di dette compagnie. Potendo ogn'uno esser eletto alli carichj, che si distribuirano in esse ridutionj.

xviij:o   Che quando occorerà mancamento d'alcuno sonatore in alcuna delle compagnie sudette: il capo con li compagni della medesima compagnia possi far elettione d'un'altro in luogo di quello, che mancerà, senza haver obligo di participar con altre compagnie di simile elettione.

xix:o   Che trovandosi doj, o tre compagnie insieme debba il capo maggiore ordinar luj. Dispensando però li concertj alle altre compagnie, come farà alla sua propria.

xx.o   Che trovandosj l'atre due compagnie insieme senza il capo maggiore, in quel caso quella compagnia à chi tocherà sia quella che dispensi li concertj: Dando però sodisfattione all'altra compagnia.

xxj.o   Che ogni doi mesi si debba eleger un cassiero per ciascuna compagnia; si che siano tre cassieri. Dovendo ogni compagnia ballotar il suo separatamente, et possi esser eletto à tal carico anco uno delli capi. Et quelli che saranno elettj possino esser confirmatj per via di ballotacione quante volte parerà ad esse compagnie.

xxxij.   Che uno, o più compagni di qual si voglia della compagnie sopranominate non possino in particolare andar à sonar in alcun loco di chiesa, overo scola senza licenza delli suoi capi. Et se per aventura occoresce, che alcuno, o più di loro fossero necessitatj andar à sonar cosi all'improviso, che per la scarsezza del tempo non havessero commodità di farlo sapere alli suoj capi siano nondimeno tenutj ricevendo mercede à metterla in compagnia.

xxiij.   Che non potendo per qualche suo incomodo trovarsi il cassiero presente per scuoder li danarj di quella festa della sua compagnia. Et occorendo, ch'un'altro compagno li scodesse, debba quel tale subito consignar il danaro al detto suo cassiero sotto pena di doi ducatj per ogni volta, che mancasse. Havendo anco il cassiero carico di dar ad ogn'uno un pocco di danarj fino al fine del mese: Andando però esso cassiero circospetto di non esser intoccato.

xxiiij.   Che se à caso il cassiero d'alcuna delle compagnie darà danaro di più allj soij compagni, ciò sia senza pregiudizio degl'altri cassierj. Dovendosj ogni mese far conto per dar sodisfattione ad ogn'uno.

xxv.   Che se alcuno delli sudetti sej sonatori di sua Serenità sarà seduttore, o seminatore di discordie tra di loro doverà esser severamente punito, et incorerà nella disgratia di sua serenità.

xxvj.   Che tutte le cose contenute nelli soprascritti Capitolj debbano esser osservate, et esseguite da tuttj, et da cadauno delli sej sonatori antedettj sotto quelle pene (oltra le espresse, et comminate in essi capitolj) cosi pessimarie come altre maggiori, che pareranno all'arbitrio della Giustizia di sua Serenità havuto risguardo alla qualità della trasgressione. Et in oltre dovranno procurar loro sei se ben divisi nelle tre compagnie, come di sopra, cioè Bassani, Udenj, et Bonfantj, di tener in pace, et unitj quelli compagni delle dette sue compagnie che dipenderanno da loro. Li quali compagni potranno ancor essi haver voce attiva, et passiva in dette compagnie, quando però staranno unitj con quelle et accordar quanto li paresse per beneficio di esse. Dovendosi ballotar l'opinione di qual si voglio compagno, et ogn'uno sarà tenuto all'osservanza di detti Capitolj.

Veduta per l'Illustrissimo et Reverendissimo monsignore Giovanni Tiepolo primicerio di San Marco la commissione, et deligatione predetta et uditj più volte Don Zuanne Bassano capo dei concertj dei Trombonj, et Pifari, Don Nicolò da Udine, Francesco Bonfante, Giacomo Roeta, Pietro Loschj, et Battista Fabri trombonj et pifari di sua Serenità et della sua Ducal capella, et chiesa di San Marco sopra le cose contenute in quella. Veduti li sottoscritti sette capitoli da loro propostj et concordemente ricercatj quelli per l'aiuta à sua Signore Illustrissima concesse come di sopra aggionge, lauda, et conferma in tutte le sue partj. cioè.

xxvij.   Che altrj che li tre sinidici delle compagnia non possino far mercato nell'occasionj d'andar à sonare cioè almeno doi di loro, sotto pena à quelli capi, o sindicj di qual si voglia che manderà, o anderà con la sua propria compagnia, o con altre à sonar senza far prima mercato di ducato uno per ogni volta che contrafacesse; et di non poter haver portione alcuna di quel sonar, che si farà di quel giorno; cosi in detto loco, come altrove, et quando per qualche conveniente urgentia, o rispetto paresse à tuttj tre essi sindicj unitj che si andasse à sonar in qualche loco senza far mercato, questo si possi far senza la predetta pena.

xxviiij.   Che partendo qual si voglia compagno delle dette tre compagnie dalla sua compagnia, non possino li altri Doi capi accettar quello, o quelli compagni nella loro compagnia; sotto pena à quel capo; che accettasse compagni, che non sono destinatj alla sua compagnia di pagar del suo per ogni volta doj ducatj. Et cosi resti condannato il compagno, che partisse in un ducato. Et hoc toties quoties, cosi l'uno come l'altro. Dovendo tornar subito nella sua compagnia sotto pena di privatione del suo guadagno; salve legittime cause, da esser conosciute dalla Giusticia.

xxix.   Che tutti li compagni, che sono sanj debbano sonar prontamente dove li sarà imposto dalli suoj capi, non solo con la compagnia, ma per occasione di far molte altre compagnie in accidente di bisogno debba ogni compagno obedir il suo capo, et non lo facendo caschi in pena per ogni volta d'uno ducato.

xxx.   Che venendo in cognitione di qual si voglia compagno che andasse à sonar senza licenza del suo capo; oltre che doverà metter tutto il danaro guadagnato in compagnia; resti condannato in uno ducato per ogni volta, et luogo, dove andasse à sonar senza tal licenza.

xxxj.   Che li tre capi ogn'un di loro ò unitj, o separatj possino dimandar riduttione per cose occorentj per beneficio delle compagnie. Et habbi ogn'uno di essj autorità di metter pena alli compagni di torvarsj nella riduttione di lire doi per compagno ogni volta, che sarà chiamato. Se però il capo, che chiamerà riduttione non li desse licenza.

xxxij. Che niuno delli capi, et molto meno delli Compagni, che sono stipendiatj, et serveno [*sic*] nella capella Ducale di *San* Marco possi separarsi da questa compagnia sotto pena di perder tutte le sue utilità certe, et anco d'altre maggiori pene ad arbitrio della Giusticia di sua Ser*eni*tà.

xxxiij. Che tuttj li danarj delle pene sop*radet*te siano applicatj al corpo della co*m*pagnia, da esser divisi tra tuttj: eccettuatj però quelli che havessero trasgredito li quali no*n* possino participar di quelle pene, che loro havessero pagate.

et cosi ha detto, aggionto, et dicchiarito esso mon*signore* Ill*ustrissi*mo Primic*eri*o adi 22. Ottobre. 1616. in casa della sua solita ressidenza appresso *San* Filippo et Giacomo....

Doc. 64: A.S.V., San Marco, Procuratia de Supra, Registro 144 (Chiesa Actorum, 1639–48)

1645 Adi 29 Ottobre

Che siano accettati p*er* sonar li doi organetti, ch*e* s'attrovano sop*ra* li Nichi in Chiesa di San Marco ogni volta, ch*e* saranno chiamati dal Mastro n*ost*ro di Capella con ducati dodeci p*er* cadauno all'anno, gl'infrascritti, cioè—
Pa*d*re Gio*vanni* Batt*ist*a Volpe; et Gio*vanni* Batt*ist*a Gualtieri

Doc. 65: A.S.V., San Marco, Procuratia de Supra, Busta 87, Processo 193 (Sottocanonici), fascicolo 1, f. 19r–20v

Cantori

Il Maestro	d*uca*ti 300
Il Vice Maestro	d*uca*ti 100
Don Paulo Fiume Negro	d*uca*ti 100
Il Padre Agustin Fasuol	d*uca*ti 100
M*e*s*se*r Mattio Faccini	d*uca*ti 70
M*e*s*se*r Paulo Veraldo	d*uca*ti 90
M*e*s*se*r Steffano Rivieri	d*uca*ti 100
M*e*s*se*r Batt*ist*a Contralto	d*uca*ti 70
Pa*d*re Antonio Sarti	d*uca*ti 60
M*e*s*se*r Zuanne Arzignan	d*uca*ti 80
M*e*s*se*r Nicolò Vandali	d*uca*ti 90
M*e*s*se*r Piero Francese	d*uca*ti 100
M*e*s*se*r Lucio Mora	d*uca*ti 90
M*e*s*se*r Torquato Bolognese	d*uca*ti 70
M*e*s*se*r Zuanne Strambali	d*uca*ti 80
M*e*s*se*r Zorzi Gardassin	d*uca*ti 60
M*e*s*se*r Bened*ett*o Pappi	d*uca*ti 70
M*e*s*se*r Domenego Aldegati	d*uca*ti 80
M*e*s*se*r Lunardo Simonetti	d*uca*ti 70
M*e*s*se*r Flaminio Corraddi	d*uca*ti 80
M*e*s*se*r Giacomo Macabressa	d*uca*ti 80
Pa*d*re Ghirardo Biancosi	d*uca*ti 60
Pa*d*re Bortolo Strambali	d*uca*ti 60

Padre Francesco Rosso	ducati 60
Padre Francesco Castigliano	ducati 80
Messer Gotardo Menegotto	ducati 100....

Capi di Coro
| Padre Gasparo Locadello | ducati 18 |
| Padre Nicolò Fransich | ducati 18 |

Organisti, et Concerti
Paulo Zusto organista	ducati 140
D. Paulo di Savij organista	ducati 140
Zuane da Udene	ducati 60
Zuane da Bassan	ducati 90
Victorio Calina per conza li organi	ducati 11
Andrea alzafoli	ducati 6
Victorio alzafoli	ducati 6

Sonadori
| Pasqualin Savioni | à ducati 15 per uno all'anno fanno |
| Antonio Padovano | in tutti ducati 240 |

Francesco Bonifante
Zuanne Chilese
Piero Loschi
Alvise Grani
Fantin Bassan
Zanetto Sanson
Bastian Mellegazzo
Battista Fabri
Zuanne de giacomo
Toni Melegazzo
Gerolamo Coltrer
Zuanne Moschettj
Antonio Almi
Biasio Marini

Doc. 66: A.S.V., San Marco, Procuratia de Supra, Registro 141 (Chiesa Actorum, 1614–20)

1615. 19 Gennaro [*more veneto*]

Vedendo l'Illustrissimi Signori Procuratori, che Isepo, et Bortolo Fioli da Paulo Roman cantor et Zuane Battista Fiol da Pier'Antonio Bevilaqua, tutti tre zaghi in San Marco, se ben sono di tenera età sono introdotti nella musica in modo, che cantano il soprano sicuramente, et che quando si fa capella serve aver loro à far corpo alla musica, come ha fatto feste il Maestro di capella Hanno terminato che della casse della chiesa siano tutti ducati dodeci per donativo à cadauno de loro per una volta tanto, et questo per darli animo di attender con maggior spirito ad amaestrarsi per poter poi riuscir boni musici da condur al servitio della chiesa.

Doc. 67: A.S.V., San Marco, Procuratia de Supra, Registro 141 (Chiesa Actorum, 1614–20)

1614. 6. Aprile

Havendo il Maestro di Capella della chiesa nostra di San Marco raccordato, che si trovano se non alcuno pochi boni da cantar la Messa in capella à 4. 5. et. 6. nelli giorni feriali tutto il tempo dell'anno come è l'ordinario per brevità, et che sarà bene per servitio della chiesa haverne delli altri, per mutar, et non cantar sempre l'istesso, considerando appresso, che darne scriver a pena, o sue compositioni, o di altri sarebbe di molta spesa, et che ritrovandosene di stampata in Roma di diversi auttori famosi, giudicarebbe esser meglio per hora pigliar sei libri di queste Messe à 4. 5. 6. et otto voci il che da SS. SS. Illustrissimi et Eccellentissimi Procuratori, et considerato, et fatto portar alla loro presentia di questi libri stampati, et trattatto accordo con il Gardano libraro hanno concluso mercato del 2.o et 5.to libro delle messe del Palestrina à 4. 5. et 6., dell primo libro à 4. di Francesco Soriano, delle messe à 6. et otto da Orlando Lasso; de Gerolamo Lambardi à 4., et del primo libro de Paulo Paciotto à 4. et 5., tutti ligati in carta carton grosso, et saldo con la bergamina de sopra azura come la nostra à lui datta con le sue cordele azure in ducati quaranta quatro, et cosi hanno à bossoli et balloti comitato.

Doc. 68: A.S.V., San Marco, Procuratia de Supra, Registro 140 (Chiesa Actorum, 1607–14)

1607. 22. April.

Havendo SS. SS. Illustrissime datto ordine già anni tre, che siano copiati diversi libri di musica della capella di San Marco, di quali si era restato d'accordo in [lire] 2 della carta imperial dandole ancora la carta, et essendo portati à logo dalli scrittori et essendosi rapresentata occassione di doi libri di messe stampati in Anversa uno di [carte] 270. di messi otto in carta papal di auttori singolari, cioè Orlando Lassus, Ciprano da Rore, Tomas Crequilon, et Josquin, et l'altro di carta real di messi dieci di Clemens non papa, Tomas Crequilon et Orlando Lassus, et uno di motetti similmente di Carta real di [carte] 272 di Henrico Isac, et Josquin le quali veduti dal Maestro di capella, et havendone fatto cantar in Capella diverse ha rifferito esser riuscite bone, dottisime, et breve et che però sarà se non bene à pigliarle per haverne bisogno essendo quelli che si adoperavano in pezzi molti di loro, et havutta s.a ciò informatione del valor di quelli, et considerato che uno solo il più grande che è di [carte] 270 costerea à scriverlo à pena [lire] 540 à [lire] 2 la carta come si è rimasto d'accordo con li scrittori di quelli di sopra dichiariti, oltra il pagar la carta, si che havendo questi tutti tre per minor P.io sarà di beneffficio alla procuratoria et riuscirano di maggior satisfattione per la stampa, Perciò hanno à bossoli et balloti terminato, che di tutti tre li detti libri siano pagatti alla procuratia ducati sessanta, Dovendo esserli poste le sue tavole per maggior fattezza, et siano consignati al Zago di libri, il qual debba haver cura di quelli con li altri conforme al suo obligo.

Doc. 69: A.S.V., San Marco, Procuratia de Supra, Registro 12 (Giornali Cassier, 1639–48)

1640 a di 30 Giugno

Per spese detto//à Cassa ducati quindici contadi à [blank space] librer à San Zulian per haver religato in curame et accomodati libri tre scritti à pena, intitolati il Magnificat del Morales, de gl'Himni....

Doc. 70: A.S.V., San Marco, Procuratia de Supra, Registro 144 (Chiesa Actorum, 1637–48)

1640. 28 Ottobre

Che à Don Angelo Rigoni Crociffero sijno dati *ducati* 19 *denari* 9 per sue mercedi di haver rescrito in Musica in carta reale Messe del Maestro Monteverdi et Palestrina.... per servitio del Coro della Chiesa di San Marco.

Doc. 71: A.S.V., San Marco, Procuratia de Supra, Registro 144 (Chiesa Actorum, 1637–48)

1642. 21 Aprile

Che a Don Angelo Rigoni Crociffero sijno date *lire* 124 per sue mercede di haver rescritto in Musica in carta reale due Compiete; una del Maestro Monteverde, et l'altra del Chiozoto.... per servicio del coro della Chiesa di San Marco.

Doc. 72: A.S.V., San Marco, Procuratia de Supra, Registro 12 (Giornali Cassier, 1639–48)

Laus Deo 1645 à di 31. Marzo

Per spese per la chiesa//à Cassa *ducati* cinque *denari* 5, contadi al mastro di Cappella per due copie vespri a 8. voci in stampa del Chiozotto....

Doc. 73: A.S.V., San Marco, Procuratia de Supra, Registro 99 (Ceremoniali), f. 191r–192v.

1631: primo Aprile; Funzione Fatta per Ordine dell'Eccelso Senato in poner la prima Pietra nel luoco destinato per formarvi la Chiesa intitolata Santa Maria della Salute per in Voto fatto dall'istesso Senato per imporare il Divino ajiuto [sic] ne presenti Bisogni.

Doveasi tal Solennità eseguire il giorno dell'Annuntiatione della Beatissima Vergine, giorno di felicissimi Auspizii à tutto il genere umano, acciochè si come in esso, hebbe già ne tempi andati questa Città il suo glorioso nascimento, cosi potesse nelli anni avenire nel medesimo gloriarsi della sua reparazione per intercessione di quella sopra lui profonda humiltà, fù dall'Altissimo nell'istesso di eretta la gran fabrica della nostra Redentione, mà per l'impedimento d'una lunga pioggia, fù trasportata al giorno dell'Ottava.

Fabricatasi à questo effetto un ponte di Tavole sopra barche che cominciando alla fine della Cale dà Ca' Giustiniano à San Moisè distendendosi per il longo del Canal Grande, andava à terminare al luogo destinato per la fabrica della nuova chiesa, nella cui avea fatta già spatiosa, et eguale per la rovina della habitazioni, che prima vi erano; per questa cerimonia era stata eretta una Chiesa di tavole in modo di Croce con il suo Coro, adornata di Cuori d'Oro, e colonne dipinte, e vagamente distinte con molte finestre di vero, coperta di telle rosse, et bianche, con il suolo similmente di tavole capace di mille persone incirca, la porta era fatta di due colonne di legno intagliate, e dipinte con suoi Pedestali, e Capitelli che sostenevano un'Arco sopra, sopra il quale in un'assai largo campo era dipinta l'imagine di Maria Santissima con una colombina significante lo Spirito Santo; Nel lato destro del Coro spatioso, e gratiosamente adornato, era preparato il Solio per il Sereniss/mo Prencipe, e Signoria; Nel lato sinistro era una porta dalla quale per molti gradi se discendeva nella fossa de fondamenti già cavati, dove si doveva mettere la prima pietra....

.... Dà S/an Marco s'incaminò al luogo desinato, processionalmente con il solito ordine, cioè precedeva la Croce, e li Giovani del Seminario gregoriano di poi li Cantori, cantando con divota melodia le Littanie....

.... fù posto la prima Pietra al suo luogo, et messevi dal Vice Doge le sopra nominate Medalzie, e coperta, si cominciò im/mediatemente à fabricarvi sopra, sendendovi anche altri Senatori, e mettendovi altri Doppie, altri Cecchini con altre pietre, ò calcina sopra, fù seguitata la Fabrica, cantando li Cantori Hinni, e Salmi al Signore, dopo il che dà Sua Signoria Ill/ustrissima fù celebrata la Messa con la mede/sima Musica, finita la quale con il mede/simo ordine et strepito de Artiglierie, e di Campane, ritornò la Sere/nissima Signoria, piena di somma fiducia à S/an Marco.

Doc. 74: A.S.V., San Marco, Procuratia de Supra, Registro 144 (Chiesa Actorum, 1637–48)

1640. 8 Luglio

Essendosi dismisso già molto te/mpo il sonar nelli concerti, che si fano in Chiesa di S/an Marco, et in tutta la Città l'instrumento del Corneto, che soleva re/nder armonia molto grata, et di com/pita sodisfatt/ione, et desiderando gli Ecc/ellentissi/mi Sig/nori Proc/urato/ri di rittornar à ravvivare detto instrumento e essendo informati della molta fattica che co/nviene fare quelli che lo vogliono esercitare, han/no p/er dar animo cosi alli presenti come ad altri che volessero attenderci, terminato che à Pietro Furlan al pre/se/nte Concerto ordin/ario in Chiesa siano agio/nti *ducati* 15 all'an/no, et à Marco Coradini C/antor ordinario pure in Chiesa siano dati altri *ducati* 15 all'an/no co/n obligo à tutti doi di dover nelle Musiche che si faran/no in detta Chiesa, et sempre, che li sarà ordinato dal Maestro di Capella sonar il detto Corneto, esercitandovi/si p/er dover riussire sempre migliori et ciò a beneplacito di SS: SS: Ecc/ellentissi/mi, dovendo nel resto adempir l'obligo che han/no in detta Chiesa questa le loro co/ndotte.

Doc. 75: A.S.V., San Marco, Procuratia de Supra, Registro 144 (Chiesa Actorum, 1637–48)

A di 25. Ottobre 1643

Che à P/adre Marco Pellegrini, che suona il violino in S/an Marco, sia assignato d/uca/ti vinti all'anno p/er insignar à sonar il cornetto.

Doc. 76: A.S.V., San Marco, Procuratia de Supra, Registro 12 (Giornali Cassier, 1639–48)

1644. 27 Luglio

Per spese diverse//à Cassa *ducati* nuove contadi à Zuan*n*e Babin et [Domenico] dei Martini, che imparano à suonare di cornetto per comparar libri, et instrumenti come per term*inazione* del giorno d'hieri.

Doc. 77: A.S.V., San Marco, Procuratia de Supra, Registro 144 (Chiesa Actorum, 1637–48)

1645 Adi 24: April

Che Zuane Babin sia condotto in Capella p*er* Cornetto con ducati dieci all'anno.

Doc. 78: A.S.V., San Marco, Procuratia de Supra, Registro 144 (Chiesa Actorum, 1637–48)

1646: Adi 23 Aprile

Che à Domenico de Martin stante la prova fatta di concerto Cornetto le sia concesso di salario ducati diese all'anno.

Doc. 79: A.S.V., San Marco, Procuratia de Supra, Registro 144 (Chiesa Actorum, 1637–48)

1642 P*rimo* Luglio

Anda*n*do creditori diversi Cantori Concerti et altri di paghe p*er* l'an*n*o passatto 1641 come appar nel libro delle paghe tenuto dal già Fra*n*cesco Badoer fu Gastaldo dell'importar delle quali paghe havendosi detto Badoer rimborsato del danaro tutto che no*n* li habbi effetivamente esborsati, essendo p*er* ciò stato formato deb*ito*r delle paghe p*er* dette come sop*ra* non corrispose da detto Badoer sotto li 22 Aprile passatto et essendo conveniente che à creditori di quelle che ne fan*n*o insta*n*za sij esborsato qua*n*to se gli deve Per ciò SS: SS: Ecc*ellentissi*me veduto il debito già formato al nome del sudetto Badoer. Han*n*o ordinato à D: Giacomo Lazari Gastaldo alla Cassa della Chiesa, che debba corrisponder le paghe à quelli che viene dechiarito nella partita sopradetta non esser stati sodisfatti gira*n*do la scrittura necessaria.

Doc. 80: Fausto Ciro, *Venetia Festiva* (Venice: Baba, 1638), pp. 22–23

Prima di tutte l'altre cose dispose d'incominciar dal Cielo per ringratiarlo delle larghe benedittioni diluviate sopra la Francia: Commandò all'Illustriss*imo* Sig*nor* Conte Vidale Cavaliere di S*an* Michele e mastro della posta di Francia in Venetia, che ordinasse tutto quello ch'era di bisogno per far celebrare una solennissima Messa, e cantare il Te Deum in rendimento di gratie. Fu eletta la Chiesa di S*an* Giorgio Maggiore de Monaci Cassinensi per questa solennità; e per la qualità del sito, e per la magnifice*n*tia della fabrica, e per altre considerationi, giudicata la più proportionata al bisogno, di quante se ne trovano in Venetia. Il Signor Conte Vidale non mancò di diligenza acciò la festa seguisse con quella pompa maggiore, che ricercava una tanta ceremonia. Fece per l'apparato della Chiesa, e per la dispositione della Musica erigere doi grandissimi et vasti palchi tra le colonne, che sostentano la Cuba della Chiesa; questi furono tutti coperti con bellissimi raseti di vario colore.

Doc. 81: Ibid., p. 26

Finita la salva de' Mortari e de' cannoni, principiarono à stridere le trombe, rumoreggiare tamburi, e risuonare i piffari, e le Viole, accompagnando sù nobile e numerosa comitiva alla porta della Chiesa.

Doc. 82: Ibid., p. 28

Nel spuntare S*ua* Ec*cellenza* in Chiesa incominciarono la melodia, gli Organi sonanti; il direttore della Musica chiamò in questo mentre al concerto le voci canore, e gl'istromenti sonori. Arrivata poi nel mezzo della Chiesa fù intonato da' Cantori il Te Deum. Prima in suono dimesso, e lento, indi con pieno et altissimo concento s'udi l'armonia. Erano i ripieni sì soavi che rapivano gli animi de gli uditori, quali riputavano à grandissima fortuna l'essersi incontrati in un spettacolo sì memorabile e gioco*n*do. Pareva loro d'ascoltare delle Sirene il choro.

Doc. 83: Ibid., p. 30

Fù poi dalli Musici dato principio à ca*n*tare la Messa, e fù stimata la Musica delle più eccelle*n*ti di quante per gran tempo si siano udite in Venetia. Da questa meravigliosa armonia di soavi accenti, da sovrano stupore erano stupefatti in maniera gli animi de gli uditori, che rassembravano tutti come in estasi rapiti....

La melodia in vero di questo ammirabile canto arrestava coloro, ch'erano dalle loro facende violentati alla partenza. Da varie voci concordi s'udiva farsi, soave la Musica. Si temprava col duro il molle, e con l'acuto il grave. Si sentivano brillar d'alta allegria gli spiriti all'udito di si soave sinfonia. Haveva certo un spirito dissona*n*te, et un'anima affatto sorda, chi dalla soave armonia di voci si grate, o dal dolce ca*n*to che solleticava l'orecchio, non si sentiva rapito.

Doc. 84: Ibid., p. 32–33

Frà gli altri si quadagnò l'applauso del popolo un Musico sopranomato il Mantovano, il quale quando con preste fughe, quando con tardi riposi, ò con piacevoli respiri cangiava in tante maniere la voce, quante forme d'animali cambiava Proteo. Hora troncava la voce, poi la ripigliava. La fermava, la ritorceva. Hor scema, hor piena gorgheggiando fuora la mandava. La mormorava talvolta grave, poi l'assottigliava. Raddoppiava con bellissimi passaggi le difference de' suoni, e del concento; e sempre con egual melodia si sentivano le vezzose e dilettevoli nime. Variava lo stile, le pause affrenava, affrettando poscia le fughe: e della gola lusinghiera e dolce fatta lunga et articolata scala, ondeggiando per gradi quell'armonia, fuora della bocca l'effalava; formando di trillo un dolce contrapunto, e trasformando la sua lingua, in mille lingue. Questo cigno canoro con garula armonia, con soave suono abbellendo il canto di mille contrapunti rapiva con dolcezza tale gli animi de gli ascoltatori, che estatichi ne divenivano. E qual più grata melodia, ò più dilettevole suono del suo canto; che ora con lieti accenti in mezzo à i pianti faceva eccitare le risai ora tra le risa scaturire da gli occhi per tenerezza il pianto.

Si godeva ancora dalla discordante concordia dell'acuto e del grave de' sonori instrumenti una soave sinfonia. Il Signor Bernardello eccellentissimo sonatore de Liuto tra gli altri instrumenti musicali si segnalava. Velocemente grattando con l'ugna le dolci linee, cominciava à ricercare sopra il Liuto del più difficile tuono i tasti; e con crome in fuga, e sincope traversate variava il verso. E con veloce corso trascorneva con i deti del cavo istromento il manico. Alle volte s'abbassava, poi si sublimava, e tal'hora trillando al canto acuto se ne passava. Volava sù per le corde, e la mano spedita alla radice, et alla cima del manico quasi nell'istesso tempo si vedeva. Balenando le leggiere dita, nelle dotte sonate tutta l'arte della musica gentilmente esprimeva.

Continuò sempre questa si grata armonia per tutta la Messa. Al cantare dell'Evangelio, et alla elevatione del Santissimo comparvero dodeci paggi di *Sua Eccellenza* con grossissimi doppieri di cera bianca accesi, lasciati poi in dono alla Sagrestia; mentre nell'istesso tempo su'l campo eccheggiava l'aria dal sonoro rimbombo de' pifari, tamburi, trombe, et violoni. Nel medesimo punto i Bombardieri con i mortari, et i marinari Francesi col cannone fecero una strepitosa salva. Pareva s'abbassasse il Mondo dal gran fragore. Ultimata la Messa si partì dal Santuario *Sua Eccellenza* osservandosi l'istesso ordine nel uscire di Chiesa, che si fece nell'entrata. All'hora i Musici con un'armonioso concerto cantarono il Salmo. Omnes gentes plaudite manibus. Tenevano con l'alternare del bel concento tutte l'orecchie atte*n*te. Delle belliche squille parimente su'l campo il suono rimbombava. Nel montare in Gondola, e nel tragittare il gran Canale, rassembrava il Cielo tutto pieno di spaventevoli tuoni per le frequentissimi tiri di mortari, e del canone.

Doc. 85: Ibid., p. 34

Risuonava il Palagio d'armoniosi strepiti di viole, pifari, et altri musicali instrumenti, mentre le tavole erano imbandite dalli scalchi....

Doc. 86: Ibid., p. 37

Mentre si mangiava sonavano nell'istessa sala le viole et altri instromenti Musicali; e nel Cortile si facevano di lontano sentire le trombe, i tamburi, et i piffari....

Nell'invitare che si fece la prima volta, e nel bere alla salute del Re furono sparati nell'istesso punto da ottanta grossi mortari. Stridevano parimente le trombe, rimbombavano i tamburi, e si facevano in maniera sentire i pifari, e le viole, che pareva, tutto il Mondo commosso al giubilo et all'allegrezza, che si faceva al gratissimo nome di s*u*a M*a*iesta.

Doc. 87: Biblioteca del Civico Museo Correr, Codice Cicogna 3118, fascicoli 44–50

Illustrissimɔ et Eccellentissimo Signor Procuratore Cassier

Havendo Vostra Eccellenza commandato à me Giovanni Rovetta Maestro di Cappella, e
commesso espressamente ch'io debba raccordare quello che fusse più à proposito, e
necessario per il buon servitio della Chiesa di San Marco circa la Musica, dico che non
ritrovandosi al presente altro che venti otto Cantori salariati, cioè

Bassi	8
Tenori	9
Alti	5
Mezzi Soprani	3
Falsetti	2
Soprani	1
	28

Et essendo altre volte stati al numero di 40 sarebbe bene giungere almeno al numero di
32., cioè otto per parte, che così per il concerto, come per il servicio continuo riusirà di
decoro alla medesima Chiesa, e di sodisfattione à Vostra Eccellenza, alla quale
humilissime Io sopradetto m'inchino.

Doc. 88: Biblioteca del Civico Museo Correr, Codice Cicogna 3118, fascicoli 44–50

1653

Obligationi aggiunte alli Cantori di San Marco doppo la Peste senza accrescimento di
salario, che mancando rigorosamente puntati—

Le Processioni di tutti le sabati, dove si consuma quasi tutta la mattina	numero 52
Processione alla Salute	numero 1
Messe da Morto in San Marco	numero 12
Offitij tre per il San Lorenzo	numero 3
Per il Santo sudetto à Castello volte	numero 1
Processioni per il Santo di Padova alla Salute mattina, e sera	numero 2
Messa à San Paternian	numero 1

I punti, che si dividevano inter praesentes sono stati levati per Vesti alli Zaghi, ch'era
stimolo al ben servicio.
Due volte l'espositione del Santissimo tre giorni per volta con le due Processioni alla
sera, che sono ufficij   numero 8
Altre ad libitum Serenissimi

In tutto uffitij numero 80

Si lamentano li Cantori, che li punti, che per parte del Maggiore venivano distribuiti fra
loro, com'ancora si stila colli Canonici gli siano stati levati per fare le Cotte, e Vesti alli
Zaghi.
Che oltre l'obligationi ordinarie, che ascendono al numero di 525 gli sono state aggiunte
dalla presa Parte 12. Officij numero 80, come si vede qui avanti.

Doc. 89: A.S.V., San Marco, Procuratia de Supra, Registro 146 (Chiesa Actorum, 1655–74)

Adi 27 Febraro 1669 [*more veneto*]

Hanno similmente gl'Ill*ustrissi*mi et Ecc*ellentissi*mi Sig*nori* Proc*urato*ri antedetti terminato, che de danari della Cassa della Chiesa sia pagata una poliza de lire quarantuna à P*ad*re Lorenzo Rossi per saldo della carta reale presa per ricopiarli motteti della messa della Caccia, ligatura de un libro, et altro giusto la polizza sudetto sottoscritta da D*omi*ne Francesco Cavalli Maestro di Capella....

Doc. 90: A.S.V., San Marco, Procuratia de Supra, Registro 146 (Chiesa Actorum, 1655–74)

Adi 11 Genaro 1670 [*more veneto*]

Inoltre hanno gli sudetti Ill*ustrissi*mi et Ecc*ellentissi*mi Sig*no*ri Procuratori terminato, che de danari della Cassa della Chiesa sia pagata una poliza de lire trenta quatro soldi disisette à D*omi*no Francesco Caletto detto Cavalli Maestro di Capella in sodisfatione della carta, ligatura, et copia della messa detta della Caccia per l'anno corrente giusto la sua poliza del giorno sopradetto....

Doc. 91: A.S.V., San Marco, Procuratia de Supra, Registro 98 (Ceremoniali), f. 6r–v

. . . In die Iovis praedicta semper Cantores cantant quondam Missam iucundam, et inchoabant olim a Kyrie Eleison. Hodie cantant Missam, quae dicitur della Battaglia, quae composita fuit ab Victoriam Christianissimi Regis Francorum de Elvetijs, et dic pulsata Media Tertia cum Gloria, et Credo cum Cereis, Cruce, et incenso ad Altare *maiore* ut in duplici feria.

Missa supradicta dicitur pr*o*pter Victoriam habitam contra Patriarcam Aquileiensem, etc. ut notatum est de alijs Victorijs.

Doc. 92: Biblioteca Ambrosiana, MS A. 328 inf., f. 20v

Il Giovedi Grasso si canta la Messa Grande à hora di Terza composta da un Todesco sopra le ricercate dell'organo molto allegra, e si chiama la Messa della Battaglia, se bene de presente la chiamano la Messa della Cazza. Questa fu composta per la Vittoria del Rè di Francia contro l'Elvetij [in margin: Svizzeri]: Si canta con Gloria, Credo, et ogn'altra cosa *more duplici*.

Doc. 93: Biblioteca del Civico Museo Correr, Codice Cicogna 3118, fascicoli 44–50; second copy in A.S.V., San Marco, Procuratia de Supra, Busta 91, Processo 208, fasicolo 2, f. 11r

Laus Deo 1677

Nota di tutti li Sig*no*ri Musici, che dall'anno 1665 sino al tempo pr*ese*nte hanno abbandonato il servitio di San Marco, e preso quello d'altri Prencipi

Soprani:

Novembre 1664. Il Signor Gabriel Batistini partì, et andò al servitio dell'Elettore di Sassonia
Giugno 1673. Il Signor Giacometto Riccardini detto del Sagredo andò al servitio di Brandemburgo
Novembre 1669. Il Signor Antonio....[sic] detto Tonin da Muran andò al servitio di Sassonia poi ritornè à Venezia per curarsi, e poi morì.
Maggio 1675. Il Signor Antonio Masserotti andò al servitio di Loreto
Agosto 1675. Il Signor Antonio Bissoni andò al servitio di Parma
Novembre 1674. Il Signor Antonio Bussi andò al servitio di Modena
Settembre 1669. Il Signor Sebastian Cioni, detto Bastianello andò al servizio di Modena

Alti:

Il Signor D, Carlo Procerati andò al servitio di Padova
Il Signor D. Giovanni Antonio Forni andò al servitio della Maestà dell'Imperatore
Il Signor Sebastiano Moratello andà al medesimo
Settembre 1670. Il Signor Pietro Benedetti detto Piloncino andò al servitio di Polonia

Tenori:

Dicembre 1668. Il Signor D. Stefano Boni andò al servitio della Maestà dell'Imperatore
Agosto 1674. Il Signor Antonio Farina andò al servitio di Napoli
Aprile 1677. Il Signor Francesco detto....[sic] detto Mutio andò al servitio di Bransuich
Settembre 1665. Il Signor Giovanni Sebenico andò al servitio d'Inghilterra
Febraro 1675. Il Signor Giovanni Mosselli andò al servitio di Bransuich
1671 Il Signor Giovanni Batista Filiberi andò al servitio d'Inghilterra
Dicembre 1673. Il Signor Francesco Pio andò al servitio di Roma
Maggio 1671. Il Signor Lodovico Zuari andò al servitio di Verona
Febraro 1666. Il Signor Francesco Medardo andò al servitio di Loreto

Bassi:

Febraro 1675. Il Signor Francesco Gallo andò al servitio d'Inghilterra
Il Signor....[sic] Todesco andò al servitio di Naiburgh
Il Signor Rugier Fedeli andò al servitio di Bergamo

Doc. 94: A.S.V., San Marco, Procuratia de Supra, Registro 98 (Ceremoniali), f. 70r–v; another copy: f. 30v

De psalmis canendis in omnibus solemnitatibus

In omnibus solemnitatibus, olim psalmi cantabantur a capella parva, et a cantoribus qui ex practica cantant, si habeantur sic dicebantur cantare, more Georgiano, hodie hic mos canendi abijt in dissuetudinem et Cantores maioris capellae cantant omnes Psalmos, et reliqua, et psalmos cantant divisi in duobus choris, videlicet quatuor cantores in uno choro, et reliqui omnes, in altero, quia capella parva non extat.

Doc. 95: A.S.V., San Marco, Procuratia de Supra, Registro 98 (Ceremoniali), f. 26v.

Post prandium hora solita aperta solemni Palla, Vesp*eri* canta*ntur* cum o*mni* pompa, ut in No*st*ris Libris. Psalmi o*mn*es Laudate, sub hac Ant*iphon*a: Veni S*an*cte Sp*irit*us, et Psalmi cantant Cantores divisi in 2. Choris, *videlicet* 4 Cantores in uno Choro, et reliqui o*mn*es in alt*er*o ut moris est in solemnitatibus.

Doc. 96: Sansovino-Stringa, *Venetia città nobilissima* (Venice, 1604), f. 44v.

Cap. LXXIII. Del pergolo dei Musici

All'incontro de i due soprascritti pulpiti, ne i quali, come s'è detto, il Vengelo, et l'Epistola si cantano, è posto, et collocato il pergolo de i Musici, il quale è in forma ottangola, et in aria da sette colonne di finissima pietra sostenuto; e due altre mediocri vi si veggono vicino al muro poste, che ancor esse qualche parte sua sostengono. Sopra questo quasi per l'ordinario, e specialmente nelle feste solenni, e quando discende la Signoria in Chiesa, cantano i Musici alla Messa maggiore, et al vespro gli ufficij divini. Et viene anch'egli, come è predetti, coperto, e vestito all'intorno di un drappo di veluto cremesino, con riccami di panno d'oro.

Doc. 97: Sansovino-Martinioni, *Venetia città nobilissima* (Venice, 1663), p. 101

Da i lati del parapetto sono due pulpiti alla usanza greca della destra, et della sinistra. L'uno altissimo, et fatto in due suoli in forma piramidale, finisce in cuba. L'altro è di forma ottangola, ma molto più basso. In quello si canta in Vangelo, et talhora si predica nei più solenni giorni dell'anno, in questo si appresenta al popolo il Doge creato di nuovo, et per l'ordinario, quando la Signoria va in chiesa, vi stanno i Musici à cantar gli officii divini.

Doc. 98: A.S.V., San Marco, Procuratia de Supra, Busta 91, f. 13r–v

1589 adi 12. Ott*obre*

.... Io andai in coro a portar in pergolo un salmista nel qual era un salmo che mancava nelli ordinarij per poter dir il vesporo doppio come me havea detto il M*aest*ro di Coro, et così vene in pergola esso M*e*s*ser* Bald*isse*ra e disse alli cantori che dovessero cantar a dui cori il vesporo, che così havea ordi*na*to il m*aest*ro di coro. Risposero tutti uno ore, che non volevono cantar a dui cori che non erano obligati, e Incominciornò a venir giù del pergolo per venir dal S*igno*r Cassi*er* et mentre venivano giù sentirno che in coro si rispondeva al vesporo che havea intonato il Can*oni*co Dove tornarono in pergolo, e come fu finito fino alla—[special symbol] vene in pergolo il m*aest*ro di Coro ordinando che si cantasse a dui cori....

Doc. 99: Biblioteca Ambrosiana, MS A. 328 inf., f. 14r

La Vigilia dell'Epifania si apre la Palla hoggi, et à tutti due li offitij di dimani. Si cantano li Vesperi in 5.o et dalli Cantori à due Chori li Salmi à 8 in Bigonzo.

Chapter IV

Doc. 100: Preface to Giovanni Rovetta's *Salmi a otto voci* (Venice: Vincenti, 1644).

Appena honorato dalla benignità dell'Eccell*enze* Vostre di questa nobilissima carica, sentendo in me lo stimolo della gratitudine, e del debito, hò dato fine ad alcune compositioni, delle quali hò pensato haver più di bisogno il servitio della Serenissima Real Capella di S*an* Marco.

Doc. 101: Biblioteca Ambrosiana, MS A. 328 inf., Dedication

In questa Ducal Basilica si stabiliì il suo Clero con ammirabile direttione, et con ordine hierarchica e p*er*che ogni chiesa possiede e le sue Cerimonie, et il suo Rito, da sommi Pontefici anche tolerato nell'officiatura, giusto la Bolla di Pio 5.o 1568, quando però eccedi il corso di anni 200—

Resta stabilir, et decretar p*er* regola propria perpetua, et immutabile della med*esi*ma Ducal Capella, e risvegliare al Mondo nuovo Ceremoniale secondo il Rito di S*an* Marco....

Doc. 102: A.S.V., Cancelleria Inferiore, Registro 81 (Atti dei Dogi, (1623–45), p. 47

.... Essendo mia ferma intentione, che nella Chiesa, et Capella mia di S*an* Marco nella celebratione delle Santissime messe cantate et de tutti li altri Sacri, et Divini offizij che si Celebrano tutto l'anno sijno, tutto, e p*er* tutto osservate, et fatte osservar tutte qu*el*le sacre Ceremonie, che p*er* antiqui ordeni, et consuetudini si sogliono osservare et tanto mossi da quel giusto zelo, che in cio si conviene con la solita authorità, che habbiamo in detta Chiesa, et Capella nostra commettemo à voi p*ad*re Cesare Vergaro Canonico, et maestro di Coro della d*et*ta alli successori vostri, et ad altri à cui speta che sempre et in qual si voglia tempo, ch*e* sara*n*no ca*n*tate, e Celebrate le dette messe, et Divini offizij vi dobbiate rittrovar presente ordinando, et operando, che tutte le sacre Ceremonie sijno fatte, et osservate secondo il rito, forma, et uso antico di d*et*ta Chiesa senza pur minima inovatione, et questo doverete eseguire, et far osservar sotto tutte quelle pene, che in caso di transgressione a noi parerà convenienti p*er* Giustitia contra li inobedienti....

.... 27 Junij 1628
Zuane Corner Doge

Doc. 103: Biblioteca del Civico Mueso Correr, Codice Cicogna 3118, fascicoli 44–50.

.... Bisogna dunque sapere, che l'uso e rito vecchio della Chiesa di Dio nell'affare, del qual'hora si tratta, era, che il Celebrante (chiunque egli fosse) faceva, o recitava insieme col Prelato la Confessione delle Messe cantate, secondo che si raccoglie dà Ceremoniali Romani stampati prima delle ultime riforme, e specialmente da quello di Clemente VIII in più suoi luoghi. Però anch'circa à questo la Regia Capella di V*ostra* Seren*i*tà ha mantenuto il suo vetustissimo uso, divenuto poi prerogativa, di non ammettere alterazioni....

.... Vede dunque V*ostra* Sere*ni*tà che in caso di qualche novità in simil proposito, bisognerebbe ceder con la Corte di Roma ad una tal prerogativa della sua Chiesa di S*an* Marco; e non solo alla prerogativa di recitar la confessione della Messa insieme co' Nucij; ma quel che più importa alla prerogativa di non ammetter riforme nella Sua Capella....

Doc. 104: A.S.V., Cancelleria Inferiore, Registro 81 (Atti dei Dogi, 1623–45), f. 70

1630. Adi. 10 Zugno

Nicolò Contarini per la Dio Gra*ti*a Doge di Venetia et cet. Essendo noi tenuti in virtù della permissione no*st*ra Ducale alla Conservatione, et augmento della Capella N*ost*ra di S*an* Marco della quale siamo soli Patroni, et insieme invigilare con ogni Spirito, che il Culto d*el* S*igno*r Iddio con resti defondato, et havendo noi inteso con gra*nde* dispiacenza dell'animo no*st*ro co*me* sono introdotte molte novità, et abusi circa li Divini Offitij, che in quella si celebrano, il che non si deve in modo alcuno tolerare, però col tenore delle presenti ordiniamo, et comandiamo ad'ogn'uno della no*st*ra Capella.

P*rimo*. Che nel Celebrar li Divini Offitij in de*t*ta Chiesa siano Osservate le Rubriche, Riti, Usi, et Cirimonie descritte nel libro chiamato Orationale, et in quanto da quello si fosse in qualche parte deviato si debbano tralasciar dette Novità, et osservar quello pontualme*n*te p*er* decoro dell'antichità, et Laudevoli usi di de*t*ta Chiesa; volendo, et commandando alli Sacristani, Mastro di Coro, et altri Offitiali in de*t*ta Chiesa, che debbano con ogni diligenza osservare, et far pontualme*n*te eseguire la presente ordinatione sotto q*ue*lle pen*n*e, che à Noi paeran*n*o espedienti.

Doc. 105: A.S.V., Procuratia de Supra, San Marco, Registro 141 (Chiesa Actorum, 1614–20)

1614. 19 Luglio

Che siano pagati d*uca*ti dieci, p*er* Marco Cassini librer p*er* haver religato doi Antifonari grandi da coro di carta Bergamina.... Ite*m* rafatto il Rational ch*e* si adopera in coro alla Messa grande, e vesperi indorado tutto coperto di cuoro cremesina....

Doc. 106: A.S.V., Cancelleria Inferiore, Registro 79 (Atti dei Dogi, 1605–1615), f. 87v–88r

Marcus Ant*onius* Memo Dei gr*atia* Dux Venet*iarum* et cet*era*
Considerando quanto neccessario sij alla dignità, et al decoro della p*er*sona et della Repub*lica* no*st*ra, che le cerimonie ecclesiastiche, che giornalmente occoreno farsj n*on* solo nelle chiese alla capella no*st*ra di S*an* Marco annesse, et dipendentj, ma in altre, ove p*er* publiche ordinationj, o votj, o p*er* particolare divotione siamo solitj andare co*n* publica pompa accompagnatj siano bene, et condecentemente osservate. Et vedendo noj, che p*er* non vi essere chi fuori della prede*t*ta no*st*ra capella habbia di ciò cura particolare

possono ben spesso seguire degl'errori, et dellj inconvenientj di non pocco momento. Per tanto mossi da quel Zelo di pietosa honorificenza ch'à noj incombe statuimo, et terminiamo, et terminando commettemo à voi Padre Cesare Vergaro canonico et maestro di choro nella sudetta nostra capella, et alli successorj vostrj in detto carico: Che sempre ch'occorerà à noj, et alli Serenissimi successorj nostrj overo alla Serenissima signoria d'andare con publica pompa alla visita d'alcuna chiesa com'è predetto dobbiate personalmente nell'habito vostro in simili occasionj consueto accompagnarij con li sei canonici nostri di San Marco ch'in dettj casi ci accompagnano. Assistendo con essi loro dal principio fino al fine à tuttj li divinj officij ch'in dette chiese occorerano farsj. Disponendo però, voi, et ordinando intorno le sacre cerimonie nella medesima maniera, et coll'istessa facoltà, che solete et che dovete nella predetta chiesa di San Marco nostra capella. Dall'uso, et dal cerimoniale della quale non intendemo, che vi dobbiate in modo alcuno discostare. Commandando per ciò à qualunque ch'havesse cura in alcuna delle predette chiese di cerimoniare che nelle sudette occasionj circa le sacre cerimonie debbano in pena dell'indignatione nostra obedire detto nostro maestro dj choro senza contraditione alcuna. Ordinando all'infrascritto nostro cancelliero che cosj debba notare. Dandone copia à detto maestro, et ad altrj sempre, che farà bisogno.

Datur in nostro Ducale Palazzo die prima Januarij 1612 [*more veneto*]

Doc. 107: A.S.V., San Marco, Procuratia de Supra, Busta 88 (Ceremoniere), Processo 195, fascicolo 1, f. 105r

Copia
1659:   3 Genaro [*more veneto*] In Collegio En Ceremoniale

Dovendosi prendere qualche deliberazione quanto espose giù nel Collegio nostro Monsignor Illustrissima Patriarca circa le Cerimonie che sono state praticate l'anno passato nella Patriarcale di Castello nel giorno del Beato Lorenzo;

Sia preso che in tutte le Chiese che doveranno esser visitate del Serenissimo Prencipe, e dalla Serenissima Signoria sia incombenza del maestro di Coro della Chiesa Ducal di San Marco ordinar e diriger le Cerimonie nella maniera stesso e con la stessa autorità che fà nella detta Chiesa di San Marco, dal uso e cerimonial della quale, dove intervengono il Serenissimo Prencipe ò la Signoria nostra non è di ragione, di decoro, e di convenienza il di partirsi.

Doc. 108: A.S.V., San Marco, Procuratia de Supra, Registro 140 (Chiesa Actorum, 1607–14)

Adi 17 Luglio 1608

Havendo il maestro di coro raccordato, che li salterij secondo il rito della chiesa di San Marco, quale s'adoperano di continuo in coro, sono in pessimo statto, et che attrovandosene un solo che possi anco malamente adoperar sarrà bene quello renovar o con farne scriver à pena o con farli stampar. Considerando, che il farli scriver à pena costerea uno solo di essi ducati cinquanta, et più, et che in capo di pochi anni bisognerà farne delli altri consummandosi per il continuo uso, onde stampandoli si potrà haverne

copie cinqua*n*ta co*n* ducati dosento inc*irc*a computata la carta, havendosi offerto il d*ett*o
Maestro di coro di riveder esso salterio, et facendo bisogno, notarli quelle aggio*n*te,
ch*e* giudicarà dover servir in d*ett*a opera, Però il tutti inteso et co*n*siderato, han*n*o à
boss*oli* et ball*oti* ter*min*a to ch*e* p*er* l'Ill*u*strissi*mo* Cassi*er* sia fatto mercato co*n* qualch*e*
stampar, ch*e* si offerirà servir co*n* più ava*n*taggio, acio ch*e* ne siano stampate copie
cinqua*n*ta, d*e*lle quali una sia ligata in tola, et uno secondo l'ordinario, et li altre siano
semate in procuratia in loco ch*e* siano ben custodite.

Doc. 109: A.S.V., San Marco, Procuratia de Supra, Registro 140 (Chiesa Actorum,
1607–14)

1608. 4. Genaro [*more veneto*]

Che della cassa della chiesa siano datti d*uca*ti cinquanta per una volta tanto, cioè
cinquanta à m*esse*r P*adre* Zuane Stringa maestro di coro atesa l'util servitio, che lui
presta, cosi nel carico suo come nella revision del salterio, che si stampa p*er* servitio
della chiesa di S*an* Marco cosi di haver aggio*n*to come corretto diverse cose p*er*tenente à
quello.

Doc. 110: A.S.V., San Marco, Procuratia de Supra, Registro 139 (Chiesa Actorum,
1598–1607)

1600. 26. Sett*emb*re

Che à gloria del G*ra*n Dio et d*i* S*an* Marco Prottettor n*os*tro sia abbracciatta la supp*li*ca
infra*scri*tta d*a* M*e*ss*er* P*adre* Zuane Stringa Can*oni*co di S*an* M*ar*co, et le siano datti
ducati vinticin*que* p*er* stampar l'opera in essa supp*li*ca co*n*tenuta co*n* questo ch*e* d*e*bba
insieme stampar anco l'off*ic*io d*e*lla vita d*i* S*an* Marco, per ch*e* non si ne trovano più
et co*n* obligo ch*e* di esse stampe ne siano datte una p*er* cad*auno* a que lli
dell'Ecc*ellentissi*mo Senato.

Doc. 111: A.S.V., Santo Ufficio, Busta 156, Processo 1, unpaginated folio

Stampatori dell'officio nuovo.

Giacomo Lioncini à Sant'Apostolo su'l capo d*e*lla Casa.
Gerlamo Bella barba è S*an* Stephano apresso la casa del q*uondam* Sig*no*r Rocco
cathaneo.
Domenigo Nicolini à S*anta* Maria formosa in calle Longa.
Francesco Rampazetto in calle dalle rasse.
Domenigo Faris à S*an* Ant*oni*o.

Doc. 112: Biblioteca Nazionale Marciana, Inc. Ven. 854, f. 129v

In sup*er* notandum q*uasi* semp*er* in primis vesperis festor*um* duplicium et cum pleno
officio ps*almi* i*n*frascripti videlicet. Laudate pueri do*minu*m. Laudate do*minu*m om*ne*s
gentes. Lauda a*nima* mea. Laudate do*minu*m q*uonia*m. Lauda hierusale*m*.

Doc. 113: Gioseffe Zarlino, *Institutioni Harmoniche* (Venice: Senese, 1573), pp. 329–30

Alcuni avertimenti intorno le Compositioni, che si fanno à più di Tre voci.

.... Et benche si rendi alquanto difficule, non si debbe però schivare la fatica: percioche è cosa molto lodevole et virtuosa; et tale difficultà si farà alquanto più facile, quando si haverà essaminato le dotte compositioni di esso Adriano; come sono quelli Salmi: Confitebor tibi domine in toto corde meo in consilio iustorum: Laudate pueri dominum: Lauda Ierusalem Dominum: De profundis: Memento Domine David, et molti altri; tra i quali sono i Salmi: Dixit Dominus Domino meo: Laudate pueri Dominum: Laudate Dominum omnes gentes: Lauda anima mea Dominum: Laudate Dominum quoniam bonus est Psalmus: Lauda Ierusalem Dominum; et il Cantico della Beata Vergine; Magnificat anima mea Dominum, il quale composi già molti anni à tre Chori.

Doc. 114: A.S.V., San Marco, Procuratia de Supra, Registro 98 (Ceremoniali), f. 27r

Sabbato post Pentecostes. In hac Vigilia et in die Psalmi cantantur cum omni pompa . . . Psalmi in primis Vesperis sunt: Levavi oculos meos, Ad te levavi, De profundis, Memento, Laudate nomen Domini.

Doc. 115: A.S.V., San Marco, Procuratia de Supra, Busta 88 (Ceremoniere), f. 60r

adi. 26. detto [i.e., August 1600]

Messer Padre Zuane Chiozoto fatto venir in procuratia de ordine ut supra.... Interrogado se esso maestro ha alterato, et fatto mutatione dalli ordini antichi circa l'officio. Rispondit ha alterato nell'officiatura del primo Vespero della Santissima Trinità, quale lui voleva che si cantasse à doi chori, et non vi sono li salmi, ne mai sono statti fatti da alcuno delli Maestri di capella, et noi per non far scandolo li cantassimo in falso bordon et fui chiamato da un senator, che hora non mi soviene et mi interogò di questa novità, che si cantasse in Capella di San Marco falso bordon.

Doc. 116: A.S.V., San Marco, Procuratia de Supra, Busta 91, Processo 208, fascicolo 1, f. 17v

[13 Ottobre 1589]

Fra Bernardo [Andeli] minoritano fatto venir in Procuratia de Supra.... li fu detto Domenica passata che era la sagra di San Marco andate in chiesa a vesporo Rispose Signor si Interrogato che vesporo coreva quel Zorno Rispose della sagra della chiesa di San Marco Interrogato andavelo detto ugnolo ò a dui cori. Rispose Ugnolo, che in 25 anni che servo mai si è cantato a dui cori, ne manco dalli maestri di Capella passati che è statto Messer Adrian, Messer Ciprian e Reverendo Padre Isepo Zerlino mai han fatto un salmo che manca....

Doc. 117: A.S.V., San Marco, Procuratia de Supra, Busta 91, Processo 208, fascicolo 1, f. 20v

[16 Ottobre 1589]

Int*errogato* ess*endo* fatto questo segno dal m*aest*ro di capella che è capo et ess*endo* ch*e* vi era il segno, et havendolo ord*inato* il m*aest*ro di coro perche non cantar et obedir. R*ispose* perche non è solito il cantarlo doppio ne manco vi è il salmo si come sono tutti li altri vespori a dui cori fatti p*er* mano de M*e*ss*er* Adria*n* che se questo fosse statto ord*ina*rio mancandovi un solo salmo lo havrebe fatto ne manco lo ha fatto M*e*ss*er* Cipria*n* successor suo ne il *prese*nte M*aest*ro M*e*ss*er* P*adre* Isepo perche se l'havesse voluto che'l se cantasse a dui cori lo haverebbe fatto....

Doc. 118: A.S.V., San Marco, Procuratia de Supra, Busta 88 (Ceremoniere), f. 56r

[16 Agosto 1600]

M*e*ss*er* Vielmo francese cantar soprano in chiesa di S*an* Marco.... Interogado se esso maestro ha alterato, et fatto mutatione delli ordini antichi cir*c*a l'off*ic*io R*ispond*it di questo ne ha fatto cantar li salmi in falso bordo*n* il giorno de*l*la sacra, cosa che non si ha mai più fatto, crida*n*do al maestro di capella p*erc*he no*n* componeva q*ue*sti salmi et il maestro di capella li rispose, ch*e* se Adria*n, n*e Cipria*n* no*n* li hanno mai fatti, ne meno il Zerlino che no*n* sapea, p*erc*he volesse ch*e* lui li facesse no*n* ess*en*do ordinario.

Doc. 119: Biblioteca Ambrosiana, MS A. 328 inf., f. 56r

La Vigilia dell'Assuntione di Maria Vergine s'apre la Palla, sonato che sij il Vespro. Si porta la B. V. sopra l'Altar more solito con li Candelieri, e Torzi avanti, et da dietro con li Cantori, che cantano *Quem Terra*, overo *O Gloriosa Domina*.

Doc. 120: Biblioteca Ambrosiana, MS A. 328 inf., f. 62r

Il doppo pranso pur a palla aperta si canta in 5.o, et li Cantori a due Cori con li Salmi a 8; et cantano p*er* Mottetto Laudate Dominum de caelis.

Doc. 121: Biblioteca Ambrosiana, MS A. 328 inf., f. 73v

Ogni volta, che s'apre la Palla, e che non venghi il Ser*enissi*mo li Cantori sono tenuti cantar un Motetto in Organo à due voci, ò come pare al loro Maestro.

Doc. 122: Biblioteca del Civico Museo Correr, Codice Cicogna 2853, fascicolo 2, f. 33v

1628

cir*c*a Musicos

Gio*vanni* Tiepolo Patriarcha di Ven*etia*

De Mandato di sua Sig*nor*ia Ill*ustrissi*ma e R*everendissi*ma si commette a netti li Piovani, Cappellani, Sagrestani, et a qualunque, che haverà cura dell'Officiature delle Chiese di questa Città alla giurisdizione di sua Signoria Illustrissima sottoposte et così anco alli Confessori, et Capellani delle Chiese di monache della medesima Giurisdizione, che non hebbino permettere che nelle lor Chiese Oratorj, o Capelle, nelle Musiche che si faranno si cantino altre parole, che quelle della Sacra scrittura admesse dalla Santa Chiesa Cattolica Romana, seguenti una doppo l'altra come che stanno nel Testo istesso senza trasposizione di una inanti dell'altra, et senza concatenazione di varie parole raccolte da più, e varij luochi di essa Sacra Scrittura, Breviarij, et Messali, et cosi anco, che non debbino permettere che in tali musiche cantino o suonino i Ciechi, come con molto scandalo et poca edificazione vi è fin hora introdotto, dovendo del resto impedire essi musiche et novità, con far sapere alli Musici et Cantori, che si assenghino dalla contrafazione delle cose sudette, et vedendo che da essi non si obedisca, debbano tralasciar li officij incominciati, et ritirarsi del tutto dall'assistervi, et darne subito conto a Sua Signoria Illustrissima e Reverendissima in pena della suspensione à Divinis quando vi assistessero o mancassero di dar detto avviso, et altre pene ad arbitrio nostro.

Doc. 123: Biblioteca del Civico Museo Correr, Codice Cicogna 2853, fascicolo 1, f. 190r

Ordini da osservarsi nelle Musiche che si fanno nelle Chiesa di Monache publicati di Ordine dell'Eccellentissimo et Reverendissimo Signor Cardinal Cornaro Patriarca di Venezia

1. Si ordina che le parole che si cantano siano tolte puramente dalla sacra scrittura eccetuate però la Cantica, la quale si proibisce del tutto nelle Musiche.
2. Che dovendosi cantare altre parole che della sacra scrittura si vedino prima, et si ammettino da Sua Eccellenza o dal suo Vicario sopra le Monache.
3. Che si possino adoperare tutti gli stromenti dal Liuto, Tiorba, ed Arpa in poi.
4. Che non si replichi il Gloria in excelsis Deo, nè il Credo in Deum ma si seguiti subito dove ha terminato il celebrante. Il simile dei Salmi, Inni et ogna altra cosa.
5. Che si portino i nomi de Musici a Sua Eccellenza affine che li possa si conoscere et approvare per le chiese di Monache se meriteranno.
6. Che li musici usino quella riverenza che ricerca la Santità del luoco dove si trovano e quella modestia ch'è propria dell'officio che essercitano, altrimenti saranno privi di più poter cantare, o sonare in Chiese di Monache.
7. Che li Palchi della Musica non si possino fabricare vicini alle seriate delle Monache, ma più lontani che sarà possibile.
8. Che nel dar le Monache la mercede a Musici, ò nel regolar li di qualche gentilezza non si cagioni streppiti con scandalo delle persone religiose et pie.

Dati dal Palazzo Patriarcale il di 16. Zugno 1633.

Doc. 124: A.S.V., Provveditori di Comun, Busta 47, "Terminationi et Ordini per il buon governo delle Scuole, Riduttioni, Sovegni, Traghetti et Arti sottoposte al loro illustrissimo Magistrato" (1637–68) (Venice: Gio. Pietro Pinelli), pp. 52–53

1639. 1 Aprile.

L'Illustrissimi Signor Iseppo Moresini, Mattio Zen, et Bernardo Sagredo honorandi Proveditori di Commun havendo dall'espositione fattali per parte della Corte Patriarchale

di questa Città conosciuto quanto con zello proprio di christiana Religione si procuri di
ridur le musiche solite farsi nelle solennità festive à quella regola decorata, che ben
corrisponda alla pietà publica, mentre massime sono passati gli abusi à tal segno, che non
sono gli habiti de Musici medesimi, ma etiamdio ne gli Instromenti musicali, e nelle
parole, che si cantano, si vede, anci riguardarsi, il diletto degli ascoltanti, che la
divotione, alla quale è ordinato l'institutio pio di simili solennità. Hanno sue Signorie
Illustrissime confirmandosi con la religiosa applicatione della Corte medesima Patriarchale
ordinato, che in avvenire siano tenuti li Guardiani, Gastaldi, et ogni altra sorte di Capi di
dette Scole al nostro Magistrato sogette, nelle solennità di musiche non permettere, che
siano usati Instromenti, se non gli ordinarij usitati nelle Chiese, astenendosi
particolarmente dall'uso d'Istromenti bellici, come sono Trombe, Tamburi, et simili più
accomodati ad usarli nelli Eserciti, che nella Casa di Dio; similmente obligandoli
medesimamente à fare, che li Musici tutti, così Ecclesiastici, come secolari vadino vestiti
con le Cotte habito proprio da usarsi nelle Chiese, et finalmente à non permettere, che
in esse musiche sia fatte tragsportatione di parole, overo cantate parole inventate da
nuovo, et non descritte sopra Libri Sacri, salvo che all'offertorio, all'elevatione, e doppo
l'Agnus Dei, et così alli Vesperi, trà li Salmi si possano cantar mottetti di parole pie, et
divote, et che siano cavate da libri sacri, et auttori Ecclesiastici, sopra il qual particolare
potranno, et doveranno quelli, che non havessero cognitione bastevole ricevere
l'instruttioni da Reverendi Parochi, e Sacerdoti delle Chiese, o altre persone intelligenti,
sotto pena per cadauna volta contravenendo de Ducati 25. applicati alla Cassa delle
Fabriche, et altre pene ad arbitrio di sue Signorie Illustrissime ordinando, che la presente
Terminatione sij registrata sopra tutte le Matricole di dette Scole.

Iseppo Moresini.	Proveditor di Commun.
Mattio Zen.	Proveditor di Commun.
Bernardo Sagredo	Proveditor di Commun.

Chapter V

Doc. 125: A.S.V., San Marco, Procuratia de Supra, Registro 142 (Chiesa Actorum,
1620–29)

Adi 18 Ottobre 1624

L'Illustrissimi Signori Procuratori tutti tre in numero hanno terminato che sij intimato il
presente loro ordine à Messer Carlo Fillago, et Giovanni Pietro Berti tutti due organisti in
San Marco che debbano conforme all'uso antico di chiesa di San Marco ritrovarsi tutte
le Dominiche et le feste comandate tutti doi sopra li organi di chiesa et sonar alle Messe
et Vespri rispondendosi un verso per uno à tutti li salmi.

Doc. 126: Michele Bauldry, *Manuale Sacrarum Caeremoniarum, iuxta Ritum S. Romanae
Ecclesiae* (Venice: Balleonius, 1689), p. 93

Versus Gloria Patri, potest solemniori modulatione decantari, et finito quolibet Psalmo,
Antiphona cum Organo repeti, ut capite proprio diximus, et tunc unus ex clericis
deputatus intelligibili voce in medio chori recitat ea, quae pulsantur per Organa.

Doc. 127: Ibid.

. . . et expleto per chorum *Alleluia*, vel *Laus tibi Domine*, et non prius, praeintonat illi primam Antiphonam primi Psalmi, clara, et sonora voce, et ab omnibus de choro intelligibili qua per celebrantem repetita, et non prius, ipse assistens iterum ipsi, et Altari debitam facit reverentiam, et cum Caeremoniario ad sedilia pro se, et alijs Assistentibus, parata, recedit ubi stat cum alijs.

    XIV. Expleta per chorum Antiphona, ipsi assistentes, iam fere ubique ex consuetudine recepta, inchoan primum versum Psalmi usque ad medium . . .

Doc. 128: *Caeremoniale Episcoporum iussu Clementis VIII* (Rome, 1600), p. 152

. . . et si placuerit, finito quolibet Psalmo, poterit Antiphona per organum repeti, dum tamen per aliquos Mansionarios, aut alios ad id deputatos eadem antiphona clara voce repetatur. Et, si quis esset, qui cum organo cantare vellet, nihil aliud cantet, quam ipsam Antiphonam . . .

Doc. 129: Ibid., pp. 151–52

. . . Subdiaconus praeintonat primam Antiphonam: et donec per Episcopum non fuerit praeintonatio repetita, caerimoniarius, et Subdiaconus praeintonator expectant ibidem stantes; ea autem repetita intelligibili voce, sive ex libro, sive memoriter, prout magis Episcopo placuerit, facta iterum profunda inclinatione, inde discedunt, et cum debita reverentia ante altare ad sua loca redeunt. Episcopus vero sic perstat, donec, expleta per chorum Antiphona, inceptus fuerit primus Psalmus . . .

Doc. 130: Adriano Banchieri, *L'Organo suonarino* (Venice: Amadino, 1605), p. 43

Pensiero utile, et studioso dell'Autore.

Le intuonationi mostrate di sopra sono veramente le reali nell'Organo per lasciare in voce il Choro, ma si possono però (a chi ne ha intelligenza) trasportare, alte et basse in diverse corde, si come hò sentito con grandissimo gusto nell'Illustrissima Città di Venetia (mentre ivi son dimorato alcuni giorni per interesse di far stampare questa mia fatica) da gl'Eccellentissimi Musici, et Organisti nella Chiesa di San Marco, il Signor Giovanni Gabrielli; et Signor Paolo Giusto la dove in questo proposito per mia curiosità, utile et studiosa sia bene vedere, che gl'otto Tuoni, possino havere la corda finale, nella positione D. la, sol, re, et questi per naturalità et accidenti, di b. b. molli et diesis X X come qui sotto saranno realmente trasportati: Praticati sono gustosi da sonare, et comodi al Choro, ma non praticati niuno si ponghi all'impresa, atteso che potria dirsi con il Poeta Mantovano Oibo vasselli.

Doc. 131: Biblioteca Nazionale Marciana 171. D. 199. *Officium Hebdomadae Sanctae, Secundum consuetudinem Ducalis Ecclesiae S. Marci Venetiarum . . . ad Antiquum ritum et integritatem restitutum.* (Venice: Prodocimus, 1716), pp. 392–93; 394–95

Psalm. Dixit Dominus. ut supra fol. 52. Confitebor, et Psal. Beatus vir. ut supra. fol. 62. cantantur cum Organi pulsatione, quibus finitis, repetitur Antiph. Vespere autem Sabbati

. . . Postea reliqui duo psalmi in canto plano à choro cantantur alternatim videlicet Psalmus. Laudate pueri D*omi*n*u*m. fol. 53. Psalmus. In exitu Israel, ex Aegypto. fol. 64.

Doc. 132: Biblioteca Ambrosiana, MS A. 328 inf., f. 53r

A primo Luglio Visitatio B. V. s'apre la Palla, e s'espone con li Cantori la B. V. sopra l'altar, come l'altre volte.... Si canta il Vespro in 5.o da un Can*oni*co cui p*er turnum* et con Cantori a due Cori con li Salmi a 8. come il solito....

(following day)
.... Il doppo pranso pur con Palla aperta si canta Vespro in 5.o da un Can*oni*co et con Cantori a due Cori con li Salmi a 8. Doppo si cantano le Litanie, e si transporta la B. V. sopra il suo Altare....

Doc. 133: Biblioteca Ambrosiana, MS A. 328 inf., f. 63r

La Vigilia della Presentatione della B.V. .... Si canta Vespro da un Can*oni*co in 5.o con Cantori a due Cori; et li Salmi a 8.

(following day)
Il doppo pranso cantata il Vespro in 5.o dal Can*oni*co cui; et dalli Cantori a 8 more solito a Palla aperta si dicono le Litanie e si pone more solito la B. V. sopra il suo Altar aggiustato è stà aperto, e la Chiesa sino a 24 hore, così hieri come hoggi.

Doc. 134: Biblioteca Ambrosiana, MS A. 328 inf., f. 64v

La Vigilia della Concettione della B. V. s'apre la Palla.... Intuona il Vespro un Can*oni*co cui, et c*etera*, et li Cantori cantano a due Cori li Salmi a 8.

(following day)
.... così il 2.o Vespero.... dopo il quale cantate le Litanie si ripone la B. V. et resta la Chiesa aperta, come hieri, così hoggi sino le 24. hore.

Doc. 135: A.S.V., San Marco, Procuratia de Supra, Registro 99 (Ceremoniali), f. 158r

26 *Otto*bre 1630

.... feci segno al Ill*ustrissi*mo e R*everendissi*mo M*e*s*ser* Ant*oni*o Cornaro Primicerio Nostro.... che intonasse le Litanie, cominciando *Exaudi nos Domine*: e li Cantori à 2. Cori incominciarono le Litanie con quella maggiore divot*ione* che fù mai possibile.

Doc. 136: A.S.V., San Marco, Procuratia de Supra, Registro 99 (Ceremoniali), f. 437r

1644: il 3 Maggio

Festum Inventionis Sanctissimae Crucis

.... subito il R*everendissi*mo Sig*no*r sottocanonico intuonò *Exaudi nos Domine* cum Gloria Patri, et c*etera* et dà soli quattro Cantori, come è solito hieri, et hoggi furono cantate le

Littanie, et fatta la Procession del Mercoledi con il doppio delle Campane, et fatto ritorno in Coro si cantò Salmo con tutte le Preci, ut in Libello Litaniarum....

Doc. 137: A.S.V., San Marco, Procuratia de Supra, Busta 91, Processo 208, fascicolo 1, f. 16v

Interrogato. Sapete che sia una tolela in sacrestia nella qual è notato li vesperi che si devono cantar così ugnoli come a dui cori.
Rispose. Signor si lo so.
Interrogato. Havete veduto che vi sia segni del cantar a dui cori.
Rispose. ho visto certi segni ma non li ho fatto fantasia.

Doc. 138: A.S.V., San Marco, Procuratia de Supra, Busta 91, Processo 208, fascicolo 1, f. 14v

Interrogato. Senteste che'l maestro di coro ordinasse che'l vesporo si dicesse a dui cori.
Rispose. Io sentei il Maestro di Coro quando fu Intonato il vesporo che disse verso li cantori che cantasse, e respondessero li quali tutti risposero, che non erano obligati per la tariffa cantare,
Ei dictum. che tariffa vi è in questa materia.
Rispose. vi è una tolela in sacrestia nella qual vi è un segno quando si canta a dui Cori.

Doc. 139: A.S.V., San Marco, Procuratia de Supra, Registro 98, f. 68r–70r

Tabula descriptionis dierum totius Anni in quibus Cantores et Organistae tenentur ad Nostram Ecclesiam Sancti Marci convenire pro suis officijs de more exequendis de mandato Serenissimi Domini Duci Leonardi Lauredani inclyti Duci nostri, et cl:morum [sic] dictae Ecclesiae Sancti Marci Procuratorum DD. Marci Bollani, Antonij Grimani et Andrea Gritti instaurata, et in melius reformata. Anno Incarnationis Domini 1515.

Januarius
1. In Missa et Vesperis pro Circumcisione Domini. Hymnus *Christe* Redemptor
5. In Vesperis Hymnus Hostis Herodes
6. In Missa, et Vesperis pro Epiphania Domini.
16. In Vesperis Hymnus Iste Confessor
17. In Messa et Vesperis pro Sancto Antonio Abbate
19. In Vesperis Hymnus Sanctorum meritis
20. In Missa et Vesperis pro Sanctis Fabiano et Sebastiano
24. In Vesperis Hymnus Doctor egregie
25. In Missa et Vesperis pro Conversione Sancti Pauli
30. In Missa et Vesperis Hymnus Natos in tono Hymni Exultet caelum
31. In Missa et Vesperis pro Translatione Corporis Sancti Marci.

Februarius.
1. In Vesperis cum Dominis [sic] in Santa Maria Formosa Hymnus Ave maris stella.
2. In Missa et Vesperis pro Purificatione B. M. V.

21. In Vesperis Hymnus Doctor egregie. Iam bone.
22. In Missa et Vesperis pro Cathreda Sancti Petri Hymnus Deus tuorum
23. In Missa et Vesperis pro Sancto Gerardo Hymnus Exultet
24. In Missa et Vesperis pro Sancto Matthia Apostolo

Martius
11. In Vesperis Hymnus Iste confessor
12. In Missa et Vesperis pro Sancto Gregorio.
18. In Vesperis Hymnus Iste confessor
19. In Missa et Vesperis pro Sancto Iosepho
20. In Vesperis Hymnus Iste confessor
21. In Missa et Vesperis pro Sancto Benedicto.
24. In Vesperis Hymnus Ave maris tum est proprius
25. In Missa Vesperis et Completorio pro Annunciatione B. M. V.

Aprilis
15. In Vesperis Hymnus Deus tuorum militum
    Si post Pascha hymnus Vita sanctorum in tono Iste confessor
16. In Missa, processione, et Vesperis pro Translatione Corporis Sancti Isydori.
22. In Vesperis Hymnus vita Sanctorum in tono Iste Confessor
23. In Missa et Vesperis pro Sancto Georgio.
24. In Missa Litaniarum cum 2. Choris et Vesperis Hymnus Athleta Christi in tono Ad caenam
25. In Missa et Vesperis pro Sancto Marco.
30. In Vesperis Hymnus Iustes erant in tono Ad caenam

Maius
1. In Missa et Vesperis pro Sanctis Philippo et Iacobo in utraque Ecclesia cum Cottis.
2. In Vesperis Hymnus Crux mundi in tono Ad caenam
3. In Missa et Vesperis pro Inventione Sanctae Crucis
5. In Vesperis Hymnus Tristes erant in tono Hymni Ad caenam.
6. In Missa tantum pro Sancto Ioanne ante portam Latinam
7. In Vesperis Hymnus Tibi Christe in tono Pange lingua
8. In Missa tantum pro Apparitione Sancti Michaelis
14. In Vesperis Hymnus Vita sanctorum in tono Iste confessor
15. In Missa et Vesperis pro Sancto Isydoro.
19. In Vesperis Hymnus Iste confessor
20. In Missa, et Vesperis pro Sancto Bernardino

Junius.
10. In Vesperis Hymnus Exultet caelum
11. In Missa tantum pro Sancto Barnaba Apostolo.
[f. 68v]
12. In Vesperis Hymnus Iste confessor.
13. In Missa et Vesperis pro Sancto Antonio de Padua
14. In Vesperis Hymnus Vita sanctorum in tempore Paschali Sanctorum meritis alio tempore.
15. In Processione Missa et Vesperis pro Sanctis Vito et Modesto
23. In Vesperis Hymnus Ut queant laxis.
24. In Missa et Vesperis et Matutino in quo cantatur Te deum et Deo gratias pro Apparitione Corporis Sancti Marci. Hymnus Hodie festis, in tono Iste confessor.

25. In Missa Processione et Vesperis
28. In Vesperis Hymnus Aurea luce.
29. In Missa et Vesperis pro Sanctis Petro et Paolo Hymnus Doctor egregie.
30. In Missa tantum pro Commemoratione Sancti Pauli Apostoli.

Julius.
  1. In Vesperis Hymnus In Mariae vita in tono O Gloriosa Domina
  2. In Missa et Vesperis pro Visitatione Sanctae Mariae
 11. In Vesperis Hymnus Omnes ad haec in tono Hymni Exultet caelum
 12. In Missa tantum pro Sanctis Hermacora et Fortunato
 16. In Vesperis Hymnus Gloria Patri virginis proles in tono Iste confessor.
 17. In Processione Missa et Vesperis pro Sancta Marina
 21. In Vesperis Hymnus Maria mater Domini in tono Hymni Magno salutis gaudio.
 22. In Missa et Vesperis pro Sancta Maria Magdalena
 24. In Vesperis Hymnus Exultet caelum
 25. In Missa et Vesperis pro Sancto Iacobo Apostolo
 31. In Vesperis Hymnus Petrus Beatus in tono Hymni Doctor egregie.

Augustus.
  1. In Missa tantum pro Sancto Petro ad Vincula
  4. In Vesperis Hymnus Ave maris.
  5. In Missa et Vesperis pro Sancta Maria de Nive Hymnus Fons pietatis, in tono Hymni O Gloriosa Domina
  6. In Missa et Vesperis pro Transfiguratione Domini.
  9. In Vesperis Hymnus proprius in tono Hymni Iste confessor.
 10. In Missa et Vesperis pro Sancto Laurentio.
 14. In Vesperis Hymnus Ave maris stella.
 15. In Missa et Vesperis pro Assumptione B. M. V.
 16. In Missa et Vesperis pro S. Rocho Hymnus Ave maris stella.
 23. In Vesperis Hymnus Exultet caelum
 24. In Missa et Vesperis pro Sancto Bartholomeo Apostolo.
 27. In Vesperis Hymnus Iste confessor vel proprius.
 28. In Missa et Vesperis pro Sancto Augustino Hymnus Deus tuorum
 29. In Missa, et Vesperis pro Decollatione Sancti Ioannis Baptistae

September.
  7. In Vesperis Hymnus Ave maris stella.
  8. In Missa et Vesperis pro Nativitate B. M. V.
 13. In Vesperis Hymnus Signum Crucis in tono Hymni proprij
 14. In Missa et Vesperis pro Exaltatione Sancti Crucis.
 17. In Vesperis Hymnus Deus tuorum militum.
 18. In Missa tantum pro Sancto Victore.
 20. In Vesperis Hymnus Exultet caelum
 21. In Missa et Vesperis pro Sancto Mattheo.
 28. In Vesperis Hymnus Tibi Christe in tono Pange lingua
 29. In Missa et Vesperis pro Sancto Michaele Hymnus Iste Confessor
 30. In Missa et Vesperis pro Sancto Hyeronimo.

October.
  3. In Vesperis Hymnus Iste confessor
  4. In Missa et Vesperis pro Sancto Francesco

5. In Vesperis Hymnus Iste confessor
6. In Missa et Vesperis pro Sancto Magno Hymnus Sanctorum meritis
7. In Missa et Vesperis pro Sanctis Sergio et Baccho Hymnus Urbs beata in tono Pange lingua
Santa Iustina dup: processione
8. In Missa et Vesperis pro Dedicatione huius Ecclesiae
17. In Vesperis Hymnus Exultet caelum
18. In Missa et Vesperis pro Sancto Luca
27. In Vesperis Hymnus Exultet
28. In Missa et Vesperis pro Sanctis Simone et Iuda
31. In Vesperis Hymnus Christe Redemptor omnium

[f. 69r]

November.
1. In Missa et Vesperis pro Commemoratione omnium Sanctorum
2. In Missa etc. pro Commemoratione omnium Fidelium Defunctorum
5. In Vesperis Hymnus Iste confessor.
6. In Missa tantum pro Sancto Leonardo.
8. In Vesperis Hymnus Deus tuorum militum.
9. In Missa et Vesperis pro Sancto Theodoro.
10. In Vesperis Hymnus Rex Christe Martini in tono Hymni Exultet caelum
11. In Missa et Vesperis pro Sancto Martino
20. In Vesperis Hymnus Ave maris stella.
21. In Missa et Vesperis pro Praescentatione B. M. V.
22. In Vesperis Hymnus Deus tuorum militum
23. In Missa tantum pro Sancto Clemente.
24. In Vesperis Hymnus Catharina mira in tono O Gloriosa Domina
25. In Missa et Vesperis pro Sancta Catharina
29. In Vesperis Hymnus Exultet caelum laudibus
30. In Missa et Vesperis pro Sancto Andrea Apostolo.

December.
5. In Vesperis in Palatio ut moris est. Hymnus proprius
6. In Missa et Vesperis Hymnus Iste confessor pro Sancto Nicolao
7. In Missa et Vesperis pro Sancto Ambrosio Hymnus Ave maris stella
8. In Missa et Vesperis pro Conceptione B. M. V.
12. In Vesperis Hymnus Virginis proles in tono Iste confessor
13. In Missa et Vesperis pro Sancta Lucia
20. In Vesperis Hymnus Exultet caelum.
21. In Missa et Vesperis pro Sancto Thomas Apostolo
24. In Vesperis, Matutino et Missa Hymnus Christe Redemptor.
25. In Missa et Vesperis pro Nativitate Domini.
26. In Missa et Vesperis pro Sancto Stephano. Hymnus Deus tuorum militum
27. In Missa et Vesperis pro Sancto Ioanne. Hymnus Exultet caelum.
28. In Missa et Vesperis pro Sanctis Innocentibus Hymnus Caterua gloria, Sanctorum meritis
30. In Vesperis Hymnus Iste confessor
31. In Missa et Vesperis pro Sancto Sylvestro Hymnus Christe Redemptor.

In omnibus Processionibus Magnis de ordine Eccellentissimi Consilij X.
In omnibus Sabbatis Quadragesimae in Vesperis

—In majori hebdomada—
In Dominica Palmarum etiam ad Passionem
Feria 4. in Matutino in mane ad Passionem
Feria 5. in Missa et Matutino
Feria 6. in Missa et Passione, Processione, et Matutino
Sabbato Sancto in Missa etc. de more

Dies Festorum Mobilium
In die Sancto Paschae et 2. sequentibus diebus
In Missa et Vesperis et Processionibus ad Fontem et Sepulcrum.
In Dominica Apostolorum in Processione a Palatio ad Sanctum Geminianum et in Missa
et Vesperis in Nostra Ecclesia.
A die Iovis ante Ascensionem usque ad diem Iovis post Ascensionem inclusive quotidie
in Vesperis ut moris est.

In Litanijs majoribus die Lunae, et Martij ante Ascensionem cum 4 Cantoribus tantum in
Processione solum
In Vigilia Ascensionis in Missa 3: et in Vesperis et Litanijs majoribus cum 2 Choris.
In die Ascensionis cum Serenissimo Duce ad Benedictionem Maris in Missa in Sancto
Nicolao de Littore, et Vesperis in Nostra Ecclesia.
In Vigilia Pentecostes in Missa et Vesperis
In die Sancto Pentecostes, et 2. sequentis diebus in Missis, et Vesperis
In Festo Sanctissimae Trinitatis in utrisque vesperis et Missa.
In Vigilia Sanctissimae Corporis Christi in Vesperis et Matutino.
In die Sacratissimae Corporis Christi in Missa Processione et Vesperis.
[f. 69v]
In omnibus Dominicis totius Anni in Missis et Vesperis et semper cantant Deo gratias
exceptis Dominicis Quadragesimae in quibus cantant ad Completorium Ave regina
caelorum.
In omnibus simplicibus diebus totius Anni in Missis ut moris est; exceptis diebus Veneris
et Sabbati dumodo in talibus diebus Festum aliquod de supradictis non occurrat
excepta etiam Feria 2.a 3.a et 4:a majoris hebdomadae
Sed postquam Capella parva non extat Cantores cantant Missam de Dominica in die
Sabbati loco cuius habent exemptionem die Iovis, nisi sit Festum.

In die Creationis serenissimi Domini Ducis ad Missam.

Rubrica seu Regula de Organistis Ecclesiae Sancti Marci.
Organistae semper veniunt et sonant in omnibus supradictis diebus exceptis simplicibus
diebus et Dominicis Adventus et a Dominica Septuagesimae usque ad Dominicam
Palmarum inclusive dumodo in talibus diebus Festum aliquod de suprascriptis non
occurrat, excepta etiam Feria 2.a, 3.a, 4:a, et 6:a majoris hebdomadae ut moris est.

Si Festum aliquod de praedictis transferatur Cantores et Organistae in die qua fit de
Festo translato venire tenentur ut supra—

Cum Capella Magna in Sancto Nicolao Palatij In Sancta Maria Formosa, et in Sancto
Georgio cantat: Capella parva supplet in Nostra Ecclesia.
Sed Hodie Capella parva non extat et canimus in cantu plano nisi dividantur Cantores, ut
moris est.

Doc. 140:   Biblioteca del Civico Museo Correr, Codice Cicogna 3118, fascicoli 44–50

Laus Deo 1677

Nota delle obligationi, che tengono le *Signori* Cantori nella Chiesa di *San* Marco

Month	Date	Feast	Vespero	Messa	Ser:mo	Vespero	
Genaro Palla	Adi p:mo	Circoncis.ne	Vespero	Messa	Ser:mo	Vespero	
	à 5. 6.	Epifania	Vespero	Messa	Ser:mo	Vespero	
	7. 8.	S. Lorenzo	Vespero	Messa	Ser:mo	Vespero	
	16. 17.	S. Antonio	Vespero	Messa	—	Vespero	
	19. 20.	S. Bastian	Vespero	Messa	—	Vespero	
	24. 25.	S. Paulo	Vespero	Messa	—	—	
	30. 31.	S. Marco	Vespero	Messa	—	Vespero	
Palla	Feb.o p.mo 2.	Purificat.ne	Vespero	Messa	Ser:mo	Vespero	
	21. 22.	Cattedra	Vespero	Messa	—	Vespero	
	23. 24.	S. Girardo	—	—	—	Vespero	
	25. —	S. Mattia	—	Messa	—	Vespero	
Marzo	11. 12.	S. Gregorio	Vespero	Messa	—	Vespero	
	18. 19.	S. Iseppo	Vespero	Messa	—	Vespero	
	20. 21.	S. Benedetto	Vespero	Messa	—	Vespero	
	24. 25.	Anon.n B. V.	Vespero	Messa	Ser:mo	Vespero	Compieta
Aple	15. 16.	S. Isidoro	Vespero	Messa	Ser:mo	Vespero	Procession
	22. 23.	S. Giorgio	Vespero	Messa	—	Vespero	Procession
Tesoro	24. 25.	S. Marco	Vespero	Messa	Ser:mo	Vespero	
Maggio	30. p.mo		due Vesperi due Messe		Ser:mo	2. Vesperi	
	2.		Vesperi 2. per la Croce				
	3.	L'esponse il Preciossiss.mo Sangue, Motetti, e Procession matt.a, e sera					
	5.	S. Gio: in Olio	Vespero	Messa	—	—	—

Month	Date	Feast	Vespero	Messa	Ser.mo	Vespero	Procession
	7. 8.	S. Michiel	Vespero	Messa	—	—	
	14. 15.	S. Isidoro	Vespero	Messa	—	—	
	19. 20.	S. Bernard.n	Vespero	Messa	—	Vespero	Vespero
		Si fà l'essequie del S.re Cardinal Zen					Procession
Giugno	10. 11.	S. Barnaba	Vespero	Messa	Ser.mo	—	Procession
	12. 13.	S. Ant.o da Pad.a	Vespero	Messa	Ser.mo	Procession	Procession
	14. 15.	S. Vito	Vespero	Messa	—	Vespero	
	23. 24.	S. Gio. Battis.ra	Vespero	Messa	Ser.mo	Vespero	
Palla	25. —	Apar.n di S. M.co	—	Messa	Ser.mo	Vespero	Procession
Palla	26. —	SS. Gio: Paulo	—	Messa	Ser.mo	Vespero	Procession
	28. 29.	S. Pietro	Vespero	Messa	—	Vespero	
Palla	30. —	S. Paulo Com.n	—	Messa	—	—	
Luglio	p.mo 2.	Visit.n B. V.	Vespero	Messa	—	Vespero	
	10. —		—	Messa à S. Paternian	—	—	
	11. 12.	SS. Hermacora For.o	Vesp.o	Messe 2.	Ser.mo	Vespero	Procession
	16. 17.	S. Marina	Vespero	Messa	—	Vespero	
	21. 22.	S. M.a Mad.a	Vespero	Messa	—	Vespero	
	24. 25.	S. Giacomo	Vespero	Messa	—	—	
	26. —	S. Anna	Vespero	Messa	—		
	31. —	S. Piet.o in Vin.la	Vespero	La 3.a Dom.ca al Redentor Mottetti	—	Vespero	
Agosto	p.mo —	S. Pietro	Vespero	Messa	—	Vespero	
	4. 5.	La mad.a dlla Neve	Vesp.o	Messa	—	Vespero	
	6. —	La Transfig.n	—	Messa	—	Vespero	
	9. 10.	S. Lorenzo	Vespero	Messa	—	Vespero	
Palla	14. 15.	Assunt.n B. V.	Vespero	Messa	Ser.mo	Vespero	

Mese	Giorno	Festa	Vespero	Messa	Ser.mo	Vespero	Procession
	16. —	S. Rocco	—	Messa	—	Vespero	
	23. 24.	S. Bart.o	Vespero	Messa	—	Vespero	
	27. 28.	S. Agostin	Vespero	Messa	—	Vespero	
	29. —	Decolation d S. Gio: Batti*s*ta		Messa	—	Vespero	
		Si fà l'Essequie dl S.r Morosini Ninfa					
Sett.e	7. 8.	Nat.a B. V.	Vespero	Messa	Ser.mo	Vespero	
	13. 14.	La Croce	Vespero	Messa	—	Vespero	
	17. 18.	S. Vettor	Vespero	Messa	—	—	
	20. 21.	S. Mattia	Vespero	Messa	—	Vespero	
	28. 29.	S. Michiel	Vespero	Messa	—	Vespero	
Ott.e	3. 4.	S. Fran.co	Vespero	Messa	—	Vespero	
	5. 6.	S. Magno	Vespero	Messa	—	Vespero	
	7. 8.	S. Giustina	Vespero	Messa	Ser.mo	Vespero	Procession
	17. 18.	S. Luca	Vespero	Messa	—	Vespero	
	27. 28.	S. Simon Iuda	Vespero	Messa	—	Vespero	
	31. —	Vig.a d'ogni SS.ti	Vespero	—	—	—	
Nov.e	p.mo —	Giorni d'ogni SS.ti	—	Messa	Ser.mo	Vespero	Procession
	2. —	Com.n de Morti	—	Messa	—	—	
	5. 6.	S. Leonardo	Vespero	Messa	—	Vespero	
	8. 9.	S. Teodoro	Vespero	Messa	—	Vespero	
Palla	11. 12.	S. Martin	Vespero	Messa	—	Vespero	
Palla	20. 21.	M.a dlla Salute	Vespero	Messa	Ser.mo	Vespero	Procession
	22. 23.	S. Clemente	Vespero	Messa	—	Vespero	
	24. 25.	S. Catterina	Vespero	Messa	—	Vespero	
	29. 30.	S. And.a	Vespero	Messa	—	Vespero	
Dec.e	5. 6	S. Nicolò	Vespero	Messa	—	Vespero	
	7. —	S. Ambrogio	—	Messa	—	Vespero	
Palla	8. —	La Concet.ne	—	Messa	—	Vespero	

Festa					
12. 13. S. Lucia	Vespero	Messa	—	Vespero	—
20. 21. S. Tomaso	Vespero	Messa	—	Vespero	—
Palla 24. Natale di N. S.	Vespero	Ser.mo	Vespero	Mattutin	—
Palla 25. Giorno di Natal	—	Messa	—	Vespero	—
Palla 26. S. Gio. Evang.ta	—	Messa	—	Vespero	—
Palla 27. S. Steffano	—	Messa	—	Vespero	—
28. Innocenti	—	Messa	—	Vespero	—
30. 31. S. Silvestro	Vespero	Messa	—	Vespero	—
Dom.ca dlle Palme	—	Messa	Ser.mo	Vespero	Compieta
Martedi Santo	—	Passio	—	—	Mattutino
Mercordi Santo	—	—	Ser.mo	—	Mattutino
Giovedi Santo	—	—	Ser.mo	—	Mattutino
Venerdi Santo	—	Messa	Ser.mo	—	—
Sabbato Santo	—	Messa	Ser.mo	Vespero	—
Dom.ca di Resurett.n	—	Messa	Ser.mo	Vespero	—
Palla 2.a Festa	—	Messa	—	Vespero	—
Palla 3.a Festa	—	Messa	—	Vespero	—
Alcune Feste Mobili					
Palla Dom.ca ottava di Pasqua	—	Messa	Ser.mo	Vespero	—
Giorni 15. alli Vesperi p la Solennità dell'Ascensione del Sig.re	—	Messa	Ser.mo	Vespero	—
Palla Vig.a dell'Ascensione	—	Messa	Ser.mo	Vespero	—
Giorno dell'Ascensione à S. Nicolò di Lido	—	Messa	Ser.mo	Vespero al Banchetto	—
Palla Vig.a delle Pentecoste	—	Messa	—	Vespero	—
Dom.ca delle Pentecoste	—	Messa	Ser.mo	Vespero	—
Palla 2.a Festa M. V. Palla 3.a Festa	Vespero	Messa	—	Vespero	—
Palla Sabb.o della Trinità	Vespero	Dom.ca dlla Trinità	—	Messa Vespero	—
Palla Vig.a dl Corpus Domini Giorno dl Corpus Domini	Vespero	Messa	Ser.mo	Vespero	Procession

Tutti li Sabbati dell'anno la Messa dlla Mad.a sono n.o 47

Tutte le Domeniche dell'anno Messa, e Vespero sono n.o 45

Tutte le Domeniche dlla Quadragesima si cantano le Compiete sono n.o 5

Le Rogationi, Lunedi, Martedi, et Mercordi Messe 3. Procession 3.

Il Terzo Venerdi di Marzo s'espone il miracoloso Sangue portato di Candia

La vig.a dell'Ascensione s'espone il Sangue precioso con Musici

Il Giovedi Santo all'Espositione dl Sangue miracoloso con Musici

Nella morte de SS.mi Dogi si cantano tre Messe una al *giorno* et Mattutin

Process.ne nel portar il Ser.mo alla Sepoltura cantando il Miserere

Nel Possesio di tutti gl'Ecc.mi SS.ri Proc.ri si cantano motetti

Nella morte d'un Ecc.mo S.r Proc.re si canta Messa

Nel Possesio del Ser.mo si canta Messa solenne

Nell'annual del Ser.mo si canta Messa solenne

Nell'elett.ne dl Pontefice si canta Messa

Nella morte dl Pontefice si cantano tre Messa una al giorno

Nelle morte de SS.ri Cannonici si canta Messa

Nella morte di Mons.re *Illustrissimo* Primicerio si canta Messa

Ad arbitrio di S. Ser.ta. tutte le processioni p li tempi, e p le guerre

Vesperi inclusi le Domeniche	n.o	210
Messe incluse le Domeniche	n.o	239
Compiete	n.o	7
Mattutini	n.o	4
Essequij ordinarij	n.o	2
Processioni	n.o	11
Rogationi, Messe, Processioni	n.o	6
Vig.a dell'Ascension, e Giovedi S.to	n.o	2
Sabbati dlla Quadragesima Vesp.i	n.o	6
Venerdi Santo Procession	n.o	1
		492

Doc. 141: Biblioteca Ambrosiana, MS A. 328 inf., f. 163r–165r

Oblighi de Cantori, et Organisti

Ogni volta che vengono cantori sono obligati ancò li Organisti come segue

Gennaro

Alla Messa e tutti li Vesperi della Circoncisione
Alla Messa e tutti due li Vesperi dell'Epifania
Alla Messa e tutti due li Vesperi per il S. Lorenzo Giustiniano
Alla Messa e tutti due li Vesperi per S. Antonio Abbate
Alla Messa e tutti due li Vesperi per SS. Fabiano e Sebastiano
Alla Messa e tutti li Vesperi per la Conversion di S. Paolo
Alla Messa e tutti li Vesperi per la Traslazion di S. Marco

Febraro

Alla Messa e tutti due li Vesperi per Purification della B. V.
Alla Messa e tutti li Vesperi per la Cattedra di S. Pietro
Alla Messa e tutti li Vesperi per S. Girardo Sagredo
Alla Messa e tutti li Vesperi per S. Matthia

Marzo

Alla Messa e tutti due li Vesperi per S. Gregorio Papa
Alla Messa e tutti li Vesperi per S. Gioseffo
Alla Messa e tutti li Vesperi per S. Benedetto Abbate
Alla Messa e tutti li Vesperi e Compieta per l'Annunciata

Aprile

Alla Messa e tutti due li Vespri e Processione per la Traslazione del Corpo di S. Isidoro
Alla Messa e tutti li Vespri per S. Giorgio
Alla Messa delle Rogazioni per la Vigilia di S. Marco
Alla Messa e tutti due li Vespri il giorno di S. Marco

Maggio

Alla Messa e Vespri della Chiesa di S. Marco, e SS. Filippo e Giacomo et alle Vergini
Alla Messa e tutti due li Vespri per S. Gio: ante Portam Latinam
Al Primo Vespro, et alla Messa tantam per l'Apparition di S. Michele
Alla Messa e tutti due li Vespri per S. Isidoro
Alla Messa e tutti li Vespri per S. Bernardino
[f. 163v]
Giugno

Al Primo Vespro e Messa tantum per S. Barnaba
Alla Messa Processione e tutti due li Vespri per S. Ant:o di Padova
Alla Messa e tutti due li Vespri per la Festività di S. Gio. Batt*ista*
Alla Messa Processione e tutti li Vesperi per SS. Vito e Modesto

Alla Messa Procession e tutti due li Vespri per l'Aparizion del Corpo di S. Marco
Alla Messa e Procession per SS. Gio. e Paolo
Alla Messa e tutti li Vespri per SS. Pietro e Paolo
Alla Messa tantum per la Comemorazione di S. Paolo

Luglio

Alla Messa e tutti due li Vespri per la Visitazione della B. V.
Al Vespro e Messa tantum per SS. Ermagora e Fortunato
Alla Messa, Processione, e tutti due li Vespri per S. Marina
Alla Messa e tutti due li Vespri per S. Maria Madalena
Alla Messa e tutti due li Vespri per S. Giacomo
Alla Messa e tutti due li Vespri per S. Anna

Agosto

Alla Messa tantum per S. Pietro in vincula
Alla Messa e tutti due li Vespri per la B. V. ad Nives
Alla Messa e tutti due li Vespri per la Trasfigurazione del Signore
Alla Messa e tutti due li Vespri per S. Lorenzo
Alla Messa e tutti due li Vespri per l'Assunta
Alla Messa e tutti due li Vespri per S. Rocco
Alla Messa e tutti due li Vespri per S. Bartolomeo
Alla Messa e tutti due li Vespri per S. Agostino
Alla Messa e tutti due li Vespri per la Decollatione di S. Gio: Battista

Settembre

Alla Messa e tutti due li Vespri per la Natività della B. V.
Alla Messa e tutti due li Vespri per l'Esalt*atione* della Croce
Al Primo Vespro e Messa tantum per S. Vettore
[f. 164r]
Alla Messa, e tutti due li Vesperi p S. Matteo.
Alla Messa, e tutti due li Vespri p S. Michiele.
Alla Messa, e tutti due li Vespri p S. Girolamo.

Ottobre

Alla Messa, e tutti due li Vespri p S. Fran.co
Alla [Messa] e tutti due li Vesperi p S. Magno.
Alla Messa, Processione, e tutti due li Vespri p S. Giustina
Alla Messa, e tutti due li Vesperi p la Dedicat.ne della Chiesa
Alla Messa tantu*m* p SS. Sergio, e Bacco.
Alla Messa, e tutti due li Vesperi p S. Luca
Alla Messa, e tutti due li Vesperi p SS. Simeone, e Giuda.

Novembre

Alla Messa, e tutti due li Vesperi p la festa di tutti li Santi
Alla Messa tantum il giorno de Morti.
Primo Vespero, et Messa tantu*m* p S. Lunardo.
Alla Messa, e tutti due li Vesperi p S. Theodoro.

Alla Messa, e tutti due li Vesperi p S. Martino.

Alla Messa, Processione, e tutti due li Vesperi p la Present:ne della B. V.

Al primo Vespro, et Messa tantum p S. Clemente.

Alla Messa, e tutti due li Vesperi p S. Cattarina.

Alla Messa, e tutti due li Vespri p S. Andrea.

Decembre.

Alla Messa e tutti due li Vesperi p S. Nicolò

Alla Messa, e tutti due li Vesperi p S. Ambroso.

Alla Messa, e tutti due li Vespri p la Concettione.

Alla Messa, e tutti due li Vespri p S.ta Lucia.

Alla Messa, e tutti due li Vesperi p S. Tomà.

Al Vespero, Matutino, e Messa La Notte di Natale.

Alla Messa, et Vespro il giorno di Natale.

Alla Messa, et Vespro il giorno di S. Steffano.

Alla Messa, et Vespro il giorno di S. Giovanni

Alla Messa, et Vespero il giorno de gl'Innocenti.

[f. 164v]

Alla Messa, e tutti due li Vespri p S. Silvestro.

Sono obligati esser presenti à tutte le Processioni commandate dal Ser:mo, e dal Senato, tutti li Sabbati non impediti da Santo Doppio à cantar la Messa della B. V., tutti li Sabbati di Quaresima al Vespero, il Martedi Santo alla Passione, il Mercordi al Matutino, il Venerdi alla Messa, Procession, et Matutino, il Sabbato Santo alla Messa, et c.

Il giorno di Pascha con le due Seguenti Feste alle Messe, Vesperi, Procession alla Fonte, et Sepolcro.

Nella Dom.ca in Albis, alla Messa, et Processione.

Li quindeci giorni del Perdon nell'Ascensione alli Vespri

La Vigilia dell'Ascensione alla Processione, Messa, et Vespro.

Il giorno dell'Ascensione in Bucintoro col Ser:mo, et poi à cantar Messa à S. Nicolò del Lido, et Vespro nella nostra Chiesa.

La Vigilia delle Pentecoste Messa, et Vespero.

Il giorno delle Pentecoste con le due festi seguenti alle Messe, e tutti li Vespri.

Il giorno della SS:ma Trinità alla Messa, e tutti due li Vespri.

La Vigilia del Corpo di Christo al Vespero, et Matutino.

Il giorno alla Messa, Processione, et al Vespero.

In tutte la Domeniche dell'anno alle Messe, et alli Vesperi, et nelle Domeniche di Quaresima anco à Compieta.

La 3.a Dom.ca di Luglio alla Processione del Redentore, et alla Messa nella nostra Chiesa.

Nel giorno della Creatione del Ser:mo, e nel suo annuale ogn'anno alla Messa.

La Domenica di Sexagesima à Messa.

Ogni volta, che si apre la Palla sono obligati Cantare à due Chori con li Salmi à 8. li Vesperi, et alle Messe cantar un Motetto nell'Organo.

[f. 165r]

Sono parimente obligati à venire nelli giorni delle Traslationi di qualcheduno delli Sopradetti Santi. Sono obligati andar tutti insieme à Cantare nella Capella di San Nicolò in Palazzo, à S. M.a Formosa, et in S. Giorgio.

Si espone il Thesoro sopra l'Altar Magg.re la Mattina di Natale, la Mattina di Pasqua di Ressurrettione [*sic*], al primo Vespro dell'Ascensione

Doc. 142: A.S.V., San Marco, Procuratia de Supra, Registro 99 (Ceremoniali), f. 409r–413r

Giorni nelli quali intervengono li Musici nella Chiesa di S. Marco

Gennaro.

1: 2: 3: all'Esposizione del Santis*si*mo Sagramento con Mottetti tutti il giorno, e nel terzo giorno alla Processione senza istrumenti con il solo Organo.
5: al Vespero à Capella in due Chori nel Bigonzo.
6: alla Messa cantata in Bigonzo à capella con la presenza del Prencipe.
7: Vespero senza Pala Aperta.
8: Messa à Capella nella Chiesa di S. Pietro di Castello ò pure in *San* Marco
[f. 409v]
    Vespero in S. Marco.
14: Messa con tutti li Organi, Palchetti, et istrumenti; il Vespero nelli due organi à Capella senza istrumenti.
16: Vespero senza Palla.
17: Messa à Capella in Bigonzo; e Vespero senza Palla.
19: Vespero senza Palla.
20: Messa à Capella in Bigonzo, e Vespero senza Palla.
30: Vespero con Palla Aperta à Capella in Bigonzo.
31: Messa à Capella in Bigonzo, e Vespero con Palla Aperta.

Febraro

1: Vespero in Santa Maria Formosa, dove vanno la mettà de Musici; à Capela e Vespero in S. Marco, con l'altra mettà de Musici à Capella con Palla Aperta.
2: Messa in Bigonzo à Capella, e Vespero con Palla Aperta.
21: Vespero senza Palla.
22: Messa in Bigonzo, e Vespero senza Palla.
23: Vespero senza Palla.
24: Messa in Bigonzo, e Vespero senza Palla.

Marzo

11: Vespero senza Palla.
12: Messa in Bigonzo e Vespero senza Palla.
18: Vespero senza Palla.
19: Messa in Bigonzo, e Vespero senza Palla
20: Vespero senza Palla.
21: Messa in Bigonzo, e Vespero senza Palla.
24: Vespero con Palla à due Cori in Bigonzo.
25: Messa in Musica negl'Organi, e Palchetti con istrumenti, e Vespero senza Instrumenti.
Nel terzo Giovedi di Marzo primo Vespero del Sangue Prezioso con Palla à due Cori nel Bigonzo.

Nel terzo Venerdì di Marzo all'Esposizione, Mottetti, e Reposizione del Sangue Pretioso senza Instrumenti col solo Organo.

Aprile

15: Vespero senza Palla.
16: Messa in Bigonzo à Capella, Littanie in Processione à due Cori, e Vespero senza Palla.
[f. 410r]
22: Vespero senza Palla.
23: Messa à Capella nel Bigonzo, Vespero senza Palla.
24: Vespero Solenne nelli Organi, e Palchetti con tutti li istrumenti.
25: Messa Solenne, con tutti li Organi, Palchetti, et istrumenti, et il Vespero con Palla.
30: Vespero in S. Marco senza Palla, e dopo quello di S. Marco altro Vespero simile in S.S. Filippo, e Giacomo.

Maggio.

1: Messa à Capella in S. Marco con la mettà de Musici, poi altra Messa simile in S.S. Filippo, e Giacomo; con la stessa mettà de Musici; in detto giorno con l'altra mettà de Musici Messa Solenne in musica con tutti li strumenti alle Vergini, con l'intervento del Serenis*si*mo Prencipe.
2: Vespero in S. Marco senza Palla.
3: Esposizione, Processione, e Mottetti in Organo per il Sangue Prezioso.
5: Vespero senza Palla.
6: Messa à Capella in Bigonzo, e Vespero senza Palla.
7: Vespero senza Palla.
8: Messa à Capella in Bigonzo, e Vespero senza Palla.
14: Vespero senza Palla.
15: Messa à Capella in Bigonzo, e Vespero senza Palla.
19: Vespero senza Palla.
20: Messa à Capella in Bigonzo, e Vespero senza Palla.

Giugno.

10: Vespero senza Palla.
11: Messa à Capella in Bigonzo, e Vespero senza Palla.
12: Vespero senza Palla.
13: Messa à Capella in Bigonzo, e Vespero senza Palla. La Messa sudetta si fà in S. Marco, quando il tempo non permettesse al Serenis*si*mo Prencipe d'andare alla Salute, dove si canta la Messa in un Palco Posticcio [*sic*] dalli Musici con due Organi, e tutti li istrumenti di Capella.
14: Vespero senza Palla.
15: Messa à Capella in Bigonzo con Palla; in case che il Doge non andasse alla Chiesa di S:S: Vito, e Modesto; dove si canta la Messa à Capella; Vespero in S. Marco senza Palla.
23: Vespero à due Cori con Palla nel Bigonzo.
24: Messa à Capella in Bigonzo, e Vespero à due Cori con Palla.
[f. 410v]
25: Messa con Palla à Capella in Bigonzo con l'intervento del Prencipe, e Vespero à due Cori con Palla.

26: Messa con Palla in Bigonzo alla Presenza del Prencipe; quando non potesse andare alla Chiesa di S.S. Gio*vanni* e Paolo, dove si canta Messa à Capella; et il Vespero in S. Marco senza Palla.
28: Vespero con Palla à Capella.
29: Messa à Capella con Palla, e Vespero à due Cori à Capella con Palla.
30: Messa à Capella senza Palla.

Luglio.

  1: Vespero à Capella con Palla.
  2: Messa, e Vespero con Palla.
10: Messa à Capella in S. Paternian.
11: Vespero à Capella senza Palla.
12: Messa à Capella in Bigonzo.
16: Messa à Capella in Chiesa alle Terese [*sic*], e Vespero in S. Marco senza Palla.
17: Messa à Capella in Chiesa di S. Marco alla presenza del Sereni*ssi*mo e due Mottetti à Capella in Chiesa di Santa Marina, Vespero senza Palla.
21: Vespero à due Cori con Palla.
22: Messa à Capella con Palla, e Vespero à due Cori con Palla.
23: Vespero senza Palla.
25: Messa senza Palla à Capella, e Vespero senza Palla.
26: Messa e Vespero senza Palla.
31. Vespero senza Palla
    Vigilia del Redentor Vespero à due Cori con Palla.
    Giorno del Redentor Messa in S. Marco con Palla à Capella; e due Mottetti nella Chiesa del Redentor à Capella, e Vespero in S. Marco con Palla à due Cori.

Agosto.

  1: Messa à Capella in Bigonzo.
  4: Vespero senza Palla.
  5: Messa à Capella, e Vespero con Palla à due Cori.
  6: Messa con Palla, e Vespero con Palla.
  9: Vespero senza Palla.
10: Messa e Vespero senza Palla.
14: Vespero senza Palla.
15: Messa negl'Organi, e Palchetti con tutti l'istrumenti, e Vespero à due Cori con Palla.
16: Vespero senza Palla.
23: Vespero senza Palla.
24: Messa, e Vespero senza Palla.
27: Vespero senza Palla.
28: Messa, e Vespero senza Palla.
29: Messa, e Vespero senza Palla.

Settembre.

  7: Vespero con Palla.
  8: Messa negl'Organi soli senza Palchetti con gl'istrumenti alla Presenza del Prencipe, e Vespero con Palla à due Cori. [f. 411r]
13: Vespero senza Palla.
14: Messa, e Vespero senza Palla.
16: Vespero senza Palla.

17: Messa senza Palla.
20: Vespero senza Palla.
21: Messa, e Vespero senza Palla.
25. Vespero senza Palla.
26: Messa à Capella in Bigonzo senza Palla.
28: Vespero senza Palla.
29: Messa, e Vespero senza Palla.
30: Messa, e Vespero senza Palla.

Ottobre

3: Vespero senza Palla.
4: Messa, e Vespero senza Palla.
5: Vespero con Palla à due Cori.
6: Messa con Palla à Capella, e Vespero à due Cori con Palla.
7: Messa in S. Marco à Capella, quando il Serenissimo non potesse andare alla Chiesa di Santa Giustina, dove si canta la Messa à Capella; e Vespero con Palla in S. Marco, à due Cori.
8: Messa, e Vespero con Palla à due Cori.
9: Messa à Capella in Bigonzo senza Palla.
17: Vespero senza Palla.
18: Messa e Vespero senza Palla.
27: Vespero senza Palla.
28: Messa e Vespero senza Palla.
31: Vespero con Palla à due Cori.
[f. 411v]
Novembre

1: Messa à Capella alla presenza del Prencipe, e Vespero con Palla à due Cori.
2: Messa de Requiem in Bigonzo.
5: Vespero senza Palla.
6: Messa à Capella.
8: Vespero con Palla à due Cori.
9: Messa à Capella, e Vespero con Palla à due Cori.
10: Vespero senza Palla.
11: Messa, e Vespero senza Palla.
20: Vespero à due Cori con Palla.
21: Messa in S. Marco alla presenza del Prencipe in Bigonzo con Palla e due Mottetti à Capella in Chiesa alla Salute; Vespero con Palla à due Cori.
22: Vespero senza Palla.
23: Messa à Capella in Bigonzo
24: Vespero senza Palla.
25: Messa, e Vespero senza Palla.
29: Vespero senza Palla.
30: Messa, e Vespero senza Palla.

Decembre.

5: Vespero senza Palla.
6: Messa nella Capella di S. Nicoletto alla presenza del Prencipe à Capella, e Vespero senza Palla.

7:   Messa à Capella, e Vespero con Palla à due Cori.
8:   Messa à Capella, e Vespero con Palla à due Cori.
12: Vespero senza Palla.
13: Messa, e Vespero senza Palla.
20: Vespero senza Palla.
21: Messa, e Vespero senza Palla.
24: Vespero negl'Organi senza li stromenti, senza Palchetti, e Messa Solenne nelle Notte di Natale con Organi, Strumenti, e Palchetti.
25: Messa Solenne con Organi, istrumenti, e Palchetti, e Vespro negl'Organi senza istrumenti.
26: Mettà de Musici in S. Marco alla Messa à Capella, e mettà de Musici in S. Giorgio Maggiore; alla Messa à Capella; e se il tempo piovoso non permettesse al Prencipe di andare à S. Giorgio tutti li Musici canteranno in S. Marco, et il Vespero à Capella in due Cori.
27: Messa à Capella con Palla, e Vespero con Palla à due Cori.
28: Messa, e Vespero senza Palla.
[f. 412r]
30: Vespero senza Palla.
31: Messa à Capella in Bigonzo.

Oltre li sudetti giorni tutte le Domeniche dell'Anno si canta Messa delli Musici in Bigonzo, et li Vesperi senza Palla.

Similmente cantano Messa à Capella in Bigonzo tutti li Sabati dell'Anno, purche sii in essi semidoppio.

In tutti li Sabbati di Quadragesima le Musici vengono al Vespero senza Palla nella Mattina.
Vengono otto giorni innanzi all'Ascensione, et otto giorni dopo l'Ascensione senza Palla; quando non accada in essi giorni qualche Santo per il quale si celebri con Palla alli Vesperi.
Nella Vigilia dell'Ascensione vengono alla Processione delle Rogazioni, et alla Messa à Capella, e nel dopo pranzo al Vespero, con organi, Palchetti, et istrumenti.
Nelli due primi giorni delle Rogazioni, il Lunedi, e Martedi, quattro soli Musici vengono alle Litanie, e nella Vigilia di S. Marco tutti li Musici alle Rogazioni, e Messa.
Nel Giorno dell'Ascensione cantano Messa à Capella al Lido, un madrigale à Capella nel Bucintoro; e se il tempo fosse piovoso cantano Messa à Capella in S. Marco con l'intervento del Prencipe, et il Vespero à due Cori senza istrumenti con Palla.
La Vigilia delle Pentecoste cantano la Messa in Bigonzo, à Capella, et il Vespero con Palla Aperta à due Cori.
Nel giorno di Pasqua delle Pentecoste cantano Messa nelli due Organi con l'istrumenti senza Palchetti, con l'intervento del Prencipe, et il Vespero à due Cori con Palla.
Nella Prima, e Seconda Festa, Messa, e Vespero con Palla.
Nella Vigilia della Santis*s*ima Trinità Messa, e Vespero à due Cori con Palla.
Nella Vigilia del Corpus Domini Vespero à due Cori con Palla, e Messa nel giorno del Corpus Domini à Capella con l'intervento del Prencipe nella Processione l'inno à due Cori, et il Vespero à due Cori con Palla.
Nel Mercordi Santo il dopo pranzo alli Matutini, e nel Martedi Santo al solo Passio.
[f. 412]
Nel Giovedi Santo alla Messa, e Mattutini; e nella sera all'Esposizione del Sangue soli quattro.

Nel Venerdi Santo alla Messa, cioè il Passio, Processione nel dopo pranzo, et alli Matutini.

Nel Sabbato Santo alla Messa à Capella, et al Vespero à Capella.

Nel giorno di Pasqua alla Messa con gl'Organi, Palchetti, et istrumenti con l'intervento del Prencipe, et alcuni alla Cerimonia della Porta, et nel dopo pranso la mettà in S. Marco al Vespero à due Cori, e l'altra mettà al Vespero di S. Zaccaria, à due Cori.

Nell'Ottava di Pasqua alla Messa in S. Giminiano con l'intervento del Prencipe à Capella, e se ivi non fosse cantata Messa, Mà solamente detta Messa Bassa canteranno due Motetti à Capella e due Musici saranno alla Pietra in mezzo la Piazza, cantando la solita Antifona.

Nel Giovedi Grasso di mattina alla Messa à Capella.

Nella Domenica delle Palme cantano il Passio e la Messa; e nel dopo pranso cantano come nelli Vesperi senza Palla, e la Compieta à Capella.

In tutte le Domeniche di Quadragesima dopo il Vespero cantano la Compieta à Capella.

Nel Martedi Santo cantano il Passio solamente.

Nelle due Feste, seconda, e Terza di Pasqua Messa e Vesperi con Palla.

Circa gl'Organisti.

Gl'Organisti quando si suoni un solo Organo in S. Marco vengono li due principali una settimana per cadauno.

Intervengono in tutti li giorni, che vengono li Musici, e suonano anche quando non intervengono Musici nelle seguenti Funzioni; cioè.

Nella Benedizione delle Aque; Nella Vigilia dell'Epifania; Alli Matutini di S. Gio: Batt*ist*a; dell'Aparizion di S. Marco, e di S. Pietro Apostolo; et alli Matutini della Vigilia del Corpus Domini.

Nella Settimana Santa alli Matutini delli tre giorni l'Organista di settimana viene ad'accompagnare le tre Lamentazioni che cantano di Musici con la Spinetta nel Palchetto; intervengono anche un Suonatore di Violoncello, et uno di Violone per detti tre giorni.

[f. 413r]

Tanto li Musici, quanto li suonatori, et ogn'altro inserviente della Chiesa di S. Marco di qualunque grado nuin eccetuatto, oltre le sopradette Funzioni, devono intervenire à tutte quelle che fossero com*m*andate dal Serenissimo Prencipe, per le quali il Maestro di Coro, e di Cerimonie della Chiesa di S. Marco espone l'invitto, e scrive le necessarie deputazioni sopra le Polizze, che vengono affisse dallo stesso nella Sagrestia di S. Marco.

Doc. 143: A.S.V., San Marco, Procuratia de Supra, Busta 91, large, unpaginated folio.

(device [picture of the Lion of St. Mark's]) /TAVOLA/Dei Giorni di tutto l'Anno, nei quali li Cantori, Organisti, e Sonatori devono intervenire/ nella Nostra Chiesa di S. Marco, per esercitar giusto il solito il proprio Officio:

Formata d'Ordine del Serenissimo D. D. LUNARDO LOREDAN Inclito Doge Nostro, e degl'Eccellentissimi Procuratori di detta Chiesa di S. Marco,/ Mis. MARCO BOLLANI, Mis. ANTONIO GRIMANI, e Mis. ANDREA GRITTI; et in miglior modo riformata l'Anno 1515., poi pubblicamente/esposta d'Ordine del Serenissimo D. D. DOMENICO CONTARINI Inclito Doge Nostro, e degl'Eccellentissimi Procuratori di detta Chiesa,

Mis./ANTONIO BERNARDO Cassier, e Colleghe l'Anno 1661., e nuovamente trascritta l'Anno 1694.

Nel Presente Anno 1761., attese le Funzioni sopravvenute, di nuovo riformata, ed esposta in Sacrestia di S. Marco a cognizione/universale, d'Ordine del Serenissimo D. D. Inclito Doge Nostro FRANCESCO LOREDAN, e degl'Eccellentissimi Procuratori della Chie-/sa di S. Marco Mis. ZAN BATTISTA ALBRICI, Mis. MARCO FOSCARINI Cav., Mis. ALMORO PISANO 3.o, Mis. FRANCESCO MOROSINI 2.o/Cav., e Mis. D./ LODOVICO REZZONICO Cav.

GENNARO.

1. 2. 3. Esposizione del Santissimo Sacramento, con Motetti tutto il giorno, coll'Organo solo: la sera del terzo: Processione.
6. Epifania: primo, e secondo Vespero con Palla; e Messa a Capella in Bigonzo.
8. S. Lorenzo Giustinian: primo, e secondo Vespero senza Palla; e Messa a Capella in S. Pietro di Castello: non andandosi: Messa a Capella a S. Marco.
14. S. Pietro Orseolo: Messa solenne negl'Organi, co' Palchetti, e Stromenti; Vespero negl'Organi, senza Stromenti, e Palchetti.
17. S. Antonio Abbate: primo, e secondo Vespero senza Palla: Messa a Capella in Bigonzo.
20. S. Bastian: primo, e secondo Vespero senza Palla; Messa a Capella in Bigonzo.
25. Conversion di S. Paolo: primo, e secondo Vespero senza Palla; Messa a Capella in Bigonzo.
31. Translazion di S. Marco: primo, e secondo Vespero con Palla; Messa a Capella in Bigonzo.

FEBRARO.

1. Vespero a Capella a S. Maria Formosa con metà de' Musici: e con l'altra metà: Vespero con Palla a S. Marco.
2. Purificazione della B. V. Messa a Capella in Bigonzo: Vespero con Palla.
22. Cattedra di S. Pietro: primo, e secondo Vespero senza Palla: Messa a Capella in Bigonzo.
24., o 25. S. Mattia Apostolo: primo, e secondo Vespero senza Palla; Messa a Capella in Bigonzo.

MARZO

12. S. Gregorio P.: primo, e secondo Vespero senza Palla; Messa a Capella in Bigonzo.
19. S. Giuseppe: primo, e secondo Vespero senza Palla: Messa a Capella in Bigonzo.
21. S. Benedetto: Primo, e secondo Vespero senza Palla; Messa a Capella in Bigonzo.
24. Vigilia dell'Annunciata: Vespero con Palla.
25. Santissima Annunciata: Messa, e Vespero, come in S. Pietro Orseolo, e Compieta in Quaresima.
Terzo Giovedì di Marzo: Vespero del Sangue Prezioso con Palla.
Terzo Venerdì di Marzo: Esposizione del Sangue Prezioso, Motetti, e Reposizione, come il terzo dì dell'Anno con Processione.

APRILE

16. Traslazion di S. Isidoro: primo, e secondo Vespero senza Palla; Messa a Capella in Bigonzo; Processione colle Litanie de' Santi.
23. S. Zorzi: primo, e secondo Vespero senza Palla; Messa a Capella in Bigonzo.
24. Vigilia di S. Marco: Vespero negl'Organi, co' Palchetti, e Stromenti.
25. S. Marco: Messa solenne, come il primo Vespero: secondo Vespero con Palla.
30. Vigilia de Ss. Filippo, e Giacomo: Vespero a S. Marco senza Palla; Vespero simile a Ss. Filippo, e Giacomo.

MAGGIO

1. Ss. Filippo, e Giacomo: Messa a Capella in S. Marco con metà de' Musici, destinati dal Maestro di Capella; e la stessa metà, Messa simile a Ss. Filippo, e Giacomo: dall'altra metà, Messa co' Stromenti alle Vergini: li secondi Vesperi, come il dì precedente.
2. Vigilia dell'Invenzion della Croce: Vespero senza Palla.
3. Invenzion della Croce: Esposizione del Sangue Prezioso etc. come il terzo Venerdì di Marzo.
6. S. Gio: in Oglio: primo, e secondo Vespero senza Palla; Messa a Capella in Bigonzo.
8. Apparizione di S. Michele: primo, e secondo Vespero senza Palla; Messa a Capella in Bigonzo.
16. Natività di S. Isidoro: primo, e secondo Vespero senza Palla; Messa a Capella, nella Capella del Santo.
20. S. Bernardino: primo, e secondo Vespero senza Palla: Messa a Capella in Bigonzo.

GIUGNO.

11. S. Barnaba: primo, e secondo Vespero senza Palla; Messa a Capella in Bigonzo.
12. Vigilia di S. Antonio: Vespero senza Palla.
13. S. Antonio: Processione alla Salute con Litanie de' Santi: Messa in Palco con due Organi, e Stromenti: non andandosi: Messa a Capella in Bigonzo; Vespero come la Vigilia.
14. Vigilia di S. Vito: Vespero senza Palla.
15. S. Vito: Messa a Capella a S. Vito; indi Processione col *Te Deum*: non andandosi: Messa a Capella in Bigonzo: Vespero come la Vigilia.
24. S. Gio: Battista: primo, e secondo Vespero con Palla; Messa a Capella in Bigonzo.
25. Apparizion di S. Marco: Messa a Capella in Bigonzo; Processione colle Litanie de' Santi; Vespero con Palla.
26. Ss. Gio: e Paolo: Messa a Capella a Ss. Gio: e Paolo; indi Processione con le Litanie de' Santi; non andandosi: Messa a Capella in Bigonzo; Vespero senza Palla.
29. Ss. Pietro, e Paolo Ap. primo, e secondo Vespero con Palla: Messa a Capella in Bigonzo.
30. Com. di S. Paolo: Messa a Capella in Bigonzo.

LUGLIO.

2. Visitazione di M. V. primo, e secondo Vespero con Palla; Messa a Capella in Bigonzo.
10. Messa a Capella in S. Paternian.
12. S. Ermagora: primo Vespero senza Palla; e Messa a Capella in Bigonzo.

16. Festa del Carmine: Messa a Capella alle Terese; quando vada il Serenissimo: trasferendosi la Festa del Carmine; Messa a Capella in Bigonzo; Vespero senza Palla.
17. S. Marina: Motetti due alla Messa bassa in S. Marina: Processione colle Litanie de' Santi: Messa a Capella in Bigonzo; Vespero come il dì precedente.
22. S. Maria Maddalena: primo, e secondo Vespero con Palla; Messa a Capella in Bigonzo.
25. S. Giacomo Apostolo: primo, e secondo Vespero senza Palla; Messa a Capella in Bigonzo.
26. S. Anna: Messa a Capella in Bigonzo; Vespero senza Palla.

Vigilia del Redentor. Vespero con Palla.

Giorno del Redentor. Motetti due alla Messa bassa al Redentor; Processione col *Te Deum*; Messa a Capella in Bigonzo; Vespero come la Vigilia.

AGOSTO.

1. S. Pietro in Vincola: primo Vespero senza Palla; Messa a Capella in Bigonzo.
4. S. Domenico: Vespero senza Palla.
5. Madonna della Neve: Messa a Capella in Bigonzo; Vespero con Palla.
6. Trasfigurazion del Signor: Messa a Capella in Bigonzo; Vespero con Palla.
10. S. Lorenzo: primo, e secondo Vespero senza Palla; Messa a Capella in Bigonzo.
15. Assunta: primo, e secondo Vespero con Palla; Messa negl'Organi, co' Stromenti, e Palchetti.
16. S. Rocco: Vespero senza Palla.
24. S. Bartolomeo Apostolo: primo, e secondo Vespero senza Palla; Messa a Capella in Bigonzo.
28. S. Agostino: primo, e secondo Vespero senza Palla; Messa a Capella in Bigonzo; il secondo al Battisterio.
29. Decollazione di S. Gio: Battista: Messa a Capella, al Battisterio. Vespero senza Palla in Bigonzo.

SETTEMBRE.

8. Natività della B. V. primo, e secondo Vespero con Palla: Messa negl'Organi, co' Stromenti, senza Palchetti.
14. Esaltazione della Croce: primo, e secondo Vespero senza Palla; Messa a Capella in Bigonzo.
18. S. Vettor: primo Vespero senza Palla; Messa a Capella in Bigonzo.
21. S. Matteo Apostolo: primo, e secondo Vespero-senza Palla; Messa a Capella in Bigonzo.
26. S. Gerardo Sagredo: primo Vespero senza Palla; Messa a Capella in Bigonzo.
29. S. Michele: primo, e secondo Vespero senza Palla; Messa a Capella in Bigonzo.
30. S. Girolamo: Messa a Capella in Bigonzo; Vespero senza Palla.

OTTOBRE.

4. S. Francesco: primo, e secondo Vespero senza Palla; Messa a Capella in Bigonzo.
6. S. Magno: primo, e secondo Vespero con Palla; Messa a Capella in Bigonzo.
7. S. Giustina: Messa a Capella in S. Giustina; indi Processione colle Litanie de' Santi: non andandosi: Messa a Capella in Bigonzo: Vespero con Palla.
8. Dedicazion di S. Marco: Messa a Capella in Bigonzo; Vespero con Palla.

9. Ss. Sergio, e Bacco: Messa a Capella in Bigonzo.
18. S. Luca Evangelista: primo, e secondo Vespero senza Palla; Messa a Capella in Bigonzo.
28. Ss. Simon, e Giuda Ap.: primo, e secondo Vespero senza Palla: Messa a Capella in Bigonzo.

NOVEMBRE.

1. Tutti li Santi: primo, e secondo Vespero con Palla, Messa a Capella in Bigonzo.
2. Morti: Messa de *Requiem* a Capella in Bigonzo.
6. S. Lunardo: primo Vespero senza Palla: Messa a Capella in Bigonzo.
9. S. Teodoro: primo, e secondo Vespero con Palla; Messa a Capella in Bigonzo.
11. S. Martin: primo, e secondo Vespero senza Palla; Messa a Capella in Bigonzo.
20. Vigilia della Salute: Vespero con Palla.
21. Madonna della Salute: Motetti due alla Messa bassa alla Salute; Processione col *Te Deum*; Messa a Capella in Bigonzo; Vespero come nella Vigilia.
23. S. Clemente: primo Vespero senza Palla; Messa a Capella in Bigonzo.
25. S. Catterina: primo, e secondo Vespero senza Palla; Messa a Capella in Bigonzo.
30. S. Andrea Apostolo: primo, e secondo Vespero senza Palla; Messa a Capella in Bigonzo.

DECEMBRE.

6. S. Nicolò: primo, e secondo Vespero senza Palla; Messa a Capella in Palazzo.
7. S. Ambroso: Messa a Capella in Bigonzo.
8. Concezione della B. V.: primo, e secondo Vespero con Palla; Messa a Capella in Bigonzo, Processione colle Litanie della B. V.
13. S. Lucia: primo, e secondo Vespero senza Palla; Messa a Capella in Bigonzo.
21. S. Tommaso Apostolo: primo, e secondo Vespero senza Palla; Messa a Capella in Bigonzo.
24. Vigilia di Natale; Vespero negl'Organi, senza Palchetti, o Stromenti: Prime Lezione del Mattutino; Messa negl'Organi, co' Palchetti, e Stromenti; dopo la Messa *Te Deum*.
25. Giorno di Natale: Messa come la sera antecedente; senza *Te Deum*, Vespero negli Organi, senza Palchetti, o Stromenti.
26. S. Stefano: Messa a Capella a S. Zorzi con metà de' Musici; l'altra metà: Messa simile in Bigonzo: non andandosi a S. Zorzi; tutti li Musici cantano in S. Marco: Vespero con Palla.
27. S. Giovanni Evangelista: Messa a Capella in Bigonzo; Vespero come il dì precedente.
28. Innocenti: Messa a Capella al Battisterio: Vespero senza Palla.
31. S. Silvestro: primo Vespero senza Palla; Messa a Capella in Bigonzo.

Oltre li sudetti giorni devono intervenire li Musici.

Tutte le Domeniche dell'Anno: Messa, e Vespero in Bigonzo.
Tutti li Sabbati, ne' quali deva cantarsi Messa della B. V. si di rito semidoppio, che doppio: Messa a Capella in Bigonzo.
Giovedì Grasso: Messa a Capella in Bigonzo.
Li Sabbati di Quaresima la mattina: Vespero in Bigonzo.
Le Domeniche di Quaresima dopo pranso: Vespero in Bigonzo, e Compieta a Capella.

Domenica delle Palme: dopo l'Antifone al getto degl' Uccelli, e alla Porta; *Passio*, e Messa a Capella in Bigonzo: Vespero in Bigonzo, e Compieta a Capella.

Martedì Santo: il solo *Passio*.

Mercordì Santo alli Mattutini: le tre prime Lezioni, li Responsorj, il *Benedictus*, il *Miserere*.

Giovedì Santo: Messa a Capella in Bigonzo; Inno alla Communione, e Processione in Sacrestia: Mattutini come il dì precedente; la sera: quattro all'Inno nell'Esposizione del Sangue.

Venerdì Santo: Tratti dopo le Profezie; *Passio*; quattro Religiosi in Pivial Rosso per l'Inno all'adorazion della Croce: la sera: Improperj alla Processione, a due Cori; Mattutini, come ne' dì precedenti.

Sabbato Santo: Tratti alle Profezie, da quattro Religiosi in Pivial Rosso; da cui pure l'Inno *Rex Sanctorum*; indi Messa, e Vespero a Capella in Bigonzo.

Giorno di Pasqua: Musici alla Cerimonia alla Porta; Messa negl'Organi, co' Palchetti, e Stromenti: Vespero con Palla da metà de Musici in Bigonzo, e dall'altra metà, Vespero simile a S. Zaccaria.

Seconda, e Terza Festa: Messa a Capella in Bigonzo; Vespero con Palla.

Ottava di Pasqua: Messa a Capella a S. Giminiano; ovvero due Motetti alla Messa bassa: nel ritorno da S. Giminiano del Serenissimo: due Religiosi in Piviale, cantano l'Antifona *Dum transisset* alla Pietra Rossa.

Vigilia di S. Marco: Rogazioni, e Messa a Capella in Bigonzo.

Li primi due giorni delle Rogazioni dell'Ascensione: quattro Musici alle Litanie.

Vigilia dell'Ascensione: tutti alle Rogazioni, e Messa a Capella in Bigonzo; Vespero negl'Organi, co' Palchetti, e Stromenti.

Giorno dell'Ascensione: Madrigale in Bucintoro; Messa a Capella al Lido: non andandosi: Messa a Capella in Bigonzo; Vespero con Palla in Bigonzo.

Otto giorni avanti, e otto giorni dopo l'Ascensione: Vespero in Bigonzo.

Vigilia di Pentecoste: Messa a Capella in Bigonzo; Vespero con Palla in Bigonzo.

Giorno di Pentecoste: Messa negl'Organi, co' Stromenti, senza Palchetti; Vespero come il dì precedente.

Seconda, e Terza Festa: Messa a Capella in Bigonzo; Vespero come ne' dì precedenti.

Giorno della Santissima Trinità: Primo, e secondo Vespero, e Messa, con Palla in Bigonzo.

Giorno del *Corpus Domini*: primo, e secondo Vespero, e Messa, con Palla in Bigonzo: dopo Messa Processione coll'Inno; quattro Musici alle Pause, e al *Tantum ergo* prima della Benedizione.

Le Domeniche semidoppie dopo le Pentecoste: li soliti Versetti alle Pause della *Salve Regina*.

Ne' Trasporti dell'Imagine della B. V. dal proprio all' Altar Maggiore: l'Inno *O Gloriosa Domina*.

Ad ogni Messa con Palla: Motetto a tre in Organo.

Tutti quei giorni, in cui si trasportano solennità del Signore, B.V., o Santi; perchè nel proprio non possono celebrarsi: tutta la stessa Funzione del giorno proprio.

Ne' Tridui della B. V. Processione colle sue Litanie, e Preci, e Messa, e Vespero in Bigonzo, secondo il Comando Pubblico.

Se li Tridui si differiscono alli Ottavarj: Messe, e Vesperi, come sopra, per tutto l'Ottavario, et anche di più, se fosse comandato.

Nell'elezione de' Pontefici: Messa solenne, e *Te Deum*.

Nel dì seguente alla Coronazione de' Serenissimi: Messa, e *Te Deum* come la Vigilia di Natale.

Nel dì Anniversario della loro Coronazione: tutto come sopra.
Nell'Ingresso degl'Eccellentissimi Procuratori: due Motetti a pieno in Organo.
Nel Possesso de Canonici, sì Ressidenti, che Piovani: Messa con Palla a Capella in Bigonzo.
Nella Morte de' Pontefici: Messa de *Requiem* etc. a Capella in Bigonzo nel Triduo, che stà esposta la Statua: nel dopo pranso della Sepultura: Officio de' Morti, (come il solito) e *Miserere* in Processione.
Nelle Sepultura della Statua de' Patriarchi: *Miserere* in Processione.
Negl'Anniversarj dell'Em. C. Zen, e di S. E. Cav. Morosini: Messa de *Requiem* etc. a Capella in Bigonzo.
Ne' Funerali de' Primicerj, Procuratorj, Canonici Ressidenti, Maestri di Coro, di Capella, e Musici: Messa de *Requiem* etc. a Capella in Bigonzo.
In ogn'altro Giorno, e Funzione estraordinaria, ordinata dal Maestro di Coro per Publico Comando.

Obblighi degli Organisti.

Quando si suoni un solo Organo; le due principali suonano alternativamente una Settimana per cadauno.
Suonano tutti li giorni, ne' quali cantano, o devono cantare li Musici, eccetto li Sabbati semidoppi, e quelle Domeniche di Avvento, e Quaresima; nelle quali secondo il rito della Chiesa non suonansi gl' Organi, e quando si canti fuori di Coro.
Oltre li giorni, che cantano i Musici: suonano alla Benedizione delle Acque la Vigilia dell'Epifania; e alli Mattutini del *Corpus Domini*, S. Gio: Battista, Apparizion di S. Marco, S. Pietro Apostolo.
La Settimana Santa: Accompagnano con la Spinetta le tre prime Lezioni de' Mattutini, che si cantano da' Musici; che pur si accompagnano da un Violoncello, e Violone di Capella.

Obblighi de' Suonatori.

Oltre li giorni soprascritti, ne' quali cadono Messe, o Vesperi co' Stromenti; fanno suonata dopo l'Epistola ne' giorni seguenti:

 6. Gennaro: Epifania del Signore.
 2. Febraro: Purificazione della B. V.
16. Aprile: S. Isidoro.
25. Giugno: Apparizion di S. Marco.
 1. Novembre: Tutti li Santi.
Giorno del *Corpus Domini*.

Stampata per li Figliuoli del qu: Z. Antonio Pinelli, Stampatori Ducali.

Manuscript copies of the above table appear in A.S.V., Procuratia de Supra, Registro 100 (Ceremoniali), f. 358r–361r and f. 365v–368r. A set of *corrigenda* is included on f. 361r:

Correzzioni di errori corsi nella Stampa della soprascritta Tavola degli Oblighi di Musici

2 Marzo—S. Gregorio—12 Marzo
16 Maggio—S. Isidoro—15 Maggio

9 Ottobre—SS.i Sergio e Bacco—12 Ottobre,
primo Vespero senza Palla; Messa a Capella
in Bigonzo.

Doc. 144: Biblioteca Nazionale Marciana, Cod. Lat. III-172 (-2276), f. 114r.

Dies in quibus cantantur ad vesperas duobus choris

Mensis Januarij

Die 1 Circumcisionis Domini
Die 6 Epiphaniae Domini

Februarij

Die 1 pridie purificationis quando non itur ad ecclesiam Santa Maria Formosa
Die 2 Purificationis Beatae Mariae

Martij

Die 24 pridie Annuntiationis Beatae Mariae
Die 25 Annuntiationis Beatae Mariae

Aprilis

Die 24 pridie Festi Sancti Marci
Die 25 Festi Sancti Marci Evangelistae

Junij

Die 24 Sancti Joannis Baptistae Nocti
Die 25 Marci Evangelistae Apparisionis
Die 29 Sanctorum Petri, et Pauli Apostolij

Julij

Die 2 Visitationis Sanctae Mariae

Augusti

Die 14 Vigiliae Asumptionis Beatae Mariae
Die 15 Asumptionis virginae Mariae

Septembris

Die 7 Vigilia nativititatis Sanctae Mariae
Die 8 Nativitatis Beatae Mariae

Octobris

Die 8 Dedicationis Ecclesiae Sancti Marci
Die 31 Vigiliae Festi Omnis Sanctorum

Novembris

Die 1 In festo omnium *Sanctorum*

Decembris

Die 8 Conceptionis Beatae Mariae
Die 24 Vig*ilia* Nativitatis
Die 25 Nativitatis D*omi*ni
Die 26 Sancti Stephanis *pro*to m*artyris*
Die 27 S*ancti* Joannis Eva*n*gelist*ae*
Die 31 Pr*i*die circo*n*cisionis D*omi*ni

In festis mobilibus verò

In Die S*ancti* Paschalis, e duobus sequentibus
In Vig*ilia* Asce*n*sionis, et in Die
In Vig*ilia* Pe*n*tecostis et in tribus diebus sequentibus
In Festo S*anctissi*me Trinitatis

Trata dalla tarifa d*e*l Maestro di capella M*e.s.ser* Iseppo Zerlino, et fu de ordine
d*e*ll'Ill*ustrissi*mo Co*n*tarini procurator....

Doc. 145: A.S.V., San Marco, Procuratia de Supra, Registro 98 (Ceremoniali), f. 69v–70r

Diebus quibus Palla aperitur.
Polizza nel Mazzo [in a later hand]
Quando cantant*ur* Psalmi p*er* Cantores

Januarius
  1. In Miss*a* et Vesp*eris*
  5. In Vesp*eris*
  6. In Miss*a* et Vesp*eris*
30. In Vesp*eris*
31. In Miss*a* et Vesp*eris*

Februarius
  1. In Vesp*eris* in S*anta* Mar*i*a Formosa
  2. In Miss*a*, et Vesp*eris*

Martius
24. In Vesp*eris*
25. In Miss*a*, Ves*p*eris et Complet*ori*o

Aprilis
16. In Miss*a*, et Processione
24. In Vesp*eris*
25. In Missa, et Vesp*eris*

Maius

Junius
15. In Processione
23. In Vesperis
24. In Missa, et Vesperis et Matutino, quando non cantant Te Deum
25. In Missa, Processione et Vesperis
28. In Vesperis
29. In Missa et Vesperis

Julius
1. In Vesperis
2. In Missa et Vesperis si placet Magistro vel proprio Senat:
17. In Processione, et Missa
21. In Vesperis
22. In Missa, et Vesperis

Augusti
5. In Vesperis
6. In Missa et Vesperis
14. In Vesperis
15. In Missa et Vesperis

Septembris
7. In Vesperis
8. In Missa et Vesperis

Octobris
5. In Vesperis
6. In Missa et Vesperis
7. In Vesperis
8. In Missa et Vesperis
31. In Vesperis

Novembris
1. In Missa et Vesperis
8. In Vesperis
9. In Missa et Vesperis

Decembris
7. In Vesperis
8. In Missa et Vesperis
24. In Vesperis Matutino, et Missa
25. In Missa et Vesperis
26. In Missa et Vesperis
31. In Vesperis

In omnibus Processionibus Magnis de ordine Excellentissimi Consilij X
In Majori hebdomada
Feria 5.   ⎫
              ⎬ in Missa
Sabbato Sancto ⎭

Dies Festorum Mobilium

In die Sanctae Paschae et 2 sequentibus diebus In Missis, et Vesperis
In Domenica Apostolorum in Missa
In Vigilia Ascensionis in Vesperis in die in Vesperis
In die Sancto Pentecostes in utrisque Vesperis et Missa etiam Palla anterior aperitur et 2. sequentibus diebus in Missis et Vesperis
In Festo Sanctissimae Trinitatis in utrisque Vesperis et Missa
In Vigilia Sacratissimi Corporis Christi in Vesperis et Matutino in die in Missa Processione et Vesperis
In die Creationis Serenissimi Domini Ducis ad Missam.
Quando datur possessus Reverendissimi Domini Primicerij Nostrae Ecclesiae

Notandum est quod si Festum aliquod de predicto transferatur in Vigilia, et in die qua fit de Festo Translato aperire tenetur ut supra.

Thessauris exponitur super Aaltre majori in Vigilia diei Nativitatis et Resurrectionis Domini in primis Vesperis et Missa Sancti Marci Apostoli, et in 1 Vesperis Ascensionis Domini tantum et semper aperitur anterior Palla Altarij.

Doc. 146: A.S.V., San Marco, Procuratia de Supra, Busta 91, fascicolo 1, f. 21v

Interrogato. sapete che il maestro di coro ordinasse a Messer Baldissera che facesse cantar a due cori. Rispose. non mi ritrovai in sacrestia a questo ordine, ma quando fu cominciato il vesporo fino al gloria patri, il maestro di coro fece tacer li preti, et vene in pergolo ordinando che si cantasse a dui cori, dove le fu respostoda tutti insieme che non erano tenuti cantar a dui cori, et che non vi era un salmo. Interrogato. perche non cantar a dui cori et il salmo in falso bordon. Rispose. perche non e solito mai se non la quadragesima cantarsi in falso bordon et sono 13 anni che Io servo ne mai mi ricordo che tal giorno si cantasse a dui cori.

Doc. 147: A.S.V., San Marco, Procuratia de Supra, Busta 91, fascicolo 1, f. 20v

Messer Padre Zuane Chiozoto fatto venir in Procuratia.... /il fo detto domenica passata che era la sagra di San Marco andaste in chiesa. Rispose. Signor si. Interrogato. che vesporo coreva quel Zorno. Rispose. quel della sagra. Interrogato. andavelo detto ugnolo o a dui cori. Rispose. li 17 è più anni che io son in capella di San Marco ne mai mi ricordo che sij statto cantato doppio ne mai ho cantato falso bordon in capella di San Marco se non la quaresema et quel Zorno.

Doc. 148: A.S.V., San Marco, Procuratia de Supra, Registro 12 (Giornali Cassier, 1639–1648)

1640. adi 19. Maggio

Per spese dette//à Cassa ducati vinti grossi 8 contadi à 12 cantori estraordinarij à lire 3 grossi 10 l'uno, et à 12 Sonatori à lire 7 l'uno tolti per agiunti al Vespero della vigilia dell'Assentione giusto l'ordinario....

Doc. 149: A.S.V., San Marco, Procuratia de Supra, Registro 12 (Giornali Cassier, 1639–1648)

1641 adi 7 Zugno

P*er* spese p*er* la Chiesa//à Cassa *ducati* vinti doi contadi à tredesi sonatori agiunti al vespero della vigilia della Senza à *lire* 7 p*er* uno, et à tredeci cantori, come sopra, à *lire* 3 *grossi* 10 p*er* un....

Doc. 150: A.S.V., San Marco, Procuratia de Supra, Registro 12 (Giornali Cassier, 1639–1648)

1642 31 Maggio....

P*er* spese di chiesa//à Cassa *ducati* diesi *grossi* 4 contadi a musici p*er* lasso sonar violini, violi, et chitaroni la vigilia d*e*lli assensioni al vespero....

Doc. 151: A.S.V., San Marco, Procuratia de Supra, Registro 12 (Giornali Cassier, 1639–1648)

1643. 18 Maggio
Per spesi p*er* la Chiesa//à Cassa *ducati* sette *grossi* 22 contadi à sonadori agionti n*ume*ro 7 p*er* il Vesporo della Vigilia della Assensione à *lire* 7 l'uno iusta l'Ordinario....

Doc. 152: A.S.V., San Marco, Procuratia de Supra, Registro 12 (Giornali Cassier, 1639–1648)

Laus Deo 1644. à di 6 Maggio

Per spesi per la chiesa//à Cassa *ducati* quindesi *grossi* 19 contadi à diversi musici, sonadori, et cantori aggionti agl'altri p*er* cantar la messa sollene il giorno della publicat*ione* della pace, et per il vespro della vigilia dell'Ascension....

Doc. 153: Sansovino-Martinioni, *Venetia città nobilissim*a (Venice: Curti, 1663), p. 516

Andate diverse in certi giorni dell'anno.

La prima adunque è nella Vigilia di Natale: .... intona Vespro, che con canti, et suoni soavissimi viene cantato da i Musici di Chiesa salariati, et da altri, che vengono tolti a posta per far maggior numero, poiche si canta in tal sera à otto, dieci, dodici, e sedici cori, con stupore, et maraviglia di ciascuno, et specialmente de i forestieri, i quali confessano non udirsi musica più rara, nè più singolar di questa in molte parti del mondo: et dicono il vero; poiche i Musici, e di voce, et di suono trovansi quivi Eccellentissimi, havendo specialmente per Maestri, et Capi loro quei tre famosi giovani, cotanto nominati al mondo, Croce, detto Chiozotto, Gabrielli, e da Bassano.

Appendix II
Obligations of the Singers of the
Cappella Marciana,
1515–1761

For a discussion of the sources from which this Appendix is compiled, see pp. 183–84.

January 1, Circumcision of Our Lord
1515:	Mass	Vespers (unspecified)	
1677:	Mass	First Vespers	Second Vespers
1678:	Mass	First Vespers	Second Vespers
1755:	Singing motets all day during the display of the Most Holy Sacrament		
1761:	Singing motets all day during the display of the Most Holy Sacrament		

January 2
1515:	——
1677:	——
1678:	——
1755:	Singing motets all day during the display of the Most Holy Sacrament
1761:	Singing motets all day during the display of the Most Holy Sacrament

January 3
1515:	——
1677:	——
1678:	——
1755:	Singing motets all day during the display of the Most Holy Sacrament
1761:	Singing motets all day during the display of the Most Holy Sacrament

January 6, The Epiphany of Our Lord[401]
1515:	Mass	First Vespers	Second Vespers
1677:	Mass	First Vespers	Second Vespers
1678:	Mass	First Vespers	Second Vespers
1755:	Mass	First Vespers	Second Vespers
1761:	Mass	First Vespers	Second Vespers

January 8, San Lorenzo Giustiniani
1515:	——		
1677:	Mass	First Vespers	Second Vespers
1678:	Mass	First Vespers	Second Vespers
1755:	Mass	First Vespers	Second Vespers
1761:	Mass	First Vespers	Second Vespers

January 14, St. Peter Orseolo
   1515:   ——
   1677:   ——
   1678:   ——
   1755:   Mass   Second Vespers
   1761:   Mass   Second Vespers

January 17, St. Anthony, Abbot
   1515:   Mass   First Vespers   Second Vespers
   1677:   Mass   First Vespers   Second Vespers
   1678:   Mass   First Vespers   Second Vespers
   1755:   Mass   First Vespers   Second Vespers
   1761:   Mass   First Vespers   Second Vespers

January 20, St. Fabian, Pope and Martyr, and St. Sebastian, Martyr
   1515:   Mass   First Vespers   Second Vespers
   1677:   Mass   First Vespers   Second Vespers
   1678:   Mass   First Vespers   Second Vespers
   1755:   Mass   First Vespers   Second Vespers
   1761:   Mass   First Vespers   Second Vespers

January 25, Conversion of St. Paul
   1515:   Mass   First Vespers   Second Vespers
   1677:   Mass   First Vespers   ——
   1678:   Mass   First Vespers   Second Vespers
   1755:   ——   ——   ——
   1761:   Mass   First Vespers   Second Vespers

January 30, St. Justinian
   1515:   Mass   ——   ——
   1677:   ——   ——   ——
   1678:   ——   ——   ——
   1755:   ——   ——   ——
   1761:   ——   ——   ——

January 31, Translation of the Body of St. Mark
   1515:   Mass   First Vespers   Second Vespers
   1677:   Mass   First Vespers   Second Vespers
   1678:   Mass   First Vespers   Second Vespers
   1755:   Mass   First Vespers   Second Vespers
   1761:   Mass   First Vespers   Second Vespers

February 2, Purification of the B. V. M.
   1515:   Mass   First Vespers   Second Vespers
   1677:   Mass   First Vespers   Second Vespers
   1678:   Mass   First Vespers   Second Vespers
   1755:   Mass   First Vespers   Second Vespers
   1761:   Mass   First Vespers   Second Vespers

February 22, St. Peter's Chair at Antioch
   1515:   Mass   First Vespers   Second Vespers

1677:	Mass	First Vespers	Second Vespers
1678:	Mass	First Vespers	Second Vespers
1755:	Mass	First Vespers	Second Vespers
1761:	Mass	First Vespers	Second Vespers

February 24, St. Gerard of Csanad[402]

1515:	Mass	——	Second Vespers
1677:	Mass	——	Second Vespers
1678:	Mass	——	Second Vespers
1755:	——	——	——
1761:	——	——	——

February 24 or 25, St. Matthias, Apostle

1515:	Mass	——	Second Vespers
1677:	Mass	——	Second Vespers
1678:	Mass	First Vespers	Second Vespers
1755:	Mass	First Vespers	Second Vespers
1761:	Mass	First Vespers	Second Vespers

March 12, St. Gregory the Great

1515:	Mass	First Vespers	Second Vespers
1677:	Mass	First Vespers	Second Vespers
1678:	Mass	First Vespers	Second Vespers
1755:	Mass	First Vespers	Second Vespers
1761:	Mass	First Vespers	Second Vespers

March 19, St. Joseph

1515:	Mass	First Vespers	Second Vespers
1677:	Mass	First Vespers	Second Vespers
1678:	Mass	First Vespers	Second Vespers
1755:	Mass	First Vespers	Second Vespers
1761:	Mass	First Vespers	Second Vespers

March 21, St. Benedict, Abbot

1515:	Mass	First Vespers	Second Vespers
1677:	Mass	First Vespers	Second Vespers
1678:	Mass	First Vespers	Second Vespers
1755:	Mass	First Vespers	Second Vespers
1761:	Mass	First Vespers	Second Vespers

March 25, Annunciation of the B. V. M

1515:	Mass	First Vespers	Second Vespers	——
1677:	Mass	First Vespers	Second Vespers	Compline
1678:	Mass	First Vespers	Second Vespers	Compline
1755:	Mass	First Vespers	Second Vespers	——
1761:	Mass	First Vespers	Second Vespers	Compline

Third Thursday of March

1515:	——	
1677:	——	Display of the Most Precious Blood
1678:	——	

| 1755: | —— | Vespers of the Most Precious Blood |
| 1761: | —— | Vespers of the Most Precious Blood |

Third Friday of March
1515:	——
1677:	——
1678:	——
1755:	Motets for the exposition and reposition of the Most Precious Blood
1761:	Motets for the exposition and reposition of the Most Precious Blood, as on the third day of the year.

April 16, Translation of the Body of St. Isidore
1515:	Mass	First Vespers	Second Vespers	Procession
1677:	Mass	First Vespers	Second Vespers	Procession
1678:	Mass	First Vespers	Second Vespers	Procession
1755:	Mass	First Vespers	Second Vespers	Procession[403]
1761:	Mass	First Vespers	Second Vespers	Procession[404]

April 23, St. George, Martyr
1515:	Mass	First Vespers	Second Vespers	
1677:	Mass	First Vespers	Second Vespers	Procession
1678:	Mass	First Vespers	Second Vespers	
1755:	Mass	First Vespers	Second Vespers	
1761:	Mass	First Vespers	Second Vespers	

April 24, Vigil of St. Mark
1515:	Mass[405]
1677:	Mass
1678:	Mass
1755:	Mass, Rogations[406]
1761:	Mass, Rogations[406]

April 25, St. Mark, Evangelist
1515:	Mass	First Vespers	Second Vespers
1677:	Mass	First Vespers	Second Vespers
1678:	Mass	First Vespers	Second Vespers
1755:	Mass	First Vespers	Second Vespers
1761:	Mass	First Vespers	Second Vespers

May 1, SS. Philip and James
1515:	Mass	First Vespers	Second Vespers[407]
1677:	Mass	First Vespers	Second Vespers
1678:	Mass	First Vespers	Second Vespers
1755:	Mass	First Vespers	Second Vespers
1761:	Mass	First Vespers	Second Vespers

May 3, Finding of Holy Cross
| 1515: | Mass | First Vespers | Second Vespers |
| 1677: | —— | First Vespers | Second Vespers[408] |

The display of the Most Precious Blood; motets and procession, morning and evening

1678:   ——   ——   ——

1755:   ——   First Vespers   ——

Display of the Most Precious Blood, procession, and motets

1761:   ——   First Vespers   ——

Display of the Most Precious Blood, as on the third Friday of March

May 6, St. John before the Latin Gate

1515:	Mass	First Vespers	——
1677:[409]	Mass	First Vespers	——
1678:	Mass	First Vespers	Second Vespers
1755:	Mass	First Vespers	Second Vespers
1761:	Mass	First Vespers	Second Vespers

May 8, Apparition of St. Michael, the Archangel

1515:	Mass	First Vespers	——
1677:	Mass	First Vespers	——
1678:	Mass	First Vespers	——
1755:	Mass	First Vespers	Second Vespers
1761:	Mass	First Vespers	Second Vespers

May 15, The Nativity of St. Isidore

1515:	Mass	First Vespers	Second Vespers
1677:	Mass	First Vespers	——
1678:	Mass	First Vespers	Second Vespers
1755:	Mass	First Vespers	Second Vespers
1761:[410]	Mass	First Vespers	Second Vespers

May 20, St. Bernardine of Siena, Confessor

1515:	Mass	First Vespers	Second Vespers
1677:	Mass	First Vespers	Second Vespers[411]
1678:	Mass	First Vespers	Second Vespers
1755:	Mass	First Vespers	Second Vespers
1761:	Mass	First Vespers	Second Vespers

June 11, St. Barnabas, Apostle

1515:	Mass	First Vespers	Second Vespers
1677:	Mass	First Vespers	——
1678:	Mass	First Vespers	——
1755:	Mass	First Vespers	Second Vespers
1761:	Mass	First Vespers	Second Vespers

June 13, St. Anthony of Padua, Confessor and Doctor of the Church

1515:	Mass	First Vespers	Second Vespers	
1677:	Mass	First Vespers	Second Vespers	Procession
1678:	Mass	First Vespers	Second Vespers	Procession
1755:	Mass	First Vespers	Second Vespers	[Procession][412]
1761:	Mass	First Vespers	Second Vespers	Procession

June 15, Ss. Vitus and Modestus, Martyrs

1515:	Mass	First Vespers	Second Vespers	Procession
1677:	Mass	First Vespers	Second Vespers	Procession

1678:	Mass	First Vespers	Second Vespers	Procession
1755:	Mass	First Vespers	Second Vespers	[Procession][412]
1761:	Mass	First Vespers	Second Vespers	Procession

June 24, Nativity of St. John the Baptist

1515:	Mass	First Vespers	Second Vespers	Matins[413]
1677:	Mass	First Vespers	Second Vespers	
1678:	——	——	——	
1755:	Mass	First Vespers	Second Vespers	
1761:	Mass	First Vespers	Second Vespers	

June 25, Feast of the Apparition of the Body of St. Mark

1515:	Mass	——	Second Vespers	Procession
1677:	Mass	——	Second Vespers	Procession
1678:	Mass	——	Second Vespers	——
1755:	Mass	——	Second Vespers	——
1761:	Mass	——	Second Vespers	Procession

June 26, Ss. John and Paul, Martyrs

1515:	——	——	——	——
1677:	Mass	——	——	Procession
1678:	Mass	——	——	Procession
1755:	Mass	——	Second Vespers	[Procession][414]
1761:	Mass	——	Second Vespers	Procession

June 29, Holy Apostles Peter and Paul

1515:	Mass	First Vespers	Second Vespers
1677:	Mass	First Vespers	Second Vespers
1678:	Mass	First Vespers	Second Vespers
1755:	Mass	First Vespers	Second Vespers
1761:	Mass	First Vespers	Second Vespers

June 30, Commemoration of St. Paul, Apostle

1515:	Mass	——	——
1677:	Mass	——	——
1678:	Mass	——	——
1755:	Mass	——	——
1761:	Mass	——	——

July 2, Visitation of the Blessed Virgin Mary

1515:	Mass	First Vespers	Second Vespers
1677:	Mass	First Vespers	Second Vespers
1678:	Mass	First Vespers	Second Vespers
1755:	Mass	First Vespers	Second Vespers
1761:	Mass	First Vespers	Second Vespers

July 10, St. Paternian

1515:	——	——	——
1677:	Mass	——	——
1678:	——	——	——
1755:	Mass[415]	——	——
1761:	Mass	——	——

July 12, Ss. Hermagoras and Fortunatus

1515:	Mass	First Vespers	——
1677:	Mass	First Vespers	——
1678:	Mass	First Vespers	——
1755:	Mass	First Vespers	——
1761:	Mass	First Vespers	——

July 16, Our Blessed Lady of Mount Carmel

1515:	——
1677:	——
1678:	——
1755:	Mass[416]
1761:	Mass[416]

July 17, St. Marina

1515:	Mass	First Vespers	Second Vespers	Procession
1677:	Mass[417]	First Vespers	Second Vespers	Procession
1678:	Mass	First Vespers	Second Vespers	Procession
1755:	Mass[418]	First Vespers	Second Vespers	Procession
1761:	Mass[419]	First Vespers	Second Vespers	Procession

July 22, St. Mary Magdalen, Penitent

1515:	Mass	First Vespers	Second Vespers
1677:	Mass	First Vespers	Second Vespers
1678:	Mass	First Vespers	Second Vespers
1755:	Mass	First Vespers	Second Vespers
1761:	Mass	First Vespers	Second Vespers

July 25, St. James, Apostle

1515:	Mass	First Vespers	Second Vespers
1677:	Mass	First Vespers	Second Vespers
1678:	Mass	First Vespers	Second Vespers
1755:	Mass	First Vespers	Second Vespers
1761:	Mass	First Vespers	Second Vespers

July 26, St. Anne, Mother of the B. V. M.

1515:	——	——	
1677:	Mass	First Vespers[420]	——
1678:	Mass	First Vespers[420]	Second Vespers
1755:	Mass	——	Second Vespers
1761:	Mass	——	Second Vespers

Third Sunday in July, Feast of the Redeemer

1515:	——	——	——	
1677:	Motetti			
1678:	——	——	——	
1755:	Mass	First Vespers	Second Vespers	Two motets in the Chiesa del Redentore

| 1761: | Mass | First Vespers | Second Vespers | Procession with *Te Deum*; two motets at Low Mass at the Chiesa del Redentore |

August 1, St. Peter's Chair

1515:	Mass	First Vespers	——
1677:	Mass	First Vespers	——
1678:	Mass	First Vespers	——
1755:	Mass	First Vespers	——
1761:	Mass	First Vespers	——

August 5, Our Lady of the Snow

1515:	Mass	First Vespers	Second Vespers
1677:	Mass	First Vespers	Second Vespers
1678:	Mass	First Vespers	Second Vespers
1755:	Mass	First Vespers	Second Vespers
1761:	Mass	First Vespers	Second Vespers[421]

August 6, Transfiguration of Our Lord Jesus Christ

1515:	Mass	——	Second Vespers
1677:	Mass	——	Second Vespers
1678:	Mass	——	Second Vespers
1755:	Mass	——	Second Vespers
1761:	Mass	——	Second Vespers

August 10, St. Lawrence, Martyr

1515:	Mass	First Vespers	Second Vespers
1677:	Mass	First Vespers	Second Vespers
1678:	Mass	First Vespers	Second Vespers
1755:	Mass	First Vespers	Second Vespers
1761:	Mass	First Vespers	Second Vespers

August 15, Assumption of the Blessed Virgin Mary

1515:	Mass	First Vespers	Second Vespers
1677:	Mass	First Vespers	Second Vespers
1678:	Mass	First Vespers	Second Vespers
1755:	Mass	First Vespers	Second Vespers
1761:	Mass	First Vespers	Second Vespers

August 16, St. Roche

1515:	Mass	——	Second Vespers
1677:	Mass	——	Second Vespers
1678:	Mass	——	Second Vespers
1755:	——	——	Second Vespers
1761:	——	——	Second Vespers

August 24, St. Bartholomew, Apostle

1515:	Mass	First Vespers	Second Vespers
1677:	Mass	First Vespers	Second Vespers
1678:	Mass	First Vespers	Second Vespers
1755:	Mass	First Vespers	Second Vespers
1761:	Mass	First Vespers	Second Vespers

August 28, St. Augustine, Bishop, Confessor and Doctor of the Church

1515:	Mass	First Vespers	Second Vespers
1677:	Mass	First Vespers	Second Vespers
1678:	Mass	First Vespers	Second Vespers
1755:	Mass	First Vespers	Second Vespers
1761:	Mass	First Vespers	Second Vespers

August 29, Beheading of St. John the Baptist

1515:	Mass	——	Second Vespers
1677:	Mass	——	Second Vespers
1678:	Mass	——	Second Vespers[422]
1755:	Mass	——	Second Vespers
1761:	Mass	——	Second Vespers

September 8, Nativity of the Blessed Virgin Mary

1515:	Mass	First Vespers	Second Vespers
1677:	Mass	First Vespers	Second Vespers
1678:	Mass	First Vespers	Second Vespers
1755:	Mass	First Vespers	Second Vespers
1761:	Mass	First Vespers	Second Vespers

September 14, Exaltation of the Holy Cross

1515:	Mass	First Vespers	Second Vespers
1677:	Mass	First Vespers	Second Vespers
1678:	Mass	First Vespers	Second Vespers
1755:	Mass	First Vespers	Second Vespers
1761:	Mass	First Vespers	Second Vespers

September 18, St. Victor

1515:	Mass	First Vespers	——
1677:	Mass	First Vespers	——
1678:	Mass	First Vespers	——
1755:	Mass	First Vespers	——[423]
1761:	Mass	First Vespers	——

September 21, St. Matthew, Apostle and Evangelist

1515:	Mass	First Vespers	Second Vespers
1677:	Mass	First Vespers	Second Vespers
1678:	Mass	First Vespers	Second Vespers
1755:	Mass	First Vespers	Second Vespers
1761:	Mass	First Vespers	Second Vespers

September 29, Dedication of the Church of St. Michael, the Archangel

1515:	Mass	First Vespers	Second Vespers
1677:	Mass	First Vespers	Second Vespers
1678:	Mass	First Vespers	Second Vespers
1755:	Mass	First Vespers	Second Vespers
1761:	Mass	First Vespers	Second Vespers

September 30, St. Jerome, Priest, Confessor and Doctor of the Church

1515:	Mass	——	Second Vespers

1677:	——	——	——
1678:	Mass	——	Second Vespers
1755:	Mass	——	Second Vespers
1761:	Mass	——	Second Vespers

October 4, St. Francis, Confessor

1515:	Mass	First Vespers	Second Vespers
1677:	Mass	First Vespers	Second Vespers
1678:	Mass	First Vespers	Second Vespers
1755:	Mass	First Vespers	Second Vespers
1761:	Mass	First Vespers	Second Vespers

October 6, St. Magnus

1515:	Mass	First Vespers	Second Vespers
1677:	Mass	First Vespers	Second Vespers
1678:	Mass	First Vespers	Second Vespers
1755:	Mass	First Vespers	Second Vespers
1761:	Mass	First Vespers	Second Vespers

October 7, St. Giustina

1515:	Mass	——	——	Procession
1677:	Mass	First Vespers	Second Vespers	Procession
1678:	Mass	——	——	Procession
1755:	Mass	——	Second Vespers	Procession
1761:	Mass	——	Second Vespers	Procession

October 8, Dedication of the Church of St. Mark

1515:	Mass	——	Second Vespers
1677:	——	——	——
1678:	Mass	First Vespers	Second Vespers
1755:	Mass	——	Second Vespers
1761:	Mass	——	Second Vespers

October 9, Ss. Sergius and Bacchus[424]

1515:	Mass	——	Second Vespers
1677:	——	——	——
1678:	Mass	——	——
1755:	Mass	——	——
1761:	Mass	——	——

October 18, St. Luke, Evangelist

1515:	Mass	First Vespers	Second Vespers
1677:	Mass	First Vespers	Second Vespers
1678:	Mass	First Vespers	Second Vespers
1755:	Mass	First Vespers	Second Vespers
1761:	Mass	First Vespers	Second Vespers

October 28, Ss. Simon and Jude, Apostles

1515:	Mass	First Vespers	Second Vespers
1677:	Mass	First Vespers	Second Vespers
1678:	Mass	First Vespers	Second Vespers

| 1755: | Mass | First Vespers | Second Vespers | |
| 1761: | Mass | First Vespers | Second Vespers | |

November 1, Feast of All Saints

1515:	Mass	First Vespers	Second Vespers	
1677:	Mass	First Vespers	Second Vespers	
1678:	Mass	First Vespers	Second Vespers	
1755:	Mass	First Vespers	Second Vespers	
1761:	Mass	First Vespers	Second Vespers	

November 2, Commemoration of All the Faithful Departed

1515:	Mass	——	——	
1677:	Mass	——	——	Procession
1678:	Mass	——	——	——
1755:	Requiem	——	——	——
1761:	Requiem	——	——	——

November 6, St. Leonardo

1515:	Mass	First Vespers	——
1677:	Mass	First Vespers	Second Vespers
1678:	Mass	First Vespers	——
1755:	Mass	First Vespers	——
1761:	Mass	First Vespers	——

November 9, St. Theodore

1515:	Mass	First Vespers	Second Vespers
1677:	Mass	First Vespers	Second Vespers
1678:	Mass	First Vespers	Second Vespers
1755:	Mass	First Vespers	Second Vespers
1761:	Mass	First Vespers	Second Vespers

November 11, St. Martin, Bishop and Confessor

1515:	Mass	First Vespers	Second Vespers
1677:	Mass	First Vespers	Second Vespers[425]
1678:	Mass	First Vespers	Second Vespers
1755:	Mass	First Vespers	Second Vespers
1761:	Mass	First Vespers	Second Vespers

November 21, The Presentation of the Blessed Virgin Mary[426]

1515:	Mass	First Vespers	Second Vespers	Procession
1677:	Mass	First Vespers	Second Vespers	Procession
1678:	Mass	First Vespers	Second Vespers	Procession
1755:	Mass	First Vespers	Second Vespers	[Procession]

Two motets *à Capella* in Santa Maria della Salute

| 1761: | Mass | First Vespers | Second Vespers | Procession[427] |

Motets at Low Mass in Santa Maria della Salute

November 23, St. Clement, Pope and Martyr

1515:	Mass	First Vespers	——
1677:	Mass	First Vespers	——
1678:	Mass	First Vespers	——

| 1755: | Mass | First Vespers | —— |
| 1761: | Mass | First Vespers | —— |

November 25, St. Catherine, Virgin and Martyr

1515:	Mass	First Vespers	Second Vespers
1677:	Mass	First Vespers	Second Vespers
1678:	Mass	First Vespers	Second Vespers
1755:	Mass	First Vespers	Second Vespers
1761:	Mass	First Vespers	Second Vespers

November 30, St. Andrew, Apostle

1515:	Mass	First Vespers	Second Vespers
1677:	Mass	First Vespers	Second Vespers
1678:	Mass	First Vespers	Second Vespers
1755:	Mass	First Vespers	Second Vespers
1761:	Mass	First Vespers	Second Vespers

December 5, St. Nicholas, Bishop and Confessor

1515:	Mass	First Vespers[428]	Second Vespers
1677:	Mass	First Vespers	Second Vespers
1678:	Mass	First Vespers	Second Vespers
1755:	Mass[429]	First Vespers	Second Vespers
1761:	Mass[430]	First Vespers	Second Vespers

December 7, St. Ambrose, Bishop, Confessor and Doctor of the Church

1515:	Mass	——	——
1677:	Mass	——	——
1678:	Mass	——	——
1755:	Mass	——	——
1761:	Mass	——	——

December 8, Feast of the Immaculate Conception of the B. V. M.

1515:	Mass	First Vespers	Second Vespers	
1677:	Mass	First Vespers	Second Vespers	
1678:	Mass	First Vespers	Second Vespers	
1755:	Mass	First Vespers	Second Vespers	
1761:	Mass	First Vespers	Second Vespers	Procession[431]

December 13, St. Lucy, Virgin and Martyr

1515:	Mass	First Vespers	Second Vespers
1677:	Mass	First Vespers	Second Vespers
1678:	Mass	First Vespers	Second Vespers
1755:	Mass	First Vespers	Second Vespers
1761:	Mass	First Vespers	Second Vespers

December 21, St. Thomas, Apostle

1515:	Mass	First Vespers	Second Vespers
1677:	Mass	First Vespers	Second Vespers
1678:	Mass	First Vespers	Second Vespers
1755:	Mass	First Vespers	Second Vespers
1761:	Mass	First Vespers	Second Vespers

December 24, Christmas Eve

1515:	Mass	First Vespers[432]	——	Matins
1677:	Mass	First Vespers	——	Matins[433]
1678:	Mass	First Vespers	——	Matins
1755:	Mass	First Vespers	——	——
1761:	Mass	First Vespers	——	Matins

December 25, Nativity of Our Lord, Christmas Day

1515:	Mass	——	Second Vespers
1677:	Mass	——	Second Vespers[433]
1678:	Mass	——	Second Vespers
1755:	Mass	——	Second Vespers
1761:	Mass	——	Second Vespers

December 26, St. Stephen, the First Martyr

1515:	Mass	——	Second Vespers
1677:	Mass	——	Second Vespers[434]
1678:	Mass	——	Second Vespers
1755:	Mass	——	Second Vespers
1761:	Mass	——	Second Vespers

December 27, St. John, Apostle and Evangelist

1515:	Mass	——	Second Vespers
1677:	Mass	——	Second Vespers[435]
1678:	Mass	——	Second Vespers
1755:	Mass	——	Second Vespers
1761:	Mass	——	Second Vespers

December 28, Feast of the Holy Innocents

1515:	Mass	——	Second Vespers
1677:	Mass	——	Second Vespers
1678:	Mass	——	Second Vespers
1755:	Mass	——	Second Vespers
1761:	Mass	——	Second Vespers

December 31, St. Silvester, Pope and Confessor

1515:	Mass	First Vespers	Second Vespers
1677:	Mass	First Vespers	Second Vespers
1678:	Mass	First Vespers	Second Vespers
1755:	Mass	First Vespers	——
1761:	Mass	First Vespers	——

All Sundays of the year

1515:	Mass	——	Second Vespers
1677:	Mass	——	Second Vespers
1678:	Mass	——	Second Vespers
1755:	Mass	——	Second Vespers
1761:	Mass	——	Second Vespers

All Sundays of Lent

1515:	——	——	Second Vespers	Compline

1677:	—	—	—	Compline
1678:	Mass	—	Second Vespers	Compline
1755:	—	—	Second Vespers	Compline
1761:	—	—	Second Vespers	Compline

All Saturdays on which a Mass of the Virgin is sung:

1515:	—
1677:	Mass (specified as 47 Saturdays per year)
1678:	Mass[435]
1755:	Mass
1761:	Mass

Thursday before Lent

1515:	—[436]
1677:	—
1678:	—[436]
1755:	Mass
1761:	Mass

All Saturdays of Lent

1515:	—	—	Second Vespers
1677:	—	—	—
1678:	—	—	Second Vespers
1755:	—	—	Second Vespers
1761:	—	—	Second Vespers

Palm Sunday

1515:	—	—	—	—
	Passion[437]			
1677:	Mass	—	Second Vespers	Compline
1678:	—	—	—	—
1755:	Mass	—	Second Vespers	Compline
	Passion			
1761:	Mass	—	Second Vespers	Compline

After the antiphon during the ceremony of throwing out the birds and the ceremony at the church door[438]

Tuesday in Holy Week

1515:	—	—	—	—
1677:	Passion	—	—	—
1678:	Passion	—	—	—
1755:	Passion	—	—	—
1761:	Passion	—	—	—

Wednesday in Holy Week

1515:	—	—	—	Matins
1677:	—	—	—	Matins
1678:	—	—	—	Matins
1755:	—	—	—	Matins
1761:	—	—	—	Matins: first three lessons, *Benedictus* and *Miserere*

Maundy Thursday
1515:	Mass	——	——	Matins
1677:	Display of the Most Precious Blood			Matins
1678:	——	——	——	——
1755:	Mass	——	——	Matins

Exposition of the Most Precious Blood, four singers only[439]
| 1761: | Mass | —— | —— | Matins, Procession |

Communion Hymn; four [singers] for the Hymn for the Exposition of the Most Precious Blood[440]

Good Friday
1515:	Mass	——	——	Matins, Procession
	Passion			
1677:	Mass	——	——	Matins, ——
1678:	Mass	——	——	Matins, Procession
1755:	Mass	——	——	Matins, Procession
	Passion			
1761:	Responsories after the prophecies			Matins, Procession
	Passion			Reproaches in two
	Four singers for the hymn at the Adoration of the Cross			choirs

Holy Saturday
1515:	Mass[441]	——	——	
1677:	Mass	——	——	
1678:	Mass[442]	——	——	
1755:	Mass	——	Second Vespers	
1761:	Responsories after the prophecies			
	Hymn *Rex Sanctorum*			
	Mass	Second Vespers		

Easter Sunday
1515:	Mass	——	Second Vespers	Procession[443]
1677:	Mass	——	Second Vespers	——
1678:	Mass	——	Second Vespers	Procession[444]
1755:	Mass	——	Second Vespers	Ceremonia della Porta
1761:	Mass	——	Second Vespers	Ceremonia della Porta

Easter Monday, Easter Tuesday
1515:	Mass	——	Second Vespers	Procession
1677:	Mass	——	Second Vespers	——
1678:	Mass	——	Second Vespers	Procession[444]
1755:	Mass	——	Second Vespers	
1761:	Mass	——	Second Vespers	

Low Sunday
1515:	Mass	——	Second Vespers	Procession
1677:	Mass	——	Second Vespers	——
1678:	Mass	——	——	Procession
1755:	Mass	——	——	Procession with
	or two motets[445]			antiphon

1761:	Mass	——	——	Procession with antiphon *Dum transisset*

Eight days before and eight days after the Feast of the Ascension

1515:	——	——	Second Vespers	
1677:	——	——	Second Vespers	
1678:	——	——	Second Vespers	
1755:	——	——	Second Vespers	
1761:	——	——	Second Vespers	

Monday and Tuesday before Ascension

1515:	——	——	——	Greater Litanies with four singers in procession
1677:	Mass	——	——	Procession
1678:	——	——	——	——
1755:	——	——	——	Four singers for Litanies
1761:	——	——	——	Four singers for Litanies

Vigil of the Ascension

1515:	Mass	——	Second Vespers	Greater Litanies
1677:	Mass	——	Second Vespers	——
	Display of the Most Precious Blood			
1678:	Mass	——	Second Vespers	Procession
1755:	Mass	——	Second Vespers	Procession of the Rogations
1761:	Mass	——	Second Vespers	Rogations

Ascension of Our Lord

1515:	Benediction of the Sea at Mass in San Nicolò on the Lido	Second Vespers	——
1677:	Mass in San Nicolò	Second Vespers	——
1678:	Mass in San Nicolò	Second Vespers	Bucintoro ceremony
1755:	Mass in San Nicolò	Second Vespers	Bucintoro ceremony
1761:	Mass in San Nicolò	Second Vespers	Bucintoro ceremony[446]

Vigil of Pentecost

1515:	Mass	——	Second Vespers
1677:	Mass	——	Second Vespers
1678:	Mass	——	Second Vespers
1755:	Mass	——	Second Vespers
1761:	Mass	——	Second Vespers

Feast of Pentecost

1515:	Mass	——	Second Vespers
1677:	Mass	——	Second Vespers
1678:	Mass	——	Second Vespers
1755:	Mass	——	Second Vespers
1761:	Mass	——	Second Vespers

Monday and Tuesday in Whitsun Week

1515:	Mass	——	Second Vespers
1677:	Mass	——	Second Vespers
1678:	Mass	——	Second Vespers
1755:	Mass	——	Second Vespers
1761:	Mass	——	Second Vespers

Feast of the Blessed Trinity

1515:	Mass	First Vespers	Second Vespers
1677:	Mass	First Vespers	Second Vespers
1678:	Mass	First Vespers	Second Vespers
1755:	Mass	First Vespers	Second Vespers
1761:	Mass	First Vespers	Second Vespers

Corpus Christi

1515:	Mass	First Vespers	Second Vespers	Matins
1677:	Mass	First Vespers	Second Vespers	——
1678:	Mass	First Vespers	Second Vespers	Matins
1755:	Mass	First Vespers	Second Vespers	——
1761:	Mass	First Vespers	Second Vespers	——

1515:	Procession
1677:	Procession
1678:	Procession
1755:	Procession, hymn in two choirs
1761:	Procession with hymn; four singers at the pauses, and at the *Tantum ergo* before the Benediction [of the Blessed Sacrament].

1515:

In all simple feasts of the entire year at Mass, as is the custom, except Friday and Saturday, provided that one of the above-mentioned feasts does not occur, [and] with the exception of Monday, Tuesday and Wednesday of Holy Week.

But when the Little Chapel is not present, the singers sing Sunday Mass on Saturday, in which case they are exempt from service on Thursday unless there be a feast.

1761:

Sundays of semi-double rank after Pentecost; the usual *versetti* during the pauses in the *Salve Regina*.[447]

During the carrying of the picture of the Virgin from its usual place up to the main altar: the hymn *O Gloriosa Domina*.

All the days to which feasts of the Lord, the Virgin, or the Saints are transferred if they cannot be celebrated on the proper day.

The Tridua of the Virgin:

| Mass | —— | Vespers | Procession with Litanies and prayers according to public command. |

If the Tridua are deferred by an Octave, Mass and Vespers for the entire
Octave, and longer if it is commanded.

The election of a Pope:
   1677:   Mass
   1761:   Mass and *Te Deum*

Death of a Pope
   1677:   Three Masses, one per day
   1761:   Messa da *Requiem* for the triduum
              Office of the Dead
              Misere in procession

Election of the procurators:
   1677:   motets
   1761:   two motets *a pieno* with the organ

Day of the coronation of the Doge
   1515:   Mass
   1677:   Mass
   1678:   Mass
   1755:   ——
   1761:   Mass and Te Deum as in the Christmas Vigil[448]

Anniversary of the coronation of the Doge
   1515:   ——
   1677:   Mass
   1678:   Mass
   1755:   ——
   1761:   Mass and *Te Deum* as in the Christmas Vigil

Death of a Doge
   1515:   ——
   1677:   Three Masses, one per day   Matins   Procession, carrying the Doge to the tomb, singing the *Miserere*

   1678:   ——
   1755:   ——
   1761:   ——

Notes

Chapter I

1. Heinrich Schütz, *Symphoniae Sacrae* (Venice: Gardano/Magni, 1629): ". . . Venetijs apus veteres amicos commoratus, cognovi modulandi rationem non nihil immutatam antiquos numeros ex parte deposuisse, hodernis auribus recenti allusuram titillatione; ad cuius ego normam ut aliqua tibi de meae industriae penu pro instituto depromerem, hunc animum, et vires adieci."

2. See in particular Martin Seelkopf, "Italienische Elemente in den Kleinen geistlichen Konzerten von Heinrich Schütz," *Musikforschung* XXV (1972): 452–64; Jerome Roche, "What Schütz learnt from Grandi in 1629," *Musical Times* CXIII (1972): 1074–75; Denis Arnold, "Monteverdi: some Colleagues and Pupils," *The Monteverdi Companion* (New York: Norton, 1968), p. 127; Hans Joachim Moser, *Heinrich Schütz: Sein Leben und Werk*, 2nd ed. (Kassel and Basel: Bärenreiter, 1954).

3. Leo Schrade, *Monteverdi, the Creator of Modern Music* (New York: Norton, 1950): 315–16; see also Arnold, "Formal Design in Monteverdi's Church Music," *Congresso internazionale sul tema Claudio Monteverdi e il suo tempo* (Venice, Mantua, Cremona, 1968), p. 187.

4. There are, of course, collections from the seventeenth century which mix these two categories and are organized around individual feasts, as Stephen Bonta has noted ("Liturgical Problems in Monteverdi's Marian Vespers," *Journal of the American Musicological Society* XX [1967]: 104). However, even in the seventeenth century these collections are exceptional, and the collections which contain either Vespers psalms and Magnificats or *motetti* are the more numerous. See Jeffrey Kurtzman, *Essays on the Monteverdi Mass and Vespers of 1610* (Rice University Studies, Vol. 64, No. 4, 1978) and James Armstrong, "The *Antiphonae, seu Sacrae Cantiones* (1613) of Francesco Anerio: A Liturgical Study," *Analecta Musicologica* XIV (1974): 89–150.

5. For a discussion of the idiom of these works, see Jerome Roche, "Monteverdi and the *Prima Prattica*," *The Monteverdi Companion*, ed. Denis Arnold and Nigel Fortune (New York: Norton, 1968), pp. 187–89.

6. The biographical information on Grandi, first assembled by Caffi, has since been expanded by both Denis Arnold ("Alessandro Grandi, A Disciple of Monteverdi," *Musical Quarterly* XLIII (1957): 171–86) and Jerome Roche ("Music at Santa Maria Maggiore in Bergamo, 1614–43," *Music and Letters* XLVII (1966): 296–312). The best summary

to date is found in Martin Seelkopf, "Das Geistliche Schaffen von Alessandro Grandi," unpublished Ph.D. dissertation, Julius-Maximilians-Universität zu Würzburg, 1973.

7. Ferrara, Biblioteca Ariostea, Collezione Antonelli, MS 22. Cited in Arnold, "Grandi/Disciple," p. 171 and in Seelkopf, "Schaffen/Grandi," p. 5.

8. Reproduced in Seelkopf, "Schaffen/Grandi," p. 6.

9. Since the Venetian calendar began on 1 March, January and February were still dated according to the preceding year. Thus, the Venetian version (*more veneto*) of all dates in January and February is one year earlier than the modern version. Modern dating has been used throughout the text of this study, though documents quoted in the appendix have been quoted in their original form.

10. Stephen Bonta has thrown considerable doubt on the reliability of Biblioteca Ariostea, Collezione Antonelli, MS 22. He states that the manuscript was compiled sometime between 1693 and 1712, that nothing is known about its origin or compiler, and that the information occasionally conflicts with more certain sources. (Stephen Bonta, "The Church Sonatas of Giovanni Legrenzi," unpublished Ph.D. dissertation, Harvard, 1964, p. 32).

11. Arnold, "Grandi/Disciple," p. 171.

12. It is possible, of course, that the Ferrarese and Venetian documents refer to two musicians with the same name, but we have no evidence for the existence of two separate figures at this time. There *does* seem to have been another Alessandro Grandi later in the century, represented by Bolognese publications of 1680, 1693 and 1707. However, the dates of his publications and the style of his music put him out of consideration in this discussion. See Arnold, *loc. cit.*

13. Hans Joachim Moser, *Heinrich Schütz: His Life and Work*, trans. Carl F. Pfatteicher (St. Louis: Concordia, 1959), p. 28.

14. See Roche, "What Schütz learnt from Grandi in 1629," *Musical Times* CXIII (1972): 1074–75.

15. On the two *accademie* served by Grandi see Arnold, "Grandi/Disciple," p. 172 and Seelkopf, "Schaffen/Grandi," p. 7. The regulations of both academies are extant in the Biblioteca Ariostea in Ferrara: Carlo Festini, *Ordini Stabiliti per il buon governo dell'Accademia dello Santo Spirito di Ferrara* (G. Gironi, Stampator'Episcopale, Ferrara, 1636) and *Ordini Stabiliti per lo governo dell'Accademia della Compagnia della Morte in Ferrara* (G. Gironi, Stampator'Episcopale, Ferrara, 1648). According to Arnold, the academies seem not to have been associations of intellectuals but rather charitable and religious organizations, not unlike the Venetian *scuole*. Musicians took a subordinate, subservient position in both of them and were not considered "academici." The permanent musical employees consisted of a *maestro di cappella*, organist, and what seem to be four solo singers: soprano, alto, tenor and bass. The musicians employed include some notable figures; both Luzzaschi and Frescobaldi were employed by the Accademia della Morte. See also Michele Maylender, *Storia delle Accademie d'Italia* IV: 61–62; and V: 248. Contrary to Arnold's view, Maylender says that both institutions are listed among the *accademie musicali* in Girolamo Baruffaldi, *Notizie Istoriche delle Accademie Letterarie Ferraresi* (Ferrara, 1787).

16. The Accademia degli Intrepidi was established in 1601 to fill the social and cultural position which the Este court had held before the death of Alfonso II in 1597. Further information on the Accademia is contained in Girolamo Baruffaldi, *op. cit.* 25-31; see also Seelkopf, "Schaffen/Grandi," p. 8.

17. Arnold, article "Grandi" in *Die Musik in Geschichte und Gegenwart*, V, col. 1380.

18. Roche, "Music/Bergamo," p. 306. Grandi left Venice sometime before his appointment at Bergamo. An act of the Procurators of 31 March 1626 names a successor to Grandi as *maestro di canto* for the seminary.

19. Roche, "Music/Bergamo," pp. 300, 307-8. There is much material on the musical establishment at Santa Maria Maggiore during the mid-seventeenth century which still awaits publication. I am indebted to Stephen Bonta and John Westcott for allowing me to examine reproductions of a number of seventeenth-century documents from the Misericordia Maggiore, and to Mr. Westcott for allowing me to read his unpublished study, "Music at Santa Maria Maggiore under Alessandro Grandi, 1627-1630."

20. See the Archives of the Misericordia Maggiore, *Inventarium* (LXXIX-1), ff. 129-30: Adi 13 Gennaro 1628. Inventario de' libri del canto figurato consegnati in mano del S.r Alessandro Grandi Maestro/di Capella in S. Maria Maggiore fatto adi 13 Gennaro 1628. (Quoted in Jerome Roche, "An Inventory of Choirbooks at S. Maria Maggiore, Bergamo, January 1628," *R. M. A. Research Chronicle* No. 5 [1965], pp. 47-51).

21. Donati-Pettini, *L'Arte della Musica in Bergamo* (Bergamo, 1930), p. 16; quoted in Seelkopf, "Schaffen/Grandi," p. 12.

22. Renate Günther, "Motette und Geistliches Konzert im Schaffen von Alessandro Grandi (ca. 1577-1630)," unpublished Ph.D. dissertation, Freie Universität Berlin, 1958, p. 17.

23. The possibilities of a relationship between Croce and Grandi are discussed in Arnold, "Giovanni Croce and the *Concertato* Style," *Musical Quarterly* XXXIX (1953): 37-48.

24. See Arnold, "Grandi/Disciple," pp. 182-85; and idem, "Monteverdi: some Colleagues and Pupils," pp. 123-27.

25. Günther, op. cit., p. 17.

26. LA VENETIA EDIFICATA/POEMA EROICO/DI GIULIO STROZZI/Con gli Argomenti/Del Sig. Francesco Cortesi/In Venetia appresso Girolamo Piuti .... IN VENETIA, MDCXXVI./Di Ordine dell'Autore./Appresso Girolamo Piuti./Al Monte Parnaso. Strozzi's poem is a sort of Venetian *Aeneid* for the "Città, che regna ancor Donna dell'acuqe" (Canto Primo, Stanza 2), which traces the city back to its origins at the time of Attila the Hun. Grandi and Monteverdi are mentioned in the following passage (1626 edition, p. 396):

> S'il *Grandi* allor, s'il *Monteverde* a gara
> In vestir sacri, o lascivetti carmi
> Con dolce canto, e sinfonia sì rara
> Stati in quella stagion fossero in armi.
> Qual dalle lor discordie illustre, e cara
> Consonanza nascea dentro à que'marmi,

Dove la Maga in quelle fiamme estive
S'ingegna d'allettar l'alme più schive.

If Grandi, then, in competition with Monteverdi
in sacred garb and [secular] song
with sweet melody and delicious symphonies
had been in arms in that season,
which of the illustrious discords and sweet
consonances was born within those marble [walls]
where the sorceress in those estival flames
strives to make the downcast souls happy?

27. Arnold, "Monteverdi: some Colleagues and Pupils," p. 123.

28. Arnold, *Monteverdi* (London: Dent, 1975), p. 30.

29. Domenico de' Paoli, ed., *Claudio Monteverdi: Lettere, Dediche e Prefazioni* (Rome: Edizioni de Santis, 1973), p. 149. ".... che in capella non si acetta cantore che prima non pigliono il parere del Maestro di capella, nè vogliono altra relatione di cause de cantori che quella del Maestro di Capella, nè accettano, nè organisti nè Vicemaestro, se non hanno il parere et la relatione da esso Maestro di Capella...."

30. Decree appointing Bartolo Moresini as first *vice-maestro di cappella* of St. Mark's. A.S.V., San Marco, Procuratia de Supra, Registro 139, f. 180v.

31. Arnold, article "Rovetta" in *Die Musik in Geschichte und Gegenwart* XI, col. 1020.

32. Caffi misquotes this date as 17 December 1623. Rovetta was presented to the Doge on 24 December 1623 (Document 6).

33. A.S.V., San Marco, Procuratia de Supra, Registro 141, decree of 7 December 1614.

34. A.S.V., San Marco, Procuratia de Supra, Registro 141, decree of 12 March 1617.

35. Misdated as 1630 in Jane Glover, *Cavalli* (New York: St. Martin's Press, 1978), p. 122.

36. See A.S.V., San Marco, Procuratia de Supra, Registro 143 (entry of 22 March 1635) and Registro 144 (entries of 28 March 1640 and 1 March 1642).

37. Biblioteca Nazionale Marciana, Misc. 180. 17. VENETIA FESTIVA/PER GLI POMPOSI SPETTACOLI/FATTI RAPPRESENTARE/Dall'Illustriss*imo* et Eccellentiss*imo* Sig*nor* d'Husè/Ambasciatore di S*ua* Maest*à* Christianissima,/PER LA NASCITA DEL REAL DELFINO DI FRANCIA.... IN VENETIA, MDCXXXVIII.... Appresso Andrea Baba. I am grateful to Ellen Rosand for drawing my attention to this volume.

38. Istituzioni di Ricovero e di Educazione Venezia, *Arte e Musica all'Ospedaletto. Schede d'archivio sull'attività musicale degli ospedali dei Derelitti e dei Mendicanti di Venezia* (sec. XVI–XVIII) (Venice: Stamperia di Venezia Editrice, 1978), p. 43.

39. Ibid., pp. 157, 168.

40. A.S.V., Fondo Monastero Spirito Santo. I am indebted to Thomas Walker for this information.

41. Caffi misquotes this date as 21 July 1643.

42. A.S.V., San Marco, Procuratia de Supra, Busta 90, Processo 204. Selected passages from a few of the letters are published in Arnold, "The Monteverdian Succession at St. Mark's," *Music and Letters* XLII (1961): 205–11.

43. Arnold erroneously cites him as an organist rather than as *maestro di cappella*.

44. See letter from Jacomo Razzi, a singer at St. Mark's, to Carissimi in Thomas D. Culley, S. F., *Jesuits and Music: A Study of the Musicians connected with the German College in Rome during the Seventeenth Century and of their Activities in Northern Europe* (Rome and St. Louis: Jesuit Historical Institute, 1970), pp. 185–87; 332–33.

45. A.S.V., San Marco, Procuratia de Supra, Busta 90, Processo 204, f. 56r.

46. ERCOLE/IN/LIDIA/Dramma/Del Signor Conte/MAIOLINO BISACCIONI/ Gentil'huomo della Camera/del RE Christianissimo./Rappresentata nel Teatro Novissimo/Nell'Anno 1645./(device)/IN VENETIA, MDCXIV./Per Giovanni Vecellio, e Matteo Leni/Con Licenza de' Superiori, e Privilegi.

    ARGIOPE/FAVOLA MUSICALE/Di N. [*sic*] e DI/GIO: BATTISTA FUSCONI./Consacrata/AL CHIARO MERITO/Della Signora/ANNA RENZI/(device)/IN VENETIA, M. DC. XLIX./Appresso Gio: Pietro Pinelli,/Con Licenza, de' Superiori, et Privilegio.

47. John Evelyn, *Diary* I: 202. Quoted in Donald Grout, *A Short History of Opera*, 2nd ed. (New York: Columbia University Press, 1965), p. 99.

48. On Anna Renzi as well as the Venetian operatic scene in the 1640s, see Claudio Sartori, "Un fantomatico compositore per un'opera che forse non era un'opera," *Nuova Rivista Musicale Italiana* V (1971): 788–98.

49. W. Gurlitt, "Ein Briefwechzel zwischen Paul Hainlein und L. Friedrich Behaim aus den Jahren 1647–48," *Sammelbände der internationalen Musikgesellschaft* IV (1912–13): 491–99.

50. See, among other documents, A.S.V., San Marco, Procuratia de Supra, Registro 12, payment list for 3 April 1645; special payments on 15 March 1645. Rovetta kept these positions until the end of his life; see A.S.V., San Marco, Procuratia de Supra, Registro 146, two entries of 24 October 1668.

51. A.S.V., Archivio Notarile, Testamenti, Busta 281 (Francesco Ciola), Testamento n.o 113.

52. The Requiem must have been composed before 1663, for the Procurators authorized 22 ducats, 16 grossi for its copying and binding on 28 May 1663. See Document 15.

53. These two compositions are preserved in Biblioteca Nazionale Marciana, Cod. It. IV-1134 (-10949), fascicolo 2.

54. Caffi's statement (I: 266) that Rovetta died sometime in August was a mere assumption, evidently based on the date of registration of the will.

55. *Salmi concertati* (Venice: Magni, 1627).

56. de' Paoli, *Lettere*, p. 275: "…. faccio poi in capella quello voglio io; poichè vi è il sotto maestro adimandato Vice Maestro di Capella …."

57. Reproduced in Gaspari's catalogue of what is now the Civico Museo Bibliografico Musicale, Bologna, III: 165.

58. The most important contributions to Cavalli's biography after Caffi are Taddeo Wiel, "Francesco Cavalli e la sua musica scenica," *Nuovo Archivio Veneto*, nuova serie, XXVIII (1914): 106–50; Henry Prunières, *Cavalli et l'opéra vénitien au XVIIe siècle* (Paris: Editions Riediers, 1931); Denis Arnold, "Francesco Cavalli: some recently discovered documents," *Music and Letters* XLVI (1965): 50–55. A complete synthesis of the biographical material is found in Lorenzo Bianconi, "Caletti (Caletti-Bruni)," *Dizionario biografico degli italiani* (Rome: Istituto della Enciclopedia Italiana, 1973), 686–696. An English synthesis of the material is found in Jane Glover, *Cavalli* (New York: St. Martin's Press, 1978), 11–39. Those events of Cavalli's life recorded in autograph documents are discussed in Peter Jeffrey, "The Autograph Manuscripts of Francesco Cavalli," unpublished Ph.D. dissertation, Princeton University, 1980.

59. The document as given was emended by a contemporary clerk. Originally the passage refers to "soprani eunuchi." Evidently the ducal secretary mistook Cavalli for a *castrato* initially and the document had to be corrected afterwards.

60. These audition trials seem to have dropped out of use sometime in the seventeenth century, though it is difficult to determine exactly when they became obsolete. In Giovanni Pace's *Ceremoniale Magnum* (1678), the table of contents lists the item "Ballotat*ione* d'Organista non più pratticata," though this material does not actually appear in the body of the volume.

61. Two writers have recognized Caffi's error, in part. Lorenzo Bianconi, noting the discrepancies between a number of the documents, concludes that Cavalli may have inherited the duties of first organist in 1645 while Neri held the title (Bianconi, op. cit., 686). Selfridge-Field tentatively lists Cavalli as first organist in 1645 but expresses reservations (Eleanor Selfridge-Field, *Venetian Instrumental Music from Gabrieli to Vivaldi* [New York: Praeger, 1975], 295).

62. A.S.V., San Marco, Procuratia de Supra, Registro 12.

63. Quoted in Francesco Bussi, "La produzione sacra di Cavalli e i suoi rapporti con quella di Monteverdi," *Rivista Italiana di Musicologia* II (1967): 233.

64. Gurlitt, op. cit., 491–99. Letter of 13 December 1647: "Was Organisten betrifft, wirtt des *Frescobaldi* gleichen nit mehr anzutreffen sein, und lest sich der jenige, so ein gutter practicus, nit allezeit hören, so wohl alss hier *Sig: Cavalli* in *S: Marco*." Letter of 1 November 1647: "Ist auch dess schlagen nit so gemein, alss wie in Teutschlandt an Bäbstischen orten, dan man in der wochen keine Orgeln rühren thut, auch die Sonabent nit, ess falle dan ein fest mit ein, lest sich auch der beste organist namens *Sig: Gaballi* [sic] in *S: Marco* nit hören, es sey den den hertzog dabey, welches doch selten geschicht."

65. Arnold, "Francesco Cavalli: some recently discovered documents," *Music and Letters* XLVI (1965): 50–55.

66. A.S.V., Fondo Monastero Spirito Santo and Reg. Monialium Archivio Curia Patriarcale. I am indebted to Thomas Walker for information on these two services.

67. Quoted in Prunières, *Cavalli*, pp. 36–37.

68. On the request for Cavalli's departure, see also A.S.V., Collegio, Esposizioni Principi, Filza 75, f. 43r and Registro 70, f. 7v.

69. Most sources list the fourteenth as the date of death, but this is the date Cavalli's will was notarized and when, according to the notary Paulini, he was still "sano, Merce del Signore, di mente, et intelleto se ben amalato essendo in letto in casa della sua habitatione posta nelle Canoniche di San Marco." Prunières gives the seventeenth as the date of death, but it is not clear from the listing in the *necrologio* of the *Provveditori alla Sanità* that the numeral 17 refers to a date. The entry itself is dated 25 January.

70. Wiel, "Francesco Cavalli e la sua musica scenica," pp. 142–50. A number of copies of the will are preserved in A.S.V., San Lorenzo di Venezia, Busta 23, fascicolo 21 (L) and Busta 24, fascicolo CC. The original, the first half of which is in Cavalli's own hand, is found in A.S.V., Archivio Notarile, Busta 488 (Testamenti Garzoni Paulini Domenico), no. 206.

71. Wiel, op. cit., p. 148.

72. See, for example, Prunières, *Cavalli*, p. 42.

73. "Havendo però riguardo di congrua recognitione ad essa Signor Maestro di Capella, ò altro, che havesse l'incombenza della Compositione di essa Messa: à distintione delli altri Musici, e Suonatori."

74. The work is preserved in five manuscripts: Dresden, Sächsische Landesbibliothek, 1702 MS, Dl; Münster, Bischöfliche Bibliothek Santini, Sant. Hs. 1024; Biblioteca Nazionale Marciana, Cod. It. IV-711 (10351); Berlin, Deutsche Staatsbibliothek; Vienna, Oesterreichische Nationalbibliothek. Francesco Bussi cites these five sources in his "Storia, Tradizione e Arte nel 'Requiem' di Cavalli," *Nuova rivista musicale italiana* X (1976): 49–77. The article is primarily a long, descriptive analysis of the double-choir Requiem. Bussi tries to apply the instrumentation listed in Cavalli's will to this work; he does not see that Cavalli is speaking of two different works in the will.

75. The canon of Cavalli's works has recently been reduced from the list of over 40 operas formerly ascribed to him. See Thomas Walker, "Gli errori di 'Minerva al tavolino': osservazioni sulla cronologia delle prime opere veneziane," *Venezia e il melodramma nel Seicento* (Venice: Fondazione Giorgio Cini, 1972).

76. A.S.V., Scuola Grande di San Marco, Busta 194, ff. 266r–267r. See also Glover, op. cit., 23, and Jeffrey, op. cit.

77. See below, Volume II, no. 22.

78. See Wolfgang Osthoff, "Neue Beobachtungen zu Quellen und Geschichte von Monteverdi's 'Incoronazione di Poppea,'" *Musikforschung* XI (1958): 129–38. For quite a different interpretation of the same facts, see Anna Mondolfi Bossarelli, "Ancora intorno al codice napoletano della *Incoronazione di Poppea*," *Rivista Italiana di Mu-

sicologia II (1967): 294–313. Peter Jeffrey has recently identified the hand of Acts I and III of the manuscript as that of a Cavalli copyist, Maria Cavalli, and one of the hands which provide *marginalia* as that of Cavalli himself. See Jeffrey, op. cit.

Chapter II

79. There are two exceptions to this principle among the prints studied. Rovetta's *Salmi concertati* (Venice: Magni, 1627) contains four motets (two of them Marian antiphons); Cavalli's *Musiche Sacre* (Venice: Vincenti, 1656) contains five hymn settings as well as all four Marian antiphons. These, however, are contrary to the general rule.

80. The chief secondary sources here are, for Grandi: Seelkopf, "Schaffen/Grandi," pp. 18–19, 34; for Rovetta: Adam Adrio, "Ambrosius Profe (1589–1661) als Herausgeber italienischer Musik seiner Zeit," *Festschrift Karl Gustav Fellerer zum Sechzigsten Geburtstag* (Regensburg: Bosse Verlag, 1962), pp. 20–27.

81. Arnold, "Grandi/Disciple," p. 183.

82. All contents are taken from the basso continuo partbook, unless otherwise stated.

83. Contents of print published in Francesco Bussi, *Piacenza, Archivio del Duomo: Catalogo del Fondo Musicale*, Biblioteca Musicae V (Milan, 1967): 54.

84. The use of the term *concertato* in the title of this collection seems analogous to its use in collections such as Rovetta's *motetti concertati*—works written for a group of soloists with basso continuo accompaniment but without any obbligato instruments.

85. Roche, "Music/Bergamo," p. 307.

86. Seelkopf, "Schaffen/Grandi," p. 267.

87. Biblioteca Nazionale Marciana. 230. d. 26. PSALTERIUM/DAVIDICUM./PER HEBDOMADAM DISPOSITUM./AD USUM ECCLESIAE DUCALIS SANCTI MARCI VENETIARUM./Cum omnibus, quae pro Psalmis, Hymnis, et Antiphonis, in Divinis Officijs necessaria sunt . . . VENETIIS. M DC IX.

88. ".... divisi in duobus choris, viz, quatuor cantores in uno choro, et reliqui omnes in altero ...." Biblioteca Nazionale Marciana, Cod. Lat. III-172 (-2276), f. 37r. See below for a further discussion of the significance of this document and a complete transcription of its contents (Document 94). It is a statement which has been overlooked by scholars so far and which, obviously, has great implications for the performance of double-choir psalms in St. Mark's.

89. See Denis Arnold, "Giovanni Croce and the *Concertato* Style," *Musical Quarterly* XXXIX (1953): 37–48.

90. Copy listed in RISM but not included in Bernard Huys, *Catalogue des Imprimés des XVe, XVIe, et XVIIe siècles. Fonds Général.* (Brussels: Bibliothèque Royale de Belgique, 1965).

91. Contents published in Claudio Sartori, *Bibliografia della musica strumentale in Italia fino al 1700* (Florence: Olschki, 1968) II, item 1617j.

92. Listed in RISM but not included in Huys, op. cit.

93. Contents published in Sartori, op. cit., I, 1621e.

94. Contents listed in Bussi, Piacenza catalogue, ut supra.

95. Contents published: Sartori 1637b.

96. Contents published: Sartori 1629b.

97. Contents listed in Bussi, Piacenza catalogue, 53.

98. Contents listed in Bussi, Piacenza catalogue, 53–54.

99. Contents listed in Rafael Mitjana, *Catalogue Critique et Descriptif des Imprimés de Musique des XVIe et XVIIe siècles conservés à la Bibliothèque de l'Université Royale d'Upsala* (Uppsala: Almquist et Wiksell, 1911) I, col. 129.

100. Seelkopf, "Schaffen/Grandi," pp. 18–19, 34.

101. I should make one addition to the list on p. 19 of Seelkopf, "Schaffen/Grandi." The second part of Johann Donfried's *Promptuarium musicum* (Strassburg: Ledertz, 1623) contains four motets of Grandi. "Cantabo Domino," "Caro mea vere est cibus," and "Quam dilecta tabernacula" are from his *Primo Libro de Motetti* (Venice, 1610); "In dedicatione templi" is from the *Terzo Libro* (Venice, 1614).

102. The following discussion enumerates the sources of the major manuscript copies of Grandi's works.
     The extensive series of manuscripts in the Biblioteca del Seminario in Lucca (Emilio Maggini, *Lucca, Biblioteca del Seminario, Catalogo delle Musiche Stampate e Manoscritte del Fondo Antico* [Milano, 1965], pp. 267–68) are actually transcriptions into score of the works of a second Alessandro Grandi, whose three prints appeared between 1680 and 1693 (see RISM, *Einzeldrucke*, III: 323). The manuscripts in the Library of Christ Church College, Oxford, are from the first, second, fourth and sixth books of motets, though the setting of "O bone Jesu" was surely taken from Playford's *Cantica Sacra* (1662) rather than from Grandi's second book itself (see G. E. P. Arkwright, *Catalogue of Music in the Library of Christ Church College, Oxford*, Part I [London: Oxford University Press, 1915], p. 55).
     Of the manuscript works listed by Eitner (*Quellenlexikon*, III: 336), all seem to be copies of existing works. The works Eitner cites in Breslau (Wroclaw) are taken from the *Ghirlanda Sacra* (1625) and from the fourth book of Grandi's motets (Emil Bohn, *Die musikalischen Handschriften des XVI. und XVII. Jahrhunderts in der Stadtbibliothek zu Breslau. Ein Beitrag zur Geschichte der Musik in XVI. und XVIII. Jahrhundert.* [Breslau: Hainauer, 1890], p. 138). The source citation in the index (p. 304) seems to be incorrect. The two works in manuscript in the Fitzwilliam Library, Cambridge, are taken from the first and second books of motets (J. A. Fuller-Maitland and A. H. Mann, *Catalogue of Music in the Fitzwilliam Museum* [London: Cambridge Press, 1893], p. 123). The "Cantabo" from Oxford Christ Church library is from the *Ghirlanda Sacra*. The manuscripts from Kremsmünster are most likely transcriptions from the printed collections of Grandi which are found there (Altman Kellner, *Musikgeschichte des Stiftes Kremsmünster* . . . [Kassel und Basel: Bärenreiter, 1956], pp. 203, 218).

103. Contents published: Sartori 1626a.

104. See LU, 282 and 1773, 285 and 1742; *Antiphonale Monasticum* (Paris, Tournai, Rome: Desclée, 1934), p. 143.

105. "…. hò dato fine ad'alcune compositioni, delle quali hò pensato haver più di bisogno il servitio della Serenissima Real Capella di S. Marco."

106. There is little doubt that the Procurators are, in fact, speaking of the *Salmi a otto voci* of 1662 in this document. That they refer to "alcune messe e salmi" when the 1662 collection contains only psalms is, I think, merely one of the inaccuracies that sometimes creep into the proceedings. Let us not forget that Cavalli was first described as a eunuch in the document relating his presentation to the Doge!

107. Contents listed in Maggini, op. cit., pp. 183–84.

108. Contents listed in Huys, op. cit., p. 360.

109. Contents listed in Mitjana, op. cit., col. 392–93.

110. Contents listed in Huys, op. cit., 360–61.

111. Contents listed in Claudio Sartori, *Assisi, La Cappella della Basilica di S. Francesco, I—Catalogo del Fondo Musicale nella Biblioteca comunale di Assisi* (Milan, 1962; Bibliotheca Musicae I), p. 118.

112. Contents listed in Huys, op. cit., p. 361.

113. See below, Volume II, no. 19.

114. A partial inventory of the materials in the archive contains the following works of Rovetta: Volume II—Turbe delli Passij per la Domenica della Palme, Martedi et Venerdi, del Roetta; Volume III—Missa Feriae Quintae Sexagesimae, R[ovetta?]; Volume IV—Due Inni, probabilmente del Rovetta; Volume XV—Missa Brevis Quattro Vocibus, Rovetta. Other composers represented in the inventory are Natale Monferrato, Antonio Lotti, and Giovanni Croce. Volumes VII through IX are missing from the inventory, and Volumes XI through XIV contain anonymous works. Indeed, Volumes XIII and XIV contain anonymous Magnificats, one of which may be the source of the transcription in the Biblioteca Marciana.

115. Let me summarize briefly the remaining works in anthologies and manuscripts:
    Essentially, one can divide this music into three categories: works preserved in Italian sacred anthologies; works preserved in German sacred anthologies; and works preserved in manuscript alone.
    Fourteen works of Rovetta are contained in six Italian sacred anthologies printed between 1620 and 1668 (see RISM, *Recueils imprimés*). To judge from the compositions of Monteverdi, Grandi, and Cavalli in analogous publications, most are probably *unica*, not found in the prints of Rovetta's works alone. While it is possible that there are Vespers compositions among these works, such anthologies often consist mainly of non-liturgical texts. Even where liturgical associations do exist, it is often impossible to assign the work to a specific feast. For example, Rovetta's motet "Nigra sum" included in the *Sacra Corona* (Venice: Magni, 1656) is actually a setting of psalm and

Magnificat antiphons connected with three different Marian feasts; it is doubtful, however, that this centonized text was used as part of the liturgy of any of these feasts (see Chapter IV).

Over 30 works of Rovetta appear in German anthologies of the seventeenth century. Certainly the most important reprinting of Rovetta's sacred works is found in the 4 prints of "geistlicher Concerten und Harmonien" which Ambrosius Profe published in Leipzig between 1641 and 1646 (RISM 1641/2, 1641/2, 1642/4, 1646/4), as well as in Profe's later *Corollarium* (RISM 1649/6). These 5 prints contain 27 works of Rovetta (despite conflicting figures given in RISM). All of the works in the four volumes of "Concerten und Harmonien" are traceable to the prints of Rovetta's works published in Italy (see Adam Adrio, "Ambrosius Profe [1589–1661] als Herausgeber italienischer Musik seiner Zeit," *Festschrift Karl Gustav Fellerer* [Regensburg: Bosse Verlag, 1962], pp. 20–27). While the 3 works of Rovetta in the *Corollarium* bear titles which are not found in the Italian prints of his works, it is likely that these are *contrafacta* of his madrigals, for 7 madrigals of Monteverdi are parodied in the same volume, both in Latin and German (see Arnold, *Monteverdi*, p. 194).

With the exception of the manuscripts in the Biblioteca Nazionale Marciana, cited above, Rovetta's manuscript works seem all to be copies of existing compositions. The most extensive source is the large set of works in Königsberg (now Kalinengrad, U.S.S.R.), listed in the published catalogue as a collection of 31 compositions of Rovetta (Joseph Müller, *Die musikalischen Schätze der Königlichen- und Universitäts-Bibliothek zu Königsberg in Preussen* [Bonn: Marcus, 1870; reprint: Hildesheim and New York: Georg Olms, 1971], p. 310). All are taken from Profe's anthologies, though two, erroneously cited in the catalogue as by Rovetta, are actually by Monteverdi. Similarly, the manuscript of Rovetta's works in the Bibliothèque nationale, Paris (J. Ecorcheville, *Catalogue du fonds de musique ancienne de la Bibliothèque nationale* [Paris: Terquem et C.ie, 1914] VII: 201) consists of works taken from Profe's anthologies. An elaborate manuscript collection of Vespers music in the Gesellschaft der Musikfreunde, Vienna, is a transcription of the *Salmi concertati* of 1627.

All of the manuscripts listed by Eitner (*Quellenlexikon*) which contain Vespers music are connected fairly certainly (on the basis of titles and number of voices of specific works) with Rovetta's Italian prints or with the German anthologies. The three psalms in Kassel (*Murhardsche Bibliothek der Stadt Kassel und Landesbibliothek: Katalog der Musikalien der Landesbibliothek* [Kassel: Lange, 1920], item 51) match forces with those in Part III of Profe's "Concerten und Harmonien." The manuscript works in Darmstadt (*Die Musikalien der Grossherzoglichen Hofbibliothek in Darmstadt*[Darmstadt: L. C. W. H., 1873], p. 24) seem to be drawn from the *Messa e Salmi* of 1639. The two settings of *Salve Regina*, à 4 and à 5 (Leipzig) are most likely the two works for those forces from Rovetta's first book of *Motetti concertati* (1635). The two Magnificats in Wroclaw (Bohn, op. cit., p. 168) would seem to be those from Rovetta's psalm collections of 1627 and 1639. The works of Rovetta in the Düben Collection in Uppsala can all be identified with compositions in his Venetian publications of psalms and of motets (see Bruno Grusnick, "Die Dübensammlung: Ein Versuch ihren chronologischen Ordnung," *Svensk tidskrift för musikforskning* XLVI (1964): 27–82 and XLVIII (1966): 63–186).

116. This according to Caffi, I: 292; the original document is preserved in A.S.V., San Marco, Procuratia de Supra, Registro 148, entry of 28 April 1675.

117. See especially the chorus of the Furies from *La Calisto* (Biblioteca Nazionale Marciana, Cod. It. IV-353 [-9877], ff. 97v-98r) and the two versions of *Erismena* (Cod. It.

IV-360 and Cod. It. IV-417). On the whole question of the revision of Cavalli's works, see Jeffrey, op. cit.

118. LO STAMPATORE ALLI Signori Virtuosi .... Presto si daran*n*o altre Opere alle stampe di questo Eccelentissimo Virtuoso .... (*Musiche Sacre*, 1656).

119. See below, Volume II, no. 7.

120. Arnold, "Cavalli/Documents," p. 53.

121. Kurtzman, *Essays*, pp. 123ff.

122. The most complete listing of Cavalli's sacred works is found in Francesco Bussi, "La produzione sacra di Cavalli e i suoi rapporti con quella di Monteverdi," *Rivista Italiana di Musicologia* II (1967): 229–54. Two items are missing from Bussi's list. One is the manuscript *Confitebor* just cited. The other is a second printing of the motet "Cantate Domino" from the *Ghirlanda Sacra* (1625). It appears under the name "Pietro Francesco" in the Erster Theil Geistlicher/CONCERTEN/und Harmonien . . . Ausz den berühmbsten Italienischen/und andern Autoribus . . . /Leipzig/. . . M. DC. XL. (RISM 1641/2). The same two works are missing from the list in Glover, op. cit., pp. 163–64.

Chapter III

123. Henry Prunières, *Monteverdi, His Life and Work*, trans. Mackie (New York: E. P. Dutton, 1926), p. 213.

124. The *Procuratia de Supra* is not part of the *Cancelleria Inferiore* but a separate archive altogether. In any event, the volumes cited by Prunières are not in the *Procuratia de Supra* at all but in the series *Atti dei Dogi*.

125. René Lenaerts, "La Chapelle de Saint-Marc à Venise sous Adriaen Willaert (1527–1562)," *Bulletin de l'institut historique belge de Rome*, fasc. XIX (1938): 205–55.

126. See especially Arnold, "The Monteverdi Succession at St. Mark's." *loc. cit.*; idem, "Towards a Biography of Giovanni Gabrieli," *Musica Disciplina* XV (1961): 199–207; and idem, *Giovanni Gabrieli and the Music of the Venetian High Renaissance* (London: Oxford University Press, 1979).

127. Selfridge-Field, *Venetian Instrumental Music*. See especially Chapter I: "Instrumental Music at San Marco" as well as the Appendix on the "Musical Staff of the Basilica of San Marco."

128. See, for example, Arnold, "Instruments in Church: Some Facts and Figures," *Monthly Musical Record* LXXXV (1955): 33, where one of the documents cited by Prunières is partially quoted and translated; and idem "Towards a Biography of Giovanni Gabrieli," 206–7.

129. Arnold, "Biography/Gabrieli," p. 205; idem, "Francesco Cavalli/Documents," p. 53; idem, *Gabrieli/Venetian High Renaissance*; idem, "Venetian Motets and their Singers," *Musical Times* CXIX (1978): 319–21.

130. Arnold, "Francesco Cavalli/Documents," p. 51; idem, "Music at the Scuola di San Rocco," p. 234; see also, for a very general treatment, idem, "Ceremonial Music in Venice at the Time of the Gabrielis," *Proceedings of the Royal Musical Association* LXXXII (1955–56): 47–59.

131. There are three brief lists of the materials on music in the *Procuratia de supra*. The first, published by Lenaerts in his article on the *cappella* at the time of Willaert, is a list of sixteenth-century materials (1486–1589); the second, part of the appendix to Selfridge-Field's study of Venetian instrumental music, is a selective list of seventeenth- and eighteenth-century materials. The third, published as part of Lorenzo Bianconi's article "Caletti-Bruni" in the *Dizionario biografico degli italiani*, cited above, is a list of those sources which relate directly to Cavalli. In no case, however, is there more than a list of *busta* numbers. There has been no overview of the available materials with a description of their contents.

132. While the modern Italian term would be *procuratoria*, the Venetian *procuratia* is so ubiquitous in the documents that it is retained in this study. The best seventeenth-century description of the government of the basilica is Giovanni Stringa's 1604 revision of Sansovino's *Venetia città nobilissima*. The best modern treatment in musicological literature is found in Prunières, *Monteverdi*, pp. 102–3, and in Winterfeld, op. cit. The latter has been translated and augmented in Egon Kenton, *Giovanni Gabrieli* (Rome: American Institute of Musicology, 1967), pp. 9–37.

133. The organization of the archive of the *Procuratia de Supra* is explained in A.S.V., catalogue 285.

134. Archival designations are given according to the following categories: specific archive within the A.S.V., series, subseries, and finally a description of the documentary item.

135. The volumes are listed according to the so-called "red numbers" from A.S.V., catalogue 285. At present the material is numbered in two large systems, one for the *registri* (red numbers) and one for the *buste* (blue numbers). The catalogue contains a series of blue numbers for the *registri* as well, but these are now obsolete.

136. See Winterfeld's tables of the various musical offices in St. Mark's. They contain the same errors as do Caffi's. See especially Winterfeld, I: 197–99; Caffi, I: 53–58.

137. See, for example, the confusion over the date at which Cavalli was promoted from second to first organist, discussed above, p. 20.

138. Wolfgang Osthoff, article "Cavalli" in *La Musica, Enciclopedia Storica* (Turin: UTET, 1966) I: 825–31.

139. Some of the information in this *busta* has been published in Sandro dalla Libera, *L'Arte degli Organi a Venezia* (Venice: Instituto per la collaborazione culturale, 1962) and in Renato Lunelli, *Studi e Documenti di Storia Organaria Veneta* (Florence: Olschki, 1973).

140. Some of these documents have been cited already in print. See Thomas Walker, "Francesco Cavalli and the beginnings of opera in Venice," cited above; R. Giazotto, "La guerra dei palchi.... " *Nuova Rivista musicale italiana* I (1967): 245–86, 465–508; Denis Arnold, " 'L'Incoronazione di Poppea' and its orchestral requirements" in *Musical*

Times CIV (1963): 176–78; Janet E. Beat, "Monteverdi and the Opera Orchestra of his Time," *The Monteverdi Companion*, pp. 284–85; Carl Schmidt, "An Episode in the History of Venetian Opera: The *Tito* Commission," *Journal of the American Musicological Society* XXXI (1978): 442–66; Glover, op. cit.; Jeffrey, op. cit.

141. A number of documents originally in this *fondo* are now found in the archive of Santa Maria a Malamocco (A.S.V.).

142. Decree of 1595 cited by Arnold, "Biography/Gabrieli," p. 205.

143. The date of the manuscript reads "MDCLXXVIII," but another "I" has been added in a different color ink. Within the volume, the phrase "In quest'anno 1679.... " is found. However, other copies of the *ceremoniale* are dated 1678 without comment.

144. Antonio Pasini lists two additional *ceremoniali* in the archive of the *Consulatore in Jure*, Registri 556 and 557. From the title pages he quotes, these seem to be exact copies of items 11 and 12. I have not been able to check these volumes, but if Pasini is to be trusted, Registri 98, 99 and 100 of the *Procuratia de Supra* of St. Mark's are equivalent to Registri 555, 556 and 557 of the *Consulatore in Jure*. (Antonio Pasini, "Il Rito antico ed il Cerimoniale della Basilica di San Marco," *La Basilica di S. Marco in Venezia* [Venice: Emiliana, 1888]; English version by W. Scott, 1888).

145. Pace's *ceremoniale* is cited in Pasini, op. cit., and in Denis Arnold, "Vivaldi's Church Music: an introduction," *Early Music* I (1973), 71.

146. Biblioteca Correr, Codice Cicogna 2770, p. 146; Cicogna 1295, p. 137.

147. Documents in A.S.V., Procuratia de Supra, Busta 88, Processo 195 provide the basic details of Bonifacio's appointment at St. Mark's. He was elected to the office of *maestro di coro* on 2 September 1552, without having served as either a canon or subcanon beforehand. His salary was raised in 1555 and twice in 1563. He was replaced in his office by Benedetto Manzini on 18 August 1564.

148. ".... caduco, postillato e confuso." A.S.V., San Marco, Procuratia de Supra, Busta 88 (Ceremoniere), Processo 195, fascicolo 1, f. 69r. The date 1609 is open to question, for it is not in Stringa's hand but in the hand which wrote the pagination for the *busta*. At any rate, the letter cannot be later than 1609, for it speaks of a projected publication of the psalter of St. Mark's, a work which was printed in that very year.

149. A.S.V., San Marco, Procuratia de Supra, Busta 88 (Ceremoniere), Processo 195, fascicolo 1, f. 69r.

150. A.S.V., San Marco, Procuratia de Supra, Busta 88 (Ceremoniere), Processo 195, fascicolo 1, f. 69r. ".... et queste sono il Cerimoniale, il Salterio, et il Messale, secondo l'uso di detta Chiesa, in diverse cose differente dal Romano: essendo cosa affatto necessaria, et conveniente, che il Cerimoniale, per trovarsi tutto caduco, postillato, et confuso, sia da me di proprio pugno rescritto, riordinato, et riformato in molti luoghi, al che fare son stato anco dall'istesso Sere*nissi*mo Principe esortato, et ne ho di già dato principio...."

151. Bonifacio's *ceremoniale* was not unknown to early scholars of Venetian ecclesiastical history. It is cited by Flaminio Corner (*Ecclesiae venetae antiquis monumentis*, 1739)

and by Marco Foscarini (*Della letteratura veneziana*, 1752). Both Foscarini and Emmanuale Cicogna (*Bibliografia veneziana*, 1847) cite the author erroneously as one Nicolò Moravio, "piovano di S. Pantaleone e Vicario di S. Marco," though they cite this on the authority of others. Clearly, they must not have known of items 7 or 11, which list Bonifacio on their title pages, but rather knew the text from items 9 or 10. Antonio Pasini mistakenly identifies Bonifacio as a thirteenth-century *Magister Ceremoniarum* (Pasini, op. cit.); his error is repeated in Otto Denus, *The Church of San Marco in Venice* (Washington: Dumbarton Oaks [Harvard University], 1960).

152. CAEREMONIALE/EPISCOPORUM/IUSSU CLEMENTIS VIII. PONT./novissime reformatum./Omnibus Ecclesijs, praecipue au-/tem Metropolitanis Cathe-/dralis et collegiatis perutile ac ne-/cessarium./(device)/ROMAE./Ex Typographia linguarum externarum./Cum licentia Superiorum, et Privilegio Sanctissimi Pon-/tificis, et aliorum Principum per decennium./Anni Iubilaei M D C. Mense Octobris.

153. See also A.S.V., San Marco, Procuratia de Supra, Registro 30 (Libri di Scontro, 1614–23), entry of 1 June 1620.

154. A.S.V., San Marco, Procuratia de Supra, Registro 139, entry of 9 July 1603. For the details surrounding Monteverdi's appointment, see Arnold, "The Monteverdi Succession at St. Mark's," *Music and Letters* XLII (1961): 205–11.

155. On the disciplinary problems of the singers under Donati, see the letter of Contarini cited above: ".... spesso con li bichieri di vino in mano cantando canzonete d'andar à bere alle fontane fraponendovi in queste bottezze il bere delli bichieri che tengono in mano."

156. This document as well as the next few are cited by Arnold in "Venetian Motets and their Singers," and in idem, *Gabrieli/ Venetian High Renaissance,* pp. 32ff.

157. See A.S.V., San Marco, Procuratia de Supra, Busta 91, Processo 208, fascicolo 2, f. 27r, 28r 29r.

158. Ibid., f. 39r: "Io ho tanto cercato che finalmente ho rubbato un basso al Domo di questa Città, è giovane di 18 anni et è un strupote che vadi tanto profondo come và, et ha una voce tanto grande che fa risonar tutta questa Chiesa, che dev'esser 4. volte più grande che San Marco."

159. See Biblioteca Correr, MS P.D. 303/C, fascicolo 4, f. 84-v for the statement of their acceptance. They are identified here as "Zuanne Grisard cantor soprano francese," and "Piero Peren cantor basso francese." See also f. 22r-v and 23r for the details of the journey, including the expense accounts. See also A.S.V., San Marco, Procuratia de Supra, Busta 91, Processo 208, fascicolo 1, f. 43r.

160. Ibid., from the testimony of Guglielmo *francese*: "Bassi numero 4. Tenori numero 5. Contr'alti numero 5 compresso la mia persona, et un puto, Soprani numero 3., et il Padre Bressano tolto ultimamente che può servir per bariton cioè che canta 3 voci."

161. A.S.V., San Marco, Procuratia de Supra, Busta 91, Processo 208, fascicolo 1, f. 62r.

162. A.S.V., Cancelleria Inferiore, Registro 79, f. 54r.–56v. The entry is dated 4 November 1601.

163. Ibid., f. 54v: "Che nel sedere, nel raggionare, nel governare, et dar licenza si tenghi quest'ordine, il *primo* luogo il Re*veren*do me*sser* Pa*d*re Zuane Croce capo maggiore, poi il vice capo, et poi il più vecchio cantore di mano in mano secondo l'elettione fatta dalli Ill*ustrissi*mi Sig*no*ri Procuratori...."

164. Cf. Prunières, *Monteverdi*, p. 105.

165. A.S.V., Cancelleria Inferiore, Registro 79, f. 138r-v. See Documents 50 and 51.

166. This document is reproduced in Prunières, *Monteverdi*, p. 213, in a very corrupt transcription which contains a number of misreadings and added phrases. Prunières also misdates the document by 10 years: 1623 instead of 1633.

167. See A.S.V., San Marco, Procuratia de Supra, Registro 139, entry of 29 July 1606: "…. udito più volte, cosi nella capella come nelli organi solo...."

168. See letter of Francesco Spagnoletto to the Procurators, A.S.V., San Marco, Procuratia de Supra, Busta 91, f. 80r: "…. essendo io uno de tre Soprani, tra quali, uno ha Ducati 100, et l'altro 80.... "; although the letter is not dated, it is included among the documents for the first decade of the century. Moreover, Francesco states that he has been in the *cappella* for 10 years: "…. havendo io servito *per* soprano questa Sere*nissi*ma Sig*no*ria diece anni.... "; and he is almost certainly the Spanish castrato which the Roman Ambassador had picked up in 1595: "…. ho parlato io stesso ad uno spagnolo eunuco già prima conosciuto da me, il quale haveva pensiero per altri suoi negotij di venirsene dapri Pasqua à Venetia...." (Ibid., f. 28r).

169. A.S.V., San Marco, Procuratia de Supra, Registro 140, entry of 3 January 1611.

170. Giovanni Stringa, revision of Sansovino's *Venetia città nobilissima* (Venice, 1604), f. 79v-84v.

171. Ibid., 84v: "I giovani di coro sono tenuti anch'essi ad assister cottidianamente al coro, et in quello cantare, e salmeggiare.... "

172. Ibid., 81r: "Ma il carico, et obligo de i Residenti, oltre il predetto, è di recitar in Chiesa ogni giorno tutte le hore canoniche.... "; f. 84r: (speaking of the *sottocanonici*) "Cantano Messa, et intonano Vespro uno per settimana così nei giorni feriali come nelle feste, che non sono più che solenni, nelli quali i canonici soli per honorevolezza intonano."

173. On the constitution of the instrumental forces in St. Mark's during the *seicento*, see Eleanor Selfridge-Field, *Venetian Instrumental Music from Gabrieli to Vivaldi* (New York: Praeger, 1974), pp. 3–25; see also her "Bassano and the orchestra of St. Mark's," *Early Music* IV (1976): 153–58. Much of the information on instruments in this chapter necessarily overlaps with that presented by Selfridge-Field, although I have tried to concentrate on aspects of the instrumental ensemble she chooses not to treat and to reproduce documents she does not discuss.

174. A.S.V., San Marco, Procuratia de Supra, Busta 90, Processo 208, fascicolo 1, f. 56r: "…. Quattro Sonatori di piffero et tro*m*boni et cornetti.... "; cf. Selfridge-Field, *Venetian Instrumental Music*, 15.

175. See Selfridge-Field, "Bassano," p. 153.

176. A.S.V., San Marco, Procuratia de Supra, Registro 6, entry of 3 January 1603 (*more veneto*).

177. See A.S.V., San Marco, Procuratia de Supra, Registro 6, entries of 9 January 1604 (*more veneto*), 29 March 1604, 28 April 1604.

178. On ceremonies involving the Doge's *piffari e tromboni*, see Biblioteca Correr, MS Donà dalle Rose 58, in particular f. 84, 16v and following; see also the engraving of Mattio Pagan, now in the Museo Civico of Bassano, which shows both the *piffari e tromboni* as well as the *sei trombe d'argento*. Despite some problems in terminology, it seems that the *piffari e trombone* must have been used in church, not the long silver trumpets which led ducal processions. However, in a description of the Mass for the coronation of Doge Giovanni Bembo on 3 December 1615, we are told that "…. udita la Messa col suono delle Trombe all'Elevatione…. Il Doge…. andò in Chiesa per la porta del loro, et andò subito nel Bergamo dei Cantori ove fù presentato al Popolo…. " (Biblioteca Correr, MS Donà dalle Rose 58, f. 19v). The *trombe* referred to here may merely be a generic term used by the ducal chronicler.

179. Selfridge-Field, "Bassano," p. 156. Selfridge-Field has equated the 26 services required of the instrumentalists in 1614 with the feast listed as requiring instruments on the large ecclesiastical calendar with the duties of the instrumentalists published in 1761 and found in A.S.V., San Marco, Procuratia de Supra, Busta 91. I think, however, that there is a danger in assuming that the services listed in 1761 are those which required music in 1614, particularly since the instrumental emphasis changed from Vespers to Mass during the late seventeenth and early eighteenth centuries. See Chapter V; the ecclesiastical calendar of 1761 is reproduced in the Appendix as Document 143.

180. A.S.V., Cancelleria Inferiore, Registro 80, entry of 27 September 1625; Registro 81, entry of 9 March 1645.

181. Sansovino-Stringa, *Venetia città nobilissima*, f. 31v: "Il suono di questo organo è soavissimo; e tanto più è soave, quanto che viene dal più eccellente Organista, c'habbia hoggdi la nostra Italia sonato; e questi- è Giovanni Gabrielli, degno d'ogni lode per la rara, et singolar virtù, che regna in lui simil professione." On the organs of St. Mark's, see Selfridge-Field, *Venetian Instrumental Music*, p. 8–13 and idem, "Gabrieli and the Organ," *The Organ Yearbook* VIII (1977): 2–19; see also Sandro dalla Libera, *L'Arte degli Organi a Venezia* (Venice and Rome: Istituto per la collaborazione culturale, 1962), and Arnold, *Gabrieli/Venetian High Renaissance*, pp. 41–43.

182. Biblioteca Ambrosiana, MS A. 328 inf., f. 31r: "…. Si canta à due Cori nelli Organi Maggiori, et nelli minori con sonate."

183. A.S.V., San Marco, Procuratia de Supra, Registro 141, entry of 11 April 1615: "…. così in capella, come nelli concerti sopra li organi et la tiorba…."

184. This picture is discussed in more detail below. It has, of course, much more information to offer on performance practice at St. Mark's than hints on the performance of *concertato* motets.

185. A.S.V., San Marco, Procuratia de Supra, Registro 146, entry of 25 July 1655: "…. per concerto per sonar il Violon sopra gl'organetti, et altrove in Chiesa de San Marco…."

186. A.S.V., San Marco, Procuratia de Supra, Registro 141, entry of 4 January 1617 (*more veneto*): "…. franceschin fiol del Maestro di capella, che ha cantato le profitie con la tiorba la notte di Nadal, et la mattina."

187. A.S.V., San Marco, Procuratia de Supra, Registro 142, entry of 6 July 1623.

188. Biblioteca Ambrosiana, MS A. 328 inf., f. 31r: "Si dice il Matutino, et tutte queste sere le prime lettioni sono cantate dalli Cantori con le Spinette…."

189. See A.S.V., San Marco, Procuratia de Supra, Registro 141, entries of 11 December 1613, 11 April 1615, 18 December 1616, 20 January 1616 (*more veneto*), 18 December 1619 and 5 April 1620.

190. Monteverdi also bolstered the soprano section of the *cappella* by occasionally using clerics from the seminary on the top vocal part (see Document 66).

191. Cited and summarized in Arnold, *Monteverdi*, 29. See also Domenico de' Paoli, *Claudio Monteverdi* (Milan, 1945), 192.

192. The Procurators' statement that the works were all "stampata a Roma di diversi auttori famosi" seems to be in error.

193. See Alphonse Goovaerts, *Histoire et Bibliographie de la Typographie Musicale dans les Pays-Bas* (1877), p. 253: also Gustave Reese, *Music in the Renaissance* (New York: Norton, 1959), p. 511. I am indebted to Howard Mayer Brown for this identification.

194. On the popularity of Morales' Magnificats during the late sixteenth century, see Mary Stuart Lewis, "Antonio Gardane and his Publications of Sacred Music, 1538–1555," unpublished Ph.D. dissertation, Brandeis University, 1979, pp. 172–73, 256–57.

195. Thus, Denis Stevens' recent statement that "Monteverdi did not set the proper psalms of Compline" must be amended. (See Stevens, *Monteverdi: Sacred, Secular, and Occasional Music* [Rutherford, Madison, Teaneck: Fairleigh Dickinson University Press, 1978], pp. 94–97).

196. Croce's works in a modern style seem to have had even greater longevity. A 1662 edition of Doglioni's *Le cose notabili…. della città di Venetia* states that Croce's *cantilene* are still performed. (See Arnold, "Giovanni Croce and the *Concertato* Style," *Musical Quarterly* XXXIX [1953]: 48).

197. See Selfridge-Field, *Venetian Instrumental Music*, p. 16–17.

198. See Arnold, *Monteverdi*, 32; Schrade, *Monteverdi*, 320; Monterosso, ed., *Claudio Monteverdi e il suo tempo*, pp. 433–34. Pamphlets describing the first two were published (see items 14 and 15 of the bibliography of *ceremoniali* above). The third is described in a letter of the cleric Antonio de' Vescovi of 29 November 1631, reproduced in Doglioni's *Le cose notabili di Venezia* (Venice, 1675), 106.

199. Although *giovani di coro* are not mentioned in Document 73, they are listed in a supplementary description of the same ceremonies; see A.S.V., San Marco, Procuratia de Supra, Registro 99, f. 95v–96r: Relazione della Fonzione, e Cerimonia nel poner

la prima Pietra alla Chiesa intitolata Santa Maria della Salute con alcune particolarità non comprese nell'altra Relazione. 1613 [*sic*]: Primo Aprile.

200. This manner of performance is discussed in more detail below; see pp. 98–99.

201. A miscellaneous payment to one "Z. Batista Ferro Cornetto in Palazzo" may indicate an attempt to engage one of the Doge's *piffari* for *ad hoc* service in the church during these years (see A.S.V., San Marco Procuratia de Supra, Registro 12, entry of 15 September 1641).

202. See Selfridge-Field, *Venetian Instrumental Music*, pp. 149–50.

203. Uppsala MS 33:12: "Missa ab. 8 (Giovan Rovetta); 2. Corn. 2 Cant. A. 2. Ten. è Basso," Bruno Grusnick has dated the manuscript 1671. See Grusnick, "Die Düben-sammlung: Ein Versuch ihren chronologischen Ordnung," Part II, *Svensk tidskrift för musikforskning* XLVIII (1966): p. 139.

204. "Von *Cornet*isten wirdt gar nichts gehört." Gurlitt, op. cit., p. 493.

205. A.S.V., San Marco, Procuratia de Supra, Registro 141, entry of 30 April 1617: ".... esser obligati sonar de tutti quell'instrumenti che sapranno sonar, si come le sarà imposto dal capo dei concerti et dal Maestro di cappella...."

206. A.S.V., San Marco, Procuratia de Supra, Registro 99 (Cerimoniali), f. 307: "La Messa fù cantata sontuosamente dal Signor Maestro Roetta con piena musica."

207. A.S.V., San Marco, Procuratia de Supra, Registro 146, entry of 20 January 1668 (*more veneto*).

208. See Michel Brenet (Marie Bobillier), *Musique et Musiciens de la Vieille France* (Paris: Félix Alcan, 1911), p. 130.

209. See Alvin Johnson, "The Liturgical Music of Cipriano da Rore," unpublished Ph.D. dissertation, Yale University, 1954, p. 146.

210. A.S.V., San Marco, Procuratia de Supra, Registro 146, entry of 29 August 1671.

211. Cf. A.S.V., San Marco, Procuratia de Supra, Busta 91, Processo 208, fascicolo 2; and Biblioteca Correr, Codice Cicogna 3118, fascicoli 44–56. Since the folios in the Correr copies are not numbered, I have referred to the copies in the A.S.V. whenever possible.

212. Cf. Caffi II, 46. He erroneously dates the starting point of this list as 1655 and states that it represents departures over a period of 22 years. He also gets only 22 singers out of the list, for he leaves off 2 names and then treats "Sr. Antonio.... detto Tonin da Muran" as 2 different singers.

213. The passports for a number of these singers are preserved in A.S.V., Collegio, Lettere, Filza 194.

214. Biblioteca Correr, Codice Cicogna 3118, fascicolo 46. See also Arnold, "Venetian Motets and their Singers," p. 320.

215. On the reforms of Legrenzi, see Stephen Bonta, "The Church Sonatas of Giovanni Legrenzi," unpublished Ph.D. dissertation, Harvard University, 1964, pp. 94–95.

216. Selfridge-Field, *Venetian Instrumental Music*, pp. 303–5.

217. See documents accepting Gerardo Biancosi and Francesco Barbarino *detto* il Pesarino into the *cappella*, A.S.V., San Marco, Procuratia de Supra, Registro 141, entry of 18 March 1614 and 25 May 1617.

218. See Volume II, nos. 11 and 15.

219. Psalms from these three collections are found in Volume II as nos. 12, 13, 18 and 21.

220. Just which group of singers is meant by the references to the "small chapel" (*capella parva*) in Document 94 is not clear. A *capella piccola* was established under Willaert on 12 October 1562 to train *zaghi* to sing in the *capella grande* and to substitute for the senior chapel when its members followed the Doge to other churches in the city. (See A.S.V., San Marco, Procuratia de Supra, Registro 129, entries of 12 October, 14 October, 11 November, 29 November and 30 November 1562). It was not a success and was disbanded on 21 April 1565 (A.S.V., San Marco, Procuratia de Supra, Registro 30, entry of 21 April 1565), a date which is somewhat enigmatic in view of the statements in Bonifacio's *ceremoniale* of 1564 that "capella parva non extat." Thus, Bonifacio may be referring to a much earlier division of the *cappella* into two groups, a *capella parva* and *capella magna*, which scholars have found in the documents of the first part of the sixteenth century. See Frank A. D'Accone, "The Performance of Sacred Music in Italy during Josquin's Time," *Josquin des Prez: Proceedings of the International Josquin Festival-Conference*, ed. Lowinsky (London: Oxford University Press, 1976), p. 607; and Jonathan Glixon, "Music at the Venetian "Scuole Grandi,' 1440–1540," unpublished Ph.D. dissertation, Princeton University, 1979, pp. 16–20.

221. A.S.V., San Marco, Procuratia de Supra, Registro 98 (Ceremoniali), f. 28v: ".... vanno li Cantori, cantando in 2. Cori *Pange lingua gloriosi*, la turma avanti li 4. dapoi...."

222. Ibid., f. 97v: "Polliza della Procession con la Madonna Ad pluviam petendam, vel ad serenitatem petendam: .... Poi li Preti, Zoveni, Diaconi, e Suddiaconi, poi li Cantori, la turma, poi li 4. Cantori, Maistro de Capella, el Maistro del Coro.... "; f. 114v: "Procession con la Madonna Pro Peste, et Mortalitate: .... poi li Zoveni, e la Turma delli Cantori, poi li 4 Cantori, poi li Sotto Canonici.... "; f. 90r: "Polizza del Sabbato Santo: ....E Poi si va alla Fonte in *que*sto ord*ine* videlicet.... poi li Diaconi, e Suddiac*oni*, poi li Cantori con le Cotte, poi li 4. Cantori...."

223. See Volume II, no. 3.

224. W. Gurlitt, op. cit., p. 497.

225. That the *pergola* and *bigonzo* refer to the self-same structure seems clear from the contexts in which they are used. However, the connection is made explicit in Pace's pamphlet, the *Nucleus Ceremoniarum*, Biblioteca Correr, Codice Cicogna 559, f. 10r: ".... sopra il Bigonzo, cioè Pergolo de Cantori.... " The choirlofts, on the other hand, are referred to in the documents as *cantorie*, and performances in which the singers stood in them are often described simply as occurring *negli organi*.

226. See also Martinioni's paraphrase of Stringa, Document 97.

227. See, inter alia, the testimony of Zorzi Polacco, Document 98.

228. A.S.V., San Marco, Procuratia de Supra, Busta 91, Processo 208, large unpaginated folio (see Document 143).

229. W. G. Constable, *Canaletto: Giovanni Antonio Canal, 1697–1768* (Oxford: Clarendon, 1962), items 556 through 561; 577 through 579.

230. Reproduced in Ferdinando Ongania, ed., *La Basilica di San Marco a Venezia* (Venice, 1888) VII, facsimile 109: "Ceremonia della consegna del pileo e dello stocco, donati dal pontefice Alessandro VIII a doge Francesco Morosini il Peloponnesiaco; fatta nel presbiterio della Basilica il 7 maggio 1690."

231. See A.S.V., San Marco, Procuratia de Supra, Registro 139, entry of 2 April 1607.

Chapter IV

232. For the complete contents of this collection, p. 46.

233. *Di Adriano et di Iachet. I Salmi appertinenti alli Vesperi per tutte le feste dell'anno, parte a versi, et parte spezzadi. Accomodati da cantare a uno et a duoi chori....* (Venice: Gardane, 1550).

234. See above p. 47, for the contents of the collection.

235. On the breviary reforms following the Council of Trent see the following: Pierre Batiffol, *History of the Breviary*, trans. Baylay (London and New York: Longmans, Green and Co., 1912); and Suitbert Bäumer, *Geschichte des Breviers* (Freiburg: Herder, 1895).

236. Hans Bohatta, *Bibliographie der Breviere, 1501–1850* (Leipzig: Hiersemann, 1937), p. 31.

237. Ibid., p. 41.

238. Ibid., p. 46.

239. Biblioteca del Civico Museo Correr, Codice Cicogna 3118, fascicoli 44-56, unpaginated folio. I would date the letter sometime after 1632, since it refers to ceremonies "secondo che si raccoglie dà Ceremoniali Romani stampati prima delle ultime riforme, e specialmente da quello di Clemente VIII in più suoi luoghi." Since the *Ceremoniale Episcoporum* of Clement VIII, published in a number of editions from 1600 onward, is cited as one of the "Roman ceremonials printed before the latest reforms," the reforms referred to are probably those of Urban VIII, which resulted in a new breviary in 1632. At any rate, the letter is found in the Correr with a group of seventeenth-century documents.

240. "…. il libro delle cerimonie et quell'altro detto Orationale nelle sue rubriche." Sansovino-Martinioni, *Venetia*, p. 517.

241. The *Orationale* may also be the volume referred to in a document of 19 July 1614, where payment is made to "Marco Cassini librer" for having bound two antiphonaries and having rebound the "Rational" for use in Mass and Vespers (Document 105). The reference to "Mass and Vespers" is a bit confusing, since the *Orationale* would not have been used during Mass and contains the texts for other offices in addition to Vespers. The document may simply be inaccurate, as are a number of the Procurators' decrees, which throw liturgical terms around in a loose fashion.

242. A ducal decree of 1 January 1613 discusses ceremonies in the "chiese alla capella n*ostr*a di Sa*n* Marco a*n*nesse, et dipendenti" as well as those "in altre, ove p*er* publiche ordinationj, o votj, o p*er* particolare divotione siamo solitj andare." In all cases, *maestro di coro* Cesare Vergaro and six canons are to attend and oversee the ceremonies, just as they do in St. Mark's "dall'uso, et dal cerimoniale della quale non intendemo, che vi dobbiate in alcuno discostare." (See Document 106.) This decree was reiterated by the Collegio in 1660. (See Document 107.)

243. Mario dal Tin, "Note di liturgia patriarchina e canti tradionali della Basilica di S. Marco a Venezia," *Jucunda Laudatio* I–IV (1973), p. 91.

244. Emmanuele Cicogna, *Saggio di bibliografia veneziana* (Venice: G. B. Merlo, 1847).

245. Joan Anne Long, "The Motets, Psalms and Hymns of Adrian Willaert: A Liturgico-Musical Study," unpublished Ph.D. dissertation, Columbia University, 1971; Staale Sinding-Larsen, *Christ in the Council Hall: Studies in the Religious Iconography of the Venetian Republic* (Rome: L'Erma di Bretschneider, 1974); Jane Weidensaul, "The Polyphonic Hymns of Adrian Willaert," unpublished Ph.D. dissertation, Rutgers University, 1978; David Bryant, "Liturgia e musica liturgica nella fenomenologia del 'Mito di Venezia'," *Mitologie* (Venice: Edizioni La Biennale di Venezia, 1979), 205–14.

246. Madan Falconer, *A Summary Catalogue of Western Manuscripts in the Bodleian Library at Oxford* (Oxford: Clarendon Press, 1897), IV: 381. See also W. H. Frère, *Bibliotheca musica liturgica* (London, 1901), p. 24.

247. Cicogna, *Bibliografia veneziana*, p. 30, item 223. Cicogna does not list the edition of 1722 but, instead, an edition of 1759.

248. Ibid., item 224. Cicogna cites only an edition of 1759.

249. Cf. Ibid., item 228. Cicogna's citation gives a slightly different title and no publisher nor date of publication. Could he be referring to some unknown manuscript source?

250. Ibid., item 221. Cicogna cites later editions after 1693 as well as one by Pinelli in 1753.

251. Ibid., pp. 29–30, item 220. Cicogna cites eight editions, from 1597 through 1791.

252. Ibid., item 225.

253. Ibid., p. 30, item 225. Cicogna cites a print (Venice: Rosa, 1806) with the same title as this manuscript.

254. In her discussion of the liturgy of St. Mark's, Joan Anne Long has overlooked the fact that a number of saints were added to the calendar at a later date and erroneously

treats the *Orationale* as a unified volume. Item no. 2 is cited briefly in Van Dijk and Walker, *The Origins of the Modern Roman Liturgy: The Liturgy of the Papal Court and the Franciscan Order in the Thirteenth Century.* (London: Darton, Longman and Todd, 1960), p. 325.

255. See Hans Bohatta, *Liturgische Bibliographie des XV. Jahrhunderts* (Vienna: Gilhofer und Ranschburg, 1911), p. 5. Although a number of manuscript Aquileian breviaries exist in the Biblioteca Nazionale Marciana, only two editions ever came to press. The Marciana also has a manuscript Aquileian missal, Cod. Lat. III-125 (-2407).

256. Cicogna also lists three prints for the liturgy of St. Mark's which I have not been able to locate. The first contains ceremonies for the Feast of the Most Precious Blood of Our Lord (Venice: Pinelli, 1737, 1784); the second, prayers for the processions on Rogation days (Venice: 1762, 1765, 1779, 1788); the third, Matins for Quadragesima Sunday (Venice: 1796). See Cicogna, op. cit., p. 30, items 222, 226, and 227. These prints may have been part of Cicogna's personal library and have never found their way into public collections; or, they may still be hidden the haphazard catalogues of the Biblioteca Correr.

257. See inter alia: "In prima Domenica Adventu omnia fiunt ut in Orationali et nostris Antiphonarijs." (A.S.V., San Marco, Procuratia de Supra, Registro 98, f. 2v); ". . . Ad Vesperas omnia dicunt ut in Orationalis et Antiphonarijs Nostris." (Ibid.)

258. Because of recent exhibits of archival materials in the A.S.V., I have not been able to see these documents myself. Their contents were communicated to me by Don Gastone Vio of the A.S.V.

259. See Joseph Valentinelli, *Bibliotheca Manuscripta ad S. Marci Venetiarum* . . . (Venice: Ex Typographia Commercii, 1868).

260. Long, op. cit., p. 76.

261. See A.S.V., San Marco, Procuratia de Supra, Registro 98, f. 37r.

262. Printed missals were also used in St. Mark's. See A.S.V., San Marco, Procuratia de Supra, Registro 140, entry of 26 March 1613: "Che siano comprati quatro messali da quelli ristampati de novo per uso della chiesa di San Marco."

263. A.S.V., San Marco, Procuratia de Supra, Busta 88, fascicolo 195, ff. 75r-v: "1630. Adi 30 Genaro. In Procuratia. Inventario delli libri, et altro come qui sotto consegnati al molto Reverendo Padre Zorzi Minaccia Canonico di San Marco, et elletto heri Maestro di Coro."

264. A.S.V., San Marco, Procuratia de Supra, Registro 98, f. 86v, 97v, et alia.

265. Ironically, the one breviary which does not figure in this study is the most famous of all, the Tridentine breviary of Pius V. While a pre-Tridentine breviary must be used to compare with the *Orationale*, all of the music in this study was published between 1610 and 1675. Thus, the breviaries of Clement VIII and Urban VIII are the relevant Roman sources.

266. A.S.V., San Marco, Procuratia de Supra, Busta 88, Processo 195, fascicolo 1, f. 66r-v: "Messali, Breviarij, et Psalterij segondo il rito di San Marco. Breviarij reformati

almeno sei perfino si faccino li sopradetti secondo il rito di *San* Marco.... Un Pontificale dei reformati per quando canta messa qualche Prelato che n'è grand*issi*mo bisogna et vergogna."

267. See Volumes IX–X, pp. 204–15.

268. Ibid., p. 205: "Ingentis molis Codex inter publica documenta asservatur ordinem rituum ecclesiasticorum pro Ducali Basilica continens, quem diligentius ab initio ad calcem excussimus, nihilque in eo diversum invenire potuimus ab iis, quibus ante correctionem Breviarii, et Missalis a Sancto Pio V peractam, Ecclesia Romana utebatur."

269. Sansovino-Martinioni, *Venetia*, p. 210: "L'ordine di officiar questo Sacrario è secondo l'uso della Chiesa Constantinopolitana, ma non però molto differente dalla Romana." Giovanni Pace made a similar claim a century later (Biblioteca Ambrosiana, MS A. 328 inf., f. [7v]: ".... ad imitatione del Primicerio dell'Imp*erato*re di Costantinopoli, da che trasse l'origine anche il nostro Rito, poco lontano dal Rito Romano.... ").

270. Marco Foscarini, *Della letteratura veneziana* (Venice: Manfrè, 1752), p. 192, note 254. The page numbers of Foscarini's citations on liturgy are given in Egon, Kenton, *Giovanni Gabrieli* (Rome: American Institute of Musicology, 1967), pp. 25–27. However, Kenton erroneously cites the book as Michele Foscarini's *Historia della Republica Veneta* (Venice, 1696), a military history which chronicles the war in Candia during the last half of the *seicento*.

271. Giovanni Diclich, *Rito Veneto Antico detto Patriarchino* (Venice: Rizzi, 1825); Antonio Pasini, op. cit.

272. See Pasini, op. cit. (English version), p. 175; and Diclich, op. cit., p. 18. This, too, seems to have entered Venetian tradition through Sansovino: ".... che gli divini officij di questo giorno, quanto di tutti gli altri dell'anno siano recitati con ordine, et regola, conforme all'antichissimo, et venerando rito Alessandrino di questa Chiesa, et che è molte cose dal Romano differente.... " (Sansovino-Martinioni, *Venetia*, p. 516). His views were later taken up by St. Didier: "Upon the Principal Solemnities of the Year, especially in the Holy Week, they follow the *Rituals* of the Church of *Alexandria*; for according to Ancient Tradition the Body of St. *Mark* was brought from thence, which hath given occasion to this Custom ever since, in observing several particular Ceremonies." (St. Didier, *The City and the Republick of Venice* [London: Char. Brome, 1699; originally published in Paris, 1680], p. 32).

273. For the sake of simplicity, I shall refer to it simply as the "Aquileian rite."

274. *New Catholic Encyclopedia* (New York: McGraw-Hill, 1967), I: 711.

275. On the connections between Venice and Aquileia-Grado, see Pasini, op. cit.; much of his material is summarized in Demus, op. cit.; see also Biblioteca Nazionale Marciana, 394. D. 1: Bernardo Maria de Rubeis, *Monumenta Ecclesiae Aquilejensis* (Argentinae: Ordinis Praedicatorum, 1740).

276. See Pasini, op. cit.

277. Indeed, the calendars in the two complete copies of the *Orationale* differ from one another. The following saints are included in Biblioteca Correr, Codice Cicogna 1602

but not in Oxford Bodleian MS Canon. Liturg. 323: St. Felician (24 January); Cyrus and John (31 January); Joseph of Arithmatia (17 March); Leodogarius (2 October); Charles Borromeo (4 November). The following are in the Bodleian manuscript, some clearly inserted at a later date, but not in the Correr copy: Francis de Sales (29 January); Romuald (7 February); Andrew (26 February); Aphrodisius (22 March); Secundus (30 March); Stanislaus of Cracow (7 May); Basil (14 June); Bonaventure (14 July). Gerard of Csanad is listed on 23 February in the Bodleian manuscript, but in the Correr manuscript he has been moved to 25 September.

In her discussion of the liturgical calendar of St. Mark's, Long does not recognize that the calendar of the Oxford *Orationale* is a composite calendar from a number of different periods. Several of the variants she cites between the rites of St. Mark's and of Rome for the period of Willaert actually involve saints who were added to the calendar during the seventeenth century.

278. This calendar has been overlooked by liturgical scholars. For example, Giuseppe Cappelletti (*Storia della Chiesa di Venezia dalla sua Fondazione sino ai nostri giorni* [Venice: S. Lazzaro, 1853] III: 477) states that Lorenzo Giustiniani's commemoration was established by Patriarch Badoaro in 1691; however, Giustiniani is present on Pace's calendar of 1678.

279. Act of the Senate, 19 December 1628, quoted in Cappelletti, op. cit., III: 478.

280. Act of the Senate, 24 January 1652 (*more veneto*). Ibid., p. 479. The *stampator ducale*, Francesco Rampazetto, seems to have profited from both sides of the dispute. He not only printed the liturgical books for St. Mark's but was also one of the first printers in Venice of the reformed office. (See Document 111.)

281. The calendars of the two printed Aquileian breviaries differ to a certain extent and are incomplete. One must examine the body of the breviary to determine all of the feasts which were observed.

282. Much of the following information is drawn from S. Tramontin *et al, Culto dei Santi a Venezia* (Venice: Edizioni Studium Cattolico Veneziano, 1965).

283. While the feast of the Translation was observed in Aquileia, that of the Apparition was not.

284. Giovanni Tiepolo, *Trattato sulle Santissime Reliquie* (Venice, 1617), quoted in Tramontin, op. cit., p. 14.

285. Biblioteca Ambrosiana, MS A. 328 inf., f. 75v: "Li Vespri di Pasqua sino la Domenica in Albis exclusive si cominciano per Chirie eleison, et non si dice Deus in Adiutorium." See also the Paschal section of the *Orationale*.

286. Suitbert Bäumer, *Histoire du Bréviaire*, trans. Réginald Biron (Paris: Letouzey et Ané, 1905), II: 28.

287. On Septuagesima Sunday, *alleluia*s were inserted after each hemistich of the Magnificat at St. Mark's, viz., *Magnificat alleluia, alleluia, alleluia; anima mea Dominum alleluia, alleluia, alleluia.* See Biblioteca Correr, Codice Cicogna 1602, f. 30v. This is not part of the pre-Tridentine Roman liturgy, nor does it seem to stem from Aquileia. See also Biblioteca Ambrosiana, MS A. 328 inf., f. 20v: "Nel Sabbato avanti la Settuagesima

ad ogni Versetto del Magnificat à mezzo si dicono 3 Alleluia, et nel fine altri 3 Alleluia V. G. Magnificat Alleluia, Alleluia, Alleluia, anima mea Dominum Alleluia, Alleluia, Alleluia, et sic de singulis.... "

288. Cf. *Psalterium Davidicum*, f. 83r and following, and the *Breviarium Romanum* (Venice: Variscum, 1562), f. 47v and following.

289. See *LU*, pp. 280ff.

290. Pasini, op. cit. (English version), p. 78.

291. They are found, however, in the *salmi spezzati* of Willaert included in the 1550 collection of Willaert and Jachet of Mantua; the other settings in the collection use the standard Vulgate.

292. The Venetian liturgical books of the sixteenth and seventeenth centuries often differ from modern Roman sources in stating just where the Vigil of a feast ends and the feast itself begins. Indeed, the service which is called First Vespers of a feast in modern Roman terminology is often called the Vespers of the Vigil in Venetian sources, although it is clear from its placement that the service on the eve of the feast itself is the one under consideration. I have followed the Venetian sources throughout this study rather than try to make all terminology conform with modern Roman usage, a practice which would clash with the Venetian service books at every turn.

293. The third and fifth antiphons are interchanged, however, in Roman practice.

294. I find Jeffrey Kurtzman's terminology to be a convenient shorthand in dealing with the two most common sets of Vespers psalms (See Jeffrey Kurtzman, "Some Historical Perspectives on the Monteverdi Vespers," *Analecta Music.* XV [1975]: 29–86). The male *cursus* refers to those five psalms used on the most important feasts of Our Lord and of many male saints: *Dixit Dominus, Confitebor, Beatus vir, Laudate pueri* and *Laudate Dominum omnes gentes*. The female *cursus* refers to those psalms for feasts of the Virgin and important female saints: *Dixit Dominus, Laudate pueri, Laetatus sum, Nisi Dominus* and *Lauda Jerusalem*.

295. This is the first time that the liturgical significance of the *Cinque Laudate* Vespers service has been identified. See the queries about its significance in Denis Arnold, "Cavalli at St. Mark's," *Early Music* IV (1976): 266–74 and in Jane Glover, op. cit., p. 147, note 14. The service for First Vespers of Christmas which Denis Stevens has published under the title *Claudio Monteverdi, Christmas Vespers* (London: Novello, 1979) is, ironically, a service which would not have been used on Christmas Eve in St. Mark's, although it would have been appropriate for churches using the Roman rite. See also Denis Stevens, "Monteverdi's other Vespers," *Musical Times* CXX (1979): 732–37.

296. Biblioteca Correr, Codice Cicogna 1602, f. 51r. The *Orationale* states that the sequence of five *Laudate* psalms was once used for Holy Saturday but that now the antiphons are sung with a single psalm, *Laudate Dominum omnes gentes*, a practice which agrees with both Aquileian and Roman sources.

297. The *Cinque Laudate* were not, however, used on the Second Vespers of Corpus Christi in Aquileia. This practice seems to have been exclusively that of St. Mark's.

298. See Ludwig Eisenhofer and Joseph Lechner, *The Liturgy of the Roman Rite* (London: Nelson, 1961), p. 470. See also the following liturgical publications, inter alia: Francis Procter and Christopher Wordsworth, *Breviarium ad usum insignis Ecclesiae Sarum* (Cambridge, 1882); Walter Howard Frere and Langton E. G. Brown, *The Hereford Breviary: edited from the Rouen edition of 1505 with collation of manuscripts* (London, 1904, 1911, 1915) III, 266–68; *Breviarium augustanum* (Augsburg: Ratdolt, 1495); *Breviarium ad usum alme Ecclesie Salzburgensis* (Salzburg, 1518); *Breviarium secundum Ordinem sancti Dominici* (Venice: Joannis de Colonia, Nicolai Jenson sociorumque, 1481); Benedict Zimmerman, *Ordinaire de l'ordre de Notre-Dame du Mont Carmel par Sibert de Beka (vers 1312)* (Paris: Picard, 1910).

299. Roman Flury's claim that Zarlino composed the *Cinque Laudate* seems to be based on a misreading of Zarlino's statement. See Flury, *Gioseffo Zarlino als Komponist* (Wintherthur: Keller, 1962), pp. 27–28, 80.

300. Biblioteca Correr, Codice Cicogna 596, p. 54.

301. The musical archives are located in the cloister of Sant'Apollonia. There is no published catalogue of the archives, but I have assembled a manuscript catalogue of their contents. Four settings of *Laudate* psalms, all for double choir, are shelved alongside a number of other works of Galuppi. They are located on the shelves opposite the windows which look out onto the Bridge of Sighs and the back of the Doge's palace; they are on the next-to-the-bottom shelf, on the right side. They are labeled as follows: 1) Laudate pueri Dominum a due cori di Baldassare Galuppi detto il Buranello, 1774; 2) Laudate concertat o con Istromenti à due cori di Baldassare Galuppi detto il Buranello 1763; 3) Laudate Dominum quoniam bonus à 8 voci e Violini di Baidassare Galuppi Anno 1780; 4) Lauda anima mea Dominum à due cori di Baldassare Galuppi da Burano 1789.

302. Polyphonic settings of the *Cinque Laudate* designed for liturgies other than that of St. Mark's are extremely rare during the seventeenth century. However, Jeffrey Kurtzman has drawn my attention to two collections of Lorenzo Penna which contain the psalms *Laudate Dominum quoniam bonus est* and *Lauda anima mea Dominum*, with the rubric "ad uso Carmelitano": *Psalmorum totius anni modulatio . . .* (Bologna: Monti, 1669); and *Il Sacro Parnasso delli salmi e brevi....* (Bologna: Monti, 1677). For the exact use of this service in the post-Tridentine Carmelite rite, see *Breviarium Carmelitarum* (Antwerp: Parys, 1672).

303. See also Biblioteca Correr, Codice Cicogna 1602, f. 61v.

304. See A.S.V., San Marco, Procuratia de Supra, Registro 98, f. 53r; also Biblioteca Correr, Codice Cicogna 1602, f. 119r.

305. A.S.V., San Marco, Procuratia de Supra, Registro 98, f. 70r.

306. A.S.V., San Marco, Procuratia de Supra, Busta 91, Processo 208, fascicolo 1, f. 12r–25r; Ibid., Busta 88, Processo 195, f. 53r–61r.

307. Biblioteca Correr, Codice Cicogna 1602, f. 100v, 127r; it is also listed as an alternate service for the Common of a Martyr, f. 131r.

308. In the modern Roman liturgy, this series has been transferred to Holy Saturday; see *LU*, p. 776B.

309. This is stated as a general rule in the *Commune Sanctorum* section of the *Orationale*. See Biblioteca Correr, Codice Cicogna 1602, f. 129r.

310. The Roman hymns cited by Stringa make it clear that he is using the breviary of Clement VIII, published in 1602, as his control. On the origins of *Festum nunc celebre*, see Batiffol, op. cit., p. 143. On the topic of special hymns for St. Mark's, see Weidensaul, op. cit., p. 156–63.

311. While St. Mark's uses *Vexilla regis* as the hymn for Passion Sunday, as does Rome, the version in the *Psalterium Davidicum* differs from that in the breviary of Clement VIII through the insertion of a new strophe right after the opening one: Confixa clavis visera:/Tendens manus vestigia:/Redemptionis gratia/Haec immolata est hostia. See *Psalterium Davidicum*, f. 112r.

312. There are, however, manuscript sources for a number of the others. See Ulysse Chevalier, *Repertorium Hymnologicum* (Louvain: Lefever, 1892) for the following texts: *Festum nunc celebre*, I: 375 (item 6264); *Maria mater Domini*, II: 78 (item 11110); *Fons pietatis culmina*, I: 386 (item 6446); and *Deus qui mundum crimine*, I: 270 (item 4494).

313. The situation is somewhat ambiguous here, for all of the hymns in the *Selva Morale* are taken from the *Commune Sanctorum*. Since the choice of hymns for the *Commune Sanctorum* in St. Mark's did not differ from the Roman hymns, it is possible that Monteverdi was merely setting those texts in Clement VIII's breviary without intending that they be used expressly for St. Mark's. However, it seems unlikely that such an astute businessman as Magni, who married into the Gardane family, took over the firm, and finally changed its name to his own, would let a collection go to press in 1640 with obsolete hymn texts unless he were consciously publishing the texts presently used in the basilica.

314. One text which seems to be a hymn is *O Jesu mi dulcissime*, set in Grandi's *Motetti con sinfonie*, Book II (1625). The text is the third stanza of the hymn *Jesu decus angelicus*, which is the hymn for the Feast of the Most Holy Name of Jesus in the modern Roman liturgy. However, the feast was not a part of the liturgy in the seventeenth century, either in St. Mark's or in the Roman rite. Thus, the text must have had a non-liturgical use in St. Mark's.

315. ".... sopra alla qual aria si potranno cantare anche altri Hinni però che siino dello stesso metro." This is actually an old practice in St. Mark's. Bonifacio's *ceremoniale* cites numerous occasions on which the text of one hymn is to be performed to the melody of another (Document 139).

316. The service is described not only in the *Orationale* but also in Biblioteca Correr, Codice Cicogna 1006, f. 24r–30v. The service was also part of the early Roman liturgy and retained in England and in the Gallican breviary; see Batiffol, op. cit., p. 97.

317. These ceremonies are not described in the *Orationale* but are found in Biblioteca Correr, Codice Cicogna 1006, f. 24r–30v and Codice Cicogna 1595, f. 34v. The details

of the ceremonies are slightly different in the two sources. See also A.S.V., San Marco, Procuratia de Supra, Registro 116, f. 50r–v for the texts of the service with plainchant and Biblioteca Nazionale Marciana 171. D. 199. for a printed description of the service in detail.

318. Biblioteca Correr, Inc. I. 31, f. 185v–186r.

319. Oxford Bodleian, MS Canon. Liturg. 323, f. 113r, Magnificat antiphon for Second Vespers of the Feast of St. Mark: "O quam beata urbs, habitatio Venetia*rum*, in qua gloriosa mem*bra* Marci in pace sepulta sunt . . . "; Biblioteca Nazionale Marciana, 136. D. 175., p. 42, Magnificat antiphon for First Vespers of the Feast of the Translation of the Body of St. Mark: "O quam felix et gloriosa es Urbs beata Venetorum; quae tam dignum, et gloriosum hodie meruisti suscipere Patronum, alleluia, alleluia."

320. The iconography of the mosiacs is described in detail in Pierre Saccardo, *Les mosaïques de Saint-Marc à Venise* (Venice: Ongania, 1896), pp. 216–83. Saccardo also reproduces all of the Latin inscriptions which identify the figures.

321. For an elaboration of this theme with regard to the iconography of the ducal palace, see Staale Sinding-Larsen, *Christ in the Council Hall: Studies in the Religious Iconography of the Venetian Republic* (Rome: L'Erma di Bretschneider, 1974). A number of the figures whose feasts have a special liturgy in St. Mark's and who are represented prominently among the mosaics of the church are also found in Tintoretto's monumental *Paradise* which dominates the *Sala del Maggior Consilio*. See Sinding-Larsen, p. 65.

322. St. Clement is also prominent among the mosaics of the church. He is portrayed above one of the doors to the church, above one of the choirlofts, and a number of scenes from his life adorn the so-called "chapel of St. Clement."

323. The Roman antiphons overlap only in the case of the fifth text: *Isti sunt Sancti, Sancti per fidem, Sanctorum velut aquilae, Absterget deus, In caelestibus regnis.*

324. Only the second of the Roman texts overlaps with St. Mark's: *Haec est virgo sapiens et una de numero, Haec est virgo sapiens quam Dominus, Haec est qui nescivit, Veni electa mea, Ista est speciosa.*

325. The first of the Roman antiphons overlaps with those of St. Mark's: *Ecce sacerdos magnus, Non est inventus, Ideo iure iurando, Sacerdotes dei, Serve bone.*

326. The frequency is even higher if one considers the series of antiphons for the Saturdays following Pentecost. Of 32 Magnificat antiphons listed in the *Orationale* for this period, fully 20 are not found in Variscum's *Breviarium Romanum*, and 11 of these can be traced to Aquileia.

327. See Biblioteca Ambrosiana, MS A. 328 inf., f. 74r: "Le 8 Antifone Maggiori si dicono 8 giorni avanti la Vigilia di Natale, eccetto che nelle Domeniche." See also Biblioteca Correr, Codice Cicogna 1602, f. 5r–12v.

328. While one is tempted to leave Grandi's first five books off the list, since he was working in Ferrara during their publication, I have chosen to include them; for my discovery of the documents proving Grandi's presence at St. Mark's during the first decade of the seventeenth century demonstrates that some of the works published in these books could easily date from these early years in Venice.

329. See, inter alia, Volume II, nos. 8 and 14.

330. See Volume II, no. 10.

331. *Salmi della Madonna.... di Paolo Agostini.... Libro Primo* (Rome: Luca Antonio Soldi, 1619). Contents listed in Jeffrey Kurtzman, "Some Historical Perspectives on the Monteverdi Vespers," *Analecta Musicologica* XV (1975): 35.

332. *Virgo prudentissima, Sub tuum praesidium, Cantate Domino, Gaudeamus omnes.* The other two texts associated with psalms are *Beata es Virgo* and *Veni in hortum meum.*

333. See James Armstrong, "*The Antiphonae, seu Sacrae Cantiones* (1613) of Giovanni Francesco Anerio: A Liturgical Study," *Analecta Musicologica* XIV (1974): 89–150.

334. See also Biblioteca Ambrosiana, MS A. 328 inf., f. 17r, a description of the Feast of the Purification: "Si espone la B*eata* V*ergine* sopra l'Altar Maggior.... Li Cantori cantano O Gloriosa Domina.... "; and A.S.V., San Marco, Procuratia de Supra, Busta 91, large ecclesiastical calendar (reproduced below as Document 143): "Ne' Trasporti dell'Imagine della B*eata* V*ergine* dal proprio all'Altar Maggiore: l'Inno *O Gloriosa Domina.*" While the texts serve as the hymns for Matins and Lauds on a number of Marian feasts in St. Mark's, their use as processional hymns is para-liturgical.

335. A.S.V., San Marco, Procuratia de Supra, Registro 98, f. 4r: "In Vigilia Epiphani*ae* . . . In p*ri*mis Vesp*eris* . . . Et Dicta orat*ione* dum pulsa*tur* organum et Cantores cantant Motetum pro Deo Gra*tias* . . ."

336. W. Gurlitt, "Ein Briefwechsel zwischen Paul Hainlein und L. Friedrich Behaim aus den Jahren 1647–48," *Sammelbände der internationalen Musikgesellschaft* IV (1912–13): 493, 497. Letter of 11 October 1647: "Wirdt aber allezeit zwischen einen iedwetern *psalm* ein *Sonata* oder *Motteten* gemacht, unter andern ein Romaner, welchen ein *Bass*ist mit seinen knaben dergleichen gesungen mit schöner Manier . . ." Letter of 13 December 1647: "Aber zwischen jedweter *psalm* ein *Motetten* oder *Sonata* gemacht, darunter ein *Bass*ist und *Discant*ist, welche von *Rom* eine gesungen, von der *Madona*, sendt auch wort auss dem 46 psalm genomen worden dieses inhalts, dass sie dess Türcken macht zerstöhren, bögen und schildt zerbrechen, schiff und Galleen verbrennen und seine Gantze macht in den abgrundt dess Meers stürzen wolle."

337. See Mario dal Tin, "Note di liturgia patriarchina e canti tradizionali della basilica di S. Marco a Venezia," *Jucunda Laudatio* I–IV (1973): 90ff.

338. See inter alia, A.S.V., San Marco, Procuratia de Supra, Registro 99, f. 149r: "1656 1.o Agosto. P*er* la gran Vittoria havuta dall'Armata N*ost*ra contro il Turco sin sotto il di 26. Zugno del sud*etto* Anno.... Fu nel fine cantata l'*in principio erat Verbum*, qual finito il Celebrante intonò l'*Exaudi nos Domine*, cantandosi dalli Cantori Nostri le Litanie al S*ant*a Maria.... "

339. Biblioteca Correr, Codice Cicogna 1602, f. 1r: "In primo Sabbato de Adventu Domini ad Vesperas . . . fit quotidie commemoratio de Sancta Maria in vesperis et laudibus, quando non fit de festo duplici usque dum ponitur."

Chapter V

340. See Pace's explanation of the role of the campanile in the ceremonial life of the basilica, Biblioteca Ambrosiana, MS A. 328 inf., f. 165r and following. See also Biblioteca Correr, Codice Cicogna 2711, fascicolo 2 and A.S.V., San Marco, Procuratia de Supra, Registro 98, f. 116v.

341. Gurlitt, loc. cit.

342. See inter alia Biblioteca Ambrosiana MS A. 328 inf., f. 44r: "La Vigilia del Corpus Domini s'apre la Palla, si canta Vespro in 5.o da un Canonico cui *per Turnum*, et dalli Cantori à due Cori li Salmi a 8."

343. See A.S.V., San Marco, Procuratia de Supra, Registro 140, entry of 24 April 1607: ".... *Padre Francesco* Brissiani canonico, il qual havea da intonar il Vespro della Vigilia di *San Marco.*" See also ibid., Busta 91, Processo 208, fascicolo 1, f. 21r: ".... doppo detto il deus in adiutorium et risposto dalli canonici domine ad adiuvandum, etc." Stringa mentions that subcanons assumed this duty on ferial days and on minor feasts. Pace reports that the Primicerio intoned Vespers on certain major feasts and that the Vicario intoned them on some lesser feasts (Biblioteca Ambrosiana, MS A. 328 inf., f. 72r–v).

344. See Volume II, no. 11.

345. A.S.V., San Marco, Procuratia de Supra, Busta 88, Processo 195, f. 55v: ".... et in tanto ordinò che si cantassero quelli salmi che mancavano in falso bordon, cosa che non si convien à una capella del Serenissimo Principe cantar falso bordon.... "; ibid., f. 58r: ".... et quando non si trovava salmi che fossero statti composti li faceva cantar in falso bordon, il che è con gran vergogna della chiesa."

346. For the afternoon offices of Holy Week, however, the duty of intoning the antiphons and psalms was eventually taken over by the two *capi di coro*; see Biblioteca Ambrosiana MS A. 328 inf., f. 207v: "E offitio delli Capi di Coro l'intonar li Salmi, et Antiphone nelli Offitij il doppo pranso la Settimana Santa; cioè Mercordi, Giovedi et Venerdi Santo."

347. Biblioteca Ambrosiana, MS A. 328 inf., f. 77r: "Se il Diacono intona un Salmo per un'altro; si seguiti il primo verso intonato dal Choro; mà nel secondo s'aggiusti il Choro al Salmo, che si doveva intonare. Se intuona un tuono per un'altro, si seguiti il tuono intonato per non far conoscer l'errore." See also A.S.V., San Marco, Procuratia de Supra, Processo 204, fascicolo 2, f. 61v: Constitutiones Ecclesiae Sancti Marci . . .De corrigendo errore in choro.

348. On the *Pala d'oro*, see especially Rodolfo Gallo, *Il Tesoro di S. Marco e la sua storia* (Venice: Instituto per la collaborazione culturale, n. d.), pp. 157–91.

349. See, inter alia, Biblioteca Ambrosiana MS A. 328 inf., f. 164v; see Document 29.

350. Biblioteca Ambrosiana, MS A. 328 inf., f. 208r: "Li Cantori erano obligati à cantar il Te Deum. Furono licentiati dalli Ecc*ellentissi*mi Proc*urato*ri da questo obligo, cum hoc, che cantassero li Salmi à Otto, in due Chori, ogni volta, che fosse aperta la Palla."

351. A.S.V., San Marco, Procuratia de Supra, Registro 98, f. 70r–v; another copy of the same document: ibid., f. 30v (see Document 94). Bonifacio also describes the same agreement with the Procurators that Pace relates over a century later. See A.S.V., Consulatore in jure, Registro 55, f. 63r: (speaking of the Feast of the Apparition of the Body of St. Mark) "Quando vero Cantores sunt licentiati propter Te Deu*m* laudamus a D*omi*nis Procuratoribus loco Te Deu*m* cantant*ur* a duobus Choris psalmi in primis Vesperis; psalmi vero de A*posto*lis, ut quando*que* accidit, sed nunc in choro in utris*que* Vesperis s*anc*ti Jo*ann*is psal*mi* cantant in duobus Choris."

352. The following information is presented in more detail in Stephen Bonta, "Liturgical Problems in Monteverdi's Marian Vespers," *Journal of the American Musicological Society* XX (1967): 87–106.

353. A.S.V., San Marco, Procuratia de Supra, Registro 98, f. 21v: "Cantatis 3. psalm*is*, et in fine unius cuiusq*ue* pulsato organo . . . ."

354. See James Armstrong, "The Vespers and Magnificats of Maurizio Cazzati" (unpublished Ph.D. dissertation, Harvard University, 1969), I: 32–33.

355. Giovanni Croce, *Magnificat omnium tonorum, cum sex vocibus* (Venice: G. Vincenti, 1605) RISM C 4461.

356. See Adriano Banchieri, *L'Organo suonarino* (Venice: Amadino, 1605), p. 42; idem, *Cartella musicale* (Venice: Vincenti, 1614), pp. 84ff.

357. Grandi, *Salmi a otto brevi* (1629); Rovetta, *Salmi a otto voci* (1644); Rovetta, *Delli Salmi a otto voci* (1662); Cavalli, *Vesperi* (1675).

358. The three items in brackets do not have modal designations in the prints, but the mode is clear from the musical setting.

359. "Quisi suona un poco con l'Organo, et serve per l'aversetto che segue, poi si ripiglia da capo, principiando dalla proportione, et cosi l'altre volte." Giovanni Rovetta, *Motetti concertati* (Venice: Vincenti, 1635).

360. See Volume II, no. 6. Cavalli's setting is not, however, an *alternatim* setting. The ritornelli merely separate the verses and do not substitute for any of the text. Denis Arnold's suggestion that the two verses which are not printed in the collection were to be performed in plainchant is a bit far-fetched (Arnold, "A Background Note on Monteverdi's Hymn Settings," *Scritti in Onore di Luigi Ronga* [Milan: Ricciardi, 1973], p. 38). Since hymn settings from this period are usually adaptable to any text in the proper meter, it would seem clear that any verses not actually printed in the partbooks could be sung to the musical settings provided.

361. Biblioteca Ambrosiana, MS A. 328 inf., f. 51r: "Al Magnificat di questo Vespro si fà l'Asperges p*er* tutta la Chiesa con acqua d'Angeli in memoria della fragranza sentita nel girrno dell'Apparitione di S*an* Marco nella Colonna alla Croce...."

362. Sansovino-Martinioni, *Venetia città nobilissima*, p. 507.

363. See Biblioteca Correr, Codice Cicogna 1006, f. 24r–30v and Codice Cicogna 1595; see also A.S.V., San Marco, Procuratia de Supra, Registro 116, f. 50r–v and Registro 98, f. 21r.

364. It seems clear that the large *Surrexit Christus* for voices and instruments in Giovanni Gabrieli's second book of *Symphoniae Sacrae* (1615) must have been written for this service. However, its text does not exactly follow the one reproduced in Cicogna 1006 and 1595.

365. Bonta, "Liturgical Problems," p. 101.

366. See Volume II, no. 9.

367. David Rosand and Michelangelo Muraro have pointed out that there is nothing which identifies this procession necessarily with Palm Sunday (Rosand and Muraro, *Tiziano e la silografia Veneziana del Cinquecento* [Venice: Pozza, 1976], p. 148); indeed, Palm Sunday is not one of the days on which a procession took place according to the liturgical calendars of the sixteenth, seventeenth and eighteenth centuries. On the place of processions in the ceremonial life of Venice as well as the place of music in Venetian politico-religious life, see Ellen Rosand, "Music and the Myth of Venice," *Renaissance Quarterly* XXX (1977): 511–37.

368. See, inter alia, A.S.V., San Marco, Procuratia de Supra, Registro 12, entries of 30 April 1639, 13 October 1639, 27 November 1639, 17 April 1640, 16 June 1640, 30 June 1640.

369. See letter of Monteverdi to Ercole Marigliani, 21 April 1618: ".... essendo che giobbia ventura che sarà il giorno di Santa Croce, si esponerà il Santissimo sangue, et mi converà essere preparato d'una messa concertata, et motetti per tutto il giorno.... " de' Paoli, op. cit., 106–7.

370. See Biblioteca Ambrosiana, MS A. 328 inf., f. 42r–v. Pace states that the singing of "qualche cosa d'allegro" on the return to Venice is actually an earlier custom and, by 1678, the singers sang nothing during the return trip. Monteverdi also speaks of composing "una certa cantata in lode di sua Serenità, qual si stilla cantarsi ogni anno in bucintoro mentre va con tutta la Signoria a sposare il mare nel giorno de la Sensa...." de' Paoli, loc. cit.

371. A.S.V., San Marco, Procuratia de Supra, Registro 141, entry of 3 July 1616.

372. A.S.V., San Marco, Procuratia de Supra, Registro 142, entries of 10 February 1620 (*more veneto*) and 21 May 1622.

373. Selfridge-Field, *Venetian Instrumental Music*, p. 22.

374. The days on which the Doge attended Vespers in St. Mark's are recorded in at least three places: the ecclesiastical calendar with the days and services of musicians, preserved in Biblioteca Correr, Codice Cicogna 3118, fascicoli 44–50; Biblioteca Ambrosiana, MS A. 328 inf., f. 113r–v; and Sansovino-Martinioni, pp. 492–526. The information in Table V-2 is drawn mainly from Cicogna 3118, although this has been checked

against other sources. Not to be trusted, I think, is the list in A.S.V., San Marco, Procuratia de Supra, Registro 99, ff. 503v–504r, an eighteenth-century source which differs from the other three sources in a number of respects.

375. A.S.V., San Marco, Procuratia de Supra, Registro 140, entry of 7 December 1614.

376. I would assert this despite the fact that the list attributed to Zarlino (see item 3) is less extensive than this one. Zarlino's list is not an integral part of the *ceremoniale* but an independent document copied into the final pages of the volume; it may well be inaccurate and incomplete.

377. See Table V-3; the numerals 1 and 2 stand for First and Second Vespers. In general, the lists of the dates on which the *Pala d'oro* is opened do not seem to have been made with much care, and in the discussion of the liturgical propriety of collections of double-choir music, I have often had to "take a reading" of all of the sources rather than follow any one religiously. The two lists of 1677 and 1678 are particularly problematic. The list of 1677 is a somewhat scrappy affair which does not even discriminate between First and Second Vespers; the designations in parentheses are my own. The list of 1678 is actually my own compilation from Pace's detailed descriptions of individual feasts, and Pace clearly lavishes more attention on some feasts than on others, regardless of their relative importance.

378. See Biblioteca Nazionale Marciana, Cod. It. VII-1269 (-9573), f. 66v: "In Vigilia Corporis Christi non cantabatur Vesper à Cantoribus ad vitanda*m* prolixitatem. Nunc solemniori Ritu aperitur Palla, et Cantatur à duobus Choris Cantorum."

379. The collections are named in a shorthand which gives merely the composer and the year of the collection. Two titles need a brief explanation: Grandi 1630/1 refers to the *Messa e salmi concertati a tre voci* (Venice: Vincenti, 1630); Grandi 1630/2 refers to Leonardo Simonetti's *Raccolta Terza* (Venice: Magni, 1630).

380. James Armstrong has used a method similar to mine in his discussion of the liturgical propriety of the psalm collections of Maurizio Cazzati ("The Vespers and Magnificats of Maurizio Cazzati," I: 36ff.). However, since he is dealing with the Roman liturgy and does not have to take into account the special role of double-choir music, his categories are somewhat different from my own.

381. The psalms which the *Orationale* prescribes for Second Vespers on the Feast of St. Martin (Dixit, Confitebor, Beatus vir, In convertendo and Memento) may well be a mis-copying of this service. St. Martin is listed as a Confessor Bishop, and there seems no reason to assume he would have a special service of his own. Moreover, the psalms listed in the *Orationale* cannot be drawn from any one source in single-choir settings.

382. On the liturgical propriety of Monteverdi's *Selva Morale* as a source for the Vespers of saints' days, see Giuseppe Biella, "I 'Vesperi dei Santi' di Claudio Monteverdi," *Musica Sacra*, serie seconda, VI (1966): 144–53.

383. There is one earlier collection which contains this Vespers sequence and which seems at first to clash with the entire tradition under discussion here. It is the large liturgical compendium for Vespers and Compline by Willaert, first published by Gardane in 1555 and 1561, re-issued by "li figliuoli di Antonio Gardano" in 1571, and published by

Francesco Rampazetto in 1565 as follows: SACRI E SANTI SALMI/CHE SI CAN-
TANO A VESPRO ET COMPIETA,/CON LI SUOI HINNI, RESPONSORII, ET
BENEDICAMUS,/COMPOSTI DA L'ECCELLENTISSIMO MUSICO
ADRIANO/VVILLAERT A UNO CHORO, ET A QUATRO VOCI/Novamente Ris-
tampato, Con la gionta di dui Magnificat./A QUATRO (device) VOCI/IN VENETIA,
Appresso Francesco Rampazetto.

This print contains two complete Vespers services, those for Second Vespers of
Christmas (Sequence VI) and for the Blessed Virgin (Sequence II); for each service,
alternate verses of the psalms are set for a single four-part choir. This seems to be a
most unlikely setting for Sequence VI, for of the feasts listed above, only the Holy
Innocents and St. Silvester would demand these psalms in settings for a single choir.
It may be that the tradition of pairing a double-choir Vespers service with the opening
of the *Pala d'oro* was not strictly established by 1555; after all, Bonifacio's *ceremoniale*
of 1564 contains the first documentation for the practice. It is also possible that the
collection was not designed with St. Mark's itself in mind; the psalms do not use the
translation of the *Psalterium Davidicum*, as do the *salmi spezzati* in Willaert's 1550
collection, and the publication of four editions in a decade and a half clearly points to
a large commercial market. While Rampazetto was, indeed, the ducal printer, he also
published with a larger market in mind (see Document 111), so his edition was not
necessarily destined for the ducal chapel.

While the designation "a uno choro, et a quatro voci" might first seem to echo
Bonifacio's "quatuor cantores in uno choro et reliqui omnes in altero" (see Document 94), I think it is merely a variant statement of the designation "a quattro voci a
uno choro," as Gardane described his 1555 publication of the four-part psalms of
Dominico Phinot (see Lewis, op. cit., II: 537); for all of the settings in Willaert's *Sacri
e santi salmi* are of alternate psalms verses for a single, four-part choir and could not
be considered double-choir settings, even if a second group of singers sang the alternate verses in plainchant. Indeed, the terminology which Gardane used on the title
page of Willaert's earlier psalm collection makes this clear. The *Salmi appertinenti alli
Vesperi per tutte le solennità dell'anno* (Venice: Gardane, 1550) have the description
"parte a versi, et parte spezzadi, accomodati da cantare a uno et a duoi chori." It
seems clear that the psalms designated "uno choro" are those whose alternate verses
are set for a single four-part choir (like those in the *Sacri e santi salmi*) while those
designated "duoi chori" are those for which all the verses are set polyphonically and
distributed between two choirs, either verse by verse or in the form of *salmi spezzati*.

384. Biblioteca Ambrosiana, MS A. 328 inf., f. 60r–v.

385. See A.S.V., San Marco, Procuratia de Supra, Busta 88, Processo 195, f. 53r–61r.

386. There is some ambiguity about the exact service for which musicians were hired on
24 December. Martinioni states that it was for the First Vespers of Christmas and says
that the music was sung in up to 16 choirs—he may mean 16 *parts*, i.e. 4 four-part
choirs (Document 153). The payment records for the Giornali Cassier, however, indicate that the musicians may have been brought in for the Masses of the Christmas
Vigil and Christmas Day rather than for Vespers. See A.S.V., San Marco, Procuratia
de Supra, Registro 12, entries of 29 December 1639, 31 December 1640, 30 December
1641 and 2 January 1642 (*more veneto*).

387. See Volume II, nos. 1, 5 and 7.

388. The double-choir setting of *Beatus vir* which is sandwiched into Rovetta's collection of 1639 is not a *concertato* work at all but, rather, similar in style to the works of Rovetta's collection of 1644.

389. See Armstrong, "The Vespers and Magnificats of Maurizio Cazzati," p. 53; and Roche, "Music at Santa Maria Maggiore, 1614–1643," p. 298.

390. Giuseppe Biella, "I 'Vespri dei Santi' di Claudio Monteverdi," *Musica Sacra*, serie seconda, VI (1966): 144–53.

391. For a rather different view on the possibilities of drawing complete services from the collection, see Denis Stevens, *Monteverdi: Sacred, Secular and Occasional Music*, pp. 83–84.

392. On Scacchi himself, see Claude Palisca, "Marco Scacchi's Defense of Modern Music (1649)," *Words and Music: The Scholar's View* (Cambridge: Harvard University Press, 1972), pp. 189–235. On Scacchi's place in seventeenth-century style-critical theory, see Erich Katz, *Die musikalischen Stilbegriffe des 17. Jahrhunderts* (Freiburg, 1926); on Christoph Bernhard, see Joseph Müller-Blattau, *Die Kompositionslehre Heinrich Schützens in der Fassung seines Schülers Chr. Bernhard* (Leipzig: Breitkopf und Härtel, 1969). Scacchi's typology is discussed with allusions to Italian music of the early seventeenth century in Palisca, *Baroque Music* (Englewood Cliffs: Prentice-Hall, 1968).

393. See Palisca, "Scacchi's Defense," p. 191; see also letter of Scacchi to C. S. Werner quoted in Katz, op. cit., p. 83: "Ecclesiasticus in quatuor iterum stylus dividitur. Primusque comprehendit Missas, Motetta, et similes Cantilenas 4. 5. 6. 8. vocum, absque Organo. Secundus easdem Cantilenas, adiuncto Organo, ita, ut plures etiam chori pleni possint constitui. Tertius similes Cantilenas in concerto. Quartus demum Motetta juxta usum modernum."

394. Biblioteca Nazionale Marciana, Cod. It. IV-1134 (-10949).

395. See Volume II, no. 4.

396. See Jerome Roche, "Northern Italian Liturgical Music in the Early Seventeenth Century, its Evolution around 1600 and its Development until the Death of Monteverdi," unpublished Ph.D. dissertation, Cambridge University, 1968, pp. 197ff.: "The Venetian Motet after Gabrieli's Death."

397. The setting of the *Salve Regina* in Rovetta's *Motetti Concertati, Libro III* (1647), a work which was lifted by Tunder and published as a *contrafactum*, is really no exception to this rule. (See Volume II, no. 14). Although it involves a five-part string accompaniment, the essential framework of the piece is still voice vs. basso continuo, and the string parts could be left out if need be without disturbing the essential contour of the work. See Roche, "Rovetta and Tunder—misattribution or plagiarism?" *Early Music* III (1975): 58–60.

398. Arnold, "Venetian Motets and their Singers," p. 320.

399. See Volume II, no. 17.

400. Biblioteca Correr, Codice Cicogna 1602, f. 51r: "Superdictis vesperor*um* ordo antiq*ui*tus servabatur. Sed modo canta*n*tur sup*er* dict*a*e q*ui*nque an*tiphonae* cum solo psalmo. Laudate dominu*m* o*mn*es ge*n*tes ut in Ordinario habetur."

Appendix II

401. The sources are inconsistent in their placement of First Vespers. Some list the service under the previous day, others under the date of the feast itself. I have included First Vespers under the date of the feast itself unless there are special ceremonies for the vigil in addition to the Vespers service itself.

402. Listed as 23 February in 1515; without a date in 1678.

403. "Littanie in Processione à due Cori.... "

404. "Processione colle Litanie de' Santi."

405. Cited specifically as a Rogation Mass in the documents: "Missa Litaniaru*m* cum 2. Choris" (1515); "Messa delle Rogazioni" (1678).

406. Listed under the moveable feasts rather than in the first part of the liturgical calendar. It would seem this is an oversight.

407. All documents prescribe two celebrations of the Mass and two of each Vespers service.

408. "Vesperi 2. per la Croce."

409. Feast is listed as 5 May in 1677 source only.

410. Listed as 16 May in 1761 source only.

411. The following entry also occurs for this date: "Si fà l'essequie del S*igno*re Cardinal Zen."

412. Procession not listed but implied by the description of Vespers in churches other than St. Mark's.

413. Although listed under the twenty-fifth, this Matins is connected with the Feast of the Apparition of the body of St. Mark, 25 June (". . . in quo cantat*ur* Te deu*m* et Deo grat*ia*s pro Apparit*ion*e Corporis S*ancti* Marci").

414. Implied by description of Mass in Ss. Giovanni e Paolo.

415. Mass in San Paternian, not in St. Mark's.

416. Mass in the Chiesa delle Terese, not in St. Mark's.

417. "Messe 2."

418. 1755: "due Mottetti à Capella in Chiesa di Santa Marina."

419. 1761: "Motetti due alla Messa bassa in S. Marina."

420. It would seem this is a mistake. Second Vespers rather than First should be celebrated, since the First Vespers for St. Anne coincides with the Second Vespers for St. James.

421. August 4th is listed as "*San*Domenico" in 1761 only; I have assumed, however, that the "Vespero senza Palla" specified is actually the First Vespers for the Feast of Our Lady of the Snow, since this would correspond with all other sources. Moreover, there is no easy explanation for the celebration of *only* Second Vespers on the Feast of St. Dominic.

422. The following entry also occurs under this date: "Si fà l'Essequie d*el* Si*gno*r Morosini Ninfa."

423. Listed as 16 and 17 September instead of 17 and 18 September in 1755 only.

424. Listed as 7 October, along with St. Giustina, in 1515 as well as in the ecclesiastical calendars in both copies of the *Orationale*.

425. The 1677 source gives 12 November as the date of the feast. This is actually the date of the Feast of St. Martin I, Pope and Martyr. While both feasts of St. Martin appear in the *Orationale*, none of the other calendars names the latter feast as a day of obligation for the singers.

426. Feast called "M*adonn*a d*e*lla Salute" in 1677 and in 1761.

427. "Processione col *Te Deum*."

428. To be celebrated in the Doge's palace (".... in Palatio.... ")

429. ".... Messa nella Capella di S. Nicoletto alla presenza del Prencipe.... "

430. ".... Messa a Capella in Palazzo...."

431. "Processione colle Litanie della B. V."

432. First Vespers of Christmas Day.

433. The services listed here for 1677 reflect my interpretation of the original data. The document itself is rather confused: "Vespero" is written in the column for First Vespers, "Ser.mo" in the column for Mass, "Vespero" in the column usually reserved to mark the presence of the Doge, and "Mattutin" in the column for Second Vespers. I have interpreted the material as follows: the singers perform at First Vespers of Christmas Day; the Doge attends the Mass of the Christmas Vigil with the singers; the singers also perform at Matins and at Second Vespers *on Christmas Day*. This is contrary to the document, but the presence of *two* Vespers services on 24 December makes no sense; moreover, there is a blank space in the document (not the usual horizontal dash to indicate a service without the singers) for Second Vespers on 25 December. Thus, I think the document is faulty at this point, and I have assumed it should agree with the other four lists.

434. In 1677 "S. Gio. Evang.ta" is listed as 26 December, "S. Steffano" as the twenty-seventh. This is clearly an error, as it accords with no other of the documents, nor with the *Orationale*.

435. 1677 and 1755: singers sing the Mass of the Blessed Virgin only if it is not displaced by a saint's day of double rank; 1761 specifies the Mass of the Virgin "sì di rito semidoppio, che doppio."

436. Mass not specified on the calendar but described elsewhere in the *ceremoniali* from which the calendars are drawn.

437. Other services are implied, for the singers are to be present *even* at the singing of the Passion (". . . In Domenica Palmarum etiam ad Passionem").

438. ".... dopo l'Antifone al getto degl'Uccelli, e alla Porta.... "

439. ".... e nella sera all'Esposizione del Sangue soli quattro.... "

440. ".... Messa a Capella in Bigonzo; Inno alla Communione, e Processione in Sacrestia: Mattutini come il dì precedente; la sera: quattro all'Inno nell'Esposizione del Sangue.... "

441. ". . . Missa etc. ut more"; thus, other ceremonies are implied.

442. ".... alla Messa, et c."

443. ".... Processione ad Fontem et Sepulcrum."

444. ".... Procession alla Fonte, et Sepolcro."

445. ".... e si ivi non fosse cantata Messa, m:a solamente detta Messa Bassa cantaranno due Mottetti à Capella e due Musici saranno alla Pietra in mezzo la Piazza, cantando la solita Antifona."

446. "Madrigale in Bucintoro."

447. This statement is somewhat enigmatic. Just what is meant by the "pause della *Salve Regina*" and what are the "soliti Versetti" which are to be performed? I know of no *Salve Regina* in the seventeenth-century repertoire from St. Mark's in which extra text is set between the sections of the antiphon, nor any setting which could be performed *alternatim*. There are paraphrase texts, of course, such as Monteverdi's first *Salve Regina* in the *Selva Morale*, but the gloss is so extensive that it cannot easily be separated from the antiphon text itself. Moreover, the arrangement described in 1761 seems to be one where figural music is sung for the "versetti" only, with the *Salve* performed in plainchant or recited.

   The document may describe a composition along the lines of the *Salve Regina* duet for canto and tenor from Lodovico Viadana's *Cento Concerti' Ecclesiastici* (1602), in which portions of the work are set as a vocal duet and other sections are notated in plain-chant. A large number of settings of the *Salve Regina* are preserved in the eighteenth-century musical archives of St. Mark's in the cloister of Sant' Apollonia; some of them may be along the lines of Viadana's setting.

448. In 1761, this is specified as the day *after* the Doge's coronation; 1515, 1677 and 1678 specify the day of the coronation itself.

Bibliography

Primary Sources: Prints

(Items marked B3 or B4 are listed in more detail in the archival bibliography in Chapter III, pp. 68–71, or in the liturgical bibliography in Chapter IV, pp. 114–17).

Banchieri, Adriano. *Cartella musicale nel canto figurato, fermo, et contrapunto*.... *Terza impressione*.... Venice: G. Vincenti, 1614.

_____. *Conclusioni nel suono dell'organo*. Bologna: Heredi di G. Rossi, 1609.

_____. *L'Organo suonarino*. Venice: Amadino, 1605. Second edition: Venice: Amadino, 1611. Third edition: Venice: Vincenti, 1622. Reprints: Bologna: Forni; Amsterdam: Fritz Knuf.

Bauldry, Michele. *Manuale Sacrarum Caeremoniarum, iuxta Ritum S. Romanae Ecclesiae*. Venice: Balleonius, 1689.

Bisaccioni, Maiolino. *Ercole in Lidia*. Venice: Vecellio et Leni, 1645.

Benedictio aquae quae sit in nocte Epiphaniae, juxta consuetudinem Ecclesiae Ducalis Sancti Marci Venetiarum. Venice: Poleti, 1722. [B4]

Breviarium Romanum. Venice: Variscum, 1562.

Breviarium Romanum ex decreto Sacrosancti Concilij Tridentini restitutum, Pij Quinti Pont. Max. iussu editum, et Clementis VIII. auctoritate recognitum. Paris: Dionysius de la Noüe, 1625.

Breviarium Romanum ex decreto Sacrosancti Concilij Tridentini restitutum. Pii. V. Pont. Max. iussu editum. et Clementis VIII primum. nunc denuo Urbani Pp. VIII. auctoritate recognitum. Paris: Regia, 1647.

Breviarium secundum ritum et consuetudinem alme ecclesiae Aquileiensis. Venice: Franciscus de Hailbrun, 1481. [B4]

Breviarium secundum usum Aquileiae. Venice: Andreas de Torresanis de Asula, 1496. [B4]

Caeremoniale Episcoporum iussu Clementis VIII. Rome, 1600.

Ciro, Fausto. *Venetia Festiva*. Venice: Baba, 1638. [B3]

Corner, Flaminio. *Ecclesiae venetae antiquis monumentis*. Venice, 1739.

Foscarini, Marco. *Della letteratura veneziana*. Venice: Manfrè, 1752.

Fusconi, Gio. Battista. *Argiope, Favola Musicale*. Venice: Pinelli, 1649.

Litania secundum consuetudinem ducalis ecclesiae Sancti Marci Venetiarum. Venice: Pinelli, 1719. [B4]

Officium hebdomadae sanctae secundum consuetudinem ducalis ecclesiae Sancti Marci Venetiarum. Venice: Prodocinus, 1716. [B4]

Officium in nocte nativitatis Domini ad matutinum secundum consuetudinem ducalis ecclesiae Sancti Marci Venetiarum. Venice: Poleti, 1722. [B4]

Psalterium Davidicum per hebdomadam dispositum ad usum Ecclesiae Ducalis Sancti Marci Venetiarum. Venice: Rampazetto, 1609. [B4]

Rubeis, Bernardo Maria de. *Monumenta Ecclesiae Aquilejensis*. Argentinae: Ordinis Praedicatorum, 1740.

Sansovino, Francesco. *Venetia città nobilissima et singolare*. Original edition 1581. Revised by Giovanni Stringa, 1604. Second revision by Giustiniano Martinioni in 1663.

St. Didier, M. de. *The City and Republick of Venice*. London: Char. Brone, 1699; originally published: Paris, 1680.

Stringa, Giovanni. *La Chiesa di San Marco*. Venice: Rampazetto, 1610.

Strozzi, Giulio. *Esequie fatte in Venetia dalla Natione Fiorentina al Ser.mo D. Cosimo II. Quarto Gran Duca di Toscana, il di 25 di Maggio 1621*. Venice: Ciotti, 1621. [B3]

_____. *La Venetia Edificata, Poema eroico*. Venice: Piuti, 1626.

Supplicationes ad Sanctissimam Virginem Mariam tempore belli secundum consuetudinem ducalis basilicae S. Marci Venetiarum. Venice: Pinelli, 1695. [B4]

Vergaro, Giulio Cesare. *Racconto dell'apparato, et solennità fatta nella Ducal Chiesa de San Marco di Venetia.... li 28, Maggio 1617*. Venice: Pinelli, 1617. [B3]

Primary Sources: Manuscripts

(Items marked B3 or B4 are listed in more detail in the archival bibliography in Chapter III, pp. 68–71, or in the liturgical bibliography in Chapter IV, pp. 114–17.)

Venice, Archivio di Stato (A.S.V.)
San Marco, Procuratia de Supra

Registri	5–17	(Giornali Cassier)	[B3]
	29–37	(Scontro)	[B3]
	52–55	(Quaderni)	[B3]
	98–100	(Ceremoniali)	[B3]
	113–119	(Libri Corali)	[B4]
	120–122	(Missals, Breviaries)	[B4]
Buste	4	(Rubricari delle Terminazioni)	[B3]
	87–89	(Cariche ed Impiegati del Clero)	[B3]
	90–91	(Cariche ed Impiegati di Capella)	[B3]

Cancelleria Inferiore, Atti dei Dogi

Registri	78–83	[B3]

Collegio
Esposizioni Principi, Filza 75; Registro 70
Ceremoniali, Registro III
Lettere, Filza 194
Archivio Notarile, Testamenti

Buste	281	(Francesco Ciola), Testamento 113
	488	(Garzoni Paulini Domenico), Testamento 206

San Lorenzo di Venezia

Buste	23	[B3]
	24	[B3]

Scuola Grande di San Marco

Buste	188	[B3]
	194	[B3]

Consulatore in Jure

Registri	555	(Bonifacio)	[B3]
	556		
	557		

Santo Ufficio
Busta   156
Provveditori di Comun
Busta   47
Fondo Monastero Spirito Santo and Reg. Monialium Archivio Curia Patriarcale

Venice, Biblioteca Nationale Marciana

Cod. It. VII-1269	(-9573)	(Pace)	[B3]
Cod. It. VII-396	(-7423)	(Pace)	[B3]
Cod. It. IV-762	(-10467)	(Caffi)	[B3]
Cod. Lat. III-172	(-2276)	(Bonifacio)	[B3]
Cod. Lat. III-44	(-2742)	(Missal)	[B4]
Cod. Lat. III-45	(-2444)	(Missal)	[B4]
Cod. Lat. III-46	(-2099)	(Missal)	[B4]
Cod. Lat. III-47	(-2100)	(Missal)	[B4]
Cod. Lat. III-48	(-2291)	(Missal)	[B4]
Cod. Lat. III-111	(-2116)	(Missal)	[B4]

Venice, Biblioteca del Civico Museo Correr

Codici Cicogna	559	(Pace)	[B3]
	596		[B4]
	801		[B3]
	1006		[B4]
	1295		[B3]
	1595		[B4]
	1602		[B4]
	1605		[B4]
	2583		[B3]
	2711, fasc. 2		[B3]
	2768	(Bonifacio)	[B3]
	2769	(Pace)	[B3]
	2770	(Pace)	[B3]
	3118, fasc. 44-56		[B3]

MS P.D. 303/C, fasc. 4
MS Donà delle Rose 58

Milan, Biblioteca Ambrosiana
MS A. 328 inf. (Pace) [B3]

Oxford, Bodleian
MS Canon. Liturg. 323 [B4]

Musical Sources: Prints

Alessandro Grandi

Salmi a otto brevi con il primo choro concertato. Venice: Vincenti, 1629.
Messa e salmi concertati a tre voci. Venice: Vincenti, 1630.
Raccolta terza di Leonardo Simonetti.... de messa et salmi del Sig. Alessandro Grandi. Venice: Magni, 1630.
Il Primo Libro de Motetti. Venice: G. Vincenti, 1610.
Reprints: 1617, 1618, 1621 and 1628 (Alessandro Vincenti)
Il Secondo Libro de Motetti. Venice: G. Vincenti, 1613.
Reprints: 1617, 1619, 1623 and 1628 (Alessandro Vincenti)

Il Terzo Libro de Motetti. Venice: G. Vincenti, 1618.
  Reprints: 1621, 1636 (Alessandro Vincenti)
Il Quarto Libro di Motetti. Venice: G. Vincenti, 1616.
  Reprints: 1618, 1620 (Palermo: Maringo); 1621 and 1628 (Alessandro Vincenti)
Celesti fiori.... Libro Quinto. Venice: Magni, 1619.
  Reprints: 1620, 1625, 1638
Il Sesto Libro de Motetti. Venice: Vincenti, 1630
  Reprints: 1637, 1640 (Phalèse).
Motetti a una et due voci con sinfonie d'istromenti. Venice: Vincenti, 1621.
  Reprints: 1626, 1637
Motetti a una, due, e quattro voci con sinfonie d'istromenti.... Libro Secondo. Venice: Vincenti, 1625.
  Reprint: 1637.
Motetti a una, et due voci con sinfonie di due violini.... Libro Terzo. Venice: Vincenti, 1629.
  Reprints: 1637; 1637 (Phalèse)
Motetti a cinque voci. Ferrara: Baldini, 1614.
  Reprint: 1620 (Magni); second reprint as:
Motetti a cinque voci.... Con l'Aggionta di Motetti di diversi Auttori. Venice: Vincenti, 1620.
Motetti a voce sola. Venice: Magni, 1621.

For a discussion of Grandi's works in printed anthologies, see above, p. 42.

Giovanni Rovetta

Salmi concertati. Venice: Magni, 1627.
Messa e salmi. Venice: Vincenti, 1639.
Salmi a tre et quattro voci. Venice: Vincenti, 1642.
Salmi a otto voci. Venice: Vincenti, 1644.
Delli Salmi a 8. voci. Venice: Magni, 1662.
Motetti concertati. Venice: Vincenti, 1635
  Reprint: 1640; partial reprint: 1648 and 1668 (Phalèse); partial reprint: 1649 (Phalèse)
Motetti concertati. Venice: Vincenti, 1639
  Reprint: 1640, 1648 (Phalèse); 1648 (Vincenti)
Motetti concertati.... Libro Terzo. Venice: Vincenti, 1647.
  Reprint: 1648 (Phalèse)
Motetti a due, tre e quattro.... Libro Quattro. Venice: Vincenti, 1650.
  Reprint: 1653 (Phalèse)

For a discussion of Rovetta's works in printed anthologies, see above, note 115.

Francesco Cavalli

Musiche Sacre. Venice: Vincenti, 1656.
Vesperi a otto voci. Venice: Gardane, 1675.
Anthologies containing sacred works of Cavalli:
Messa a quattro voci e salmi.... del Signor Claudio Monteverde. Venice: Vincenti, 1651.
  Ghirlanda Sacra. Venice, 1625.
    Reprint: 1636

Erster Theil Geistlicher Concerten und Harmonien. Leipzig, 1640.
Motetti a voce sola di diversi Eccelentissimi Autori. Venice, 1645.
Sacri concerti overo motetti. Bologna: Monti, 1668.
Sacra corona. Venice: Magni, 1656.

Musical Sources: Manuscripts

Alessandro Grandi

See the discussion of the manuscript sources of Grandi's sacred works Chapter II, note 102.

Giovanni Rovetta

Venice, Biblioteca Nazionale Marciana. Cod. It. IV-1134 (Magnificat, Requiem)
Venice, Biblioteca Nazionale Marciana. Cod. It. IV-1135 (Motets)
Venice, Archive of the Procurators of St. Mark's. Uncatalogued choirbooks (see discussion of these volumes, Chapter II, note 114).
Venice, Archive of St. Mark's (Sant'Apollonia). Uncatalogued manuscripts. (Passio D. N. J. C. secundum Mattheum, Passio secundum Joannem, Turbae per la settimana santa, motetti, Missa pro Defunctis octo vocibus [1655], Missa a Cape*l*la a 4 voci).

For additional manuscript sources of Rovetta's sacred works, see the discussion in Chapter II, note 115.

Francesco Cavalli

Dresden, Sächsische Landesbibliothek, 1702 MS, D1	(Requiem)
Münster, Bischöfliche Bibliothek Santini, Sant. Hs. 1024	(Requiem)
Venice, Biblioteca Nazionale Marciana, Cod. It. IV-711 (-10351	(Requiem)
Berlin, Deutsche Staatsbibliothek (Landsberg)	(Requiem)
Vienna, Oesterreichische Nationalbibliothek (Kiesewetter)	(Requiem)
Berlin Staatsbibliothek der Stiftung Preussicher Kulturbesitz	(Confitebor)

Secondary Sources: Books and Articles

Abert, Anna Amalie. "Cavalli" in *Die Musik in Geschichte und Gegenwart*. Kassel and Basel: Bärenreiter, 1951. Vol. II, col. 926–934.

Adrio, Adam. *Die Anfänge des Geistlichen Konzerts*. Berlin: Junker und Dünnhaupt Verlag, 1935.

————. "Heinrich Schütz und Italien," *Bekenntnis zu Heinrich Schütz*. Kassel and Basel: Bärenreiter, 1954.

————."Ambrosius Profe (1589–1661) als Herausgeber italienischer Musik seiner Zeit," *Festschrift Karl Gustav Fellerer zum Sechzigsten Geburtstag am 7. Juli 1962*. Regensburg: Gustav Bosse Verlag, 1962. pp. 20–27.

Apel, Willi. "Probleme der Alternierung in der liturgischen Orgelmusik bis 1600," *Congresso Internationale sul tema Claudio Monteverdi e il suo tempo: Relazioni e Comunicazioni*. Ed. Rafaello Monterosso, Venice, Mantua and Cremona, 1968.

Armstrong, James. "The *Antiphonae, seu Sacre Cantiones* (1613) of Francesco Anerio: A Liturgical Study," *Analecta Musicologica* XIV (1974): 89–150.

————. "The Vespers and Magnificats of Maurizio Cazzati." Unpublished Ph.D. dissertation, Harvard University, 1969.

————. "How to Compose a Psalm: Ponzio and Cerone Compared," *Studi Musicali* VII (1978): 103–41.

Arnold, Denis. *Giovanni Gabrieli.* London: Oxford University Press, 1974.

————. *Giovanni Gabrieli and the Music of the Venetian High Renaissance.* London: Oxford University Press, 1979.

————. "Giovanni Croce and the Concertato Style," *Musical Quarterly* XXXIX (1953): 37–48.

————. "The Monteverdi Succession at St. Mark's," *Music and Letters* XLII (1961): 205–11.

————. "Towards a Biography of Giovanni Gabrieli," *Musica Disciplina* XV (1961): 199–207.

————. "Ceremonial Music in Venice at the Time of the Gabrielis," *Proceedings of the Royal Musical Association* LXXXII (1955/56): 47–59.

————. "Monteverdi's Church Music: Some Venetian Traits," *Monthly Musical Record* LXXXVIII (1958): 83ff.

————. "Cavalli at St. Mark's," *Early Music* IV (1976): 266–74.

————. "Notes on Two Movements of the Monteverdi 'Vespers,' " *Monthly Musical Record* LXXXIV (1954): 59ff.

————. "Formal Design in Monteverdi's Church Music," *Claudio Monteverdi e il suo tempo*, pp. 187–216.

————. "Alessandro Grandi, A Disciple of Monteverdi," *Musical Quarterly* XLIII (1957): 171–186.

————. "Francesco Cavalli: Some Recently Discovered Documents," *Music and Letters* XLVI (1965): 50–55.

————. "Instruments in Church: Some Facts and Figures," *Monthly Musical Record* LXXXV (1955): 32–38.

————. *Monteverdi.* London: Dent, 1963. Revised edition, 1975.

————. "Music at a Venetian Confraternity in the Renaissance," *Acta Musicologica* XXXVII (1965): 62ff.

————. "Music at the Scuola di San Rocco," *Music and Letters* XL (1959): 229ff.

————. "The Significance of 'Cori Spezzati'," *Music and Letters* XL (1959): 4–14.

————. "A Background Note on Monteverdi's Hymn Settings," *Scritti in Onore di Luigi Ronga.* Milan: Ricciardi, 1973, pp. 33–44.

————. "Vivaldi's Church Music," *Early Music* I (1973): 66–75.

————. "Monteverdi, Some Colleagues and Pupils," *The Monteverdi Companion.* Ed. Denis Arnold and Nigel Fortune. New York: Norton, c. 1968, pp. 110–30.

————. "Andrea Gabrieli und die Entwicklung der 'cori-spezzati'-Technik," *Die Musikforschung* XII (1959): 258ff.

————. "Venetian Motets and their Singers," *Musical Times* (April, 1978): 320ff.

————. "Brass Instruments in Italian Church Music of the Sixteenth and Early Seventeenth Centuries," *Brass Quarterly* I (1957): 81–92.

Barblan, Guido; Gallico, Claudio; Pannain, Guido. *Claudio Monteverdi nel quarto centenario della nascita.* Torino: Edizioni radiotelevisione italiana, c. 1967.

Battiffol, Pierre. *History of the Roman Breviary.* Trans. Atwell Baylay. London: Longmans, Green and Co., 1912.

Bäumer, Suitbert. *Histoire du Bréviaire.* Trans. Réginald Biron. Paris: Letouzey et Ané, 1905. 2 volumes.

Beat, Janet E. "Monteverdi and the Opera Orchestra of his Time," *The Monteverdi Companion*, 277–304.

Benvenuti, Giacomo. *Andrea e Giovanni Gabrieli e la musica strumentale a San Marco*. Milan: Ricordi, 1931–32.

Bergin, Anne-Marie. "The *Salmi Concertati* (1626) of Giovanni Rovetta." Unpublished Masters thesis, University of Otago (New Zealand), 1967.

Bianconi, Lorenzo. "Caletti (Caletti-Bruni), Pietro Francesco, detto Cavalli," *Dizionario biografico degli italiani*. Rome: Instituto della Enciclopedia Italiana, 1973, pp. 686–96.

Biella, Giuseppe. "La 'Messa' il 'Vespro' e i 'Sacri Concenti' di Claudio Monteverdi," *Musica Sacra*, serie seconda, IX (1964): 105–15.

_____. "I 'Vespri dei Santi' di Claudio Monteverdi," *Musica Sacra*, serie seconda VI (1966): 144–53.

Boito, Camillo. *The Basilica of St. Mark's in Venice*. Trans. W. Scott. Venice: Ongania, 1888.

Bohatta, Hans. *Bibliographie der Breviere*, 1501–1850. Leipzig: Hiersemann, 1937.

_____. *Liturgische Bibliographie des XV. Jahrhunderts*. Vienna: Gilhofer und Rauschburg, 1911.

Bohn, Emil. *Die musikalischen Handschriften des XVI. und XVII. Jahrhunderts in der Stadtbibliothek zu Breslaw*. Breslau: Hainauer, 1890.

Bonta, Stephen. "The Uses of the *Sonata da chiesa*," *Journal of the American Musicological Society* XXII (1969): 54–84.

_____. "Liturgical Problems in Monteverdi's Marian Vespers," *Journal of the American Musicological Society* XX (1967): 87–106.

_____. "The Church Sonatas of Giovanni Legrenzi." Unpublished Ph.D. dissertation, Harvard University, 1964.

Borgir, Tharald. "The Performance of the Basso Continuo in Seventeenth-Century Italian Music." Unpublished Ph.D. dissertation, University of California (Berkeley), 1971.

Bossarelli, Anna Mondolfi, "Ancora intorno al Codice napoletano dell' *Incoronazione*," *Rivista Italiana di Musicologia* II (1967): 294–313.

Boyden, David. "When Is a Concerto Not a Concerto?" *Musical Quarterly* XLIII (1957): 220–32.

Bradshaw, Murray. *The Falsobordone: A Study in Renaissance and Baroque Music*. American Institute of Musicology, 1978. (Musicological Studies and Documents, no. 34).

_____. *The Origins of the Toccata*. Rome: American Institute of Musicology, 1972.

Brenet, Michel (Marie Bobillier), *Musique et Musiciens de la Vieille France*. Paris: Félix Alcan, 1911.

Brindle, Reginald Smith. "Monteverdi's G-minor Mass: An Experiment in Construction," *Musical Quarterly* LIV (1968): 352–60.

Bryant, David. "Liturgia e musica liturgica nella fenomenologia del 'Mito di Venezia,' " *Mitologie* (Venice: Edizioni La Biennale di Venezia, 1979), pp. 205–14.

Burkley, Francis. "Priest-Composers of the Baroque: A Sacred-Secular Conflict," *Musical Quarterly* LIV (1968): 169–84.

Bussi, Francesco. "La produzione sacra di Cavalli e i suoi rapporti con quella di Monteverdi," *Rivista Italiana di Musicologia* II (1967): 229–54.

_____. "Storia, tradizione e arte del 'Requiem' di Cavalli," *Nuova Rivista Musicale Italiana* X (1976): 49–77.

_____. *Piacenza, Archivio del Duomo: Catalogo del Fondo Musicale* (Biblioteca Musicae V). Milan, 1967.

Caffi, Francesco. *Storia della Musica Sacra nella già Cappella Ducale di San Marco in Venezia dal 1318 al 1797*. Venice: Antonelli, 1854. Reprint: Milan: Bollettino Bibliografico Musicale, 1931.

Cappelletti, Giuseppe. *Storia della Chiesa di Venezia dalla sua Fondazione sino ai nostri giorni*. Venice: S. Lazzaro, 1853.

Chevalier, Ulysse. *Repertorium Hymnologicum*. Louvain: Lefever, 1892.

Cicogna, Emmanuele. *Saggio di bibliografia veneziana* (Venice: G. B. Merlo, 1847).

Constable, W. G. *Canaletto: Giovanni Antonio Canal, 1697–1768* (Oxford: Clarendon, 1962).

Culley, Thomas. *Jesuits and Music: A study of the musicians connected with the German College in Rome during the seventeenth century and of their activities in Northern Europe*. Rome: Jesuit Historical Institute, 1970.

Dalhaus, Carl, ed. *Riemann Musiklexikon. Ergänzungsband. Personenteil*. Mainz: Schott, 1972.

Demus, Otto. *The Church of St. Mark's in Venice*. Washington: Dumbarton Oaks (Harvard University), 1960.

Diclich, Giovanni. *Rito Veneto Antico detto Patriarchino*. Venice: Dalla Tipografia di Vincenzo Rizzi, 1823.

Donati-Petteno, G. *L'arte della musica in Bergamo*. Bergamo: Edito per cura della Banca mutua popolare, 1930.

Ecorcheville, J. *Catalogue du fonds de musique ancienne de la Bibliothèque nationale*. Paris: Terquem et Compagnie, 1914.

Eisenhofer, Ludwig and Lechner, Joseph. *The Liturgy of the Roman Rite*. London: Nelson, 1961.

Eitner, Robert. *Biographisch-bibliographisches Quellen-Lexikon der Musiker und Musikgelehrten der christlichen Zeitrechnung bis zur Mitte des 19. Jahrhunderts*. Leipzig: Breitkopf und Härtel, 1898–1904. 10 volumes.

————. *Bibliographie der Musik-Sammelwerke des XVI. und XVII. Jahrhunderts*. Berlin: L. Liepmannssohn, 1877.

Falconer, Madan. *A Summary Catalogue of Western Manuscripts in the Bodleian Library at Oxford*. Oxford: Clarendon Press, 1897.

Fano, Fabio. "Il Monteverdi sacro, la 'prima prattica' e la scuola veneziana," *Rivista Italiana di Musicologia* II (1967): 264–69.

Fasoli, Gina. "Liturgia e cerimoniale," *Scritti di storia medioevale*. Bologna: La Fotocromo Emiliana, 1974, pp. 529–66.

Federhofer, Hellmuth. "Die Dissonanzbehandlung in Monteverdis Kirchen-musikalischen Werken und die Figurenlehre von Christoph Bernhard," *Claudio Monteverdi e il suo tempo*, 435–78.

Fellerer, Karl Gustav. "Guidetti" in *Die Musik in Geschichte und Gegenwart*. Kassel and Basel: Bärenreiter, 1951. Vol. V, col. 1070–71.

Flury, Roman. *Gioseffo Zarlino als Komponist*. Wintherthur: Keller, 1962.

Fortescue, Adrian. *The Ceremonies of the Roman Rite Described*. Fifth Edition. London: Burns, Oates and Washbourne, Ltd., 1934.

Frere, Walter Howard. *Bibliotheca musico-liturgica*. London: Plainsong and Medieval Music Society, 1894. Reprint: Hildesheim: Olms, 1967.

Fuller-Maitland, J. A. and Mann, A. H. *Catalogue of Music in the Fitzwilliam Museum*. London: Cambridge Press, 1898.

Gallo, Rodolfo. *Il Tesoro di S. Marco e la sua storia*. Venice: Istituto per la collaborazione culturale (Florence, Olschki), n.d.

Gaspari, Gaetano. *Catalogo della Biblioteca del Liceo Musicale di Bologna*. Bologna: Libreria Romagnoli dall'Aqua, 1892. Vol. II: Musica Vocale Religiosa. Reprinted as *Catalogo della Biblioteca Musicale G. B. Martini di Bologna*. Bologna: Forni, 1961.

Giazotto, R. "La guerra dei palchi...." *Nuova Rivista Musicale Italiana* I (1967): 245–86, 465–508.

Glixon, Jonathan. "Music at the Venetian 'Scuole Grandi,' 1440–1540." Unpublished Ph.D. dissertation, Princeton University, 1979.

Glover, Jane. *Cavalli*. New York: St. Martin's Press, 1978.

Goovaerts, Alphonse. *Histoire et bibliographie de la typographie musicale dans les Pays-Bas*. n.p., 1877.

Ghisi, Federico. "Alcuni aspetti stilistici della musica sacra monteverdiana in Giacomo Carissimi," *Claudio Monteverdi e il suo tempo*, pp. 305–12.

Grusnick, Bruno. "Die Dübensammlung. Ein Versuch ihrer chronologischen Ordnung," *Svensk tidskrift för musikforskning* XLVIII (1966): 63–186; XLVI (1964): 27–86.

Günther, Renate. "Motette und geistliches Konzert im Schaffen von Alessandro Grandi (ca. 1577–1630)." Unpublished Ph.D. dissertation, Freie-Universität Berlin, 1958.

Gurlitt, W. "Ein Briefwechzel zwischen Paul Hainlein und L. Friedrich Behaim aus den Jahren 1647–48," *Sammelbände der internationalen Musikgesellschaft* IV (1912–13): 491–99.

Horsley, Imogene. "Symposium on Seventeenth-Century Music Theory: Italy," *Journal of Music Theory* XVI (1972): 51–61.

Huys, Bernard. *Catalogue des Imprimés des XVe, XVIe, et XVIIe siècles. Fonds Général*. Brussels: Bibliothèque Royale de Belgique, 1965.

Istituto di Ricovero e di Educazione, Venezia. *Arte e Musica all'Ospedaletto. Schede d'archivio sull'attività musicale degli ospedali dei Derelitti e dei Mendicanti di Venezia* (sec. XVI–XVIII). Venice: Stamperia di Venezia Editrice, 1978.

Jeffrey, Peter. "The Autograph Manuscripts of Francesco Cavalli." Unpublished Ph.D. dissertation, Princeton University, 1980.

Jürgens, Jürgen. "Urtext und Aufführungspraxis bei Monteverdis *Orfeo* und *Marien-Vesper*," *Claudio Monteverdi e il suo tempo*, pp. 269–304.

Jungmann, S. J., Rev. Joseph A. *The Mass of the Roman Rite: Its Origin and Development (Missarum Sollemnia)*. Trans. Rev. Francis A. Brunner. New York: Benzinger Bros., 1959.

Katz, Erich. *Die musikalischen Stilbegriffe des 17. Jahrhunderts*. Freiburg, 1926.

Kellner, Altman. *Musikgeschichte des Stiftes Kremsmünster*. Kassel and Basel: Bärenreiter, 1956.

Kenton, Egon. *Life and Works of Giovanni Gabrieli*. New York: American Institute of Musicology, 1967.

————. "The Late Style of Giovanni Gabrieli," *Musical Quarterly* XLVIII (1962): 427ff.

Kimmel, William B. "Polychoral Music and the Venetian School." Unpublished Ph.D. dissertation, University of Rochester, 1942.

King, Archdale. *Liturgy of the Roman Church*. London: Longmans, Green and Co., 1957.

Kunze, Stefan. "Die Entstehung des Concertoprinzips im Spätwerk Giovanni Gabrielis," *Archiv für Musikwissenschaft* XXI (1964): 81–110.

Kurtzman, Jeffrey G. "The Monteverdi Vespers of 1610 and their Relationship with Italian Sacred Music of the Early Seventeenth Century." Unpublished Ph.D. dissertation, University of Illinois, 1972.

————. "Some Historical Perspectives on the Monteverdi Vespers," *Analecta Musicologica* XV (1975): 29–86.

————. *Essays on the Monteverdi Mass and Vespers of 1610*. Rice University Studies, Vol. 64, No. 4 (1978).

Lampl, Hans. *Praetorius, Michael, Syntagma Musicum III*. Unpublished Ph.D. dissertation, University of Southern California, 1957.

Leichtentritt, Hugo. *Geschichte der Motette* (Kleine Handbücher der Musikgeschichte nach Gattungen, Band II), Leipzig, 1908.

Lenaerts, René. "La Chapelle de Saint-Marc à Venise sous Adriaen Willaert (1527–1562)," *Bulletin de l'institut historique belge de Rome*, fasc. XIX (1938): 205–55.

Lewis, Mary Stuart. "Antonio Gardane and his Publications of Sacred Music, 1535–1555." Unpublished Ph.D. dissertation, Brandeis University, 1979.

Libera, Sandro della. "Cronologia musicale della Basilica di San Marco a Venezia," *Musica Sacra*, seconda serie LXXXV (1961): 25–27; 88–91; 135–36.

—————. *L'Arte degli Organi a Venezia*. Venice: Istituto per la collaborazione culturale, 1962.

Long, Joan Anne. "The Motets, Psalms and Hymns of Adrian Willaert: A Liturgico-Musical Study." Unpublished Ph.D. dissertation, Columbia University, 1971.

Lunelli, Renato. *Studi e documenti di storia organaria veneta*. Florence: Olschki, 1973.

Malipiero, Gian Francesco. *Claudio Monteverdi*. Milan: Fratelli Treves, 1929.

Maggini, Emilio. *Lucca, Biblioteca del Seminario, Catalogo delle Musiche Stampate e Manoscritte del Fondo Antico*. Milan, 1965.

Mason, Wilton. "The Architecture of St. Mark's Cathedral and the Venetian Polychoral Style: A Clarification," *Studies in Musicology*, Chapel Hill: University of North Carolina Press, c. 1969.

Mitjana, Rafael. *Catalogue critique et descriptif des imprimés de musique des XVIe et XVIIe siècles conservés à la Bibliothèque de l'Université Royale d'Uppsala*. Uppsala: Almquist et Wiksell, 1911.

Mompellio, Federico. *Lodovico Viadana*. Florence: Olschki, 1967.

Moser, Hans. *Heinrich Schütz: Sein Leben und Werk*. Second edition. Kassel and Basel: Bärenreiter, 1954. English translation by Carl P. Pfatteicher, St. Louis: Concordia, 1959.

Mosto, Andrea da. *L'Archivio di Stato di Venezia, indice generale, storico, descrittivo ed analitico*. Rome: Biblioteca d'arte editrice, 1937. 2 volumes.

Müller, Joseph. *Die musikalischen Schätze der Königlichen- und Universitäts-Bibliothek zu Königsberg in Preussen*. Bonn: Marcus, 1870. Reprint: Hildesheim: Olms, 1971.

Müller-Blattau, Joseph. *Die Kompositionslehre Heinrich Schützens in der Fassung seines Schülers Christoph Bernhard*. Leipzig, 1926. Second edition: Kassel, 1963.

New Catholic Encyclopedia. New York: McGraw-Hill Co., c. 1967.

Ongania, Ferdinando, ed. *La Basilica di San Marco a Venezia*. Venice: Ongania, 1888.

Osthoff, Wolfgang. "Cavalli" in *La Musica: enciclopedia storica*. Turin: UTET, n.d., pp. 825–34.

—————. "Unita Liturgica e Artistica nei 'Vespri' del 1610," *Rivista Italiana di Musicologia* II (1967): 314–27.

—————. "Neue Beobachtungen zu Quellen und Geschichte von Monteverdis 'Incoronazione di Poppea,' " *Die Musikforschung* XI (1958): 129–38.

Palisca, Claude V. "Marco Scacchi's Defense of Modern Music," *Words and Music: The Scholar's View*. Cambridge: Harvard University Press, 1972.

—————. *Baroque Music*. Englewood Cliffs: Prentice-Hall, 1968.

Pasini. "Il Rito Antico ed il Cerimoniale della Basilica di San Marco," in Camillo Boito, ed., *La Basilica di S. Marco in Venezia*. Venice: Tipografia Emiliana, 1888.

Prunières, Henry. *Monteverdi: His Life and Work*. Trans. Marie D. Mackie. New York: Dutton, 1926. Reprinted: New York: Dover, 1972.

—————. *Cavalli et l'opera vénitien au XVII siècle*. Paris: Editions Riediers, 1931.

Paoli, Domenico de'. *Claudio Monteverdi: Lettere, Dediche e Prefazioni.* Rome: Edizioni de Santis, 1973.

Redlich, Hans. *Claudio Monteverdi: Life and Works.* Trans. Kathleen Dale. London: Oxford University Press, 1952.

_____. "Claudio Monteverdi: Some Problems of Textual Interpretation," *Musical Quarterly* XLI (1955): 68ff.

_____. "Early Baroque Church Music," *New Oxford History of Music, IV: The Age of Humanism*, 1540–1630. London: Oxford University Press, 1968, pp. 520–49.

Roche, Jerome. "Anthologies and the Dissemination of Early Baroque Sacred Music," *Soundings* IV (1974): 11–12.

_____. "The Duet in Early Seventeenth-century Italian Church Music," *Proceedings of the Royal Musical Association* (1966–67): 33–50.

_____. "Music at Santa Maria Maggiore in Bergamo, 1614–43," *Music and Letters* XLVII (1966): 296–312.

_____. "Northern Italian Liturgical Music in the Early Seventeenth Century, its Evolution around 1600 and its Development until the Death of Monteverdi." Unpublished Ph.D. dissertation, Cambridge University, 1967.

_____. "Giovanni Antonio Rigatti and the Development of Venetian Church Music in the 1640s," *Music and Letters* LVII (1976): 256–67.

_____. "Rovetta and Tunder—misattribution or plagiarism?" *Early Music* III (1975): 58–60.

_____. "What Schütz learnt from Grandi in 1629," *Musical Times* CXIII (1972): 1074–75.

_____. "Monteverdi and the *Prima Prattica*," *The Monteverdi Companion*, pp. 167–91.

_____. "An Inventory of Choirbooks at S. Maria Maggiore, Bergamo, January 1628," *R. M. A. Research Chronicle* No. 5 (1965): 47–51.

Rosand, David and Muraro, Michelangelo. *Tiziano e la silografia veneziana del cinquecento.* Venice: Pozza, 1976.

Rosand, Ellen. "Music and the Myth of Venice," *Renaissance Quarterly* XXX (1977): 511–37.

Saccardo, Pierre. *Les mosaïques de Saint-Marc à Venise.* Venice: Ongania, 1896.

Sander, Hans Adolf. "Beiträge zur Geschichte der Barockmesse," *Kirchen-musikalisches Jahrbuch* XXVIII (1933): 77–129.

Sartori, Claudio. *Dizionario degli Editori Musicali Italiani.* Florence: Olschki, 1958.

_____. "Monteverdiana," *Musical Quarterly* XXXVIII (1952): 412ff.

_____. *Bibliografia della Musica Strumentale Italiana Stampata in Italia fino al 1700.* Florence, Olschki, 1952. *Volume secondo di aggiunte e correzioni con nuovi indici.* Florence, Olschki, 1958.

_____. "Un fantomatico compositore per un'opera che forse non era un'opera," *Nuova Rivista Musicale Italiana* V (1971): 788–98.

_____. *Assisi, La Cappella della Basilica di S. Francesco, I—Catalogo del Fondo Musicale nella Biblioteca comunale di Assisi.* (Biblioteca musicae I). Milan, 1962.

Schmitz, E. *Geschichte der Kantate und des geistlichen Konzerts.* Leipzig, 1914.

Schneider, Louis. *Claudio Monteverdi (1567–1643).* Paris: Perrin et Compagnie, 1921.

Schnoebelen, Mary Nicole. "The Concerted Mass at San Petronio in Bologna, ca. 1660–1730: A Documentary and Analytical Study." Unpublished Ph.D. dissertation, University of Illinois, 1966.

Schrade, Leo. *Monteverdi, Creator of Modern Music.* New York: Norton, 1950.

Seelkopf, Martin. "Das Geistliche Schaffen von Alessandro Grandi," Ph.D. dissertation, University of Würzburg, 1973. 2 volumes.

—————. "Italienische Elemente in den Kleinen geistlichen Konzerten von Heinrich Schütz," *Die Musikforschung* XXV (1972): 452–64.

Selfridge-Field, Eleanor. *Venetian Instrumental Music from Gabrieli to Vivaldi*. Praeger: New York, 1975.

—————. "Gabrieli and the Organ," *The Organ Yearbook* VIII (1977): 2–19.

—————. "Bassano and the Orchestra of St. Mark's," *Early Music* IV (1976): 153–58.

Schmidt, Carl. "An Episode in the History of Venetian Opera: The *Tito* Commission," *Journal of the American Musicological Society* (1978): 442–66.

Sinding-Larsen, Staale. *Christ in the Council Hall: Studies in the Religious Iconography of the Venetian Republic*. Rome: L'Erma di Bretschneider, 1974.

Spinelli, Gianfranco. "Confronto fra le registrazioni organistiche dei Vespri di Monteverdi e quelle dell'*Arte organica* di Antegnanti," *Claudio Monteverdi e il suo tempo*, 479–88.

Stäblein, Bruno. Foreword to *Francesco Cavalli, Vier Marianische Antiphonen* (1656). Regensburg: Pustet, 1950.

Steele, John. Foreword to *Claudio Monteverdi, Gloria Concertata (Selva Morale)*. University Park and London: Pennsylvania State University Press, c. 1968.

Stevens, Denis and Steele, John. Foreword to *Claudio Monteverdi, Magnificat (Selva Morale)*. London: Novello, 1969.

Stevens, Denis. "Monteverdi's Venetian Church Music," *Musical Times* CVIII (1967).

—————. "Monteverdi's Vespers Verified," *Musical Times* CII (1961).

—————. "Claudio Monteverdi: 'Selva Morale e Spirituale,' " *Claudio Monteverdi e il suo tempo*.

—————. "Monteverdi's Necklace," *Musical Quarterly* LIX (1973): 370–81.

—————. "Where Are the Vespers of Yesteryear?" *Musical Quarterly* XLVII (1961): 315–30.

—————. Preface to *Claudio Monteverdi, Christmas Vespers*. London: Novello, 1979.

—————. "Monteverdi's other Vespers," *Musical Times* CXX (1979): 732–37.

Tagliavini, L. F. "Registrazioni organistiche nei 'Vespri,' " *Rivista Italiana di Musicologia* II (1967).

Tagmann, Pierre M. "The Palace Church of Santa Barbara in Mantua, and Monteverdi's Relationship to its Liturgy," *Festival Essays for Pauline Alderman*. Provo: Brigham Young University Press, 1976.

Testi, Flavio. *La Musica italiana nel seicento*. Milan: Bramante, 1972. Vol. II.

Tin, Mario dal. "Note di liturgia patriarchina e canti tradizionali della Basilica di S. Marco a Venezia," *Jucunda Laudatio* I–IV (1973): 90–131.

Tramontin, S. *et al*. *Culto dei Santi a Venezia*. Venice: Edizioni Studium Cattolico Veneziano, 1965.

Valentinelli, Joseph. *Bibliotheca Manuscripta ad S. Marci Venetiarum*. Venice: Ex Typographia Commercii, 1868.

Van Dijk, S. D. P. and Walker, J. Hazelden. *The Origins of the Modern Roman Liturgy: The Liturgy of the Papal Court and the Franciscan Order in the Thirteenth Century*. London: Darton, Longman and Todd, 1960.

Vogel, Emil. "Claudio Monteverdi," *Vierteljahrschrift für Musikwissenschaft* III (1887): 315–450.

Walker, Thomas. "Gli Errori di 'Minerva al Tavolino': Osservazioni sulla cronologia delle prime opere veneziane," *Venezia e il melodramma nel seicento*. Florence: Olschki, 1976.

Weidensaul, Jane. "The Polyphonic Hymns of Adrian Willaert." Unpublished Ph.D. dissertation, Rutgers University, 1978.

Wheelock, Gretchen A. Fahlund. "The Solo Motets of Alessandro Grandi (d. 1630): A Stylistic Analysis." Masters thesis, Yale University, 1966.

Wiel, Taddio. "Francesco Cavalli (1602–1676) e la sua musica scenica," *Nuovo Archivio Veneto*, Nuova Serie, XXVIII (1914). Partial translation in *Musical Antiquary*, 1912, pp. 1–19.

Winterfeld, Carl von. *Johannes Gabrieli und sein Zeitalter*. Berlin, 1834. Reprint: Hildesheim: Olms, 1965.

Witzenmann, W. "Stile antico e stile nuovo nella musica sacra di Claudio Monteverdi," *Rivista Italiana di Musicologia* II (1967): 371–81.

―――――. "Die italienische Kirchenmusik des Barocks. Ein Bericht über die Literatur aus den Jahren 1945 bis 1974. Teil I: Der Frühbarock," *Acta Musicologica* XLVIII (1976): 77–103.

Secondary Sources: Musical Editions

Alessandro Grandi

Bartha, D., ed. *A Zenetörtenet Antologiaja*. Budapest, 1948.
    "Plorabo die ac nocte"

Blume, Friedrich, ed. *Das Chorwerk*. XL. Wolfenbüttel: Möseler, 1936.
    "Deus qui nos in tantis periculis"
    "Plorabo die ac nocte"
    "Ave Regina caelorum"

Corte, Andrea della, ed. *Scelta di musiche per lo studio della storia*. Milan: Ricordi, 1949.
    "Quam pulchra es"

Ewerhart, Rudolf. *Cantio Sacra*. Cologne: Bieler, 1960.
    "O quam tu pulchra es"
    "Jesu mi dulcissime"
    "Cantabo Domino"
    "Egredimini, filiae"
"O quam tu pulchra es"

Gunther, Renate. Transcriptions in appendix to "Motette und Geistliches Konzert im Schaffen von Alessandro Grandi (ca. 1577–1630)." Ph.D. dissertation, Freie-Universität Berlin, 1958.

Pineau, Charles, ed. *Musique d'église des XVIIe et XVIIIe siècles*, in *Répertoire classique de musique religieuse et spirituelle* (ed. Henry Expert). Paris: Senart, 1913–14.
    "O quam tu pulchra es"
    "Quam tu pulchra es"

Roche, Jerome. "The Duet in Early Seventeenth-Century Italian Church Music," *Proceedings of the Royal Musical Association*. (1966–67), pp. 33–50.
    "Hodie nobis de caelo"
    "Anima Christi"

―――――. *Faber Baroque Choral Series*. London: Faber, 1968.
    "Exaudi Deus orationem meam"
    "Veniat dilectus meus"

Seelkopf, Martin. Transcriptions in Volume II of "Das Geistliche Schaffen von Alessandro Grandi." Ph.D. dissertation, Julius-Maximilians-Universität zu Würzburg. 1973.

Giovanni Rovetta

Leichtentritt, Hugo. *Geschichte der Motette*. Leipzig, 1908.
   "Salve Regina" (excerpts)
Roche, Jerome. "Rovetta and Tunder—mis-attribution or plagiarism?" *Early Music* III (1975): 58–60.
   "Salve Regina" (Basso continuo part only)
Seiffert, Max. Franz Tunder, *Gesangswerke*. *Denkmäler Deutscher Tonkunst* III.
"Salve Regina"; music identical to Rovetta's except for Basso continuo part; variants in text.

Francesco Cavalli

Leppard, R. J. ed. *Messa Concertata*. London: Faber, 1966.
————. *Laudate Dominum*. London: Faber, 1969.
————. *Laetatus sum*. London: Faber, 1969.
————. *Salve Regina*. London: Faber, 1969.
————. *Magnificat*. London: Faber, 1969.
Nielsen, Riccardo, ed. *Musiche Sacre*. Canzonas à 6 and à 12. Bologna, 1955.
Piccioli, G., ed. *Vesperi a otto voci* (1675). Milan, 1960.
   Three Magnificats
Stäblein, Bruno. *Musiche Sacre. Vier Marianische Antiphonen. Musica Divina*, 1–4. Regensburg, 1950.
Vatielli, F. *Antichi cantate spirituali*. Turin, 1922.
   "Cantate Domino"

Index

The page references below cover the body of the text only, pp. 1-230. The documents in Appendix I, pp. 231-312, are all cited in the body of the text, and those documents in a particular topic can be located by referring to the pages of the text cited in the index.